Isaiah among the Ancient Near Eastern Prophets

Supplements
to the
Vetus Testamentum

VOLUME 117

Isaiah among the Ancient Near Eastern Prophets

A Comparative Study of the Earliest Stages of the Isaiah Tradition and the Neo-Assyrian Prophecies

By

Matthijs J. de Jong

BRILL

LEIDEN • BOSTON
2007

This book is printed on acid-free paper.

A C.I.P. record for this book is available from the Library of Congress.

ISSN   0083-5889
ISBN   978 90 04 16161 0

To Elske

CONTENTS

CONCLUSION

ACKNOWLEDGEMENTS

This volume is a revised version of my doctoral dissertation accepted by the Faculty of Theology at Leiden University in December 2006. The present work benefited from comments and suggestions of various scholars who read the manuscript of the dissertation. I also took the opportunity to make use of some new literature, to polish the manuscript, and to provide indexes.

I am grateful to Helen Richardson-Hewitt who corrected the English of the manuscript.

I began my study of Isaiah and the Assyrian prophecies during my M.A.-study of theology in Leiden under the supervision of prof. Karel van der Toorn. Thanks to his views on comparative study and to prof. Klaas Veenhof's willingness to devote a reading class to the Assyrian prophecies, I was able to start out a comparison between Isaiah 6-8 and the Assyrian prophecies, which resulted in a M.A.-thesis in 1999 under the supervision of prof. Arie van der Kooij.

A grant of the talents programme of the NUFFIC (Netherlands Organization for International Cooperation in Higher Education) enabled me to study in Oxford during the year 2000/01. Under the supervision of dr. Stephanie Dalley I completed a Master of Studies in Oriental Studies, focusing on the Assyrian prophetic literature. From autumn 2001 to spring 2006, I was in the privileged position to carry out a doctoral study at the Faculty of Theology in Leiden thanks to the Council of the Humanities of the Netherlands Organisation for Scientific Research (NWO).

First of all I would like to thank prof. Arie van der Kooij, under whose direction I have written my dissertation. I am very grateful for his guidance and helpful suggestions. His unremitting trust in the success of the project has been a great support. I also thank prof. Wilfred van Soldt, as second supervisor, who guided me through the field of Assyriology. I have greatly enjoyed his interest in the project and his help.

Since we met in Oxford in 2000, Stephanie Dalley has been a constant adviser and friend. Her views on the Assyrian texts, Assyriology, and scholarship in general, have made a strong impression of me, for which I am grateful. While studying in Oxford, I also enjoyed the classes of prof. Hugh Williamson. I greatly appreciate his willingness to read drafts of my dissertation, despite our different approaches to First Isaiah. The present work has profited from his comments and insights.

Prof. Manfred Weippert, in his role as external referee of my dissertation, offered many valuable comments and suggestions. I thank him for his thorough assessment of my study and his interest in its subject.

I also want to include dr. Johannes Tromp in my appreciation, whose plain but ever sincere criticism helped me to keep on the right track at some critical points. Finally, I want to thank prof. Henk Jan de Jonge. Among the many things he taught me was to acquire an academic attitude. This will be of lasting value no matter what field of study lies ahead.

This book is dedicated to the person I love most, Elske Burger.

The English quotations from the Old Testament are based on the *New Revised Standard Version. Anglicized Edition* (Oxford 1995); occasional alternative translations are not explicitly indicated.

For the Assyrian prophecies, I largely follow Simo Parpola's edition, *Assyrian Prophecies, State Archives of Assyria* 9 (Helsinki 1997), but usually offer my own translation of the prophetic texts. Transcriptions of the Assyrian prophetic texts are mostly based on Martti Nissinen et al., *Prophets and Prophecy in the Ancient Near East* (Atlanta 2003).

INTRODUCTION

CHAPTER ONE

INTRODUCTION

'It is an irony of the present situation in Old Testament study that, just as newer methods of reading and discussing texts, prophetic and other, are being applied, our greatly increased knowledge of prophecy in its wider Near Eastern setting requires that we pay renewed attention to Israelite prophecy as an historical phenomenon with precursors and parallels in sibling Near Eastern cultures.'[1]

The present study focuses on prophecy as a historical phenomenon by offering a comparison between parts of First Isaiah and the Assyrian prophecies.[2] In the first part of this study the material from First Isaiah and from seventh-century Assyria is investigated in its own right, in order to create the conditions for a valid and fruitful comparison between parts of the book of Isaiah and the Assyrian prophecies. The second part of this study contains a comparison of the Isaiah tradition in its earliest shape and the prophetic material from seventh-century Assyria. The comparison consists of three elements: the interrelation of prophetic oracles and historical events; the functions of the prophets; and the literary development of prophecy. The present study aims to contribute to three issues relating to prophecy:

1) This study deals with the question of which parts of First Isaiah can be dated to the Assyrian period, i.e. the eighth to the seventh century BCE. It offers an exploration of the earliest stages of the Isaiah tradition, its origin and development in the Assyrian period, long before it was expanded into the prophetic book as we have it. This is of importance for the question of the character of the prophet described in the earliest, prophetic material. What kind of prophet was the historical Isaiah, and how did he develop into one of the great prophetic figures? Recently, Uwe Becker has formulated the question like this:

---

[1]   Gordon 1995: 29.
[2]   The Assyrian prophecies are often referred to as the 'Neo-Assyrian prophecies', since they date from the Neo-Assyrian period. This study refers to these prophecies as 'Assyrian prophecies' and to the Neo-Assyrian period as the 'Assyrian period'.

> War Jesaja der "klassische" Gerichtsprophet des 8.Jh.s, für den man ihn
> gewöhnlich hält? .... War Jesaja im Kontext der vorexilischen
> judäischen Staatsreligion wirklich ein Außenseiter, ein einsamer Rufer?
> Die Beantwortung dieser Fragen fällt heute schwerer denn je, und sie
> kann gewiß nicht allein am Jesajabuch entschieden werden.[3]

New insights gained from redaction-historical and literary focus on
the book of Isaiah have challenged the traditional understanding of
First Isaiah as representing essentially the preaching of the historical
prophet. The issue of the earliest stages of the Isaiah tradition has to
be addressed anew, and cannot be solved by the exegetical study of
the book of Isaiah alone.[4] The present study intends to provide a new
answer to this question.

2) This study furthermore aims to contribute to the question: how
does biblical prophecy relate to prophecy as a socio-historical phenomenon? The relation between the biblical images of the prophets, in
particular that of the 'classical prophets', and the prophetic figures that
functioned in ancient Judah and Israel, is a complex issue. The present
study attempts to answer this question with regard to the prophet
Isaiah.

3) The main interest of this study is of a comparative nature. The
study deals with the prophetic material from First Isaiah and the phenomenon of prophecy in Judah from a comparative perspective. As a
counterpart, the prophetic material from seventh-century Assyria is
dealt with. The comparative aim is to illuminate the earliest stages of
the Isaiah tradition, to increase our understanding of the prophetic material of seventh-century Assyria, and to develop further the comparative study of prophecy by taking one of the prophetic books into the
focus of attention.

In this introduction, I present an overview of the recent developments in the study of First Isaiah (1.1) and in the study of prophecy
(1.2). The final section of this chapter deals with the aim and focus of
the present study.

---

[3]   Becker 1999: 152. See also Steck 1996: 6-7; Köckert 2003: 112-114.
[4]   For similar views, see Nissinen 1993: 249-250, Rösel 2003: 121, and Höffken
2004:144, who concludes: 'Rein buchintern verfahrende Analysen sind auf die Dauer
sehr unbefriedigend.'

1.1 Recent Developments in the Study of First Isaiah

1.1.1 Shifts of Focus

The last three decades of research on the book of Isaiah are character-ised by an increasing diversity in scholarly approach.[5] The eighth-century core of the book and the view taken of the historical prophet have become more and more a matter of controversy.[6] Two major changes in the recent study of Isaiah can be singled out. First, empha-sis on Isaiah as a prophetic personality has changed into an emphasis on the book of Isaiah. Second, as the focus of interpretation had shifted to the book as a whole, the strictly tripartite division of the book was challenged.

Following Bernhard Duhm's theory of three independent Isaiahs, First, Second and Third Isaiah, most twentieth-century exegetes ap-proached First Isaiah in relative isolation from the rest of the book.[7] During most of the twentieth century, the exegesis of First Isaiah was marked by a relative consensus. The main exegetical task was to iden-tify and to describe the views and preaching of the historical prophet. To this end, scholars distinguished between 'authentic' and 'unauthen-tic' material within First Isaiah.[8] The approach was largely atomistic: the core of First Isaiah was perceived as being a collection of eighth-century texts to which divergent fragments had been added in the ex-ilic and post-exilic periods. The understanding of the prophet's life and ministry was important for the exegesis. Isaiah was perceived as one of the great prophets, who lived and worked in eighth-century Je-rusalem (c. 740-701 BCE). His forty-year-long ministry was usually divided into several stages.[9] Isaiah was described as a genius, a poet, and a great theologian.[10] The presumed 'life of the prophet' functioned as a starting point for the exegesis: passages from First Isaiah were connected with the various stages of his career. As one of the classical

---

[5] Steck 1996: 5-6. Becker (1999: 151) describes the current research on Isaiah as 'eines methodisches beliebigen, diffusen Nebeneinanders von Richtungen und Positionen'. For an overview of the history of research on the book of Isaiah, see Becker 1999; Hardmeier 1986; Höffken 2004; Seebaß 1995; Seitz 1992; Tate 1996.

[6] Becker 1999: 4.

[7] Höffken 2004: 27.

[8] Becker 1968: 44-68.

[9] Höffken 2004: 22.

[10] See e.g. Von Rad's qualification: 'Die Verkündigung Jesajas ist das gewaltigste theologische Phänomen des ganzen Alten Testamentes' (1960: 158).

eighth-century prophets, Isaiah was regarded as having been essentially a prophet of judgement,[11] whose preaching was, at least in certain respects, radically new.[12] Since Isaiah was regarded as being
essentially a prophet of judgement, passages from First Isaiah that
promise salvation were disputed. Some exegetes held that Isaiah only
preached judgement and doom and that words of salvation had to be
unauthentic.[13] Others, taking a subtler view, argued that although he
was a prophet of judgement, he spoke certain words of salvation as
well.[14] In any case, the material of First Isaiah was analysed and reconstructed in conformity with the supposed spirit and teaching of the
prophetic personality. The context of ancient Near Eastern prophecy
played no role of importance for the study of First Isaiah.

In the second half of the twentieth century, the rise of redaction
criticism led to an increased attention to the literary afterlife of the
prophetic texts.[15] Scholarly focus moved from Isaiah as a prophetic
personality to the book of Isaiah as a literary product. Whereas Hans
Wildberger's commentary on First Isaiah,[16] focusing on Isaiah as a
prophet-theologian,[17] can be characterised as the culmination of the
earlier approach, Otto Kaiser's revised edition of his commentary on
Isaiah 1-12 principally shifted the focus to the history of development
of the book of Isaiah, away from the eighth-century prophet.[18]

Among scholars the insight grew that the various parts of the book
of Isaiah were more intertwined than a strict application of the theory
of a tripartite division allowed for.[19] The exegetical focus turned to the
book of Isaiah as a whole, and the issue of the compositional, redactional and theological unity of the book became central to research.[20]
As a result, the independent existence of Third Isaiah is usually re-

---

[11]   E.g. Becker 1968: 9; Herrmann 1965; Kilian 1983: 95; Kraus 1982: 464; Von
Rad 1933: 109-121; 1960: 182-194; Würthwein 1952.
[12]   E.g. Von Rad 1960: 421. See Kratz (2003b: 1-6) for the positions of Wellhausen, Duhm, Von Rad and Albertz on this issue.
[13]   E.g. Kilian 1983: 96; Seebaß 1995: 315.
[14]   E.g. Becker 1968: 13.
[15]   Kraus 1982: 467; Kilian 1983: 139.
[16]   Wildberger 1965-1982.
[17]   Wildberger's commentary concludes with a synthesis of the prophetic ministry
of Isaiah and his preaching (1965-82: 1577-1667). See Becker 1999: 135-136.
[18]   Kaiser 1981.
[19]   Becker 2004: 40.
[20]   Steck 1996: 11-14; Becker 1999: 3-4.

jected,[21] and the redactional relationship between a first and a second main part of the book has become a major issue.[22] These developments were consequential for the study of First Isaiah. It became accepted that this part of the book does not only contain early material, but also material from later, even from the latest, redactional stages. Furthermore, whereas scholars had previously focused on the prophetic personality, it was recently argued that the image of the prophets which emerges from the books called after them is first and foremost of a literary character.[23] Scholars have become increasingly aware of the gap between the books and the historical prophets, and some have even claimed the impossibility of bridging it.[24]

1.1.2 Approaches to the Book of Isaiah

Assyria Redaction

Whereas the exegesis of First Isaiah previously concentrated on the identification of the Isaianic material, implying that the 'unauthentic' texts were theologically less interesting, the rise of redaction criticism stimulated the appreciation of texts representing later developments of the prophetic tradition. One of the first major redaction-critical contributions to First Isaiah is Hermann Barth's study *Die Jesaja-Worte in der Josiazeit*.[25] Barth dealt with texts from First Isaiah relating to the contemporary Assyrian empire, which were, according to the scholarly majority of his time, not from Isaiah. Barth interpreted these texts as a coherent redaction of the earlier, Isaianic texts and situated them in the reign of Josiah (640/39-609 BCE).[26] By distinguishing between the Isaianic view of Assyria and a later, seventh-century view, Barth relieved the prophet Isaiah of a heavy burden, and proposed a coherent

---

[21] E.g. Steck's argument (1989: 361-406) that Isaiah 56-66 is not an independent composition but a series of textual expansions relating to the development of a 'Großjesaja'; similarly Rendtorff 1984: 295-320; Berges 1998: 13.

[22] E.g. Steck (1985: 80) argues that Isa 35 forms a redactional bridge between two formerly independent collections (a First and Second Isaiah), as part of a 'Great Isaiah redaction' to be dated to the Hellenistic period. Williamson (1994: 113) qualifies Second Isaiah as a literary expansion to, and elaboration on, an earlier version of First Isaiah, by an author who both depended on First Isaiah and edited it.

[23] Steck 1996: 9; Becker 1999: 6; 2004: 31; Ben Zvi 2003.

[24] E.g. Auld 1983; Carroll 1983; and effectively Kaiser 1981.

[25] Barth 1977.

[26] The main passages from First Isaiah which Barth attributes to the Assyria Redaction are 8:9-10; 8:23b-9:6; 10:16-19; 14:24-27; 17:12-14; 28:23-29; 30:27-33; 31:5.8b-9 and 32:1-5.15-20.

solution to a range of ambiguous passages. Barth explained them as a
literary continuation of the Isaiah tradition: an Assyria Redaction during the reign of Josiah. The value of his study lies in the interpretation
of a series of passages regarded as non-Isaianic but nevertheless of
importance. Barth remained within the boundaries of previous scholarship: he saw Isaiah as a classical prophet of judgement and he attributed a great number of texts from First Isaiah to the historical
prophet. As a result, Barth reckoned with the existence of an earlier
version of First Isaiah, a 'Proto-Isaiah booklet', consisting of Isa 2-
32*, in the late seventh century. Barth's ideas have found much scholarly approval, though in most cases with modifications.[27]

Jacques Vermeylen proposed a similar view in his study *Du prophète Isaïe à l'apocalyptique*.[28] He identified several collections of
eighth-century prophetic sayings as the core of the book of Isaiah.[29] As
a result of elaborations on these collections during the reigns of Manasseh and Josiah, a Proto-Isaiah booklet (Isa 2-33*) came into existence at the end of the pre-exilic period.[30] Various later redactions,
continuing into the second century BCE, ultimately produced the book
of Isaiah. Ronald Clements adopted Barth's hypothesis in his commentary on First Isaiah. He modified Barth's view to some extent,[31]
and characterised the seventh-century redaction as the Josiah Redaction.[32] Furthermore, in his study *Isaiah and the Deliverance of Jerusalem*, he qualified the story of 2 Kgs 18:17-19:37 (Isa 36-38) as a
product of the same circles responsible for the Josiah Redaction.[33]
With regard to the eighth-century material in First Isaiah, Clements
maintained a traditional position. Though acknowledging that decisive
criteria for dating prophecies to the eighth century are often lacking,[34]

---

[27]   For an overview of the positions of Barth, Vermeylen and Clements, see
Höffken 2004: 29-33. Earlier, Mowinckel, in various studies (e.g. 1933), proposed a
seventh-century development of the Isaiah tradition as being the work of a so-called
Isaiah-school.

[28]   Vermeylen 1977-78.

[29]   See Vermeylen 1977-78: 656-657.

[30]   See Vermeylen 1977-78: 673-692.

[31]   Clements' main modifications consist of the attribution of 8:23b-9:6 to Isaiah
himself, and the qualification of Isa 2-4 as resulting from a later, exilic redaction. This
leads to a seventh-century Proto-Isaiah booklet of Isa 5-32*.

[32]   The main passages from First Isaiah which Clements attributes to the Josiah
Redaction are 8:9-10; 10:16-27.33-34; 14:24-27; 17:12-14; 28:23-29; 29:5-8; 30:27-
33; 31:5.8-9 and 32:1-5.15-20.

[33]   Clements 1980b: 95; cf. Clements, 1980a: 6.

[34]   Clements, 1980a: 7.

he nevertheless assumed the Isaianic character of many passages traditionally attributed to Isaiah. According to Clements, Isaiah himself
laid the foundation for the book as he composed his memoirs of the
Syro-Ephraimitic crisis, in Isa 6:1-8:18.[35] Furthermore, Clements described the prophet Isaiah in traditional terms, as 'one of the greatest
figures of the religious and political story of ancient Israel'.[36]

Recent studies have elaborated on the hypothesis of a seventh-
century redaction.[37] Erich Bosshard-Nepustil followed the suggestion
of an Assyria Redaction and added an exilic Assyria-Babylonia Redaction that announced salvation after punishment, and a post-exilic
Babylonia Redaction concerned with restoration.[38] In this way, he produced a detailed redaction history of First Isaiah.[39] Furthermore, Jörg
Barthel in his study *Prophetenwort und Geschichte* adopted Barth's
thesis.[40] Barthel's study focused on Isa 6-8 and 28-31, which are regarded in their literary core (Isa 6-8*, 28-31*) as stemming from the
hand of Isaiah. In opposition to the proponents of a radical redaction
criticism (see below), Barthel aimed to vindicate the historical Isaiah,
but in a way that transcends the traditional, exegetical approach.[41] He
made a principal distinction between the original, oral messages of
Isaiah, relating to specific historical situations, and the later stage in
which the messages were cast into written form by the prophet himself, thereby creating a new literary context for the prophecies. According to Barthel, the literary record of the prophetic words involved
interpretation, which produced a literary context with its own constellation of meaning.[42] In addition, Barthel adopted Barth's theory of a
seventh-century Assyria Redaction, which led to the assumption of a
Proto-Isaiah booklet (Isa 1-32*) in the late pre-exilic period. Among
the recent commentaries on First Isaiah that have adopted the suggestion of a seventh-century Assyria Redaction, are those of Marvin
Sweeney,[43] Joseph Blenkinsopp,[44] and Wim Beuken.[45]

---

[35] Clements, 1980a: 4.
[36] Clements, 1980a: 11.
[37] E.g. L'Heureux 1984; Sheppard 1985; Gonçalves 1986; Sweeney 1996b.
[38] Bosshard-Nepustil 1997.
[39] Bosshard-Nepustil 1997: 234-267.
[40] Barthel 1997.
[41] Barthel 1997: 465.
[42] Barthel 1997: 27; cf. 1997: 459, as a 'Sinnentwurf sui generis'.
[43] Sweeney (1996a) discerns an eighth-century Isaianic layer of 5:1-10:34; 14:24-
27, and 28-32*, and a seventh-century Josianic edition, consisting of Isa 5-12; 14-23*;
27; 28-32; 36-37.

Barth's position built on earlier scholarship, since the question he aimed to solve was based on a majority view among exegetes with regard to the issue of which texts from First Isaiah were Isaianic and which were not. Barth intended to clarify certain ambiguous passages that seemed to be of pre-exilic origin but that were difficult to harmonise with the preconceived picture of the prophet Isaiah. Thus, Barth provided a new answer to an old question.[46] Scholars who adopted the Assyria Redaction, on the one hand contributed to the new approach to the book of Isaiah by addressing the literary and redactional development of the prophetic heritage. On the other hand, they did not fundamentally question the traditional view of the earliest stage of the Isaiah tradition: the prophet Isaiah and his preaching.

Radical Redaction Criticism
An important shift in the exegesis of Isaiah was achieved by Otto Kaiser's revised commentary on Isaiah 1-12, in which he presented a radical redaction-critical analysis.[47] In Kaiser's view, the book of Isaiah is a product from the post-exilic period. Although he identified a small collection of earlier prophetic words, consisting of critical sayings and announcements of judgement, he attributed them to anonymous prophets from the late pre-exilic period rather than to Isaiah.[48] Kaiser's view was based on his understanding of Isa 6-8, the so-called *Denkschrift*, usually attributed to the eighth-century prophet, but regarded by Kaiser as a literary text from the fifth century.[49] From this understanding it followed that the other literary complexes within First Isaiah dated from a similarly late, or even later, period. Kaiser formulates his approach as: 'die Forderung [...], dem Propheten

---

[44]   Blenkinsopp 2000a. Blenkinsopp (2000a: 73-74) shows awareness of the recent shifts of focus in the study of Isaiah in qualifying the book as essentially a post-exilic literary construct, but nevertheless presumes a significant Isaianic substratum within First Isaiah. For the seventh-century Assyria Redaction, see Blenkinsopp 2000a: 91-92. Blenkinsopp (2000a: 88) reckons with the existence of a Proto-Isaiah booklet, an earlier version of First Isaiah in the pre-exilic period, with which, as he assumes, the author of Second Isaiah was familiar.

[45]   Beuken on Isa 28-39 (Beuken 2000). Beuken proposes that the Assyria Redaction incorporated the Isaianic material, consisting of the units 28:1-29, 29:1-14, 29:15-24, 30:1-33 and 31:1-9, and considers the narratives of Isa 36-39 to be influenced by the Assyria Redaction.

[46]   For a critical review of Barth's thesis, Becker 1997: 212-219; 1999: 128-130.

[47]   Kaiser 1981.

[48]   Kaiser 1981: 19-20. Later, Kaiser adopted a milder view, acknowledging the existence of a small collection of Isaianic sayings (Kaiser 1983: 4; 1994: 29-66).

[49]   Kaiser 1981: 119.

grundsätzlich jedes Wort abzusprechen, das auch aus einer anderen Zeit erklärt werden kann'.[50] This principle and Kaiser's exegetical position have been strongly criticised.[51]

Uwe Becker strengthened the radically critical position in his study *Jesaja—von der Botschaft zum Buch*.[52] First, he made a stronger and more consistent case for a late dating of most parts of First Isaiah. According to Becker, the earliest, eighth-century material from First Isaiah is limited to a handful of passages, among them 6:1-8* and 8:1-4*.[53] The earliest redaction of these texts consisted of 6:9-11 and 8:5-8, and this redaction dates from the early post-exilic period. As a consequence, the rest of the book of Isaiah is of a still later date. Among the late redactional material we find Isa 1-4, qualified by Becker as various successive introductions, an anti-Assyrian Redaction, less extensive and dated considerably later than by Barth, and Isa 28-31, which according to Becker is dependent on the stories of Isa 36-38.[54] Becker's study changes the image of the historical Isaiah. The fragments identified as Isaianic, portray Isaiah as a prophet of salvation closely connected to the court and cult of Jerusalem, who announced the destruction of Judah's enemies. It was only with the first (post-exilic) redaction of the Isaianic material (e.g. 6:9-11 and 8:5-8) that the prophet was turned into a preacher of judgement.[55] In this way, Becker turned the tradition view of the prophet Isaiah upside down.

Becker's study has been criticised, but also praised as a 'Zäsur in der Jesajaforschung' providing a basis for further research.[56] It may be noted that Becker, despite his critical position, still accepts the historicity of the prophet Isaiah and the possibility of approaching the historical prophet through redaction-historical analysis. Becker's position has been criticised, and rightly so in my view, for the two hundred-year gap that is assumed to exist between the Isaianic material

---

[50]   Kaiser 1983: 4.
[51]   See e.g. Hardmeier 1986: 19. Hardmeier (1986: 5, 14-19) criticises the 'neo-literary-critical approach' of Kaiser and others for the radically late dating based on linguistic and stylistic observations and on claims of literary dependency of Isaiah on other texts (such as Second Isaiah and Jeremiah). Hardmeier (1986: 17-18) criticises Kaiser's claim that Isa 7:1-9, and by extension the complete Isaiah tradition in its early version, was influenced by Deuteronomistic theology.
[52]   Becker 1997.
[53]   Becker further accepts 17:1b.3*; 18:1-2*; 20:3-4*; 28:1-4*.7-10* as Isaianic.
[54]   Becker 1997: 227.
[55]   Becker 1997: 286-287.
[56]   Dietrich 1999: 335 and 337.

and its earliest redaction.[57] It may be more likely that the Isaianic material had already been developed in the late pre-exilic and exilic period, rather than having remained dormant for two centuries.

The Book of Isaiah as a Literary Unity

Recent contributions, mainly by Anglo-American scholars, approach the book of Isaiah as a compositional and redactional unity.[58] Whereas some scholars have abandoned the historical-critical approach altogether in favour of a literary, synchronic approach,[59] others have combined a literary approach with a redaction-historical interest.[60] David Carr has described the recent search for thematic or intertextual unity within the book of Isaiah.[61] He discussed various macro-structural proposals regarding the book of Isaiah as a textual unity, such as chapter 35 or chapters 36-39 as a transition between two different parts of the book,[62] and chapters 1 and 65-66 as a cohesively paired introduction and conclusion to the book of Isaiah as a whole.[63] Carr argued that no single structural perspective successfully organises the book as a whole,[64] since redactors have added material without exhaustively integrating it or adapting the existing tradition to their conceptions.[65] Unity in the book of Isaiah is of a necessarily complex character,[66] or, in the words of Ulrich Berges, a 'disziplinierter Chaos'.[67]

Further contributions to the study of the book of Isaiah as a whole and the search for unity within the book include the publications of Rolf Rendtorff,[68] and the study by Berges, *Das Buch Jesaja*, in which a synchronic and a diachronic analysis of the book of Isaiah are combined.[69] Berges argued that the literary study of the book of Isaiah in its final form cannot be separated from redaction-critical study focus-

---

[57]   Dietrich 1999: 336-337; Barthel 2003: 135.
[58]   Melugin and Sweeney (eds) 1996; Broyles and Evans (eds) 1997; Tate 1996.
[59]   E.g. Watts 1985; 1987; O'Connell 1994.
[60]   E.g. Seitz (1991) attempts to explain the development of the Isaiah tradition by considering Isa 36-39 as a bridge between a First and a Second Isaiah.
[61]   Carr 1993.
[62]   Isa 35: Steck 1985. Isa 36-39: Ackroyd 1982; Clements 1982; Sweeney 1988: 32-34; Laato 1998.
[63]   Sweeney 1988: 21-24, 97-98; Tomasino 1993.
[64]   Carr 1993: 70-71.
[65]   Carr 1993: 77-78.
[66]   Rendtorff 1996.
[67]   Berges 1998: 46.
[68]   Rendtorff 1984; 1989.
[69]   Berges 1998. For an overview of Berges' study, see Höffken 2004: 74-78.

ing on the intentions of the final editors, the community of intended readers, and on the question of the historical development of the book of Isaiah.[70] The unity of the book is the result of a long process.

It has become generally acknowledged that priority should be given to the text, i.e. to the book of Isaiah in its final form. This twofold change of focus, from the prophet to the text and from parts of the text to the whole, has been called a paradigm shift in the study of Isaiah.[71] The study of the text however must also include the historical question of how the text has come into being, i.e. the question concerning the development of the Isaiah tradition into the book. Scholars have rightly argued that the point of exegetical departure must be what we have, the text of Isaiah, and not any preconception about the historical prophet and his preaching. However, exploration of the origins and earliest development of the Isaiah tradition remains part of the exegetical agenda.[72]

1.1.3   Approaches to the Prophet

Isaiah the Eighth-Century Prophet
With regard to the study of the prophet Isaiah, it may be observed that the shifts of focus discussed above have hardly altered the view of Isaiah as a classical prophet at all. In the words of Uwe Becker: 'das Interesse an der Prophetenperson und ihrem "Ausnahmecharakter" [ist] ungebrochen'.[73] The nineteenth-century understanding of the preaching of the great prophets as 'ethical monotheism' (Kuenen, Wellhausen, Duhm) may have been replaced by labels such as social criticism and the uncompromising preaching of judgement, the great prophets and their preaching generally maintain a unique status.[74]

Scholars with a historical interest tend to attribute a maximum of texts to the historical Isaiah.[75] Walter Dietrich, for instance, aiming to

---

[70]   See also Deist 1989: 12-13.
[71]   E.g. Berges 1998: 11; Blenkinsopp 2000a: 73; Becker 2004: 31. See further Gordon 1995; Deist 1989; Steck 1996: 7-14.
[72]   According to Berges, redaction-historical analysis is a necessary part of the study of Isaiah, and 'der hypothesenartige Charakter der zu erzielenden Ergebnisse sollte nicht abschrecken, sondern gehört zu den Lasten jeder Wissenschaft' (1998: 47). Similarly Steck 1996: 122.
[73]   Becker 2004: 33; cf. 2002a: 12.
[74]   Becker 2004: 33-34.
[75]   See also Becker 1999: 132.

describe Isaiah's political theology,[76] discerned three political crises during Isaiah's ministry, 734-733, 713-711 and 705-701 BCE, and argued that Isaiah prophesied both the punishment of Assyria which implied salvation for Judah, and the punishment of Judah because of the anti-Assyrian policy. Dietrich solved the apparent contradiction by assuming a radical change in Isaiah's preaching from a prophecy of salvation to a prophecy of judgement.[77] Jesper Høgenhaven, who in his study *Gott und Volk bei Jesaja* explored Isaiah's theological position,[78] also suggested biographic explanations to apparent contradictions within the proposed corpus of Isaianic texts. Though the prophet announced salvation for Judah until the destruction of the Northern Kingdom, afterwards, provoked by Hezekiah's anti-Assyrian policy, his message changed to announcements of judgement and doom. In a similar way Antti Laato in his study *Who is Immanuel?* explained the origin of the messianic expectation against the background of Isaiah's biography.[79] By taking 9:1-6 and 11:1-9 as Isaianic, Laato suggested Isaiah's messianic hope was born in a situation of crisis (734-733).[80]

These studies work from the basic assumption that Isaiah is one of the classical prophets from the eighth century, who stood in opposition to the establishment of his time. This assumption however is at least to some extent at odds with recent exegetical developments focusing on the prophetic books. The new approach to the book of Isaiah certainly leaves room for a historical prophet, but requires reconsidering the traditional preconceptions concerning the historical prophet and his preaching.

Judgement and Salvation

The joint occurrence of prophecies of salvation and prophecies of judgement within First Isaiah has been a subject of discussion. Among the solutions proposed, we find theological, rhetorical, biographical and literary-critical explanations.[81] Wildberger attempted to bring both

---

[76] Dietrich 1976.
[77] Dietrich 1976: 101-114.
[78] Høgenhaven 1988.
[79] Laato 1988.
[80] Some extreme examples of the tendency to attribute as much as possible from First Isaiah to the historical prophet are Hayes and Irvine 1987 and Gitay 1991.
[81] Köckert (2003: 105-111) provides an overview of solutions suggested by Von Rad, Wildberger, Fohrer, Kilian and Joachim Becker. The latter suggested that prophecy of salvation was a fundamental aspect of Isaiah's repertoire (Isa 7:10-16, 8:1-4, 9:1-6, 11:1-5), and concluded 'daß man dem Propheten den Character eines

perspectives together on a theological level.[82] Others explained it as part of the prophet's rhetoric, for instance Georg Fohrer, who considered Isaiah a prophet of repentance whose words of judgement had a pedagogic intention.[83] The converse was supported by Hans Walter Wolff who saw Isaiah as a prophet of judgement whose call for repentance referred to a stage already past.[84] Others tried to solve the contradiction against the background of changes during the life of the prophet, who initially preached salvation and later on judgement. This was the argument of Høgenhaven (above) and Hans Werner Hoffmann, who suggested that Isaiah called for repentance, until he understood in that Judah had lost its chance of escaping judgement.[85]

Rudolf Kilian attempted to solve the matter by arguing that all passages proclaiming salvation and repentance were by definition not Isaianic. In his view, Isaiah had 'nie etwas verkündet, was mit einem Verstockungsauftrag von allem Anfang an nicht vereinbar wäre'.[86] Similarly, Wolfgang Werner argued that Isaiah is the 'Prophet der Verstockung Israels',[87] whereas all mentions of salvation are of post-exilic origin.[88] This position has been criticised for being a *petitio principii*.[89] Most scholars accepted that prophecy of salvation in one way or another was part of Isaiah's prophetic preaching. However, it was generally agreed that prophecy of judgement played the decisive role in his preaching. Isaiah was essentially, although according to most scholars not exclusively, a prophet of judgement.[90]

In recent contributions, the battlefield has to some extent been shifted from the level of the historical prophet to later, redactional stages. Jürgen Werlitz, for instance, exploring Isa 7:1-17 and 29:1-8, two texts combining themes of salvation and punishment, argued that these passages originate from the exilic period or later. In the case of

---

Heilspropheten im üblichen Sinne nicht absprechen kann' (Becker 1968: 29). Yet, according to Joachim Becker, Isaiah also prophesied Judah's punishment.

[82]   Similarly Barth 1977: 52, 189; Hardmeier 1986: 27-31.

[83]   For Fohrer, the aim of preaching judgement was repentance: 'Es wird kein Gericht geben, wenn der Mensch von seinem bösen Wege auf den Weg des göttlichen Willens umkehrt! Das steht im Hintergrund aller Worte des Propheten' (1960: 37).

[84]   Wolff 1977; similarly Schmidt 1977.

[85]   Hoffmann 1974.

[86]   Kilian 1983: 130. For the term *Verstockungsauftrag*, see 'The Isaiah Memoir' below.

[87]   Werner 1982: 12.

[88]   Werner 1982: 197.

[89]   Becker 1999: 29; cf. Gordon 1995: 15.

[90]   Deck 1991.

29:1-8, he discerned a literary-critical distinction between words of judgement, from an exilic origin, and words of salvation, from a post-exilic origin.[91] Furthermore, 7:1-17, in Werlitz's view, is in its literary core an exilic composition that deliberately juxtaposes salvation and judgement.[92] However, even among adherents of a radical redaction-historical approach, the debate concerning the character of the histori-cal Isaiah continued. Whereas Kaiser maintained the image of Isaiah as a prophet of judgement, Becker described him as a prophet of sal-vation.[93]

The joint occurrence of prophecy of salvation and prophecy of judgement within First Isaiah has not been decisively solved, and no image of the prophet Isaiah can be taken for granted. A possible indi-cator of a solution may be pointed out here. It has been broadly ac-cepted that Isaiah's message contained *some* positive aspects, such as the Immanuel prophecy (7:14-16) and the announcement of destruc-tion of Judah's enemies (8:1-4, 28:1-4). A popular way of dealing with these positive aspects was to suggest that they had been part of Isaiah's preaching but had been, in one way or another, overruled. Ei-ther the positive message had been conditional from the outset and thus implicitly overruled by the disbelief of the recipients, or Isaiah's message had initially (partly) been positive, but at a later stage during his prophetic career changed into prophecy of judgement. In any case, the positive aspects represent an earlier, superseded stage, whereas prophecy of judgement, characterising Isaiah as a classical prophet, became decisive for Isaiah's message. This transition from 'earlier' (positive) to 'later' (negative) has traditionally been projected onto the life of the prophet. However, given the recent shift in the exegesis of Isaiah, it would be natural to suggest that this transition may have taken place at some stage in the redactional development of the Isaiah tradition. In Becker's words: 'Ist die 'unheilstheologische Wende' *biographisch-psychologisch* aus dem Leben des Propheten heraus oder aber *literarisch-redaktionsgeschichtlich* mit der Buchwerdung zu erklären?'[94]

In my view, the second alternative merits serious attention (though I would like to stress that this need not result in a one-dimensional

---

[91]   Werlitz 1992: 307-320.
[92]   Werlitz 1992: 213-250.
[93]   Becker 1997: 286-287.
[94]   Becker 2004: 57; similarly Collins 1993: 13.

picture of the historical Isaiah as a 'Heilsprophet'). The exegetical issue of what kind of prophet emerges from the earliest layer of the
Isaiah tradition, is of course related to a broader, religious-historical
question: are the 'classical prophets' a specific type of prophets, or do
they represent a specific image of prophets, which exists in the biblical
literature but not in the ancient world? Again, the second alternative
deserves consideration (see 1.2.4 below).

The Isaiah Memoir

Isa 6-8, traditionally called the Isaiah memoir (*Denkschrift*), has
played a decisive role in scholarly views of the relation between the
historical Isaiah and the text of First Isaiah. For a great scholarly majority, Isaiah is the author of an early version of Isa 6-8. This perception defines the view of Isaiah as a 'writing prophet', which
subsequently can be used as a model for the rest of First Isaiah. Similarly, scholars who challenged this common view, such as Kaiser and
Becker, took as their point of departure the *Denkschrift* as well; a
change of view on the *Denkschrift* led to a different assessment of
First Isaiah as a whole.[95]

Traditionally, two elements within the Isaiah memoir are considered of particular importance. In the first place, 6:9-11 is commonly
regarded as the testimony *par excellence* for Isaiah as a prophet of
judgement and, by extension, as a *locus classicus* of biblical prophecy:[96]

> He (Yahweh) said, 'Go and say to this people: Keep listening, but do
> not comprehend; keep looking, but do not understand. Make the mind
> of this people dull, and stop their ears, and shut their eyes, so that they
> may not look with their eyes, and listen with their ears (...). Then I said,
> How long, O Yahweh? And he said: Until cities lie waste without in-
> habitant, and houses without people, and the land is utterly desolate.

Secondly, 7:9b, the conclusion of a prophecy to Ahaz, 'If you do not
stand firm in faith, you shall not stand at all', was believed to identify
Isaiah as the originator of the concept of faith as a condition for salvation. This has been often interpreted as an important moment in the
history of prophecy. Whereas prophets in Israel and among other na-

---

[95]   In the preface to his commentary on Isaiah 1-12, Kaiser (1981: 9) explains that
his understanding of the *Denkschrift* was fundamental to his assessment of First Isaiah
as a whole. Once it is allowed that the *Denkschrift* is a composition reflecting the
situation of the sixth century, the rest follows almost automatically.

[96]   Becker 1999: 146.

tions, for centuries had promised salvation *tout court*, Isaiah, as one of the first classical prophets, demanded faith as a condition for salvation, and, when this condition was not met, announced Yahweh's punishment instead. It was held that the prophet Isaiah was the author of 6:1-8:18 in its literary core, and that this text represented his memoirs concerning the so-called Syro-Ephraimitic crisis (734-732 BCE).[97] This view functioned as an important pillar in twentieth-century exegesis of First Isaiah, and has remained popular.[98] The image of Isaiah following from this was that of a preacher of judgement and as an apostle of the condition of faith. This view, however, has become challenged.

First, doubt was raised by the observation that 6:9-10, the hardening order (*Verstockungsauftrag*), as it is formulated (see the quotation above) cannot be qualified as a prophetic *announcement*, but must be regarded as *reflection* on the prophetic task. Generally, scholars attempted to overcome this difficulty in either of two ways. Some proposed to distinguish between the present formulation of 6:9-10, which might be secondary, and the message of hardening as such, which from the outset was part of Isaiah's prophetic preaching.[99] More popular however has been the interpretation of 6:9-10 as the product of Isaiah's own reflection: 'Jesaja verarbeitet produktiv seine Erfahrungen des Scheiterns seiner Botschaft als gottgewollten Vorgang'.[100] In this way, 6:9-10 effectively is Isaiah's reformulation of what he during his ministry had come to understand as Yahweh's intention.[101]

The weakness of this solution is that it requires speculation on the life of the historical prophet and his psyche. Some scholars have therefore proposed a different solution. Uwe Becker and Ulrich Berges have argued on literary-critical, redaction-historical, and particularly

---

[97] For the understanding of Isa 6-8 as Isaiah's memoir, the views of Bernhard Duhm and Karl Budde have been of fundamental importance, see Barthel 1997: 38; Reventlow 1987: 62-67.

[98] E.g. Barthel 1997: 60-65; Blum 1996: 550-552; Clements 2000: 89-102.

[99] E.g. Von Rad 1960: 158-162.

[100] Höffken 2004: 119. This is the position of Wildberger 1965-82: 242. Furthermore, Hardmeier (1986: 24 and 28) qualifies the announcement of hardening (*Verstockung*) in 6:9-10 as fictive, and reflective of the failure of Isaiah's preceding preaching, but nevertheless maintains Isaiah's authorship of 6:1-8:18. See further Hardmeier 1986: 22: 'allein schon die Textform von Jes 6,1-8,8* [weist] das Dargestellte als Retrospektive aus'.

[101] This has sometimes been designated as a retrojection of Isaiah's negative experiences as a prophet. For this discussion, see Hardmeier 1986: 21-24.

intent-critical grounds, that the 'message' of 6:9-11 must be separated from the vision report preceding it (6:1-8). They believe that the vision report in an earlier version was reinterpreted and reworked from a judgement-theological perspective in the exilic or post-exilic period (6:9-11).

A second point of doubt follows from the interpretation of 7:1-17. Whereas Isa 6 and 8 are first-person accounts (Isaiah is narrator), 7:1-17 is a third-person account about Isaiah.[102] Furthermore, it has become clear that 7:1-17 is related to other texts, such as 2 Kgs 16 and 2 Kgs 18-20 (Isa 36-39). Various scholars, such as Kaiser, Becker and Werlitz, have suggested a (post)exilic origin for 7:1-17, interpreting the account as reflecting the Hezekiah stories of 2 Kgs 18-20 (Isa 36-38) and as presenting Ahaz as the antitype of Hezekiah.[103] This does not exclude the possibility that 7:1-17 embodies earlier, prophetic material, but it renders the view of 7:1-17 as an account written by Isaiah unlikely.

Once it is realised that Isa 6-8 is not a literary unity *aus einem Guß* but a redactional composition, the authorship of Isaiah needs to be reconsidered. The Isaianic provenance of the hardening order (6:9-10) and the principle of the condition of faith (7:9b) are to be reconsidered too. The *Denkschrift*-hypothesis can no longer function as a pillar of the exegesis of First Isaiah.[104]

1.1.4   The Current State of Affairs

The discussion between Uwe Becker and Jörg Barthel illustrates the current state of affairs with regard to the prophetic books in general and that of Isaiah in particular.[105] Whereas Becker's minimum of early

---

[102] The proposal to change 7:1-17 into a first-person account has to be rejected. E.g. Barthel 1997: 120; Reventlow 1987: 65.

[103] Kaiser 1981: 143-144; Werlitz 1992: 225-231; Becker 1997: 24-60. Among the scholars that have suggested a connection between 7:1-17 and 2 Kgs 18-20 (Isa 36-38) also Ackroyd (1982; 1984) and Blenkinsopp (2000b) can be mentioned.

[104] Cf. Reventlow 1987: 67.

[105] Becker 2003; Barthel 2003. Recently, Wagner (2006) published a monograph on Isa 6:1-9:6. In his view, the earliest, eighth-century layer of the *Denkschrift* consists of 7:2-8a.9-14.16-17; 8:1-4.6-8, whereas 6:1-11*, 7:20 and 9:1-6, which he equally considers as Isaianic material, were added to it during later stages. Whereas Wagner's assessment of Isa 6:1-9:6 to an important extent (in particular with regard to Isa 6 and 8) resembles that of Barthel 1997, I find Barthel's analysis of 7:1-17 as a later reworking of early oracular material, and of 9:1-6 as part of a seventh-century redaction, more convincing than that of Wagner. In general, Wagner remains close to

material characterises Isaiah as a 'Heilsprophet',[106] Barthel reckons that a substantial literary layer within Isa 6-8 and 28-31 can be attributed to the hand of Isaiah or one of his disciples.[107] Becker and Barthel agree however on various important issues: 1) The search for the origins of the prophetic books, and thus for the earliest stages of the prophetic traditions, is an indispensable aspect of critical exegesis.[108] 2) The point of departure for this search can only be what we have to hand: the written texts of the prophetic books, and not what we have in mind: concepts of the historical prophet and his preaching.[109] 3) The words of Isaiah are not directly accessible since they have been integrated in written compositions. Their *Sitz im Leben* is overshadowed by their *Sitz in der Literatur*.[110]

Becker and Barthel agree that Isa 6-8, the *Denkschrift*, in its literary core (6:1-11, 7:1-17, 8:1-18) is 'eine gewachsene Größe'.[111] Within Isa 6 and 8, both make a distinction between *prophetic material* representing the initial preaching of Isaiah—i.e. the vision of Isa 6*[112] and a prophecy against Ephraim and Aram in 8:1-4—and *reflective material* that belongs to the literary level of Isa 6 and 8 as written compositions, e.g. 6:9-10 and 8:5-8.[113] However, Barthel and Becker fundamentally disagree with regard to the provenance of the earliest composition, 6:1-11 and 8:1-18. According to Barthel, Isaiah himself wrote it shortly after the events of 734-732 BCE, affected by the rejection of his words by the people. The compositions 6:1-11 and 8:1-18 are marked by the prophet's later insight that the rejection of his

---

the traditional position by attributing the following aspects to the preaching of the historical prophet: 1) an initially supportive message; 2) announcements of judgement over Judah; and 3) a vision of future peace. The importance of Wagner's study lies in the traditio-historical investigation of the material included in Isa 6:1-9:6.

[106] Becker 1997: 286; Becker 2003: 119, 123.
[107] For an overview of their positions, see Köckert 2003: 114-116.
[108] Becker 2003: 117; Barthel 2003: 133.
[109] Becker 2003: 123; Barthel 2003: 125, 133.
[110] Becker 2003: 123; Barthel 2003: 133. In this respect, Barthel and Becker stand in opposition to the assumption by earlier scholarship that prophetic words can be lifted up from their literary context with relative ease (cf. Höffken 2004: 23). According to Barthel, the prophetic words cannot be easily grasped, since the basic literary context in which they are included is already characterised by reflection on, and interpretation of, the prophetic words.
[111] Becker 2003: 122; Barthel 2003: 130.
[112] Whereas Becker discerns an original vision report (6:1-8*), Barthel acknowledges an original visionary *experience* of Isaiah behind 6:1-8, but not an original report.
[113] Becker 2003: 120-122; Barthel 2003: 129-132.

words was due to Yahweh's will and that the punishment of the people had become irreversible.[114] The *Verstockungsauftrag* (6:9-10), in Barthel's view, is not part of the original visionary experience, nor is it fictitious (contra Becker). Instead, it follows from Isaiah's reflection on the rejection of his words.[115] Within 6:1-11, two radically different experiences of Isaiah merge: an earlier visionary experience (behind 6:1-8), and a later experience that the people rejected his message (behind 6:9-11). Yet, Barthel does not accept a literary-critical distinction between 6:1-8 and 6:9-11.[116]

Becker suggests the existence of a small collection of Isaianic words (6:1-8*, 8:1-4*, and some further texts), preserved in a Jerusalem archive. Some time after the collapse of the Judaean state in the sixth century, these prophetic words underwent a literary reworking, marked by *Unheilstheologie* (e.g. 6:9-11*, 8:5-8*). This reworking represented the birth of prophecy of judgement and formed the initial stage of the development of the prophetic books.[117] Whereas the 'unheilstheologische Wende' between 8:1-4 and 8:5-8 is obvious,[118] the case of 6:1-11 is more ambiguous. On the one hand, a literary-critical distinction between 6:1-8 and 6:9-11 cannot be decisively proven.[119] On the other, 6:9-10 is evidently formulated secondarily, and attempts to attribute it to the level of the historical Isaiah are equally uncertain.[120]

Barthel and Becker both regard 7:1-17 as a *Fremdkörper* within Isa 6-8.[121] Barthel qualifies 7:1-17 as a 'Neugestaltung' of earlier, prophetic words, which is marked by a dynastic-critical tendency and which reacts to the disastrous events of 701 BCE.[122] Becker, by con-

---

[114] Barthel 1997: 81, 109-110. For a similar position, see Blum 1996; 1997.
[115] Barthel 1997: 106-107; 2003: 129.
[116] Barthel 2003: 128-129.
[117] Becker 2003: 120-122.
[118] Becker 2003: 120; Barthel 2003: 131-133.
[119] Barthel 2003: 128. Becker's main trump is the intent-critical argument that 6:9-11 aims to explain the sixth-century disasters as having been caused by Yahweh himself. Becker (2003: 121) characterises this as a 'Versuch einer Theodicee', which is criticised by Barthel 2003: 128.
[120] According to Barthel (2003: 129), Isa 6:1-11 combines Isaiah's memories of a visionary experience in the past (his commission as a prophet) and his later experience that the message he preached was rejected. Barthel argues that the *Verstockungsauftrag* resolves the conflict between intent and effect of the prophetic message by attributing it to Yahweh, but has to admit: 'aber auf der Ebene der prophetischen Erfahrung bleibt er ungelöst'.
[121] Becker 2003: 122; Barthel 2003: 130.
[122] Barthel 1997: 151-153.

trast, proposes the literary dependency of 7:1-17 on the Hezekiah stories, 2 Kgs 18-20 // Isa 36-39, and argues that 7:1-17 deliberately pictures Ahaz as an antitype of Hezekiah.[123] In my view, Becker is right to
regard 7:1-17 as mirroring the Hezekiah stories: Ahaz is purposefully
portrayed as an antitype of Hezekiah, and Barthel's argument for regarding 7:1-17 as the earlier composition is unconvincing.[124] Barthel
on the other hand is right to distinguish within 7:1-17 between the
composition and the earlier prophetic material included in it. Whereas
the 'unheilsprophetische' outlook of 7:1-17 presents Yahweh's
judgement on the Davidic dynasty as a whole (7:9b, 7:13-14a.17), the
'heilprophetische' oracles are addressed to Ahaz as an individual (7:4-
9a, 7:14b.16).[125] The essence of Becker's approach to Isa 6 and 8 is the
distinction between the original 'heilprophetische' words and their
later 'unheilstheologische' edition. It is difficult to understand why
Becker does not apply a similar approach to 7:1-17. That 7:1-17 as a
composition reflects the Hezekiah stories, does not exclude the possibility that it incorporates earlier prophetic material. The composition
7:1-17 has a profoundly negative tendency,[126] but it incorporates prophetic words that are marked by a positive tone.

Both Barthel and Becker make a distinction within Isa 6-8 between
the earliest material representing prophetic activity and a later,
reflective, literary context. Whereas the early material has a positive
nature, the later reflective material has a markedly negative nature.
The question is however how to qualify the basic literary compositions of Isa 6:1-11 and 8:1-18. In his recent contribution, Barthel no
longer explicitly identifies Isaiah as the author, but he still argues for
an early date close to the prophetic preaching. His first argument is
that Becker's explanation, which assumes a two hundred-year gap between the prophetic words in the eighth century and their first literary
reworking in the early post-exilic period, is inadequate.[127] In this, I
agree with Barthel (see below). Secondly, Barthel argues that the more

---

[123]   Becker 2003: 122-123; see further Becker 1997: 21-60.

[124]   Barthel (2003: 130) argues that since the announcement of 7:17 relates to the
events of 701 BCE, and since it depicts the events as disastrous, 7:1-17 cannot be dependent on the Hezekiah stories, which present the events of 701 from a focus on Jerusalem's salvation. However, the question of whether 7:1-17 depends on the
Hezekiah stories must be decided through textual analysis (see chapter 2.1.2) and the
connection between 7:1-17 and 701 BCE does not hold.

[125]   Barthel 2003: 130.

[126]   Contra Becker 2003: 123.

[127]   Barthel 2003: 135.

we explain the prophetic books as products of later reflection, the more we lose the incalculable speaking and acting of God which the prophets announced and which determines the beginning and direction of the tradition process. The biblical God of history is then killed by reflection, and becomes a God of theory.[128] This theological argument ignores the fact that the entire prophetic tradition is presented in the shape of 'nachträgliche theologische Reflexion', be it from the hand of Isaiah himself or from (much) later redactors.[129] More importantly, this argument reveals a theological *parti pris*.[130] Barthel, in the end, demands an exceptional status for the biblical prophets such as Isaiah.[131] This is at odds with the view that the point of departure for the exegesis cannot be a perception of the historical prophet, but only the text.

Becker defends a principal distinction between the prophetic words and their literary edition. He reinforces his argument by pointing out the analogy between Isaiah and the Assyrian prophets as being both *Heilspropheten*.[132] Barthel opposes this by stating that the issue of the 'proprium' of Old Testament prophecy is oversimplified when similarity with ancient Near Eastern prophecy becomes the criterion for the exegetical analysis.[133] As an appeal for methodological care, this criticism is justified (see 1.3.1 below).

Neither Barthel's nor Becker's position is fully convincing. Becker's main thesis falters since it is incomprehensible why a post-exilic author would suddenly pick up some fragments of ancient *Heilsprophetie* kept away for two centuries, in order to rework them into compositions of *Unheilstheologie*.[134] Barthel's portrayal of Isaiah as not only a deliverer of prophetic words but also as an interpreter

---

[128]   Barthel 2003: 135.

[129]   Becker 2004: 47-48.

[130]   Cf. Barthel's disqualification of critical exegesis as an exponent of a general 'säkularisierten Bewusstseins' (2003: 135).

[131]   Isaiah's words may somewhat resemble the ancient Near Eastern oracles but the driving force behind his 'Heilsworten' is not the well-being of the state, the dynasty or the temple, but 'die Wahrnehmung des "Heiligen Israels" als der Tiefendimension aller Geschichte' (Barthel 2003: 132-133).

[132]   Becker 2003: 117-119; cf. 1997: 287.

[133]   Barthel 2003: 134. Further criticism relates to Becker's dependence on terminological argumentation and 'Sprachstatistik', and the ease of dating passages from First Isaiah late by claiming literary dependence on parts from other biblical books; see Barthel 2003: 133. Hardmeier's criticism (1986: 5, 14-19) against the 'neo-literary-criticism' of Kaiser, to a great extent applies to Becker too (see note 51).

[134]   Dietrich 1999: 336; Barthel (2003: 135) states: 'die Frage, warum das schmale jesajanische Erbe überhaupt eine geradezu explosionsartig sich entwickelnde literarische Arbeit freigesetz hat, bleibt ungeklärt'.

who afterwards reflected on his own message and reworked it into literary compositions, has not been made historically plausible either. A critical review of their respective positions however shows a direction for further study.

1) The discussion of the positions of Barthel and Becker leads to the suggestion that a distinction can be made between early *prophetic material* (6:1-8, 7:4-9a, 7:14b.16, 8:1-4) on the one hand, and later *reflective material* (6:9-11, 7:9b, 7:13-14a.17; 8:5-8) that marks the literary composition of Isa 6-8 in its basic form on the other. Isa 6-8* is a literary composition in which earlier prophetic words are incorporated, and the intent of the literary composition clearly differs from the earlier, prophetic words.

2) The literary Isaiah presented in the book must be carefully distinguished from the historical prophet, who can only be a result of reconstruction.[135] The search for the historical prophet, the words to be attributed to him, and their earliest, literary development, should however not only be a literary-critical, but also a historical exercise. The literary development of the prophetic tradition must be illuminated from a historical perspective, and the reconstruction of the historical prophet must be historically plausible. Exegetical analysis should be guided by historical awareness, and not by a theological *parti pris*.[136]

3) The historical question about the eighth-century prophet cannot be solved by the study of the book of Isaiah alone.[137] It is not unreasonable to expect that the historical prophets, to a greater or lesser extent, resembled their ancient Near Eastern counterparts.[138] It is however of methodological importance to bring in the analogy at the right moment, i.e. *after* the exegetical and historical analysis, and not as a criterion for it, and to carry out a complete comparison instead of just claiming similarity.

---

[135] Barthel 2003: 126-127.
[136] Contra Barthel 2003: 135.
[137] Becker 1999: 152.
[138] Becker 2003: 119.

1.2   Recent Developments in the Study of Prophecy

1.2.1   The Rise of the Comparative Study of Prophecy

With the discovery of the royal archives of Nineveh at the end of the nineteenth century, the first direct evidence of Mesopotamian prophecy became available: the Assyrian prophecies from the seventh century BCE. Despite their availability in transliteration and translation,[139] the Assyrian prophecies for many decades hardly received any attention. Their neglect—in Manfred Weippert's words their "Aschenputteldasein"—continued into the 1970s.[140]

It was the prophecies in the Old Babylonian letters from Mari, discovered since the 1930s, which effectuated an important shift in the study of prophecy. Some time after the first discoveries it had become widely recognised that the Mari archives contained a number of letters reporting prophetic oracles that formed a counterpart to Israelite prophecy.[141] Martin Noth, for instance, pointed out that the similarities between prophecy in Mari and in the Old Testament were undeniable and significant, because 'etwas wirklich Vergleichbares sich sonst in der ganzen Welt des alten Orients bisher nicht gefunden hat'.[142] This not only confirms that the Assyrian prophecies were often ignored as a counterpart to Israelite prophecy, but it also shows how the Mari prophecies fitted into a concept of historical development as a forerunner of Israelite prophecy. In Noth's view it could not be doubted that the Mari prophets to some extent paralleled the Old Testament prophets, since both functioned as messengers of the divine. The Mari prophets however represented a preceding stage of prophecy.[143]

The Mari prophecies were held to provide insight into the prehistory of prophecy and to resemble Israelite prophecy on the level of primitive, pre-classical, ecstatic prophecy.[144] However, with regard to the content of the prophetic messages, the gap between Mari and the Old Testament was regarded as huge, especially with regard to the great prophets. For Noth, any comparison in content between the bib-

---

[139]   For the earliest publications, see Parpola's bibliography (1997: CIX-CX).
[140]   Weippert 1985: 56; 2001a: 32-33. Notable exceptions are Greßmann 1914; Langdon 1914: 146; Guillaume 1938: 48; Herrmann 1965: 55-59.
[141]   Schmitt 1982: 7; cf. already Haldar 1945: 90.
[142]   Noth 1957: 239.
[143]   Noth 1957: 239.
[144]   For an overview of the literature on Mari, including studies dealing with prophecy, see Heintz 1990: 17-124, and subsequent updates, Heinz 1992-98.

lical prophecies and the Mari prophecies was out of the question.[145] As formulated in his *Geschichte Israels*: 'Wir kennen zu dieser Erscheinung der "Prophetie" (i.e. biblical prophecy) kein wirkliches Gegenstück aus der Geschichte der Menschheit.'[146] This represented a common view of biblical scholarship. The classical prophets from the eighth-century onwards, it was held, had no counterpart in the ancient Near Eastern world. As formulated by Hans-Joachim Kraus:

> Dominant ist also die Gerichtsbotschaft. Ob überhaupt und in welchem Ausmaß Heilsankündigungen mit der Gerichtsbotschaft der vorexilischen Propheten verbunden waren, wird von Fall zu Fall sorgfältig zu ermitteln sein. Eines ist gewiß: Zu diesem Auftreten der alttestamentlichen Propheten gibt es kein wirkliche Parallele in der Geschichte der Religionen, allenfalls partielle Berührungspunkte.[147]

The Mari prophecies effected a change within the study of prophecy, which the Assyrian prophecies had failed to do. Several reasons may be mentioned for this. First, the Assyrian prophecies were ignored partly because they were in most cases not clearly presented as prophecies.[148] Second, the Mari prophecies were more easily accessible.[149] Third, the early provenance of the Mari prophecies, in the eighteenth century BCE, helped their popularity as the example of extra-biblical prophecy *par excellence*, whereas the seventh-century date of the Assyrian oracles added to their marginality. The Mari prophecies conveniently fitted in a historical scheme of development representing a kind of primitive, pre-classical prophecy, far removed in time from the great classical prophets. The Assyrian prophecies, by contrast, dated from what was considered the heyday of classical prophecy, which according to scholarly preconceptions was beyond comparison. A fourth reason for the neglect of the Assyrian oracles may lie in the fact that prophetic activity was considered to be typical of West-Semitic culture and alien to Mesopotamian culture.[150] This worked well for the Mari prophecies, which were explained as being influenced by the West-Semitic population stratum of northern Meso-

---

[145] Noth 1957: 241.
[146] Noth 1956: 232.
[147] Kraus 1982: 542. See further e.g. Schmökel 1951: 55-56; Herrmann 1965: 13-15, 306-308; Malamat 1966: 208; Nötscher 1966: 187; Huffmon 1968: 101-124; Saggs 1978: 144-152, 187; Schmitt 1982: 129; Koch 1995: 14, 17.
[148] They were often presented as 'priestly oracles' or as 'oracles', see e.g. Pfeiffer 1955; Biggs 1969.
[149] See Nissinen 1993: 218.
[150] E.g. Oppenheim 1977: 222.

potamia. Again, the Assyrian prophecies did not fit into the scholarly concepts.[151]

The uniqueness of the classical prophets was usually related to their social criticism and their prophecy of judgement. Furthermore, it was often held that their unique preaching grounded in their perception of history as the playground of the realisation of Yahweh's plan. The prophetic perception of history was regarded as unparalleled.[152] This has been criticised by Bertil Albrektson who demonstrated that the concept of God's purposeful control of history and the belief in the course of events as a realisation of divine intentions were common notions in the ancient Near East.[153] Henry Saggs, building on the views of Albrektson, qualified both the Mari prophecies and the Assyrian prophecies as counterparts of Old Testament prophecy.[154] Yet, he did not challenge the common view: 'although uniqueness cannot be claimed on grounds of mechanism, when we come to look at the nature of the message, it may be possible to see a significant difference'.[155] Whereas the Mesopotamian prophecies relate to royal affairs, the classical prophets in Israel address the people as a whole. Their messages transcended the immediate historical context, being universal statements about God's nature and his demands upon man. In this way, the canonical prophets transcended the limitations of ancient Near Eastern religion, including traditional Yahwism. So, if there is one unique aspect of Israel's religion, it is, according to Saggs, 'canonical prophecy'.[156]

Until today, the classical prophets are often granted a *status aparte*. They are held to represent a high-spirited and moral prophecy of judgement, whereas the ancient Near East offers parallels for a more primitive 'pre-classical' type of prophecy. Some notable exceptions to the common view can however be mentioned. Morton Smith, in a sketch of the common religion in the ancient Near East, also mentions the prophets who 'everywhere claimed to know by revelation the

---

[151] See Ellis 1989: 145. In the 1970s and 1980s the view dominated that the oracular activity of the prophets had been imported to Assyria from the West.

[152] See e.g. Lindblom 1962: 106, 325; Saggs 1978: 67; Barthel 2003: 132-133.

[153] Albrektson 1967: 96. Albrektson points out that what may be regarded as 'unique' from the perspective of the religious commitment of modern exegetes, is not necessarily 'unique' in the context of the ancient Near East. See Lambert 1970 for a critical review of Albrektson's study.

[154] Saggs 1978: 139-152.

[155] Saggs 1978: 149.

[156] Saggs 1978: 187.

country's state of obedience or disobedience and the rewards or punishments soon to be allotted'.[157] Similarly, Friedrich Ellermeier rejected a sharp distinction between prophets of salvation and prophets
of judgement, arguing that the Mari prophets show traces normally
considered as typical of the classical prophets of the Old Testament.[158]
These dissenting voices deserve renewed attention.

1.2.2   Recent Study of Biblical Prophecy

Recent study on biblical prophecy has not fundamentally challenged
the traditional view. Klaus Koch's study of the classical prophets
aimed to comprehend them as theologians and to display their
'geistiges Eigenprofil'.[159] In Koch's presentation, the great eighth-
century   prophets   are   representatives   of   'Unwiderrufliche
Unheilsprophetie'. Their radical social criticism and announcements
of judgement are without parallel in the ancient Near East.[160] Isaiah is
depicted   along   traditional   lines   and   characterised   as   the
'wortgewaltigste' among the classical prophets.[161] Isaiah's *geistiges
Eigenprofil* is a theological synthesis of main themes found within
First Isaiah. Joseph Blenkinsopp, rejecting the conventional distinction between 'primitive' and 'classical' prophecy,[162] nevertheless described the eighth-century prophets as representing a new type of
intellectual leadership, marking a decisive turning-point in Israel's
history.[163] Despite his statement that the prophetic books are post-
exilic compositions, Blenkinsopp proceeds with apparent ease from
the books to the historical prophets and accepts a traditional picture of
Isaiah's life.[164]

In a programmatic contribution, Ferdinand Deist indicated future
directions for the study of prophecy.[165] In his view, the traditional
paradigm focusing on the personalities of great prophets whose words

---

[157] Smith 1952: 145.
[158] Ellermeier 1968: 165-223, esp. 172. According to Ellermeier (1968: 217) the
principal difference does not lie in the content of the prophecies, but in the fact that
the messages of the biblical prophets are considered to be still theologically relevant,
whereas the Mari prophecies are not.
[159] Koch 1995: 9.
[160] Koch 1995: 14.
[161] Koch 1995: 119.
[162] Blenkinsopp 1995: 140; 1996: 66.
[163] Blenkinsopp 1995: 141; 1996: 82.
[164] Blenkinsopp 1996: 97-110.
[165] Deist 1989.

and deeds were recorded in the books bearing their names was to be abandoned. Whereas historical-critical analysis remains necessary for reconstructing the development of the prophetic books,[166] Deist's suggested grounding a new paradigm for the study of the prophets in the socio-anthropological approach to ancient Israelite society.[167] However, this program of situating the prophets within a reconstruction of ancient Israel based on archaeology and shaped by socio-anthropological theory, has met with difficulties.

Robert Wilson's study *Prophecy and Society* (1980) has become a famous monument rather than the beginning of a new paradigm.[168] Wilson described the Old Testament prophets from a socio-anthropological point of view, dividing them into peripheral prophets and prophets taking a central position in society. However, Wilson did not deal with the question of the extent to which the biblical material could be accepted as a reliable source for pre-exilic prophecy.[169] Studies in the fields of new archaeology and socio-anthropology have made great progress, but it has proved difficult to deploy them for the study of Israelite prophecy.[170] Paula McNutt's assessment of prophecy, in the context of the reconstruction of ancient Israel, may illustrate this: 'we are still far from understanding the nature and functions of prophets in ancient Israel and Judah'.[171]

During the last few decades, biblical scholars have displayed an increased uneasiness with regard to historical prophecy. It is broadly recognised that the depiction of prophecy in the Hebrew Bible is historically questionable. As the historical and prophetic books of the Old Testament nowadays are most often approached as being first and foremost literary compositions from the Persian and Hellenistic period, they can no longer be regarded as straightforward sources of prophecy as a historical phenomenon in pre-exilic Israel. Some schol-

---

[166] Deist 1989: 16.

[167] Deist 1989: 14-18.

[168] See Kselman 1985: 124.

[169] Wilson's study, an important contribution to Israelite prophecy from a socio-anthropological angle, does not distinguish between an analysis of the portrayal of prophets in the Old Testament and the reconstruction of prophecy as a socio-historical phenomenon. Wilson offers a sociological analysis of biblical depictions of prophets, which are first and foremost literary images.

[170] Socio-anthropological depictions of Israelite prophecy have often been based on the views of Max Weber; e.g. McNutt 1999: 179-181; Blenkinsopp 1995: 115-119. For serious criticism of the application of Weber's concepts to prophecy in Israel and the ancient Near East, see Petersen 1981: 9-15.

[171] McNutt 1999: 179.

ars have even raised the question of whether the biblical prophetic books have anything to do with the phenomenon of prophecy in pre-exilic Israel at all.[172] Hans Barstad described this trend as follows:

> [B]y reducing what we find in the 'prophetic writings' of the Hebrew Bible to postexilic literary creations with little or no connection at all back into the history that went before, it may seem that recent scholarship has postulated an impassable tradition gap, and made whatever pre-exilic prophetic activity there was quite unavailable to us.[173]

The difficulty can be overcome by acknowledging that prophetic texts such as First Isaiah are not pure poetry but rather the outcome of a literary and redactional development. In order to decide to what extent it is 'prophetic', the earliest stages of the Isaiah tradition have to be explored, at first through exegetical and historical analysis, and secondly also from a comparative perspective which includes ancient Near Eastern prophecy.[174] The comparative study adds to our understanding of prophecy and supplies analogies that may confirm the exegetical and historical analysis. The route from the biblical texts to prophecy as a socio-historical phenomenon in pre-exilic Israel runs through exegesis and historical analysis on the one hand, and comparative study on the other.

1.2.3   Recent Comparative Study of Prophecy

The Assyrian prophecies have become the subject of comparative research since the 1970s, initially through the contributions of Manfred Dietrich, Herbert Huffmon, and Manfred Weippert.[175] The comparative studies were based on the view that Mesopotamian prophecy belonged to the same cultural-historical world as its Israelite counterpart preserved in the Old Testament. Prophecies from Mari and Assyria were the most obvious sources for comparative study, as they represent the only two corpora of prophetic oracles outside the Bible.[176]

---

[172] Various scholars have emphasised the gap between the prophetic books as literary products of the post-exilic period and the phenomenon of pre-exilic prophecy. For a critical review of this position, see Barstad 1993a; Heintz 1997.

[173] Barstad 1993a: 43.

[174] Cf. Barstad 1993a: 46.

[175] See the bibliography in Parpola 1997: CX-CXI.

[176] Nissinen 1993: 217.

Preliminary Issues

An important issue was the definition of prophecy. The following definition of Weippert has found scholarly approval:

> Prophecy is at stake when 'a person (a) through a cognitive experience (a vision, an auditory experience, an audio-visual appearance, a dream or the like) becomes the subject of the revelation of a deity, or several deities and, in addition, (b) is conscious of being commissioned by the deity or deities in question to convey the revelation in a verbal form (as a "prophecy" or a "prophetic speech"), or through nonverbal communicative acts ("symbolic acts"), to a third party who constitutes the actual addressee of the message'.[177]

This definition concentrates on the prophetic experience and consciousness, which are however beyond our control.[178] A simpler definition that focuses on the prophetic function as messenger of the god(s) would be: 'The prophet is a mediator who claims to receive messages direct from a divinity, by various means, and communicates these messages to recipients.'[179]

According to a recent insight, the notion of prophets as intermediaries is applicable to prophecy throughout the ancient Near East.[180] Furthermore, some facets shared by Mesopotamian, Syrian and Israelite prophets have been formulated which can tentatively function as a point of departure for comparative study: 1) prophets present communications from the divine world and serve as mediators; 2) they can draw upon inspiration through ecstasy, dreams, or visions; 3) their messages are immediately understandable; 4) they offer assurance but can also admonish or exhort the addressee.[181]

In many recent publications on prophecy enumerations of the non-biblical prophetic material can be found.[182] The evidence mainly stems from Mesopotamia and from West-Semitic areas.[183] Previously, the

---

[177] Weippert 2001b: 197; translation by Nissinen 1998: 5. For a slightly different version, see Weippert 1988: 289-290; Barstad 1993a: 46.

[178] Petersen 2000: 41.

[179] Grabbe 1995: 107.

[180] Petersen 2000: 39.

[181] See Huffmon 2000: 48.

[182] E.g. Ringgren 1982; Weippert 1988: 294-305; Ellis 1989: 134-145; Malamat 1989: 70-121; Huffmon 1992; Lemaire 1996: 427-429; Nissinen 2000a: 235-237; Nissinen 2004: 25-28. See in particular the recent sourcebook on ancient Near Eastern prophecy, Nissinen 2003a.

[183] Ancient Egypt generally falls outside the scope of comparative study of prophecy. Although various literary compositions from ancient Egypt have been qualified as 'prophetic literature', it has been argued by Shupak (1990) that prophetic oracles

dominant view was that prophetic activity was typical of West-Semitic culture, and 'deeply alien' to Mesopotamian culture,[184] where it was introduced only in eighth to seventh-century Assyria due to western influence.[185] However, a growing amount of examples of non-biblical prophecy and the widespread attestation of prophetic oracles and references to prophetic figures in time and place, has stimulated the view that prophecy was at home in the ancient Near East as one of the common forms of divination, in the West-Semitic areas as well as in Mesopotamia.[186] According to a recent understanding, there were, generally speaking, prophets in the ancient Near East, although not necessarily everywhere and at every time, who delivered oracles, although not necessarily always in the same way. They did not, however, always get attention, nor would their messages necessarily have been recorded.[187]

Comparisons

Some of the main topics that have become the subject of comparative study of prophecy may be mentioned.

Similarities between the Assyrian prophecies and parts of Second Isaiah, noticed long ago,[188] became a popular issue of comparative study.[189] Both sides represent prophecy of salvation, in which a deity presents itself (e.g. 'I am Yahweh'), in which the formula 'Fear not!' occurs, and in which salvation through divine intervention is promised. Whereas it was previously held that Second Isaiah depended on

---

are not attested in ancient Egypt: 'The image of a prophet functioning as divine messenger is absent in ancient Egypt. We look in vain for divinely inspired prophecy, or prophecy associated with symbolic revelations and visions' (1990: 24). For similar views, see Nötscher 1966: 163-170; Ben Zvi 2000: 2, note 3.

[184]   Oppenheim 1977: 222.
[185]   Tadmor 1975; 1982; Spieckermann 1982: 302; Von Soden 1985: 187; Hutter 1996: 107; Malamat 1997: 315-317. See Gordon 1993: 64-67, for a discussion of this hypothesis.
[186]   Millard 1985: 133-134; Ellis 1989: 130-135, 144-146; Nissinen 1993: 222-224; Parpola 1997: LXVII; Durand 1997: 118; Sasson 1998: 115-116; Pongratz-Leisten 1999: 49-51; Weippert 2001a: 58; Charpin 2002: 32-33.
[187]   See Nissinen 1993: 223; Nissinen 2003a: 4.
[188]   Greßmann 1914.
[189]   The similarities between the Assyrian prophecies and Second Isaiah became more generally acknowledged only much later, in particular through the work of Dijkstra (1980: 136-170), a first form-critical study to make fully use of the Assyrian prophecies, and through Spieckermann 1982: 302; Van der Toorn 1987: 95; Weippert 1982; Nissinen 1993: 235-236. For an overview, see Weippert 2001a: 37; 1988: 311, note 49.

the Assyrian sources,[190] Weippert established the view that the Assyrian oracles and the salvation oracles in Second Isaiah are examples of
a similar genre, 'oracles for the king'.[191] Isa 45:1-7, addressing King
Cyrus, is a pure form of the genre, whereas in the other salvation oracles in Second Isaiah the role traditionally taken by the king had been
shifted to the people.[192]

A further point of comparison was found in the connection of
prophecy with the royal office. Prophetic oracles provide ideological
support of the royal dynasty, both in Israel (2 Sam 7:5-17), in Mari,[193]
and in Assyria.[194] Among the shared themes we find the concepts of
the king's divine election, the divine promise to destroy the king's
enemies, the promise of peace for the land, royal succession, and the
divine paternity of the king.[195]

Various similarities in prophetic designations have been noted. The
Hebrew term *nābî'* has a counterpart in the designation *nabûm*, which
occurs in Mari and in Emar.[196] The term *nābî'* further occurs in the Lachish ostraca.[197] The title *ḥōzeh*, 'visionary', is attested on the Zakkur
Stele and in the Deir 'Allā plaster texts.[198] Furthermore, scholars have
suggested that throughout the ancient Near East, including Israel,
prophets functioned as divine messengers or intermediaries,[199] operated
in groups,[200] were connected with the royal court,[201] and could perform
symbolic actions to support their message.[202] The close relation between prophetic oracles on the one hand, and dreams and visions on
the other has been pointed out.[203] It has been noted that throughout the
ancient Near East, prophecy often relates to foreign politics and politi-

---

[190] Greßmann 1914: 289-290.
[191] Weippert 1982. According to Weippert (1972), this oracular genre had its
original *Sitz im Leben* in the ancient Near Eastern ideology of holy war; cf. Heintz
1969; Dion 1970; Van der Toorn 1987; Kang 1989. In Weippert's view, this genre
was at home in pre-exilic Israel as well (1981: 105-108; 1982: 11; 2001a: 58).
[192] Weippert 1981: 92-111; 1982: 9-11; 1988: 304-314.
[193] Malamat 1980: 79-82.
[194] Ishida 1977: 90-92.
[195] See Nissinen 1993: 233-234.
[196] Fleming 1993a: 1993b.
[197] Parker 1994.
[198] Huffmon 2000: 65; Dijkstra 1995; Lemaire 2001b.
[199] E.g. Polley 1980: 149-150; Gordon 1993: 74-75; Petersen 2000: 37-39.
[200] Huffmon 2000: 64.
[201] Huffmon 2000: 64-65.
[202] Anbar 1993: 3; Huffmon 2000: 67.
[203] Gordon 1993: 69-74.

cal-military situations, in particular situations of crisis.[204] Furthermore, reactions to prophetic messages from the ruling officials have been the subject of investigation.[205]

The earlier thesis that certain Psalms are to be qualified as cultic prophecies has been revived with the help of the Assyrian prophecies. John Hilber explored Ps 110,[206] and a range of further Psalms, such as Ps 2; 81; 89; 132,[207] from a comparative perspective, taking into account the Assyrian prophecies from the seventh century. On the basis of similarities between the Psalms and the Assyrian prophetic oracles, with regard to style, form, theme and ideology, Hilber aimed to demonstrate that these Psalms have a prophetic character.[208]

In addition to similarities, scholars have pointed out differences between Israel and its *Umwelt* with regard to prophecy. In particular differences in the content of the prophetic messages and differences with regard to the function and status of prophets have been emphasised.[209]

Most recently, the comparative study of prophecy has resulted in a range of collective volumes.[210] In particular Martti Nissinen put the Assyrian prophecies on the comparative agenda,[211] and published a sourcebook of ancient Near Eastern prophecies, *Prophets and Prophecy in the Ancient Near East* (2003). Because of the influx of comparative contributions dealing with the material from Mari and Assyria, the phenomenon of ancient Near Eastern prophecy has become well known.

The role of the biblical prophetic books in the comparative study of prophecy has however remained very limited. These books have received attention mainly on the level of expressions, metaphors and

---

[204] Anbar 1993.

[205] Parker 1993; Roberts 1997a.

[206] Hilber 2003; 2005: 76-88.

[207] Hilber 2005.

[208] Hilber (2003) concludes that Ps 110 is a cultic enthronement prophecy from the monarchic period. Furthermore Hilber (2005) concludes that the origin of the psalms containing first-person divine speech is to be explained from the model of cultic prophecy.

[209] Malamat 1998: 62; Huffmon 2000: 63-64. McFadden (1983: 133) referring to Oppenheim, argues that prophecy was dominant in Israel and technical forms of divination in Mesopotamia.

[210] Nissinen (ed.) 2000; Ben Zvi and Floyd (eds) 2000; Grabbe and Haak (eds) 2001; Lemaire (ed.) 2001; Kaltner and Stulman (eds) 2004.

[211] See bibliography.

similes.[212] Moshe Weinfeld, for instance, discerned a range of literary patterns and motifs in the prophetic books, for which he tried to provide counterparts in ancient Near Eastern texts.[213] The prophetic books however have not been studied from the angle perhaps most expected: as prophecy that has been developed into literary texts. The prophetic books have been established in biblical scholarship as literary compositions based on prophetic traditions that were developed over the course of time. For this reason, one would expect comparisons not only with Mesopotamian prophecies, but also with literary texts from the ancient Near East, in particular literary texts with a prophetic imprint or closely resembling the genre of prophecy. This kind of comparative study has however not been undertaken. Literary prophetic texts from the ancient Near East are nevertheless available. First, there is a range of texts from seventh-century Assyria that can be qualified as prophetic compositions. These texts are based on, or inspired by, prophetic oracles, but are to be regarded as literary compositions.[214] A second category is formed by the so-called literary-predictive texts, which have received due scholarly attention since the 1960s.[215] These texts however have hardly been exploited in a comparative study to prophecy:

> Unfortunately, the literary prophecies are often dissociated from OT prophecy because they are literary. This ignores the fact that much OT prophetic literature may well be literary in origin rather than merely the recording of oral prophecies. It is here that the Akkadian literary prophecies are very relevant to a study of OT prophecy: they demonstrate that written prophecies can be *scribal* creations.[216]

---

[212] Nissinen 1993: 242-247; 1991: 268-294; Weippert (1985) discusses similes from the Assyrian oracles that depict the goddesses Ištar and Mullissu as protectors of the king, comparable to Old Testament passages where Yahweh is pictured as the protector of his people.

[213] Weinfeld (1977) points to mouth-purification (Isa 6 and the *mīs pî* ritual), dreams and visions, the motif of morality versus cult, and the motif of violation of morality as a cause for destruction.

[214] Examples are SAA 9 3 and 9, SAA 3 13 and 44-47; for these texts, see chapter 6.2.1 and 6.2.2.

[215] These texts include the Šulgi and Marduk prophecies (Borger 1971); the Dynastic prophecy (Grayson 1975b); and the Uruk prophecy (Hunger and Kaufman 1975). On these texts, see Ellis 1979; 1989: 157; Grabbe 1995: 92-94. These texts are to be distinguished from prophetic oracles since they do not have an oral background, and are to be qualified as literary compositions (Grayson 1975: 13; Ellis 1989: 147).

[216] Grabbe 1995: 94. So far, the literary prophecies have only been related to biblical apocalyptic texts; see Grayson 1980: 184; Kaufman 1977; Lambert 1978; Ringgren 1983; Tadmor 1981; cf. Ellis 1989: 147, 172.

The reason why the prophetic books have not been fully included in the comparative study of prophecy is probably the common view that these books form a literary genre *sui generis*.[217] However, the recent exegetical approach to the prophetic books from a perspective of literary expansion and redactional development calls for a new step in the comparative study of prophecy. The literary afterlife of prophecy, in particular the issue of the transition from prophecy to literature, should become a subject of comparative study.

1.2.4   *The Classical Prophets Revisited*

The comparative study of prophecy has left the opinion concerning the classical prophets mostly unaltered. The preaching of the classical prophets was and is generally considered as something without parallel in the history of the ancient Near East. The image of the classical prophets as true prophets, opposed to the wicked establishment of their time and characterised by prophecy of judgement and a sharp rejection of moral abuse, functioned as one of the pillars of the commonly accepted view of Israel's religion and Old Testament theology.[218] Because of this, the status of the classical prophets as historical figures was hardly questioned at all.

The classical prophets were clearly distinguished, both from their adversaries, the false prophets, and their predecessors, the pre-classical prophets. Weippert, for instance, held that the history of Israel and Judah was marked by the controversy between prophets who promised salvation and the classical prophets who foretold punishment. He regarded the Mesopotamian prophecies as being important for a better insight into the phenomenon of salvation prophecy in Israel that had disappeared together with the dynasties it had supported, whereas the messages of the oppositional prophets had been considered worth preserving and finally resulted in the prophetic books.[219] Furthermore, the view of a transition from the early, pre-classical prophets to the classical prophets as an important change, taking place during the ministry of the prophet Amos, was again defended by Jörg

---

[217] E.g. McFadden 1983: 128.
[218] For a critical assessment of this common view, see Cryer 1991: 79.
[219] Weippert 1988: 310-311.

Jeremias.[220] Scholars still widely hold that the classical prophets began to write down their messages themselves in response to the dismissive reaction of the people to their preaching, and that this was how the genre of the prophetic books originated.[221] In this way, scholars have remained inclined to accept a vital connection between the historical prophets and their preaching, and the prophetic books named after them.

Recently however some scholars have questioned the historical validity of the image of the classical prophets. Following the recent shift of focus from the prophetic personalities to the prophetic books as literary products, the prophetic books are regarded, first and foremost, as compilations from the Persian period or later. Instead of reading the prophetic books as having emerged from the mind of prophetic personalities, they are now approached as the end-result of a lengthy development of prophetic traditions. Nissinen has expressed his doubts whether the biblical images of the great prophets represented the situation of prophecy as a socio-historical phenomenon in pre-exilic Israel and Judah.[222] Others completely rejected the image of the classical prophets as a historical reality.[223] Uwe Becker concluded his monograph on First Isaiah with the thesis that the historical Isaiah was a prophet of salvation.[224] In a further study, he argued that the classical prophecy of judgement was never a historical phenomenon, but a literary creation from post-exilic times. Only in the course of the development of the prophetic books was the image of the classical prophets of judgement created:

> Am Anfang stand vielmehr die "vorklassische" Heils- und Mahnprophetie […]. Die Art der Prophetie ist aber nur noch sehr gebrochen in den Büchern der Propheten enthalten, weil diese in der erkennbaren Absicht entstanden sind, das eingetretene Unheil rückblickend als Erfüllung längst zuvor ergangener prophetischer Unheilsansagen zu begründen.[225]

---

[220] Jeremias 1996: 496: 'Der Wandel von den "früheren" zu den "späteren" Propheten, der in der Entstehung der neuen Literaturgattung Prophetenbuch seinen Ausdruck fand, hat sich in der Biographie des Amos selber vollzogen.'

[221] Jeremias 1996: 484-485. This is also a main thesis of Barthel 1997.

[222] Nissinen 1993: 253.

[223] E.g. Loretz 1992.

[224] Becker 1997: 286-287.

[225] Becker 2001: 162. See also Kratz 1997: 22.

The recent view that the prophetic books are the end-result of lengthy and complicated literary-redactional developments leaves room for the following suggestion. At the basis of the traditions that ultimately developed into the prophetic books may have lain short prophetic words that initially were orally delivered. It is this earliest stage of the prophetic traditions that may be compared to the examples of ancient Near Eastern prophecy.[226] In this light, it may be considered whether the classical prophets as ethical preachers and foretellers of judgement might be a later, exilic or post-exilic image.[227] These suggestions, although not yet sufficient to establish a new understanding of prophecy in ancient Israel, merit serious attention.

1.3   Aim and Focus of the Present Study

1.3.1   Question of Research

The history of research presented above leads to the following conclusions.

1) An unbroken scholarly tradition takes First Isaiah as a direct source for pre-exilic prophecy and the figure presented in it as one of the great historical prophets. However, we have also seen that the recent shift of focus to the book as a whole, has rendered problematic the relationship between the book and the phenomenon of pre-exilic prophecy. The question of the historicity of the figures behind the prophetic books has become a matter of debate.

2) We have seen that the comparative study of prophecy has recently become a fruitful enterprise. However, one major field still not explored is a comparative study focusing on the prophetic books. There is furthermore discussion with regard to the classical prophets as historical figures, the phenomenon of prophecy in ancient Israel, and the earliest stages of the traditions that ultimately resulted in the prophetic books.

The best way to deal with these issues is undertaking a comparative study of prophecy that includes the earliest layers of the prophetic tra-

---

[226]   See Kratz 2003: 54-67; cf. Lemaire 2001a: 15.
[227]   Cf. Collins 1993: 13: 'Something happened which removed biblical prophecy from that whole area (i.e. ancient Near Eastern divination), and it is my contention ... that the 'something' was a literary development rather than a sociological or an anthropological one.' See also Weippert 2003: 286.

ditions behind the biblical prophetic books. The first step must be the exploration of the origin of the prophetic traditions and their initial developments, long before they resulted in the books as we have them. The second step is to include these early prophetic traditions in a comparative study of prophecy in the ancient Near East. The present study aims to contribute to this project. First, it explores the origin and earliest development of the Isaiah tradition. Second, it includes this in a comparative study of prophecy, focusing on the seventh-century Assyrian prophecies. This study has an analytical part (I), consisting of chapters 2 and 3, and a comparative part (II), consisting of chapters 4, 5 and 6. The reason for the division into two parts is that the prophetic material from First Isaiah and from seventh-century Assyria must be investigated in its own right before a comparison is undertaken. In particular for the Isaiah material this is important from a methodological point of view: one must determine on exegetical and historical, and not on comparative grounds, which parts of the book represent the earliest prophetic tradition and its first development in the Assyrian period. Only after the earliest stages of the Isaiah tradition have been identified and the prophetic material explored, can it be studied from a comparative perspective.

1.3.2   *Analytical Part*

Part I of the study consists of a description of the material, which is used for the comparison carried out in the second part. Chapter 2 presents an exegetical analysis of First Isaiah as a source of pre-exilic prophecy and its earliest development. Chapter 3 consists of a description of the Assyrian sources relating to prophecy.

Traditionally, First Isaiah has been seen as an obvious source for the Assyrian period. Although First Isaiah was believed to include later elements as well, its natural background was regarded to be the pre-exilic period. Exegesis aimed at identifying a 'Proto-Isaiah', a version of First Isaiah from the eighth or seventh century, written by the historical prophet or his followers.

Following the recent shift of perspective as regards the book as a whole, the first part of the book no longer can be regarded as consisting of an eighth-century 'Proto-Isaiah' plus a series of later extras. Instead, the book must be regarded as a literary product of a much later period. Throughout the book we find evidence of redactional attempts to establish literary structures within the book as a whole, which implies that passages within First Isaiah may belong to the latest redactions.[228] Furthermore, the Isaiah tradition has undergone a complex development in the course of time. Not only was new material added at various stages, but existing material was also reworked and reinterpreted. First Isaiah is not an anthology of pre-exilic material supplemented by later elaborations, but part of an extensively edited literary compilation from post-exilic times that contains material from several ages. We should reckon with an ongoing tradition that through a series of formative stages resulted in the book of Isaiah, which may be visualised in the following schema.[229]

Emergence and development of the Isaiah tradition				Development into the book of Isaiah		
1	2	3	4	5	6	7
historical prophet	collection of oracles	first literary elaboration	substantial literary complex	redactions, addition of new complexes	final redactions	book of Isaiah
Assyrian period			Babylonian period		Persian-Hellenistic period	

Point of departure

My research question differs from that of the earlier exegesis. In the past, scholars searched for 'authentic' passages in order to explain them as aspects of the preaching of a prophetic personality, who, as a great prophet of judgement belonged to a decisive stage in Israel's religious development. My research question is also different from that of recent scholars who primarily have a literary interest in the book of Isaiah. Instead, my question is a historical one: which parts of First Isaiah can be plausibly dated to the Assyrian period? The aim of the exegetical chapter is not to present a redaction history of First Isaiah, but to decide which material from First Isaiah can be dated to the Assyrian period.

It is generally acknowledged that the earliest material within the book of Isaiah stems from the Assyrian period, and that this material is to be found within the first part of the book. However, scholars hold different views with regard to the question of which parts of First

---

[228] Clements 2002: 116.
[229] For a similar description of this process of development, see Collins 1993:16.

Isaiah stem from the Assyrian period, and they have ended up with increasingly different results.[230] Since the pre-exilic origin of the material involved no longer can be taken for granted, the question regarding the earliest material within First Isaiah has to be addressed anew.[231] Instead of assuming that material from First Isaiah originates from the Assyrian period, scholars must adduce grounds that make this plausible. The divergence of scholarly positions shows that exegetical analysis does not produce indisputable answers. Exegesis rather provides a set of tools to be used to support a particular view, to render it plausible and convincing. My approach to the Isaiah tradition in the Assyrian period, worked out in chapter 2, consists of three steps.

1) For the identification of the material belonging to the Assyrian period I take as a point of departure references to historical entities and circumstances of the eighth and seventh centuries. Texts within First Isaiah display a profoundly historical interest in various episodes of the Assyrian period, which can hardly be considered as being complete literary inventions of later times.[232] The historical clues are the following:

i) The names Ephraim (i.e. Northern Israel) and its capital Samaria occur in oracles predicting the downfall of Northern Israel (7:4-9; 8:1-4; 17:1-3; 28:1-4). Most of these oracles refer to Aram and Damascus as well, the point being that Israel and Aram would be punished for their aggression against Judah. These passages make most sense in the later part of the eighth century.

---

[230] Williamson (2004: 181-182) points out that earlier scholars generally accepted the Isaianic character of a fair amount of material from First Isaiah. Recently however the amount of uncontestedly Isaianic material has diminished. As a result, fewer 'certain' passages remain with which more disputed passages can be compared. In the end, 'less and less can be securely regarded as original'. See also Barthel 1997: 25.

[231] Williamson (2004: 183) states: 'The current situation demands the adoption of a whole new agenda.' Similarly Steck 1996: 69-70.

[232] The abundance of historical figures mentioned within First Isaiah is in marked contrast to the rest of the book. Apart from Isaiah (1:1; 2:1; 7:3, 13; 13:1; 20:2, 3; ch. 37-39 passim), the following are mentioned: Uzziah (1:1; 6:1; 7:1); Jotham (1:1; 7:1); Ahaz (1:1; 7:1-17 passim; 14:28; 38:8) and Hezekiah (1:1; ch. 36-39 passim); the Aramaean king Rezin (7:1, 4, 8; 8:6); the Israelite king Pekah, son of Remaliah (7:1, 4, 5, 9; 8:6); a certain Ben Tabeel (7:6); three 'sons': Shear-jashub (7:3), Immanuel (7:14; 8:8, 10), and Maher-shalal-hash-baz (8:3); the two witnesses, Uriah and Zechariah (8:2); the officials Shebna (22:15; 36:3, 11, 22; 37:2), Eliakim (22:20; 36:3, 11, 22; 37:2) and Joash (36:3, 11, 22); the Assyrian kings Sargon (20:1) and Sennacherib (36:1; 37:17, 21, 37); Sennacherib's sons Adrammelech, Sharezer and Esarhaddon (37:38); the Cushite king Taharqa (37:9); and the Babylonian king Merodach-baladan (39:1). By contrast, the only historical figure mentioned by name in the second part of the book is Cyrus (45:1).

ii) References to 'Cush' (Nubia) also point to the Assyrian period since the Cushite (25th) Dynasty ruled over Egypt from the later part of the eighth century until 669 BCE. Although the term Cush appears in later texts as well,[233] references to the Cushite empire as a political and military power are likely to reflect the situation of the late eighth or early seventh century (18:1; 20:3-5; 37:9). Furthermore, references to Cush and Egypt in the context of prophetic warnings against Judah's search for assistance from them against Assyria probably stem from the Assyrian period. Military alliances with Egypt under Cushite rule were a historical reality in the late eighth century. Passages from First Isaiah that warn against such an alliance are likely to date from the Assyrian period, i.e. the earliest version of 18:1-6; 19:1-4; 20:1-6; 30:1-5 and 31:1-3.

iii) References to 'Assyria' are a further indication of early material.[234] The view that 'Assyria' in First Isaiah is a *chiffre* for a later empire (Babylonia or Persia) has to be rejected.[235] Within First Isaiah, Assyria and Babylonia are distinguished as different powers (23:13; 14:22-23 and 14:24-27).[236] Furthermore, since the Isaiah tradition is rooted in the Assyrian period it is reasonable to attempt to understand 'Assyria' as Assyria.[237] In particular those passages describing Assyria as a political-military superpower fit in with the Assyrian period.[238] The passages that, in all likelihood, refer to the Assyrian empire from a contemporary perspective are the earliest forms of 7:20; 8:1-4; 10:5-34; 14:24-27; 20:1-6; 30:27-33 and 31:8-9.

iv) First Isaiah contains various historical dating formulae, some of which presumably belong to an early layer introducing material that originates from the Assyrian period. Isa 6:1 introduces a vision report;

---

[233] E.g. Isa 43:3; 45:14; Jer 46:9; Ezek 30, also in Isa 11:11, usually regarded as part of a late passage, 11:10-16.

[234] 7:17, 18, 20; 8:4, 7; 10:5, 12, 24; 11:11, 16; 14:25; 19:23, 24, 25; 20:1, 4, 6; 23:13; 27:13; 30:31; 31:8; chapter 36-37 *passim*.

[235] Höffken 2004: 133-134.

[236] The name *'aššûr* is mentioned in several later texts as well, but these are to be distinguished from the earlier passages. The later occurrences partly consist of glosses and additions to earlier passages, such as 7:17b, 7:18, 8:7 and 10:12. In various other cases *'aššûr* functions as a geographical description, no longer as the name of a current superpower (11:16; 19:23-25; 27:13.); for this and other reasons these passages are generally considered as of a late date.

[237] Contra e.g. Werner 1982: 171-178, 190-193; 1988: 33.

[238] See Machinist 1983a.

14:28 introduces an oracle against the Philistines; and 20:1 introduces a report of a prophetic performance.[239]

v) Finally, the accounts of 7:1-17, 20:1-6 and 36-39 describe activities of the prophet Isaiah situated in the Assyrian period. These accounts contain material that to some extent corresponds to contemporary external sources.[240] Although they are in their present shape marked by a later elaboration, these accounts are probably rooted in the Assyrian period.[241]

As appears from the historical clues, the main issue in the second half of the eighth century in Judah was the question of whether or not to resist Assyrian imperialism. In the periods 734-732, 722-720, and 713-711 BCE, several of Judah's neighbour states resisted Assyrian dominance, and in 705-701 BCE Judah attempted to free itself from Assyria's rule. Material from First Isaiah that can be connected with these major political events can with some confidence be dated to the latest part of the eighth century.[242] The most secure ground for identifying the earliest stratum within First Isaiah is the political controversy of the late eighth century.[243] The earliest layer of the Isaiah tradition in my assessment consists of prophetic words relating to particular, historical contexts from the eighth century.

A second identifiable layer of the Isaiah tradition consists of passages dealing with the destruction of Assyria and the restoration of Judah. In these passages it is emphasised that it is Yahweh who carries out Assyria's destruction (10:16-19; 10:26a.27a; 10:33-34; 14:24-27; 30:27-33; 31:4-5.8-9), as part of his dealings with the entire world (14:26-27; 30:27-28; cf. 8:9-10; 17:12-14; 18:1-6). Closely related to

---

[239] By contrast, the dating formulae in 1:1 and 7:1 are to be regarded as late. For 1:1, see Sweeney 1996a: 71-72; for 7:1 (dependent on 2 Kgs 16:5), see chapter 2.1.2.

[240] Williamson (2004: 184) mentions as a main principle in the search for pre-exilic material within First Isaiah: 'where the account of a purportedly early event for which there is no other direct evidence in the biblical text is corroborated by some contemporary external source which could not, in all probability, have been known to a later biblical writer'. In such cases a pre-exilic origin is plausible.

[241] Cf. Williamson 2004: 185-186. I deal with Isa 7:1-17 and 20:1-6 in chapter 2; Isa 36-37 is dealt with in chapter 6.

[242] Related to 734-732 BCE are the oracles of Isa 7*, 8:1-4 and 17:1-3; related to 722-720 BCE are the oracles of 28:1-4, 14:28-32, and Isa 10*; related to 713-711 BCE is Isa 20*; related to 705-701 BCE are the sayings within Isa 28-31*, the critical sayings of Isa 5* and 10:1-2 and Isa 18-19*, 22*. This will be worked out in particular in chapter 4.1.

[243] This is also the position of Høgenhaven (1990: 351) and Höffken (2004: 144): 'Nach meinem Eindruck sprechen gerade ältere Schichten in PJ die Politsprache der damaligen Zeit, wie sie assyrische Königsinschriften (usw.) dokumentieren'.

the theme of Assyria's destruction is that of Judah's restoration: the reign of a new, ideal, Judaean king, in 9:1-6, 11:1-5 and 32:1-2. The themes of Assyria's downfall and the reign of the ideal king are two sides of the same coin, as both result from Yahweh's intervention. These passages in all likelihood date to the Assyrian period. Yet they clearly differ from the eighth-century prophetic material (as will be worked out in 6.1.3 and 6.1.4). I suggest regarding them as the product of a revision of the Isaiah tradition in the late seventh century.[244]

2) The second step of my assessment of the Isaiah tradition in the Assyrian period is based on the fundamental difference that can be perceived between the Isaiah tradition in the Assyrian period—the eighth-century prophetic material and the seventh-century revision—on the one hand, and the later transformation of the Isaiah tradition on the other. In particular within Isa 6-8 and 28-32, the prophetic material and its first revision can be distinguished from a later elaboration that put a decisive mark on these chapters. Isa 6-8 and 28-32 in their basic literary version represent textual complexes in which the earlier Isaiah tradition is extensively reworked and in which a new view of Isaiah's prophetic ministry is presented.[245] These literary complexes represent a thorough reworking of the Isaiah tradition in the light of the events of the early sixth century. The suggestion that the disastrous events of the early sixth century left their marks on the Isaiah tradition is not new (e.g. Clements 1980c). However, in my view these marks are much more decisive than scholars have previously acknowledged (in this respect I agree by and large with Becker 1997). The disastrous events of the sixth century—the fall of Jerusalem, the collapse of the state, the end of the dynasty, the Babylonian exile—led to a profound reconsid-

---

[244]   See also Collins 1993: 38-39.

[245]   For a similar approach to the Amos tradition, see Kratz 2003a. Kratz (2003a: 54-67) distinguishes between the basic literary layer (*Grundbestand*) and the presumed original prophetic words. The prophetic words, transmitted orally or in writing, are rooted in a particular historical context in which they were originally understood. They were however reinterpreted in the literary context of the developing prophetic tradition. According to Kratz (2003a: 67-89), the *Grundbestand* of Amos 3-6 is marked by the main characteristic of the literary prophetic tradition: unconditional judgement. Within the *Grundbestand* Kratz identifies sayings that originated as independent prophetic words (3:12; 4:1*; 5:2.3.7.18*.19.20; 6:1a.3-6a.13). The sayings originally related to specific historical situations but received a new role within the literary composition. The sayings, referring to a situation of great international tension and military threat, are to be situated in the eighth century. They aimed to prevent a national catastrophe. The words of the 'historical Amos' thus differ fundamentally from the 'literary Amos', the latter being a product of an ongoing prophetic tradition.

eration of the past. Far from being given up, the Isaiah tradition was thoroughly reworked in order to get it into lines with a new view of Israel's past and in order to use the authority of the figure of Isaiah as a spokesman of the new view. This view was essentially that the destruction of Judah and Jerusalem was the result of Yahweh's punishment because of the sinful disobedience of the people. It was this transformation of the Isaiah tradition, presumably in the sixth century, which created the image of Isaiah as a prophet of judgement.

The eighth-century prophetic material within First Isaiah and its earliest elaboration in the Assyrian period however are distinctly different from what is supposedly the main characteristic of biblical prophecy: the proclamation of unconditional judgement. The eighth-century prophetic material is partly marked by positive aspects (e.g. Isa 7*, 8*, 28:12*, 30:15*), and the critical sayings apply to a specific group of people; furthermore, the seventh-century revision is of an unambiguously positive tone. Isa 6-8 and 28-32 in their later literary version however present the positive message as a superseded stage: the positive message was rejected and what remains is the preaching of judgement, applied to the people as a whole.[246] This important transition must not be projected onto the prophetic biography. Rather, it betrays a later stage of development of the Isaiah tradition.

3) The final step of my assessment of the Isaiah tradition in the Assyrian period relates to the forms of the material. The eighth-century prophetic material consists of oracles and sayings that in all likelihood originally were orally delivered. This material can be qualified as prophetic in a strict sense. The passages that in my view belong to the seventh-century revision of the Isaianic material do not have an oral background but are literary from the outset. With regard to the nature of the seventh-century revision, the following may be observed. The eighth-century prophetic material can essentially be connected with three historical periods: 734-732, 723-720 and 705-701 BCE. The material relating to each period was probably preserved in the form of a collection of prophetic words, and each of these three collections was probably revised in the late seventh century. The revision turned the collections into editions consisting of eighth-century prophetic words on the one hand, and of new material on the other. In the analysis of the texts (chapter 2.4, chapter 6.1) I will attempt to make plausible

---

[246] See also Collins 1993: 49-50.

that the seventh-century revision took the form of three compilations, each revising a small collection of prophetic words. Furthermore, each compilation followed a similar pattern of dating formula and prophetic commission, followed by the prophetic words to which some comments were added, and concluding with a portrayal of the reign of the ideal king.

These three steps form my conception of the Isaiah tradition in the Assyrian period. In chapter 2, I will attempt to demonstrate that this is the most plausible way to deal with the earliest stages of the Isaiah tradition.

Chapter 3 needs less introduction. For the non-biblical prophecy, I focus on the prophetic material from seventh-century Assyria. There are several reasons for giving priority to the Assyrian prophecies over other extra-biblical prophecies. The first reason is the relative abundance of prophetic material from seventh-century Assyria. Second, perhaps even more important than the relative wealth of material, is the integration of prophetic oracles and references to prophets in the literature of that period, such as letters, royal inscriptions, and literary texts. Third, the Assyrian prophecies are close to the period of Isaiah. Whereas the Mari prophecies date from the eighteenth century, the Assyrian prophecies stem from the first half of the seventh century. This is close to the earliest prophetic material within First Isaiah, which dates from the late eighth century.[247] The Assyrian material consists of collections of prophetic oracles, single oracles, oracles reported or quoted in letters, oracles included in royal inscriptions, and oracles reworked into literary texts.

Whereas the emphasis is on the Assyrian prophetic material in a strict sense (chapters 4 and 5), some further texts will be taken into account in order to explore the transition from prophecy to literature (chapter 6). These additional texts consist of two groups. The first group is formed by texts that stem from seventh-century Assyria. These texts can be qualified as prophetic compositions. They are closely related to the prophetic oracles, in particular to the oracles that are reworked into literary texts.[248] The second group of texts consists

---

[247]   The prophetic material in West-Semitic sources from the first millennium BCE will occasionally be taken into account in this study (for these texts, see Nissinen 2003a: 201-218).
[248]   See also note 214 above.

of the so-called literary-predictive texts (sometimes called literary prophecies or pseudo-prophecies).[249]

1.3.3 *Comparative Part*

The second part of this study contains a comparison of the Isaiah tradition in its earliest shape on the one hand, and the prophetic material from seventh-century Assyria on the other.[250]

The comparison focuses on three aspects: the interrelation between prophecy and historical events in Judah and Assyria (chapter 4), the functions of the prophetic figures (chapter 5), and the secondary adaptation and elaboration (the 'literary afterlife') of prophecy (chapter 6). A necessary condition for an adequate comparison is clarity with regard to procedure and significance.[251] The kind of comparison to be carried out in this study is a historical comparison.[252] The rationale for a historical comparison is the relative closeness, geographically and historically, of the societies to which the units of comparison belong, their mutual influence on one another, and their shared cultural aspects.[253] The various ancient Near Eastern cultures have a common ground, shared by Judah and Israel as well,[254] and prophecy forms one aspect of this.[255] The material from First Isaiah and the Assyrian prophecies, comply with the conditions for historical comparison: there is similarity or analogy between the observed phenomena; there is a certain dissimilarity between the environments in which the phenomena occurred;[256] and though the phenomena occur at approximately the same point of time, they are independent of each other rather than causally related.[257]

---

[249] See also note 215 above.

[250] Whereas the focus of this study is on the prophetic material from seventh-century Assyria, other examples of ancient Near Eastern prophecy are occasionally taken into account as well.

[251] Etzioni and DuBow (1970: 7) define comparative study as 'a design whereby the same process of data-collection and data-analysis is carried out within a number of spatial units'.

[252] To be distinguished from a phenomenological or typological comparison; see Bloch 1970; Barstad 2000: 5-6; Talmon 1978: 325.

[253] Bloch 1970: 41.

[254] E.g. Vriezen 1969: 14-15; cf. Van der Toorn 1994: 1-2.

[255] Cf. Weippert (2001a: 58) for the view 'daß es eine gemeinaltorientalische— oder wenigstens syrisch-mesopotamische—prophetische Sprache gab, an der sowohl die assyrischen Prophet(inn)en als auch Deuterojesaja partizipierten'.

[256] These conditions are formulated by Bloch 1970: 39.

[257] This condition is formulated by Etzioni and DuBow 1970: 11.

Comparative Procedure
For a valid comparison it is important to compare 'like with like'.[258] In
their final version the biblical books do not resemble the Assyrian
texts, which are of a more rudimentary state. Neither does it make
sense to compare prophetic oracles from Mesopotamia to the multi-
layered textual complex of First Isaiah. However, after a careful distinction between prophetic oracles and sayings—orally delivered messages going back to prophetic activity—on the one hand, and the
literary development of the prophetic tradition on the other, it is possible to compare 'like with like'. First, prophetic material, preserved
within First Isaiah, can be compared with extra-biblical prophetic oracles. Second, the literary extensions to the prophetic material can be
compared with literary prophetic texts from the ancient Near East,
which likewise have a literary *Sitz im Leben.*

The procedure of a historical comparison implies the selection of
apparently analogous phenomena, in this case texts from First Isaiah
and the Assyrian prophecies, a description of how they resemble or
differ from each other, and an explanation of the similarities and differences.[259] Several fallacies are to be avoided. First, the phenomena in
question have to be explored in their own right. Instead of explaining
aspects of Judaean prophecy through the Assyrian prophecy or *vice
versa*, both phenomena have to be explained within their own historical contexts, and compared from their respective contexts.[260] Secondly,
the comparative study, instead of merely listing similarities or dissimi-
larities, must take into account the cultural context in order to establish the significance of apparent parallels.[261] Both in Judah and in
Assyria, prophecy was part of the cultural, religious and social system.
Given the shared ancient Near Eastern tradition on the one hand, and
the particular circumstances of Judah and Assyria on the other, one
would expect to find both similarities and differences, the significance
of which can be established within a contextual interpretation.[262]

---

[258] Cf. Saggs 1978: 79.
[259] Bloch 1970: 39.
[260] Cf. the consideration expressed by Saggs 1978: 17.
[261] Barstad 2000: 8.
[262] For the contextual approach, see Hallo 1990. For the term 'context' and the
'contextual approach', see Hallo 1997: XXV: the context of a text is '... the geographical, historical, religious, political and literary setting in which it was created and
disseminated. The contextual approach tries to reconstruct and evaluate this setting,
whether for a biblical text or one from the rest of the ancient Near East.'

Comparative Aim

The comparison is carried out on the basis of texts. Furthermore an attempt will be made to proceed to a further stage of comparison, consisting of an analysis of the socio-historical phenomena behind the texts.[263]

Chapter 4 offers a comparison between the Isaianic material and the Assyrian prophecies with regard to the relationship between prophecy and historical events. The Assyrian prophecies relate to various historical situations during the reigns of Esarhaddon and Ashurbanipal. The prophecies from First Isaiah dating from the Assyrian period relate to specific historical situations as well. A comparison will be carried out with regard to the way in which the prophecies functioned in their respective historical contexts.

Chapter 5 deals with the functions of the prophetic figures in Judah and Assyria. The position of the Assyrian prophets and the Judaean prophets within their respective societies is not evident. Whereas the latter have been the subject of ongoing debate, the former have not received much attention.[264] One of the questions I will address is: are the classical prophets a specific type of prophets, or rather a specific prophetic image, present in the biblical literature but not in the biblical world? With regard to Isaiah, it will be argued that he was not a classical prophet in the traditional sense. Instead, he resembled prophets elsewhere in the ancient Near East to the extent that he was principally supportive of the Judaean state (which does *not* mean that he was a *Heilsprophet*).

Chapter 6 describes the adaptation, elaboration and reworking of the prophetic oracles. Many of the Assyrian prophecies enjoyed a (literary) 'afterlife'. They were quoted in letters, re-applied to new situations, and republished and reworked for new occasions. Furthermore, various kinds of literary texts were composed, based on the genre of prophetic oracles. The literary functioning of Assyrian prophetic texts will be compared with the earliest literary revision of the prophetic oracles in First Isaiah in the Assyrian period. The suggestion of a revision of the Isaiah tradition in the late seventh century will play an important role in this respect.

---

[263] Cf. Barstad 2000: 11.
[264] A notable exception is Nissinen 2000b.

1.3.4   *Conclusion*

This study aims to provide a depiction of the Isaiah tradition in the Assyrian period (chapter 2), and to give a presentation of the prophetic material from seventh-century Assyria (chapter 3). The main purpose of this study is to present a comparative perspective on the Isaiah tradition in the Assyrian period and the prophetic material from Assyria which sheds light on three issues: the interrelation between prophecy and historical circumstances (chapter 4), the functions of the prophets (chapter 5), and the literary development of prophecy (chapter 6).

PART ONE

CHAPTER TWO

THE ISAIAH TRADITION IN THE ASSYRIAN PERIOD

This chapter deals with the issue of which parts of First Isaiah can be dated to the Assyrian period, i.e. the eighth-seventh century. The chapter begins with an analysis of Isa 6-8 and Isa 28-32, because these two complexes play a key role with regard to the question of the extent to which one may find early prophetic words within First Isaiah.[1] In this way, these complexes provide an ideal battleground for defending my views against the radical position (as taken by Kaiser and Becker) and the more traditional position (as taken by Wildberger and Barthel). My main thesis is that within both complexes a distinction can be made between material from the Assyrian period on the one hand, and a thorough reworking of this material on the other. This reworking, which is of a literary and redactional character, can in my view be plausibly situated in the period following the downfall of the Judaean state in the sixth century. It will be demonstrated that the Isaiah tradition in the Assyrian period has a quite different profile than its later, probably exilic, reworking.

After analysing Isa 6-8 and Isa 28-32, I deal with the rest of First Isaiah in search of early material. Instead of dealing with every chapter, I concentrate on parts of Isa 5, 9-11 and 13-23.[2] The analysis fo-

---

[1]   Barthel 1997: 25; similarly Höffken 2004: 139.

[2]   Isa 12, 24-27, 33, and 34-35 are left out, because these are usually perceived as late texts. Furthermore, Isa 36-39 will not be discussed here, since an analysis of these chapters would exceed the bounds of this study. Isa 36-37 (2 Kgs 18-19) however will be taken into account in chapter 6.1.2. Isa 1-5, finally, is a somewhat complicated case. Although, in my view, parts from ch. 5 date from the Assyrian period (the *woe*-sayings, discussed in section 2.3.1), most of the material of these chapters belongs to later redactional stages. With regard to ch. 1, I agree with those who see it as a text from a late stage in the growth of the book of Isaiah as a whole (cf. Williamson: 2006, 15, 28). Although ch. 1 may include 'earlier material' (earlier compared to the very late date of ch. 1 as a whole), I am not convinced that parts from it can be traced back to the Assyrian period. A case in point is 1:4-8, a unit which in my view postdates the Assyrian period (discussed in section 2.3.7). The *woe*-sayings of ch. 5 are dressed in a later (probably exilic) redaction focusing on judgement and disaster, to which at a still later stage 5:1-7 was added. Similarly, ch. 2-4 in my view mainly consist of later material. Although I would not principally exclude the possibility that some early mate-

cuses on the supposedly early material included within these chapters in relation to its later literary-redactional context. The chapter concludes with a presentation of the Isaiah tradition in the Assyrian period, which in my view originated as a series of prophetic words that were preserved in the form of small collections, and that, in the seventh-century were revised in the form of three textual compilations.

2.1   Isaiah 6-8

2.1.1   Isaiah 6:1-8:18 as a Literary Composition

Isa 6:1-8:18 is traditionally perceived as a memoir of the prophet Isaiah, written in the aftermath of the Syro-Ephraimitic crisis.[3] Nowadays, this textual unit is generally considered to be a redactional complex, but there are good reasons to regard 6:1-8:18 to some extent as a unit on its own. First, 6:1 begins with a first-person account, which ends in 8:18. Second, 8:18 presumes Isa 7 in some form as it refers to the children's names (7:3, 7:14, 8:3).[4] Third, sometime during the development of the Isaiah tradition, a compositional ring of material has been arranged around Isa 6-8.[5] If one takes for a moment 6:1-8:18 as an independent unit, one may be struck by the insight that this text presents itself as an account of Isaiah's prophetic ministry *as such*.[6] It gives an account of Isaiah's prophetic career from its beginning to its end, starting with Isaiah's commissioning in Isa 6 and ending with his withdrawal from public life after having fulfilled his prophetic task (8:16-18). The presentation of Isaiah's ministry in 6:1-8:18 is of a reflective, interpretative character. It presents a view of Isaiah the prophet in retrospect. This portrayal of Isaiah, in my view, has become

---

rial has been preserved here (perhaps e.g. in 3:1-7*) or in some other chapter, I have chosen to focus on those parts of First Isaiah where a distinction between the 'Assyrian' Isaiah tradition and its later development can be made plausible.

[3]   Barthel 1997: 38.

[4]   Barthel 1997: 232.

[5]   See Sheppard 1985. The apparent oddity that Isaiah's commission is narrated only in chapter 6 can be explained from the redactional development of the Isaiah tradition. Barthel (1997: 83) suggests that the material in Isa 1-5 does not represent a stage of Isaiah's career prior to the vision of Isa 6, but contains a complex based on Isaianic prophecies that is structured around the *Denkschrift*.

[6]   Becker (1997: 73) argues that Isa 6 and 8 present a (later) picture of Isaiah's *'gesamte* prophetische Wirken'.

of fundamental importance in the development of the Isaiah tradition as a whole.

The composition presents Isaiah as having been ordered by Yahweh *from the outset* to announce judgement to the people (6:9-11). According to the compositional perspective, Isaiah's ministry started with the announcement of judgement (6:11), and ended with its realisation (8:17).[7] Uwe Becker, in my view, is right to qualify 6:11 and 8:17 as 'eine sachliche wie literarische Klammer, die den Hauptinhalt des jesajanischen Predigt umschließt'.[8] In other words, the account ranges from Isaiah's commission to proclaim disaster (6:9-11), to his withdrawal when the task had been completed (8:17).

6:9-11 describes the disaster as a divine punishment because of the people's refusal to listen. Furthermore, the passage explains that the people rejected Isaiah's message because Yahweh made them unsusceptible. Isaiah's commission, prepared for by the vision in 6:1-8, is presented in 6:9-11 as directed against the people. Isaiah is depicted as standing in opposition to the people, referred to as 'this people' (הָעָם הַזֶּה). This is, as elsewhere, a pejorative depiction. The same term occurs in 8:11, stating that it was Yahweh who forced Isaiah to dissociate himself from 'this people'. This refers to the vision of Isa 6, understood from the perspective of 6:9-11. Both 6:9-11 and 8:11 imply that the vision led to a radical reorientation of the prophet: Yahweh positioned him opposite to 'this people' and commissioned him with a message of doom for 'this people'.[9] The identity of the recipients of the prophetic message, 'this people' in 6:9-10 and 8:6, 11-12, must be sought within the compositional perspective. Within the depiction of Isa 6 and 8, הָעָם הַזֶּה refers to the people in general as standing in opposition to Isaiah and his followers (8:16).[10] According to 8:11-15, the disobedience of 'this people' caused the destruction of both Northern Israel and Judah. This suggests that 'this people' is not a precise identification but a general category. It depicts the disobedient people that are punished by Yahweh because they have rejected his words delivered by the prophet.[11]

---

[7]   Becker 1997: 73.

[8]   Becker 1997: 75.

[9]   Jones 1993: 158-159.

[10]   The other occurrences of this motif in First Isaiah (9:15, 28:11, 28:14, and 29:13-14) confirm that הָעָם הַזֶּה refers to the people as a whole.

[11]   The designation 'this people' (הָעָם הַזֶּה) functions as a pejorative depiction in First Isaiah. In a similar way, it occurs frequently within two other complexes, in

8:16-18 is formulated as a conclusion to Isa 6-8. Isaiah is presented as withdrawing from public life after he has delivered Yahweh's message of judgement. The message is to be sealed and preserved (8:16).[12] Meanwhile, now the fate of the people has been destined and Yahweh's judgement has become irreversible, Isaiah is presented as waiting and hoping for Yahweh's salvation (8:17).[13] The phrase 'Yahweh is hiding his face' (8:17) indicates not only the hopelessness of the situation, but also the interruption of communication between Yahweh and the people after the prophet's resignation.[14] 8:16-18 presents Isaiah as having fulfilled his prophetic task. The image of the prophet as presented in 8:16-18 is evidently a literary construct.[15]

The depiction of Isaiah's prophetic ministry in 6:1-8:18 is likely to be from a later hand. The text gives an interpretation of Isaiah's prophetic activity. Because it has become part of a much larger complex, it is tempting to read Isa 6-8 as representing one stage of Isaiah's prophetic career. However, it is still discernable that at some stage in the course of development, Isa 6-8 presented an account of Isaiah's prophetic ministry *as such*. The account presents a retrospective view on Isaiah's ministry. It reflects on disastrous events that are interpreted as a divine punishment for the disobedience of the people, announced by the prophet Isaiah. Whereas 6:1-11 and 8:1-18 focus on the disobedient people (הָעָם הַזֶּה), 7:1-17, as will be argued below, presents Ahaz, representative of the Davidic dynasty, as an example of the disobedience mentioned in 6:9-10.

Although 6:1-8:18 as a redactional composition is of a later date, it contains earlier material. Beneath the compositional surface another

---

Jeremiah and in the Pentateuch traditions, that equally deal with the disobedience and stubbornness of Israel. The occurrences of this motif in First Isaiah, Jeremiah and the Pentateuch traditions, are characterised by a remarkable uniformity. In all cases, Yahweh's anger is aroused against his people because of their disobedient and stubborn rejection of his blessings, and the prophet (Moses, Isaiah, Jeremiah) is positioned between the people and God. Although Moses is depicted as a successful intercessor, the Pentateuch traditions make clear that the destruction of the people is eventually unavoidable (Exod 32:34; Deut 31). This becomes a reality within First Isaiah and Jeremiah. The development of the motif of הָעָם הַזֶּה, in my view, lies in the reflection on the disasters that had befallen Judah and Jerusalem in the early sixth century.

[12]   Isa 8:16 intends to suggest that Isaiah's testimony was faithfully transmitted from generation to generation. See Kaiser 1981: 190.

[13]   The phrase 'I will wait for Yahweh, I will hope in him', expresses hope for salvation in a hopeless situation. See Williamson 1994: 99-100; Barthel 1997: 237; contra Becker 1997: 75.

[14]   See particularly Ezek 39:23-29, and the explanation by Renz 1999: 120-121.

[15]   Cf. Barthel 1997: 233, with regard to 8:18.

layer is discernible, most clearly so within 7:1-17 and 8:1-18. It cannot be denied that 7:1-17 and 8:1-18 contain prophetic sayings of a remarkably positive character, namely 7:4-9a, 7:14b.16 and 8:1-4. Furthermore, it is evident that these positive sayings have been embedded in a literary context displaying a negative tendency (7:9b, 13-14a.17; 8:5-8). The most convincing explanation is that within 7:1-17 and 8:1-18 earlier prophetic sayings have been provided with a new literary context. The early prophecies have some distinct characteristics: they display a positive message for Judah and its king Ahaz, they are associated with 'sons' bearing symbolic names (7:3; 7:14; 8:3), and they are historically related to a particular situation, the Syro-Ephraimitic crisis (734-732 BCE). By contrast, the later literary context in which they have been integrated is marked by a negative tendency. Furthermore, the reworking disconnected the prophetic activity from the original historical situation, turning it into a more general presentation of Isaiah's prophetic ministry. The profiles of the prophetic material and the literary context are clearly distinctive. Furthermore, the text gives cause for a literary-critical separation between an earlier level of prophetic material and a later level of literary composition.

The distinction between earlier, prophetic material and later, compositional passages can be applied further. Isa 8:9-10 is a fragment that can be associated with the earlier, prophetic oracles included in 7:1-17 and 8:1-18. Furthermore, the vision report of 6:1-8 can be interpreted against the background of this early material. The prophetic oracles intend to encourage Ahaz (and the Judaeans) during a political crisis. The vision report of 6:1-8 can be read against the background of these oracles, as being intended to affirm Isaiah's legitimacy as a prophet who proclaimed encouragement in a critical situation. By contrast, a range of passages from Isa 6-8 can be identified as having been composed as part of the literary-redactional reworking of the earlier material, i.e. 6:9-11, 7:9b, 7:13-14a.17, 8:5-8, 8:11-15, and 8:16-18. Whereas the early material in origin related to a particular historical situation, the composition of Isa 6-8 transcended these particular events and presented Isaiah's activities as a paradigm for his prophetic activity as an announcer of divine judgement.

2.1.2   *Isaiah 7:1-17*

Oracular Material

7:1-17 is a narration about the prophet Isaiah and King Ahaz, in which
Ahaz is depicted as an example of the disobedience mentioned in 6:9-
10.[16] Two textual markers indicate the relation between 6:1-11 and
7:1-17. In the first place, the reference to Uzziah in 7:1 makes a connection with 6:1 and suggests in this way that the events heralded in
6:9-11 begin to take place in 7:1-17. Secondly, the exclamation שִׁמְעוּ in
7:13 echoes 6:9. 7:1-17 can be regarded as a composition with a dynastic-critical tendency. Various indications suggest however that it is
not a textual unity *aus einem Guß*.

1) 7:1 refers to a war (מִלְחָמָה) waged by Aram and Israel against Jerusalem, which however failed. The following verses describe however the *threat* that Aram posed to Ahaz and his people by settling on
Ephraim (7:2), and the *plan* of Aram to invade Judah in order to replace Ahaz (7:6). The oracle however insists that this plan will not
come true (7:7). Whereas the oracle deals with Aram's aggressive intent, the narrative introduction in 7:1 goes further by referring to an
actual assault.

2) 7:9b and 7:13-14a quite unexpectedly address a plural subject,
whereas Ahaz is addressed in the singular throughout (7:4, 5, 11, 14b,
16). The oracles addressed to Ahaz in singular forms (7:4-9a, 14b.16)
are encouraging. The plural passages however display a profoundly
dynastic-critical tendency.

An explanation for these apparent disparities may start with 7:10,
'Yahweh went on to speak to Ahaz'. This clearly stems from the compositor's hand. Although the phrase contrasts with the immediate context where Isaiah is speaking, it is less clumsy than sometimes
suggested,[17] since it continues 7:3 (וַיֹּאמֶר יהוה). The phrase 'Yahweh
said' in 7:3 introduces a first encounter between Isaiah and Ahaz,
whereas the phrase 'Yahweh went on to speak' in 7:10, creates a sec-

---

[16]   Isa 7:18-25 contains additional material, marked by the redactional formula
וְהָיָה בַּיּוֹם הַהוּא (7:18, 21, 23). 7:20, introduced by the formula בַּיּוֹם הַהוּא, may go back
to an earlier prophetic announcement, and can be associated with the oracles of 7:4-
9a, 7:14b.16 and 8:1-4 (Wagner 2006: 250-252, 293). Isa 7:18-19 is likely to stem
from a later redaction (Wagner 2006: 250). The expression 'land of Assyria' in juxtaposition with Egypt is suggestive of a later provenance (cf. Isa 11:16; 19:23-25;
27:13; Jer 2:18.36; Lam 5:6; Hos 7:11; 9:3; 11:5.11; 12:1; Zech 10:10-11).

[17]   Wildberger 1972-82: 268: 'V. 10 [erweckt] den Eindruck einer (eher unge-
schickten) redaktionellen Naht'. Cf. Werlitz 1992: 169, 170, 173.

ond scene, parallel to the first one. This arrangement is indicative of an editor/composer who neatly arranged the material at his disposal, the oracles of 7:4-9a and 7:14b.16. The earliest material embodied within 7:1-17 consists of two oracles to Ahaz. The oracles do not reflect any criticism against Ahaz, but rather encourage him in a straightforward way. They were however incorporated in a composition that displays a theme of threat and disaster.[18]

In the following, I will discuss how the oracles have been reworked into a new composition. 7:1-17 consists of two scenes, 1-9 and 10-17, each of which has at its core an oracle addressed to Ahaz. The first oracle, 7:4-9a, probably consisted of the following text:

> [4*] Take heed, be quiet, do not fear, and do not let your heart be faint because of these two smouldering stumps of firebrands.
> [5*] Because Aram has plotted evil against you, saying,
> [6] Let us invade Judah, terrify it, and cleave it open for ourselves and make the son of Tabeel[19] king in it![20]
> [7] therefore thus says the Lord Yahweh: It shall not stand, and it shall not come to pass.
> [8a] For the head of Aram is Damascus, and the head of Damascus is Rezin,
> [9a] and the head of Ephraim is Samaria, and the head of Samaria is the son of Remaliah.

The original word is an oracle of encouragement for Ahaz. The prophet encourages the king in a threatening situation, which can be inferred from the oracle itself. Furthermore, the threat is described in 7:2-3a, an early note on the historical setting of the oracle.[21] The oracle has been expanded in various ways. Some minor additions were made in 7:4 and 5 to explicitly identify the aggressors as Rezin and Pekah.[22]

---

[18]   Barthel 1997: 63, 151-153.

[19]   טָבְאַל, 'good for nothing', is usually understood as a tendentious vocalisation of original טָבְאֵל, 'God is good', as in Ezra 4:7; cf. Zech 6:10, 14, and Isa 7:6 LXX.

[20]   The suffixes are feminine, suggesting that Judah here means the land of Judah, rather than the people of Judah; see JM § 134g.

[21]   According to 7:2 the army of Aram is camping in the country of Ephraim, which corresponds to Aram's plan to invade Judah in 7:6. The house of David is referred to in the singular (contrary to 7:13). Furthermore, the name of Isaiah's son, Shear-jashub (7:3a), is likely to represent an early tradition (Barthel 1997: 166). It forms a clear analogy with the 'sons' with symbolic names in 7:14 and 8:3. The name Shear-jashub can be interpreted as alluding to the destruction of Judah's enemies Ephraim and Aram (Høgenhaven 1988: 82; Wagner 2006: 141, note 45; the interpretation of 10:21 is secondary).

[22]   7:4b explicitly mentions Rezin and Pekah as the referents of 'these two smouldering stumps of firebrands', see Werlitz 1992: 215, 219; Barthel 1997: 133. Further-

A further addition consisted of 7:8b, 'within sixty-five years Ephraim will be shattered, no longer a people', which interrupts the coherence of 7:8a and 9a and does not make sense within the scope of the oracle.[23] The most significant addition to the oracle is 7:9b: 'If you do not stand firm in faith, you shall not stand at all'. It is unlikely that 7:9b belonged to the original oracle. First, it addresses a plural subject, in contrast to the oracle, which is addressed to Ahaz in the singular (7:4, 5 suffix).[24] Second, the conditional threat expressed in 7:9b contrasts with 7:4-9a as an oracle of encouragement. The oracle exhorts Ahaz to persist in his policy of neutrality and not to give in to the pressure of the anti-Assyrian coalition.[25] 7:9b on the other hand introduces a condition of faith addressed to a plural subject. The terminology of 7:9b suggests the following explanation. The verb אמן alludes to Yahweh's promise to the Davidic dynasty.[26] In 2 Sam 7:16, Yahweh says: 'Your house and your kingdom shall be made sure (אמן ni.) forever before me; your throne shall be established forever'.[27] 7:9b reformulates the Davidic covenant by changing the promise into a negative condition. In this way, it gives a new twist to the oracle to Ahaz.[28]

The second scene, 7:10-17, can be equally explained from the suggestion that an original oracle of salvation was secondarily reworked into a context of threat. The birth oracle concerning Immanuel is a straightforward announcement of salvation.[29] Its immediate context however consists of threatening words that announce judgement over the house of David.[30] The original oracle consisted of 7:14b.16. By contrast, 7:15 is a later *relecture* of the oracle that focuses on the

---

more, the grammatical correspondence of אֲרָם and יָעַץ suggests that 5bα is a later addition too, see Irvine 1990: 152.

[23] Werlitz 1992: 199, 214, 250. The possibility of 7:8b as a seventh-century addition will be discussed in 2.4 below.

[24] Werlitz (1992: 160) notes that 7:9b in recent literary-critical contributions often is taken as secondary to 9a. Hardmeier (1979: 48-54; 1981: 236-238) argues that 7:9b addresses Isaiah's disciples, who are, in his view, the real recipients of the *Denkschrift*.

[25] Barthel 1997: 165-166.

[26] With regard to 7:9b, MT has the most original reading (with e.g. Symmachus, Theodion). Some of the versions (e.g. LXX) appear to reflect a variant Hebrew text, reading תבינו (בין hi.) instead of תאמנו (אמן ni.). This can be explained as a secondary reading, which attempted to make sense of the corrupted reading preserved in 1QIsa^a (אם לוא תאמינו כי לוא תאמינו), as was argued by Menzies (1998).

[27] See also 1 Sam 25:28 and 1 Kgs 11:38.

[28] Barthel 1997: 133-139.

[29] Barthel 1997: 141.

[30] Barthel 1997: 139.

figure of Immanuel himself rather than on the events of which he was a portent.[31]

> [14b] Look, the young woman is pregnant and is about to bear a son,
> and you must name him Immanuel,
> [16] for before the child knows how to refuse the evil and choose the good,
> the land before whose two kings you are terrified will be deserted.

7:14b.16 is the announcement of a sign, which takes the form of a birth oracle. It consists of the following elements: 1) statement (or announcement) of pregnancy, beginning with הִנֵּה; 2) announcement of the birth of a son; 3) order for name-giving; 4) explanation of the portentous meaning of the name, beginning with כִּי.[32]

Ahaz is the recipient of the birth oracle (אַתָּה, 7:16). Since within birth oracles the order of the name-giving is always directed to the addressee of the oracle,[33] the subject of the ambivalent form וְקָרָאת in 7:14b must be Ahaz.[34] The form is to be read as וְקָרָאתָ 'you must name'. The much-adopted reading of a third person feminine singular is to be rejected on form-critical grounds. Besides, the feminine form would normally be וְקָרְאָה.[35] The reading of a third person feminine singular corresponds with the later *relecture* of the birth oracle. Immanuel was disconnected from Ahaz as name-giver in order to make the announcement valid for later times. Whereas in the original oracle Yahweh's benevolence implied by the name Immanuel applies to Ahaz, the alternative reading 'she will name him' creates the possibility of interpreting Yahweh's benevolence as referring to a circle different from the king and the sinful people.[36]

---

[31]   7:15 is a later interpretation of 7:16; see Werlitz 1992: 182-186; Barthel 1997: 142; Wagner 2005: 75-76; 2006: 73. Whereas the phrase in 7:15 is interpreted as indication of moral responsibility, its original meaning (7:16) refers to the age of discrimination (Herbert 1973: 65). According to 7:15, Immanuel must suffer hardship in order to be able to choose the good and to reject the evil.

[32]   Barthel 1997: 141-142; Wildberger 1972-82: 289; contra Höffken 1980: 323, note 5.

[33]   Barthel 1997: 141-145.

[34]   Barthel 1997: 122; Müller 1974: 39.

[35]   Cf. Gen 29:35; 30:6; 1 Chron 4:9. MT וְקָרָאת is a second person feminine (cf. e.g. Gen 16:11), which is impossible in this context. 1QIsaᵃ וקרא is likely to be an adaptation to Isa 8:3 (or 9:5). The readings of the versions derive either from MT וקראת, read as second person masculine or third person feminine, or from 1QIsaᵃ וקרא, imperative or third person singular (impersonal). Note however that in the Siloam inscription the form הית seems to occur as a third person feminine form (see HAE I: 187, with note 9).

[36]   Barthel 1997: 178, 180.

The two oracles of encouragement, 7:4-9a and 7:14b.16, are closely related. Both address Ahaz and are intended to support him in an urgent situation. The name Immanuel refers to the imminent rescue from the aggressor and reinforces the exhortation to resist the anti-Assyrian coalition and the promise of salvation by Yahweh. The verb קוּם in 6 and 16 establishes a connection,[37] and the 'son Immanuel' forms a contrastive parallel with the 'son of Tabeel'.

The birth oracle of 7:14b.16 is a straightforward announcement of salvation for Ahaz.[38] 7:14a (לָכֵן) however seems to introduce a word of judgement in reaction to Ahaz's disbelief.[39] Within the composition, 7:13 functions as an accusation against Ahaz, which is followed by an announcement of judgement introduced with לָכֵן (7:14-17). In this way, the birth oracle is incorporated in a literary context that gives the oracle a new twist. Isaiah's critical encounter with Ahaz in 7:10-13 is followed by an announcement of judgement in 7:14-17. The plural addressee in 7:13-14a evidently disrupts the dialogue between Isaiah and Ahaz. These verses give a negative twist to the oracle of salvation. The house of David, addressed in plural, is accused of stubbornness. The exclamation שִׁמְעוּ in 7:13 echoes 6:9. The Davidic dynasty, represented by Ahaz, is accused of the kind of behaviour mentioned in 6:9. The plural forms imply that the criticism applies not only to Ahaz, but also to the Davidic dynasty as a whole. The composition reflects the view that the kings of Judah, represented by Ahaz, by their continuous disobedience and lack of trust have exhausted the patience of Yahweh and his prophets, represented by Isaiah.[40] 7:13-14a is connected with 7:9b. Both passages are in the plural and display a dynastic-critical tendency. So, both scenes, 7:1-9 and 7:10-17, contain an oracle of salvation for Ahaz that is enclosed in a literary framework characterised by threat and criticism.[41] Whereas the oracles address Ahaz, the plural

---

[37] The meaning of וּנְקִיצֶנָּה in 7:6 is disputed. The root קוּץ II hi. is supposed to mean 'to demolish' (KB); however, derivation from קוּץ I hi. 'to frighten', 'to horrify' is perhaps preferable, see Wildberger 1972-82: 266; Barthel 1997: 120.

[38] So also Wagner 2005.

[39] Barthel 1997: 146.

[40] See Barthel 1997: 172-173. The reference to 'my God' in 7:13 points at a break between Yahweh and Isaiah on the one hand and the Davidic dynasty on the other; Wildberger 1972-82: 288; Wagner 2006: 161.

[41] See Barthel 1997: 150.

passages address the Davidic dynasty as a whole.[42] Isaiah's opposition to the Davidic dynasty in 7:1-17 parallels his opposition to the people (הָעָם הַזֶּה) in 6:9-10 and 8:6, 11-12. To some extent, the people are included in the compositional perspective of 7:1-17 as well. The lack of faith, exemplified by Ahaz, will cause disaster both for the dynasty *and* for the people (7:17).[43] The criticism in 7:1-17 is not directed at Ahaz's foreign policy in particular, but to the policy of the Davidic dynasty in general, which ultimately resulted in disaster.

Literary Composition
7:1-17 contains two oracles addressed to Ahaz that were reworked into a composition that criticises the Davidic dynasty, exemplified by Ahaz, and announces its destruction. In the following, I will demonstrate that 7:1-17 has been composed with an eye to the descriptions of Ahaz and Hezekiah found in 2 Kings. In three cases, a connection can be established.
1) 7:1 is almost completely identical to 2 Kgs 16:5.

2 Kgs 16:5	Isa 7:1
Then	In the days of Ahaz son of Jotham son of Uzziah, king of Judah
came up	came up
King Rezin of Aram and King Pekah son of Remaliah of Israel	King Rezin of Aram and King Pekah son of Remaliah of Israel
to wage war on Jerusalem; they besieged Ahaz	to Jerusalem to attack it,
but could not	but could not[44]
prevail over him.	mount an attack against it.

It is mostly agreed that 7:1 is dependent on 2 Kgs 16:5. A clear indication for this is that in 7:1-17 the Northern Kingdom is referred to as 'Ephraim' (7:2, 5, 8, 9, 17), and its king as the 'son of Remaliah' (7:4, 5, 9), whereas in 7:1 the names 'Israel' and 'Pekah, son of Remaliah'

---

[42]   Williamson (1998b: 251) notes that the plural form of address 'suggests that the whole "house of David" is in view, not just Ahaz as an individual'. 7:1-17 adds a further dimension to 6:9-10 (1998b: 250).

[43]   7:9b alludes to the motif of the disobedient people. The condition of trust means trust in Yahweh. The accusation of lacking trust in Yahweh occurs especially with regard to the people of Israel in the wilderness (Num 14:11; Deut 1:32; 9:23; 2 Kgs 17:14; Ps 78:22, 32, 37; 106:24). Despite the signs Yahweh showed them the people did not believe (e.g. Num 14:11). In Isa 7:1-17, the lack of trust (אמן hi.) is indirectly connected with the 'sign' (אות) given by Yahweh.

[44]   Contrary to 2 Kgs 16:5 (יָכְלוּ), Isa 7:1 continues the singular (יָכֹל).

are used, following the common usage of the book of Kings. With the narrative introduction of 7:1 based on 2 Kgs 16:5, the editor/composer of 7:1-17 gave a slightly different twist to the events. The prophetic material at his disposal, 7:2-3a.4-9a and 7:14b.16, deals with the *threat* posed to Ahaz by Aram and Ephraim, and leaves open whether an actual assault took place. The report of 2 Kgs 16:5, taken up in Isa 7:1, makes things more explicit by referring to a military assault by Aram and Israel. The editor/composer of 7:1-17 however changed the report of 2 Kgs 16:5, by turning the focus from Ahaz to Jerusalem. In 2 Kgs 16:5, the object of assault is Ahaz: 'they besieged Ahaz, but could not prevail over him'.[45] In 7:1, the assault is launched against Jerusalem.[46] This change of focus from Ahaz to Jerusalem can be explained as part of the royal-critical tendency of 7:1-17. The assault was thwarted, not because of Ahaz's merits, but for the sake of Yahweh's city Jerusalem.

The connection with 2 Kgs 16 reveals more. The beginning of 16:5 אָז ('then') continues the dating of 16:1, 'In the seventeenth year of Pekah son of Remaliah, Ahaz son of Jotham king of Judah began to reign.' Whereas 2 Kgs 16:1 refers to 'Ahaz son of Jotham', Isa 7:1 extends this to 'Ahaz, son of Jotham, son of Uzziah'. This is remarkable, since it is highly unusual that a third generation is mentioned in a dating formula. This exceptional feature reveals a specific meaning of the reference to Uzziah. Its purpose is to create a link with Isa 6, which dates Isaiah's vision to 'the year King Uzziah died' (6:1). The connection suggests that the events announced in Isa 6, particularly in 6:9-11, begin to take place in 7:1-17.[47]

2) The two other parallels are with the Hezekiah stories of 2 Kgs 18-20 (Isa 36-38). The first is the detailed description of the location where Isaiah is to meet Ahaz, 7:3b. This resembles the location of 2 Kgs 18:17 (Isa 36:2) where the Assyrian delegation takes up position: '(at the end of) the conduit of the upper pool on the highway to the Fuller's Field'. Such detailed topographical indications are exceptional in the Hebrew Bible and the close similarity in wording points

---

[45] יכל in combination with לחם means 'to prevail (over)' and refers to a human being (Num 22:11; 1 Sam 17:9, 33; Jer 1:19; 15:20), except in Isa 7:1.

[46] לחם עַל is frequently used with respect to cities (Deut 20:10, 19; 2 Kgs 12:17; 19:8; Jer 32:29; 34:1, 7, 22).

[47] This resembles the interpretation of Williamson (1998b: 244-254, 269-270) who understands 7:1-17 as reflecting on the fall of the Davidic dynasty in 586 BCE and as intending to explain the disasters in the light of the announcement of 6:9-10.

to a relation of literary dependency. The description has its natural position within the context of 2 Kgs 18:17 (Isa 36:2). In this story, the exact locality is of utmost significance. The Assyrian delegation is posted outside the city of Jerusalem (18:17), and a Judaean delegation gets out of the city to negotiate (18:18). Their conversation is however audible for the Judaean people on the city wall (18:26). The credibility of this scene depends on the precise position of the Assyrian delegation at a strategic spot, outside, but close to, the city wall. For Isa 7:1-17, by contrast, the place where Isaiah is to meet Ahaz is hardly relevant at first sight. Its significance lies in the parallel it creates with the Hezekiah story. The similarity in location establishes a comparison between Hezekiah and Ahaz, who both face an enemy assault, and who are both put to the test: trusting in Yahweh or not.

3) The third connection relates to the אות, the sign for Ahaz.[48] Ahaz is ordered to ask for a sign (7:11), and the sign given to him is the birth of a son to be named Immanuel (7:14b.16). However, the description of the sign in 7:11 does not correspond to the sign actually given. 7:11 refers to a confirmatory sign, a sign confirming the accompanying prophetic message, and the qualification 'deep as Sheol or high as heaven', points to its miraculous character.[49] This resembles the receding shadow (2 Kgs 20:8-11; Isa 38:7-8, 22), a confirmatory sign of a miraculous character, requested by Hezekiah. The actual sign of 7:14b.16 is of a different character.[50] It is not an unusual feature of the child's conception or birth, but sets a time-limit for the fulfilment of the announcement, before the child reaches the age of discretion.[51] The description of the sign as a miracle by the editor/composer (7:11) hardly evolved from the material at his disposal (the birth oracle), but can be explained as a purposeful reference to 2 Kgs 20 (Isa 38), where Hezekiah asks for a sign from God. The argument between Isaiah and Ahaz concerning the request for an אות (7:11-14) deliberately contrasts with Hezekiah's pious request for a sign.[52]

---

[48]   See Ackroyd 1982: 17-18.
[49]   Barthel 1997: 171-172.
[50]   Berges 1998: 111.
[51]   Roberts 1977a: 477. The character of the אות mentioned in 2 Kgs 19:29 (Isa 37:30), which also sets a time-limit (within three years), is comparable to the sign of the newborn son Immanuel (7:14b.16).
[52]   Contra Barthel 1997: 171.

In these three cases, 7:1-17 borrows from 2 Kgs 16 and 18-20 (Isa 36-38).[53] The two latter cases show that 7:1-17 deliberately mirrors the Hezekiah stories. The disobedient Ahaz is contrasted with the faithful Hezekiah.[54] Hezekiah trusted in Yahweh and asked for a sign, Ahaz refused a sign and did not trust. Isa 7:1-17 uses the example of the disobedient Ahaz, who represents the Davidic dynasty as a whole, to explain the disaster that overcame both dynasty and people.

Early Material versus Later Composition
Although 7:1-17 to some extent is a *Fremdkörper* within Isa 6-8, several cross-references point to the unity of Isa 6-8 on a redactional-compositional level. The reference to Uzziah in 7:1 links the composition of 7:1-17 to Isa 6. This connection is corroborated by the parallel between 7:13 and 6:9 (שִׁמְעוּ). The prophet stands in opposition to the disobedient people ('this people', Isa 6 and 8), and to the disobedient royal house (Isa 7). Furthermore, the characterisation of Isaiah's sons as 'signs' in 8:18, not only refers to Maher-shalal-hash-baz (8:3), but also to Shear-jashub (7:3) and probably to Immanuel (7:14) as well.[55] A third connection is found in 8:10, which summarises the prophetic words of 7:5, 7:7 and 7:14 (see below).

The connections between 7:1-17 and Isa 6 and 8 lie on two levels. First, on a compositional level, Isa 6-8 forms a redactional unity. Whereas 6:1-11 and 8:1-18 focus on the disobedient people (הָעָם הַזֶּה), Isa 7 presents Ahaz, representing the Davidic dynasty, as an example of the disobedience announced in 6:9-10. The message of the composition is that Yahweh brings destruction and disaster over the people of Judah and the royal house, because of their stubborn, recalcitrant attitude and lack of trust. Secondly, both Isa 7, and 6 and 8, have at their core, material that can be related to actual prophetic activity in the eighth century. 8:1-4 lies on the same level as 7:4-9a and 7:14b.16, and 8:9-10 is to be associated with this material as well; finally it will be argued that 6:1-8 belongs to this earliest level too.

---

[53] Kaiser 1981: 143-144, 164; Werlitz 1992: 225-231; Becker 1997: 29-31, 36-38, 40-41; Ackroyd 1982: 19-20, tentatively. By contrast, Barthel (1997: 63) holds that 2 Kgs 18-20 (Isa 36-39) is dependent on Isa 7:1-17, and uses this as an argument for a pre-exilic dating of 7:1-17 (cf. Barthel 1997: 135, note 74).

[54] The thesis that 7:1-17 depicts Ahaz as an antitype of Hezekiah was proposed by Kaiser (1981: 143), and worked out by Becker (1997: 24-60). According to Becker (1997: 47), 7:1-17 aims to show that Ahaz's disbelief caused the end of the dynasty.

[55] Only Immanuel is explicitly referred to as a 'sign' (7:14a); 8:18 apparently takes Immanuel as another son of Isaiah.

Because 7:1-17 builds upon other material, in particular the Hezekiah stories, the composition cannot date from an early period. Furthermore, since 7:1-17 depicts Ahaz as the negative counterpart to Hezekiah, it is highly unlikely that it was composed shortly after the events of 701, caused by Hezekiah's foreign policy.[56] Instead, the composition is likely to refer to the disastrous events of the early sixth century, the collapse of the state of Judah and the end of the Davidic dynasty. Ahaz typifies the disbelief of the Davidic dynasty, and 7:9b, 13 and 17 are to be read from an *ex eventu* perspective that explains the end of the dynasty as due to lack of faith and disobedience.[57]

7:1-17 concludes with an announcement of judgement (7:17).[58] The phrase 'Ephraim's removal from Judah' (סוּר אֶפְרַיִם מֵעַל יְהוּדָה), refers to the division of the Davidic Kingdom (cf. 1 Kgs 12).[59] Something worse is announced here: the destruction of Judah and the end of the Davidic dynasty. In 7:17, finally, the oracles of encouragement (7:4-9a, 14b.16) are turned upside down completely.

2.1.3   Isaiah 8:1-18

Oracular Material

It is commonly agreed that 8:1-4 relates to the activity of the prophet Isaiah. The passage consists of two parts, 8:1-2 and 8:3-4, both focusing on the symbolic name or phrase Maher-shalal-hash-baz. This means something like 'quick booty, fast spoil'.[60]

---

[56]   Contra Barthel 1997: 155-157.

[57]   Werlitz 1992: 229-230. The depiction of Ahaz in Isa 7 (his disobedience functions as an explanation for the downfall of the dynasty and disaster for the nation) is paralleled to some extent by the portrait of Manasseh in 2 Kings, whose wicked behaviour effectuated the disaster (2 Kgs 21:11-15; 23:26-27; 24:2).

[58]   Barthel (1997: 181) argues that 7:17 announces judgement not only for Aram and Ephraim but also for Judah's king and people. The expression בוא hi. plus עַל with Yahweh as subject denotes disaster for the addressees (Barthel 1997: 146). The combination of בוא (qal or hi.) plus עַל and יוֹם, with Yahweh as instigator, always refers to disaster: Jer 51:47, 52; Amos 4:2 (cf. 1 Kgs 21:29; Jer 9:24; 17:18; 46:21; Zeph 2:2). 7:17b, 'the king of Assyria', is a later, historicising, addition.

[59]   A parallel expression is found in 2 Kgs 17:21, 'when Yahweh had torn Israel from the house of David (קָרַע מֵעַל בֵּית דָּוִד)'. In that context, Israel's separation from Judah and its exile are connected as a first and second step of the same process: separation led to exile (see 2 Kgs 17:22). In 7:17 a similar association between separation and exile may be implied.

[60]   The name has been explained from Egyptian military language; Wagner 2006: 168.

> [1] Then Yahweh said to me, Take a large tablet[61] and write on it in common characters,[62] 'Maher-shalal-hash-baz'.
> [2] And I took[63] reliable witnesses, the priest Uriah and Zechariah son of Jeberechiah.
> [3] And I went to the prophetess, and she conceived and bore a son. Then Yahweh said to me, Name him Maher-shalal-hash-baz;
> [4] for before the child knows how to say 'father' or 'mother', the wealth of Damascus and the spoil of Samaria will be carried away by the king of Assyria.

The historical background of this material is the Syro-Ephraimitic crisis (734-732 BCE), which is similar to that of the oracles within 7:1-17.[64] The announcement of disaster for Aram and Ephraim effectively encourages Ahaz and the people of Judah. In 8:1 Isaiah is commanded to perform a symbolic act. The prophetic message on the large tablet probably was for public display. The function of the two witnesses probably was to be able to testify afterwards that Isaiah indeed had predicted the punishment of Aram and Ephraim beforehand.[65] 8:3-4 resembles 7:14b.16, and the intent of the two oracles is similar too: Aram and Ephraim will be punished by Assyria because of their threat against Judah. The imminence of the punishment is even more strongly emphasised than in 7:16.[66] The correspondence between 7:14b.16 and 8:3-4 can be explained by the fact that both are birth oracles. In both cases a newborn son receives an auspicious name, which encourages king and people in a threatening situation.

Later Material

This section concentrates on 8:5-8 and 8:11-15 (for 8:16-18, see 2.1.1 and 2.1.5). As in 7:1-17, where the earlier oracles 7:4-9a and 14b.16 were incorporated in a new literary context, 8:1-4 received a twist with the extended passage 8:5-8. The phrase 'Yahweh spoke to me again' (8:5) is a compositional bridge introducing a new prophecy. 8:6-8 is a literary extension to the earlier word (8:1-4) from the hand of the editor/composer. The announcement against Judah's enemies was complemented with an announcement of punishment against

---

[61]   For a discussion of the term גִּלָּיוֹן, see Wagner 2006: 50 note 30.
[62]   Cf. Gray 1912: 142-143, 'an ordinary stylus', which would mean that Isaiah is ordered to write in ordinary letters.
[63]   For this translation, see Barthel 1997: 184, 186.
[64]   Barthel 1997: 187-188.
[65]   Cf. Wildberger 1972-82: 317.
[66]   The time indication of 8:4 means: before the child speaks its first words.

Judah itself. The additional 'prophecy' has a fine balance between accusation and announcement, both in metaphoric language:

> Because this people have refused the waters of Shiloah that flow gently
> and smoothly,[67] Therefore, the Lord is bringing up against them the wa-
> ters of the River mighty and many.

This passage reflects the rejection of the prophetic message by the
people.[68] The expression 'waters of Shiloah' is a metaphor for Yahweh's blessings: the people are accused of having rejected Yahweh
and his blessings.[69] A similar accusation is found in Jer 2:13, 'my people have forsaken me, the fountain of living water'. The accusation is
followed by the announcement that the people will be consumed by
raging water.[70] 8:7b-8 continues the announcement of 8:7a. 8:8a takes
up the threat against Judah introduced in 8:7. The phrase 'to reach up
to the neck' does not indicate deliverance, but stresses the dangerous
depth of the flood.[71] 8:8b carries on with the image of the river as referring to the Mesopotamian king, 'its wings' probably meaning the
riverbanks that stand for the flanks of the king's army.[72]

The person addressed in 8:8b 'your land' (אַרְצְךָ) must be Immanuel,[73] likely to represent the Davidic dynasty.[74] In this way, the announcement of 8:8b corresponds to the dynastic-critical tendency of

---

[67] Cf. Clements 1980a: 96. Both accusation and announcement contain a water
metaphor, with 'gently and smoothly' (taking מְשׁוֹשׂ as a by-form of מְסוֹס) paralleling
'mighty and many'. The phrases 'Rezin and the son of Remaliah' (8:6bβ) and 'the
king of Assyria and all his glory' (8:7aβ) are later, historicising additions, aiming to
establish a link with the situation as depicted in 7:1-17; cf. Dietrich 1976: 65, and see
note 137 below.

[68] Barthel (1997: 196) acknowledges the reflective character of 8:6-8, but regards
it as reflection by Isaiah himself on the lack of effect of his words.

[69] See Nielsen 1989: 45; Wildberger 1972-82: 324. The 'waters of Shiloah' do
not stand for the Davidic monarchy (contra Barthel 1997: 203; Irvine 1990: 190-191).
Various passages from First Isaiah contain similar accusations with מאס, 'to reject':
5:24, the people have rejected Yahweh's torah, and 30:12, the people have rejected
Yahweh's word.

[70] For the image of the destructive flood depicting an enemy invasion, see Isa
28:15-18; Jer 47:2; Nah 1:8. Isa 30:28 depicts Yahweh as a raging flood that destroys
Assyria.

[71] Wong 1999: 426-427.

[72] Barthel 1997: 207; Wong 1999: 427.

[73] Wong's suggestions (1999: 429) to separate אַרְצְךָ from the immediately
following עִמָּנוּ אֵל, and to regard Isaiah as the addressee, are unconvincing. The
prophet functions as the mediator of the oracle, not as the recipient. Moreover, עִמָּנוּ אֵל
does not make sense in an isolated position.

[74] According to Barthel (1997: 207-208), Immanuel is a fictive addressee;
Sweeney (1996a: 173) suggests Immanuel symbolising Judah.

Isa 7 (especially 7:17). 8:5-8 forms a conceptual unity: the introduction (8:5) is followed by a balanced accusation and announcement (8:6-7a), an extension of the announcement (8:7b-8a), and a concluding remark (8:8b). The depiction of disaster does not correspond to the situation of Judah's submission to Tiglath-pileser III in 734. Instead, it may refer to a disastrous situation as a *vaticinium ex eventu*. The prophecy against Judah in 8:5-8 is a later expansion of the oracle against Ephraim and Aram, from the perspective that what counts for Ephraim counts for Judah as well. This is indicative of a later view, when both kingdoms had come to an end, and historical parallels were drawn (cf. 8:14 below).

The announcement of judgement in 8:5-8 must be interpreted in connection with 6:9-11: 'this people' will be punished because of their disobedience. The designation 'this people' functions on the level of the redactional composition of Isa 6-8, not within a supposed eighth-century setting.[75] By referring to הָעָם הַזֶּה, 8:11 takes up the theme of 8:5-8. The passage 8:11-15 is composed from a later point of view as well.[76] The depiction in 8:11 of Yahweh's hand overpowering Isaiah and preventing him from going the way of the people refers to the vision report of Isa 6,[77] from the perspective of 6:9-11. The vision is presented here as illustrating Isaiah's opposition to the disobedient people ('this people') to whom he announces disaster.[78] In 8:11 Isaiah is warned not to go the way of the people, which implies that they have gone astray.[79] Whereas in 8:5-8 Judah's destruction is announced, 8:11-15 describes two reactions to this announcement of disaster. 8:12-13 addresses a plural subject, not explicitly identified, but to be designated as 'the faithful'. They stand in opposition to 'this people', i.e. the sinful nation. The faithful probably are the same as the prophet's 'disciples' mentioned in 8:16. They are summoned not to

---

[75] According to Barthel (1997: 201-202), הָעָם הַזֶּה refers to the Judaeans who supported the plot of Rezin and Pekah against Ahaz. The conspiracy mentioned in 8:12 is then taken as referring to this plot. See Barthel 1997: 224; Irvine 1990: 203. However, the 'waters of Shiloah' (8:6) refer to Yahweh's blessings, not to the Davidic dynasty, and 8:12 cannot be convincingly understood as referring to a conspiracy against Ahaz.

[76] Becker 1997: 111.

[77] Barthel 1997: 87. Cf. 'the hand of Yahweh was strong upon me' (Ezek 3:14); 'the hand of Yahweh was upon …', as introducing a visionary experience (Ezek 1:3; 3:22; 8:1; 37:1; 40:1; cf. 2 Kgs 3:15).

[78] Barthel 1997: 220.

[79] See also Isa 30:11; and cf. Isa 65:2; Jer 7:23-24; 18:15.

call קֶשֶׁר, 'conspiracy' or 'high treason' what the sinful people call קֶשֶׁר. This represents the reaction of the sinful people to the announcement of judgement (8:5-8). The people reject the prophecy of judgement and the prophet proclaiming it. They call it 'high treason', an offence against the state. Similar reactions to 'true prophecy of judgement' are found in Amos 7:10 and Jer 38:1-4. The true prophet of judgement is accused of conspiracy against the state. The point of 8:11-15 is that this is the wrong reaction to the prophetic message. The faithful, in opposition to 'this people', are therefore summoned to refrain from this reaction and from fearing the wrong thing. The sinful people fear the foreign enemy and regard the prophetic announcement that the enemy will destroy them as high treason. However, they do not realise that the foreign enemy is an agent of Yahweh, who is determined to destroy the people. The faithful are urged to fear Yahweh; then they will be saved. Whereas for them Yahweh will be a sanctuary, a safe place (8:14),[80] he will be a stone of stumbling, a cause for destruction for the sinful people of Israel and Judah.[81]

Far from being a report of an eighth-century controversy, 8:11-15 deals with the right view of history. It explains that Yahweh himself brought disaster over 'the two houses of Israel'. Behind the Assyrians and the Babylonians stands Yahweh, who was determined to punish the sinful people. Instead of qualifying this view as high treason, conspiracy against the state, the readers or hearers of the message should focus on Yahweh as the real actor in history. The wrong reaction of the sinful people to the announcement of judgement and the right reaction of the faithful, is part of the reflection of the composition of Isa 6-8.

The disasters are no longer restricted to Judah's enemies (8:1-4), but affect Judah and Jerusalem. This extension reveals a later perspective, far exceeding the Syro-Ephraimitic crisis.[82] 8:14-15 explicitly states that the destruction includes Northern Israel, Judah, and the inhabitants of Jerusalem. Whereas Northern Israel was dealt with in 8:1-4, the extension of 8:5-8.11-15 makes clear that Yahweh's judgement similarly applies to Judah and Jerusalem.

---

[80]   MT 8:14 makes sense and must not to be changed; so also Wagner 2006: 52 note 37.

[81]   Barthel (1997: 227) shows that this announcement of judgement turns the traditional depictions of Yahweh (i.e. Yahweh as rock of rescue) upside down.

[82]   This is agreed by Barthel 1997: 225.

The expressions 'stone of blow' and 'rock of stumbling' are paralleled in Jer 6:21, Ezek 7:19 and 44:12.[83] The phrase 'both houses of Israel', which occurs only here, implies the view of Israel and Judah as being twin nations, and refers to the collapse of both national states. It was probably after the termination of the national states of Israel and Judah (i.e. after 586 BCE) that such historical parallels were drawn.

Isa 8:9-10

The passage 8:9-10 is a *Fremdkörper* between 8:5-8 and 8:11-15:

> [9] Band together,[84] you peoples, and be dismayed; listen, all you far countries;
> gird yourselves and be dismayed; gird yourselves and be dismayed!
> [10] Take counsel together, but it shall be brought to naught;
> speak a word, but it will not stand, for God is with us.

Enclosed within the announcements of judgement against Judah, the nations of the world are addressed. The change of perspective is indicated by the use of the terms עַם and אֶרֶץ: contrary to הָעָם הַזֶּה in 8:6, 11-12 (the people of Judah), עַמִּים refers to foreign nations, and contrary to אֶרֶץ in 8:8b (the land of Judah), אֶרֶץ in 8:9 means 'world'. Furthermore, 8:9-10 takes up the oracles of encouragement of 7:1-17.[85] 8:10 is a construction of three phrases from the oracles: יַעַן כִּי יָעַץ ... רָעָה (7:5), לֹא תָקוּם (7:7) and עִמָּנוּ אֵל (7:14). This suggests that 8:9-10 is close to the oracles concerning the Syro-Ephraimitic crisis. The fact that 8:10 quotes only from the oracles of encouragement suggests that 8:9-10 preceded the literary reworking of Isa 6-8 focusing on the people's disobedience and subsequent disaster. 8:9-10 is to be related to the oracles of encouragement. Various authors have attributed 8:9-10 to an Assyria Redaction.[86] The Assyria Redaction is regarded a redactional revision of earlier, Isaianic material, dating from the later part of the seventh century, against the background of Assyria's loss of

---

[83] Cf. esp. Jer 6:21: 'See, I (Yahweh) am laying before this people (הָעָם הַזֶּה) stumbling blocks against which they shall stumble; parents and children together, neighbour and friend shall perish'.

[84] רעו can be derived from רעה II 'to band together' (Wildberger 1972-82: 329), or from an otherwise unknown qal of רוע 'erhebt den Kriegsruf!' (Müller 1974: 47), or from רעע 'to be evil' (Barthel 1997: 195-196).

[85] See Müller 1974: 47-48; Irvine 1990: 193-194. The language of 8:9 reflects the motif of the *Völkerkampf*, a mythical depiction belonging to the Zion tradition.

[86] See Barthel 1997: 208-212, following Barth.

imperial power. The case of 8:9-10 however is somewhat different, since Assyria is not mentioned. Nevertheless, 8:9-10 is characterised by the same euphoric voice found in passages probably belonging to the Assyria Redaction, which proclaim the downfall of Assyria (14:24-27, 30:27-33, 31:4-5.8-9).

Early Material versus Later Composition

8:1-4, representing early prophetic material, and 8:9-10, a passage close to the prophetic material, have been reworked into the larger literary unit of 8:1-18. Whereas the early material is supportive and positive (Judah's enemies will be destroyed), the later reworking is characterised by a perspective of judgement against Judah. My analysis of 8:1-18 resembles that of Kratz (2003b: 11-13). Kratz regards 8:1-4 as representing the earliest layer. This material, in his view, identifies Isaiah as a prophet of salvation. At a secondary stage, Isaiah was turned into a prophet of judgement:

> Erst im Rückblick, im Rahmen der weiteren literarischen Überlieferung, ist aus dem Heilspropheten ein Gerichtsprophet und aus dem Heilsorakel ein Mittel zur Verstockung des Volkes geworden. Der Übergang vom einen zum andern ist in der Fortsetzung von Jes 8,1-4 in 8,5-8 mit Händen zu greifen.[87]

In the opinion of Kratz, 8:5-8 and the *Denkschrift* as a redactional unit in general have turned the original meaning of the oracles of salvation upside down.[88]

2.1.4   *Isaiah 6:1-11*

Connection between Isa 6:1-8 and 6:9-11

My analysis of Isa 6 focuses on the character of the connection between 6:1-8, the vision report, and the following verses 6:9-11, the 'message' Isaiah is to deliver. Before discussing this issue, however, I deal with the later update of the message in 6:12-13abα.[89] This passage is usually considered as displaying a late perspective.[90] 6:12-13abα is an addition to 6:11, which gives a more explicit account of the total

---

[87]   Kratz 2003b: 12.
[88]   Kratz 2003b: 13.
[89]   6:10bβ and 6:13bβ are generally considered to be late additions, introducing a hopeful perspective in a context of judgement (e.g. Wagner 2006: 66).
[90]   Williamson 1994: 35-36; Barthel 1997: 75-77, 93; Wagner 2006: 252-255.

destruction of Judah and the deportation of the people.[91] If 6:12-13abα
is a *relecture* of 6:1-11, the latter is of course from an earlier date than
the former. Various scholars have argued that 6:1-11 must be of a pre-
exilic origin, since the addition of 6:12-13abα, reflecting the events of
586 BCE, is to be exilic.[92] This argument, in my view, is not convincing. That 6:12-13abα is later than 6:11 does not mean that 6:11 must
be pre-exilic. Both 6:11 and 6:12-13abα imply the disastrous events of
the sixth century. Whereas 6:11 focuses on the destruction in rather
general terms, 6:12-13abα makes a different point, emphasising the
complete emptiness of the land. 6:12-13abα may date from a late exilic, but also from a post-exilic period,[93] and 6:9-11 can be equally
dated to after 586 BCE.[94] That 6:12-13abα dates to after 586 BCE and
that 6:9-11 dates to before 6:12-13abα, does not imply that 6:9-11
dates to before 586 BCE.[95] The question remains of whether 6:1-11 is
a literary unity or whether a distinction is to be made between 6:1-8
and 6:9-11.[96] A plain reading of 6:1-11 gives the impression that Isaiah
volunteers to go before he knows what an impossible message he is to
deliver. Furthermore, as it is formulated the message of 6:9-10 is
hardly communicable at all. Scholars therefore widely agree that 6:9-
10 is not really a prophetic message, but either a reformulation of
what was from the outset the message Isaiah was to deliver, or a revision of his prophetic message based on his reflection on the lack of
effect of his ministry.[97] Either way, scholars maintain the Isaianic
character of 6:9-11.

A recent proposal by Joosten illustrates this line of argumentation.
Joosten takes 6:9-10 as a pseudo-quotation;[98] instead of being a real

---

[91]   Kaiser 1981: 134; Becker 1997: 64-65.

[92]   Williamson 2004: 195-197; Wagner 2006: 119.

[93]   The motif of the emptiness of the land played a role in the post-exilic period
(see Lipschits 2005: 374). The verb רקק pi. is attested in Jer 27:10; Ezek 11:16 and
Joel 4:6.

[94]   I agree with Williamson (2004: 195-197) that in view of 6:12-13abα as a later
addition, the position of Kaiser and Becker that 6:9-11 is of post-exilic origin, is
unlikely (see Kaiser 1981: 134; Becker 1997: 64-65). This does not imply however
that 6:1-11 in its entirety must be pre-exilic.

[95]   This is important to emphasise, since according to Wagner (2006: 119) the
relatively earlier date of 6:1-11 compared to 6:12-13abα is the only argument on
which a pre-exilic dating of 6:1-11 in its entirety can be based.

[96]   6:10 is sometimes regarded as a later extension to 6:9.11 (Becker 1997: 81-82),
but this is not entirely convincing.

[97]   See Barthel 1997: 87-94.

[98]   Joosten 2001.

word of Yahweh, it represents what Isaiah, through his experience of a long and ineffective ministry, had discerned to be Yahweh's intention.[99] 6:11, on the other hand, is taken as reporting a real conversation between Isaiah and Yahweh, which initially followed Yahweh's original message that later was replaced by its revision (6:9-10). The original word of Yahweh (replaced by the reflection of 6:9-10) was a prophecy of judgement against Judah.[100] This line of argument—taking 6:1-8 and 6:11 as direct encounters between Yahweh and Isaiah, and 6:9-10 as a reflection from the hand of Isaiah at a later point in his career—apparently rescues 6:1-11 as Isaianic. However, the argumentation fails to convince. 6:9-10 can only be regarded as Isaiah's reflection on his failed ministry if his ministry aimed at repentance. Yet, 6:11 clearly suggests his prophetic message consisted of announcements of punishment and destruction. More importantly, this line of thought requires extensive speculation. On the part of the recipients it must be speculated that they did not listen (which in the case of the Syro-Ephraimitic crisis is hardly plausible). Moreover, on the part of the prophet it must be speculated that Isaiah, forced by his own experiences, no longer was able to take Yahweh's words in their plain sense, but pondered upon Yahweh's real intentions behind them. In my view, 6:9-10 cannot be read as a real message, but neither as Isaiah's own reflection on his prophetic ministry. The latter view turns Isaiah into a theologian who became the interpreter of his own prophetic message. Others have suggested that 6:9-11 represents Isaiah's reflection on his own ministry, provoked by his experience that the people had rejected his message. Isaiah learned to understand that his preaching was ineffective through Yahweh, and reinterpreted his mission as to harden the people in order to effectuate the coming judgement.[101] This would however imply that Isaiah became rather cynical, believing that Yahweh had made the people unsusceptible in order to punish them.

---

[99] Joosten 2001: 239-242.

[100] Joosten 2001: 239-242.

[101] This argument is called the *Rückprojizierungsthese*, see Hesse 1955: 84: 'So, wie Jesajas Verkündigung tatsächlich aussieht, ist sie nicht zu verstehen, wenn man Kap. 6,9f wörtlich nimmt'. According to Barthel (1997: 110), Isaiah solved the difficulty of his message being rejected by explaining his prophetic failure as due to the paradoxical intervention of Yahweh. Barthel 1997: 92: 'Die faktische *Wirkung* des Prophetenwortes erscheint im Verstockungsauftrag *fiktiv als Zweck* und wird auf diese Weise in Jahwes vorgängiger, planvoller Absicht verankert'. Cf. also Hardmeier 1981: 248.

On the contrary, 6:9-11 makes sense if understood as a reflection on the disasters of the early sixth century. The passage makes clear that the disasters are to be understood as Yahweh's punishment, which was not accidental but inevitable. According to 6:9-11, Yahweh was determined to punish his people, because of their sins, and the prophet had to announce the unimaginable. The likeliest origin of the thought that Yahweh was determined to destroy his land and people is the experience of destruction and disaster of the early sixth century BCE.

Isa 6:1-8 as an Independent Unit

Whereas the vision report is intended to legitimise Isaiah as a speaker and actor on behalf of Yahweh, the subsequent passage, 6:9-11, reflects on the disasters as divine punishment for the disobedience of the people. It is difficult to ascribe the different intentions of 6:1-8 and 6:9-11 to a common denominator.[102] Many scholars acknowledge that 6:1-11 goes back to two entirely different experiences: the first being Isaiah's visionary experience as the basis for 6:1-8, the second Isaiah's later experience of the ineffectiveness of his prophetic ministry as the basis for 6:9-11. They maintain nevertheless the literary unity of 6:1-11.[103] Some scholars however have proposed a distinction between 6:1-8 and 6:9-11, on literary-critical, redaction-critical, and mainly intent-critical grounds.[104]

In my view, 6:9-11 belongs to the literary reworking of the earlier material within Isa 6-8. 6:1-8, on the other hand, represents an earlier stage. Although at present the hardening order of 6:9-10 takes a central position within Isa 6,[105] the vision report can very well be read as

---

[102]   See in particular Berges 1998: 98-99.

[103]   E.g. Barthel (1997: 106) admits that the vision report displays a purpose of its own (the '*Begegnung* Jesajas mit Jahwe') and was included in the larger literary composition by a shift of focus to Isaiah's '*Beteiligung* am Vorhaben Jahwes mit "diesem Volk".' With respect to the vision report, Barthel (1997: 107, note 187) acknowledges: 'daß die Erinnerung der ursprünglichen Erfahrung hier ein stärkeres Eigengewicht bewahrt hat'. Barthel (1997: 103) furthermore agrees that the vision report does not anticipate the harsh message of 6:9-11. Nevertheless, Barthel refuses to regard the vision report independently of its literary context. In my opinion, Barthel has not applied to Isa 6 a similar, critical approach to the one he successfully applies to 7:1-17.

[104]   See Berges 1998: 94-102; Becker 1997: 81-89. Becker (1997: 81) points out that Kaiser's arguments to regard 6:1-11 as later theological reflection (1981: 121-123, 133) in fact apply to 6:9-11. See further the considerations of Deck 1991: 168.

[105]   Cf. Barthel 1997: 72-73.

an independent unit.[106] The report describes a visionary experience pinpointed to a specific moment, the year Uzziah died (6:1). Furthermore, the report has a theme of its own: Isaiah's encounter with the holy Lord, which resulted in the prophet's transformation. From a dramatic perspective, the vision report consists of two scenes: 6:1-4 and 6:5-8. The first scene describes Yahweh as a powerful and majestic king; the second describes an act of purification involving Isaiah. Whereas in the first scene Isaiah is a spectator, he becomes a participant in the second. The first scene is marked by an inclusion of הַהֵיכָל and הַבַּיִת (6:1 and 4) both referring to the temple. The second scene is marked by an inclusion of וָאֹמַר (6:5 and 8). The action taken by the seraph purifies Isaiah, and Yahweh includes him in the heavenly court. If we focus on the pattern built by the narrative forms, the composition of the vision report appears to be the following:

A	6:1	וָאֶרְאֶה		וָאֶשְׁמַע	6:8	A'
B	6:2	seraph description יְעוֹפֵף		seraph description וַיָּעָף	6:6	B'
C	6:3	seraph shouts: *holy*		seraph says: *purified*	6:7	C'
D	6:4	קוֹל הַקּוֹרֵא		קוֹל אֲדֹנָי	6:8	D'
E	6:5	וָאֹמַר אוֹי לִי כִּי נִדְמֵיתִי		וָאֹמַר הִנְנִי שְׁלָחֵנִי	6:8	E'

The narrative pattern discloses a focus on Isaiah's transition. At first, he sees Yahweh worshipped by the seraphs, and reacts: 'woe is me! I am lost'. After having been purified by the act of a seraph however he hears Yahweh speaking, and reacts: 'Here am I; send me!' This contrast indicates the aim of the report as to present Isaiah as the legitimate speaker and actor on behalf of Yahweh.[107] The vision report is intended to present Isaiah as being commissioned by Yahweh: Isaiah speaks and acts on behalf of Yahweh, the great king.[108]

---

[106] No argument based on the literary form of Isa 6:1-11 can be raised against a distinction between 6:1-8 and 6:9-11, since 6:1-11 does not apply to any *Gattung* (1 Kgs 22:19-22 is not a helpful parallel; see Wagner 2006: 115-116).

[107] Berges 1998: 97. Barthel's suggestion (1997: 96-105) to restrict the vision report in a strict sense to 6:1-7, eliminates its climax.

[108] Cf. Brueggemann 1998: 59-60: 'The throne room of God is the policy room of world government. There is business to conduct. ... There are messages to be sent. The government of Yahweh ... needs a carrier.' According to Deck (1991: 168), if the function of the report was to confirm the prophet's legitimacy over against his hearers, 6:8 forms a good conclusion.

The imagery of 6:1-8 is suggestive of a temple setting.[109] Yahweh is depicted as a king on a throne of huge dimensions.[110] The seraphs in attendance around him are to be understood as uraeus-like figures, divine figures in the form of winged snakes.[111] The accompanying shaking and smoke (6:4) are indicative of Yahweh's epiphany.[112] Isaiah, initially terrified, is purified by the act of one of the seraphs, and in this way he is prepared for being commissioned.[113] This is not a vision of judgement as some have argued.[114] On the contrary, the imagery supports the interpretation of 6:1-8 as a vision with a positive, encouraging, intent. First of all, the seraphs are protective figures.[115] Furthermore, the image of Yahweh's fearsome radiance (6:1-4) does not necessarily imply that Yahweh is angry with his own people.[116] It is much more likely that Yahweh's fearsome appearance as sovereign king points to his decision to take action against Judah's enemies. The motif of Yahweh's lordship, paralleled in texts such as Ps 24:7-10 and Ps 29, indicates 'die Kriegsmächtigkeit Jahwes im Streit gegen andere Völker'.[117] Yahweh's epiphany as a mighty and fearsome king in texts resembling the imagery of 6:1-4, such as Ps 18:6-17, deals with Yahweh's violent actions against Judah's enemies. Understood in this way, the vision of 6:1-8 completely corresponds with the earlier pro-

---

[109]   Keel 1977: 47-56; Wagner 2006: 87.
[110]   See Podella 1996: 189; Keel 1977: 124.
[111]   For the seraphs, see Keel 1977: 70-115; Mettinger 1999; Provençal 2005; Wagner 2006: 87-95. The background of the seraph motif is the Egyptian uraeus serpent, well attested in eighth-century Palestine on seals, as was demonstrated by Keel (1977). The position of the seraphs as standing above Yahweh (6:2), is reminiscent of the image of the uraei as protective figures on Egyptian and Phoenician chapel friezes. In Isa 6, the seraphs use their wings to cover themselves from Yahweh's consuming holiness, which underscores Yahweh's supreme holiness (Mettinger 1999: 743). Provençal (2005) shows that in the ancient Near East deities were depicted as surrounded by lower deities, often in the form of serpents or dragons, whose function was to protect. In Egypt, the uraeus-snake was such a figure, part of the Pharaoh's regalia. The uraei serpents are cobras mythologically portrayed with wings (2005: 373-375).
[112]   Keel 1977: 121-123.
[113]   Wagner 2006: 94-95.
[114]   Contra Knierim 1968: 55; Hartenstein 1997: 3, 26-29.
[115]   Keel 1977: 54, note 43; Wagner 2006: 92-93. Sass (1993: 213) notes regarding the uraeus-figures on pre-exilic Hebrew seals: 'the being was meant to hover over the name, providing divine protection'.
[116]   Becker 1999: 149-150; cf. Hardmeier 1981: 241.
[117]   Wagner 2006: 102. Related to Yahweh's violent actions against Judah's enemies are his benefactions for, and protection of his people (Wagner 2006: 102, 109). For the motif of Yahweh's lordship in connection with Ps 24:7-10 and 29, see Wagner 2006: 99-102.

phetic material, discussed above: 7:4-9a, 7:14b.16 and 8:1-4.[118] In 6:5-8, Isaiah, who is one of the people, not someone opposed to them, is purified and commissioned as Yahweh's envoy to the people. This adds to the expectation of an encouraging message.[119]

The vision report (6:1-8) proclaims Isaiah's legitimacy as Yahweh's envoy. Its role in the Isaiah tradition was to underscore the prophet's credentials as a spokesman of Yahweh.[120] Isa 6:1-8 is to be understood in relation to the early prophecies of 7:4-9a, 7:14b.16 and 8:1-4. The prophecies encourage King Ahaz and the people of Judah and announce the destruction of Judah's enemies. The vision report portrays the bearer of these messages as Yahweh's trustworthy envoy.

The Vision turned Upside Down

The account of Isaiah's commissioning (6:1-8) is likely to date from the Assyrian period.[121] In its later version, the vision has been given a new twist. Whereas the function of the account of Isaiah's commissioning was to present Isaiah as Yahweh's legitimised messenger, 6:9-11 focuses on the people's lack of attention and their punishment. In 6:5-8, Isaiah is pictured as one of his people. 6:9-11, on the contrary, presents Isaiah in opposition to the people. This turn of focus is marked by the introduction of a new category, הָעָם הַזֶּה. The pejorative designation displays the perspective that the disasters that befell Judah are to be understood as Yahweh's punishment because of the people's disobedience. In this way, 6:9-11 changed the original meaning of the vision report in exactly the same way as the composition of 7:1-17 changed the original meaning of the oracles included, and as 8:1-18 gave a twist to the original meaning of 8:1-4. 6:9-11 reflects on a disastrous situation, as does 7:1-17, which focuses on the end of the Davidic dynasty, and 8:1-18, which refers to the destruction of Judah and Jerusalem (8:14-15). The prophetic figure presented in 6:1-8:18 is to announce the incomprehensible until it has become a reality (6:11).

---

[118] The motif of Yahweh as king of the whole earth in 6:3 (see Wagner 2006: 105, 107), particularly resembles 8:9-10, which is close to the prophetic material within Isa 7* and 8*.

[119] Keel 1977: 55, note 43: 'Man könnte sogar sagen, daß Jesaja, nachdem er Jahwe geschaut hatte und am Leben geblieben, ja von seiner Unreinheit (...) gnädig befreit worden war, eher eine Heilsbotschaft erwartete und sich deshalb so willig zur Verfügung stellte.'

[120] Berges 1998: 97.

[121] The imagery, in particular the seraphs, points to the Assyrian period; see Wagner 2006: 121-122.

When his ministry is completed he hopes and waits for Yahweh's salvation in the midst of disaster (8:17). This line of thought is far removed from the eighth-century prophet and must be qualified as a
product of later interpretation.

2.1.5   *Evaluation*

In this section I have argued that within Isa 6:1-8:18 two basic layers
are to be discerned, the one represented by early prophetic material
(7:2-3a.4-9a; 7:14b.16; 7:20; 8:1-4, to which 8:9-10 and 6:1-8 are to
be related) the other consisting of a later, literary reworking of the
prophetic material.[122] The two layers can be shortly characterised by
8:1 on the one hand, and 8:16 on the other. In 8:1, Isaiah appears as a
prophet who performs a symbolic act, whereas in 8:16 he is portrayed
as having codified his message as a testimony for future times.
Whereas the earliest level in all probability relates to the activity of a
historical prophet, the later account is a literary elaboration that displays a new view of the prophet and his commission. In 8:1, Isaiah is
to write down a single saying on a tablet; 8:16 deals with the
codification of the prophetic preaching as such, which functions as a
testimony for future generations. The testimony and teaching (תְּעוּדָה,
תּוֹרָה) mentioned in 8:16 are likely to refer to the composition of Isa 6-
8 itself.[123]

The earliest layer consists of prophecies of encouragement. Isaiah's
role during the Syro-Ephraimitic crisis as inferred from these prophecies to a great extent resembles the role the figure of Isaiah plays in
the Hezekiah story of 2 Kgs 18-19 (Isa 36-37).[124] The earliest version
of the Hezekiah story is likely to date from the seventh century.[125] This
story pictures Isaiah as a prophet proclaiming salvation to the king in a
situation of national disaster. This resembles the role Isaiah played
according to the earliest material within Isa 6-8. Although the Hezekiah story in its earliest version is not an historical account, the corre-

---

[122]   This distinction builds on earlier publications. Various scholars have made a
more or less similar distinction between earlier and later material within Isa 6-8:
Barthel 1997: 118-183; Becker 1997: 21-123; Berges 1998: 94-117; Clements 1980a:
96-100; Hardmeier 1979.
[123]   Barthel 1997: 236.
[124]   Barthel 1997: 166.
[125]   Gonçalves 1986: 441. The earliest version, usually referred to as the B1-story,
consists of 2 Kgs 18:17-19:9a.36-37; see chapter 6.1.2.

spondence of the portrayal of Isaiah with the early material in Isa 6-8 is of traditio-historical relevance. It confirms that in the seventh century, the prophet Isaiah was not yet known as a prophet of judgement.

The composition of Isa 6:1-8:18 refers to a terrible situation for Judah and Jerusalem (8:14-15), which implies the devastation in the early sixth century, resulting in the destruction of Jerusalem, the collapse of the Judaean state, the end of the Davidic monarchy and the exile of the upper class. The view that Isaiah was the author of Isa 6-8, either shortly after the Syro-Ephraimitic crisis or at a later stage in his career, is to be rejected.[126] Neither can the composition be explained as a reflection on the events of 701.[127] The way in which Isaiah is presented in Isa 6-8, in particular 6:9-11 and 8:16-18 suggests a later compositional milieu. The prophet is presented as still hoping for Yahweh in the midst of a situation in which disaster has become inevitable. The composition is intended to show that the disaster was not due to the failure of the prophetic message, but the result of the people's disobedience decided on by God: the punishment was inevitable.[128] The disasters that befell Judah in the sixth century, interpreted as divine punishment for the disobedience of the people and the royal dynasty, induced theological reflection, which resulted in a new image of the prophet as messenger from Yahweh to warn the people, and, as his message was rejected, to announce Yahweh's judgement.[129]

The literary composition of Isa 6-8 is in all probability to be dated to after 586.[130] The text presents a reworking of the prophetic tradition

---

[126] If the oracles of 7:4-9a, 14b.16 and 8:1-4 represent Isaiah's message during the Syro-Ephraimitic crisis, it is difficult to imagine how the king or the people could have rejected it. 6:9-11 and 8:5-8 are better understood as the product of later reflection. It is unlikely that Isaiah himself was responsible for the new interpretation that turned the original meaning of the oracles upside down. The image of Isaiah as a prophet *and* the interpreter of his prophetic message telescopes two different stages that are better explained separately. The view of Isaiah as a prophet-theologian may be attractive from a biblical theological point of view, but is exegetically and historically implausible.

[127] The announcement of disaster over the Davidic dynasty (7:17) and the inclusion of Jerusalem in the disasters announced (8:14-15) cannot be explained from a 701-perspective. Besides, the seventh-century reception of 701 is marked by a positive and glorifying tone: Jerusalem's deliverance is emphasised rather than the destruction of the land.

[128] Berges (1998: 101) points out that 6:9-10 is not a theodicy (contra Becker 1997: 85-86), but an evaluation of the prophetic commissioning in reaction to the disastrous situation of the Babylonian exile.

[129] Collins 1993: 49-50.

[130] Becker 1997: 78-79.

resulting from the reflection provoked by the disasters of 586, and is best situated in the exilic period.[131] The exilic dating of Isa 6:1-8:18 is furthermore confirmed by terms and concepts used in the reflective, literary passages within Isa 6-8. The clearest case is 6:11. The exclamation 'how long, O Lord?' reflects a situation of crisis. The expression occurs as lamentation in Psalms and as outcry in the prophetic books, and indicates a time of tribulation.[132] In the answer of Yahweh, the utter destruction of the cities and the land is announced in terms that elsewhere refer to the destruction of Judah and Jerusalem by the Babylonians. The following parallels may be noted: 'cities without inhabitants' (עָרִים מֵאֵין יוֹשֵׁב);[133] the verb שאה referring to the devastation of cities and land;[134] desolation 'without human beings' (מֵאֵין אָדָם);[135] the land becoming a desolation (שְׁמָמָה).[136] The correspondence does not only consist of the use of similar terms, but also of a similar theme: it is Yahweh's will that Judah is devastated, because of its disobedience.

The depiction of the prophet Isaiah as a preacher of disaster to a disobedient people is the product of theological reflection and came into being through an extensive reworking of the Isaiah tradition in the exilic period. Within the process of the exilic reworking of the Isaiah tradition, the composition of Isa 6:1-8:18 probably takes a relatively early place. The literary reworking of the earlier, prophetic material

---

[131] Williamson (2004: 193-195) rightly points out that Becker's arguments for dating 6:9.11 and 8:5-8.17 to the early post-exilic period (Becker 1997: 78, 87) are problematic. This does not however imply that we have to assume a pre-exilic dating for 6:9-11 and related passages. A late exilic or early post-exilic dating of the *Grundbestand* of Second Isaiah (which takes up the theme of 6:9-10) leaves room for a post-586 dating of the complex 6:1-11, 7:1-17, 8:1-18, and comparable literary complexes of the earlier prophetic material. I agree with Berges (1998: 99), who suggests that the order of hardening in 6:9-10 is to be seen as an exilic reflection aiming to excuse Yahweh's prophet.

[132] See Ps 6:4; 13:2; 74:10; 79:5; 80:5; 82:2; 89:47; 90:13; 94:3 and Jer 4:21; 12:4; Dan 8:13; 12:6; Hab 1:2; Zech 1:2. Cf. Roberts 1977a, with examples from Mesopotamian lament.

[133] Cf. Jer 2:15; 4:7, 29; 9:10; 33:10; 34:22; 44:2 (referring to the cities of Judah) and Jer 26:9 (referring to Jerusalem).

[134] The verb in this meaning further occurs only in 2 Kgs 19:25 (Isa 37:26). That passage is part of the later, exilic, extension to the Hezekiah story of 701. The twofold occurrence of this verb in 6:11 has led to the suggestion that תִּשָּׁאֶה is a corruption of תִּשָּׁאֵר, 'the land is left desolate' (Williamson 1994: 249).

[135] Cf. Jer 32:43; 33:10, 12, referring to the land of Judah.

[136] The combination of שְׁמָמָה with הָאֲדָמָה only occurs in Isa 1:7 and 6:11. More frequently it is the combination of שְׁמָמָה with אֶרֶץ, referring to the land of Judah becoming a desolation: Jer 4:27; 10:22; 12:11; Ezek 6:14; 12:20; 15:8; 33:28-29 (cf. Lev 26:33).

not only revised the original meaning of the prophecies, but also disconnected them from the events of 734-732, in order to provide an account of Isaiah's prophetic ministry from beginning to end. The literary reworking of Isa 6-8 dehistoricised the earlier material.[137] It is likely that 6:1-8:18 to some extent functioned as a model for similar reworkings of other parts of the Isaiah tradition, such as Isa 28-32. In the rest of this chapter, I attempt to demonstrate that the reworking of Isa 6-8 does not stand in isolation, but can be compared to various other texts within First Isaiah that announce the destruction of Judah and Jerusalem.

2.2   Isaiah 28-32

2.2.1   Isaiah 28-32 as a Literary Complex

The literary complex of Isa 28-32 is the result of redactional elaboration and contains different kinds of material.[138] Previously, scholars have identified three kinds of material. a) A basic literary layer, believed to consist of words of Isaiah: 28:1-4.7-22; 29:1-4.9-10.13-16; 30:1-16; 31:1-4. b) Passages belonging to a seventh-century redaction: 29:5-7(8); 30:27-33; 31:5.8-9; 32:1-5.15-20. c) A post-exilic edition proclaiming salvation after the punishment: 28:5-6; 29:17-24; 30:18-26.[139] In general, I agree with this view on Isa 28-32. However, I propose a refinement of the passages of category a), by distinguishing between the early prophetic material and its literary reworking or transformation in response to the sixth-century disasters.[140] This re-

---

[137]   At a later stage, when the composition of Isa 6-8 had become part of a larger literary complex, it became to some extent rehistoricised through a series of additions. This section of the book was presented as focusing on the fate of the Northern Kingdom and as relating to the events of 734-732. In order to create this connection, a series of historical identifications was added: 7:4b ('because of the fierce anger of Rezin and Aram and the son of Remaliah'), 7:5bα ('with Ephraim and the son of Remaliah'), 7:17b ('the king of Assyria'), 8:6bβ ('and melt in fear before Rezin and the son of Remaliah'), 8:7aβ ('the king of Assyria and all his glory'), similarly 9:8aβ ('Ephraim and the inhabitants of Samaria'), 9:10a ('Rezin').

[138]   Barthel 1997: 255.

[139]   See the overview in Stansell 1996: 68-69.

[140]   Cf. for instance Beuken's division of Isaiah 30 into three main blocks (Beuken 1997). Beuken attributes 30:1-17 to Isaiah and regards 30:18-26 as a post-exilic, written composition. 30:27-33, in his view, may be earlier than 30:18-26. I accept Beuken's threefold division (in my view, 30:27-33 is part of the seventh-century revision). With respect to 30:1-17, I propose however a refinement of Beuken's posi-

working probably is to be dated in the exilic period and was a formative stage of the Isaiah tradition. A certain number of reflective texts,
traditionally attributed to the 'writer-prophet Isaiah', in fact belong to
a later reworking of the Isaiah tradition. Whereas the Isaiah tradition
in the seventh-century revision probably developed into several small
textual compilations, it was in all likelihood the literary reworking of
the exilic period that first created some substantial literary complexes.
I therefore propose a distinction between a) material deriving from
eighth-century prophetic activity, b) a seventh-century revision addressing the theme of Yahweh's destruction of Assyria, c) a literary-
redactional reworking of the earlier material, situated in the exilic period, and d) a post-exilic edition proclaiming eschatalogical salvation:

a) prophetic sayings and ora-cles	b) seventh-century Assyria revision	c) 'disobedience-judgement' exilic reworking	d) post-exilic edition
28:1-4		28:7a.11-13	28:5-6
28:7b-10, 12		28:14-22	
28:14-18*		29:1-4(6).9-10	29:7-8
29:15		29:13-16	29:17-24
30:1-5*. 6-8		30:9-11.12-14	
30:15	30:27-33	30:15-17	30:18-26
31:1-3*	31:4-5.8-9 + 32:1-2	32:9-14	32:15-20

The passages from category d), from the post-exilic period,[141] are not
taken into account here. Category c) is where I depart from the traditional position. The literary complexity of the passages of category c)
renders their attribution to Isaiah unlikely in my view. The passages
not only have a reflective character, but also contain indications of
literary elaboration. Whereas I agree that Isa 28-32 in its core contains
material deriving from prophetic activity,[142] this early material is to be
distinguished from its later literary reworking. Before discussing the
presumedly early material I will argue that an analogy can be drawn
between Isa 28-32 and Isa 6-8. In both cases, prophetic material has

---

tion. On the one hand, this unit clearly contains sayings that can be connected with the
situation of 705-701 BCE. On the other, these sayings are presented in a reworked
form, which postdates the Assyrian period.
[141]   Barthel 1997: 259.
[142]   Becker (1997: 223-268) challenges the common view that Isa 28-32 contains
early, prophetic material, by arguing that Isa 28-32 (apart from 28:1-4*.7b-10*) is in
its core a late (post-exilic) complex. See Williamson 2004: 198-199, for a critical
review of this position.

been incorporated within a literary complex that is marked by reflection and elaboration on the earlier material. Various characteristic features of the literary reworking are pointed out:

1) 28:12-13 and 30:15-17 present a vision on prophecy. First, in both passages a quotation is included that is to represent 'prophecy of old':

> ²⁸:¹² This is the resting place—give rest to the weary; this is the place of repose.
> ³⁰:¹⁵ Thus says the Lord Yahweh, the Holy One of Israel: In sitting and rest you shall be saved; in quietness and trust shall be your strength.

The immediate context however insists that this 'prophecy of old' has been replaced by a prophecy of judgement. In 28:12b-13 and 30:15b-17 it is stated that because the people refused to listen they would be severely punished by Yahweh. Both passages present the 'prophecy of old', which promises salvation, as a passed stage. In this way, they reveal a retrospective point of view. According to this view, prophecy has become prophecy of judgement. This forms an analogy to the transition visible in Isa 6-8, where the earlier positive, encouraging prophetic words at a later stage were turned upside down. Passages belonging to this stage probably reflect on the sixth-century disasters, explaining Judah's terrible fate as being due to Yahweh's punishment because of the people's disobedience.

2) 30:8 is of significance for the transition from the earlier material to the later literary reworking. On the one hand, 30:8 concludes the passage 30:6-8, an early note concerning a prophetic act of inscribing a symbolic name. On the other, at a later stage, 30:8 was extended with 30:9-11: the message is to be preserved as a testimony to the people's stubborn disobedience. The documentation functions as proof of the rejection of the message by the people (cf. 6:9-10). The original act of inscribing a saying has been generalised into the written documentation of the prophetic message as such. The expression עַם מְרִי in 30:9 refers to the motif of the recalcitrance of the people and their long-lasting rebellion against Yahweh.¹⁴³ The refusal to listen occurs in

---

¹⁴³ The terminology and concepts in 30:9-11 confirm a later (probably exilic) provenance: 1) מְרִי indicates the stubbornness of the people (cf. Deut 31:27; Neh 9:17; Ezek 2:5-8; 3:26-27; 12:2-3, 9, 25; 17:12; 24:3; 44:6). 2) For כְּחָשׁ ('lying'), cf. Jer 5:12. 3) The accusation that the people did not obey Yahweh's torah, is paralleled in Isa 1:10; 5:24. 4) אבה שמע 'they refused to listen (i.e. to Yahweh's torah)' is paralleled in Isa 1:19; 28:12; 42:24; Lev 26:21; Ezek 3:7; 20:8 (cf. Ps 81:12). 5) For סור מן דֶּרֶךְ cf. Exod 32:8; Deut 9:12, 16; 31:29; Mal 2:8. 6) The reference to 'seers and

confrontation with the prophetic word. The transition from 30:8 as the conclusion of 30:6-8 to its *relecture* in 30:9-11 forms an analogous case to the transition from 8:1, concerning the inscription of a single symbolic name, to 8:16, concerning the documentation of the prophetic message of judgement as such.

3) Within the literary context of Isa 28-32, the *woe*-word against Samaria (28:1-4) is juxtaposed by that against Jerusalem (29:1-4). Taken together, the two *woe*-words indicate the view that what counts for Samaria (28:1-4) counts for Jerusalem as well (29:1-4). This juxtaposition can be compared to 8:1-4 and its extension in 8:5-8. In the course of the literary development of the Isaiah tradition, earlier prophetic sayings against Ephraim and Samaria (8:1-4, 28:1-4) were complemented by words announcing judgement over Judah and Jerusalem (8:5-8, 29:1-4).

Apart from these indications of a distinction between the earlier prophetic sayings and their later literary reworking, a more general account of the reflective character of the literary complex of Isa 28-32 (passages of category c, above) can be given. Whereas the complex probably ended in 32:9-14 with a description of the disasters that befell Jerusalem in the sixth century ('the palace will be forsaken, the populous city deserted', 32:14), this conclusion is prepared for in various preceding passages with a reflective character. In some of these passages the motif of הָעָם הַזֶּה, 'this people' occurs again (28:11, 14; 29:13-14). 28:11-13 in various ways displays a literary, reflective character. First, it appears to present a *relecture* of the preceding saying, 28:7b-10, which is an earlier prophetic word. The 'unintelligible speech' (28:10) is reinterpreted as an utterance in a foreign language, indicating the invasion of an enemy army. Furthermore, whereas the preceding saying is addressed to (part of) the religious establishment, the announcement of disaster in 28:11-13 is addressed to the people (הָעָם הַזֶּה). The people are accused of having rejected Yahweh's blessings (represented by a quotation of 'prophecy of old') and their severe punishment is announced. The following oracle, 28:15-18, originally directed at the political leaders of Jerusalem, has begun to function as an announcement of disaster in a more general sense. Through the motif of הָעָם הַזֶּה taken up in 28:14, the political leaders are connected

---

prophets' implies the concept of a long-lasting rejection of the prophetic message by the people. These elements are characteristic of the later motif of the disobedient people.

with the people accused in 28:11-13, and the extended, literary re-working of the oracle in 28:19.21-22 renders a more general sense to the announcement.

Further literary-reflective passages are 29:9-10 and 29:13-14. 29:9-10 is thematically related to 6:9-11, as it expresses the relation between the recalcitrance of the people as their own action and their recalcitrance as caused by Yahweh.[144] In the present literary context the imperative plural of 29:9 seems to address the foreign nations of 29:7, but this is a secondary reading, which became possible only in the course of the redactional process, when 29:7 and 8 had been added to 29:1-6. 29:9-10 is intended to address the same subject as 6:9-11: 'this people', that is the people as a disobedient and sinful entity, which is in agreement with the intent of 29:1-6. The people are described as being unable to read the signs of the imminent judgement (they are stupefied and blind). 29:13-16 begins with a word of Yahweh addressed to 'this people' (הָעָם הַזֶּה). The term refers to the people as a sinful entity. Various indications point to the redactional character of 29:13-14. First, the saying has a parallel in 8:6-8. In both cases, the people are accused of having offended Yahweh. The accusation that their hearts are far from Yahweh (29:13) concurs with passages condemning them because of their evil and stubborn hearts.[145] Furthermore, the phrase 'I will again do amazing things (יוֹסִף לְהַפְלִיא)' in 29:14 suggests this is not an isolated oracle, but a literary passage referring to another passage. The connection may be found within the literary complex of Isa 28-32, either 28:21 (with פלא) or perhaps the announcements of 28:11-13 or 29:1-4.[146] Yahweh's wondrous dealings with his people refer to the disasters that befell Judah as being Yahweh's work.[147] A major point of the literary reworking of the Isaiah tradition was to demonstrate that the unimaginable—Yahweh himself was to destroy Judah and Jerusalem—had been announced by the prophet Isaiah (e.g. 6:9-11, 29:1-4, 29:13-14). All this shows that 29:13-14 was composed for the literary context of Isa 28-32.

---

[144] The verb שׁעע occurs only in Isa 6:10; 29:9 (and 32:3): Yahweh himself blinds the people to prevent them escaping his judgement.

[145] See Num 32:7, 9; Jer 5:21, 23; 7:24; 9:13; 13:10; 16:12; Ezek 33:31. The accusation of the pretension of piety, is paralleled in Jer 3:10: 'Yet for all this her false sister Judah did not return to me with her whole heart, but only in pretence, says Yahweh'.

[146] Cf. Barthel 1997: 387.

[147] The parallel expression in Joel 2:25-26 also refers to the disasters that befell Judah.

A final passage to be mentioned here is 30:12-14.15-17. The accusation in 30:12, 'because you reject this word', indicates the redactional character of the passage, as 'this word' (דָּבָר הַזֶּה) is a literary reference, probably to 30:15.[148] The image of the broken jar in 30:14 illustrates the inevitability of the judgement.[149] Like the preceding passage (30:9-11), 30:12-14 focuses on the people's rejection of the prophetic message. The point is similar to that of Isa 6-8: the disasters that befell the people are to be understood as Yahweh's punishment of the people's disobedience: they kept rejecting Yahweh's blessings.

These passages, 28:11-13, 29:9-10.13-14 and 30:12-14.15-17 were composed as part of a literary reworking of the Isaiah tradition, and form the basic literary complex of Isa 28-32. This outline suggests that a principal distinction has to made between the earlier material incorporated within Isa 28-32 on the one hand, and the basic literary complex of Isa 28-32 on the other. The suggestion that either Isaiah or one of his disciples composed the basic literary complex of Isa 28-32 becomes quite unlikely when the character of this literary complex is taken into account.[150] The complex refers to the fall of Jerusalem and the disasters that befell Judah in the sixth century (i.e. 29:1-4, 32:14), and reflects on this by explaining the disasters as Yahweh's punishment of the disobedience of the people.

This overview concludes with a characterisation of the presumed earlier material incorporated within Isa 28-32. Barthel has demonstrated that the prophetic words to a considerable degree have been integrated into a compositional context.[151] The earlier sayings to some extent cannot be simply 'lifted up' from their context, but rather have to be 'peeled out'. In the following analysis, I will discuss 28:1-4, 7b-10, 12, 14-18*, 29:15, 30:1-5*, 6b-8, 15 and 31:1-3* as representing the prophetic material. These sayings derive from prophetic activity in the later part of the eighth century. Besides an announcement of Samaria's downfall in 28:1-4, we find sayings characterised by an encouraging and positive tendency (28:12, 30:15) and sayings criticizing a particular group of people, i.e. the leading figures of Jerusalem (28:7b-10, 14-18*; 29:15; 30:1-5*, 6b-8; 31:1-3*).

---

[148] Barthel 1997: 419-420.
[149] Barthel (1997: 421) points to several parallels, among them Jer 19:10-11.
[150] Contra Barthel 1997: 245-454.
[151] Barthel 1997: 245-454.

Within Isa 28-32, 30:27-33 and 31:4-5.8-9 stand out as texts that deal with Yahweh's destruction of Assyria, reflecting on the downfall of the Assyrian empire. These passages are to be considered as part of a revision of the earlier prophetic material to be situated in the second half of the seventh century.[152] Furthermore, I will argue that 31:4-5.8-9 is to be connected with the beginning of Isa 32. The theme of Assyria's downfall is to be related to the motif of the reign of a righteous Judaean king. I regard it as likely that these texts are part of a revision of the earlier prophetic material that was provoked by a new situation, the decline of the Assyrian empire in the later part of the seventh century.

2.2.2   The Woe-Words in Isaiah 28-31

Although the *woe*-words form part of the basic literary structure of Isa 28-32, they need not all go back to sayings from Isaiah. It will be argued that 28:1-4, 29:15, 30:1-5 and 31:1-3 in their core go back to earlier prophetic material, whereas 29:1-6 does not. Before discussing the sayings some remarks with regard to *woe*-sayings in general are necessary.

Woe-Sayings in the Prophetic Books
The *woe*-sayings as found in the biblical prophetic books probably derive from funerary lament.[153] Whereas the funerary lament expresses grief and mourning, in the prophetic *woe*-saying this is turned into accusation and threat.[154] The *woe*-saying consists of the exclamation הוֹי, 'woe!', which is followed either by a general or proper noun (if the addressees form a well-defined entity), or by a participle (if the addressees are characterized by a certain behaviour that is condemned).[155] Whereas funerary *woe*-cries express lament over the dead, the *woe*-sayings in the prophetic literature utter severe threat to the addressees: from the perspective of the speaker the addressees are as good as

---

[152]   Since Barth (1977), Isa 29:5-7; 30:27-33 and 31:5.8-9 are often considered as part of a so-called Assyria redaction. This section demonstrates that this applies to 30:27-33 and 31:4-5.8-9 plus 32:1-2, but not to 29:5-7.

[153]   Werlitz 1992: 293; Janzen 1972; Wanke 1966b: 217-218.

[154]   See Janzen 1972: 39-40.

[155]   Janzen 1972: 81.

dead.[156] Some characteristics of the *woe*-sayings found in the prophetic books may be mentioned:[157]

1) The saying begins with the particle הוֹי, which denotes threat to the subject involved; הוֹי introduces a new saying, independently of what precedes it.[158] 2) The addressees are represented by an active participle, or by a general or proper noun. 3) The *woe*-sayings usually are not divine speech, as they frequently refer to Yahweh in the third person.[159] 4) The *woe*-sayings condemn the subject involved for a particular offence. The exclamation הוֹי implies a threat of disaster for the subject: the subject is doomed because of this wicked behaviour.[160] 5) In the sayings, the exclamation הוֹי is usually followed by several (parallel) clauses. 6) The addressee is normally referred to in the third person. In many sayings, suffixes point to a third person reference to the addressee.[161] 7) Various indications suggest that *woe*-sayings are independent sayings, i.e. sayings standing on their own. In some cases the immediate context makes clear that the preceding *woe*-word stands on its own as an independent saying,[162] either because it is followed by a formula that introduces another, divine word, or because what follows is not directly connected with the saying.[163]

In their basic form, the *woe*-sayings contain both an accusing aspect (the behaviour of the addressees is condemned) and an aspect of

---

[156] Werlitz 1992: 296.

[157] The *woe*-sayings may be divided into three groups. 1) Sayings that conform to a range of shared characteristics: Isa 5:8-23*; 10:1-2; 29:15; 30:1-2*; 31:1*; 45:9, 10; Amos 6:1; Mic 2:1-2; Hab 2:6, 9, 12, 15, 19a. 2) Sayings that show minor variations to this: Isa 1:4; 17:12-14; 18:1-2a; 28:1-4; Jer 22:13-14; 23:1; Ezek 13:3; Amos 5:18; Nah 3:1; Zeph 3:1. 3) Words that begin with *hôy* but are not *woe*-sayings in a strict sense: Isa 10:5-15; 29:1-4; 33:1; Jer 47:6; 48:1; 50:27; Ezek 13:18; 34:2; Zeph 2:5; Zech 11:17.

[158] In Isa 5:8; 10:5; 17:12; 18:1; 28:1; 29:1; 31:1; 33:1; Jer 23:1; Amos 6:1; Mic 2:1; Hab 2:6b; Zeph 3:1, הוֹי introduces a new speech.

[159] Isa 1:4; 5:19; 28:2; 29:15; 31:1*; Amos 5:18; Zeph 2:5; 3:2. Exceptions may be Isa 10:1-2 and Jer 23:1.

[160] Werlitz 1992: 298; Janzen 1972: 90.

[161] Isa 5:11, 21; 10:2; 17:13; 28:1; 29:15; 45:9; Jer 22:13; 50:27; Ezek 13:3; 34:2; Amos 6:1; Mic 2:1; Hab 2:6, 9; Zech 11:17. In some further cases the direct context refers to a third person subject (Zeph 3:1-5). In various ambivalent cases third person references are predominant. In Isa 5:8 the second person address וְהוּשַׁבְתֶּם לְבַדְּכֶם probably is a secondary expansion; Hab 2:15 חֲמָתְךָ may be a corruption (due to the second-person address of 2:16).

[162] Isa 5:9-10; 45:11-13; Jer 22:15-19; Jer 23:2; Mic 2:3-5; Nah 3:5-7.

[163] Hab 2:6a introduces a *woe*-saying consisting only of 2:6b, since 2:7a parallels 6a (הֲלוֹא). Hab 2:19b and 20 cannot be easily connected with the saying of 19a. Zech 11:17 is the conclusion of a section (17b may be a secondary explanation to the saying of 17a).

judgement (the exclamatory *hôy*). Although third-person forms pre-
dominate within the *woe*-sayings, they were apparently taken as a direct address, since the immediate context easily switches to a second-
person form of address.[164] Within the prophetic books, the character of
the *woe*-sayings may differ. On the one hand, in some cases an original *woe*-saying can be literary-critically distinguished from its immediate context. On the other hand, there are cases where an exclamatory
hôy begins a larger literary unit which is to be qualified as a literary
derivation of the original *woe*-saying. The earliest versions of 29:15,
30:1-5* and 31:1-3*, in my view, consist of original, prophetic *woe*-
sayings.

Isa 29:15
29:15 represents an early, originally independent, prophetic saying:[165]

> Woe them that deeply hide[166] their plan from Yahweh, whose deeds are
> in the dark, and who say, 'Who sees us? Who knows us?'

In 29:16 follows a comment on the *woe*-saying. Whereas 29:15 accuses certain people of making plans without taking Yahweh into account, 29:16 focuses on the principal difference between 'maker' and
'thing made' and ridicules the alleged attempt to reverse the two.[167]
The theme of the reversal of maker and thing made is connected with
the motif of wisdom: 'shall the thing formed say of the one who
formed it, "He has no understanding" (בין)?' (29:16bβ).[168] The verb בין
occurs in 29:14 too. Whereas in 29:14 it is human wisdom that will
perish, because the people have not truly honoured Yahweh (29:13),
in 29:16 it is Yahweh's wisdom that is raised beyond doubt (cf. 31:2,

---

[164]   In a range of cases, a *woe*-saying is followed by a rhetorical question addressed
to a second person. E.g. Isa 1:5; 10:3; 18:2aβ; 29:16; 30:3.
[165]   Vermeylen 1977-78: 406-407.
[166]   The verb עמק hi. has an adverbial function.
[167]   29:16, הָפְכְּכֶם, seems to be a noun, הֶפֶךְ, 'perversity' (cf. Ezek 16:34) with a
second plural suffix: 'your perversity', which may be translated as 'You turn things
upside down!' (Wildberger 1972-82: 1125: 'oh, eure Verkehrtheit!'). I agree with
Wildberger (1972-82: 1126) that none of the emendations proposed is entirely convincing (1QIsaᵃ has a slightly different text: הפך מכם 'perversity on your account').
The switch to a second-person form argues against the original connection of 29:15
and 16. Furthermore, the rhetorical question in 16 does not fit the form of the *woe*-
saying. A comparison with 10:5-15 does not help, since the latter is not a characteristic *woe*-saying (contra Williamson 1994: 62).
[168]   Cf. Isa 45:9 and Jer 18:6; the combination of עשׂה and יצר frequently occurs in
Second Isaiah.

below). 29:15, in my view, is best understood as an earlier saying that has been embedded in a later literary context of 29:13-16.

29:15, read as a saying in itself, closely parallels the *woe*-saying of 5:18-19; terms occurring in both are מַעֲשֶׂה, עֵצָה, ראה and ידע. The attitude of the subjects accused is similar too: they do not take Yahweh into account. The two questions in 29:15b resemble the questions of the evildoers in the Psalms (Ps 64:6; 94:7). By using this language, the prophet depicts his adversaries as notorious evildoers and accuses them of ignoring Yahweh and thus being godless.

Isa 30:1-5

30:1-5 is, as I will argue, a literary reworking of earlier prophetic words.

> [1] Woe, rebellious children, oracle of Yahweh,
> to carry out a plan, but not mine; to make an alliance, but against my will, in order to add sin to sin;[169]
> [2] who set out to go down to Egypt without asking for my counsel,
> to take refuge in the protection of Pharaoh, and to seek shelter in the shadow of Egypt.
> [3] But the protection of Pharaoh shall become your shame,
> and the shelter in the shadow of Egypt your humiliation.
> [4] For though his officials are at Zoan and his envoys reach Hanes,[170]
> [5] everyone comes to shame through a people that cannot profit them,
> that brings neither help nor profit, but shame and disgrace.

Within 30:1-2, two separate words seem to have been combined, a *woe*-saying and a *ně'um*-oracle.[171] There are no other examples of a saying beginning with the exclamation הוֹי followed by the subject addressed which is subsequently identified as a נְאֻם יהוה.[172] Moreover, 30:1-2 appears to contain the ingredients of both a *woe*-saying and a

---

[169] סְפוֹת is an infinitive of יסף, 'to add', cf. Num 32:14.

[170] Zoan (Tanis) and Hanes (probably Heracleopolis parva) are cities in the Egyptian delta. Both are mentioned in a list of Egyptian delta rulers installed as Assyrian vassals (BIWA: 20-21, Prism A i 95-96), see Wildberger 1972-82: 1154; Barthel 1997: 402.

[171] The formula נְאֻם יהוה 'oracle of Yahweh' mainly occurs in the prophetic books. The formula occurs twelve times in First Isaiah: either at the end of a saying, in 3:15; 17:3, 6; 19:4; 31:9, or within a saying, in 1:24; 14:22, 23; 22:25; 30:1 (37:34 is ambiguous, since the speech of 37:22-35 is a composite).

[172] The only exception is Jer 23:1 (MT), but the element נְאֻם יהוה is missing in the LXX, and was probably added, as elsewhere in Jeremiah, at a late stage of the book's development.

něʾum-oracle.[173] The *woe*-saying probably consisted of the exclamation הוֹי directly followed by the participle הַהֹלְכִים (30:2). Yahweh's first person speech originates from the *něʾum*-oracle. The phrase לְמַעַן סְפוֹת חַטָּאת עַל חַטָּאת, 'adding sin to sin', may have been added by the compositor of 30:1-5 who combined the two earlier sayings, in order to create an analogy with the *woe*-word of 29:1-6 (29:1b, 'add year to year').[174] This leads to the following *woe*-saying:

> Woe them who set out to go down to Egypt,
> but do not ask for <Yahweh's> oracle,[175]
> in order to take refuge in the protection of Pharaoh,
> and to seek shelter in the shadow of Egypt.[176]

Apart from this *woe*-saying, 30:1-2 contains a *něʾum*-oracle. 30:3-5 probably was partly composed by the editor/composer responsible for 30:1-5. 30:3 is a literary expansion, as may appear from the second person address (cf. 29:16) and the use of וְהָיָה.[177] The masculine singular suffixes in 30:4, furthermore, refer to Pharaoh and thus imply 30:3.[178] 30:5a apparently is corrupted;[179] the duplication of בֹּשׁ/בְשֶׁת and לֹא יַעַל in 30:5a and 5b in my view indicates the secondary character of 30:5a. The phrase עַל עַם לֹא יוֹעִילוּ was presumably adopted from the end of 30:6, as part of the reworking that connected the various earlier prophetic sayings within a new literary context.[180] Whereas 30:3-5a is likely to consist of expansions to the earlier sayings, added as part of a literary reworking, 30:5b presumably contains the original ending of the oracle:

---

[173] Barthel (1997: 400) recognises the doublet within 30:1-2 ('Der eigentliche Weheruf in V.1f. zeigt in sich eine auffällige Doppelung'), but refuses to distinguish between the two sayings (cf. his note 64). Deck (1991: 120-122) observes that הוֹי (30:1) probably was originally continued by 30:2.

[174] Barthel (1997: 402) argues that the parallel between 30:1b and 29:1b indicates that 30:1-5 received its present shape as part of the literary composition. This explains the second person address in 30:3.

[175] Originally, the phrase may have been וּפִי יהוה לֹא שָׁאָלוּ, whereas the present formulation 'without asking for my oracle' goes back to the composer of 30:1-5. The phrase 'to counsel Yahweh' (שָׁאַל פִּי יהוה) means 'to obtain an oracle'; cf. Josh 9:14; Judg 1:1.

[176] According to the official ideology of monarchic Jerusalem, Yahweh is the 'refuge', 'shelter', 'protection' and 'shadow' of the people.

[177] Barthel 1997: 400-401.

[178] Barthel 1997: 402.

[179] הֵבִישׁ is hi. of בוש, but the *ketib* הבאיש may be the relict of an earlier reading (e.g. כָּל הַבָּא הֹבִישׁ); Barthel 1997: 394-395. JM § 103f sees לָמוֹ as poetic form of לָהֶם 'to them'.

[180] Barthel 1997: 402.

Rebellious sons[181]—oracle of Yahweh—to carry out a plan,[182] without involving me,[183] to make an alliance,[184] but against my will,[185] not to aid and not to profit, but to bring shame and disgrace.

The two words, the *woe*-saying and the *nĕ'um*-oracle, criticise the politics of relying on Egyptian aid against Assyria, claiming that this is an alliance against Yahweh's will that will lead to nothing. 30:1-5 thus incorporates two early words which refer to a particular situation and criticise a particular group of people. The words address a political elite that advocated rebellion against Assyria in reliance on Egypt. This theme recurs in 31:1-3*, and further in 28:14-18*, 29:15, and 30:6-7. The two words have been reworked into the passage 30:1-5, which apart from making a connection with 30:6-8 in 30:5a and with 29:1-6 in 30:1b, added a more general meaning to the earlier sayings. The generalising tone is perceivable particularly in the phrase 'in order to pile up sin to sin' (30:1b) and in the element כל ('everyone comes to shame') in 30:5a.[186]

Isa 31:1-3

The common view that the earliest version of 31:1-3 is Isaianic has been challenged by Becker, who argued that 31:1-3* is dependent on 2 Kgs 18-20 (Isa 36-39).[187] In his view, 31:1-3 was composed, together with some other passages, to pave the way for the incorporation of the Hezekiah stories (Isa 36-39) within the developing book of Isaiah.[188] Williamson has objected to this that the prophetic criticism in 31:1-3 against a pro-Egyptian policy is at odds with the encouraging role

---

[181] בָּנִים סוֹרְרִים in the context of concluding a wrong treaty has a political-ideological connotation (cf. Ps 68:7, 19).

[182] Cf. 2 Sam 17:23, for the expression עָשָׂה עֵצָה, 'to carry out a plan'.

[183] Cf. Hos 8:4, וְלֹא מִנִּי, 'without involving me'.

[184] The expression נֶסֶךְ מַסֵּכָה, 'to pour out a libation', refers to the act of making a political agreement; see Wildberger 1972-82: 1148. A libation was part of the ritual meal that confirmed the agreement. Normally, the Hebrew expression would be the verb נסך in combination with נֶסֶךְ/נֵסֶךְ 'drink offering', 'libation'; מסכה may be a sub-form of נֶסֶךְ/נֵסֶךְ.

[185] The sequence of an opening clause, followed by נְאֻם יהוה, and continued by an infinitive construct, is further attested in Jer 1:19; 13:11; 30:11.

[186] Becker's suggestion (1997: 248-250) that the earliest version of 30:1-5 is a *relecture* of 31:1-3, is unconvincing.

[187] Becker 1997: 245-263.

[188] According to Becker (1997: 218-222), the passages 10:5-11* + 14:24-25a and 29:1-4a + 31:1-3*.8a were composed as a preparation for the insertion of the Hezekiah legends.

Isaiah plays in the stories of Isa 36-39.[189] An analysis of 31:1-3 may show that the phrase containing Becker's main evidence does not belong to the earliest saying.[190]

> [1] Woe them that go down to Egypt for help and who rely on horses,
> who trusted in chariots because they are many and in horsemen because they are very strong,
> but did not look to the Holy One of Israel nor consulted Yahweh!
> [2] Yet he too was wise and brings disaster; he did not call back his words, but he will rise against the house of the evildoers, and against the helpers of those who work iniquity.
> [3] The Egyptians are human, and not God; their horses are flesh, and not spirit.
> When Yahweh stretches out his hand, the helper will stumble, and the one helped will fall, and they will all perish together.

31:1a and 3a are connected through the terms מִצְרַיִם and סוּסִים. Besides, the negative element of 31:1c, וְלֹא, 'they did not account for Yahweh', has its pendant in 31:3a, וְלֹא, 'Egypt is not God' and therefore untrustworthy.[191] The structure of 31:1a.c, הוֹי plus participle plus imperfect, followed by negation plus perfect, is attested elsewhere.[192] The perfect forms (31:1c) indicate that the action described in 31:1a was based on a previous error: they had not consulted Yahweh. 30:1b, by contrast, is not tightly connected with the rest of the saying. First, the clause begins with a *wayyiqtol*-form, which is exceptional within a *woe*-saying. Secondly, whereas 31:3a takes up the element 'horses' from 1a, the chariots and horsemen of 31:1b are not referred to. 31:1b gives the impression of being an expansion of 1a: שׁען is taken further by synonymous בטח and the סוּסִים are extended with 'chariots and horsemen'.[193] 31:1b can be explained as a secondary extension to 31:1a, in the following way. 31:1b is strikingly similar to a phrase from the Hezekiah legends, where Rabshakeh scorns Judah's reliance on Egypt:

2 Kgs 18:24b (Isa 36:9b)	וַתִּבְטַח לְךָ עַל־מִצְרַיִם לְרֶכֶב וּלְפָרָשִׁים
Isa 31:1b	וַיִּבְטְחוּ עַל רֶכֶב כִּי רָב וְעַל פָּרָשִׁים כִּי עָצְמוּ מְאֹד

---

[189] Williamson 2004: 198.
[190] Williamson 2004: 198-199, referring to the analysis of Höffken 2000.
[191] Höffken 2000: 232.
[192] Isa 30:1-2*: הוֹי plus participle, followed by negation and perfect; Zeph 3:1-2: הוֹי plus participle, followed by negation and perfect.
[193] Höffken 2000: 232-233; Deck 1991: 214-215; Kaiser 1989: 58-62.

The expression עַל בטח, much less frequently attested than בְּ בטח, its
pendant, is at home in the Hezekiah legends,[194] referring to Judah's
reliance on Egypt. Moreover, בטח with רֶכֶב and פָּרָשִׁים only occurs in 2
Kgs 18:24 (Isa 36:9) and in Isa 31:1, both times with the less frequent
preposition עַל. Furthermore, both passages point out that trusting in
Egypt is senseless. Rather than being coincidental, 31:1b can be understood as a redactional extension to 31:1a. Its purpose was to explicitly establish a connection with the Hezekiah legends. This
explanation is supported by the development of Isa 31. 31:4-5.8-9,
reflecting on Jerusalem's rescue and Assyria's downfall, was added to
31:1-3* at a later stage. This passage is part of a revision of the Isaiah
tradition to be situated in the second half of the seventh century (see
2.2.4 below). A later editor explicitly connected the *woe*-saying of
31:1-3 with the Hezekiah legends in order to emphasise that it was not
Egypt with its great military power that saved Jerusalem, but Yahweh.[195]

31:3b contains an announcement of judgement by Yahweh.[196]
31:1a.c.3a emphasises that relying on Egypt instead of Yahweh is a
fatal mistake, since Egypt cannot save Judah but only Yahweh can. In
31:3b, by contrast, Yahweh himself intervenes to destroy the coalition
of helper (Egypt) and helped (Judah). The verbs indicating the destruction, כשל 'stumble', נפל 'fall', and כלה 'perish', occur elsewhere as
part of the motif of the disobedient people, particularly referring to the
disasters that befell Judah in the early sixth century.[197] 31:2, which is
often regarded as a later extension to the *woe*-saying, is on the same
level as 31:3b. It introduces a new concept: Yahweh's wisdom. Since
this is not mentioned in 31:1, the clause 'yet he too is wise' probably
alludes to another passage. This is likely to be 29:13-16, where the
fading wisdom of humans (29:14) is contrasted with Yahweh's superior wisdom (as implied by 29:16). Thus, the literary reworking of

---

[194]   2 Kgs 18:20, 21, 24 (Isa 36:5, 6, 9).

[195]   31:1b as a redactional bridge between Isa 31* and the Hezekiah stories within
Isa 36-39 does not stand in isolation. 31:5b probably is a quite similar addition, which
echoes the stories of 2 Kgs 18-19 (Isa 36-37) as well, in order to emphasise that it is
Yahweh who saves (see the analysis of 31:4-5.8-9 in 2.2.4).

[196]   Barthel (1997: 434) regards the *woe*-saying as the motivation for a subsequent
announcement of judgement in 31:3b, with 31:2 as a necessary turning-point. This
construction however does not represent the original prophetic saying, but a literary
reworking.

[197]   For the combination כשל and נפל, cf. Isa 3:8; 8:15; Jer 6:15; 8:12; for כלה, cf.
Jer 9:15; 14:12; 16:4.

31:1*.3a, consisting of 31:2.3b is comparable to the reflective passages within Isa 28-32, such as 29:13-16. According to 31:2, Yahweh brings disaster (רַע) to his people; the expression 'house of evildoers' (בֵּית מְרֵעִים) closely parallels the 'offspring of evildoers' (זֶרַע מְרֵעִים) in 1:4, where it also refers to the people as a whole.[198] The reworking of 31:2.3b focuses on the entire people: Yahweh will bring destruction for both Egypt and Judah. This contrasts with the earlier *woe*-saying, which condemns a particular group of people, the political elite relying on Egypt's military force in their anti-Assyrian politics. The earliest saying probably consisted of 31:1a.c., with 3a as an early comment:

> Woe them that go down to Egypt for help and who rely on horses,
> but did not look to the Holy One of Israel nor consulted Yahweh!
> The Egyptians are human, not divine; their horses are flesh, not spirit!

The sayings discussed so far, 29:15, 30:1-2.5b and 31:1ac.3a, can be regarded as words from the prophet Isaiah directed against the political elite of Jerusalem who advocated an anti-Assyrian policy in the period 705-701 BCE.[199] The sayings strongly deprecate them, describing their reliance on Egypt as being against Yahweh's will.

Isa 28:1-4

28:1-4 contains an announcement of judgement against Samaria, depicted as the crown of Ephraim:

> [1] Woe, proud garland of the drunkards of Ephraim, a fading flower is his glorious beauty, which is on the head of the fertile valley![200]
> [2] See, the Lord has one who is mighty and strong; like a storm of hail, a destroying tempest, like a storm of mighty, overflowing waters.
> He hurls down to the earth with his hand,
> [3] and tramples with feet[201] the proud garland of the drunkards of Ephraim,

---

[198] Isa 1:4-8 is discussed in 2.3.7 below.

[199] Wildberger 1972-82: 1127.

[200] According to Barthel (1997: 281), the final phrase of 28:4, 'those overcome with wine', is an extension taking up שִׁכֹּרֵי אֶפְרַיִם in order to make a connection with 28:7-10.

[201] The absence of a direct object for הִנִּיחַ suggests that 28:2b and 3 form a syntactical unity. Despite grammatical difficulties, the chiasm 'to hurl down with the hand' (נוח בְּיָד hi.), 'to trample with feet' (רֶגֶל רמס) is clear. Evidently, the עֲטֶרֶת is hurled down and trampled. 28:3b concludes the sentence with an inclusion to 28:1aα. Originally, the word concluded with a comparison: וְהָיְתָה plus 4b; see Barthel 1997: 281-282.

⁴ And it will be like a first-ripe fig before the summer; whoever sees it, eats it up as soon as it comes to hand.²⁰²

Since the suffix of תִּפְאַרְתּוֹ refers to Ephraim, the following clause, and 28:1-4 as a whole, is to be understood as referring to Samaria.²⁰³ Yahweh (28:2) is presented as the actor in history and Assyria, referred to in a metaphorical way, as his agent. 28:1-4 presumably is an early prophetic saying. The announcement of the destruction of Samaria makes best sense in a late eighth-century setting. In contrast to the other prophetic words within Isa 28-32, which are to be read against the background of 705-701 BCE, 28:1-4 is to be dated to around 720 BCE. Although the content does not give any decisive clues, the siege of Samaria by the Assyrians in 720 is a suitable historical background. The word presents a contrast between the joyful celebrations of the city's inhabitants and the threat posed by the enemies. Although the disaster is near (28:4), the city is careless. In various respects, 28:1-4 resembles the earlier prophecies incorporated within Isa 7 and 8. The name 'Ephraim' is used as a designation for the Northern Kingdom (7:9a; 28:1, 3), and the destruction is presented as being imminent (7:16; 8:4; 28:4).

Isa 29:1-6

This unit, often reduced to 29:1-4, is a word of judgement against 'Ariel', i.e. Jerusalem.²⁰⁴

¹ Woe, Ariel, Ariel, city where David encamped! Add year to year; let the festivals run their round.
² I will distress Ariel, and there shall be moaning and lamentation, and she shall be to me like an Ariel.
³ And like a (siege) wall (כַדּוּר)²⁰⁵ I will encamp against you;
I will enclose you with earthworks and raise siege works against you.

---

²⁰² According to Barthel (1997: 282), 28:4a probably is an expansion of 28:3 based on 28:1. The addition disrupts the original connection between וְהָיְתָה and the comparison (28:4b) and led to the form צִיצַת (feminine construct); the combination of עֲטֶרֶת גֵּאוּת and צִיצַת נֹבֵל in its turn elicited the feminine plural תִּרְמַסְנָה.
²⁰³ Barthel 1997: 280, 283.
²⁰⁴ Werlitz (1992: 309-310) and Wagner (2006: 150) argue that 'Ariel' is best explained as 'altar hearth' (cf. Ezek 43:15-16), used as a metaphor for Jerusalem. It fits the announcement of 2bβ and contrasts with the cultic celebrations referred to in 1b.
²⁰⁵ LXX ὡς Δαυιδ 'like David' (כדוד) is *lectio facilior* (cf. 29:1). MT כַדּוּר means 'like a wall'; for דוּר cf. Akk. *dūru* 'wall', as in Isa 45:2; Hoffmann 1972, 191: 'Ich lagere mich gegen/um dich wie die/eine Ringmauer'.

⁴ Then deep from the earth you shall speak, from low in the dust your words shall come; your voice shall come from the ground like the voice of a ghost, and your speech shall whisper out of the dust.
⁵ The multitude of your insolent ones (זָרָיִךְ) shall be like small dust, and the multitude of the ruthless like flying chaff.
And in an instant, suddenly,
⁶ you will be visited by Yahweh of Hosts with thunder and earthquake and great noise, with whirlwind and tempest, and the flame of a devouring fire.

In this passage, Yahweh announces that he will fiercely oppress Jerusalem. The first part of this discussion deals with 29:1-4. This passage forms a literary unity: 29:1 begins with a mourning cry over Ariel (הוֹי אֲרִיאֵל אֲרִיאֵל), which forms an inclusion to 29:4b, where Ariel is compared to a spirit of the dead.²⁰⁶ This suggests that 29:1-4 deals with the downfall of Jerusalem. 29:1-4 is often interpreted as a word of threat against Jerusalem, to be connected with the circumstances of 701, and attributed to Isaiah.²⁰⁷ The following analysis however aims to demonstrate that 29:1-4 reflects the fall of Jerusalem in the sixth century.

Various scholars have argued that Sennacherib's siege of Jerusalem in 701 BCE consisted of a blockade and not of an assault on the city with the intent of a swift capture.²⁰⁸ An important indication for this suggestion is the Assyrian description of the siege: 'Ihn (Hiskia) schloß (*esēru*) ich wie einen Käfigvogel in Jerusalem, seiner königlichen Residenz, ein, legte Befestigungsanlagen (*bīrāte rakāsu*) gegen ihn an und machte es zu einem Ding der Unmöglichkeit für ihn, aus seinem Stadtor hinauszugehen.'²⁰⁹ By common practice, cities that could not be easily captured by a frontal assault were cut off from supplies by a blockade, which would eventually force them to surrender.²¹⁰

---

²⁰⁶ Note the play with חנה, 'to dwell' in 29:1, and 'to besiege' (with עַל) in 29:3.
²⁰⁷ E.g. Barthel 1997: 355, 363, 371.
²⁰⁸ See in particular Van der Kooij 1986: 97-98.
²⁰⁹ Frahm 1997: 54, line 52 (Frahm's translation). Van der Kooij (1986: 97-98), following a suggestion of Deller, proposes to read ᵘʳᵘḫal-ṣu-meš as *bīrāte*, 'forts'. Cf. BIWA: 28, A ii 52 (siege of Tyre) and Mayer 1995: 361. Mayer (1995: 310, 360) points out that the siege of a city is normally referred to with the verb *lamû*, whereas *esēru*, 'einschließen', in this context means to deprive someone of initiative and of his space to move.
²¹⁰ According to Mayer (1995: 310, 361), *bīrāte* refers to 'Grenzbefestigungen' positioned at the entrances to the highland of Judah, as a blockade rather than a real siege.

The terminology of 29:1-4, by contrast, points to a frontal assault on Jerusalem. The expression 'to set blockades' does not occur in 29:1-4. Instead, צוק (hi.) with לְ (29:2), 'to oppress', occurs elsewhere within a description of coming disaster, in particular for Jerusalem;[211] 29:3, חנה, 'to encamp', is used with respect to Jerusalem in 2 Kgs 25:1 (with לְ), where Nebuchadnezzar attacks the city. In 2 Chron 32:1 חנה with עַל describes Sennacherib's assault on Judah's fortified cities (not Jerusalem), such as Lachish, which were taken by frontal military assault. Furthermore, צור with עַל (29:3) 'to besiege' elsewhere describes a frontal assault on a city (e.g. 2 Sam 20:15). The expression is used for the capture of Samaria in 2 Kgs 17:5 and 18:9 and for the capture of Jerusalem by the Babylonians in 2 Kgs 24:11.[212] One of the means of frontal assault was the construction of a siege wall around the city from where it could be attacked. This is referred to on the stele of Zakkur, where his enemies are said to have 'raised a wall higher than the wall of Hazr[ak]', (whrmw . šr . mn [.] šr . ḥzr[k .]).[213] The phrase 'I will besiege you like a wall' (וְחָנִיתִי כַדּוּר) in 29:3 presents a similar image. Finally, 29:3 points to the means with which Ariel is besieged. The word מצב is an object of instrument by וְצַרְתִּי עָלַיִךְ. The only other case where צור plus עַל plus suffix is followed by an instrumental object, it means 'to enclose x with y'.[214] The meaning 'to enclose her with (...)' fits 29:3, but מצב remains uncertain.[215] The phrase 'I will raise siege works against you' (וַהֲקִימֹתִי עָלַיִךְ מֻצָּרֹת)[216] resembles Ezek 4:2 'put siege works against it' (וְנָתַתָּה עָלֶיהָ מָצוֹר) and Mic 4:14 'siege is laid against us' (שָׂם עָלֵינוּ מָצוֹר). Besides, קום with עַל occurs in Ezek 26:8 'he shall set up a siege wall against you, cast up a ramp against you, and raise a roof of shields against you' (וְהֵקִים עָלַיִךְ צִנָּה). 29:1-4 thus pictures a frontal military assault on Jerusalem, leading to the downfall of the city. The passage does not reflect Sennacherib's siege of Jerusalem

---

[211] See particularly Jer 19:9 and cf. Deut 28:53, 55, 57.

[212] See also Jer 21:4, 9; 32:2; 37:5; 39:1.

[213] Zakkur Stele, line 10; edition by Seow, in: Nissinen 2003a: 204, 206. Cf. Mic 4:14: 'Now you (i.e. daughter Zion) are walled around with a wall; siege is laid against us'.

[214] Song 8:9, 'we will enclose her with boards of cedar'.

[215] מֻצָּב, vocalised as a ho. ptc. of נצב 'to be placed', is *hapax legomenon*. The vocalisation מַצָּב 'garrison' (e.g. 1 Sam 13:23; 14:1) might be possible.

[216] 1QIsa[a] has מצודות 'strongholds' (plural) and 4QIsa[f] מצור 'siege works' (singular). MT מצרת can be read as a by-form of מצור (voc. מְצָרֹת) conform 4QIsa[f] מצור, rather than as a defectively spelled plural form מְצֻרֹת. In this case, the masoretic vocalisation and 1QIsa[a] represent secondary readings.

in 701, but resembles the descriptions of the Babylonian assault on Jerusalem in the sixth century.

Various characteristics of 29:1-4 confirm this interpretation. The exclamation הוֹי does not introduce here a prophetic *woe*-saying condemning a particular form of wicked behaviour (such as 29:15, 30:1-2, 31:1.3a). Instead, it is a divine word that announces disaster against Ariel/Jerusalem. 29:1-4 contains characteristic features of city laments:[217] 1) The repetition of Ariel (הוֹי אֲרִיאֵל אֲרִיאֵל) suggests a vocative address; it is a mourning cry over the city.[218] 2) The identification of Ariel as the 'city of David' and reference to the annual festivals (29:1), prepare for a contrast with the following verses, which describe Ariel's humiliation and downfall (cf. 22:1-14, in 2.3.6 below).[219] 3) Yahweh's violent conduct causes devastation,[220] through military assault.[221] The image of Yahweh's violent attack is paralleled in Lamentations, in particularly Lam 2. Lam 2:5, for instance, contains a similar image: 'Yahweh has become like an enemy; he has destroyed Israel; He has destroyed all its palaces, laid in ruins its strongholds, and multiplied in daughter Judah mourning and lamentation.' The expression 'mourning and lamentation' (תַאֲנִיָּה וַאֲנִיָּה) occurs only in 29:2 and in Lam 2:5, both in a context of Yahweh's assault on Jerusalem. 4) Characteristic of city laments is the personification of the city as a lady.[222] Whereas 'Ariel' is not a feminine name,[223] in 29:3-4 Ariel is addressed as a lady (cf. also 29:5-6). This can be explained from the characteristics of city laments. The personification of a city as a lady in the Hebrew city lament may be reminiscent of the motif of the weeping goddess of the Mesopotamian city lament.[224] 5) Ariel is described as mourning and weeping, her voice resembling that of a ghost (29:4). This resembles the image of the weeping goddess from the Mesopotamian city lament. Ariel's voice sounds like that of a spirit

---

[217] The characteristics of city lament and their appearance in the Hebrew Bible have been explored by Dobbs-Allsopp 1993. In addition to Lamentations, Dobbs-Allsopp discusses passages from the prophetic books, which display characteristic features of city lament.

[218] Cf. Dobbs-Allsopp 1993: 90-92; Janzen 1972: 11. This resembles Marduk's cry over Babylon in the Song of Erra ('Alas, Babylon!', tablet 4:40-45).

[219] Cf. Dobbs-Allsopp 1993: 38-40.

[220] Cf. Dobbs-Allsopp 1993: 55-65.

[221] Cf. Dobbs-Allsopp 1993: 57.

[222] In Lamentations, Jerusalem is personified as a mother, a widow and especially as 'daughter Zion'.

[223] In Ezra 8:16 אֲרִיאֵל is a masculine name; both אֵל and אֲרִי are masculine words.

[224] Dobbs-Allsopp 1993: 75-90.

from the netherworld, since she lies flat on the ground in the dust, corresponding to the image of lament in Lam 2:10: 'The elders of daughter Zion sit on the ground in silence; they have thrown dust on their heads and put on sackcloth; the young girls of Jerusalem have bowed their heads to the ground.'[225] 29:1-4 exposes the disastrous fate of Jerusalem brought about by Yahweh. It is formulated as a divine word bearing characteristics of city laments, particularly close to Lam 2.

29:5-6, in my view, continues the *woe*-word against Ariel, rather than adding a new perspective.[226] In 29:5, I prefer to read זָדַיִךְ 'your insolent ones' (with 1QIsaᵃ).[227] This reading is in agreement with 29:5bβ.6, which describes a sudden attack of Yahweh against Ariel.[228] A characteristic feature of city laments is that the violent divine intervention is described in terms of the destructive powers of nature (29:6; cf. Lam 2:3; 4:11).[229] 29:5-6 is likely to be read as a continuation of 29:1-4,[230] with זָדַיִךְ, 'your insolent ones', as the original reading.[231] Whereas 29:1-4.5-6 deals with Yahweh's assault on Ariel, 29:7 evidently changed the focus to the foreign nations as the attackers of Ariel, and claims that their fighting against Ariel will come to nothing.[232] 29:7 is a *relecture* of the preceding passage, which takes up

---

[225] Cf. also Lam 3:6, 'he has made me sit in darkness like the dead of long ago', and the expression 'to put one's mouth to the dust' in Lam 2:1b, 2b and 3:16.

[226] Those who interpret 29:5-6 as a *relecture* of 29:1-4, follow MT's reading זָרַיִךְ, 'your strangers', in 29:5. 'Your strangers' must refer to the enemies that oppress Jerusalem, and by consequence 29:5-6 announces the destruction of Jerusalem's oppressors through Yahweh's intervention. If, by contrast, 1QIsaᵃ זָדַיִךְ, 'your insolent ones', is followed, Jerusalem itself suffers from Yahweh's violent intervention. In that case, 29:5-6 continues 29:1-4.

[227] Neither זָר, 'stranger' nor זֵד, 'insolent one', occurs elsewhere with a suffix. Furthermore, the parallel עָרִיץ, 'the ruthless', is not decisive, as it occurs elsewhere in juxtaposition both with זָר (Ps 54:3; Isa 25:5; Ezek 28:7) and with זֵד (Ps 86:14; Isa 13:11). However, the suffix, referring to Ariel, makes better sense within זֵדִיךְ, 'your insolent ones' (1QIsaᵃ). The variant 'your strangers' (MT) in the sense of 'your enemies', makes best sense as a relecture from the perspective of 29:7.

[228] The terminology of 29:5bβ.6 (Ariel visited by Yahweh with thunder) strongly suggests that the passage deals with the destruction of Ariel, not with her being rescued by Yahweh; see Wong 1995: 371. Contra Becker 1997: 236; Barthel 1997: 358.

[229] Cf. Dobbs-Allsopp 1993: 56-57 and 62.

[230] The motif of becoming like dust and chaff occasionally occurs within announcements of destruction (e.g. Isa 5:24; cf. Job 21:18; Ps 1:4; Hos 13:3). The terms זֵד and עָרִיץ occur in Isa 13:11, together with פקד and שפל hi., referring to total destruction: 'I will punish the world for its evil; I will put an end to the pride of the arrogant, and lay low the insolence of tyrants'.

[231] See notes 226 and 227 above.

[232] According to 29:7, the foreign enemies shall be 'like a dream, a vision of the night'. The expression כַּחֲלוֹם, 'like a dream', emphasises the vanishing of the enemies.

elements from 29:5,[233] but turns the perspective by identifying the foreign nations as Ariel's attackers.[234] MT זָרַיִךְ, 'your strangers', is probably inspired by the *relecture* of 29:7. According to the later perspective, the foreign nations that attack Ariel will be destroyed.[235]

Both 29:1-4 and its continuation 29:5-6 deal with the downfall of Jerusalem due to Yahweh's violent attack. This does not fit the situation of 701, but reflects the capture of Jerusalem in the sixth century.[236] In the process of the literary development of Isa 28-32, 29:1-6 as a word of judgement against Jerusalem, was placed in juxtaposition to 28:1-4: Jerusalem is punished for its sins, just as Samaria was punished.[237]

2.2.3 *Further Prophetic Material in Isaiah 28-31*

Isa 28:7b-10.12

The passage of 28:7-13 contains early prophetic material in a reworked, elaborated form. First, וְגַם אֵלֶּה, 'these too', in 28:7a (cf. 31:2) connects the saying that follows, 28:7b-10, with the 'the drunkards of Ephraim' of 28:1-4.[238] Furthermore, 28:13b clearly echoes 8:15.[239] Moreover, the repetition of the cryptic saying (28:10 and 13a) is an indication of literary development. Whereas 28:7b-10 goes back to an early prophetic saying,[240] 28:11-13 presents a *relecture* of this saying, marked by a different perspective.

> [7] Priest and prophet reel with strong drink, are confused with wine,
> stagger with strong drink; they err in vision, stumble in giving verdict.
> [8] All tables are covered with filth, vomit is everywhere.[241]
> [9] Whom will he (i.e. the priest) teach knowledge,

Cf. Job 20:8; Ps 73:19-20: 'How they (i.e. the wicked) are destroyed in a moment ... ! They are like a dream when one awakes'.

[233] See particularly Werlitz 1992: 307.

[234] Contra Wong 1995: 374.

[235] Barthel (1997: 358) attributes 29:5-8 to the Assyria redaction, pointing to 17:12-14 and 30:27-33 as closely related passages. However, as argued here, in 29:5-6 Yahweh's intervention is directed *against* Ariel.

[236] This interpretation of 29:1-4.5-6 generally concurs with that of Werlitz (1992: 316-320), who dates the earliest version of 29:1-7 in the exilic period. Passages from First Isaiah closely related to 29:1-6, are 22:1-14 and 32:9-14, which similarly reflect the downfall of Jerusalem in 586 BCE; see Barthel 1997: 267-268.

[237] Cf. Barthel 1997: 288.

[238] Barthel 1997: 293.

[239] Wildberger 1972-82: 1061.

[240] Becker (1997: 229) qualifies 28:7b-10 as 'eine ältere Sprucheinheit'.

[241] I take צֹאָה with the second colon; see Wildberger 1972-82: 1052-1053.

and to whom will he (i.e. the prophet) explain the message?
To those who are weaned from milk, taken away from the breast?
[10] For it is *ṣaw lāṣāw ṣaw lāṣāw qaw lāqāw qaw lāqāw*, a bit here, a bit there.

The saying refers to prophets and priests, probably in Jerusalem.[242] Since no change of voice is indicated, I take the whole saying as reflecting one point of view.[243] The point of the saying is the denouncement of the advice and messages from 'priest and prophet'. The 'priest and prophet' of 28:7b are subject of 28:9a, and the saying in 28:10 mocks what they say. The activities referred to in 28:9a, 'to teach knowledge' (יוֹרֶה דֵעָה) and 'to explain the message' (יָבִין שְׁמוּעָה) are to be associated with priests and prophets respectively.[244] The former refers to priestly instruction, the latter may belong to the technical vocabulary of prophetical divination.[245] 28:9b specifies the object mentioned in 9a, אֶת־מִי 'whom'.

According to the saying, 'priest and prophet' eat and drink excessively. In their drunkenness they deliver unreliable messages and give unintelligible advice. Their drunken speech may be good for talking with small children, but certainly not as sound advice. Their speech is mocked in 28:10. The saying denounces 'priest and prophet', in particular the divine messages and advice they give. Whereas prophets and priests are supposed to expose and interpret the divine will, the saying claims they have gone astray, being only interested in food and drink. They are talking ridiculously, as if speaking to small children. The mocking phrase of 28:10 imitates unintelligible, drunken talk. It is difficult to ascertain the precise meaning of the wording of 28:10 apart from its general sense as mocking the messages and advice of 'priest

---

[242] Contra Becker (1997: 229), who suggests that 28:7b-10 originally addressed cultic functionaries from Samaria. This is unlikely, since Isaiah's prophecies against Ephraim and Samaria (in Isa 7*, 8*, 17*, 28:1-4) do not single out any particular group of people.

[243] According to a common interpretation, 28:7-8 is a word by Isaiah denouncing his adversaries, 28:9-10 the mocking reply of his adversaries, and 28:11-13 Isaiah's harsh reaction to the scorn of his adversaries (Wildberger 1972-82: 1053-1054). However, the assumption of a change of voice between 28:8 and 9 is implausible. Furthermore, this interpretation depends on the presupposition that 28:7b-13 (or 28:7b-12) forms an Isaianic unit. Instead, 28:7b-10 is to be read as a word of criticism from one perspective, with 28:11-13 as a later *relecture*.

[244] Becker 1997: 229; Barthel 1997: 291.

[245] Van der Toorn 1988: 205. In his view שְׁמוּעָה is equivalent to Akk. *egirrû*, 'portentous utterance, oracle' (1988: 214).

and prophet'.[246] 28:7b-10 suggests that Isaiah's opponents, the leading politicians of Jerusalem, appealed to revelatory visions and inspired advice for their political position.

In its literary reworking, the earlier saying of 28:7b-10 was elaborated by 28:11-13, which added a new interpretation. 28:11 is a *relecture* of 28:10, interpreting the mocking phrase of 28:10 as a saying in a foreign language, words uttered by foreigners that the Judaeans do not understand. This turns the focus to the arrival of a foreign, enemy power.[247] According to 28:11, Yahweh no longer communicates with his people through prophets or priests, but through an invasion of foreigners; he speaks the 'language of destruction'. The motif of a devastating invasion functioning as Yahweh's message to the disobedient people, also occurs in Jer 5:15.

In the literary context of 28:7-13, verse 12 functions as a motivation for the announced judgement. It includes however an earlier saying: 'This is the resting place—give rest to the weary; this is the place of repose.' The phrase 'this is the resting place' (זֹאת הַמְּנוּחָה) also occurs in Ps 132:14, where Yahweh refers to Zion as: 'this is my resting place (זֹאת מְנוּחָתִי) for ever', continued with 'I will satisfy its poor with bread', and in Mic 2:10, 'Arise and go; for this is no place of rest (לֹא זֹאת הַמְּנוּחָה), because of uncleanness that destroys with a grievous destruction.' This is part of a passage that accuses the powerful in Jerusalem of social injustice, and the 'place of rest' points to Zion. The likeliest interpretation of 28:12 is to take זֹאת הַמְּנוּחָה and its parallel זֹאת הַמַּרְגֵּעָה as referring to Zion (or Jerusalem) as a divinely protected place,[248] where social justice is acted out. The command 'give rest to

---

[246] Many suggestions have been made, but see the caution expressed by Wildberger 1972-82: 1053-1054. Emerton (2001), discussing a variety of interpretations, regards it as possible that the phrase consists of an unintelligible jumble of words (2001: 56). Yet, it may be significant that the words צַו and קַו somewhat resemble צֹאָה 'filth' and קִיא 'vomit' in 28:8. A relationship between 28:8 and 10 (which has support in some of the early versions; Emerton 2001: 40-42, 51-55), supports my suggestion that the phrase in 28:10 mocks the 'priest and prophet' for delivering senseless messages and stupid advice. Differently, Van der Toorn (1988: 209-211) suggested that the sounds represent bird-like twittering and groans, which were believed to be uttered by the dead; 28:7b-10 may then refer to the practice of necromancy. Various scholars have suggested that צַו and קַו refer to letters of the alphabet and that the saying refers to small children learning the alphabet in school (recently Carr 2005: 124-125). I agree with Emerton (2001: 51) that this suggestion lacks firm evidence.

[247] Unintelligible language is regularly used as a characteristic of a hostile, foreign nation; Deut 28:49; Isa 33:19; Jer 5:15; Ezek 3:5-6; see Barthel 1997: 300.

[248] הַמַּרְגֵּעָה is *hapax legomenon*, but רגע hi. 'to find repose', 'to give rest' is attested (Deut 28:65; Isa 34:14; Jer 31:2; 50:34).

the weary' belongs to the sphere of social justice.[249] Whereas it is normally Yahweh who is said to give rest,[250] here, the earthly leaders are urged to do so, as a mark of good leadership.[251]

Although the saying may be a paraphrase rather than a verbal quotation of a prophetic oracle,[252] it represents a prophecy from the early period, i.e. the eighth century. According to the larger context, Zion used to be a resting place for the people, the place *par excellence* for social justice. However, this has been overruled since the people refused to listen (וְלֹא אָבוּא שְׁמוֹעַ).[253] According to 28:12, an earlier stage of prophecy, characterised by an encouraging message, has been followed by a later stage of prophecy of judgement. At some stage in the development of the Isaiah tradition, prophecy of salvation was regarded a thing of the past, whereas the present was considered as being marked by the prophecy of judgement (see also 30:15).

Isa 28:14-18

The earliest version of 28:15-18 probably represents prophetic material. 28:19-22 consists of later extensions to the oracle.[254] An important feature within the oracle of 28:15-18 is the parallel between accusation and announcement: the six clauses of 28:15 correspond to those of 28:17b-18. This is not to imply however that the passage in between, 28:16-17a, should be eliminated. 28:16aα, 'Therefore, thus says the Lord Yahweh', cannot be missed, since the transition from accusation to announcement requires some form of messenger-formula. Furthermore, as this formula is normally followed by divine speech, at least some part of 28:16-17a belongs to the original oracle.[255] Whereas 28:17b parallels 15bβ (c'-c, see below), it does not take

---

[249] Cf. Job 22:7, which is part of a catalogue of social injustice: 'You have given no water to the weary to drink, and you have withheld bread from the hungry'.

[250] MT הָנִיחוּ is imperative plural from נוח hi. A. 'to secure repose, rest'. With לְ it means 'to give rest to *x*'. Normally, the subject is Yahweh, who gives rest to the people, i.e. protection against the enemies and living without fear of foreigners. In Isa 28:12 the imperative plural addresses a human subject.

[251] Barthel (1997: 302-304) rejects the suggestion of Kaiser and Vermeylen that 28:12 bears a Deuteronomistic mark. According to Barthel, the 'rest for the tired ones' refers to a guarantee required by Yahweh for the socially weak who are suppressed by the elite.

[252] Barthel 1997: 301.

[253] The motif of the people's refusal of Yahweh's blessings further occurs in Lev 26:21; Isa 30:9; Ezek 3:7; Ezek 20:8 (cf. Isa 42:24; Ps 81:12).

[254] Barthel 1997: 313-314; Becker 1997: 233.

[255] Contra Becker 1997: 231.

up שִׂים from 15bβ; it is, on the other hand, 17a which takes up this verb, thereby forming intrinsically part of the oracle. Since 28:17a begins with a consecutive form (וְשַׂמְתִּי), the phrase הִנְנִי יֹסֵד בְּצִיּוֹן אֶבֶן (28:16) must have preceded it.[256] The construction of הנני יסד (28:16) continued by a perfect consecutive וְשַׂמְתִּי in 28:17a is naturally read as הִנְנִי יֹסֵד.[257] First, הִנְנִי is to be followed by a participle singular, as is attested in 1QIsa[b] יוסד.[258] 1QIsa[a] has a variant reading, מיסד (pi. ptc.). If יסד pi. has the specific meaning 'to lay foundations', whereas יסד qal has a broader meaning, applying to the whole process of (re)building,[259] יסד (qal ptc.) may represent the original reading, and the more specified מיסד (pi. ptc.) a secondary variant. In any case, LXX and the other versions reflect a participle form with a future tense.[260] Apart from the two *lectiones*, הנני יֹס(ו)ד, naturally read as qal ptc., and הנני מיסד, of which the former probably is *lectio difficilior*, there is the deviant vocalisation in MT. It has been pointed out that the Masoretic vocalisation was probably influenced by Isa 14:32, יהוה יִסַּד צִיּוֹן, 'Yahweh has founded Zion'.[261] The Masoretes chose for a different vocalisation in order to harmonise 28:16 with 14:32;[262] the vocalisation יִסַּד is a late development.[263]

---

[256] Barthel 1997: 315-316.

[257] Cf. JM § 119n.

[258] Defectively spelled ptc. masc. singular qal are quite common in the MT of Isaiah.

[259] See Mosis 1981: 676-677.

[260] LXX ἰδοὺ ἐγὼ ἐμβαλῶ (future) renders a participle; Aquila, Symmachus and Theodotion have a participle.

[261] Roberts 1987: 28; acknowledged by Dekker 2004: 92-93.

[262] Dekker (2004: 91) points out that because הִנְנִי יִסַּד is an anomalous construction, the Masoretes gave הנני a distinctive accent rather than the common conjunctive accent.

[263] Contra Dekker 2004: 90-104. Dekker's arguments for following MT's vocalisation יִסַּד are unconvincing. First, as Roberts (1987: 28) noted, the construction of MT is 'totally unparalleled' (Isa 29:15; 38:5, הנני יוסף, can be debated, but either is participle יוֹסֵף or imperfect יוֹסֵף, not perfect. In Jer 44:26; Ezek 25:7; 36:6, הנני is followed by a perfect first person, not a third person). MT's construction הִנְנִי יִסַּד is without parallel, even more so because it is continued by a perfect consecutive form (וְשַׂמְתִּי) in 28:17. In my view, הנני יסד ... ושמתי can only be read as a participle with future tense continued by a consecutive perfect with future tense (contra Dekker 2004: 44). Dekker's form-critical argument against הִנְנִי יֹסֵד that it is strange for an oracle of judgement to contain an announcement of salvation (2004: 93-94) is unconvincing. It cannot be taken for granted that 28:16 implies salvation, as is demonstrated by the interpretation offered here. Against Dekker's position, a form-critical observation is that Yahweh's announcement of his intervention (often punishment, sometimes restoration) in the prophetic books frequently makes use of the construction הִנְנִי plus participle (e.g. Isa 13:17; 37:7; 38:8; 43:19; 65:17, 18; Jer 1:15, 5:14, 15; 6:21; 8:17, many

The first phrase of the announcement is: 'Behold, I am about to lay a foundation stone on Zion'.[264] 28:16b in my view partly is the result of later elaboration. The words אֶבֶן בֹּחַן specify the stone Yahweh is going to lay on Zion as a 'massive stone' or perhaps a 'fortress stone' (for בֹּחַן, cf. Isa 23:13; 32:14).[265] This corresponds with an image of protection often found in psalms, referring to Yahweh as a protective rock and stronghold.[266] This may be part of the original oracle. What follows, 'a precious cornerstone, a sure foundation', is reminiscent of 1 Kgs 5:31 and 7:10, since only there does the combination of יָקָר (precious), אֶבֶן (stone) and יסד (to found) occur. This specification probably had the temple in mind (cf. esp. 1 Kgs 5:31) as being founded by Yahweh on Zion. This may be a later *relecture* of the oracle. The final phrase, הַמַּאֲמִין לֹא יָחִישׁ, probably means 'he who believes will not move'.[267] This is commonly related to 7:9b, the only other instance in Isaiah where אמן hi. is used in an absolute sense: 'If you do not stand firm in faith, you shall not stand at all'. Whereas 7:9b adds a condition of faith to the preceding oracle of salvation, 28:16bβ adds a promise for the faithful within an oracle of judgement. 28:16bβ forms a counterpart to 7:9b.[268] It is part of a later relecture referring to a group other than the addressees of the original oracle.

The recipients of the oracle are addressed in 28:14 as 'scoffers' and 'leaders' of the people.[269] From the oracle it is clear that not the people as a whole, but the political leaders of Jerusalem are addressed. The element הָעָם הַזֶּה was probably added as part of the literary reworking of the earlier prophetic material within Isa 28-32. This element has the effect of placing the oracle on a par with the other negative passages

---

more examples could be added). What one expects, from a form-critical point of view, is thus הִנְנִי plus participle.

[264] The interpretation of בְּצִיּוֹן as *bêt-essentiae*, 'I am about to lay a foundation stone: Zion', is rejected by Barthel 1997: 308-309, and Roberts 1987: 29.

[265] Roberts 1987: 33-34; Barthel 1997: 306, 309, 'Festungsstein'.

[266] Ps 18:3, 32, 47; 31:3-4; 62:3, 7-8; 71:3; 94:22.

[267] See Wildberger 1972-82: 1067-1068: 'wegeilen, weichen'; cf. the allusion to Isa 28:16 in 1QS 8, 7-8, 'its foundations ... will not move' (בל יחישו).

[268] Becker 1997: 232, with note 34. Barthel (1997: 325) suggests reading 28:16 as a positive variation on the conditional word of faith of 7:9b, which in my view is unconvincing. At this point, Barthel's interpretation is inconsistent. In his analysis of Isa 6-8, he regards 7:9b as part of a post-Isaianic elaboration of 7:4-9a, whereas in the analysis of Isa 28, he regards 28:16 as dependent on 7:9b but also as Isaianic; see Barthel 1997: 422, note 187, and 424.

[269] Some have derived מֹשְׁלֵי from מֹשֵׁל I. 'to recite', but the constructive relation with עַם suggests that it comes from מֹשֵׁל II. 'to rule'; cf. the other cases where מֹשֵׁל and עַם are combined, 'ruler of the peoples', Ps 104:20; Prov 28:15; Isa 3:12.

within Isa 28-32. The expression בִּירוּשָׁלַםִ [אֲשֶׁר] הָעָם occurs elsewhere,[270] and the phrase 'leaders of the people in Jerusalem' may be part of the original address.

> [15] Because you have said,
> (a) 'We have made a covenant with death, and with Sheol we have an agreement;[271]
> (b) when the overwhelming scourge[272] passes through it will not come to us;
> (c) for we have made lies our refuge, and in falsehood we have taken shelter';
> [16*] Therefore thus says the Lord Yahweh:
> Look, I am about to lay a foundation stone on Zion, a massive stone,
> [17] and I will make justice the line, and righteousness the plummet,
> (c) but hail will sweep away the refuge of lies, and waters will overwhelm the shelter,
> (a) [18] your covenant with death will be annulled,[273] and your agreement with Sheol will not stand;
> (b) when the overwhelming scourge passes through you will be beaten down by it.

The oracle is to be understood against the background of the actions of a pro-Egyptian (anti-Assyrian) faction in Jerusalem during 705-701.[274] The immediate cause may have been a treaty with Egypt against Assyria, regarded by the prophet as a violation of the treaty with Yahweh.[275] The position of the politicians that rely on Egypt in a revolt against Assyria is represented in the oracle by a fictive speech (28:15). It is not a trustworthy quotation (cf. כָּזָב and שֶׁקֶר), but a fictitious speech

---

[270] Jer 29:25; 34:8; 36:9.

[271] The context requires for חֹזֶה in verse 15 and חָזוּת in verse 18 the meaning 'agreement, pact'; Wildberger 1972-82: 1065; Barthel 1997: 307.

[272] The meaning of שׁוֹט (qere and 1QIsaᵃ) in 28:15, 18 (and 10:26) is disputed. It has been suggested to take שׁוֹט as 'flood' based on an Arabic cognate form (see Wildberger 1972-82: 1065). Barthel (1997: 308) however argues that 'scourge' is a metaphor for Assyria as Yahweh's agent (elsewhere 'stick, rod'), and thus fits to this phrase well (cf. 10:24.26; 30:27-33).

[273] The reading וכפר probably is a corruption (a feminine form is expected, though not required, and כפר is not used in this meaning). פרר hi. or ho. is used for annulling or cancelling an agreement; the form וְתֻפַּר may be suggested; see Barthel 1997: 310.

[274] Barthel 1997: 317.

[275] According to Barthel (1997: 320), the accusation equals that of 31:1-3*. Van der Toorn (1988: 202-203) argues that 'death' and 'netherworld' represent underworld deities, but the reference to treaty and pact suggests that death and Sheol refer to a political entity (Egypt). For a critical review of the position of Van der Toorn, see Dekker (2004: 121-128), who explains the covenant with death as an ironic typification of the coalition politics carried out by the political leaders of Jerusalem (2004: 274).

that functions as an accusation.[276] These leaders consider themselves as being protected against Assyria (שׁוֹט שׁוֹטֵף), Egypt being their refuge. The clauses designated as c and c' allude to expressions known especially from the Psalms, where Yahweh is described as the מַחֲסֶה ('refuge') and סֵתֶר ('hiding place') for his people, but turn them upside down: not Yahweh, but כָזָב and שֶׁקֶר are relied on for rescue.[277] The oracle announces that the supposed rescue will not stand, and pictures Yahweh as the real protagonist in history.[278]

28:16-17a has been often regarded as an announcement of salvation, and therefore creating a difficulty within the oracle of judgement.[279] 28:16-17a however does not so much promise salvation, but rather announces Yahweh's intervention directed against the political leaders, who are the oracle's addressees. Whereas the political leaders have gone astray, Yahweh presents himself as the true leader who establishes justice and righteousness. Yahweh announces that he will establish a standard of true leadership, characterised by justice and righteousness and providing protection (28:16-17a), whereas the bad leaders will experience Assyria's harsh repercussions. The pro-Egyptian politics of the Jerusalem leaders are rejected and associated with deception and lies. The main topic of the oracle is good versus bad leadership. Concluding a treaty with Egypt is a mark of bad leadership, whereas Yahweh's standard of justice and righteousness stands for good leadership. The bad leaders trust a deceitful refuge, but the refuge that Yahweh will establish—a strong stone in Zion, characterised by justice and righteousness—is trustworthy. The instruments of measurement 'the line and the plummet' are used as metaphors of

---

[276] Van der Toorn 1988: 201-202. For fictive quotations functioning as accusations in prophetic oracles, see Kaiser 1983: 200.

[277] Bartel 1997: 318-319. Van der Toorn (1988: 203) argues that כָזָב and שֶׁקֶר are *chiffres* for other gods (cf. Jer 10:14, Amos 2:4, Ps 40:5). In that case, the politicians are accused of having made a treaty with Egypt under the auspices of gods other than Yahweh. However, the use of כָזָב and שֶׁקֶר in the prophetic books may point to a different meaning: כָזָב and שֶׁקֶר are used in Mic 2:11 in a context of vain prophecy inspired by drinking (cf. Isa 28:7b-10). For כָזָב, see Ezek 13:6-9, 19, 22:28; Hos 12:2; שֶׁקֶר referring to 'false trust' especially with regard to unreliable prophets, frequently occurs in the book of Jeremiah.

[278] Barthel 1997: 321.

[279] Scholars have proposed different solutions to this apparent problem. Becker (1997: 231) regards 28:16-17a as out of place within the oracle and eliminates it; Dekker (2004: 90-104) argues that 29:16 refers to the past ('Heilshistorische terugblik'); others have attempted to bring the different elements together through theological interpretation (Wildberger 1972-82: 1081-1082; Barthel 1997: 326-327). I propose a different interpretation.

standard (justice and righteousness as a standard set by Yahweh),[280] whereas the 'stone' stands for the protection that follows from good leadership.[281] The announcement of destruction (28:17b-18) is directed to the political leaders: *they* will be beaten down.[282] For the recipients, the political leaders of Jerusalem trusting in Egypt, the prophecy is unambiguously negative. Yahweh's announcement to establish a standard of true leadership, characterised by justice and righteousness and providing protection (28:16-17a), may be encouraging for the people of Judah, but for the addressees it only emphasises the terrible fate they will suffer.

The oracle of 28:15-18 is likely to go back to prophetic activity in the late eighth century.[283] The oracle originally announced that Yahweh would provide a secure refuge in Zion, characterised by justice and righteousness, and contrasting with the false and deceptive shelter of the bad leaders. In later periods, the image of the foundation stone was reinterpreted. For instance, in 32:1-2, which in my view belongs to a revision of the Isaiah tradition in the seventh century (see 2.2.4), the king and his officials are compared to a protective rock. At this stage, 28:16-17a was probably interpreted as a promise of a king who would execute the values established by Yahweh. In the context of the seventh-century revision of the Isaiah tradition, 28:16 was probably read as announcing the reign of a new king, which according to this revision, had been fulfilled with Josiah's reign (32:1-2). Still later reinterpretations include the stone at Zion as imaging the temple (cf. the additional phrase in 28:16b, 'a precious cornerstone, a sure foundation'), and the foundation stone as an image of a messianic king to come.[284]

---

[280]   Van Keulen 1996: 130.

[281]   Cf. Barthel 1997: 322.

[282]   Barthel (1997: 327, note 113) and Wildberger (1972-82: 1072) acknowledge that the oracle originally announces the terrible fate that will befall the political leaders.

[283]   Instead, Becker (1997: 232-233) dates 28:14-18 in its core to the post-exilic period. In his view, the editor/composer took the judgement against the Northern Kingdom (28:1-4) as a prefiguration for Judah's judgement (28:14-18*), similar to the redactional addition of 8:5-8a to the earlier 8:1-4. However, the earliest layer of 28:14-18 does not announce a complete destruction of Judah and Jerusalem, but is directed specifically against Jerusalem's political leaders.

[284]   The stone at Zion (28:16) and its later reinterpretations form an analogy to the figure of Immanuel (7:14) and its later reinterpretations.

Isa 30:6-8

30:6-11 is characterised by a double duty of 30:8, which both con-cludes 30:6-8 and introduces 30:9-11.[285] Whereas 30:8 originally con-cluded 30:6b-8, a later redactional elaboration extended it with 30:9-11. Grammatically speaking, the suffix in כָּתְבָהּ (literally 'write her down!'), refers back to 30:7, where the content of the inscription is found: the symbolic name (30:7b).[286] The early material can be found in 30:6b-8.[287]

> [6b] Through a land of trouble and distress, where lioness and lion roar,[288] viper and serpent fly, they carry their riches on the backs of donkeys, and their treasures on the humps of camels, to a people that cannot profit them.
> [7] Yes, Egypt is wind, and vain their aid,[289] therefore I have called her, 'Rahab who sits still (רַהַב הַמָּשְׁבָּת)'.[290]
> [8] Go now, write it before them on a tablet, and inscribe it in a document, so that it may be for the time to come as a witness[291] forever.

Whereas the oracle focuses on the uselessness of Egypt's help, the criticism concerns Judah: trusting in Egypt is pointless.[292] By contrast, 30:9 does not refer to the content of the inscription, but adds a motiva-tion. The extension of 30:9-11 is to be regarded as a *relecture* which incorporated the earlier saying of 30:6-8 and changed its meaning to make it fit the negative qualification of the people. The command to inscribe a saying on a tablet is now connected with the people's rejec-tion of Yahweh's torah. In this way, 30:9-11 gives a new twist to 30:8: an occasional act of inscribing—the symbolic name—becomes exem-plary of the documentation of the prophetic preaching in general.[293] The act of inscribing was disconnected from its incidental character and became a testimony for the people's disobedience for times to

---

[285] For various positions with regard to this passage, see Williamson 1994: 86-87.

[286] Barthel 1997: 404-405.

[287] 30:6a, the heading, is likely to be secondary, based on the wild animals men-tioned in the oracle; see Barthel 1997: 403.

[288] The emendation of מהם into נֹהֵם qal ptc. (cf. Isa 5:29-30; Prov 28:15) is the best solution; see Wildberger 1972-82: 1158.

[289] Following Irwin 1977: 75.

[290] The symbolic name stresses the uselessness of Egypt as a helper to Judah (cf. Barthel 1997: 396). I prefer the emendation רַהַב הַמָּשְׁבָּת, 'Rahab who sits still', 'Ra-hab, who has lain silent' (שבת ho. ptc.), with Wildberger 1972-82: 1159; Williamson 1994: 253. For a slightly different view, see Barthel 1997: 396-397.

[291] MT לָעַד is usually revocalised into לְעֵד; cf. Isa 8:2.

[292] Barthel 1997: 415.

[293] Cf. Barthel 1997: 406.

come. Whereas in 30:6-8 Yahweh is speaking, the later reflection on the rejection of the prophetic message in 30:9-11 refers to Yahweh in the third person. The reflective and generalising character indicates its later redactional perspective.[294]

30:8, originally the conclusion of 30:6-8, became a fundamental statement on the necessity of written documentation of the rejected prophetic words, as part of a literary reworking of the earlier prophetic material. The term תּוֹרַת יהוה in 30:9, similarly to תּוֹרַת יהוה צְבָאוֹת in 5:24 (paralleled by אִמְרַת קְדוֹשׁ יִשְׂרָאֵל), refers to the message of Yahweh mediated by the prophet (cf. 30:10; 8:16).[295] The term is used in the (exilic) reworking of the Isaiah tradition in the specific sense that the people are accused of having rejected and despised Yahweh's message and having refused to listen to it (cf. 1:4, 8:6). For this, they wil be severely punished by Yahweh. The concept of the people's rejection of Yahweh and his word, mediated by the prophet, and their subsequent punishment by Yahweh, is presented in 8:16 as a prophetic testimony, and again as תּוֹרָה in 30:9. The Isaiah tradition in its reworked form presents itself as Isaiah's prophetic testimony, focusing on the disobedience of the people and their punishment by Yahweh.

The two functions of 30:8 resemble the difference between 8:1 and 8:16. Whereas 30:6-8 and 8:1-2 deal with the inscription of a single symbolic name, in 30:8-11 and 8:16 the act of inscribing refers to the documentation of the prophetic message as such.[296] Both 8:16 and 30:8-11 record the people's rejection of the prophetic message and present this as a motivation for the coming disaster.[297]

Isa 30:15

30:15-17 continues the theme of the people having rejected Yahweh's blessings, represented by earlier prophecies of salvation. Like 28:12, this passage presents a view on different stages of prophecy. In its literary context, 30:15 functions as a reminder of 'prophecy of old', presented as a passed stage. According to this depiction, Yahweh in the

---

[294] Cf. Barthel 1997: 416.

[295] Barthel (1997: 417) argues that 'torah of Yahweh' here does not mean 'the law' in a Deuteronomic-Deuteronomistic sense. However, neither does it refer to a single, concrete oracle, but rather to the prophetic message in a more general sense, from the perspective of the (exilic) reworking of the Isaiah tradition. I agree with López (1995: 611-612) that 'torah' here refers to a written document, a fixed tradition.

[296] Cf. Barthel 1997: 277.

[297] Cf. Barthel 1997: 419.

past promised to save the people, but they refused his help; they
trusted military power instead of Yahweh. Therefore Yahweh turned
against them (30:17). The passage, in my opinion, displays a retrospective view; disaster has become reality and is explained as having
been caused by the people's unwillingness to accept Yahweh's salvation promised in the earlier prophetic oracles. 30:15a is a quotation or
paraphrase representing the 'prophecy of old': 'Thus says the Lord
Yahweh, the Holy One of Israel: In staying and rest you shall be
saved; in quietness and in trust shall be your strength.'

The word שׁוּבָה (*hapax legomenon*) is often derived from שׁוב ('to re-
pent'),[298] but a derivation from ישׁב, 'to sit down', is preferable.[299]
Whereas נוח and שׁוב (or derivations) are never in juxtaposition within
the Hebrew Bible, the combination of נוח with ישׁב is attested,[300] e.g. in
Jer 27:11, which resembles 30:15 also thematically. Another related
passage is Judg 18:7, the description of the life of the people from
Lais: 'The people who were there living securely (יוֹשֶׁבֶת לָבֶטַח), after the
manner of the Sidonians, quiet and unsuspecting (שֹׁקֵט וּבֹטֵחַ).' These
descriptions point to a quiet, peaceful life, without military oppression. When the people are confronted with a foreign superpower, the
Assyrians or Babylonians, the prophetic advice is not to rebel, but to
accept the yoke and prosper. The suggestion of the word of salvation
in 30:15 is: if you accept the situation and do not revolt, you will live
in peace. This is fully in line with the other early prophecies within Isa
28-31.

In the present literary context, the quotation is followed by a
fictitious reply from the people in which Yahweh's word is rejected,
and by an announcement of judgement.[301] From the compositional perspective, 30:15a represents prophecy from a past stage. This presentation of the prophecy of old, its rejection by the people and their

---

[298] Barthel 1997: 423.

[299] Or from a supposed root שׁוב as a by-form of ישׁב; Wildberger (1972-82: 1181)
despite his preference for deriving it from שׁוב 'to return', presents strong arguments
for derivation from ישׁב. The variant of 1QIsaᵃ, שׁיבָה may likewise mean 'staying' (cf.
2 Sam 19:33).

[300] Deut 12:10; 2 Sam 7:1; Jer 27:11. For further evidence, see the texts mentioned in Wildberger 1972-82: 1181; and furthermore the Akkadian text KAR 58:19,
'quiet down (*nâhu*), sit down (*wašābu*) compose yourself, provide well-being for the
house you have entered' (CAD s.v. *nâhu*, 145).

[301] Cf. Barthel 1997: 422.

punishment by Yahweh, again indicates the retrospective character of Isa 28-32.[302]

2.2.4   *Isaiah 28-32 and the Seventh-Century Revision*

Within the complex of Isa 28-32, the designation אַשּׁוּר occurs in 30:31 and 31:8. Both 30:27-33 and 31:4-5.8-9, followed by 32:1-2, display an anti-Assyrian tendency. It is likely that these passages were part of a revision of the Isaiah tradition to be situated in the later part of the seventh century.

Isa 30:27-33

30:29 and 32 have sometimes been regarded as later additions,[303] but Beuken has argued that the unit has a balanced structure and from a thematic point of view forms a unity: Yahweh's destruction of Assyria and Judah's joyful celebration over this belong together (cf. 9:1-6).[304]

> [27] See, there comes Yahweh from far away, his nose burning, <his liver raging>[305], his lips full of indignation, his tongue like a devouring fire,
> [28] and his breath like an overflowing stream that reaches up to the neck,[306] to sift the nations with a deceptive sieve,[307]
> to place on the peoples' jaws a bridle that leads them astray.
> [29] You shall have a song as in the night when a holy festival is kept;
> and gladness of heart, as when one sets out to the sound of the flute
> to go to the mountain of Yahweh, to the Rock of Israel.

---

[302]   Cf. Barthel 1997: 423. Barthel (1997: 407, note 107) concludes with regard to 30:15-17: 'Die einfache Alternative von selbständiger mündlicher Verkündigungsein-heit und rein literarischer Bildung ist auch hier ungeeignet, die Eigenart der Komposi-tion zu erfassen'.

[303]   Wildberger 1972-82: 1215.

[304]   Beuken 1997: 384-386.

[305]   וְכֹבֶד מַשָּׂאָה (MT) is a crux. Barth (1977: 93) suggests taking it as a further qualification of אַפּוֹ, 'und läßt Menge von Rauch aufsteigen'. Wildberger (1972-82: 1208) proposes reading כָּבֵד מַשָּׂאָה, 'wuchtig ist seine Erhebung'. Evidently, it is part of Yahweh's appearance: his nose, his lips, his tongue, his breath. The structure of 30:27 suggests that the parallelism of 'his lips ...' // 'his tongue ...' is preceded by a parallelism of 'his nose burning' // וכבד משאה. Since כָּבֵד means 'liver', the expression 'his liver raging, inflamed' may be suspected behind the Hebrew phrase (cf. the Ak-kadian expression, 'his liver raging' as an expression of anger); Hummel (1957: 100) suggests the emendation שָׂאָה כְּבֵדוֹ־ם 'his liver raging' (with enclitic *mêm* after pro-noun suffix).

[306]   יֵחָצֶה from חצה 'to divide' is odd; cf. Isa 8:8 for the same expression עַד צַוָּאר.

[307]   Barth 1977: 94: נָפָה 'yoke'; but note the criticism by Beuken 1997: 388.

³⁰ Yahweh will cause his majestic voice to be heard and the descending blow of his arm to be seen,³⁰⁸ in furious anger and a flame of devouring fire, with a cloudburst and tempest and hailstones.

³¹ Assyria will be terror-stricken at Yahweh's voice, when he strikes with his rod.

³² And every stroke of the staff his punishment³⁰⁹ that Yahweh lays upon him will be to the sound of timbrels and lyres; battling with brandished arm he will fight with him.

³³ For his burning place has long been prepared;³¹⁰ its pyre made deep and wide, with fire and wood in abundance; the breath of Yahweh, like a stream of sulphur, kindles it.

The meaning of 30:27-33 is obscured by the vocalisation of 30:27a: 'See, the name of Yahweh (הִנֵּה שֵׁם־יהוה) comes from far away'. In my view, this is implausible. First, Yahweh's name never is the subject of בוא. Furthermore, Yahweh's שֵׁם within First Isaiah only occurs in texts of a late date,³¹¹ and never as subject.³¹² On the contrary, several passages can be mentioned where יהוה is the subject of בוא. Of the seven attestations within Isaiah,³¹³ 30:27 is closely resembled by 13:5 'They come (בוא) from a distant land, from the end of the heavens, Yahweh and the weapons of his indignation, to destroy the whole earth', and 19:1 'Behold, Yahweh is riding on a swift cloud and comes (בוא) to Egypt.' In 13:5, the element מֵאֶרֶץ מֶרְחָק 'from a distant land' parallels מִמֶּרְחָק, 'from afar' of 30:27.³¹⁴ MT's reading שֵׁם is implausible. The suggestion to delete it, however, leads to the difficulty that it cannot be convincingly explained as a later addition.³¹⁵ The problem is solved by vocalising שָׁם. The sequence הנה שם occurs ten times in the Hebrew

---

³⁰⁸ Wildberger (1972-82: 1209) regards נַחַת as a unique substantive of נחת 'to descend'.

³⁰⁹ For מוּסָדָה the emendation מוּסָרֹה 'his punishment' is generally accepted, see e.g. Barth 1977: 94; Wildberger 1972-82: 1209.

³¹⁰ The phrase 'truly it is made ready for the king' probably is a later addition, aiming to explicitly single out the Assyrian king as object of the violent actions (cf. 10:12).

³¹¹ Isa 12:4; 18:7; 24:15; 25:1; 26:8, 13 and 29:23.

³¹² The name of Yahweh is the subject only in a few cases; e.g. Prov 18:10, 'the name of Yahweh is a strong tower'.

³¹³ Isa 3:14; 13:5; 19:1; 40:10; 59:19, 20; 66:15.

³¹⁴ See also Deut 33:2: 'Yahweh came from Sinai (מִסִּינַי בָּא) and dawned from Seir upon us'; and Hab 3:3: 'God came from Teman (מִתֵּימָן יָבוֹא), the Holy One from Mount Paran'.

³¹⁵ Contra Wildberger 1972-82: 1214.

Bible and is (except for Isa 30:27) always vocalised הִנֵּה שָׁם.[316] In five cases, the phrase is followed by a subject and a participle:

Gen 29:2	Behold, three flocks of sheep were lying there	הִנֵּה־שָׁם שְׁלֹשָׁה עֶדְרֵי־צֹאן רֹבְצִים
1 Kgs 17:10	Behold, there was a widow gathering sticks	וְהִנֵּה־שָׁם אִשָּׁה אַלְמָנָה מְקֹשֶׁשֶׁת עֵצִים
Jer 36:12	Behold, all the officials were sitting there	וְהִנֵּה־שָׁם כָּל־הַשָּׂרִים יוֹשְׁבִים
Ezek 3:23	Behold, the glory of Yahweh stood there	וְהִנֵּה־שָׁם כְּבוֹד־יהוה עֹמֵד
Ezek 8:14	Behold, women were sitting there weeping for Tammuz	וְהִנֵּה־שָׁם הַנָּשִׁים יֹשְׁבוֹת מְבַכּוֹת אֶת־הַתַּמּוּז

The parallels show that 30:27a is to be read as 'Behold, there comes Yahweh from afar.'[317] 30:27-33 presents Yahweh's theophany as a warrior. It remains unspecified where Yahweh comes *from* (cf. Isa 13:5; Deut 33:2; Hab 3:3), but the location where he comes *to* is important for understanding the passage. The common answer that Yahweh comes to Zion,[318] makes sense. Beuken argues that 30:27-29 displays a movement concentrated on Zion: first, Yahweh comes to Zion (30:27), from where he leads the nations away (30:28). After that, the people of Judah come to Zion to celebrate (30:29). The movements result in a meeting of Yahweh, 'the rock of Israel', and the people.[319] Yahweh's theophany, the removal of the nations, punishment of Assyria, and the cultic celebration belong together.[320] The cultic celebration (חַג, 30:29) contains the following elements: a festival journey to the sanctuary, joyful song and thanksgiving, offerings and a festive meal.[321] 30:27-28 presents a mythological description of Yahweh's violent destruction of the enemy nations that threaten Zion. The terms used in 30:28, the word-pair nations and peoples, refers to the

---

[316] Gen 29:2; 2 Sam 15:36; 1 Kgs 14:2; 17:10; Jer 36:12; Ezek 3:23; 8:4, 14; 46:19.

[317] This solution has received little attention. Wildberger (1972-82: 1207), one of the few scholars mentioning it, rejects it without discussion.

[318] See Wildberger 1972-82: 1216-1217; Kaiser 1983: 244.

[319] Beuken 1997: 389-392.

[320] Beuken 1997: 395.

[321] Beuken 1997: 394-395. With regard to the question of which feast is referred to (suggestions are Passover and Tabernacles), Beuken (1997: 394) states that too little is known to take a position. He argues that 'efforts to establish the festival do not account for the fact that the schematisation of Israel's feasts in the three well known calendar celebrations (...) is a post-exilic objective. Older texts do not always lend themselves to such schemes'.

world of the nations as a whole.[322] Against this background, 30:30-33 describes Yahweh's destruction of Assyria, carried out at Zion.[323] 30:33 takes up the fire metaphor of 30:27-28. The great enemy comes to his end at the bonfire of Tophet.[324] The passage makes clear that Assyria's destruction is understood from the motif of the *Völkerkampf*: Yahweh destroys the enemy nations that threaten Zion.

30:27-33 contains various elements that allude to other early texts within First Isaiah, in particular the motif of the striking rod (cf. 10:5; 10:24; 11:4; 14:29), and the motif נוף 'to wane, to shake', which occurs in 10:15 and 10:32: Assyria shakes its fist at Yahweh (10:15) and at Jerusalem (10:32) and is punished for that.

Isa 31:4-5.8-9 and 32:1-2

31:4-5.8-9 can be read as a coherent unit. Of critical importance in this respect is 31:4. If it is an announcement of judgement against Jerusalem it cannot be read in continuity with 31:5. In that case, 31:5 is a *relecture* of 31:4.[325] In my view, 31:4 contains an announcement of salvation, and can therefore be read in continuity with 31:5. 31:4-5 forms a double portrait, to be read in connection with 31:8-9.[326]

> [4] For thus Yahweh said to me:
> Like a lion or a young lion growls over its prey, and, when a band of shepherds is called out against it, is not terrified by their shouting or daunted at their noise, so Yahweh of Hosts will descend upon Mount Zion and upon its hill to fight;
> [5] Like birds hovering overhead, so Yahweh of Hosts will protect Jerusalem; he will protect and deliver it, he will spare[327] and rescue it.[328]
> [8] Then the Assyrian shall fall by a sword, not of mortals;

---

[322] Beuken 1997: 387.

[323] 30:30 is directly linked to 30:27 by means of an inverted perfect (Beuken 1997: 392).

[324] Beuken 1997: 396.

[325] Barth (1977: 87-89) distinguishes between 31:1-3.4.8a as Isaianic and 31:5.8b-9 as belonging to the Assyria redaction; Barthel (1997: 436-443) interprets 31:4 in continuity with 1-3 as words of Isaiah, and regards 5.8-9 as belonging to the Assyria redaction.

[326] By contrast, 31:6-7 is incongruous with the rest of Isa 31. See Barthel 1997: 436-437; Wildberger 1972-82: 1239.

[327] The meaning of פסח is disputed. Barth (1977: 78) suggests 'verschonen' (cf. Exod 12:13, 23, 27). Barth (1977: 89-90) connects this with the Pesach celebration as part of the cult-reform of Josiah (621 BCE) and uses this for dating the Assyria redaction.

[328] The consecutive perfects והציל and והמליט are often revocalised as absolute infinitives (וְהַצֵּל and וְהַמְלֵט), which is possible but not necessary.

and a sword, not of humans,[329] shall devour him;
he shall flee from the sword, and his young men shall be put to forced labour.
[9] His rock shall pass away in terror,[330] and his officers despair in front of the standard.[331] Oracle of Yahweh, whose fire is in Zion, and whose[332] furnace is in Jerusalem.

The interpretation of 31:4 depends on עַל in 4b. Connected with לְצָבֹא, it means that Yahweh will fight *against* Zion, but connected with יֵרֵד, it means that Yahweh descends on mount Zion in order to fight *for* Zion.[333] In the latter case, 31:4a images Yahweh's imperturbability as Jerusalem's guard, in the former, the image mirrors the irrevocability of Jerusalem under Yahweh's judgement.[334] The suggestion that עַל goes with צבא because it immediately follows it is not valid. Since עַל is preceded by both verbs, both options are grammatically possible. The combination צבא with עַל, 'to fight against' is attested four times,[335] and once צבא plural participle is used without a preposition ('fighting men', Num 31:42). The verb ירד in connection with Yahweh's descent is a motif that occurs elsewhere too.[336] In Exod 19:11, 18-20 it is combined with עַל: 'Yahweh descended (יֵרֵד) upon Mount Sinai (עַל־הַר סִינָי).' Moreover, when ירד (qal) is followed by עַל, ירד governs עַל, even when ירד and עַל are separated from each other by another word or phrase.[337]

The simile in 31:4a pictures a lion carefully guarding its prey. 31:4 is the only case where a lion is the subject of הגה (יֶהְגֶּה is usually read

---

[329]   See JM § 160k.

[330]   Although recent commentators regard 31:9aα as an acceptable sentence, others have considered it corrupted (Barth 1977: 78).

[331]   Barthel (1997: 432) argues that 31:9aβ means 'erschrecken beim (feindlichen) Signal' (cf. ni. in 30:31; 31:4); Barth 1977: 79: to despair because of the enemy's war-signal.

[332]   1QIsa[a] (ולוא) and some of the versions have a negation here, probably to solve the apparent contradiction between 31:8a (killed by the sword) and 31:8b (flight from the sword). MT is *lectio difficilior*; see Barthel 1997: 430.

[333]   Barthel (1997: 440, notes 63 and 64) mentions representatives of both positions.

[334]   Barthel (1997: 441) argues that 31:4 is an announcement of judgement and 31:5 is a reinterpretation aiming to correct 4. Barthel claims that the image of a lion provokes an association of danger. However, the lion is depicted in its quality of watchfully guarding its prey, not as a fearsome animal.

[335]   Num 31:7; Isa 29:7, 8; Zech 14:12.

[336]   Gen 11:5, 7; 18:21; Exod 3:8; 19:11, 18, 20; 34:5; Num 11:17, 25; 12:5; Isa 31:4; 64:1, 3; Mic 1:3.

[337]   Cf. Exod 2:5, וַתֵּרֶד בַּת פַּרְעֹה לִרְחֹץ עַל הַיְאֹר, 'the daughter of Pharaoh descended into the river to bathe'; here עַל is governed by ירד (not רחץ, as 'to wash in' is רחץ בְּ, 2 Kgs 5:10).

as 'he growls' or 'he roars'),[338] and the only case where הגה governs the preposition עַל. The verb הגה denotes a total concentration accompanied by a muttering sound.[339] The lion is fully concentrated on its prey; he holds it tightly, watches it carefully, and is neither distracted nor scared off by the screaming of the herdsmen around him. The tertium comparationis is the utter concentration of a lion on its prey, the object it wants to keep. Likewise, Yahweh carefully watches over Zion.[340] From this it follows that the likeliest interpretation of 31:4 is, that Yahweh fights *for* Zion; he does not want to loose it.

The close parallel between 31:4 and 31:5 supports this interpretation of verse 4. Both 4b and 5aβ describe an action of 'Yahweh of Hosts' (descend, verse 4; protect, verse 5), as part of a simile. The actions have the same beneficiary: Yahweh will descend 'upon Mount Zion' (עַל הַר צִיּוֹן), and protect 'Jerusalem' (עַל יְרוּשָׁלָם). Both in verse 4 and 5, Yahweh intervenes in favour of Zion and Jerusalem.

Further arguments support the interpretation of 31:4-5 as a depiction of Yahweh's protection of Zion and Jerusalem. First, verses 4 and 5 are likely to belong together, since a lion is frequently paired with birds in similes.[341] Second, 31:9b, which concludes the unit of 31:4-5.8-9, again parallels 'Jerusalem' and 'Zion'. This supports the reading of 31:4 (Zion) and 5 (Jerusalem) as a pair. Finally, the verb חתת occurs both in 31:4 and 9a and functions as a contrast. The lion (Yahweh) is not scared off by the shouting of the herdsmen (Assyria) that threaten Jerusalem, but Assyria is terrified by Yahweh (31:9).[342]

31:5 compares Yahweh's protective presence for Jerusalem with the image of birds that protectively spread their wings.[343] A parallel is

---

[338] The only other animals attested as the subject of הגה are pigeons, in the expression 'to moan (mournfully) like doves' (Isa 38:14; 59:11), which does not help.

[339] Josh 1:8; Ps 1:2; 63:7; 77:12; 143:5.

[340] See Eidevall 1993: 81-82, for a similar analysis in terms of *topic* and *vehicle field*. The topic of 31:4 (and 31:5) is the descent of Yahweh upon Mount Zion and his protection of Jerusalem. The vehicle field is a lion defending its prey. The descent of Yahweh to battle against the enemies is structured as the fearless action of a lion defending its prey against a band of shepherds. Iconographically, this is supported by lion statues flanking temple entrances, serving as a protection of the temple against evildoers; see Cornelius 1989: 63-64.

[341] See Amos 3:4-5; Hos 11:10-11; and also 2 Sam 1:23; Isa 38:13-14; Job 38:39-41.

[342] Cf. the similarly contrastive parallel between 30:31 and 31:1: whereas Assyria is terrified by Yahweh's voice (מִקּוֹל יהוה יֵחַת), the Yahweh, the lion, is not terrified by the shouting of Assyria, the herdsmen (מִקּוֹלָם לֹא יֵחָת).

[343] Barth 1977: 85; Barthel 1997: 438-439.

found in 2 Kgs 19:34 (Isa 37:35), 'I will defend (נָנַן עַל) this city to save it (ישׁע hi.)', and in 2 Kgs 20:6 (Isa 38:6), 'I will deliver (נצל hi.) you and this city, and defend (נָנַן עַל) this city'.[344] The consecutive perfect of 31:8 grammatically continues 31:5. With regard to its content it continues 31:4, since 31:8 reveals the identity of the 'shepherds'. 31:8-9 mentions different aspects of military defeat, such as killing, flight and the submission to forced labour of prisoners of war.[345] The term 'his rock' in 31:9aα means 'the rock of Assyria'. It is paralleled by 'his officers' in 9aβ. In all likelihood, 'the rock of Assyria' is a designation of the Assyrian king. 31:4-5.8-9 presents Yahweh as divine warrior that defends Zion against its enemies.[346]

The unity of 31:4-5.8-9 is supported by the inclusion of the beginning of verse 4 and verse 9b. Verse 4 begins with the phrase 'for thus Yahweh said to me', and 9b concludes with 'oracle of Yahweh'. The text in between, 31:4-5.8-9, is not a divine word. However, the beginnings of verse 4 and 9b deliberately present 31:4-5.8-9 as a divine message to the prophet Isaiah. The unit 31:4-5.8-9 comments on 31:1.3a. In 31:1.3a the search for help from Egypt is criticised, with ירד 'to go down' to Egypt as indication of the sinful behaviour of the political leaders. In 31:4, Yahweh's descent (ירד) on Mount Zion images the rescue from Assyrian threat. The Egyptians cannot save, since they are human, not God (31:1.3a). Yahweh however rescues Jerusalem and Zion, since he is God. In this way, 31:8a comments on 3a.

The earliest material of 31:1.3a was commented upon by 31:4-5.8-9. The latter unit in all likelihood was part of a seventh-century revision of the Isaiah tradition. The material of Isa 31 to be dated to the Assyrian period, is to be connected with the beginning of Isa 32.[347] Although Isa 32 for the greater part postdates the Assyrian period,[348]

---

[344]   Barthel 1997: 438-439.
[345]   Cf. Wildberger 1972-82: 1239: 'Tod, Flucht, Frondienst stehen einfach neben einander'. Cf. Barthel 1997: 437-438.
[346]   So Wagner 2006: 149-151, pointing out the parallel depiction of Yahweh in Ps 76:2-8. I will argue in chapter 6.1.6 that the seventh-century Isaiah revision, of which 31:4-5.8-9 is part, has its traditio-historical roots in the official ideology of monarchic Jerusalem, of which Ps 76:2-8 is an exponent.
[347]   Barthel 1997: 266-267, 452.
[348]   32:6-8 is a later extension to 32:1-5 (Barthel 1997: 266, note 69); 32:9-14 reflects the downfall of Jerusalem in 586 BCE and is to be dated in the exilic period (Barthel 1997: 267-268, 452; Clements 1980a: 261-263; Wildberger 1972-82: 1265-1267), and 32:15-20 is a still later elaboration, depicting salvation (Barthel 1997: 268, 259-262).

the beginning of this chapter, in my view restricted to 32:1-2, is to be situated in the Assyrian period. Whereas 32:1-2 presents a portrayal of the ideal king and his officials, 32:3-5 displays a quite different interest (a reversal of the negative depiction of 6:9-10).[349]

> [1] See, a king will reign in righteousness, and officers will rule with justice.[350]
> [2] Each will be like a hiding place from the wind, a covert from the tempest, like streams of water in a dry place, like the shade of a great rock in a weary land.[351]

The 'rock' and the 'officers' of 31:9 correspond to the 'king' and the 'officers' of 32:1. Furthermore, 32:2 refers to both of them as to the protective shade of a mighty 'rock'. Although 31:9 and 32:1 are not grammatically connected, there is a strong conceptual connection between 31:4-5.8-9 and 32:1-2. After the collapse of Assyria, brought about by Yahweh's intervention, there is room for a new Judaean king. A similar double portrait of Assyria's downfall and the reign of a righteous king in Jerusalem, occurs in 10:33-34 followed by 11:1-5 (see 2.3.2 below). Furthermore, 32:1-2 begins with the exclamation *hēn*, 'See!'. This evidently relates to the exclamation *hôy* in the prophetic material of 29:15, 30:1-2, 31:1.3a. In these *woe*-sayings, the prophet Isaiah condemns the Judaean leaders, because of their policy of rebellion against Assyria. 32:1-2 adds to this the positive perspective that once Assyria is destroyed by Yahweh (31:4-5.8-9), an ideal king and his officials will rule the people of Judah in justice and righteousness.

2.2.5 Evaluation

Isa 28-32 contains a range of material deriving from the Assyrian period. However, the basic literary complex of Isa 28-32 is to be situated at a greater distance from the prophet Isaiah than is usually believed.

---

[349] Barthel (1997: 266, 267, note 71, and 452, note 122) argues that the core of 32:1-5 is limited to 32:1-2, and that 32:3-5 is to be compared to 29:17-24. For 32:3-4 echoing 6:9-10, see Williamson 1998a: 67-69.

[350] MT *lĕśārîm* is to be regarded as an error for *śārîm*, with LXX and other witnesses (cf. most translations and commentaries, see e.g. Wildberger 1972-82: 1250).

[351] Williamson (1998a: 63-65) points out the proverbial character of 32:1. In my view, 32:1 cannot be disconnected from 32:2. The proverbial character applies to 32:1-2: a depiction of the ideal king in a proverbial garb. This corresponds to the presumed scribal milieu of the seventh-century revision of the Isaiah tradition (see chapter 6.1.6).

The literary complex of Isa 28-32 is characterised by the theme that the people have rejected Yahweh's blessings (28:12; 30:15), have not truly worshipped Yahweh (29:13), have been rebellious, and have rejected Yahweh's word (30:9, 12). Because of this Yahweh punishes them with a foreign invasion (28:11-13, 19), the fall of Jerusalem (29:1-4, 32:14), and a total destruction (30:13-14). This theme of disobedience and punishment indicates later reflection: the sixth-century disasters are interpreted as Yahweh's just punishment of the sinful people. There is a strong analogy between Isa 6-8 and Isa 28-32. Both complexes contain earlier prophetic material in a reworked form. It is likely that the literary reworking of the earlier material that resulted in the basic complex of Isa 28-32 was carried out following the example of the composition of Isa 6-8.

2.3   The Rest of First Isaiah

In this section I discuss texts from the rest of First Isaiah that can be situated in the Assyrian period. The presumed early material presented in this section consists of prophetic sayings from the eighth-century, and of texts that are likely to belong to a seventh-century revision. I focus on Isa 5 and 9-11, and on the earliest layers of 13-23.

2.3.1   The Woe-Sayings in Isaiah 5:8-23* and 10:1-2

Within the prophetic literature *woe*-sayings regularly occur in series. In various cases it seems likely that small collections of *woe*-sayings received literary elaboration, such as Hab 2[352] and Amos 3-6.[353] Some scholars have argued that Isa 5:8-23 is a short collection of earlier sayings that was elaborated and integrated into the expanding literary

---

[352] Hab 2 contains five *woe*-sayings, 2:6b, 9, 12, 15 and 19a. 2:6b clearly is presented as an independent saying (2:6a characterises what follows as 'proverbial saying', 'mocking poem', 'enigmatic saying'). The *woe*-saying consists of the exclamation הוֹי followed by two substantivised participles that describe the wicked behaviour of the subject involved. Since 2:7 begins similar to 2:6a (הֲלוֹא), it does not belong to the *woe*-saying. Furthermore, the discrepancy between the sayings and their direct context suggests that the sayings have been incorporated into the present context as part of a literary reworking.

[353] For Amos 3-6 going back to a collection of early *woe*-sayings, see Kratz 2003a: 74-80.

complex of the Isaiah tradition.[354] 5:8-23 contains six *woe*-sayings, 5:8, 11, 18-19, 20, 21, and 22-23. Whereas the first two have been extended with commentary (5:9-10, 5:12-13.14-17), the others, 5:18-19, 20, 21, and 22-23, are standing on their own. This suggests that the *woe*-sayings are independent sayings and that 5:8 and 11 originally stood on their own too. The comments of 5:9-10 and 5:12-13.14-17 can be explained as later extensions that were added in the process of a literary reworking of earlier material. 5:18-19, 20, 21 and 22-23 confirm that *woe*-sayings are independent sayings, in which doom is implied, and that the explicit announcements of punishment may be secondary expansions.[355]

5:9-10 forms an extension to 5:8. The phrase 'In my hearing, Yahweh of Hosts has sworn' (5:9a) probably alludes to 6:1-11, where Yahweh reveals to Isaiah his decision to bring destruction to his people.[356] The announcement of 5:9b resembles 6:11.[357] 5:9-10 is the product of a reworking of the earlier *woe*-saying. The first extension to 5:11 consisted of 5:12-13,[358] which again contains parallels with 6:9-11. The motifs of 'not seeing' (5:12) and 'lacking insight' (5:13) as an explanation for the coming disaster correspond to 6:9-11. The other sayings stand by themselves: 5:18-19,[359] 5:20, 5:21, and 5:22-23.[360]

5:8-23 was extended by 5:24, which was composed as a conclusion to the *woe*-sayings in a reworked form. 5:24 accuses the people of rejecting (מאס) Yahweh's torah and of despising (נאץ) his word. This resembles the theme of accusation and punishment that characterises the literary reworking of Isa 6-8 and 28-32. The accusation of 5:24 is furthermore paralleled by texts reflecting the destruction caused by the Babylonians in the sixth century. For example Jer 6:19, 'they have not

---

[354] Kaiser 1981: 100-107; Vermeylen 1977-78: 170; Werner 1988: 12-13.

[355] Cf. Kaiser 1981: 102.

[356] The same phrase occurs in 22:14, there followed by an oath as well. 22:14 similarly alludes to 6:1-11. For 22:1-14, see 2.3.6 below.

[357] 5:9 and 6:11 share the terms בָּתִּים 'houses', מֵאֵין יוֹשֵׁב 'without inhabitants', שְׁמָמָה/שַׁמָּה 'ruin'; cf. Becker 1997: 137. Isa 5:9 describes a complete destruction, comparable to 1:7, 6:11 and 22:4; cf. Jer 9:19; 19:13; 32:29; 33:4.

[358] Kaiser (1981: 104) argues that 5:12-13 is a later extension of 5:11.

[359] Becker 1997: 141; contra Kaiser 1981: 104, 112; Werner 1988: 20.

[360] The *woe*-sayings within 5:8-23 find parallels in *woe*-sayings in Micah and Amos. Isa 5:8 parallels Mic 2:2 (שָׂדֶה; בַּיִת), and cf. Amos 5:11; Isa 5:11 parallels Amos 6:4-6a; Isa 5:20 resembles Amos 5:7 and 5:18-20; Isa 5:23 resembles Amos 5:12b. The parallels are however rather general. They can be explained from a similarity in genre and theme. Literary dependency cannot be convincingly demonstrated; contra Becker 1997: 134-145.

given heed to my words; and as for my torah, they have rejected (מאס)
it'.[361] Originally, the *woe*-sayings condemned a specific group of people of a particular kind of improper behaviour. The reworking of the
sayings into the unit 5:8-24 is characterised by a generalisation. It is
now the people as a whole who are accused. Furthermore, a clear announcement of total disaster is added.

10:1-4 contains a similar *woe*-saying extended with later commentary. The *woe*-saying probably consisted of 10:1-2, whereas 10:3 and
4 are to be understood as a literary elaboration.[362] The saying of 10:1-2
can be associated with those within 5:8-23. The early *woe*-sayings are
the following:

> [8] Woe them that join house to house, who add field to field,
> until there is no room left[363] in the midst of the land!
> [11] Woe them that rise early in the morning in pursuit of strong drink,
> who linger in the evening to be inflamed by wine!
> [18f] Woe them that drag iniquity along with cords of falsehood,
> who drag sin along as with cart ropes,[364]
> who say, 'Let him make haste, let him speed his work that we may see
> it; let the plan of the Holy One of Israel hasten to fulfilment, that we
> may know it!'
> [20] Woe them that call evil good and good evil, who put darkness for
> light and light for darkness, who put bitter for sweet and sweet for bit-
> ter!
> [21] Woe them that are wise in their own eyes, and shrewd in their own
> sight!
> [22f] Woe them that are heroes in drinking wine and valiant at mixing
> drink,
> who acquit the guilty for a bribe, and deprive the innocent of their
> rights!
> [10:1f] Woe them that make iniquitous decrees, who write[365] oppressive
> statutes,[366] to turn aside the needy from justice and to rob the poor of my

---

[361] The despising (נאץ) of Yahweh and his word further occurs in Isa 1:4 and Jer
23:17 (cf. Num 14:11, 23; Deut 31:20). The transgressions result in the destruction of
the people. The image of destruction in Isa 5:24 resembles that of Jer 13:24-25; cf.
also Num 11:1; Isa 29:6; Jer 5:14; 21:14; Lam 2:3; Ezek 15:7; Amos 2:5.

[362] 10:3 addresses a second person and announces judgement, by referring to the
'day of punishment'. This refers to the judgement Yahweh will bring over his people
(Jer 8:12; 10:15; Hos 9:7; Mic 7:4; cf. Jer 46:21; 50:27; 51:18). Furthermore, the term
שׁוֹאָה 'destruction' representing Yahweh's action, occurs in Isa 47:11 and Zeph 1:15.
The motif of threat coming from afar is paralleled in Jer 4:16; 5:15. For the motif of
the slain on the battlefield in 10:4, cf. Lam 2:21.

[363] The phrase וְהוּשַׁבְתֶּם לְבַדְּכֶם is to be regarded as a later addition; Becker 1997:
137.

[364] Kellermann (1987: 95) suggests: 'Wehe denen, die die Schuld herbeiziehen
mit Rinderstricken und wie mit einem Wagenseil die Versündigung'.

people[367] of their right, that widows may be their spoil, and that they may make the orphans their prey!

This series of *woe*-sayings probably formed a small collection that predated the literary complex into which it has been reworked. The sayings are to be read as criticism directed at members of the upper class of Jerusalem and Judah, who took a leading role in society. In chapter 4.1.8 it will be argued that this criticism can be understood against the background of a particular controversy. The controversy between Isaiah and his opponents, leading political figures from the upper class, was the question whether or not to rebel against Assyria in the hope of military aid from Egypt. From the critical sayings of Isaiah it appears that this was not just a political question, but a deep controversy involving issues of good versus bad leadership. Isaiah denounces his opponents as bad leaders, and his criticism covers all aspects of public life: political decisions, religious attitude, and social behaviour.

2.3.2 Isaiah 10:5-11:5

Since Isa 10 deals with Assyria as a superpower, it is mostly agreed that the earliest version of this chapter consists of material from the Assyrian period. 10:5-34, as I will argue, contains three oracles from the eighth century: 10:5-9.13-15*, 10:24-25 and 10:27b-32. These words were extended by a revision of the Isaiah tradition, to be situated in the seventh century. The revision consisted of a commentary to each of them: 10:5-9.13-15 was extended by 10:11 and 10:16-19;[368] 10:24-25 with 10:26-27; and 10:27b-32 with 10:33-34. Furthermore 10:33-34 is directly continued by 11:1-5, which forms a conclusion to 10:5-11:5 as a whole.

---

[365] כתב pi., occurring only here, may denote an iterative meaning: to do again and again.

[366] With the emendation מכתבי, plural construct of מִכְתָּר 'writing', 'document'.

[367] The expression עַמִּי 'my people' is remarkable, since the *woe*-sayings usually are prophetic words, not divine words. Either the prophet refers to the people as to 'his people', or it is due to a later development of the text influenced by the divine speech of 10:5-15.

[368] On 10:20-23 as a later expansion, see Wildberger 1972-82: 412-416.

Isa 10:5-15

10:5-15 to some extent resembles the *woe*-sayings discussed above, but it is a divine word instead of a prophetic word and also much longer than the prophetic *woe*-sayings. It may be qualified as an extensive *woe*-word, to some extent comparable to 28:1-4. At present, 10:5-15 contains two accusations against Assyria. First, Assyria is condemned for its aim to conquer the world. Whereas Yahweh ordered Assyria to punish a particular nation (10:6), Assyria planned to conquer the entire world. Assyria is condemned for its unbridled expansion. A second accusation is formulated in 10:11: Assyria aimed to conquer Jerusalem. These two different accusations represent two stages in the oracle's development: the earliest passage consists of 10:5-9.13-15, whereas 10:11 represents a revision of it.[369]

> [5] Woe, Assyria, rod of my anger, a staff (that is in their hands) is my fury![370]
> [6] Against a godless nation I send him, against the people of my wrath I command him, to take spoil and seize plunder, and to tread it down like the mire of the streets.
> [7] But this is not what he thinks he should do, nor does this accord with his intentions, for it is in his heart to destroy, and to cut off many nations.
> [8] He says: 'Are my officials not all kings?
> [9] Is not Calno like Carchemish? Is not Hamath like Arpad?
> Is not Samaria like Damascus?
> [13] By the strength of my hand I have done it, and by my wisdom, for I have understanding; I have removed the boundaries of peoples, and have taken as spoil their leaders;[371] Like a Mighty one I brought down rulers.[372]

---

[369] Wildberger 1972-82: 392; Dietrich 1976: 116-118; Kaiser 1981: 219-222; Mittmann 1989: 112. Verse 11 is part of a first revision, 10:12 was added at a still later stage.

[370] The easiest solution is to omit הוּא בְיָדָם as a gloss and to revocalise מַטֶּה as a construct: 'my rod of anger, my club of fury'. For a different solution, see Mittmann 1989: 114-115: Assyria is not only the rod in Yahweh's hand, but also carries the club in their own hand (cf. Mittmann 1989: 132, *Korrekturzusatz*).

[371] See Mittmann 1989: 120. The *qere* עַתּוּד 'leading male goat' (cf. Jer 50:8), applied to human leaders, fits the context (cf. Isa 14:9).

[372] The phrase is difficult and perhaps corrupt. I have adopted the reading suggested by Irvine 1993: 133-144 (esp. 144). Cf. Wildberger 1972-82: 391, for various solutions. Mittmann (1989: 121-123) argues that the end of 10:13 parallels the first stiche of 10:14, and suggests the reading: 'Ich brachte hinab wie Schwingen (כאבר) Thronenden', which is too far-fetched in my view.

> [14] My hand has found, like a nest, the wealth of the peoples, as one gath-
> ers eggs that have been forsaken, so I have gathered the whole earth;
> and there was no wing that fled, or opened its mouth, or chirped.'
> [15] Shall the axe vaunt itself over the one who wields it, or the saw mag-
> nify itself against the one who handles it? As if a rod raises the one who
> lifts it up, as if a staff lifts the one who is not wood!

According to 10:5-6, Yahweh ordered the 'rod of his anger', Assyria,
to punish the 'people of his anger'. The second part of 10:6 specifies
Assyria's task as the complete looting of the godless nation so that its
land is left devastated and trampled down.[373] The nation against which
Assyria is sent, designated as godless and as people of Yahweh's
wrath, can be identified as Ephraim. A parallel depiction of Ephraim is
found in 28:1-4, in particular רמס in 28:3 and מִרְמָס in 10:6. Furthermore, Ephraim is included in the announcements of 8:1-4, where similar verbs are used to those in 10:6 (שׁלל and בזז). The identification of
the nation in 10:6 as Ephraim is confirmed by the enumeration of cities in 10:9, which has its climax with Samaria, the capital of the nation against which Assyria is sent.[374]

Assyria did not act according to Yahweh's commission. Although
it conquered the nation specified by Yahweh, it also adopted a policy
of wide-scale conquest. Assyria's dissent has two aspects: instead of
spoiling and trampling down (10:6), Assyria aims at annihilation
(10:7), and instead of taking actions against one nation (Ephraim),
Assyria aims to cut off many nations (10:7).[375] Both aspects are
worked out in the following verses. The aspect of the many nations is
continued in the enumeration of 10:9, and in 10:14, 'I have gathered
the whole earth'. The aspect of complete annihilation of nations and
lands is continued in 10:13, 'I have removed their boundaries', and in
the statement of the Assyrian king: 'Are my officials not all kings?'
This refers to the eradication of national identities due to Assyria's
politics of deportation and provincialisation. The removal of boundaries, i.e. the abolition of the territorial status quo by provincialisation
and dispossession of land, implies a violation of the divine distribution
of the lands from of old.[376] According to 10:5-9.13-15, Yahweh ordered a specific action against Ephraim, but not against the whole
world, and his order involved plunder and devastation, but not depor-

---

[373]   Mittmann 1989: 115-116.
[374]   Mittmann 1989: 118-119.
[375]   Mittmann 1989: 117.
[376]   Mittmann 1989: 120; cf. Deut 32:8; Ps 74:17.

tation and abolition of territorial boundaries.[377] This word condemns
Assyria's imperialism, which was a reality during the second half of
the eighth century. The fictitious speech of the Assyrian king mirrors
various political measures that were a reality in the Assyrian period,
such as the exile of populations and the change of territorial borders.[378]

The point of 10:5-9.13-15 is the discrepancy between Yahweh's
order and Assyria's own political agenda. This discrepancy is acute, in
my view, because of Judah's involvement. Judah, although not explicitly mentioned, is implied in the phrases 'nations not few' (10:7) and
'all the earth' (10:14). It was Judah's involvement in Assyria's expansion that elicited the message of 10:5-9.13-15. Whereas the enumeration of six cities in 10:9 generally points to the reigns of Tiglath-
pileser III and Sargon II,[379] Sargon's campaign against the West in 720
is the most likely background of the prophecy of 10:5-9.13-15. First,
Hamath, Arpad, Damascus and Samaria were all involved in the revolt
against Assyria.[380] Furthermore, Assyria's military actions in Syria-
Palestine were of consequence for Judah too, as it was required to
submit to Assyria. Whereas 28:1-4 is likely to date from before 720,
10:5-9.13-15 looks back at the campaign of 720, and criticises Assyria
for its ambition for worldwide conquest. The message reflects the experience that Assyria's expansion involved Judah as well. The term
אַשּׁוּר (10:5) refers to Assyria as a political-military power, which is
personified in this oracle and represented by the king.[381]

Whereas the material within Isa 6-8 and 28-31 identified as eighth-
century prophetic oracles or sayings has an oral background, the early
version 10:5-9.13-15 looks more like a literary composition. To this
the following explanation may be suggested. 10:13-14 differs in style
from the preceding verses (10:5-9). Furthermore, 10:13-14 repeats the
accusations that contrary to Yahweh's will Assyria has turned against
many nations (10:7; cf. 10:14, 'all the earth') and has abolished terri-

---

[377] See Mittmann 1989: 131.
[378] See Wildberger 1972-82: 399-400; cf. Machinist 1983a: 725, for the motif of
the removal of boundaries.
[379] By 738 BCE, Carchemish, Calno, Arpad, Hamath, Damascus and Samaria had
either been conquered by Assyria (Arpad in 740, Calno in 738, see Millard 1994: 44,
59) or had submitted to Assyria and paid tribute (see Tadmor 1994: 54-57, 68-69).
Later, during the reigns of Tiglath-pileser III and Sargon II, further actions were taken
against several of these cities, which included measures criticised in Isa 10:5-9.13-
15*.
[380] See Fuchs 1994: 89, 200-201.
[381] Mittmann 1989: 115.

torial boundaries and national states (10:7, 8; cf. 10:13). 10:13-14 repeats 10:7-8, but more eloquently and rhetorically. The hubris of the
Assyrian king, implied by 10:7-10, is much more explicit in 10:13-14.
As 10:13-14 doubles 10:7-8, 10:15b doubles 15a. I therefore suspect
that 10:5-9.15a represents the original prophetic word. 10:13-14.15b
can be seen as a product of elaboration, a literary embellishment of the
prophecy when it was put down in writing. 10:13-14 is a typical word
of hubris.[382] The judgement over this hubris in 10:15b makes an explicit connection with 10:5: Assyria is only a tool in Yahweh's hand, a
piece of wood.

10:5-9.15a can be regarded as the record of an oracle that was once
orally delivered. It is a balanced oracle, in which the rhetorical questions of 10:8-9 are countered by a rhetorical question of Yahweh in
10:15a. The fictive quotation of the Assyrian king in 10:8-9 resembles
the fictive quotation of Rezin in 7:6 (and the fictive quotations of the
bad leaders in 5:19 and 29:15). In each case, the purpose of the quotation is to demonstrate the arrogant and self-willed behaviour of the
enemy. With regard to style, 15a with the construction אִם ... הֲ directly
responds to verse 9, הֲלֹא ... אִם־לֹא ... אִם־לֹא. 10:5-9.15a is a word of
threat against Assyria. After the threatening exclamation *hôy*, Assyria's politics and hubris is exposed, and the final rhetorical question
(10:15a) leaves little space for doubt that Assyria has gone too far and
will be punished by Yahweh. With the elaboration of 10:13-14.15b the
accusation and threat are made more explicit: Assyria is doomed.

Isa 10:11 and 16-19
10:5-9.13-15 received a revision by the insertion of 10:11.[383] This can
be regarded as a *relecture* that turns the focus to Jerusalem: 'Shall I
not do to Jerusalem and her idols what I have done to Samaria and her
images?' The *relecture* refers to Assyria's attempt to capture Jerusalem, reflecting the events of 701, when Sennacherib campaigned
against Judah and threatened Jerusalem. In its elaborated form, 10:5-
15 condemns Assyria for threatening Jerusalem, and, especially, for
regarding Yahweh as 'just another god'. The reworked unit is ex-

---

[382]   Machinist 1983a: 734.
[383]   10:10 is probably a still later addition, based on 2 Kgs 18:33-35 // Isa 36:18-
20. 10:12 forms a later relecture of 10:11: the work to be done is the abolition of
idolatry in Jerusalem.

tended by an announcement of disaster against Assyria, consisting of 10:16-19:

> [16] Therefore the Sovereign, Yahweh of Hosts, will send wasting sickness among his stout warriors, and under his glory a burning will be kindled, like the burning of fire.
> [17] The light of Israel will become a fire, and his Holy One a flame; and it will burn and devour his thorns and briers in one day.
> [18] The glory of his forest and his fruitful land Yahweh will destroy, both soul and body, and it will be as when an invalid wastes away. [384]
> [19] The remnant of the trees of his forest will be so few that a child can write them down.

This passage forms an extension to 10:5-9.13-15 and announces Assyria's destruction, as in 14:24-27, 30:27-33, and 31:8-9. In the earlier saying, 10:5-9.13-15, the punishment of Assyria was only implicit. In the seventh-century revision, this becomes explicit, as a main theme. Assyria is wood that will be burned down by Yahweh. The intensity of destruction in 10:16-19 exceeds that of the punishment implied in 10:5-15.

Isa 10:24-25

10:24-25 is often dated to the post-exilic period,[385] but for no good reasons. 10:24-27a, which deals with the liberation of the people of Zion from Assyria, consists of a divine oracle (10:24-25) followed by a commentary (10:26a.27a). In my view, 10:26a.27a belongs to the Assyria redaction and dates from the second half of the seventh century, whereas 10:24-25 is of an earlier date and reflects the military power of Assyria as a reality.

My interpretation of 10:24-25 differs from the common view with regard to two issues, בְּדֶרֶךְ מִצְרַיִם in 10:24, and וְכָלָה זַעַם in 10:25. 10:24b describes Assyria's actions as 'he smites you with a rod, he lifts up his staff against you'. The final words בְּדֶרֶךְ מִצְרַיִם are commonly translated: 'as the Egyptians did'.[386] This reading, adopted in most commentaries,[387] is in my view incorrect. The combination דֶרֶךְ and בְּ, either means literally 'on the way, on the road', or דֶרֶךְ is used metaphorically as 'way of life'. Understanding בְּדֶרֶךְ מִצְרַיִם as 'as Egypt did' is unparal-

---

[384] According to Barth (1977: 30) this phrase is corrupted.

[385] See Wildberger 1972-82: 418.

[386] Or similarly: 'in the way of Egypt', 'after the manner of Egypt', 'as it was in Egypt'.

[387] An exception is Irvine (1990: 268-269), who translates 'on the road to Egypt'.

leled.[388] The literal interpretation 'the way/road to Egypt' is much more plausible, since followed by a topographic designation, בְּדֶרֶךְ determines a location:

Gen 16:7	The spring on the way to Shur (בְּדֶרֶךְ שׁוּר)
Gen 35:19/48:7	And she was buried on the way to Ephrath (בְּדֶרֶךְ אֶפְרָתָה)
1 Sam 17:52	The Philistines fell on the way to Shaaraim (בְּדֶרֶךְ שַׁעֲרַיִם)

Furthermore, the 'way to Egypt' is a well-known route.[389] The idea that Assyria struck Judah on the way to Egypt resembles the image of Assyria as a 'passing flood', in 28:18: 'when the overwhelming scourge passes through, you will be beaten down by it'.[390]

In 10:25, many scholars follow the emendation of BHS app. crit. זַעְמִי, 'my indignation', which creates a juxtaposition of זַעְמִי and אַפִּי. Furthermore, וְכָלָה is usually translated as 'shall cease' or 'shall come to an end'. This results to the following interpretation: 'for yet a very little while, and my (Yahweh's) indignation against you (the people of Jerusalem) will be over'. In my view, the phrase has the opposite meaning. The combination of זַעַם and כלה occurs in Dan 11:36 as well, in a description of the outrageous behaviour of the foreign king: 'he shall prosper till the wrath is complete (עַד כָּלָה זַעַם), for what is determined shall be done'. This means that the king is free to act until the limit of God's indignation is reached.[391] Isa 10:25 is to be understood similarly: 'for yet a very little while and the indignation—i.e. Yah-

---

[388]   As a metaphor דֶּרֶךְ is used creatively: 'to instruct the right way' (Ps 25:8, 12) or 'the way of wisdom' (Prov 4:11), but exact parallels for 'as Egypt did' are not found. Gen 19:31 and Ezek 20:30 are rather close, but not as elliptic as the supposed reading of בְּדֶרֶךְ מִצְרַיִם. The only parallel would be Amos 4:10, 'I sent among you a pestilence after the manner of Egypt' (דֶּבֶר בְּדֶרֶךְ מִצְרַיִם). However, בְּדֶרֶךְ מִצְרַיִם probably is a corruption of כְּדֶבֶר מִצְרַיִם 'like the pestilence of Egypt', referring to one of the plagues (Exod 9:3, 15; cf. Ps 78:50). Even if this emendation is rejected, בְּדֶרֶךְ מִצְרַיִם in Amos 4:10 and Isa 10:24 would mean different things: Amos 4:10, 'I will treat you the way Egypt was treated' (genitive objective); Isa 10:24, 'Assyria acts as Egypt acted' (genitive subjective). Zehnder (1999: 324) rejects the geographical interpretation of בְּדֶרֶךְ מִצְרַיִם in 10:24 in favour of a metaphoric understanding ('Art und Weise'), but without good arguments.

[389]   This road is referred to in Deut 17:16, 28:26, and in Jer 2:18. In Exod 13:17, it is referred to as well, but from the opposite direction as the 'route to/through the land of the Philistines' (דֶּרֶךְ אֶרֶץ פְּלִשְׁתִּים), the customary route from Egypt to Palestine.

[390]   The comment of 10:26a supports the view that בְּדֶרֶךְ מִצְרַיִם in 10:24 is not intended to compare Assyria to Egypt: Assyria's behaviour and fate is compared to that of Midian, not Egypt.

[391]   See also Dan 8:19, אַחֲרִית הַזַּעַם, 'the last end of the indignation', and 8:23, כְּהָתֵם הַפֹּשְׁעִים, 'when the transgressions have reached their full measure'.

weh's indignation provoked by Assyria's wicked behaviour—will be complete'. As soon as the limit is reached, Yahweh's anger will be directed at Assyria's destruction. This leads to the following oracle:

> [24] Therefore[392] thus says the Lord Yahweh of Hosts:
> O my people, who live in Zion, do not be afraid of Assyria when it beats you with a rod and lifts up its staff against you on the way to Egypt.
> [25] For in a very little time the limit will be reached, and then my anger will be directed at their destruction.[393]

10:24-25 is an oracle of encouragement for the people in Jerusalem. They are threatened and oppressed by Assyria's imperialistic aggression. The oracle condemns Assyria for beating the Judaeans with a rod and lifting up its staff against them. The terms 'rod' and 'staff' equal those in 10:5, but there is a decisive difference: Assyria's actions against Ephraim are according to Yahweh's orders, but the actions against Judah are an act of aggression. With regard to Judah and Jerusalem, Assyria is not Yahweh's stick, but an evil aggressor that will be punished itself. Yahweh announces that the wrath against Assyria will soon be complete, and that they will be destroyed. A similar aspect of imminence is found in other early oracles as well, such as 7:16, 8:4 and 28:4 (cf. also 17:14 and 18:5).

Isa 10:26a.27a

The oracle of 10:24-25 received a commentary, consisting of 26a.27a, which probably belongs to the Assyria redaction of the seventh century:

> [26a] Yahweh of Hosts will wield a whip against them, as when he struck Midian at the rock of Oreb.
> [27a] On that day his burden will be removed from your shoulder, and his yoke will be destroyed from your neck.[394]

The first comment (10:26a) announces the destruction of Assyria, by using terms from the earlier prophetic oracles (שׁוֹט, 28:15, 18) and a motif similar to 9:3: the destruction of Assyria is compared to the de-

---

[392] לָכֵן probably functions on a (later) compositional level as a connection between the subsequent oracle and the preceding words (cf. Wildberger 1972-82: 417-418).

[393] תַּבְלִיתָם can be interpreted as a noun deriving from בלה (not further attested), meaning 'end, destruction', with suffix.

[394] Read יְחֻבַּל; MT וְחֻבַּל and 10:27b are corrupted; see Wildberger 1972-82: 417.

struction of Midian.[395] The second comment (10:27a) closely resembles 9:3 (and 14:25). 10:26a.27a comments on the oracle of 10:24-25 as 10:16-19 comments on 10:5-9.13-15. The theme of Yahweh's punishment of Assyria is worked out.

Isa 10:27b-32

10:27b-32, a third prophetic word within Isa 10, indicates the approach of an Assyrian army:

> [27b] He has marched from <Samaria>,
> [28] come to Aiath, passed through Migron. At Michmash he stores his baggage.
> [29] They have crossed over the pass: 'Geba will be our quarters for the night'. Ramah trembles, Gibeah of Saul has fled.
> [30] Cry aloud, O Bat-Gallim! Listen, O Laishah! Answer him, O Anathoth![396]
> [31] Madmenah is in flight, the inhabitants of Gebim flee for safety.
> [32] This very day he will halt at Nob, he will shake his fist at the mount of daughter Zion,[397] the hill of Jerusalem.

Although not all sites mentioned have been securely identified, it is commonly agreed that the list indicates an army approaching Jerusalem from the north.[398] This supports the restoration of the probably corrupted phrase of MT 10:27b, עַל מִפְּנֵי שֶׁמֶן, 'yoke in front of oil', into עָלָה מִפְּנֵי שֹׁמְרוֹן.[399] The Assyrian army comes from the territory of Northern Israel to Jerusalem. The places mentioned indicate that the army left the main road from Beth-El to Jerusalem in order to bypass fortified Mizpah, and approached Jerusalem along the central ridge.[400] The Assyrians did not aim to conquer Judah's fortified cities, but quickly marched to Jerusalem. At Nob (Mount Scopus) they halted in order to intimidate the people of Jerusalem.[401] This passage does not describe a huge army preparing for a siege of Jerusalem, but refers to a specific military expedition, aiming to intimidate and quickly subjugate Jerusalem and Judah to Assyria.

---

[395] 10:26b may be part of a later relecture, induced by בְּדֶרֶךְ מִצְרַיִם; Wildberger 1972-82: 418, 421.

[396] Read עֲנִיָּה in conformity with LXX.

[397] Reading *bat* for *bêt* with 1QIsa[a]; 4QIsa[c]; LXX.

[398] Sweeney 1994: 464.

[399] Wildberger 1972-82: 424.

[400] Blenkinsopp 2000a: 261; Sweeney 1994: 464; Wildberger 1972-82: 431.

[401] Sweeney 1994: 464.

Isa 10:33-34 and 11:1-5

10:33-34, directly continued by 11:1-5, presents a commentary to the preceding word of 10:27b-32:

> [33] Look, the Sovereign, Yahweh of Hosts, will lop the boughs with terrifying power; the tallest trees will be cut down, and the lofty will be brought low,
> [34] he will hack down the thickets of the forest with an axe, and Lebanon with its majestic trees will fall,

> [1] but from the stump of Jesse a shoot shall come out, and a branch shall grow out of his roots.
> [2] The spirit of Yahweh shall rest on him, the spirit of wisdom and understanding, the spirit of counsel and might, the spirit of knowledge and the fear of Yahweh.
> [3] His delight shall be in the fear of Yahweh. He shall not judge by what his eyes see, nor decide by what his ears hear;
> [4] but with righteousness he shall judge the poor, and decide with equity for the meek of the land;[402] he shall strike the oppressor[403] with the rod of his mouth, and with the breath of his lips he shall kill the wicked.
> [5] Righteousness shall be the belt around his waist, and faithfulness the belt around his loins.

Whereas 10:33-34 describes the destruction of Assyria, 11:1-5 pictures the reign of a Judaean king.[404] From a formal point of view, 10:33-34 and 11:1-5 are related by the consecutive perfect וְיָצָא in 11:1. Moreover, the passages are connected from a thematic point of view too: the power-vacuum resulting from Assyria's downfall is filled up

---

[402] For עֲנַוֵי־אָרֶץ as 'the meek of the land', cf. Amos 8:4; Job 24:4.

[403] The phrase 'he will hit the earth' is less likely ('earth' is not a parallel to 'the wicked', and the earth cannot be knocked down in the sense of being killed, cf. the parallelism). I adopt the emendation עָרִיץ 'the oppressor', which is paralleled with רָשָׁע elsewhere too (Job 15:20; 27:13; Isa 13:11). ארץ may be a corruption due to preceding עֲנַוֵי־אָרֶץ. See also Williamson 1998a: 48.

[404] Some scholars have argued that Isa 11 as a whole belongs to a seventh-century revision (Vermeylen 1977-78: 269-275; Sweeney 1996b; cf. Cole 1994, arguing that Isa 11 can be situated in the later part of Hezekiah's reign). In my view, only 11:1-5 can be plausibly situated in the seventh century. 11:6-9 is a *relecture* that no longer focuses on the king, but presents a vision of salvation in general terms; see Wagner 2006: 235-237. The issue of whether 11:11-16 goes back to an earlier passage is debated. Most scholars hold that 11:11-16 belongs to a late stage within the development of the book of Isaiah (Williamson 1994: 127). However, the triplet 'Egypt, Patros, Cush' (11:11) further only occurs in the inscriptions of Esarhaddon (see TUAT I, 398-399), which could be an indication of an earlier provenance of 11:11-16 (cf. Sweeney 1996b: 110). Nevertheless, this interpretation is uncertain, as the motif of 'gathering the dispersed' (11:12) has clear parallels in later (post 586) passages. I hold that only 11:1-5 can be plausibly situated in the seventh century.

by the righteous Judaean king. A similar double picture of Assyria's destruction and the reign of a new king of Judah occurs in 31:4-5.8-9 plus 32:1-2, and both themes are juxtaposed in 9:1-6 as well. The decline of the Assyrian empire and the revival of the Davidic dynasty are presented as two sides of a coin. The king portrayed in 11:1-5 has been identified as Josiah (see 2.4 below).[405]

The earliest words of Isa 10, 10:5-9.13-15, 10:24-25, and 10:27b-32, are likely to relate to Sargon's campaign of 720 BCE as will be elaborated on in chapter 4.1.4. These words criticise Assyria's imperialism in three ways. First, 10:5-9.13-15 condemns Assyria for its unbridled expansion: Yahweh ordered Assyria to take actions against a particular nation, Ephraim, but Assyria planned to conquer the whole world. Although Judah is not explicitly mentioned, it is likely that Judah's involvement in Assyria's conquest induced this criticism. Second, 10:24-25 specifies Assyria's aggression against Judah: Assyria struck Judah on the way to Egypt. The 'way to Egypt' refers to the coastal highway, along which the Assyrian army marched to Philistia.[406] Third, 10:27b-32 describes an Assyrian army coming from the north, which leaves the main road from Beth-El to Jerusalem in order to bypass fortified Mizpah.[407] This refers to a military expedition to Jerusalem, with the likely intention of intimidating the people of Jerusalem and forcing them to submit again to Assyria and pay tribute.[408]

2.3.3   Isaiah 9:1-6

9:1-6, as I will argue, is to be understood in the context of an anti-Assyria redaction of the Isaiah tradition in the seventh century.[409]

> [1] The people who walked in darkness have seen a great light;
> those who lived in a land of deep darkness, on them light has shined.

---

[405] So also Sweeney (1996b) and others.

[406] This was the quickest and most direct route to Philistia; Hayes and Kuan 1991: 178. This same road was taken by Sennacherib in 701 and probably by Tiglath-pileser in 734. Sweeney's objection (1994: 465) that this route would be too risky in a situation of Western revolt, is unconvincing since Sargon when he marched to Philistia had already defeated the coalition at Qarqar.

[407] Sweeney 1994: 464; Blenkinsopp 2000a: 261; Wildberger 1972-82: 431.

[408] Sweeney 1994: 464.

[409] 8:23aβb is not an original part of 9:1-6; see Vieweger 1992: 79; Wagner 2006: 81-83.

² You have multiplied the rejoicing,[410] you have increased the joy; they rejoice before you as with joy at the harvest, as people exult when dividing plunder.

³ For the yoke of their burden, and the bar across their shoulders, the rod of their oppressor, you have broken as on the day of Midian.

⁴ For every sandal he put on in roar[411] and the garments rolled in blood shall be burned as fuel for the fire.

⁵ For a child has been born for us, a son given to us; authority rests upon his shoulders; and he is named wonderful decider, mighty god, eternal father, prince of peace.

⁶ To increase the authority, to (secure) endless peace for the throne of David and his kingdom, to establish it and uphold it with justice and with righteousness from this time onward and forevermore: this the zeal of Yahweh of Hosts will accomplish.

9:1-6 is often interpreted as an accession oracle for the king. The royal appellations (9:5) are believed to reflect the throne names adopted by the Pharaoh at the Egyptian coronation ritual.[412] However, the parallel is less strong than sometimes suggested.[413] Egyptian coronation titulary consisted of a series of five names adopted at the ceremony of the throne accession. The names are of a standard character and each of them is preceded by a fixed title.[414] The names in Isa 9:5 are not five but four,[415] they do not follow the categories of Egyptian coronation names, and there are no exact parallels with the Egyptian names.[416] Furthermore, it may be questioned whether 9:1-6 refers to a royal coronation.[417] Some scholars have compared the names of 9:5 with Assyrian royal appellations.[418] Although the parallels are not close enough to exclude Egyptian influence,[419] it makes sense to see 9:1-6 as

---

[410] The well-known emendation הַגִּילָה is the best solution (read הִרְבִּיתָ הַגִּילָה); Wildberger 1972-82: 364; Williamson 1994: 249-250. הַשִּׂמְחָה (2a) is continued in שׂמח (2b), which suggests that יָגִילוּ in 2c is the continuation of הַגִּילָה (2a).

[411] The words סְאוֹן סֹאֵן do not occur further in the Hebrew Bible. Akk: šēnu, 'sandal, shoe'; šēnu, 'to put on (shoes)'.

[412] See Roberts 1997b: 115-118, discussing the studies by Von Rad 1958, and Alt 1950.

[413] For a recent discussion, see Wagner 2006: 218-222. Note however that the element of jubilation in 9:1-6 is not connected to the coronation of the king, but with Yahweh's annihilation of the enemies; contra Wagner 2006: 220, 222.

[414] See Von Beckerath 1999: 1-26.

[415] Against the suggestion that 9:5 consists of two long names each containing a theophoric element, see Wagner 2006: 217-218, note 40.

[416] Cf. the criticism by Wegner 1992: 104-107.

[417] See Wildberger 1972-82: 378-387; Barth 1977: 167-168; Clements 1980b: 41.

[418] Carlson 1974; Wagner 2006: 222-226.

[419] For the names of 9:5, see also chapter 6.1.6.

a reaction to Assyrian royal ideology (see further 6.1.6). The enemy described in 9:3-4 is Assyria.[420] The Assyrian oppression is symbolised by the metaphor of the yoke, from which Yahweh will liberate Judah (cf. 10:27; 14:25).[421] The yoke motif relates to the yoke metaphors in the Assyrian royal inscriptions as a kind of counter-propaganda.[422] Furthermore, the names of the ideal Judaean king in 9:5 to some extent parallel Assyrian royal appellations.[423]

9:3 parallels 10:26, as both share the motif of 'Midian's day'. In 9:3, the motif symbolises liberation, whereas in 10:26 it images the annihilation of the enemy.[424] As in 30:27-33 and 31:4-5.8-9, it is Yahweh who will destroy the Assyrians. The final phrase in verse 6b, 'the zeal of Yahweh of Hosts will accomplish this', indicates that 9:1-6 deals with the acknowledgement of Yahweh's actions on the political scene. 9:1-6 combines the themes of the destruction of Assyria and the reign of a new Judaean king. We have seen that the same combination is found in 10:33-34 continued by 11:1-5, and in 31:8-9 continued by 32:1-2. The passages do not present an eschatological picture, but a political reality that is idealised.[425] The king whose reign is glorified probably is Josiah.[426]

9:1-6 is traditionally connected with the *Denkschrift* (Isa 6-8), but the precise relationship with 6:1-8:18 is a debated matter.[427] In my opinion, 9:1-6 is closely connected with the early material of Isa 7 and 8 in two main respects. First, in 9:5 the form of the oracles 7:14b.16 and 8:3-4 is adopted. The ideal king is presented as a child that has been born and named with auspicious names, corresponding to the early prophetic announcements. 9:5-6 does not, in my view, specifically refer to a particular moment, either birth or enthronement.[428] Instead, it gives an idealising depiction of the reign of a Judaean king. Second, the Assyrians are not explicitly mentioned in 9:1-6. This resembles the character of the material in Isa 7, 8 (and 17). In the earliest prophetic material, Assyria is not yet presented as

---

[420] Wagner 2006: 225-226; cf. the use of the Akkadian word *šēnu* in verse 4.
[421] These verses share the words עֹל, סֵבֶל and שֶׁכֶם. 10:27 and 14:25 are especially close since the expression סוּר עֹל 'removal of the yoke', occurs only here in MT.
[422] Ruwe and Weise 2002: 299.
[423] Wagner 2006: 225-226.
[424] Ruwe and Weise 2002: 300.
[425] Cf. Wagner 2006: 246.
[426] See chapter 6.1.7; cf. Barth 1977: 141-177.
[427] See Barthel 1997: 37-65; Wagner 2006: 291-300.
[428] Wagner 2006: 230-231.

Judah's enemy. Instead, Assyria is mentioned as Yahweh's agent to destroy Judah's enemies Aram and Ephraim. The seventh-century comments on the eighth-century oracles, 8:9-10 and 17:12-14, refer to the frustration of the aggression of the enemy nations, which are unspecified. This means that it applies to Aram and Ephraim, but equally to Assyria. Similarly, 9:1-6 does not explicitly mention Assyria. 9:1-6 was probably composed as a conclusion to a revised edition of the early, prophetic material within Isa 7, 8 and 17. It formed the climax to a revised edition of earlier prophetic sayings.

2.3.4 Isaiah 14*

Isa 14 within the Complex of Isa 13-23

The complex of *maśśā'*-prophecies (Isa 13-23) is a literary construction, which is usually attributed to a redactional stage. This literary complex mainly consists of prophecies against foreign nations. Nine times a standard formula is used, with the term מַשָּׂא 'oracle',[429] followed by a designation of the nation involved.[430] The *maśśā'*-prophecies form a literary construction composed at some stage during the development of the Isaiah tradition. The theme of the collapse of Babylon (Isa 13 and 21) is important, suggesting that the *maśśā'*-complex dates from the sixth century or later. Not every part of Isa 13-23 intrinsically belongs to the complex of *maśśā'*-prophecies. Some passages are to be regarded as later extensions, such as 19:16-25.[431] Other passages however represent earlier material that was incorporated within the literary structure of the *maśśā'*-complex. This earlier material must be sought within Isa 14, 17, 18-20 and 22. The material incorporated within the *maśśā'*-complex was probably taken from various compilations of prophetic words: the material of Isa 14* (14:24-27.28-32) originally belonged to Isa 10*, the material of Isa 17* (17:1b-3.12-14) belonged to Isa 6-9*, and the material of Isa 18-20*, 22* (18:1-6, 19:1b-4, 20:1-5, 22:15-18) belonged to Isa 28-31*. The composers/editors of the *maśśā'*-complex took this material from other compilations and inserted it, because this material was useful as it critically addressed various foreign nations.

---

[429] This formula further occurs only in Nah 1:1, perhaps in imitation of Isa 13-23.

[430] Babylon 13:1; Moab 15:1; Damascus 17:1; Egypt 19:1; the Wilderness of the Sea 21:1; Dumah 21:11; the Desert Plain 21:13; the Valley of Vision 22:1; Tyre 23:1.

[431] See Blenkinsopp 2000a: 316-320.

14:24-27 and 14:28-32 are positioned as an appendix to Isa 13-14. Whereas 13:1-14:23 deals with Babylonia (13:1, 19; 14:4, 22), 14:24-27 announces the destruction of Assyria, and 14:28-32 contains an oracle against the Philistines. The heading 'oracle concerning Babylon' in 13:1 presents the text that follows as part of the complex of *maśśā'*-prophecies. 13:2-22 and 14:22-23, directed against the Babylonians, form an inclusion to 14:4b-21, which is directed against a foreign king.[432] Whereas 13:2-22 and 14:22-23 imply a setting in the late Babylonian or Persian period,[433] it is a debated issue whether or not 14:4b-21 contains an earlier poem that at a later stage was incorporated into the complex of 13:1-14:23.

Isa 14:4b-20
The poetic composition of 14:4b-20 has been qualified as a parody on the lament for the dead,[434] alluding to a variety of mythical motifs.[435] Its theme is the terrible fate of the tyrant. The first stanza tells that the tyrant is dead and that the earth rejoices (4b-8). The second (9-11) deals with the expected arrival of the tyrant in Sheol.[436] The Rephaim state that the tyrant shares their fate (he is dead). The third stanza expands on the motif of the king's ascension to heaven and his subsequent downfall (12-15). The fourth stanza forms the climax and specifies the terrible fate of the tyrant. The bystanders commenting on the tyrant's dead body (14:16-17) may be the kings of the nations (Rephaim) in Sheol, who pass their judgement on the tyrant.[437] The kings of the nations cast the tyrant from Sheol. He is not allowed to stay in their company for he has destroyed his land and killed his people (14:20). The poem concludes by stating that the 'offspring of evildoers', i.e. the offspring of the tyrant, will nevermore be named. The

---

[432]   13:2-22 and 14:22-23 are formulated as divine speech and refer to the Babylonians in the plural, whereas 14:4b-21 is a poem (not divine speech) addressing an individual king. After 14:1-2, an editorial bridge, 14:3-4a introduces the poem.

[433]   See Williamson 1994: 158-160.

[434]   Shipp 2002: 43. Wildberger 1972-82: 537. For the poetic structure of 14:4b-20, see Holladay 1999: 633-645, esp. 641. According to Wildberger (1972-82: 537) and Holladay (1999: 635-636) 14:21 is a later expansion.

[435]   Shipp 2002: 127; Schöpflin 2002b: 309. Shipp (2002: 67-127) demonstrates that there is not one particular myth behind this poem, but rather a range of mythical themes.

[436]   Schöpflin 2002b: 305.

[437]   Holladay 1999: 642-643.

downfall of the tyrant does not end with his death, but with his ejection from Sheol, and his name being erased forever.

The tyrant's fate is worse than that of the kings of the nations in Sheol. The Rephaim are buried in splendour but the tyrant is cast out,[438] and lies with those bodies without proper burial.[439] The climax of the poem is that the tyrant is not just dead, but that his remains become desecrated. This is of consequence for his position in Sheol: the tyrant does not become one of the Rephaim in the netherworld.[440]

The terrible fate of the tyrant has often been connected with the violent death of Sargon II on the battlefield in Anatolia in 705 BCE,[441] but the identification is unconvincing. It requires הָשְׁלַכְתָּ מִקִּבְרְךָ to mean 'you are cast out *far away from* your grave', which is unlikely.[442] Moreover, whereas Sargon's body was not buried because it was lost on the battlefield, the dead body of the tyrant is deliberately thrown away, cast out in dismay (תעב ni.).[443] The poem deals with a foreign king who behaved as if he was invincible and immortal. However, when sometime after his death his dynasty comes to an end, his body is disinterred from its royal tomb and the remains are desecrated.[444] Exhuming the buried remains of kings is frequently understood as an act of hostility.[445] A clear example of this is found in the inscriptions of Ashurbanipal, who narrates that he destroyed the graves of the kings

---

[438] Shipp 2002: 150.

[439] Shipp 2002: 157.

[440] According to Holladay (1999: 642-643), the phrase 'you are cast out from your grave' (14:19) on one level refers to the disinterment of the tyrant's corpse, but on a deeper level to the tyrant's ejection from Sheol.

[441] See particularly Ginsberg 1968. Many scholars have adopted this view, among them Shipp 2002: 158-163. However, this identification has not met with general approval. Wildberger (1972-82: 542-543), listing the various candidates that have been put forward, concludes that any identification is uncertain; similarly Schöpflin 2002b: 312.

[442] שלך means 'to throw (away)', 'to cast (out)', with מן 'to throw away from', 'to cast (out) from'. The ho. can mean 'to become cast out', said of corpses (cf. Isa 34:3; Jer 14:16), or 'to be thrown out' (and left), cf. Jer 36:30; Ezek 16:5. Olyan (2006: 425) pointed out that the idiom clearly means 'to be cast from locus A (to locus B)'; the body of the tyrant is cast from one locus to another (without specific mention of the second locus). For the expression 'far away' the verb רחק would be used.

[443] According to Schöpflin (2002b: 310) the phrase 'clothed with (the slain) those pierced by the sword, like a trampled corpse' (14:19) need not refer specifically to a battlefield, but more generally to killed bodies that are left unburied (cf. Isa 34:3; Jer 14:16; 22:19).

[444] This is also the view of Schöpflin 2002b: 310: the tyrant at first was properly buried but afterwards his grave was desecrated and his body thrown away.

[445] Olyan 2006: 425.

of Elam and transported their remains to Assyria in order to deny the dead kings repose in the afterlife.[446] Every king, no matter how powerful he was, ran the risk that after his death his remains would be disintered. This was considered a terrible fate.[447] A similar picture is found in Jer 8:1-2, which announces that 'the bones of the kings of Judah ... shall be brought out of their tombs ... they shall be like dung on the surface of the ground.'[448] The poem states that the tyrant is deliberately dishonoured after his death. His dead body is not left on the battlefield (like Sargon's) but his remains are cast out from his grave.

14:4a introduces the tyrant as 'the king of Babylon'. In the end, there is no reason for suggesting the poem was not composed from the outset as a taunting song concerning a Babylonian king. The poem offers ideological criticism or even wishful thinking rather than a description of actual events. As ideological criticism from a Judaean point of view, it is applicable to various Babylonian kings and certainly to Nebuchadnezzar.[449]

14:4-20 belongs to an ongoing tradition of critical address to foreign imperial powers, beginning in the Assyrian period (e.g. 10:5-9.13-15), and continuing into later periods (e.g. Isa 37:22-29). As a literary composition, the poem clearly differs from the early prophetic material within First Isaiah, which goes back to spoken words.

Isa 14:24-27

Isa 14 ends with two fragments, 14:24-27 and 14:28-32, loosely attached to the preceding unit on Babylonia. These two fragments deal with Assyria and are to be attributed to the Assyrian period. 14:24-27 focuses on the certainty of Yahweh's decision.[450] It proclaims that

---

[446] Olyan 2006: 425. For the passage, see BIWA: 55, A vi 70-76, F v 49-54 and 241: 'Die Grabstätten ihrer früheren und späteren Könige ... verwüstete und zerstörte ich ... Ihre Gebeine nahm ich mit nach Assyrien. Ihren Geistern legte ich Ruhelosigkeit auf. Totenopfer und Wasserspenden versagte ich ihnen.' (Borger's translation).

[447] Various inscriptions attest to the fear that the (royal) tomb may be desecrated and the remains removed (KAI 14, 5-6.7-12, 226, 6-10; see Olyan 2006: 425).

[448] Cf. also 2 Kgs 23:16. A rather similar fate is announced for king Jehoiakim in Jer 22:19: 'With the burial of a donkey he shall be buried; dragged off and thrown out (מִן שְׁלַךְ) beyond the gates of Jerusalem.' (cf. Jer 36:30b). Both Isa 14:20 and Jer 22:17-18 claim that the dead king's remains are desecrated because he tyrannised his own people.

[449] See Wildberger 1972-82: 542-543; Gosse 1988: 239; Holladay 1999: 638. 14:19 כְּנֵצֶר is sometimes taken as a pun on his name. However, also Nabonidus could be intended, since he is also elsewhere accused of bad treatment of his own subjects (cf. Isa 14:20).

[450] Barth 1977: 107.

Yahweh as king of the world rules from Zion and governs the international scene.[451] With regard to its theme and vocabulary, it is particularly close to Isa 10*.[452] At a later stage, it was included in the complex of *maśśā'*-prophecies, filling the need for a passage against Assyria.[453]

> [24] Yahweh of Hosts has sworn: As I have designed, so shall it be, and as I have planned, so shall it come to pass:
> [25] I will break the Assyrian in my land, I will trample on my mountains. His yoke shall be removed from them, his burden from his shoulders.
> [26] This is the plan that is planned concerning the whole earth; This is the hand that is stretched out over all the nations.
> [27] For Yahweh of Hosts has planned, and who will annul it? His hand is stretched out, and who will turn it back?

14:24-27 contains two parts, 14:24b-25 and 14:26-27. Whereas 14:24b-25 makes clear what Yahweh's plan is about—the destruction of Assyria—14:26-27 puts this in a perspective of Yahweh's plans concerning the entire world. The two parts are closely related through the term יעץ/עֵצָה in 14:24b and 26-27.[454] The transition from Assyria (14:24-25) to the whole earth and all the nations (14:26-27) makes sense from a traditio-historical point of view.[455] The theme of Assyria's downfall, which characterises the seventh-century revision of the Isaiah tradition (14:24-27, 30:27-33, 31:4-5.8-9), was based on the Jerusalem tradition of Yahweh's war against the nations that threaten Zion (the *Völkerkampf*-motif). Given this traditio-historical background, the motif of Assyria's destruction (14:24-25) and that of Yahweh's dealings with 'all the nations' (14:26-27, similarly 8:9-10 and 17:12-14) essentially belong together.

---

[451] Barth (1977: 109-117) suggests a connection between 14:26-27, Yahweh's outstretched hand, and the poetic refrain in 9:11, 16, 20 (and in 5:25 and 10:4) 'his hand is stretched out still', but the expressions are not on the same level. 14:26, הַיָּד הַנְּטוּיָה עַל, referring to the nations, differs from the refrain in Isa 9, where it is used in an absolute sense. In 14:24-27, Yahweh's outstretched hand symbolises the worldwide extension of his power: he rules the world. In the refrain of Isa 9, the motif of Yahweh's still outstretched hand refers to the continuation of the punishment of Israel and Judah. In my view, the motif of Yahweh's outstreched hand, symbolising his worldwide authority, was at a later stage applied to Israel and Judah, as to become a symbol of Yahweh's punishment of his people.

[452] 14:24-27 is often associated with Isa 10*, see Wildberger 1972-82: 568, 572.

[453] Wildberger 1972-82: 566.

[454] Barth 1977: 105.

[455] Contra Clements (1989: 256-257), who attributes 14:24-25 and 14:26-27 to two different redactional levels, qualifying 14:26-27 as part of a post-exilic apocalyptic redaction.

Within 14:24-27, verse 25b seems a bit odd, since the context provides no referent for the suffixes in מֵעֲלֵיהֶם ('from them') and שִׁכְמוֹ
('from his shoulder'), which *ad sensum* refer to the people of Judah.
The clause may be dependent on 9:3 or 10:27a, where the same motif
occurs (cf. שִׁכְמוֹ in 10:27). The intent of the addition then was to expli-
cate the positive outcome for Judah.[456]

Isa 14:28-32
The introductory formula הַמַּשָּׂא הַזֶּה in 14:28 differs from the standard
formula used in the complex of *maśśā'*-prophecies of Isa 13-23. This
can be taken as an indication of a different origin.[457] 14:28-32 shows
some traces of elaboration: the dating formula in 14:28 was added at a
later stage and 14:32 forms an extension to the preceding oracle (both
elements are discussed below). Moreover, 14:30 interrupts the coherence of verses 29.31 in several respects. Whereas 14:29 and 31 address the Philistines, 14:30 has a quite different focus.[458] The earliest
saying consisted of 14:29.31, whereas 14:28 and 32 constitute a first
revision:

> [28] In the year that King Ahaz died this oracle came:
> [29] Do not rejoice, all you Philistines, that the rod that struck you is bro-
> ken, for from the root of the snake will come forth an adder,
> and its fruit will be a flying fiery serpent.
> [31] Wail, O gate; cry, O city; melt in fear, O Philistia, all of you!
> For smoke comes out of the north, and there is no straggler[459] in its
> ranks.
> [32] What will one answer the messengers of the nation?
> 'Yahweh has founded Zion, and the needy among his people will find
> refuge in her.'

---

[456] Cf. Wildberger 1972-82: 566; Barth 1977: 105. However, 14:24-27 is a fragment which originally may have belonged to a context that did provide a reference for
the suffixes.

[457] The origin of this passage has been debated. Whereas some, following Duhm
(1922: 101), suggest a Hellenistic dating of this passage, others have kept to the
eighth-century dating suggested by 14:28.

[458] 14:30 contrasts the fate of the 'poor' and 'needy' (Judaeans?) with the ill fate
of an unspecified addressee (the Philistines?). The suffix of בְּמוֹעֲדָיו 'in his ranks' in
14:31 refers to the subject of 14:29bα, which suggests that originally, 14:31 directly
followed 14:29. Besides, 14:30 contains various late motifs; see Berges 1998: 146;
Becker 1997: 272.

[459] MT בּוֹדֵד, 1QIsaᵃ מודד; conj. נוֹדֵד 'deserter' (cf. Isa 22:3; 21:15) is a possibility;
see Wildberger 1972-82: 574.

The oracle of 14:29.31 fits well into the later part of the eighth century. The warning 'do not rejoice' (אַל שִׂמְחִי) occurs elsewhere in the context of the ill fate of enemies.[460] Philistia's enemy has fallen, but the Philistines should not rejoice, because a new and even harsher king shall rule. The exhortation to mourn directed at the gate and the city (14:31) is characteristic of city laments;[461] gate and city are, as usual in city laments, personified as a weeping lady.[462] Originally, the oracular saying did not refer to the death of Ahaz and his succession by Hezekiah, but to the death of an Assyrian king and the reign of his successor. The qualification of the king as a rod that strikes also refers to the Assyrian king in 10:5 and 24. Furthermore, the words, 'for smoke comes out of the north, and there is no straggler in its ranks', refers to the Assyrian army, not to the Judaean army. The original background of the saying is the death of an Assyrian king that could have provoked rejoicing among the Philistines. This is likely to refer to the death of Tiglath-pileser III (727 BCE), who had campaigned against Philistia in 734.[463] Against the hopeful expectation, attributed to the Philistines, that Assyria's expansion would have come to an end with Tiglath-pileser's death, the oracle announces that the Philistines will be oppressed even harder by Tiglath-pileser's successor.[464] This announcement came true, at first, in 720 with Sargon's campaign to the West.

The oracle 14:29.31 can be related to 28:1-4 and 10:5-9.13-15, 10:24-25 and 10:27b-32. 14:29.31 and 28:1-4 seem to contain announcements to be dated some time before Sargon's campaign of 720 and the final downfall of Samaria. The early material within Isa 10* looks back at the events and condemns Assyria for having exceeded the order given by Yahweh. Whereas in 28:1-4 and 14:29-31 the perspective is on Assyria's dealing with other nations, Ephraim and the Philistines, in the prophecies of Isa 10* Judah's involvement in Assyria's imperialism is taken into account.

14:28, the introduction to 14:29.31 indicates a revision of the oracle. The phrase 'In the year King Ahaz died this oracle came', sug-

---

[460] Ps 35:19, 24; Prov 24:17; Hos 9:1; Ob 1:12; Mic 7:8.
[461] Dobbs-Allsopp 1993: 133.
[462] This may explain for שַׁעַר (masculine) addressed with a feminine imperative.
[463] Wildberger 1972-82: 578-579.
[464] If 14:29bα and 29bβ are parallel, the 'adder' and 'flying fiery serpent' both refer to the successor of Tiglath-pileser (Wildberger 1972-82: 581). Alternatively, the snake, adder and flying fiery serpent may refer to a sequence of three Assyrian kings.

gests that the oracle deals with the death of Ahaz, and points to Ahaz's successor Hezekiah. This is a Judaeo-centred interpretation of the oracle, which originally referred to the death of Tiglath-pileser. It represents a revision of the original saying, which presumably imitated the introductory dating of Isa 6:1. 14:32 probably is on the same level as 14:28, adding a new dimension to the earlier oracle. 14:32b evidently reflects the Zion ideology and fits a seventh-century revision (see chapter 6.1.6). 14:28-32 forms a revision of an earlier oracle (14:29.31). Whereas the oracle announces the harsh rule of Tiglath-pileser successor, in its Judaeo-centred revision it implies Judah's dominance over Philistia. The revision makes sense, since in 705-701, Ahaz's son Hezekiah did act to some extent as overlord of Philistia (see chapter 4.1.7), as is implied by 14:28. Furthermore, the image of Zion as a place of special protection resembles the ideology of the Hezekiah stories concerning 701 (see chapter 6.1.2).

14:24-27 and 14:28-32 are likely to belong to the seventh-century revision of the Isaiah tradition, and can be connected with Isa 10:5-11:5.

2.3.5   *Isaiah 17**

Isa 17:1-3

The heading מַשָּׂא דַּמֶּשֶׂק (17:1a) suggests that what follows is part of the complex of *maśśā'*-prophecies. However, since 17:1b-3 deals with Aram and Ephraim, this may go back to an earlier prophetic word. This is confirmed by the identification of the oracle in 17:3 as נְאֻם. 17:1-3 (as 19:1-4, below) is likely to contain an earlier *nĕ'um*-oracle, which has been incorporated into the *maśśā'*-complex through the addition of the introductory formula מַשָּׂא דַּמֶּשֶׂק. The oracle begins with הִנֵּה (17:1b, cf. 19:1b), which is paralleled in *nĕ'um*-oracles, not in *maśśā'*-prophecies.[465] Thus, it is likely that 17:1b-3 (as 19:1b-4) predated the complex of *maśśā'*-prophecies.

The text of 17:1b-3 MT is particularly obscure. In particular the expression 'the cities of Aroer are deserted' (MT 17:2a) is dubious as Aroer is a city name itself and no city Aroer is known close to Damascus.[466] 17:2, although obscure, deals with the Aramaean cities: they

---

[465] E.g. Jer 1:15, 1:18-19, 5:15, 8:17, 9:24.

[466] I follow the emendation עֲזֻבוֹת עָרֶיהָ עֲדֵי עַד 'her cities are forever deserted'; Wildberger 1972-82: 635.

will be deserted and become places for flocks. The final clause is probably a later addition, as it turns away from the cities, and qualifies the flocks, 'they will lie down undisturbed.' The first line of 17:3 clearly announces the end of the kingdoms of Ephraim and Aram. The second part 'the rest of Aram will be like the glory of the Israelites' is obscure. It is not a parallelism (as is the first line of 17:3) and may be a later addition.[467] 17:1b-3a announces disaster for Aram and Ephraim:

> [1b] See, Damascus is about to cease to be a city, and to become a heap of ruins.[468]
> [2*] Her cities will be deserted for ever, and become places for flocks.
> [3*] The fortress will disappear from Ephraim, the kingdom from Damascus, says Yahweh of Hosts.

The announcement resembles the oracles of 7:4-9a, 14b.16 and 8:1-4. Therefore, 17:1b-3a is best situated in the later part of the eighth century as well, probably during the Syro-Ephraimitic crisis.[469]

Isa 17:12-14

17:12-14 can be regarded as an early commentary to 17:1-3, comparable to the way in which 8:9-10 comments on the prophetic oracles of 7:4-9a and 14b.16.[470]

> [12] Woe, thunder of many peoples, they thunder like the thundering of the sea, and roar of nations, they roar like the roaring of mighty waters!
> [13] The nations roar like the roaring of many waters.[471]
> But he will rebuke them, and they will flee far away, chased like chaff on the mountains before the wind and whirling dust before the storm.
> [14] At evening time, lo, terror! Before morning, it is gone.
> This is the fate of those who despoil us, and the lot of those who plunder us.

17:12-14 resembles 8:9-10 in various respects. Both comment on prophetic oracles against Aram and Ephraim. Furthermore, in both cases the motif of the *Völkerkampf* is used to comment on the destruction of the enemies. This motif depicts the enemies as posing a threat against

---

[467] Becker 1997: 274.

[468] MT מְעִי (*hapax legomenon*) is slightly dubious. Since עִי means 'ruin' (Ps 79:1; Jer 26:18; Mic 1:6), the reading לְעִי 'into a ruin' may be preferable.

[469] Wildberger 1972-82: 645.

[470] The rest of Isa 17 consists of later extensions marked by redactional formula and later motifs. Becker (1997: 274-275) argues that 17:4-6 is late ('Jacob', 17:4, refers to Israel as a whole, 'das gesamte Gottesvolk'). Cf. the redactional formula in 17:4, 5, 7, and 9.

[471] This phrase is often regarded as a later addition; Wildberger 1972-82: 664.

Jerusalem and Judah, but, as is implied by the tradition of the *Völker-kampf*, their actions are frustrated by Yahweh, who destroys them. 8:9-10 and 17:12-14 are particularly close to passages from First Isaiah that deal with the destruction of Assyria.

2.3.6   *Isaiah 18-22**

The earliest layer of Isa 18-22 consists of material that reflects Isaiah's opposition to the alliance with Egypt against Assyria. This material in many respects resembles the early material within Isa 28-32, consisting of polemic sayings that reflect Isaiah's position.[472] The early material was of interest to the editors/composers of the *maśśā'*-complex, since it related to Cush (18*, 20*) and Egypt (19*, 20*). The early material included an oracle against a Judaean official (22:15-18) in which the same mentality was condemned that in 22:1-14, part of the *maśśā'*-composition, functions as an explanation for the fall of Jerusalem.

Isa 18:1-6

The passage 18:1-6,[473] is likely to consist of eighth-century prophetic material in a revised form:

> ¹ Woe, land of whirring wings,[474] in the region of the rivers of Cush,[475]
> ² which sends envoys by the Nile[476] in vessels of papyrus on the waters! Go, you swift messengers, to a nation tall and smooth, to a people feared near and far, a nation mighty and conquering, whose land the rivers divide.
> ³ All you inhabitants of the world, you who live on the earth, when a signal is raised on the mountains, look! When a trumpet is blown, listen!
> ⁴ For thus Yahweh said to me: I will quietly look from my dwelling like clear heat in sunshine, like a cloud of dew on the day of harvest.[477]

---

[472]   Jenkins 1989: 248.

[473]   18:7 is a later extension, which gives a twist to 18:1-6, see Wildberger 1972-82: 681, and particularly Blenkinsopp 2000a: 311.

[474]   Or 'boats'; cf. Wildberger 1972-82: 679: 'geflügelte Boote'.

[475]   Wildberger 1972-82: 679: 'im Umkreis der Ströme von Kusch'.

[476]   יְאֹר here in all likelihood refers to the Nile (cf. Isa 19:5; Nah 3:8).

[477]   MT קָצִיר חֹם may be a corruption of חֹם יוֹם קָצִיר; חֹם, due to the preceding clause (various manuscripts and some of the versions attest the reading יוֹם, see Wildberger 1972-82: 681).

⁵ For before the harvest, when the blossom is over and the flower becomes a ripening grape, he will cut off the shoots with pruning hooks, and the spreading branches he will hew away.
⁶ They shall all be left to the birds of prey of the mountains and to the animals of the earth. And the birds of prey will summer on them, and all the animals of the earth will winter on them.

18:1-2aα can be identified as a prophetic *woe*-saying against Cush: 'Woe, land of whirring wings, in the region of the rivers of Cush, which sends envoys by the Nile in vessels of papyrus on the waters!' This probably is an eighth-century *woe*-saying, condemning Cush, i.e. the rulers of the Cushite (25th) dynasty over Egypt, for their political plotting. What follows is an extension to the saying, since no longer are the Cushites addressed. Whereas the *woe*-saying is directed at Cushite envoys (צִירִים) travelling in vessels of papyrus, the following passage addresses 'swift messengers' (מַלְאָכִים קַלִּים) that come to the Cushites for negotiation, since the description in 18:2 of 'a nation tall and smooth' in all likelihood characterises the Cushites.[478] Whereas the 'swift messengers' could be interpreted as being Judaeans, negotiating for military aid against Assyria, in the period 705-701 BCE, 18:3 explicitly broadens the perspective. The signal and trumpet blast in 18:3 are indications of military action, and the address to the whole world, suggests that the passage indicates a battle between mighty nations. 18:4-6 deals with the outcome of the battle. First it is stated that Yahweh, like clear heat or a cloud of dew, hangs above the international playground and watches. 18:5 explains that Yahweh not only watches the battle, but also intervenes: 'he will cut off the shoots, and hew away the spreading branches'. The result is that they, i.e. the fighting parties, together (יַחְדָּו) will be left to birds of prey and wild animals (18:6).

18:1-6 is marked by two perspectives. The first is characteristic of the eighth-century prophetic material, the second of the seventh-century revision of the earlier material. According to the eighth-century perspective the Cushites are condemned for their diplomatic plotting against Assyria. This relates to the controversy of 705-701, whether or not Judah should rebel against Assyria while trusting Egypt ruled by the Cushite dynasty. The eighth-century material has been revised into an international perspective, which addresses all the people of the world to attend to how Yahweh cuts down the military

---

[478] See Wildberger 1972-82: 689; Blenkinsopp 2000a: 309-310.

powers. The armies that are cut down are not explicitly identified, but
in my view not only the Egyptians and Cushites are implied, but also
the Assyrians. From a late seventh-century perspective, 18:1-6 makes
clear that Yahweh eliminates the military powers of the world, including Assyria. The image used in 18:5b parallels that of 10:33-34, where
it refers to the destruction of Assyria.

According to 18:5, the destruction of the aggressors will happen
soon, 'before harvest'. This motif of imminence occurs in the early
prophetic announcements (7:16, 8:4, 10:25 and 28:4), and is echoed in
the seventh-century revision (17:14, 18:5).

Isa 19:1-4
As in 17:1-3, the heading מַשָּׂא מִצְרַיִם in 19:1 was added secondarily in
order to incorporate the nĕ'um-oracle into the complex of maśśā'-
prophecies (cf. 17:1-3 above). 19:1b-4 contains a nĕ'um-oracle that in
all likelihood predated the maśśā'-complex.[479]

> [1b] See, Yahweh is riding on a swift cloud and comes to Egypt; the idols
> of Egypt will tremble at his presence, and the heart of the Egyptians
> will melt within them.
> [2] I will stir up Egyptians against Egyptians, and they will fight, one
> against the other, neighbour against neighbour, city against city, king-
> dom against kingdom;
> [3] the spirit of the Egyptians within them will be emptied out,
> and I will confound their plans; they will consult the idols
> and the spirits of the dead and the ghosts and the familiar spirits;
> [4] I will deliver the Egyptians into the hand of a hard master,[480]
> a fierce king will rule over them, says the Sovereign, Yahweh of Hosts.

19:1b-4 pictures a chaotic situation in Egypt. The passage focuses on
the Egyptians in general. The context is probably the same as for the
rest of the early material within Isa 18-22*, the situation of 705-701
BCE.[481] The oracle implies that the anti-Assyrian politics will lead to
disaster for the Egyptians. The 'hard master' and 'fierce king', in 19:4,

---

[479] The rest of Isa 19 probably is of a later date; 19:5-15 may have been composed
as part of the maśśā'-complex, and 19:16-25 consists of a series of very late additions.
[480] The plural אֲדֹנִים is taken ad sensum as having singular meaning (see JM §
148a).
[481] The fact that the Cushite kings are not mentioned in 19:1b-4 does not mean
that it must refer to the period before the Cushite rule over Egypt. Although the
Cushite kings in the eighth and seventh century ruled as the overlords of the Egypt,
the various Egyptian kings ruled their city-states as vassals of the Cushite overlords.

refers to the Assyrian king.[482] Whereas the original oracle may have referred to Sennacherib as the conqueror of Egypt, only his son and grandson achieved this (see chapter 4.2.4).

Isa 20*

20:1-6 looks like a story about Isaiah, comparable to Isa 7:1-17 and Isa 36-39. This is supported by the designation 'Isaiah the son of Amoz' (20:2), which, apart from the headings in 1:1, 2:1 and 13:1, only occurs in stories concerning Isaiah.[483] Furthermore, Isa 20 contains terminology that corresponds to prophetic stories from the books of Kings, such as the expression דִּבֶּר יהוה בְּיַד, 'Yahweh spoke through x', followed by a name and/or a title (20:2).[484] This phrase combined with the title עֶבֶד, 'servant' (20:3) occurs only in the books of Kings.[485] For this reason, Blenkinsopp and Williamson have argued that Isa 20, together with Isa 7:1-17 and Isa 36-39, are to be seen as 'Deuteronomistic narratives' about Isaiah's involvement in various major political affairs of his time, which were incorporated into the book of Isaiah.[486] Against this assessment however is the fact that each of the 'narratives' concerning Isaiah contains earlier material. In the case of Isa 36-39, the so-called B1-story (36:1-37:9a.37-38) predates the present narrative complex.[487] Isa 7:1-17, furthermore, is a composition that incorporates earlier prophetic material. Finally, as I will argue, Isa 20 includes an earlier report. 20:1-6 contains various indications of literary elaboration. I will discuss the three main elements of its literary reworking.

1) 20:1 begins with a dating, which resembles 6:1 and 14:28. The three datings have a similar beginning: בִּשְׁנַת followed by an infinitive construct as a dating: 6:1 'in the year that King Uzziah died' (בִּשְׁנַת מוֹת); 14:28 'In the year that King Ahaz died' (בִּשְׁנַת מוֹת); 20:1 'In the year that the *tartānu* came to Ashdod' (בִּשְׁנַת בֹּא). In 6:1 and 14:28 the temporal clause, is followed by a main clause, which introduces the subsequent unit: Isaiah's vision (6:1-8) and the prophecy against the Philistines (14:29.31). Both the *wāw*-consecutive וָאֶרְאֶה in 6:1 ('I saw

---

[482] Wildberger 1972-82: 708.
[483] 2 Kgs 19:2, 20; 20:1 (Isa 37:2, 21; 38:1), 2 Chron 26:22, 32:20, 32.
[484] Cf. 1 Kgs 8:53, 56; 12:15; 14:18; 15:29; 16:7, 12, 34; 17:16; 2 Kgs 9:36; 10:10; 14:25; 17:23; 21:10; 24:2.
[485] 1 Kgs 8:53, 56; 14:18; 15:29; 2 Kgs 9:36; 10:10; 14:25; 17:23; 21:10 and 24:2.
[486] Williamson 2004: 185; Blenkinsopp 2000a: 321-322; Blenkinsopp 2000b.
[487] Gonçalves 1986. I deal with 2 Kgs 18-19 (Isa 36-37) in chapter 6.1.2.

the Lord') and the perfect הָיָה in 14:28 ('this oracle came'), produce a main clause in the past tense. The case of 20:1-2 is somewhat complicated. The dating of 20:1a pinpoints Yahweh's order to Isaiah (20:2) in the year of the Assyrian campaign against Ashdod. In the present text however the temporal clause of 20:1a is followed by the main clause 'he (the *tartānu*) besieged Ashdod and captured it'.[488] This main clause is unexpected and has no apparent function within 20:1-6. In order to maintain the connection with the dating, 20:2 had to begin with a second temporal clause, 'at that time'. This complicated construction points to literary elaboration. 20:1-2 presents a dating formula in a reworked form. The original dating probably was: 'In the year that the *tartānu*, being sent by King Sargon of Assyria, came to Ashdod, Yahweh spoke to Isaiah' (דִּבֶּר יהוה). This dating closely resembles that of 6:1 and 14:28, with the only difference that an important moment in Isaiah's prophetic activity is dated to the year of an Assyrian campaign rather than to the year of the death of a Judaean king. The reason for this may simply be that no Judaean king died in this period. The dating of 20:1-2* originally introduced a report of a symbolic act, 20:1-5. The elaboration of 20:1b, 'he besieged Ashdod and conquered it', added a narrative element.[489] Subsequently, the temporal adverbial בָּעֵת הַהִיא had to be added in 20:2, because 1b disrupted the original connection between the dating and Yahweh's order.

2) A second mark of later reworking is found in the expression בְּיַד יְשַׁעְיָהוּ בֶן־אָמוֹץ in 20:2. Yahweh's speaking through (בְּיַד) a prophet, or prophets, is a stock phrase from the books of Kings. In this case however Yahweh does not speak *through* Isaiah, but *to* him.

3) A final indication of later reworking is found in 20:5 and 6, which present a double reaction. Both describe the reaction of those who trusted Egypt and Cush. 20:6 is likely to be a later addition. The 'inhabitants of this coastland' are in all likelihood the Philistines. In this way, 20:6 forms a deliberate inclusion with 20:1 in a reworked shape: the siege of Ashdod and the reaction of the Philistines. Furthermore, thanks to the reaction of the Philistines, 20:1-6 fits the complex of *maśśā'*-prophecies concerning the foreign nations.

---

[488] The combination of לחם (ni.) and לכד is a common way to describe a successful siege of a city ('to besiege and capture it').

[489] 20:1-2 is often translated as one sentence. However, 20:1b must be read as a main clause, since there is no finite form in 20:1a of which the consecutive forms of 20:1b could be the continuation (see JM § 118*l* and 166*l*). In 20:2 a new sentence begins.

As in the case of Isa 7:1-17, the later literary reworking added a narrative imprint to earlier material. The views of Williamson and Blenkinsopp of Isa 7, 20 and 36-39 as a series of stories on Isaiah is right to the extent that the literary reworking of Isa 7 and 20 seems to echo the narrative complex of 2 Kgs 18-20 (Isa 36-39). However, 7:1-17 and 20:1-6 in their core are not stories about Isaiah, but contain early material reflecting Isaiah's prophetic activity. The earliest version of Isa 20, probably was, more or less, the following:

> [1*] In the year that the *tartānu*, commissioned by King Sargon of Assyria, campaigned against Ashdod,
> [2*] Yahweh spoke to Isaiah: Go, and loose the sackcloth from your loins and take your sandals off your feet.
> [3*] And Yahweh said: Just as Isaiah has walked naked and barefoot for three years as a sign and a portent against Egypt and Cush,
> [4*] so shall the king of Assyria lead away the Egyptians as captives and the Cushites as exiles, both the young and the old, naked and barefoot.
> [5] And they shall be dismayed and confounded because of Cush their hope[490] and of Egypt their boast.

20:1-5* probably is an early report that reflects a symbolic act performed by the prophet. It is imaginable that a prophet really did this. More importantly, the symbolic act as described in 20:1-5* has some important similarities with 8:1-4 and 30:6-8: a public act performed by Isaiah bearing a political message. As in the case of 8:1-4, the most important part of the report is the divine announcement of destruction (8:4). Moreover, the message of 20:1-5* is wholly consistent with Isaiah's preaching as found within Isa 28-31. Especially in 30:1-5*.6-8 and 31:1.3a, the prophet makes clear that trusting on Egypt is pointless. 20:1-5* is a report of a symbolic act which belongs to the earliest stage of the Isaiah tradition. The prophet Isaiah may well have actually performed such an act around 712-711 BCE, in order to warn the Judaeans against trusting Egypt for assistance against Assyria.

As Isa 18* and 19:1b-4, 20:1-5* is particularly related to the early prophetic words within Isa 28-31. It focuses, however, on a slightly earlier period: whereas the critical prophetic sayings of Isa 28-31* (and Isa 18*, 19:1b-4, 22:15-18) directly relate to the controversy of 705-701, 20:1-5* refers to the rebellion of Ashdod (713-711 BCE). In this way, 20:1-5* prefigures the controversy of 705-701.

---

[490] MT מַבָּטָם; 1QIsaᵃ מבטחם is probably *lectio facilior*.

Isa 22:1-14

Although the core of 22:1-14 is traditionally attributed to Isaiah and
believed to be connected with the situation of 701 BCE,[491] I hold that
22:1-14 even in its earliest version reflects the events of 586 BCE.[492]
As has been pointed out by Dobbs-Allsopp, the view that 22:1b-2 and
22:12-14 describe Jerusalem's situation after the Assyrian retreat of
701,[493] has to be rejected. 22:1b-2 and 22:12-14 contain a motif of reversal, which is characteristic of city laments.[494] 22:1b does not suggest
that the city is currently jubilant, but poses the (rhetorical) question of
why the city that used to be joyful now has gone up to the housetops.
This is not an expression of joy,[495] but as in 22:12 an act of lament and
mourning in reaction to the utter destruction.[496] The motif of the glorious and jubilant city (22:2, 13) establishes a contrast of past joy versus
present grief because of destruction.[497] 22:1-2 contrasts the former
happiness of Jerusalem with its present grief. The flight of the leaders
(22:3) is paralleled in Lam 1:6 and 2:9.[498] The expression 'daughter of
my people' (בַּת עַמִּי) in 22:4 is further attested only in Jeremiah and
Lamentations.[499] The destruction (שֹׁד) of Jerusalem is closely paralleled
in Lam 2:11b, 3:48, and 4:10b (שֶׁבֶר). According to 22:5, Yahweh carries out destruction, with Elam and Kir as his instruments (22:6). This
explains the author's expression of amazement about the lament of the
people: the destruction is the will of Yahweh (22:2b). 22:8 states that
Yahweh withdrew his protection (מָסָךְ) from Judah, leaving her open to

---

[491]   22:8b-11 is often regarded a later elaboration implying the fall of Jerusalem in
586. For further reductions of the supposed Isaianic core, see Clements 1980a: 182;
Kaiser 1983: 113-114; Vermeylen 1977-78: 339.

[492]   See Barthel 1997: 268.

[493]   Clements 1980a: 183: in 22:1-3 and 22:12-14 Isaiah rebukes the people of Jerusalem who are rejoicing because of their escape from the Assyrians.

[494]   Dobbs-Allsopp 1993: 38-41, 168-169.

[495]   Contra Clements 1980a: 183.

[496]   See also Isa 15:3 and Jer 48:38. Cf. Sargon's inscription concerning his campaign against Urartu of the threat posed to the city Muṣaṣir (a city conquered by Sargon), Mayer 1983: 102-103, lines 343-344: 'Über diese Stadt ließ ich wie ᵈAddu das
fürchterliche Gebrüll meiner Truppen erschallen (...). Seine Leute, die alten Männer
und die alten Frauen stiegen auf die Dächer ihrer Häuser und weinten laut und bitter-
lich' (Mayer's translation).

[497]   Dobbs-Allsopp 1993: 38-40. See the list by Dobbs-Allsopp 1993: 180: Isa
13:19; 22:2; 23:7; Jer 48:2; 49:25; Lam 2:1b, 15c; Ezek 26:17; 27:3; Zeph 2:15; Nah
2:8a.

[498]   Cf. Dobbs-Allsopp 1993: 74.

[499]   Jer 4:11, referring to Jerusalem (cf. 4:14); 6:26; 8:11, 19, 21, 22, 23; 9:6; 14:17
and Lam 2:11; 3:48; 4:3-10.

enemy attack.[500] A parallel may be found in Lam 2:3, 'he has with-
drawn his right hand from them in the face of the enemy'.

22:1-14, as 29:1-4, emphasises that it is Yahweh who carries out
the destruction of his city Jerusalem. 22:14 presumably refers to 6:9-
11. The phrase 'Yahweh of Hosts has revealed himself in my ears'
(וְנִגְלָה בְאָזְנָי) refers to the vision of Isaiah, from the perspective of the
reworking of 6:9-11. The phrase 'this iniquity will not be forgiven you
until you die' (עַד־תְּמֻתוּן), resembles 6:11, 'until (עַד) cities lie waste ...'.
Jerusalem is addressed as the once glorious city, whose inhabitants led
a careless life. They have come to an end by Yahweh's attack: the fall
of the city is explained as Yahweh's work. This in all likelihood refers
to the fall of Jerusalem in 586 BCE.

Isa 22:15-18

The unit of 22:15-25 contains many indications of intensive elaboration, even if the latest expansions to this passage, verses 24-25, are not
taken into account.[501] First, the oracle is doubly addressed: 'to this
official' and 'to Shebna, head of the palace', (22:15), and has a double
announcement: 'death in exile' (22:17-18) and 'discharge' (22:19).
Furthermore, Shebna's discharge as head of the palace and Eliakim's
succession (22:20-23) probably relates to 2 Kgs 18-19 (Isa 36-37).[502]
In order to explain the composite text of 22:15-23, I suggest the following developments.

1) Originally, an oracle was addressed to הַסֹּכֵן הַזֶּה 'this official', an
unnamed recipient. The man is reproached for his light-heartedness,
and the oracle announces his death in exile. The essence of the oracle
lies in the contrast between the threefold פֹּה 'here' of the accusation
and the twofold שָׁמָּה 'there' of the announcement. 2) A first development probably was the designation עַל שֶׁבְנָא, which aimed to present the
whole oracle as 'concerning Shebna'.[503] This probably is an early
identification, which may be adequate. 3) A subsequent development
consisted of a literary reworking of the oracle. The reason for this
probably was that the oracle had not come true and was reshaped in
order to show that it in fact had come true. Originally, the oracle announced that the addressee, a high official of Jerusalem, would die in

[500]   Dobbs-Allsopp 1993: 143.
[501]   Cf. Willis 1993: 394-399.
[502]   2 Kgs 18:37; 19:2; Isa 36:3, 22; 37:2.
[503]   Clements 1980a: 187-188.

exile in Assyria. However, Jerusalem was not captured in 701, nor was the official in question deported. This provoked a reworking, consisting of two steps. First, a new announcement was added in 22:19: Shebna would be discharged from his position.[504] Part of this reworking was the transposition of the designation עַל שֶׁבְנָא at the end of 22:15 and the addition of the function אֲשֶׁר עַל הַבָּיִת.[505] This resulted in the text of 22:15-19 as we have it, an oracle, which indirectly is 'proven' by the story of Hezekiah in 2 Kgs 18-19 (Isa 36-37). There, Eliakim is designated 'head of the palace' and Shebna takes the lower position of secretary. In other words, the Hezekiah story 'confirms' that Shebna was discharged from his function as head of the palace, as announced by the oracle in its reworked form (22:15-19). The second step was to strengthen the connection with the Hezekiah story by the addition of 22:20-23. These verses state that Eliakim takes over Shebna's position as head of the palace.

The identification of the addressee as Shebna probably occurred at an early stage, during the Assyrian period. The further reworking of the oracle probably dates to a later stage, since it reflects the importance of the Hezekiah narratives of 2 Kgs 18-19 (Isa 36-37) for the ongoing development of the Isaiah tradition. However, it cannot be excluded that this reworking had already taken place in the seventh century. The earliest oracle probably was the following:

> [15*] Thus says the Lord Yahweh of Hosts: Come, go to this official (and say):
> [16*] What do you think you are doing *here* (פֹּה),[506]
> and whom do you think you can rely on *here* (פֹּה),
> that you have cut out a tomb for yourself *here* (פֹּה)?[507]
> [17] Look, Yahweh is about to hurl you away violently, O mighty man! He will seize firm hold on you,
> [18] whirl you round and round, and throw you like a ball into a wide land.[508]

---

[504] The announcement of 22:19, 'I will thrust you from your office, and from your station I will cast you down', is formulated as a divine word in the first person, contrary to the earlier announcement in 22:17-18. See Willis 1993: 390-391.

[505] Wildberger 1972-82: 833. עַל שֶׁבְנָא has a strained relation with the preceding בֹּא אֶל הַסֹּכֵן הַזֶּה. Willis (1993: 378-381) presents examples showing that אֶל and עַל are used interchangeably, but the difficulty is not so much with the two prepositions as with the two different titles.

[506] Cf. Judg 18:3; 1 Kgs 19:9, 13 for the same question.

[507] 22:16b, 'hewing out on a high place his tomb, cutting in the rock a habitation for himself', looks like an explanation of 22:16a, and is likely to be a later addition.

There (שָׁמָּה) you shall die, and *there* (שָׁמָּה) your splendid chariots shall lie, oh you disgrace to your master's house!

The deeds described in 22:16-17 are presented not as a ground for punishment,[509] but as a demonstration of the addressee's fundamental misconception. He thinks he will die in peace in his own country, but the prophet opens his eyes: the politics he supports will lead to a violent reaction of Assyria and end with his deportation. He will die in exile. This appears from the exclamation הִנֵּה at the beginning of the announcement, which functions to draw attention to something not expected.[510] The addressee is rebuked for his light-heartedness: the man expected to be safe and to enjoy a peaceful lifetime and die at home, as appears from the fact that he made a tomb for himself near Jerusalem. The prophet however tells him differently: he will be taken away in captivity and die far from home. The key to understanding the oracle lies in the contrast between 'here' (פֹּה) in 22:16-17, and 'there' (שָׁמָּה) in 22:18. The foreign country, described in 22:18 as a widely extended land, is Assyria. The background is the Assyrian policy to deport the political elite of a rebellious nation in order to break local resistance.[511]

The oracle is closely related to the early words within Isa 28-31*, which also criticise the anti-Assyrian politics advocated by Judah's political leaders during the reign of Hezekiah (in particular 705-701 BCE). The oracle announces the disastrous outcome of this politics of rebellion: these politicians will not enjoy a peaceful lifetime and death, but will be brought to Assyria in captivity.[512] The identity of the recipient of this oracle (הַסֹּכֵן הַזֶּה) cannot be established with certainty. The expression מַרְכְּבוֹת כְּבוֹדֶךָ 'your splendid chariots' suggests that it

---

[508] Literally 'in a land wide to both hands (sides)'. Willis (1993: 386-389) offers an alternative reading of the end of verse 17-18: 'Yea, he will roll you up tightly, he will wrap you up like a turban, he will throw you like a ball into a wide land'.

[509] Contra Barton (1995: 47-48), who suggests that the 'patrician' Isaiah condemned the 'social climber' Shebna for acquiring a family grave in Jerusalem to which he had no right.

[510] See Wildberger 1972-82: 642, with regard to Isa 17:1b.

[511] See Wildberger 1972-82: 790-791; cf. 2 Kgs 17:6; Amos 7:17; Isa 28:14-18.

[512] A similar announcement is directed against the Judaean king Coniah in Jer 22:20-30 (esp. 22:26): 'I will hurl (טול hi.) you and the mother who bore you into another country, where you were not born, and there you shall die (וְשָׁם תָּמוּתוּ)'. This refers to Coniah's deportation to Babylonia. The situation resembles that of Isa 22:15-18: anti-Assyrian or anti-Babylonian rebellion leads to deportation of the ruling class (cf. also Amos 7:17).

refs to an important official. It is possible that the characterisation of
the oracle as עַל שֶׁבְנָא 'about Shebna', is adequate.

2.3.7 The Later Perspective: Isaiah 1:4-8

In the discussion of Isa 6-8 and Isa 28-32, I have argued that the earliest material was reworked into a literary complex best situated against
an exilic background. This same, exilic, perspective is also present in
the rest of First Isaiah. In order to accentuate the distinctive profile of
the later literary reworking, I discuss 1:4-8.

1:4-8 is usually regarded as Isaianic and believed to be connected
with the situation of 701 BCE.[513] Ben Zvi has however challenged this
view, by arguing for a later, exilic, dating of this passage.[514] First, Ben
Zvi suggests that the terminology used in 1:4-9, such as שׁחת (hi.) in 1:4
and בַּת צִיּוֹן in 1:8 indicates a post-Isaianic date (although he agrees that
this alone is not decisive).[515] To this can be added that the main concepts in 1:4-8 are Israel's sin (1:4) and utter destruction as their punishment (1:6). This closely resembles the literary reworking of Isa 6-8
and Isa 28-32.[516] The main terms used for Israel's sin[517] and for Yahweh's punishment[518] occur elsewhere particularly in contexts dealing
with the disasters brought about by the Babylonians.[519] Second, Ben
Zvi argues that the assumed correspondence between 1:4-8 and the
events of 701 is far from clear.[520] His arguments can be strengthened
by the following consideration. In particular 1:8 is believed to describe the situation of 701: 'Daughter Zion is left behind like a cottage
in a vineyard, like a garden hut in a cucumber field, like a besieged

---

[513] For the adherents of this position, see Ben Zvi 1991: 95-97.

[514] Ben Zvi 1991: 98-111.

[515] Ben Zvi 1991: 98-103, שׁחת hi. cf. Deut 4:16, 25; 31:29. Ben Zvi also points
out that 1:9a is particularly close to Ps 94:17, mostly dated to the post-exilic period.
However, 1:9 may be a later addition to 1:4-8.

[516] Isa 1:7 is closely connected with 6:11; Van Peursen 1996: 101.

[517] I.e. to forsake and despise Yahweh (עזב; נאץ; cf. 1:2, to rebel against Yahweh,
פשׁע), to desert (זור), apostasy (סרה).

[518] I.e. to strike (נכה), wounds (מַכָּה).

[519] In particular the books of Jeremiah and Ezekiel, and in the Pentateuchal traditions concerning the disobedient people and their punishment by Yahweh. Cf. the
motif of the strangers consuming the produce of the fields, occurring in Deut 28:49-51
and Jer 5:17. Van Peursen (1996: 101-103) points at connections between Isa 1:2-9
and Lev 26 and Deut 28-32.

[520] Ben Zvi 1991: 103-107.

city.'[521] It is held that this refers to Jerusalem, which was besieged but not taken in 701, whereas most of Judah was overrun by the Assyrians. However, Dobbs-Allsopp has argued that the point of the simile is not that Jerusalem has been spared, but that the ravaging of the enemy left the city in ruins.[522] Parallel expressions from city laments make clear that the image of Jerusalem as a 'cottage' and a 'garden hut' does not indicate its survival but its downfall.[523] In the lamentation for Ur, for instance, the destruction of the sanctuary is described as follows: 'My house established by a faithful man, like a garden hut indeed was thrust on its side. My faithful house (…) like a tent, like a pulled-up harvest shed, like a pulled-up harvest shed indeed was exposed to wind and rain.'[524] The 'garden hut' and 'harvest shed' are temporary structures used during harvest time. The destroyed sanctuary is thus compared to 'dilapidated structures', abandoned after the harvest.[525] Jerusalem, once a proud and strong city, has become something 'akin to a frail garden hut, deteriorating after the harvest'.[526] After the siege, to be understood as Yahweh's punishment, the city is ruined and abandoned like a garden hut after harvest.[527]

This interpretation of 1:8 is supported by the use of the term 'daughter Zion', particularly at home in the book of Lamentations.[528] A final argument for connecting 1:4-8 with the destructive events of the early sixth century has been formulated by Berges. He points out that the motif of שַׁמָּה/שְׁמָמָה, 'waste', throughout the book of Isaiah refers to

---

[521] Hebrew נְצוּרָה stems either from נצר, 'to guard' (qal ptc. passive, 'guarded') or is by-form of נְצוּרָה, from צור, 'to besiege' (ni. ptc., 'besieged'). Since the preceding similes emphasise the city's desolation, the first option seems unlikely. Besides, עִיר regularly occurs in combination with צור (Deut 20:19, Judg 9:31, 2 Sam 20:15, 2 Kgs 24:11, Jer 21:4, 9, Ezek 4:3), but never with נצר 'to guard, to protect'. The likeliest reading is 'like a besieged city' (with most of the versions). For a different interpretation, see Williamson 2006: 51-52.

[522] Dobbs-Allsopp 1993: 146.

[523] Dobbs-Allsopp 1993: 146. For parallels, see Dobbs-Allsopp 1993: 69-70.

[524] Dobbs-Allsopp 1993: 69, referring to Kramer 1940, lines 122-123 and 125-129. Similar phrases are found in other Mesopotamian lamentations: 'Enlil, you have turned the faithful house into a reed hut'; Dobbs-Allsopp 1993: 69-70, referring to the text CT 42 26:13; cf. 6:20 (for the texts, Cohen 1988).

[525] Dobbs-Allsopp 1993: 70. On Lam 2:6a, perhaps containing a similar expression, cf. Dobbs-Allsopp 1993: 69-70. Cf. also Job 27:18.

[526] Dobbs-Allsopp 1993: 146.

[527] See Oesch (1994: 443) for a similar interpretation of 1:4-8.

[528] The term בַּת צִיּוֹן as part of a simile further occurs in Jer 4:31 and Lam 2:13, both relating to Jerusalem's destruction. Furthermore, devastation of the fields around the main city is regularly part of the description in city laments (e.g. Lam 2:2); see Dobbs-Allsopp 1993: 66.

the destruction brought about by the Babylonians.[529] To conclude, 1:4-8 reflects the disastrous events of the early sixth century.

The exilic reworking of the Isaiah tradition has been decisive for the character of First Isaiah and for the image of the prophet. The image of Isaiah as a prophet who preached disaster to a wicked and disobedient people resulted from theological reflection developed after the events of 586 BCE. The exilic reworking is characterised by the view that the disasters that befell Judah are to be seen as Yahweh's just punishment of the people's disobedience.[530] An important motif of this reworking is the designation הָעָם הַזֶּה 'this people', discussed in 2.1.1 above.

The exilic reworking must not be labelled Deuteronomistic. It has been rightly argued that First Isaiah hardly contains any passages that are in a strict sense Deuteronomistic.[531] However, Deuteronomistic theology was not the only form in which (post)exilic reflection on the disasters of the early sixth century was expressed. The Isaiah tradition, in my opinion, underwent a literary reworking (which was not Deuteronomistic) that reflected on the disasters of the early sixth century and is to be situated in the exilic period.

2.4   The Format of the Isaiah Tradition in the Assyrian Period

2.4.1   Material from the Eighth and Seventh Century

In this chapter I have presented an analysis of the texts from First Isaiah that can be situated in the Assyrian period.The earliest layer of the Isaiah tradition consists of prophetic sayings and oracles related to

---

[529]   Berges 1998: 62-63. According to Berges (1998: 63), 1:7 is connected with 6:9-11: the hardening of the people, announced in 6:9-10, will come to an end only after the destruction of land and people has been completed (6:11, 1:7).

[530]   Becker (1997: 283), distinguishes between an *unheilstheologische Redaktion* (6:9.11;   8:5-8a;   28:7a.11-18*) and an *Ungehorsams-Redaktion* (1:2-20*; 28:12.16aβb; 29:9f.13-16; 30:1-2.4-5a.8-13.15f.17aβb; 31:2). In his view, these redactions turned Isaiah into a prophet of judgement and produced a literary corpus, which eventually developed into a prophetic book. Whereas Becker (1997: 240) acknowledges the close affinity between both redactions, I would go a step further, and propose that the literary reworking of the earlier material, present within Isa 6-8, 28-32 and in passages from the rest of First Isaiah, is part of one redactional stage (though presumably carried out by different hands). The extensive reworking of the Isaiah tradition originated from one and the same milieu.

[531]   Perlitt 1989.

specific moments in Judah's political history of the later part of the eighth century. The early material can be related to three episodes:

1) The Syro-Ephraimitic crisis of 734-732 BCE, to which are related the oracles against Ephraim and Aram, included within Isa 7-8 (7:2-3.4-9a; 7:14b.16; 7:20; 8:1-4) and in 17:1b-3.

2) Sargon's campaign of 720 BCE, to which are related the oracles announcing threat against Philistia and Samaria (14:29.31 and 28:1-4), and the oracles condemning Assyria's imperialism within Isa 10 (10:5-9.13-15; 10:24-25; 10:27b-32).

3) The controversy about whether or not to rebel against Assyria trusting Egypt's military aid. This played a role in c. 713-711 BCE (Isa 20*) and reached a climax in 705-701 BCE. Related to this are the words against the Judaean leaders within Isa 28-31 (28:7b-10; 28:12; 28:14-18*; 29:15; 30:1-5*; 30:6b-8; 30:15; 31:1.3a), and furthermore the *woe*-sayings of 5:8-23* with 10:1-2, and the critical oracles of 18:1-6*, 19:1b-4 and 22:15-18.

It is likely, in my view, that the sayings and oracles were initially preserved in the form of small collections. The interrelation between the prophetic material and the various historical episodes will be worked out in chapter 4. The material attributed to the later part of the eighth century offers a clear picture of prophetic activity. The prophet spoke words of encouragement in situations of political-military crisis, he announced the destruction of the enemies, and he adopted a clear political position and played a public role. His consistent message was: do not resist or rebel against Assyria and do not trust Egyptian and Cushite power, but leave things to Yahweh. The prophetic function of Isaiah will be worked out in chapter 5.

A second identifiable layer of the Isaiah tradition consists of passages dealing with the destruction of Assyria and the restoration of Judah. They contain colourful descriptions of Assyria's destruction, a revision of Isa 10 (10:11.16-19, 10:26a.27a, 10:33-34), 14:24-27, 30:27-33, and 31:4-5.8-9. It is emphasised that Yahweh causes Assyria's destruction by means of cosmic powers, such as fire, flood and hailstorms. As Yahweh's actions against Assyria are set in an international perspective (14:26-27, 30:27-28), 8:9-10 and 17:12-14 are to be connected with these passages. Closely related to the motif of Assyria's destruction is the motif of Judah's restoration: the reign of a new Judaean king, who is both authoritative and righteous, in 9:1-6, 11:1-5 and 32:1-2. These two themes, Assyria's downfall and the reign of the ideal king, are like two sides of a coin, since both are the result of Yahweh's intervention. These passages in all likelihood date from the Assyrian period. Yet they clearly differ from the eighth-century prophetic material. The best position is, in my view, to regard them as the product of a revision of the Isaiah tradition in the late seventh century. This will be worked out in chapter 6.

2.4.2   *The Format of the Isaiah Tradition*

Based on the analysis of the passages from First Isaiah presented in this chapter, I suggest that the Isaiah tradition in its seventh-century revised shape took the form of three textual compilations. Each compilation contained a series of earlier prophetic oracles and sayings, which originally related to a specific historical situation: 734-732, 720 and 705-701 BCE. The early material was extended with seventh-century passages. A remarkable feature within the revision consisted of the descriptions of the reign of the ideal king: 9:1-6, 11:1-5 and 32:1-2. Notwithstanding the many later developments of the Isaiah tradition, it can still be discerned that these three passages form the end of a textual unit. 9:1-6 forms the conclusion to the unit 6:1-9:6*, which contains the prophetic words relating to 734-732. Furthermore, 11:1-5 closes the cycle of 10:5-11:5, containing the words relating to 720. Finally, the *hēn*-saying of 32:1-2 marks the end of a series of *woe*-sayings and critical sayings against the political leaders of Jerusalem relating to the situation of 705-701 in 28-31*. I suggest that these three passages, which in different terms describe the reign of an ideal king, each concluded a compilation of earlier prophetic words in a revised form. Each of them has a particular character. Significantly, the character of each portrayal of the ideal king corresponds to the nature of the compilation it concludes.

Whereas most of the material is still in place, part of it has been removed to Isa 13-23. This is a later composition of *maśśā'*-prophecies, in which earlier material was incorporated. The earlier material was taken from the existing compilations, and inserted because it contributed to the subject of the collection: the fate of foreign nations. The early material identified within Isa 13-23 can be related to the respective compilations: material from Isa 17* (17:1b-3, 12-14) belonged to compilation 1, Isa 14* (14:24-27, 28-32) to compilation 2, and Isa 18-20*, 22* (18:1-6, 19:1b-4, 20:1-5, 22:15-18) to compilation 3. To this, two minor displacements of material are to be added. 28:1-4, originally part of compilation 2, was at a later stage inserted into the complex of 28-32. It was positioned at the beginning of the unit, in order to create a parallel between the fate of Samaria (28:1-4) and that of Jerusalem (29:1-4; 28:7-22). Furthermore, the *woe*-sayings of 5:8-23* and 10:1-2, which may have formed an independent collection of prophetic sayings, are best associated with the material of compilation 3. At a later point it was integrated into the developing complex of Isa 2-12.

I suggest that the compilations adhered to a similar pattern, consisting of a dating formula and prophetic commission. This is followed by the prophetic words to which some comments are added. The compilations conclude with a portrayal of the reign of the ideal king:

	Compilation 1 Isa 6-9* (+ 17*)	Compilation 2 Isa 10-11* (+ 14*, 28:1-4)	Compilation 3 Isa 28-32* (+ 18-22*, 5:8-23*, 10:1-2)
Dating, prophetic commission	6:1-8	14:28-32	20:1-5*
Early prophetic words	7:2-9a, 7:14b.16, 7:20, 8:1-4, 17:1b-3	28:1-4, 10:5-15*, 10:24-25, 10:27b-32	28:7b-18*, 29:15, 30:1-8*, 30:15, 31:1.3a, 18:1-2, 19:1b-4, 22:15-18, 5:8-23*, 10:1-2
Comments	8:9-10, 17:12-14	14:24-27, 10:11, 10:16-19, 10:26-27, 10:33-34	18:1-6, 30:27-33, 31:4-5.8-9
Portrayal of ideal king	9:1-6	11:1-5	32:1-2

Compilation 1. Isa 6:1-9:6 (and 17:1b-3.12-14)
The compilation began with 6:1-8, a vision report concerning the commission of the prophet Isaiah, and concluded with 9:1-6, a depiction of the ideal king. Included are various prophetic oracles that originally dealt with the crisis of 734-732 BCE, i.e. 7:2-3a.4-9a, 7:14b.16, 7:20, 8:1-4, and 17:1b-3a and two short commentaries to the prophetic material, 8:9-10 and 17:12-14.

9:1-6 forms the climax of the compilation. The presentation of the ideal king in 9:1-6 adopts the style of the earlier prophetic words included in the compilation. In 9:5 the king is presented as: 'For a child has been born to us, a son given to us.' This corresponds with the birth announcements in 7:14b.16 and 8:3-4, according to which the son to be born was a hopeful sign. 9:5 echoes the terminology of 7:14b and 8:3 (קְרָא שֵׁם בֵּן, יִלֵּד). Both in the prophetic oracles and in the description of the ideal king, the son's name plays a crucial role. In the prophetic oracles the name to be given expresses salvation for Judah ('Immanuel') and the destruction of the enemies ('Maher-shalal-hash-baz'), whereas in 9:5-6 the names typify the ideal character of the new king.

A remarkable element within this compilation is the use of the first person plural ('we', 'us'). This is found in 8:10, 'for God is with us' (כִּי עִמָּנוּ אֵל) and in 17:14, 'this is the fate of those who despoil us, and the lot of those who plunder us'. The 'us' are the people of Yahweh (the Judaeans), who, according to the prophetic announcement will be saved from their enemies by Yahweh (7:14b). This is explicitly confirmed by the comments of 8:9-10 and 17:12-14. In 8:9-10 and 17:12-14 the use of the 'us' language contributes to the effect of a hymnal style. In 9:5 the first person plural is used once more, 'a child has been born to *us*, a son given to *us*'. This use of the first person plural, in 8:10, 17:14 and 9:5 relates to the name 'Immanuel' in the prophetic material (7:14b). The revisers related this symbolic name from the eighth-century prophecy to the promise that Yahweh will destroy Judah's enemies (8:9-10, 17:12-14), and that he will establish in glory a new king on the throne of David (9:5-6). In this way, the late seventh-century events, as reflected in the revision, are presented as the outcome of the earlier prophecies.[532]

Isa 6:1 dates the commission of Isaiah several years before the Syro-Ephraimitic crisis: 'In the year that King Uzziah died' (c. 740 BCE). This creates a view of Isaiah who had been commissioned by Yahweh to prophesy some time before the crisis of 734-732. This presentation probably belongs to the construction of the prophetic image of Isaiah, part of the seventh-century revision. The vision report itself (6:1-8) is difficult to date. On the one hand, it reflects a retrospective interest in the words of Isaiah. Nevertheless, it could very well predate the seventh-century revision of the Isaiah tradition and be close in origin to the eighth-century prophetic material. In any case, the arrangement of a vision report beginning with a dating (6:1-8),

---

[532] A first person plural is also found in 6:8, where Yahweh says 'whom shall I commission, who shall go for us?'. Here, 'us' represents the divine council headed by Yahweh on whose behalf Isaiah speaks.

followed by oracles and sayings and hymnal commentary (Isa 7*, 8*, 17*) and concluding with a picture of reversal—the aggressor destroyed, a new Judaean king rules in glory (9:1-6)—is best situated in the seventh century as part of a revision of the earlier prophetic material.

Within this first compilation, 8:9-10, 17:12-14, and 9:3-4 take the position of the anti-Assyria passages in the two other compilations (see below). 8:9-10 and 17:12-14 comment on the prophetic material dealing with Aram and Ephraim. The prophetic material included in the first compilation focuses on the aggression posed to Judah by Aram and Ephraim. Assyria is mentioned as the agent of Yahweh, which destroys the aggressors. The seventh-century revision presents the destruction of Judah's enemies in rather general terms (8:9-10; 17:12-14). The unspecified reference to the 'nations' applies both to Aram and Ephraim, but secondarily, from the perspective of the seventh-century redaction, also to Assyria. The unspecified character is continued in 9:1-6. Here, Assyria is not mentioned explicitly either, but certainly implied.

One further detail may be mentioned here. 7:8b, 'Within sixty-five years Ephraim will be shattered, no longer a people,' is a secondary insertion within 7:4-9a.[533] It interrupts the coherence of 8a and 9a and does not make sense within the scope of the oracle.[534] The verb חתת 'to shatter' (or elsewhere 'to dismay')[535] frequently occurs in the seventh-century revisional material (8:9; 9:3; 30:31; 31:4, 9; cf. 20:5). 7:8b, furthermore, makes sense in the context of a seventh-century revision of the Isaiah tradition. It 'announces' that Ephraim will cease to be a nation, i.e. the political state would be destroyed by the Assyrians, the

---

[533] Roberts' attempt (2004) to recover the supposedly original text of verse 8b, 'within five years Ephraim will be shattered from being a people, and within six Damascus will be removed from being a city', is unconvincing. First, it is unlikely that so much went wrong within one verse (cf. Roberts 2004: 168, for the supposed errors). Moreover, to explain the change from 'six' (שֵׁשׁ) into 'sixty' (שִׁשִּׁים), Roberts' reconstruction needs a verbal form beginning with מ. The suggestion מוּסָר, taken from 17:1 (הִנֵּה דַמֶּשֶׂק מוּסָר מֵעִיר) however ignores that in 17:1 הִנֵּה is followed by a ptc. (מוּסָר), whereas in the reconstruction of 7:8 an imperfect is needed. Thus, MT cannot be explained as a corrupted text from Roberts' suggested original.

[534] Werlitz 1992: 199, 214, 250.

[535] For חתת cf. Renz 1995: 224, suggesting to separate between ḥtt 1 (< ḤTT) 'zerbröckeln, zerbrechen, zu ende gehen', and ḥtt 2 (< ḤTT), '1. die psychische Reaktion der Furcht, des Erschreckens (im Niph.), … 3. Metonymisch wird ḥtt die Ursache dieser Reaktion angesprochen, der 'Terror', der als Sachgrund hinter dem Erschrecken steht'.

people deported, and new inhabitants brought into the land. The eradication of Ephraim as a nation in this context was presumably to imply that Judah would inherit the leftovers. This would be a seventh-century understanding of the name Shear-jashub, 'a rest will come back' (7:3). This view on Ephraim probably corresponded with the political ambitions current during Josiah's reign. Although it remains a puzzle what events the revisers had in mind by the period of 65 years,[536] the phrase can be understood as a *vaticinium ex eventu* from a late seventh-century perspective, supporting Judah's claims on northern territory.

Compilation 2. Isa 10:5-11:5 (and 14:24-27.28-32, 28:1-4)
The second compilation deals with Assyria's imperialism and expansion. 11:1-5 forms the conclusion to this compilation. The way in which the ideal king operates in 11:1-5 forms a purposeful contrast with the brutal actions of Assyria described in Isa 10*. Contrary to the pride, self-satisfaction, and godlessness of the Assyrian king stands the wisdom and piety of the ideal king. The Assyrian king boasts, 'by the strength of my hand I have done it, and by my wisdom, for I have understanding' (10:13a). The ideal king, by contrast, is endowed with the spirit of Yahweh, a 'spirit of wisdom and understanding, a spirit of counsel and might, a spirit of knowledge and fear of Yahweh' (11:2). In contrast to the brutal power of Assyria, 'the stick' (שֵׁבֶט, 10:5, 15), the ideal king rules with authority, 'the stick of his mouth' (שֵׁבֶט פִּיו, 11:4), which is a purposefully chosen image. Assyria rules with a brutal hand (יָד, 10:5, 10, 13, 14, 32), the Judaean king rules with his mouth (11:4).[537]

14:24-27, which in its present context seems to be out of place after the unit on Babylonia (13:1-14:23), resembles the theme of the 'Assyria cycle' of Isa 10. It has therefore been suggested that this passage originally belonged to the material of Isa 10.[538] The theme of the early prophecies included in the second compilation, 14:29.31, 28:1-4, 10:5-9.13-15, 10:24-25, 10:27b-32, was that Assyria as Yahweh's instrument was ordered to take action against Philistia (14:29.31) and Ephraim (28:1-4, 10:5-6), but went astray by following its own agenda of

---

[536] Younger (2002a: 309-310) suggests that 7:8b, which seems to refer to c. 669-667 BCE (65 years after 734-732), is to be connected with a repopulation of Samaria by Esarhaddon and Ashurbanipal.
[537] So also Beuken 2003: 304.
[538] E.g. Blenkinsopp 2000a: 289.

worldwide destruction, which included Judah. To this the revision added that Assyria therefore was severely punished. I suggest that the early prophetic words included in this compilation originally referred to Sargon II, in particular to his campaign of 720 BCE.

14:28-32 is to be connected with the material of this second compilation too. I have argued that the heading in 14:28 is secondary to the oracle of 14:29.31. Whereas the original oracle refers to the death of an Assyrian king (Tiglath-pileser) and his successor, 14:28 changes this to the death of Ahaz, implying that Hezekiah acted as the overlord of Philistia. This pro-Judaean presentation typically belongs to the later, seventh-century revision. The heading of 14:28 closely resembles that of 6:1. I suggest this compilation began with 14:28-32, followed by the Assyria-cycle of Isa 10 (including 28:1-4 and 14:24-27) and concluded by the portrayal of the ideal king in 11:1-5. If the suggestion that 14:28-32 formed the beginning of this compilation is right, it makes an inclusion with 11:1-5. 14:28-32 presents Hezekiah as a strong Judaean king who dominated the Philistines, with terms resembling that of 11:1, where the ideal king (Josiah) is depicted (יצא, פרה/פרי, מן שֹׁרֶשׁ).

The revisers were not interested in an accurate historical portrayal of Assyria. Whereas the prophetic words originally referred to Sargon, in the revision they became the basis for a typological presentation of the Assyrian oppression in general. What counted for the revisers was their conviction that Isaiah had rightly foretold the collapse of Assyrian rule.[539]

Compilation 3. Isa 28-32* (and 5:8-23*, 10:1-2 and ch. 18-20.22*)
The prophetic material included in this compilation dealt with the issue of rebellion against Assyria. Isaiah emphasised that trusting in Egypt for military support against Assyria was senseless and that those leaders advocating rebellion violated Yahweh's will. Whereas the prophetic material of compilation 1 announced the destruction of Aram and Ephraim, and the material of compilation 2 critically dealt with Assyria's imperialism, the third compilation contains both polemic sayings against the Judaean leaders and material denouncing Egypt. The sayings directed against the prophet's opponents, the political (and religious) leaders of Jerusalem are found in 28:7b-10;

---

[539] Sweeney 1996b: 116.

28:15-18; 29:15; 30:1-5; 31:1.3a; 5:8-23*.10:1-2; 22:15-18. Further-more, words against Egypt and Cush on which the political leaders trusted are found in 18:1b-6, 19:1b-4, 30:6-8. Finally, as a positive counterweight against the doomed politics of rebellion of the ruling elite, the prophet points to Yahweh's standards, in 28:16, 28:12, 30:15. Whereas the prophetic material of compilations 1 and 2 focuses on external enemies that threaten Judah's peace (Aram and Ephraim, and Assyria), the material of compilation 3 deals with the advocates of rebellion as internal enemies of the state, threatening Judah's peace.

The seventh-century revision dealt with the destruction of Assyria: 30:27-33 and 31:4-5.8-9. It is asserted that it is Yahweh, no human hand, that saves Judah from the Assyrian oppression. The compilation concluded with 32:1-2, another portrayal of the ideal king. Again, the depiction of the ideal king is closely related to the material incorpo-rated in the compilation. Apart from the king, the leaders or officers (שָׂרִים) are also mentioned: 'See, a king will reign in righteousness, and officers will rule with justice'. This forms a purposeful contrast to the image of the wicked leaders in the polemic words of the prophet Isaiah. In 28:15, the leaders are accused of having made lies their ref-uge and falsehood their shelter, which is a denouncement of Egypt, in which the leaders of Judah have put their trust in the rebellion against Assyria. Further, 28:17-18 announces that the leaders together with their deceptive refuge Egypt will fall. By contrast, in the portrayal of the ideal situation in 32:1-2, both the king and the leaders are pre-sented as a reliable hiding-place and a covert. The rule of the king and the princes, marked by 'justice and righteousness', is presented as the fulfilment of Yahweh's announcement in 28:16-17. In contrast to the 'Assyrian rock' (i.e. the Assyrian king) that passes away in terror (31:9), the righteous Judaean king is like a protective rock (cf. the 'foundation stone', laid by Yahweh, 28:16). Finally, the form of 32:1-2, an exclamation beginning with הֵן, 'Behold!', relates to the form of the woe-sayings (הוֹי), which dominate the prophetic material of this compilation.

The third compilation may have begun with a dating analogous to that of compilations 1 and 2. Isa 20 originally began with a dating closely resembling that of 6:1 and 14:28: 'In the year that the tartānu, commissioned by King Sargon of Assyria, campaigned against Ash-dod, Yahweh spoke to Isaiah.' This refers to the period 712-711, when the city of Ashdod rebelled against Assyria. Isa 20:1-5 prefigures the issue of Judah's rebellion of 705-701, and already points to its disastrous outcome. Therefore, the rebellion of Ashdod and Isaiah's symbolic act formed a good point of departure for the theme of the third compilation.

Each of the three compilations presumably began with a historical reference, introducing the prophetic activity and commission of the prophet Isaiah (6:1, 14:28, 20:1-2*). Moreover, each of them concluded with a portrayal of the ideal king (9:1-6, 11:1-5 and 32:1-2). These portrayals of the ideal king, the climax to the compilations, probably are indicative of the purpose of the compilations. I will argue in chapter 6 that the ideal king in all likelihood refers to Josiah, during whose reign the revision of the earlier prophetic material was undertaken. The prophetic material, included in the three compilations, probably pre-existed in the form of small collections. The new material of the seventh-century revision was only loosely attached to the earlier material included.

2.4.3   *Conclusion*

During the late seventh century the figure of Isaiah was associated with the promise that Judah would be liberated from Assyrian domination, though not through rebellion. The situation during Josiah's reign in the second half of the seventh century was regarded as proving the prophet right. The oracles attributed to Isaiah, which had been preserved, were edited and republished in the light of the new situation. In its revised version the Isaiah tradition was marked by a perspective of state ideology: the destruction of Assyria and the political restoration of Judah under Josiah are presented as both resulting from Yahweh's intervention, which, as is suggested, was already announced by the prophet Isaiah. In this way, Isaiah's reputation served the glorification of the political situation under Josiah.

The disastrous events of the early sixth century—the fall of Jerusalem, the collapse of the state, the end of the dynasty, and the Babylonian exile—led to a profound reconsideration of the past. Rather than to leave the Isaiah tradition behind, it was thoroughly reworked in order to get it into lines with the new views on Israel's past and in order to use the authority of the figure of Isaiah for the new ideas. These views were, in short, that the destruction of Judah and Jerusalem was seen as the result of Yahweh's punishment because of the sinful disobedience of the people. Among the strategies deployed for connecting the new views with the earlier material, we see first the historical analogy that as Northern Israel was punished for its sins, so Judah had been punished as well. A second strategy was the generalisation of the specific criticism against Isaiah's opponents, the leading class of Jerusalem, so as to apply it to the people as a whole. It was this transformation of the Isaiah tradition, probably situated in the sixth century, that created the image of Isaiah as a prophet of judgement.

CHAPTER THREE

THE ASSYRIAN PROPHECIES

The Assyrian prophecies date from the first half of the seventh century BCE, from the reigns of the Assyrian kings Esarhaddon (681-669 BCE) and Ashurbanipal (669-631 BCE). Most of the Assyrian prophecies have been published in Parpola's edition.[1] A further range of prophecies and texts referring to prophetic figures has been published and discussed by Nissinen (1998). Besides, Nissinen has published a source book of ancient Near Eastern prophecy (2003a), in which all prophetic material from seventh-century Assyria is included both in transcription and translation.[2] In this study, I have adopted Parpola's numbering of the oracles (as does Nissinen 1998; 2003a).

3.1   *Sources of Assyrian Prophecies*

3.1.1   *The Corpus of SAA 9 (Nissinen 2003a: 101-132)*

In Parpola's edition (SAA 9: 4-43; followed by Nissinen 2003a: 101-132) the prophetic texts are divided into two types: (a) collections of prophetic oracles (SAA 9 1-4), and (b) reports of prophetic oracles (SAA 9 5-11). According to Parpola, the single oracles, written on small horizontal tablets (*u'iltu*), are first-hand reports of oracles (type b), whereas the oracle collections (type a), written on large vertical tablets (*ṭuppu*), are second-hand compilations based on the first-hand

---

[1]   Parpola 1997 (SAA 9). Reviewers praise Parpola's edition and translation of the prophetic oracles; Weippert 2002: 39; Cooper 2000: 441. Parpola's edition of the prophecies contains many textual restorations, most of which have been adopted in Nissinen 2003a: 101-132. Many of these restorations are convincing, but not all. Furthermore, Parpola has included an introduction to Assyrian prophecy in the broader context of Assyrian religion (1997: XIII-XLIV). Parpola's views as displayed in the introduction have met with criticism from various reviewers; see Cooper 2000; Frahm 2001; Porter 2000; and Weippert 2002: 4-13.

[2]   Nissinen 2003a: 97-188. For earlier literature on the Assyrian prophecies, see Parpola 1997: CIX-CXII, Weippert 2002: 39, and particularly, Nissinen 2003a: 101-177.

reports of oracles.[3] This procedure—the content of small tablets meant for instant use at some later stage copied on larger tablets meant for archiving—is on itself plausible. However, Parpola's application of the distinction between second-hand collections and first-hand reports is misleading. Four of the seven texts labelled as report by Parpola are written on horizontal tablets (SAA 9 5-8), three on vertical tablets (SAA 9 9-11). Of the latter, SAA 9 10 and 11 could very well be letters to the king in which a prophetic oracle is reported (first-hand texts).[4] SAA 9 9 however certainly is a library copy, which presents a prophetic oracle in a literary, elaborated form.[5] The four texts on horizontal tablets (SAA 9 5-8), on the other hand, are not all straightforward, oracular reports. SAA 9 7 and 8 contain oracles but both show traces of elaboration. SAA 9 7 could be an archival copy,[6] and may combine various oracles.[7] SAA 9 8 may similarly contain various divine words, and could be an archival copy too.[8] SAA 9 5 and 6 are probably first-hand texts, but SAA 9 5 is a derivative of prophecy rather than an oracular report. This leaves only the fragment SAA 9 6 as an example of Parpola's 'reports' (small horizontal tablets containing a first-hand report of a prophecy). I suggest a different qualification of the texts from SAA 9. Oracles delivered by prophets were reported to the king either in a letter (e.g. SAA 9 10, 11; further examples below), or in a report (e.g. SAA 9 6). Such reported oracles could be archived in different ways. They could be copied by a scribe either on a large tablet as part of a collection (SAA 9 1, 2, 4) or on a smaller tablet (SAA 9 7, 8). Or they could be elaborated into a literary text (SAA 9 9, and, to some extent, SAA 9 3).

---

[3]   Parpola 1997: LIII.

[4]   The form of these tablets (see Parpola 1997: LXI-LXII) suggests they are letters. Note that these texts were included in CT 53, Parpola's copies of Assyrian letters.

[5]   Parpola correctly states that SAA 9 9 resembles SAA 9 1-4 (1997: LIII), and is a library copy rather than a report (1997: LXI). It is difficult to understand why Parpola and Nissinen nevertheless present this text as a report.

[6]   Cf. Parpola 1997: LX.

[7]   Nissinen (2000a: 247-248) points out that SAA 9 7 and 9 are examples of secondary prophecy: they are written in polished style by experienced hands on tablets intended for archival storage.

[8]   Parpola (1997: LXI) suggests this tablet may have been written by Ashurbanipal's chief scribe Ištar-šumu-ereš.

SAA 9 1

This tablet contains a collection of prophetic oracles. Nine different prophetic oracles can be identified. Of eight of them, the colophon has been preserved, in which the prophet(ess) who delivered the oracle is mentioned. The unit numbered as 1.9 presents a description of activities of Ištar of Arbela. It is not formulated as a prophetic oracle (contra Parpola and Nissinen), but the unit refers to an oracle. Ištar of Arbela is said to have sent a *šulmu*, a message of well-being, to Esarhaddon. Because the end of this unit is broken, it is unclear whether it was followed by a colophon comparable to the oracles of this collection.

SAA 9 2

The tablet contains a collection of prophetic oracles. Five straightforward prophetic oracles can be identified. In addition, the unit 2.4 seems to be a compilation of several oracles. Most of the colophons have been preserved (2.1, 2.2, 2.3, 2.4).

> 2.4 is a compilation of various oracles, consisting of an introductory remark (ii 29'), an oracle presented as *abutu* of Ištar of Arbela and *abutu* of Mullissu (ii 30'-37'), an oracle presented as *abutu* of Ištar of Arbela (ii 38'-39') [break of about two lines at the end of column ii; break of about two lines at the beginning of column iii]; continuation of an oracle (iii 1'-17'); colophon (iii 18'); ruling.

SAA 9 3

This text is to be divided in two main parts. The first part consists of a tripartite composition in which the god Aššur figures (3.1, 3.2, 3.3). The second part consists of two 'divine words' (*abutu*) of Ištar of Arbela. Parpola's presentation of this text as another oracle collection, consisting of five individual oracles, delivered by the prophet La-dagil-ili (1997: LXIII-LXIV; adopted by Nissinen 2003a: 118) is to be rejected. The colophon following the fifth unit (3.5) mentions a prophet: [*La-dagil-i*]*li raggimu* [*Arbail*]*āya*. The restoration of the name La-dagil-ili is uncertain,[9] but the unit 3.5 clearly is a prophetic oracle. The unit 3.4 can perhaps be attributed to the same prophet, be-

---

9   Although the name is almost completely lost, Parpola's arguments for this identification (1997: CVI, note 266) are rather strong: oracle 3.5 contains elements that are paralleled in the oracles 1.10 and 2.3, attributed to La-dagil-ili: 1) the phrase *atta ana ayyāši* 'as for you', occurs both in 3.5 and in 2.3; 2) both 1.10, 2.3 and 3.5 contain cultic demands from the side of the goddess. These arguments, however, only apply to 3.5 and perhaps to 3.4. There is no evidence for attributing all the units of this tablet to La-dagil-ili (contra Parpola).

cause this unit too is presented as an *abutu*, a divine word of Ištar of Arbela. However, 3.4 is not formulated as a straightforward prophetic oracle, but is rather to be qualified as a derivative of prophecy.

The first part of the text, the tripartite composition of 3.1-3.3 forms a different case. This composition is separated from the 'words' of 3.4 and 3.5 by a double ruling, which indicates that it is a different text. Moreover, this composition has its own colophon (ii 27-32), in which no prophet is mentioned. None of the individual units, 3.1, 3.2 and 3.3, is a straightforward prophetic oracle. Whereas Parpola has labelled 3.1 as an 'introduction' (1997: 22), the two following units (3.2 and 3.3) are designated as *šulmu*, 'message of well-being'. They are formulated as divine words, but not as prophetic oracles. The composition of 3.1-3.3 has been labelled as a liturgy of a ritual.[10]

SAA 9 4

The text contains a fragment of an oracle for Esarhaddon, comparable to those in SAA 9 1 and 2. The tablet may be a fragment of another collection of prophetic oracles.

SAA 9 5

This tablet contains one textual unit, presented as a divine word (*abutu*) of Ištar of Ar[bela]. Ištar speaks in the first person and refers to Esarhaddon in the third person. The text is to be qualified as a literary derivative of prophecy, comparable to unit 3.4. Parpola presents this text as an oracle addressed to the queen mother, Naqia, by restoring the first line as *abat Issār ša Arbail [ana ummi šarri]*[11] (SAA 9; adopted by Nissinen 2003a: 125). This restoration is based on the phrase *qablīki ruksī* 'gird your loins!' (line 4), addressed to a female subject. In my view, it is unlikely that Ištar of Arbela gives this command to Naqia.[12] Furthermore, the suggestion that Ištar's knees are bent for Esarhaddon (restoration in Nissinen 2003a: 125, line 2) is

---

[10]   See Van der Toorn 2000b: 73.
[11]   This goes back to the suggestion by Weippert 1981: 77.
[12]   In various prophetic oracles Naqia is addressed as representative of her son Esarhaddon (SAA 9 1.7, 1.8, and probably 2.1, 2.6). In most of these cases, Esarhaddon is addressed too (1.8, 2.1, 2.6). In 1.7 the oracle concludes with the phrase *atti attīma šarru šarrīma*, literally 'you are you, the king is my king', which means, you (Naqia) take care of yourself, I (the goddess) take care of the king. Naqia, as elsewhere Esarhaddon, is ordered to remain quiet. It is the goddess who will act. From this perspective it is unlikely that Ištar urges Naqia to 'gird her loins'. Instead, the text describes how Ištar mobilises divine help for Esarhaddon.

unlikely as well. In my view, the text presents Ištar of Arbela in her role as intercessor for Esarhaddon, who mobilises divine support for him (as in SAA 9 3.4):

> ¹ Word of Ištar of Arbela [..........]
> ² my knees are bent for [*Mullissu* ......].
> ³ Mullissu [listen] to [my] cry,
> ⁴ tie your belts, [*take action for the sake of*]
> ⁵ of Esarhaddon, king of Assyria. [..... DN and]¹³
> ⁶ Ninurta [*will go/stand*] at [my] right and left [...]
> ⁷ [...] his enemies under [his] foot [.........]
> ⁸ in/out/of the Palace of the desert [........]
> ⁹ I will give security for [Esarhaddon ......]¹⁴
> ₁₀ ⁻ ʳ·² ......
> ʳ·³ the enemy who/of [......]
> ʳ·⁴ the enemy who/of [.......]
> ʳ·⁵ Let us cast [before his feet]¹⁵ and [go] [...]
> ʳ·⁶ glorify (pl.) Mullissu!
> ʳ·⁷ [...] their [........]¹⁶

SAA 9 6

This tablet contains a single textual unit, which consists of a fragmented report of a prophecy. It is an oracle of Ištar of Arbela, delivered by the prophet Tašmetu-ereš. It is uncertain to which period this oracle can be attributed.¹⁷

SAA 9 7

This tablet contains a single textual unit, which probably consists of an elaboration of various prophetic oracles. The oracles are from the goddess Mullissu, delivered by the prophetess Mullissu-kabtat.

---

¹³ At the end of this line another god is probably mentioned, since it would be unlikely that Ninurta stands (or goes) at both sides (cf. SAA 9 1 ii 24'; 2 i 21'). See the prophetic oracle included in the Old Babylonian Epic of Zimri-Lim: 'The king goes forth with forceful heart! Adad goes at his left side, Erra, the mighty one, at his right side.' (Nissinen 2003a: 90, lines 140-142).

¹⁴ Parpola's restoration [*aš-šur*-PAB-AŠ MAN KUR-*aš-šur*] ('Esarhaddon, king of Assyria') seems too long in comparison with his interpretation of the rest of this text. A shorter alternative would be [Esarhaddon, my king].

¹⁵ Parpola convincingly restores [*ina* IGI(*pān*) GÌR.2.MEŠ(*šēpē*)-*šú*]; cf. SAA 9 1 i 44', 4:4.

¹⁶ The reading and interpretation of this line is very uncertain.

¹⁷ Parpola (SAA 9: 33, 35) presents it as an oracle for Esarhaddon.

SAA 9 8

This tablet contains a single textual unit, which may consist of an elaboration of prophetic oracles. As an alternative to Parpola's edition (SAA 9: 40; adopted by Nissinen 2003a: 129), the first two lines may be read as follows:

> ¹ Words (*dibbī*) [concerning the Elam]ites:
> ² As [Aššur?] says (*ki-i* ᵈ[*aš-šur?*])[18]

SAA 9 9

This tablet contains a textual unit, which consists of an introduction referring to two goddesses (l. 1-7), an oracle in which a goddess speaks in the first person singular (l. 8-28), a blessing of the king again referring to two goddesses (r. 1-3), and a colophon (r. 4-7). This text is to be qualified as a prophetic oracle in an elaborated literary form.

SAA 9 10

This tablet contains a single textual unit, which probably consists of a report of a prophetic oracle (comparable to SAA 9 6). The oracle is delivered by the prophetess Dunnaša-amur.

SAA 9 11

This tablet, of which the obverse is completely lost, probably is a letter in which a prophetic oracle is reported (r. 4-5).

3.1.2   *Oracles Reported in Letters*

The purpose of a report of a prophetic oracle is to inform the king of what messages from the gods, either promises or demands, have been uttered. In the cases of oracle report, the circumstances of the deliverance of the oracle, such as the situation and the name of the prophet(ess), are of importance.

SAA 10 24 (not in Nissinen 2003a)

A letter to Esarhaddon, reporting an incident in which an oracle of Marduk and Zarpanitu is delivered (r. 7-11).

---

[18]   In SAA 3 44, divine words to be attributed to the god Aššur, are identified as *dibbī* 'words' as well (SAA 3 44 r. 30). The suggestion presented here has the advantage that the god who speaks is identified.

SAA 10 352 (Nissinen 2003a: 164-166)
A letter to Esarhaddon, reporting the deliverance of two prophetic oracles in the context of a substitute king ritual (l. 22-r. 4).

SAA 13 37 (Nissinen 2003a: 167-168)
A letter to Esarhaddon, reporting the deliverance of a prophetic oracle, which contains the demand for a throne (l. 7-r. 9).

SAA 13 139 (Nissinen 2003a: 168)
A letter to Ashurbanipal, reporting a prophetic oracle, which deals with the reconciliation between Marduk, and Mullissu and Ashurbanipal (obverse).

SAA 13 144 (Nissinen 2003a: 169)
A letter to the king, reporting the deliverance of a prophetic oracle, which demands the return of certain objects (r. 7-s. 1).

SAA 13 148 (Nissinen 2003a: 169)
Fragment of a letter to the king, referring to a message (*šipirtu*) to the king, probably by Ištar of Arbela, delivered by a votary (*šēlūtu*) of the goddess.

SAA 16 59 (Nissinen 2003a: 170-172)
A letter to Esarhaddon, reporting the deliverance of a prophetic oracle (*abutu*) of Nusku, in which the kingship of a certain Sasî is proclaimed. The oracle is delivered by a female slave (ABL 1217 r. 3'-5').

3.1.3 *Oracles Quoted, Paraphrased, or Referred to in Letters*

The purpose of a quotation or paraphrase of a prophetic oracle in letters is to support the point of view of the author before the king. The divine word is used as an argument. The circumstances of the original deliverance of the oracle are not of importance; no reference to the prophet(ess) is included. The point is the argumentative force of the divine message.

SAA 10 109 (Nissinen 2003a: 152-155)
Bel-ušezib reminds Esarhaddon that he reported (*qabû*) the 'sign' (*ittu*) of Esarhaddon's kingship. This 'sign' probably was a prophetic oracle, which is quoted (l. 13'-15').

SAA 10 111 (Nissinen 2003a: 155-157)
Bel-ušezib quotes a prophetic oracle of Marduk concerning Esarhaddon's supremacy, which was delivered previously (Bel *has said*; r. 23-26).

SAA 10 174 (not in Nissinen 2003a)
Marduk-šumu-uṣur reminds Ashurbanipal of an oracle of Sin to his father Esarhaddon, announcing the conquest of Egypt (l. 10-14).

SAA 10 284 (Nissinen 2003a: 158)
Nabû-[nadin]-šumi paraphrases an oracle of Ištar of Arbela and Ištar of Nineveh concerning the destruction of Esarhaddon's enemies (r. 4-7).

SAA 16 59 (Nissinen 2003a: 170-172)
Nabû-reḫtu-uṣur, aiming to protect Esarhaddon against a supposed *coup d'état*, paraphrases an oracle, referred to as *dabābu* (word) of Nikkal (ABL 1217, l. 8-12).

SAA 16 60 (Nissinen 2003a: 172-174)
Nabû-reḫtu-uṣur, aiming to protect Esarhaddon against a supposed *coup d'état*, paraphrases an oracle, referred to as *dabābu* (word) of Mullissu (CT 53 17, l. 5-9). Furthermore he quotes an oracle of Ištar of Nineveh (CT 53 107, l. 12'-14'), paraphrases a subsequent oracle (CT 17, r. 13'-16'), and finally quotes an oracle of Bel containing a demand for gold and precious stones (CT 53 17, s. 1-2).

SAA 16 61 (Nissinen 2003a: 174-175; a fragment similar to SAA 16 60)
Nabû-reḫtu-uṣur, aiming to protect Esarhaddon against a supposed *coup d'état*, paraphrases an oracle, referred to as *dabābu* (word) of Mullissu (l. 4-9).

ABL 839[19] (not in Nissinen 2003a)
Nabû-bel-šumate quotes a prophetic oracle of Nabû and Marduk concerning Assyria's rule of Elam and the Sealand (r. 11-18).

3.1.4 *Other Messages from Deities*

Two messages addressing the king are characterised as a *šipirtu* (message) of a deity:

SAA 3 47 (not in Nissinen 2003a)
The text contains a message from Ninurta, orally delivered, recorded, and in a later stage copied onto a tablet from Ashurbanipal's library.

SAA 13 43 (not in Nissinen 2003a)
A message (*šipirtu*) from a deity (probably Aššur) to the king. Nothing points to an originally oral deliverance of this message.

3.1.5 *Oracles in Ashurbanipal's Royal Inscriptions*

It is a matter for discussion whether the prophecies in the royal inscriptions represent real prophetic oracles or rather literary creations.

Prism A (F, B, C); BIWA: 35, 221 (Nissinen 2003a: 144-145)
A word (*amātu*) of Ištar of Arbela announcing the death of Aḫšeri (iii 4-7)

Prism A (F, T); BIWA: 57-58, 242 (not in Nissinen 2003a)
A word (*amātu*) of Nanâ announcing her return to Uruk (vi 107-117)

Prism B (C); BIWA: 100, 225 (Nissinen 2003a: 146-150)
A word of Ištar of Arbela announcing the defeat of Teumman (v 47-49), followed by a dream.

Votive inscription to Marduk; BIWA: 202 (not in Nissinen 2003a)
A message (*šipru*) from Marduk announcing the defeat of the enemy (l. 24-26)

---

[19] See Mattila 1987.

3.2   *Characteristics of Prophetic Oracles*

A prophetic oracle may be defined as a direct word presented as spoken by a deity in the first person, addressed to a third party, and orally delivered by a functionary of the deity, a prophet. Indications for prophetic activity are the following.[20]

3.2.1   *Terms indicating Prophetic Activity*

1) *raggimu* (feminine *raggintu*; for the term see chapter 5.1.1) designates a prophetic figure in the Neo-Assyrian period. It is attested in the following texts:

MSL 12 226:134	lexical text	lú.šabra (PA.AL) = ŠU-*u* (*šabrû*) = *rag-gi-mu*
SAA 9 3 iv 31	prophecy (SAA 9 3.5)	*raggimu* as deliverer of oracle
SAA 9 6 r. 11	prophecy (SAA 9 6)	[*raggimu*] as deliverer of oracle
SAA 9 7:1	prophecy (SAA 9 7)	*raggintu* as deliverer of oracle
SAA 2 6:116	*adê*-text	*raggimu, maḫḫû, šā'ilu amat ili*
SAA 7 9 r. i 23	Administrative list	*raggimu*
SAA 10 109:9	letter referring to prophets	*raggimānu* and *raggimātu* spoke in favour of Esarhaddon's kingship
SAA 10 294 r. 31	letter referring to a prophet	reference to *raggimu* in obscure passage
SAA 10 352:23, r. 1	letter reporting an oracle	*raggintu* declares PN as (substitute) king
SAA 13 37:7	letter reporting an oracle	*raggintu* demands for a throne

2) The verb *ragāmu* is attested four times meaning 'to prophesy', three times in texts mentioned above (SAA 9 6 r. 6, 8, 12; SAA 10 352 e. 23 and SAA 13 37:10), and once where it identifies another oracle:

SAA 13 144 r. 7	letter reporting an oracle	woman demands return of objects

3) *maḫḫû* (fem. *maḫḫūtu*), 'ecstatic', a figure associated with prophetic activity in the Mari letters, occurs in texts from the Neo-Assyrian period as well, but mostly without reference to prophetic oracles.[21] In connection with prophecy, *maḫḫû* is attested in the ex-

---

[20]   Cf. Nissinen 1998: 9-11, for a similar set of criteria.

[21]   SAA 2 6:117, an enumeration in an *adê*-text (Nissinen 2003a: 150-151); SAA 3 34:28 and 35:31, two versions of a ritual text (Nissinen 2003a: 151-152); SAA 12 69:29, a decree for temple maintenance (Nissinen 2003a: 166-167); and SAA 3 23:5, in the phrase: 'he wailed like an ecstatic' (not in Nissinen 2003a).

pression *šipir maḫḫê*, 'messages from ecstatics', in the royal inscriptions of Esarhaddon (Assur A ii 12 and Nineveh A ii 6),[22] and Ashurbanipal (Prism B v 95 and Prism T ii 16).[23] Since the expression *šipir maḫḫê* probably refers to prophetic messages, it may be suggested that cases where a divine *šipru* is mentioned in the royal inscriptions, may refer to a prophetic oracle as well (e.g. the *šipru* of Ištar, Prism B v 78-79). In one case, a *šipru* is actually quoted: a message of Marduk to Ashurbanipal in which the god announces the destruction of Ashurbanipal's enemy.[24] SAA 9 10 s.1 refers to MÍ.GUB.BA, *maḫḫūtu*,[25] probably in connection with an oracle that is lost.[26]

3.2.2   *Oracles as Spoken Divine Words*

References to 'prophets' (*raggimu, maḫḫû*) and 'prophesying' (*ragāmu*) provide a firm criterion for identifying prophetic oracles. Further evidence can be found in references to the oral deliverance of oracles, since it is characteristic of prophecy that the deity speaks through the mouth of the mediator.

1) The oracles in the compendia SAA 9 1 and 2 are divine speeches in the first person, that come 'from the mouth' (*ša pî* of PN in SAA 9 1; *issu pî* of PN in SAA 9 2) of individuals. Although these people are not explicitly identified as *raggimu* or *maḫḫû*, the same expression is used in SAA 9 9 r. 4, *ša pî* of PN, and this woman, Dunnaša-amur, is identified as a *maḫḫūtu* in SAA 9 10 s. 1-2.

2) A designation for a divine word is *abutu* 'word' in the construction *abat* followed by a divine name. A range of oracles are introduced as *abutu* of a deity: SAA 9 2.4 (ii 30', 38'), 3.4, 3.5, 5:1, 7:2; SAA 16 59 (ABL 1217) r. 4-5; Prism A iii 4-7 (BIWA: 35, 221) and Prism A vi 113-117 (BIWA: 57-58, 242). Besides, the term *dabābu* was used (SAA 16 59 [ABL 1217] 8, 12; SAA 16 60 [CT 53 17] 8 // SAA 16 61:8).

3) In the oracles themselves, the deity often refers to other oracles as his/her *words* and to the *oral character* of the prophecies:

---

[22]   Borger 1956: 2, 45.
[23]   BIWA: 104, 141.
[24]   BIWA: 202, Votive inscription to Marduk, l. 24-26.
[25]   Cf. Parpola 1997: XLVI, CII, note 228; Parpola reads MÍ.GUB.BA here as *raggintu*.
[26]   SAA 9 10 s. 1-2: 'PN said: '[...]'; thus the prophetess, who [...]'.

SAA 9 1 i 15'-16'	Words that I have spoken to you
SAA 9 1 ii 17'-18'	I speak to you
SAA 9 1 iii 31	I have spoken to you
SAA 9 1 vi 7-8	The previous utterance I spoke to you
SAA 9 2 ii 22'-23'	Collect these words of mine in your palace
SAA 9 2 ii 34'	I will speak to the multi[tudes]
SAA 9 7:3	The things I said to you
SAA 9 7:12	(Mullissu) has said thus:
SAA 9 7:14	Secondly, let me tell you:
SAA 9 8:1	Words [concerning the Elamites]
SAA 9 8:2	As [Aššur?] says:
SAA 9 8:4	He s[ai]d it five, six times
SAA 3 47:4-5	Say to …, thus speaks DN:
SAA 10 109:8	Words (revealed by the prophets)
SAA 10 111 r. 23	Bel has said:
SAA 10 174	(the deity) said thus:
SAA 10 284	according to what Ištar of Nineveh and Ištar of Arbela have said
SAA 16 60 (CT 53 107:12')	Ištar of Nineveh says thus:
Prism A iii 7	As I (Ištar) have said
Prism A vi 117	(the word which) she had said
Prism B v 47	(Ištar) said to me

These characteristics distinguish the prophetic oracles not only from texts relating to forms of technical divination,[27] but also from closely related phenomena, such as message-dreams and prophetic compositions. Being straightforward, first person messages of a deity, prophetic oracles are distinctive from message-dreams, which involve visual experience,[28] and references to their oral deliverance distinguish the oracles from the prophetic literature, which presents a deity speaking.

Furthermore, texts that in themselves are not clearly recognisable as prophetic oracles, can be identified as such based on analogies with clearly identified oracles:

1) SAA 9 11 contains the passage: 'I will vanquish the enemy of Ashurbanipal […] Sit down! I will put the lands in orde[r …]' (r. 4-5). This can be recognised as (a report of) an oracle, given the parallels in

---

[27] Weippert 1981: 71.
[28] E.g. dreams referred to in Ashurbanipal's royal inscriptions (Prism B v 50-76; Prism A ii 95-110; Prism A iii 118-127; Prism A v 95-103) and in letters (SAA 10 361 and 365).

e.g. SAA 9 2.5 ('I will vanquish the enemies of my king. I will put Assyria in order, I will put the kin[gdom of] heaven in order').

2) The word in SAA 10 174:14 is introduced with *mā*: 'you will go and conquer (*kašādu*) the lands with them (*ina libbi*, i.e. two crowns placed on Esarhaddon's head)'. This can be accepted as a prophetic oracle based on the parallel with the oracle reported in SAA 13 37: '[L]et the [t]hrone go! I shall conquer (*kašādu*) my king's enemies with it (*ina libbi*)'.

3) SAA 16 60 (CT 53 17) r. 13-16 is identifiable as a paraphrase of a prophetic oracle, because of the expression *lā tapallaḫ* and the phrase 'Bel, Nabû and Mullissu are standing [with you]' (cf. SAA 9 1.4); besides, the phrase 'let ... die, save your life!' occurs in an oracle of the goddess Nikkal in another letter from the same author as well (SAA 16 59 [ABL 1217] 8-12).

The prophetic oracles are not abstract religious speeches, but deal with particular historical situations.[29] Many of them deal with royal legitimacy, whether addressed to the king, the crown-prince, the king's mother, a rebel, or a substitute king. In addition, they announce the defeat of the king's enemies or contain demands from the deity. The Assyrian prophecies resemble other examples of ancient Near Eastern prophecy. The prophetic material from Mari and elsewhere corroborates the oral character of prophecy.[30] Furthermore, the prophetic oracles from Mari and elsewhere support the relationship between prophecy and kingship as found in the Assyrian prophecies. This does not mean that prophetic oracles in the ancient Near East were necessarily addressed to the king. Since the evidence for ancient Near Eastern prophecy comes from royal correspondence, royal archives and steles, the relationship with kingship is obvious, but not necessarily representative of all prophecy.

---

[29] Weippert 1981: 71-72. For this, see chapter 4.2.

[30] The oracles reported in the Mari letters were orally delivered. This is indicated by the use of the verbs *qabû* and *dabābu*, 'to speak' and the noun *awātum* 'word' (see ARM 26/1). Cf. the Zakkur Stele, referring to the oracles to King Zakkur: 'Baal-šamayin answered me' (l. 11); 'and [Baal-šamayin] said to [me]' (l. 15); see Seow, in: Nissinen 2003a: 204.

3.2.3 *Characterisation of the Assyrian Prophecies*

A prophetic oracle can be recognised by several characteristics: it is a first-person message from a deity, which is addressed to a recipient (mostly the king) in the second person; it relates to the imminent future; and it is orally delivered by a prophet(ess). Oracles of this type are found in SAA 9 collections 1 and 2; oracle 3.5; the fragment of collection 4; the fragment of an oracle report, text 6; the oracles of text 7. These prophetic oracles are clearly recognisable as divine messages. In most of them the deity introduces itself with *anāku* followed by a name or a title. Ištar of Arbela appears most often, but Mullissu, Bel (Marduk), Nabû and probably Banitu and Urkittu appear as well. Other oracles are formally introduced as a 'word' (*abutu*) of the goddess (Ištar of Arbela or Mullissu).[31] In these cases, the goddess does not present herself within the oracle through the *anāku*-formula. In most oracles the king is addressed (sometimes the king's mother or the crown prince). The recipient is often, but not always, encouraged with the phrase 'fear not!' (*lā tapallaḫ*). All oracles show a concern for the imminent future, either by announcing divine action against the enemies, or by promising divine protection, restoration, reconciliation, and kingship.

Outside the corpus of SAA 9 we find prophetic oracles reported or quoted in letters to the king or embedded in royal inscriptions. None of them displays the full set of characteristics mentioned above. They are significantly shorter than the prophetic oracles of SAA 9. This might be explained by suggesting that within reports, oracles were abbreviated to what was conceived their core message. Their deviant presentation may exist in the following points:

1) The identification of the deity speaking is missing in the prophecies reported in SAA 10 352 l. 25 and r. 2-4, and SAA 13 37 l. 11-r. 9 (all delivered by a *raggintu*).

2) The second person address is missing in the oracle reported in SAA 16 59 (ABL 1217 r. 4-5, *abutu* of Nusku), in the prophecy SAA 9 8 (*dibbī* of a deity), and in several prophetic oracles embedded in Ashurbanipal's inscriptions: Prism A iii 4-7, an *amātu* (word) of Ištar

---

[31] The *abat damiqti* of Ištar of Uruk (Borger 1956: 17) probably refers to a prophetic oracle as well. The expression *abat* followed by a divine name may find a parallel in the expression *abat šarri*, if the latter is taken as referring to the verdict of the king as the most powerful authority (see Postgate 1974b: 424).

of Arbela,[32] A vi 113-115 (F, T), an *amātu* (word) of Nanâ,[33] and the votive inscription to Marduk, l. 24-25, a *šipru* of Marduk.[34]

3) An explicit promise or announcement concerning the future is missing in the oracle reported in SAA 13 139, and in the oracle in SAA 3 47, an orally delivered prophecy classified as *šipirtu* of Ninurta (r. 3).

4) No mention of a prophet, as if the deity spoke directly to the king: in SAA 10 174 (l. 14 introduces the message with *mā*), in Ashurbanipal's inscriptions B v 47-49 (C vi 46-48), *iqbâ*,[35] and in SAA 13 43, a message, *šipirtu* (r. 7), of a god to the king.

5) The king is referred to in the third person in the prophetic oracle reported in SAA 13 144 r. 8-17 (introduced with *ragāmu*, r. 7) and in SAA 10 111 r. 24-26 (oracle of Bel/Marduk).

6) Apart from omitting certain characteristics, some letters quote prophecy in a rather flexible way. SAA 10 284 r. 6-8 seems to be a rather free quotation of a prophetic oracle, and Nabû-reḫtu-uṣur paraphrases several prophetic oracles in his letters to Esarhaddon (SAA 16 59-61). SAA 10 24 reports on a man who claimed to have received a prophetic message (r. 7-11).

These messages too are to be qualified as prophetic oracles.[36] Remarkably, references to *raggimu*, 'prophet', and *ragāmu*,'to prophesy', occur more often outside the SAA 9 corpus than in texts included in SAA 9.

A further group of prophecies consist of prophetic oracles in an elaborate, literary form. In various cases, prophetic oracles have become part of a literary text. The two main examples are SAA 9 3 and 9:

1) SAA 9 3 contains a tripartite text concerning the god Aššur and the king (3.1, 3.2, 3.3), separated with a double ruling from two following units presented as an *abutu* of Ištar of Arbela. The Aššur-composition may be classified as a ceremonial-cultic text. Two passages described as *šulmu*, 'message of well-being' (3.2, 3.3) are embedded in a description of a ceremony for Aššur (3.1) and an *adê* (loyalty oath)-ceremony (ii 27-32). The purpose is the exaltation of

---

[32]   BIWA: 35.
[33]   BIWA: 57-58.
[34]   BIWA: 202.
[35]   BIWA: 100.
[36]   Two further prophetic oracles can be mentioned: SAA 9 10 s. 1-2, 'Dunnaša-amur said: '[....]'; thus the prophetess, who […]'; and SAA 13 148.

Esarhaddon as victorious king and of Aššur as king of the gods. The first *šulmu* seems to include a prophetic oracle (i 35-ii 2); the second *šulmu* consists of divine speech, but is not a prophetic oracle proper. It has been suggested that the *šulmu*-texts were recited at an enthronement ritual.[37] The following unit (3.4) presented as an *abutu* of Ištar of Arbela, describes an *adê*-ritual. The reason that these texts were put on one tablet may be found in the fact that the Aššur-composition and the first *abutu* of Ištar (3.4) both deal with an *adê*-ceremony.

2) SAA 9 9 is a literary text, which incorporates a prophetic oracle in an elaborate form.

3.3   *Literary Texts bearing a Resemblance to Prophecy*

Whereas the prophetic material introduced above is part of the focus of this study (chapter 4.2; chapter 5.1; chapter 6.2.1), some further texts will be taken into account in chapter 6 (6.2.2 and 6.2.3), dealing with the transition from prophecy into literature and with the phenomenon of literary prophecy. These additional texts consist of two groups. The first group comprises texts from seventh-century Assyria. These texts, stemming from the reign of Ashurbanipal, can be qualified as literary derivatives of prophecy. Although they probably have no oral background, they contain material closely resembling the prophetic oracles. The following examples can be mentioned:

1) The composition of SAA 3 13 contains material strongly reminiscent of the prophetic oracles, but it is a literary composition.[38]

2) The texts SAA 3 44, 45, and 46 are compositions of divine words. SAA 3 44 relates to the war of Ashurbanipal against Šamaš-šum-ukin; 3 45 consists of divine announcements that encourage Ashurbanipal in the war against Teumman; and 3 46 is a fragment of a text similar to 3 44.

Since these texts are particularly close to the prophetic oracles that received a literary elaboration, they are of importance for the investigation of the transition from prophecy into literature in seventh-century Assyria.

---

[37]   Van der Toorn 2000b: 77.
[38]   Nissinen 1993: 219; Pongratz-Leisten 1999: 75: 'literarische Kreation in Anlehnung an die Gattung der Prophetensprüche'.

A second group consists of so-called literary-predictive texts. These texts have sometimes been labelled as literary prophecies or pseudo-prophecies, but they are not prophecies in a strict sense.[39] Neverthe-less, these texts bear some resemblances to the genre of prophecy. They contain descriptions of political events cast in a predictive style. These predictions are mostly regarded as being for the greater part *va-ticinia ex eventu*. In various cases, the texts explicitly claim that the future course of events has been revealed by the gods.[40] Several of these literary-predictive texts will be taken into account in chapter 6, since they provide a counterpart to the seventh-century revision of the Isaiah tradition, which equally has a literary character. The texts dis-cussed in chapter 6 are known as the Marduk Prophecy, the Šulgi Prophecy,[41] the Uruk Prophecy,[42] and the Dynastic Prophecy.[43] These texts contain pseudo-predictions of political events, which in each case cover a broad period of time and are referred to without any men-tion of the names of rulers. A further characteristic element of these texts is their betrayal of a particular interest or agenda.[44] They aim to justify or glorify a specific situation: the reign of a particular king. To this end, the texts culminate in the description of the reign of an ideal ruler, who defeats the enemies, restores the temples and provides well-being for the people.[45]

An adequate label for these texts is literary-predictive texts.[46] They do not go back to prophetic intermediation and have no oral back-ground, but from the outset are literary compositions.[47] The fragments of the Marduk Prophecy and Šulgi Prophecy stem from Neo-Assyrian

---

[39]   Weippert 1988: 291-294.

[40]   In the Marduk Prophecy, Marduk 'reveals' the future course of events; in the Šulgi Prophecy, Šulgi claims to have received a divine revelation; the Uruk Prophecy may have been cast as a revelation by a divine speaker (see chapter 6, note 265). Fur-thermore, the Song of Erra, mentioned below, is presented as a divine revelation as well (tablet 5: 42-46).

[41]   Edited by Borger 1971.

[42]   Edited by Hunger 1976: 21-23; Hunger and Kaufman 1975.

[43]   Edited by Grayson 1975b.

[44]   Ellis 1989: 156.

[45]   Nissinen 2003c: 134-135; Beaulieu 1993: 41. These four texts can be distin-guished from the so-called text A, text B and LBAT 1543, which can be seen as some kind of astrological compositions. For the latter texts, see Biggs 1967; 1985; 1987.

[46]   Ellis 1989: 148; cf. Weippert 1988: 294. For a discussion of these texts, see Ellis 1989: 148-156; Nissinen 2003c. The label 'Akkadian apocalypses' (Hallo 1966: 240-242; Lambert 1978; Grayson 1980: 184) has been rejected by Borger (1971: 24) and Nissinen (2003c: 142-143).

[47]   Nissinen 2003c: 139-140.

archives. These texts were apparently treated as (part of) a series.[48] The Uruk Prophecy stems from Late Babylonian Uruk and displays a Neo-Babylonian interest; the Dynastic Prophecy is believed to date from, and to relate to, the Hellenistic period.

The final text that will be taken into account in chapter 6 is the Song of Erra, which bears some important resemblances to the literary-predictive texts. This poem may date from the eighth century BCE but is likely to incorporate older elements.[49] Although the literary-predictive texts and the Song of Erra are not exclusively connected with seventh-century Assyria, there was a clear seventh-century Assyrian interest in, at least, the Marduk Prophecy and the Song of Erra. The literary-predictive texts (and parts from the Song of Erra) are relevant for this study, since they show that written 'prophecies' can be scribal creations.[50] With regard to the issue of the transition from prophecy into literature and the phenomenon of literary prophecy (chapter 6), these texts provide an analogy to the literary character of the development of the Isaiah tradition.

---

[48] Borger 1971. The Marduk Prophecy is preserved as follows. Ten fragments, according to Borger's reconstruction, are presumably part of the same tablet (K 2158 +), with a colophon from Ashurbanipal's library (iv 17'-19'). A small fragment of a different copy of the text contains the first part of lines 25-36 of column i (Sm 1388), and stems also from the library of Ashurbanipal. The text Assur 13348 ek, another duplicate, contains a substantial fragment of the final part of the text. This tablet belonged to the archive of a family of exorcists in Assur. The texts from this archive mostly date from the Sargonid period (ranging from 713-612 BCE). The precise date of this fragment is uncertain (Pedersén 1986: 41-44, 56, 76).

[49] Dalley 2000: 282.

[50] Grabbe 1995: 94.

PART TWO

CHAPTER FOUR

PROPHECY IN ITS HISTORICAL SETTING

This chapter deals with the prophetic material from First Isaiah and from seventh-century Assyria in their respective historical settings and aims to illuminate the relationship between prophetic oracles and historical events. Its purpose is to explore one of the main characteristics shared by the eighth-century prophetic material from First Isaiah and the Assyrian prophecies: the fact that prophetic words relate to events of great political importance and intervene in the political scene. It will be demonstrated that, notwithstanding the immense differences between Judah and Assyria as political entities, prophecy to some extent played a similar role in situations of crucial political importance. Prophetic words and oracles take root in, and relate to, concrete historical situations. They interfere with contemporary events and seek to influence the imminent future. In order to demonstrate this, I will describe various relevant episodes in eighth-century Judah and seventh-century Assyria, and discuss the prophetic materials connected with them. The chapter contains two main parts: historical events in Judah and prophetic oracles from First Isaiah (4.1), and historical events in Assyria and the Assyrian oracles (4.2). A final section (4.3) presents a balance of similarities and differences between the ways Isaiah's oracles and the Assyrian oracles relate to their respective historical contexts.

4.1   *Historical Events in Judah and Prophecies from First Isaiah*

The first Judaean king to enter an Assyrian royal inscription is Ahaz, listed in one of the summary inscriptions of Tiglath-pileser among rulers who submitted to Assyria and offered tribute in 734 BCE.[1] By the

---

[1]   Summary inscription 7, l. 11' (ITP: 170-171), ^{m}Ia-$\acute{u}$-ha-zi ^{kur}Ia-$\acute{u}$-da-a+a, 'Jehoahaz of Judah'. The earlier view that Azriyau, a ruler defeated by Tiglath-pileser in 738 BCE, may be identified with King Azariah/Uzziah of Judah, has now mostly been abandoned. Annal 19*, l. 1-12 (ITP: 58-63), describing Azriyau's actions, present him

second half of the eighth century BCE the kingdom of Judah was a political state of modest dimensions, ruled by the royal house of David.[2] For the kingdom of Judah, the eighth-seventh century BCE proved to be an important period. Assyria's takeover of Syria-Palestine in the late eighth century opened up Judah to international trade and to neighbouring civilisations. After the downfall of Israel and the establishment of direct Assyrian rule in the North, the way for Judah was clear to become a player in regional political affairs. From the second half of the eighth century onwards Jerusalem expanded and Judah's importance increased.[3] Furthermore, Judah became integrated into the Assyrian economic sphere and played a role in the southern trade network.[4]

In the ninth century, after a period of temporary weakness (c. 1100-900 BCE), a new wave of Assyrian expansion began. The policy of westward expansion brought Assyria into conflict with the North-Syrian states on the Euphrates, and subsequently with Damascus and other Syrian states.[5] Assyria's military successes however had not resulted in permanent supremacy over the West.[6] It was Tiglath-pileser III (745-727 BCE), who by adopting a new political-military strategy 'reshaped the map of the ancient Near East.'[7] Whereas his predecessors had conquered and plundered the Neo-Hittite and Aramaean states along the west of the Euphrates and had occasionally reached as far as the Mediterranean coast, Tiglath-pileser aimed to establish a

---

as an Aramaean ruler (esp. l. 9-11). The identification with Azariah/Uzziah of Judah was based on a connection with another text, K 6205, which includes a reference to the land of Judah. However, Na'aman (1974: 36-39) has shown that K 6205 is part of a text dating to the time of Sennacherib (the Azekah inscription, discussed in 4.1.7). This implies there is no reason to identify Azriyau as a Judaean king. Instead, Annal 19* suggests he was the ruler of Hamath; so Weippert 1976-80: 205; Galil 1996: 61; Veenhof 2001: 249.

[2]   The process of state formation in Judah is a much-debated issue. For the current state of the discussion, see Vaughn and Killebrew (eds) 2003, and Herzog and Singer-Avitz 2004.

[3]   For the expansion of Jerusalem, see Geva 2003; Killebrew 2003: 335-338. Steiner (2001: 110-111) points out that in the seventh century Judah developed into a strongly centralised state, with Jerusalem taking a central position, surpassing the other cities in the region in size.

[4]   Evidence of trade relations with Greece or Cyprus, Syria and perhaps Arabia indicates that during the seventh century Jerusalem profited from international trade under the *Pax Assyriaca*; see Steiner 2001: 109-110; Zimhoni 1990: 49; Dalley 2004a: 389-390, 393.

[5]   Lambert 2004: 353; Veenhof 2001: 236-239; Na'aman 1991a: 80-83.

[6]   Veenhof 2001: 240-249.

[7]   Tadmor ITP: 9; see also Veenhof 2001: 251.

permanent rule in these regions. After the defeat of Sarduri II of
Urartu and the fall of Arpad (741/40 BCE), many Western kingdoms,
including Israel, Damascus and Tyre, were forced to submit to Assyria. This situation is probably reflected in a tribute list in Tiglath-
pileser's Iran Stele, which refers to Menahem of Israel, together with
Rezin of Damascus[8] and Tuba'il of Tyre.[9] In 738, the Assyrian army
returned to the West and defeated a coalition headed by Tutamu of
Unqi and Azriyau of Hamath.[10] The kingdom of Unqi was turned into
an Assyrian province and Hamath was reduced to a rump state ruled
by king Eni-ilu. The outcome of this campaign is reflected in another
list of rulers upon whom Tiglath-pileser imposed tribute (Annal 13*),
which mentions Menahem of Samaria together with Rezin of Damascus and Hiram of Tyre.[11] During the next stage, 734-732 BCE, Tiglath-
pileser conquered Philistia, Trans-Jordan, Israel and Aram-Damascus.

4.1.1   The Historical Events of 734-732 BCE

With the campaigns of 734-732, Tiglath-pileser aimed to achieve control over the Mediterranean coast from Phoenicia to the Egyptian border and to consolidate Assyria's hegemony in southern Syria and
Palestine.[12] Through the campaigns, Assyria gained control over both

---

[8]   The more historical spelling would be Raḫiān; see Weippert 1973: 46-47, note
83.
[9]   Iran Stele iii A l. 5 (ITP: 106-107). According to the reconstruction of Tadmor
(ITP: 267), Tuba'il was king of Tyre in 740.
[10]   See note 1 above.
[11]   Annal 13* l. 10-12 (ITP: 68-69), similar to Annal 27 (ITP: 89). By 738,
Tuba'il had been succeeded by Hiram, who was king until at least 734/733 (ITP: 267).
[12]   Two recent studies on the Syro-Ephraimite crisis are Asurmendi 1982 and Irvine 1990. Both present a survey of the Assyrian sources and the biblical material,
and both offer a reconstruction of the events (Asurmendi 1982: 48-51; Irvine 1990:
75-109). The reconstruction presented here differs from theirs in some respects. 1)
Both Asurmendi and Irvine, in my view, overestimate the scale of the anti-Assyrian
rebellion. Neither Edom nor Gaza nor Egypt actively participated in the rebellion
(contra Asurmendi 1982: 49-51; Irvine 1990: 69-70). 2) Both assert that the campaign
of 734 BCE against Philistia was a reaction against the anti-Assyrian league, just as
the campaigns of 733 and 732 BCE were; Asurmendi 1982: 48; Irvine 1990: 70: 'The
Assyrians responded to the Western revolt in 734/733 by marching against Philistia'.
This is, however, unlikely. As Tadmor (1966: 88) pointed out, with the campaign of
734 the Assyrians aimed to dominate the Mediterranean seaports. In order to remain
in control over the coastal commerce however Assyria had to consolidate its power in
Syria-Palestine. After the campaign against Philistia, it appeared that the rulers resist-
ing Assyria's supremacy, Rezin, Hiram and Pekah, could also induce others, such as
Mitinti of Ashkelon, to join their rebellion. For that reason, the Assyrians returned in
733 and 732 BCE, to break the resistance. 3) Asurmendi (1982: 48) and Irvine (1990:

routes to Egypt, 'the Transjordanian desert road which goes south from Damascus, and the Levantine road with goes south from Samaria towards the Mediterranean coast, and passes the great coastal cities of the Phoenicians and the Philistines'.[13] The Assyrian Eponym Canon mentions Philistia as the region on which the campaign of 734 was focused, and the land of Damascus as the main target of the campaigns of 733 and 732.[14] Among the remains of Tiglath-pileser's annals are some fragments that deal with the campaign of 733.[15] In addition, various summary inscriptions from Tiglath-pileser's reign deal with events of 734-732.[16]

The campaign of 734 was directed at the Mediterranean coast. The Assyrians invaded Philistia by marching south from Phoenicia along the coastal highway. One of the main events of this campaign was the conquest of Gaza.[17] The Assyrian inscriptions claim that Hanunu of Gaza fled to Egypt because of the Assyrian army, but returned after Gaza had been conquered. Tiglath-pileser restored him to the throne and imposed a large tribute upon him. The Assyrian king established a centre for international commerce (*bīt kāri*) at Gaza, and erected a royal stele in the city of the Brook of Egypt (*naḥal Muṣur*).[18] Hanunu's flight to, and return from, Egypt may suggest that he sought support against Assyria among the Egyptian rulers, but in vain.[19] Assyria achieved control over the international trade routes via the Mediterranean coast.[20] Tiglath-pileser's royal stele at the Brook of Egypt symbolised the Assyrian takeover and marked the southern border of the

108-109) situate the threat posed to Ahaz *before* Assyria's campaign against Philistia. I suggest however that the Syro-Ephaimitic crisis is best situated *after* Assyria's campaign against Philistia.
[13]   Dalley 1998: 86.
[14]   Millard 1994: 44-45.
[15]   According to Tadmor's reconstruction, 733 BCE is Tiglath-pileser's thirteenth regnal year; the annals from his twelfth and fourteenth year (734 and 732) are lost.
[16]   Unlike the annals, the summary inscriptions are not organised chronologically, but geographically or thematically; see Tadmor, ITP: 275.
[17]   Described in Summary inscription 4, 8'-15' (ITP: 138-141); Summary inscription 8, 14'-19' (ITP: 176-179); Summary inscription 9, 13-16 (ITP: 188-189). Cf. ITP: 222-225.
[18]   ITP: 223-226.
[19]   For an explanation of Hanunu's stay in Egypt and return to Gaza, see Kahn 2001: 16, note 89.
[20]   See Tadmor 1966: 88. According to Becking (1992: 9), the Assyrian aim was 'control over the overseas-trade via the Phoenician harbour-cities as well as control over trade with Egypt and the caravan-routes to the Arabian peninsula'. Economic motives were a major factor in Assyria's military expansion, see Veenhof 2001: 231.

west part of the Assyrian empire.[21] In the course of the campaign of 734, several rulers submitted to Assyria and paid tribute. Summary inscription 7 contains a list of rulers who paid tribute to Assyria, and the final part of this list concerns rulers who submitted to Assyria in 734:

> Matanbi'il of Arvad, Sanipu of Ammon, Salamanu of Moab, [...]
> [Mi]tinti of Ashkelon, Jehoahaz of Judah, Qaushmalaka of Edom [...]
> and Hanunu of Gaza.[22]

Tiglath-pileser claims to have received their tribute,[23] consisting of gold, silver and all kinds of valuable material and treasures. Ahaz's submission and tribute offered to Tiglath-pileser in 734 represents the first direct contact between Assyria and Judah. This is more or less confirmed by the biblical account of 2 Kgs 16:5-9, where Ahaz's appeal to Tiglath-pileser is presented as the beginning of Judah's servitude to Assyria. It is uncertain whether any other events mentioned in Tiglath-pileser's summary inscriptions are to be situated during the campaign of 734.[24]

Despite Assyria's successful campaign of 734, parts of southern Syria and Palestine resisted Tiglath-pileser's hegemony. During 737-735, while Assyrian forces were occupied in other areas, several rulers who had previously been subdued by Assyria, such as Rezin of Damascus and Hiram of Tyre, had thrown off the Assyrian yoke. In Israel, the usurpation of Pekah, which ended the reign of Pekahiah son of Menahem, probably marked a transition to the anti-Assyrian camp led by Rezin of Damascus (c. 736 BCE). Against this background, the remark of 2 Kgs 15:37, that during the reign of Jotham, Judah was

---

[21] Kahn 2001: 16-17.

[22] Summary inscription 7, r. 10'-12' (ITP: 170-171). The inscription was written in 729/728 BCE; the kings mentioned in the fragment quoted are the tribute-bearers of 734, see Tadmor ITP: 268. Hanunu of Gaza, mentioned in last position, apparently was the only ruler from this list who initially resisted Assyria's dominion.

[23] Summary inscription 7, r. 7', *madattu* (restored).

[24] The events described in Summary inscription 8 l. 2'-9' and 10'-13' (ITP: 176-177) are sometimes situated during the campaign of 734 BCE, since they are followed by a description of the Hanunu episode. According to Irvine (1990: 46-49) the passage deals with Arvad rather than with Tyre, but this is based on the assumption that it describes an event from the campaign of 734 because it precedes the episode of Hanunu of Gaza. However, since the summary inscriptions may list events in geographical sequence rather than chronological order (as Irvine [1990: 26] acknowledges), the passage may deal with events from the campaign of 733. It is known that Hiram of Tyre rebelled against Assyria. Lines 2'-9', dealing with a rebel king (possibly Hiram) of a Phoenician city ('in the midst of the sea', line 4') is likely to describe an event of 733/732. Similarly, lines 10'-13' are likely to reflect events of 733/732 and may deal with Israel and the killing of Pekah; so Na'aman 1986: 72-73.

troubled by Rezin of Damascus and Pekah of Israel, can be understood.[25]

In order to secure its control over the coastal commerce and its su-
premacy in Syria-Palestine, Assyria had to break the resistance. This
was the purpose of the campaigns of 733-732. In the inscriptions of
Tiglath-pileser, various rulers and states are accused of rebellion
against Assyria: the Arab queen Samsi, 'who broke her oath of
Šamaš',[26] Mitinti of Ashkelon, who broke the loyalty oath,[27] Hiram of
Tyre and Rezin of Damascus,[28] and perhaps Israel.[29] It is clear that
Rezin took a leading role. The revolts of Mitinti of Ashkelon and
Hiram of Tyre are connected with Rezin's policy.[30] The biblical material connects Pekah of Israel with Rezin's anti-Assyrian politics and
confirms Rezin's leading role. The rebellion of the Arab queen Samsi
may be connected with Rezin's politics as well, since in the annals of
733 the Assyrian measures taken against Samsi directly follow those
against Rezin.[31] The Assyrian inscriptions thus point to a joint rebellion. However, they do not refer to a coalition of joint forces against
Assyria. Apparently, no battle was fought against the coalition, but
Tiglath-pileser took action against the rebelling countries one by one.

The annals of Tiglath-pileser's thirteenth year (733 BCE) deal with
Rezin's defeat, his flight to Damascus, the siege of Damascus, the
conquest of his cities, and the annexation of his land.[32] The fragment
ends with a reference to Queen Samsi of the Arabs, who is accused of

---

[25]   Rezin's aim was not only to resist Assyria's hegemony but also to achieve his
own hegemony in the region. Pekah of Israel was under his influence, and the purpose
of the Syro-Ephraimite crisis was to appoint a ruler over Judah, who would be under
his supervision as well. In this respect, Oded (1972) rightly presented the Syro-
Ephraimite crisis as an inner-Palestinian conflict. Rezin's ambitions of course brought
him in conflict with Assyria.

[26]   ITP: 80-81.
[27]   ITP: 82-83.
[28]   ITP: 186-187, '[Hi]ram of Tyre, who plotted together with Rezin [...]'.
[29]   Na'aman 1986: 72-73.
[30]   ITP: 82-83 (Mitinti); ITP: 186-187 (Hiram).
[31]   ITP: 80-81. There is no evidence that any Egyptian ruler supported the anti-
Assyrian resistance (contra Irvine 1990: 69-70). Na'aman (1991a: 92) and Irvine
(1990: 53-54) may be right that the Assyrian campaign of 734 aimed to block off the
way for a possible Egyptian intervention in Palestine. Schipper (1999: 141) however
argues that Egypt suffered from a weak period 'in der an eine aktive Außenpolitik
Ägyptens nicht zu denken war'.
[32]   Summary inscription 9 r. 3-4 (ITP: 186-187), reads: 'The wide [land of Bit-
]Haza'ili (Aram) in its entirety, from [Mount Leb]anon *as far as the cities of Gile*[ad,
Abel ....] [on the bor]der of Bit-Humria (Israel) I *annexed* to Assyria. [I placed] *my
eunuch* [over them as governor].' (Tadmor's translation).

having violated 'the oath of Šamaš'.[33] Another fragment from the annals of 733 BCE (annals 18 and 24) deals with Israel and Ashkelon. Israel's territories in Galilee and Trans-Jordan (Gilead) were occupied and annexed, and some of the inhabitants were deported. The kingdom was reduced to a rump state consisting of the central hill country around Samaria. In the course of these events, perhaps after the fall of Damascus in 732, a regime change took place in Samaria: Pekah was killed and succeeded by Hoshea, who made obeisance to Tiglath-pileser in 731.[34]

Ashkelon's king Mitinti had submitted to Assyria in 734, but soon afterwards broke the loyalty oath. In the Assyrian annals Mitinti's rebellion is connected with the resistance of Rezin of Damascus, by stating that Mitinti became insane (or panicked) when he saw Rezin's defeat.[35] It is not clear how Mitinti fell from power, but he may have been killed by the people of Ashkelon in an effort to avert an Assyrian attack.[36] Mitinti was succeeded by Rukibtu, possibly his son. Thus, the campaign of 733, aiming to end the resistance in southern Syria and Palestine, included measures against Rezin of Aram, the Arab queen Samsi, Mitinti of Ashkelon, the Kingdom of Israel, and probably Hiram of Tyre.[37]

Since Damascus had not been captured in 733, the campaign of 732 was again focused on Rezin of Damascus. Although the annals of 732 are lost, the expected outcome is the death of Rezin.[38] The fact that Tiglath-pileser did not return to Syria-Palestine implies that he was satisfied with the accomplishments of 734-732. Furthermore, the fall

---

[33]   For the Samsi episode, ITP: 228-230.

[34]   Summary inscription 13 l. 17'-18' (ITP: 202-203) describe Israel's affairs as follows: '[the land of Bit-Humria], all of whose cities I had [devastated] in my former campaigns, [...] its livestock I had despoiled and had spared the city of Samaria alone, ... they overthrew (Peqah) their king.' (Tadmor's translation). Pekah was succeeded by Hoshea, who was recognised as ruler by Tiglath-pileser after he had offered tribute at Sarrabanu (731 BCE); see Summary inscription 9 r. 9-11 (ITP: 188-189).

[35]   Annal 18 l. 9'; annal 24 l. 14' (ITP: 82-83).

[36]   See Irvine 1990: 36. Assyria's dealings with Ashkelon may be connected with the siege of Gezer. This siege, not mentioned in the inscriptions, is known from a relief of Tiglath-pileser. The army that conquered Gezer may have had Ashkelon as its destination.

[37]   Hiram of Tyre surrendered and paid tribute. After this, he and his son Matan remained vassals of Assyria. Tiglath-pileser's actions against Tyre which led to Hiram's surrender are probably to be situated not during the campaign of 734, but during one of the subsequent campaigns of 733 and 732; Irvine 1990: 58-59.

[38]   See Tadmor ITP: 281.

of Damascus and the death of Rezin are confirmed by the account of 2
Kgs 16:5-9.

> [5] Then King Rezin of Aram and King Pekah son of Remaliah of Israel
> came up to Jerusalem for war; they enclosed Ahaz, but were unable to
> fight.
> [6] At that time the king of Edom recovered Elath for Edom, and drove
> the Judaeans from Elath; and the Edomites came to Elath, where they
> live to this day.[39]
> [7] Ahaz sent messengers to King Tiglath-pileser of Assyria, saying, 'I am
> your servant and your son. Come up, and rescue me from the hand of
> the king of Aram and from the hand of the king of Israel, who are at-
> tacking me.'
> [8] Ahaz also took the silver and gold found in the house of Yahweh and
> in the treasures of the king's house, and sent a bribe to the king of As-
> syria.
> [9] The king of Assyria listened to him; the king of Assyria marched up
> against Damascus, and took it, carrying its people captive to Kir; then
> he killed Rezin.

This account reflects various events of 734-732, but deliberately puts
them in a different light, as I will argue. 2 Kgs 16:5-9 is a composite
account.[40] First, verse 6, which is only loosely connected with the rest
of the account, is not historical but betrays a particular agenda.[41] Furthermore, 16:7-9 give the impression of continuing verse 5, but this is
misleading. Since verse 5 already reveals that Rezin and Pekah were
unsuccessful, the appeal of Ahaz to Tiglath-pileser (verse 7) does not
follow smoothly. Moreover, 16:7-9 does not mention the (ending of)
Jerusalem's siege, nor Rezin's return to Damascus, nor the fate of
Pekah of Israel.[42] Whereas verses 7-9 were composed as a continuation

---

[39] מֶלֶךְ אֱדוֹם 'king of Edom' in the original text became מֶלֶךְ אֲרָם 'king of Aram'
and the name 'Rezin' was added from verse 5; 'Edom' and 'Edomites' is to be read in
the entire verse (cf. 2 Chron 28:17). So Tadmor and Cogan 1979: 496-497.

[40] Irvine 1990: 88; Tadmor and Cogan 1979: 494.

[41] According to Tadmor and Cogan (1979: 496-498), 16:5 and 6 refer to different
events. Aram has nothing to do with the war between Edom and Judah, and the capture of Elath is not connected with the Syro-Ephraimite crisis. In Summary inscription
7, King Qaushmalaka of Edom is mentioned (just as Ahaz) among the rulers who
submitted to Tiglath-pileser in 734, and there is no evidence that he, either before or
afterwards, joined the anti-Assyrian camp. For 16:6 a seventh- or sixth-century background may be suggested. At that stage, Edom adopted a position hostile to Judah.
The insertion of verse 6 aimed to contribute to the negative depiction of King Ahaz.
For this interpretation, see Tadmor and Cogan 1979: 496-498.

[42] Cf. 2 Kgs 15:29-30 for measures of Tiglath-pileser against Pekah of Israel.

of verse 5 (as is evident from verse 7b), verse 5 once stood on its own as a short note concerning the reign of Ahaz.[43]

Verse 5 is a relatively early note concerning the Syro-Ephraimite crisis, which in itself is not negative about Ahaz. The extension of 16:7-9 refers to the events of 734-732, but deliberately puts them in a different perspective. On the one hand, it reflects Ahaz's submission to Assyria and his tribute to Tiglath-pileser in 734. On the other, it reflects Assyria's campaign against Damascus (733-732) and its outcome: Rezin's death.[44] However, whereas in the Assyrian inscriptions these events are unrelated, in 16:7-9 they have become connected. From Tiglath-pileser's inscriptions it appears that in the course of the campaign against Philistia in 734 BCE, Ahaz submitted to Assyria and paid tribute. Furthermore, in the campaigns of 733-732 BCE Assyria broke the resistance of Damascus and its allies. There was no specific connection between Ahaz's submission in 734 and the campaigns against Rezin and his allies in 733-732 BCE. This connection is however what 2 Kgs 16:7-9 adds in its interpretation of the events: it is claimed that Tiglath-pileser came to Palestine at Ahaz's request, in order to save him from the Syro-Ephraimite aggression. This presents the events of 734-732 from a Judaeo-centred perspective. Historically, Tiglath-pileser was motivated by a policy of westward expansion. From the later Judaean perspective, he came to Palestine at the request of Ahaz. Whether or not Ahaz asked for Tiglath-pileser's help while threatened after the Assyrian army had left the scene, remains uncertain.[45] It is however evident, 1) that Tiglath-pileser had his own motive for the campaigns of 733-732,[46] and 2) that 16:7-9 turned the events upside down by presenting Ahaz's tribute to Assyria of 734 as a bribe for his rescue from his enemies and by presenting the arrival of the Assyrian army in Palestine as being singularly motivated by Ahaz's request.

---

[43] Irvine 1990: 85-86.

[44] For a similar interpretation, see Irvine 1990: 88.

[45] According to Irvine (1990: 86-89 and 299) Ahaz's appeal to Tiglath-pileser is unlikely to be historical. Oded (1993) however presents a range of cases in the Assyrian royal inscriptions where the quest of help from a vassal is followed by a response of the Assyrian king.

[46] Oded (1993: 64, note 4) concedes that 'It is more likely that the connection between Ahaz's appeal and the Assyrian campaign was not causal but to a large extent chronological – the Assyrian military campaign would have taken place even without the call for help.'

Whereas 16:5 is a relatively early note, 16:7-9 is an extension from
a later hand. It describes how Assyria became involved in Judah's affairs. In 2 Kgs 16:7-9, Ahaz is depicted as a powerless king who in a
situation of crisis submits to a powerful king, begging him for help
and buying his assistance with a large sum.[47] 2 Kgs 16:7-9 is not a
neutral description. 1) Ahaz implores Tiglath-pileser to rescue him
from the hands of his enemies (יֹשַׁע מִן כַּף). This expression often denotes rescue initiated by Yahweh, but Ahaz appeals to a foreign king.[48]
2) The term שֹׁחַד ('bribe') bears a negative connotation.[49] 3) The self-
address of Ahaz to Tiglath-pileser, 'I am your servant and your son',
confirms that he chose the Assyrian king rather than Yahweh for his
rescue.[50] 16:7-9 seems to assume an ideological contrast between Ahaz
and Hezekiah. Whereas Hezekiah trusted in Yahweh and prayed to
Yahweh to rescue (יֹשִׁע) him from the hand of Sennacherib (2 Kgs
19:19), Ahaz begged Tiglath-pileser to rescue (יֹשִׁע) him from the
hands of his enemies (2 Kgs 16:7).[51] The interpretation of 16:7-9 as a
critical passage is supported by the broader picture of the relation between Judah and Assyria as found in 2 Kings. According to the presentation of 2 Kings, it was Ahaz who made Judah be subjected to
Assyria,[52] whereas it was Hezekiah who, thanks to his trust in Yahweh,
successfully threw off the Assyrian yoke. 2 Kgs 16:7-9 is not as
overtly critical of Ahaz as Isa 7:1-17, or as 2 Kings 16 in its final
shape. In the course of time the picture of Ahaz became increasingly
negative. Whereas the earliest material concerning Ahaz (the prophetic material in Isa 7* and 8*, the note of 2 Kgs 16:5, and the source
behind 2 Kgs 16:10-18a) is not negative at all towards him, the later
compositions of Isa 7:1-17 and 2 Kings 16 give, in different ways, an
increasingly negative picture of Ahaz, based on a contrast between
Ahaz and Hezekiah.[53] I would suggest that 2 Kgs 16:7-9 reflects an

---

[47]   Cf. Lemaire 2004: 371-372.
[48]   Historical appeals for help to the Assyrian king are formulated differently; see
Oded 1993: 68-69.
[49]   Tadmor and Cogan 1979: 499-500. That this bribe partly consisted of silver
and gold from the temple of Yahweh adds to the critical depiction of Ahaz; see also
Irvine 1990: 86-87.
[50]   The Davidic king was both servant and son of Yahweh; see Irvine 1990: 87-88.
[51]   In both cases, the request was granted: the king of Assyria listened to his request (2 Kgs 16:9); Yahweh listened to his request (2 Kgs 19:16, 20).
[52]   Tadmor and Cogan 1979: 505.
[53]   The contrast between Ahaz and Hezekiah reached its climax in 2 Chron 28; see
Smelik 1998: 180-182. Many commentators suggest that 2 Chron 28:7, dealing with a
coup d'état of a certain Zichri from Ephraim, which almost succeeded, derives from

early stage of this Ahaz-Hezekiah contrast: instead of buying help and becoming dependent on Assyria, Ahaz should have trusted in Yahweh, as Hezekiah did.

The events of 734-732 BCE can be summarised as follows: 1) In 734 BCE, Tiglath-pileser conquered Philistia. Ahaz, together with several other rulers from the region, submitted to Assyria and paid tribute. 2) The anti-Assyrian resistance, led by Rezin of Damascus, continued (c. 737-733 BCE). Ahaz's refusal to cooperate with the anti-Assyrian politics brought him into a critical situation. 3) In the campaigns of 733-732 BCE, Tiglath-pileser broke the resistance, which resulted in Assyrian dominance over the region, regime changes in Ashkelon and Israel, and presumably Rezin's death.

The situation mentioned under 2), reflected in the prophetic material within Isa 7* and 8*, and summarised in the note of 2 Kgs 16:5, is appropriately called the Syro-Ephraimite crisis.[54] This crisis—the plan of Rezin to kill Ahaz and to replace him with a cooperative ruler—is best situated after Assyria's campaign of 734 BCE against Philistia, for the following reasons. First, we have an analogy in the case of Mitinti of Ashkelon. Both Ahaz and Mitinti were among the kings that submitted to Tiglath-pileser in 734 BCE. Soon afterwards Mitinti broke his loyalty oath and joined the rebellion, either inspired or persuaded by Rezin of Damascus. Second, Ahaz's submission to Tiglath-pileser in 734 BCE meant that he, from Rezin's perspective, had joined the wrong camp. This would have motivated Rezin to take action against him. Third, the advice of Isaiah, reflected in the prophetic material of Isa 7* and 8* (see below), not to take action and not to give in to the pressure of Rezin and Pekah (Isa 7:4) fits into the period between the Assyrian campaigns of 734 and 733/732 BCE. In all likelihood, Ahaz had sworn a loyalty oath in 734 BCE, just as had Mitinti of Ashkelon. Ahaz's oath-enforced bond with Assyria may explain Isaiah's advice and Ahaz's persistence not to join the anti-Assyrian

an early, historical source (see Irvine 1990: 95). If this is correct, the report concerning Zichri adds to the threat that was posed to King Ahaz.

[54] The earliest layer of Isa 7:1-17 focuses on the evil intentions of Rezin and the fear of Ahaz and his people. The note of 2 Kgs 16:5 furthermore states that Rezin and Pekah came up to Jerusalem. Rezin and Pekah intended to kill Ahaz in order to get someone on the throne who would cooperate with their anti-Assyrian politics. They were however unsuccessful. Their plan to accomplish a regime change failed. Since it is uncertain how much fighting was involved, I prefer the term Syro-Ephraimite crisis, rather than Syro-Ephraimite war.

rebellion.[55] Fourth, the note in 2 Kgs 16:5 and the oracles of Isaiah suggest that the plan of Rezin failed. If there was a siege of Jerusalem it was broken off prematurely. This fits the period between Assyria's campaign to Philistia in 734 BCE and the subsequent campaign directed against the rebellious kingdoms.

4.1.2 *Prophetic Words relating to 734-732 BCE*

As can be inferred from the prophecies to be situated in this period, the prophet Isaiah played an encouraging role during the Syro-Ephraimite crisis. The prophecies to be connected with the circumstances of 734-732 BCE, are 7:4-9a, 7:14b.16, 7:20, 8:1-4 and 17:1b-3.[56]

Isa 7:4-9a*

> Take heed, be quiet, do not fear, and do not let your heart be faint because of these two smouldering stumps of firebrands. Because Aram has plotted evil against you, saying: "Let us invade Judah, terrify it, and cleave it open for ourselves and let us make the son of Tabeel king in it!", therefore thus says the Lord Yahweh: 'It shall not stand, and it shall not come to pass.' For the head of Aram is Damascus, and the head of Damascus is Rezin, and the head of Ephraim is Samaria, and the head of Samaria is the son of Remaliah.

The earliest layer of 7:1-17, consisting of 7:2-3a.4-9a.14b.16 (see chapter 2.1.2), presents a coherent picture: Rezin, with Pekah as an ally under his supervision, intends to replace Ahaz of Judah with an anti-Assyrian king, cooperative with Rezin. This policy, posing a threat to Judah, terrifies Ahaz (7:2, 4, 16). The plan to kill and replace Ahaz makes sense in the political circumstances of the period. A regime change could secure the adoption of the anti-Assyrian politics advocated by Rezin.[57] When the oracle 7:4-9a was delivered, Jerusalem was not yet under siege (cf. 7:2). This may however have happened soon afterwards (cf. 2 Kgs 16:5). Under the threatening circumstances, pictured in 7:2 and 7:6, Isaiah urges Ahaz neither to

---

[55] See also Dalley 1998: 88-89.

[56] For the exegetical analysis of the prophetic texts in this chapter, see chapter 2.

[57] Examples of such regime changes are Pekah, who took the throne from Pekahiah (loyal to Assyria) and adopted a policy of rebellion against Assyria; Hoshea who took over from Pekah (anti-Assyria), and resumed a policy of loyalty; Mitinti of Ashkelon who rebelled against Assyria, succeeded by Rukibtu who resumed a policy of loyalty.

give in to the pressure of the anti-Assyrian rulers, headed by Rezin, nor to go out to wage war against the Aramaean-Israelite army that was ready to invade Judah. Instead, he is to stay in Jerusalem and wait, for Yahweh promises him that the plan of Rezin will fail.[58] 7:6 presents a quotation from the mouth of Rezin. Quoting the adversaries is a characteristic of the prophecies of Isaiah, as appears from 5:19, 10:8-9.13-15, 28:10, 28:15, and 29:15. The quotations are fictitious, some of them evidently (10:8-9.13-15, 28:10, 28:15), others most probably.[59] The function of the fictitious quotations is rhetorical. The quotations function to reveal the self-willed and arrogant attitude of the adversary speaking. The adversary speaks as if Yahweh can be safely neglected. This reveals his hubris and anticipates his downfall and punishment.

The identity of the 'son of Tabeel' is disputed.[60] Some scholars have suggested that behind *ṭāb'al* figures the Phoenician name Itto-baal,[61] pronounced *toba'l* and deliberately changed into *ṭāb'al*, 'good for nothing', perhaps already by the prophet himself (such a de-nouncement would be characteristic of prophetic language). The at-traction of this possibility is that the predecessor of Hiram of Tyre was named Ittobaal, so that the son of Ittobaal would be a Phoenician prince related to Hiram of Tyre who took part in the rebellion of Rezin. However, since this identification remains speculative, other explanations must be taken into account as well.[62] In any case, the 'son of Tabeel' is contrasted with the 'son' Immanuel. In contrast with the candidate-king, the 'son of Tabeel', depicted as an illegitimate pre-

---

[58]   The similarities between Isa 7:4 and Deut 20:3 do not imply that 7:4-9a is a 'war oracle' (contra Williamson 1998b: 251, note 27). Oracles of encouragement, de-pending on the circumstances, may contain different promises and admonitions. Deut 20:1-4 deals with a situation of war and promises that 'it is Yahweh your God who goes with you, to fight for you against your enemies, to give you victory', whereas in Isa 7:4-9a the situation is an evil plan, which, according to the oracle will not come true.

[59]   It is quite unlikely that Isaiah knew Rezin's political agenda in detail.

[60]   The name *ṭāb'al*, 'good for nothing', is often regarded as a Masoretic distor-tion of *ṭāb'el*, 'God is good'.

[61]   See Dearman 1996 (going back to Vanel 1974; cf. Asurmendi 1982: 53-54).

[62]   Some scholars have proposed to connect the name with the 'land of Ṭab'el' (son of Ṭab'el meaning 'someone from Ṭab'el'). They point to 'Ayanûr the Ṭabelite' (ND 2773, l. 4-5, Saggs 2001). This is problematic since no convincing explanation has been provided in what way 'the Ṭabelite' was connected with the politics of Rezin and Pekah (Dearman 1996: 37-40). Since the name *ṭb'l* is attested on various seals from monarchic Judah, Wagner (2006: 139-140, note 39) proposes that the 'son of *ṭb'l*' could have been a Judaean.

tender to the throne, the prophet presents the 'son' Immanuel as a
hopeful sign for Ahaz and his dynasty. The contrast between the two
royal figures in the prophetic words is deliberate.

The oracle 7:4-9a shares various important features with extra-
biblical prophetic oracles.[63] 1) The phrase 'fear not' (7:4). Nissinen in
his study of this phrase in ancient Near Eastern texts, refers to the difference between justified 'fear' and unjustified 'anxiety'.[64] Whereas an
individual must pay reverence to a legitimate authority, royal or divine, he should not be anxious when confronting anything that should
not be feared. The phrase 'fear not' is an exhortation to show fearless-
ness before illegitimate powers and to refrain from unjustified anxiety.[65] The phrase 'fear not' prominently occurs in the Assyrian
prophecies,[66] as encouragement in the face of the enemy, or connected
with promises for future support.[67] The phrase 'fear not' in oracles
means 'trust me': the addressee is encouraged to trust in the power
and promise of the deity and not to fear any illegitimate power.[68] The
phrase is appropriately called an 'encouraging formula'.[69] The formula
functions as a sign of the divine acceptance of the king's rule.[70] This is
also the case in the prophecy on the Zakkur Stele: 'F[e]ar not, for I
have made [you] king, [and I will st]and with [you], and I will deliver
you from all [these kings who] have forced a siege against you!'[71]

2) In order to emphasise that the enemies should not be feared, they
are ridiculed by derogatory metaphors. Isa 7:4 refers to Rezin and
Pekah as to 'these two smouldering stumps of firebrands'. In the Assyrian oracles we find comparable depictions: enemies that roll as
'ripe apples' before the king's feet (SAA 9 1 i 9'-10'), enemies as
'plotting weasels and shrews' (SAA 9 1 v 3-5), and as 'butterflies'

---

[63] Conrad (1985: 52-62) discusses Isa 7:4-9 in comparison with the prophecy on
the Zakkur Stele, the prophecy for Ashurbanipal SAA 9 7, and the dream report in
Ashurbanipal's Prism B v 63-68 (BIWA: 225). Conrad argues that in 7:4-9 Ahaz is
not ordered to become actively engaged in battle: the king must remain passive; Yahweh will fight for him.

[64] Nissinen 2003b. The phrase occurs in oracles of encouragement comparable to
7:4-9a, such as Isa 10:24, 2 Kgs 19:6 (Isa 37:6) and Hag 2:5.

[65] Nissinen 2003b: 131-132.

[66] Nissinen 2003b: 148-158.

[67] Nissinen 2003b: 149.

[68] See also Weippert 1981: 78.

[69] Nissinen 2003b: 132.

[70] Nissinen 2003b: 159.

[71] Translation from: Seow, in: Nissinen 2003a: 203-207. For a reconstruction of
the historical events referred to in the oracle, see Margalit 1994.

(SAA 9 3 iii 24).[72] Prophetic oracles make abundant use of metaphors, both in Judah and Assyria, and one category consists of contemptuous depictions of the enemy. The metaphor of 7:4 is meaningful: the pieces of wood taken from the fire are not burning, but only smouldering. This implies that one must be careful not to touch them, but also that they will extinguish soon. The image underscores the message: do not act, for soon the threat will disappear.[73]

3) An important element within prophetic oracles of encouragement is the deity's assertion that he or she is the one who acts, whereas the king has to stay, to remain quiet and to leave things to the deity.[74] Similarly, Isaiah urges Ahaz to keep quiet in view of the threat. In this context, it means not to wage war, not to undertake military activity. The urge to be careful (הִשָּׁמֵר) occurs in other oracles as well.[75] The admonition to keep quiet and not to act functions as assurance that it is the deity who governs the events. The deity takes care, the king should not fear. Similarly, Isa 7:7 implies that Yahweh will take care of the situation.

4) An important theme of the oracle is Ahaz's legitimate kingship versus the illegitimate pretension of Rezin, Pekah, and the son of ṭāb'al. The illegitimacy of the latter is implied by 7:7. Verses 5 and 6 draw a contrast between Ahaz's legitimate kingship and the illegitimate throne candidate: 'Aram has plotted evil against *you* (i.e. Ahaz)' (7:5); the enemies intend to make the 'son of Tabeel' king (7:6). It has been suggested that the conclusion of the oracle (7:8a.9a) implicitly says, 'for the head of Judah is Jerusalem, and the head of Jerusalem is the son of David'.[76] Yahweh's election of Ahaz is the reason why

---

[72] See further SAA 9 7 r. 1-2, concerning the enemies: 'I will break the thorn, I will pluck the bramble into a tuft of wool, I will turn the wasps into a squash' (Parpola's translation); and SAA 3 13 r. 9-10: 'Your ill-wishers, Ashurbanipal, will fly away like *pollen* on the surface of the water. They will be squashed before your feet like *burbillātu* insects in spring!' (Livingstone's translation).

[73] Cf. Wildberger 1972-82: 279.

[74] For examples in the Assyrian prophecies: SAA 9 2 ii 18', 'I am the one who says and does!'; 2 ii 2', '[stay] in your palace' (Parpola's restoration); perhaps 9 1 i 26'-27', 'I will rise in woe, you sit down!' (see Van der Toorn 1987: 83). See further Ištar's message (in a dream) to Ashurbanipal: 'You stay here in your place! Eat food, drink beer, make merry and praise my godhead, until I go to accomplish that task, making you attain your heart's desire.' Prism B v 63-68 (BIWA: 225); translation Nissinen 2003a: 148.

[75] 2 Kgs 6:9 (cf. 1 Sam 19:2), within a prophetic oracle as a warning to take heed in a dangerous situation. The same term occurs in an oracle quoted in Lachish ostracon 3 (see Seow in: Nissinen 2003a: 214-215).

[76] See Wildberger 1972-82: 271.

Ahaz needs not to fear.[77] This reveals a contrast between Ahaz as legitimate king, and his opponents with their illegitimate candidate. A similar contrast is present in some of the Assyrian prophecies. In SAA 9 1.8 Esarhaddon's mother Naqia contrasts the illegitimate but apparently successful half-brothers of Esarhaddon, with her own son Esarhaddon, the legitimate but so-far unsuccessful, crown prince. The Assyrian prophecies continually picture the king as the legitimate ruler,[78] whose enemies will be annihilated.

Among the characteristics of oracles of encouragement, two themes stand out as particularly important: divine legitimation of the king, and self-presentation of the deity as the principal actor in history who protects the king and takes care of his enemies.[79] Isa 7:4-9a is an oracle of encouragement, a typical response from the deity delivered through the mouth of a prophet, in a situation in which the king is severely threatened his enemies.

Isa 7:14b.16

> Look, the young woman is pregnant and is about to bear a son, and you must name him Immanuel. For before the child knows how to refuse the evil and choose the good, the land before whose two kings you are terrified will be deserted.

This oracle further encourages Ahaz. In addition to 7:4-9a, this oracle indicates the moment of Yahweh's intervention. Yahweh announces that the aggressors will be annihilated before the child knows what it wants. The moment of punishment will come fast, within a few years.[80] The situation is the same as that of 7:4-9a: Judah, and Ahaz in particular, are threatened by Rezin and Pekah. The announcement of 7:16 intensifies that of 7:7. Whereas 7:7 announces that the evil plan of the enemies to replace Ahaz will not come true, 7:16 announces

---

[77] Conrad 1985: 57.

[78] E.g. SAA 9 1 iv 5-6, 20-21, 'Esarhaddon, legitimate heir (*aplu kēnu*), son of Mullissu'.

[79] See also Wagner 2006: 130-136, who presents three Assyrian prophecies (SAA 9 1.1, 1.2, 1.6) as a counterpart to Isa 7:4-9. In Wagner's estimation (2006: 141) Yahweh functions as 'Schutzgottheit der Dynastie', as does Ištar of Arbela in the Assyrian prophecies.

[80] Irvine (1990: 163) comments: 'Isaiah meant to suggest how events and circumstances would unfold in the *imminent future* (my emphasis) and so thought of the child's development within the first year or so after his birth.' If the threat posed to Ahaz was at its height soon after the return of the Assyrians following the campaign of 734, the oracles 7:4-9a and 7:14b.16 are to be situated in late 734-733.

that the enemies, within a few years, will be punished: their land will be deserted.[81] Although their display of aggression terrifies Ahaz, soon they will be annihilated. The desertion or abandonment of the land probably refers to the deportation of the inhabitants. Rezin and Pekah planned actions that involved the land of Judah (7:6); the punishment involves their own land too.

The identity of the 'young woman' is unknown. Most likely she was Ahaz's wife, and Immanuel Ahaz's son. The name Immanuel purposefully contrasts with *ben ṭāb'al* of 7:6. Whereas *ben ṭāb'al* is the desired result of Aram's *rā'â* (7:5-6), Immanuel will choose between *ṭôb* and *rā'*. The child itself is a sign of the good news, represented by his name.[82] A further link between the oracles 7:4-9a and 14b.16 is provided by the verb קוץ: 7:6 'to terrify' (hi.); 7:16 'to be terrified' (qal). The name Immanuel is an assurance that Ahaz and his people need not fear the enemy, since Yahweh is at their side. This corresponds with the ideology expressed in the Assyrian oracles, such as the phrase: 'Fear not, Bel, Nabû and Mullissu are standing [with you]'.[83] Verse 16 announces the imminent destruction of the land of the enemies, Rezin and Pekah. Although Yahweh does not explicitly announce that he himself will punish the enemies, the implicit message of the name Immanuel is that he will take care of it. The divine promise to deal with the enemies is a prominent feature in Assyrian prophecies as well (see 4.2 below).

Isa 7:20

The announcement of 7:20 makes clear how Yahweh is going to intervene to punish Aram and Israel:

> The Lord will shave with a razor hired beyond the River the head and the hair of the feet (pubic hair), and it will take off the beard as well.

The 'razor' mentioned in this announcement denotes the Assyrian king. The Assyrian king is symbolised as a hired razor in the hand of Yahweh. This resembles to some extent the depiction of Esarhaddon

---

[81]   In 7:16, the lands of Rezin and Pekah are presented as a unity. The early material within Isa 7:1-17 (7:2-3a.4-9a, 7:14b.16) presents Aram and Ephraim as one enemy.

[82]   In 7:14a Immanuel is presented as a sign (אוֹת). In some Mari letters prophetic figures are referred to as 'signs' (*ittu*) as well (ARM 26/1 207 l. 4 and 212 r. 2').

[83]   SAA 16 60 r. 14'-15'; see also the oracle on the Zakkur Stele: '[I will st]and with [you]' (see above).

in one of the Assyrian prophecies: 'Esarhaddon, king of Assyria, cup full of lye, double-bladed axe!'[84] The Assyrian king is a deadly poison and a lethal weapon.[85] In the same prophecy Ištar addresses Esarhaddon as 'Esarhaddon, true heir, son of Mullissu, angry dagger in my hand'.[86]

Yahweh has hired the Assyrian king in order to punish Ahaz's enemies,[87] to defeat and humiliate them. The expression 'hired razor' also reveals an important difference between Isaiah's oracles and the Assyrian prophecies. Whereas Ištar takes action through the hand of her own king, Yahweh intervenes by mobilising a foreign power.[88] This role of Assyria in Isaiah's prophecies of course corresponded to the current political reality. Both in the prophecies of Isaiah (7:20; 8:1-4; 10:5-6; 28:2) and in the Assyrian royal inscriptions, the Assyrian king is represented as the agent of the divine anger.[89]

The prophecy of 8:1-4 is quite explicit about what will happen to Aram and Ephraim:

> Then Yahweh said to me, Take a large tablet and write on it in common characters, 'Maher-shalal-hash-baz.' And I took reliable witnesses, the priest Uriah and Zechariah son of Jeberechiah. And I went to the prophetess, and she conceived and bore a son. Then Yahweh said to me, Name him Maher-shalal-hash-baz; for before the child knows how to say 'father' or 'mother', the wealth of Damascus and the spoil of Samaria will be carried away by the king of Assyria.

The time-span indicated in verse 4 is again more narrowly defined than in 7:16, referring to an even more imminent future. 8:1-2 points to the public role of the prophet. The large tablet with a clearly readable saying on it was probably meant for the people in Jerusalem. The reliable witnesses were to testify afterwards that it had been a genuine prediction by Isaiah. In this way, 8:1-2 illustrates the communal aspect implied by the name Immanuel, 'God is with *us*'. The announcement

---

[84] SAA 9 1 iv 5-13.

[85] In a similar way Ashurbanipal is depicted as a battleaxe in SAA 3 26 l. 3'.

[86] This passage, which is not without difficulties, is discussed in 4.2.4.

[87] Note the difference between Isaiah's prophecies and 2 Kgs 16:7-9. According to 7:20, 8:1-4, 10:5-6 and 28:2, Assyria is Yahweh's agent, summoned to punish Judah's enemies. By contrast, according to 2 Kgs 16:7-9, Ahaz appealed to the Assyrian king to save him (rather than trusting in Yahweh), and in this way brought Judah under Assyrian rule.

[88] For the motif of hiring military forces (שׂכר), cf. 2 Sam 10:6; 2 Kgs 7:6; Jer 46:21.

[89] On the motif of the Assyrian king as the 'rod of wrath in the hand of the gods', Oded 1991: 226-227.

in 8:4 is straightforward: Damascus, the capital of Aram, and Samaria, the capital of Israel, will be captured and plundered. This refers to 7:8a.9a, where the names Damascus and Samaria are mentioned as well. The point of 7:4-9a was that the plan of Rezin and Pekah would fail: they would not be able to put another king on the throne of Jerusalem, because they were not authorised to do so. Whereas Rezin and Pekah would not be able to get into Jerusalem (7:4-9a), 8:4 announces that instead their own capital would be captured and plundered. This is again an element of retribution: what they tried to accomplish in Judah, would happen to themselves as a punishment.

An important feature of the oracles from Isa 7* and 8* is their partial repetition. The announcements of 7:7, 7:16, 7:20 and 8:4 can be read as a series. There is an element of repetition, but also an element of increasing explicitness. Step-by-step the announcements reveal how and when Yahweh is going to punish the enemies for their aggression.[90] The actions of Yahweh, furthermore, mirror the plan of the enemies: over against their throne candidate *ben ṭāb'al* stands the son Immanuel; over against their plans against Judah (7:6) stands the abandonment of their own land (7:16); over against their intention to enter Jerusalem in order to kill Ahaz, stands the spoliation of their own cities (8:4).

A final announcement to be mentioned here is 17:1b-3:

> See, Damascus is about to cease to be a city, and to become a heap of ruins. Her cities will be deserted for ever, and become places for flocks. The fortress will disappear from Ephraim, the kingdom from Damascus, says Yahweh of Hosts.

The announcement fits the circumstances of 733-732. This word specifically announces the fall of Damascus and the annexation of the land of Aram into an Assyrian province, and the conquest of Israel.

The prophecies discussed in this section were probably delivered in the period 734-732. The intended regime change in Jerusalem was not accomplished, presumably because of the arrival of the Assyrian army. Furthermore, during the campaigns of 733-732, Tiglath-pileser annexed territory from Aram and Israel, which was provincialised.

---

[90] The phenomenon of repetition occurs in the Assyrian prophecies too, albeit in a somewhat different way. The deity often refers to previous words (e.g. SAA 9 1 15'-17', 'What words have I spoken to you that you could not rely upon?'; Parpola's translation) in order to increase the reliability of the oracle at stake. The element of repetition in the prophecies of Isa 7* and 8* probably served a similar goal.

Damascus was, in all likelihood, captured and plundered in 732. The only element not fulfilled as yet was the capture and spoliation of Samaria.

The prophecies discussed here can be characterised as pro-state. The oracles assert that Yahweh governs the events. He protects his legitimate king and uses Assyria as his agent. Symbolic names underscore the prophetic message of encouragement. The prophetic material cannot be qualified as royal propaganda however. It clearly adopts concepts from royal ideology, but at the same time the prophet takes his own political position. In the situation of 734-732, he supported and admonished the king through encouraging prophecies.

4.1.3 *The Historical Events of 723-720 BCE*

Tiglath-pileser was succeeded by Shalmaneser V, who ruled for a short period (727-722). In 733, Tiglath-pileser had reduced the Kingdom of Israel to a rump state consisting of the hill country surrounding Samaria. King Hoshea initially paid tribute to Assyria but at some point acted treasonably and negotiated with a king of Egypt (2 Kgs 17:3-4).[91] Shalmaneser invaded Israel and according to the Babylonian Chronicle (i 28) 'destroyed Samaria'. This apparently refers to the capture of the city of Samaria.[92] The chronicle does not mention the year, but a dating in 723 or 722 is likely.[93] Hoshea probably was taken captive to Assyria (2 Kgs 17:4).

When Shalmaneser died in 722, Sargon seized power in a struggle for the throne. During the turbulent years of 722-720, various countries and kingdoms tried to free themselves from Assyrian rule. The Chaldean prince Merodach-baladan occupied the throne in Babylonia and made an alliance with Elam. Various Syro-Palestine kingdoms and provinces, headed by the king of Hamath, rebelled against Assyria. After Sargon had settled internal affairs in his first year, Assyrian troops fought against the Babylonian-Elamite forces in his second year. The Assyrians lost the battle,[94] and Sargon left Babylonia and

---

[91] 2 Kgs 17:4 refers to 'King So' of Egypt'. This king has been identified both as Tefnakht of Sais, Osorkon IV, and the Cushite king Piye; see Schipper 1998; Kahn 2001: 14; Younger 2002a: 290, note 4. In any case, the Egyptian ruler did not come to the rescue of Hoshea; so Schipper 1999: 153.

[92] Younger 2002a: 290; Becking 1992: 24-25; Veenhof 2001: 255.

[93] Becking (1992: 53) argues that the fall of Samaria took place in 723.

[94] See Grayson 1975a: 73: 33-35.

Elam undisturbed for some ten years.[95] In his third year Sargon was able to deal with the rebellious Syro-Palestinian kingdoms.[96] At Qarqar he defeated a coalition of rebellious provinces, including Arpad, Ṣimirra, Damascus, and Samaria, which was headed by Yau-bi'di (Ilu-bi'di) of Hamath.[97] Subsequently, Samaria was captured. After that, Sargon invaded Philistia,[98] went south and defeated an Egyptian army, which had come to the aid of Hanunu of Gaza, under the command of Re'e, the *tartānu* (commander-in-chief) of Egypt. According to a recent reconstruction of the chronology of the Cushite (25th) dynasty, this was the *tartānu* of Shabaka, the Cushite king who had come to the throne in 722/21, and had conquered Egypt in 720.[99] The suggestion that Re'e, a figure not otherwise mentioned, was the *tartānu* of the Cushite ruler of Egypt,[100] is confirmed by reliefs from Sargon's palace at Khorsabad concerning the campaign of 720 on which Cushite sol-

---

[95]   Brinkman 1984: 48-49. Sargon's next campaign against Babylonia was in 710 (Brinkman 1984: 46-60).

[96]   Dalley 1985: 33-34. It has been claimed that the Assyrian scribes antedated the fall of Samaria to Sargon's first year (721). Tadmor argues they did so for ideological reasons: the first year had to contain an important achievement (Tadmor 1958: 34-39). However, the passage from the annals on which this is based is very fragmented (Fuchs 1994: 87, Annals l. 11: [^{lú.uru}*sa-me-r*]*i-na-a-a*). Becking (1992: 39-45) argues that this passage might refer to another city.

[97]   Younger 2002a: 292; Veenhof 2001: 255; Hawkins 2004.

[98]   The conquest of the cities Gibbethon and Ekron, depicted on a relief in Sargon's palace, was part of the campaign of 720 BCE; see Uehlinger 1998: 755, 766; Russell 1999: 114-123; Younger 2003: 242-243.

[99]   Kahn 2001: 1-18, esp. 11-13. Previously, the conquest of Egypt in the second year of Shabaka, was connected with the rebellion of Iamani of Ashdod in 712 (or in 711, following Fuchs 1998: 124-131); see e.g. Kitchen 1986: 148-173. However, Sargon's Tang-i Var rock inscription published by Frame 1999, shows that Shabaka's successor Shabatka reigned as early as 706. This implies that Shabaka was king in 721-707/6. The conquest of Egypt in Shabaka's second year is to be dated to 720 (February); see Kahn 2001: 11. For the Cushite dynasty, see Morkot 2000; Schipper 1999: 199-228.

[100]   Conversely Veenhof (2001: 256), who suggests that it is the *tartānu* of Tefnakht of Sais. However, according to Kahn's chronology (2001: 18), Tefnakht had already died in 726/5. Schipper (1999: 154-157) argues that Re'e was the *tartānu* of Osorkon IV, because Sargon's Display inscription, after mentioning the defeat of Re'e, continues with a tribute brought by Arab rulers and by the Pharaoh of Egypt (referring to Osorkon IV). This argument is however inconclusive. In this episode, Sargon's Display inscription brings various different events together: the defeat of Re'e (720), and the tribute of Osorkon and various Arab rulers. The Arabs were not involved in 720, and the tribute of Osorkon IV probably dates from 716 (see 4.1.5 below).

diers are depicted.[101] According to the Assyrian account, the Egyptians were defeated, Gaza was conquered, Hanunu was deported to Assyria, and the city of Raphia on the Egyptian border was captured.[102]

The capture of Samaria was thus part of a larger military campaign.[103] Sargon claims to have deported a great number of inhabitants from the capital and the district of Samaria; one inscription mentions 27,290 deportees, another 27,280.[104] The capture of Samaria and the conquest of the land were regarded as important achievements, since the events are referred to in eight different inscriptions.

Both Shalmaneser and Sargon claim to have captured Samaria. The biblical accounts of 2 Kgs 17:3-6 and 18:9-11 describe however only one fall of Samaria. Scholars have therefore suggested either that Shalmaneser claimed to have achieved what his successor accomplished, or that Sargon took the credit for what his predecessor had done.[105] Others have proposed that Shalmaneser started the siege of Samaria in 723/22, which was concluded after his death by Sargon in 720.[106] Babylonian and Assyrian sources however refer to two different captures.[107] From 2 Kgs 17:3-4 we may infer that Shalmaneser captured Samaria in 723 or 722, and took Hoshea prisoner to Assyria. This is indirectly confirmed by Sargon's inscriptions, which mention no king of Samaria.[108] It is likely that Shalmaneser had already turned the rump state of Samaria into an Assyrian province. After Shalmaneser's death, Samaria joined a coalition of rebelling provinces, supported by Yau-bi'di of Hamath. In 720, the city was captured again, and Sargon deported a number of its inhabitants to various locations throughout the Assyrian empire.[109]

---

[101] See Franklin 1994: 264-267, with figures 3, 4, and 5; Uehlinger 1998: 749-750, 766; Kahn 2001: 12.

[102] Younger 2002a: 293; Younger 2003: 237.

[103] Younger 2002a: 291, 293.

[104] Display inscription l. 24 (Fuchs 1994: 196-197); Nimrud Prism iv 31 (Gadd 1954).

[105] See Becking 1992: 33.

[106] Galil 1996: 90-92.

[107] For the suggestion of a twofold conquest, see Tadmor 1958: 34-39; Veenhof 2001: 256; and particularly Becking 1992: 21-56.

[108] Sargon in his inscriptions is frequently designated 'conqueror of the land of Omri (or Samaria)'. Mention is made of the conquest of the country and of the deportation of the inhabitants, but not of a king of Samaria.

[109] Younger 2002a: 293-301; Becking 1992: 47-56; cf. 2 Kgs 17:6 and 2 Kgs 18:11.

The report on which 2 Kgs 17:5 and 18:10 are based presumably telescoped two different sieges, that of 723/22 and that of 720, into one three-year siege. In this way, 2 Kgs 17:3-6 and 18:9-11 combine the deeds of Shalmaneser (the captivity of Hoshea which put an end to Samaria as a kingdom) and Sargon (the deportation of Samaria's population) into an account of a single king who put an end to the Northern Kingdom. This was probably done for the sake of the story: there could only be *the* fall of Samaria.[110]

Sargon's campaign against the West in all likelihood involved action against the Kingdom of Judah too. In the Nimrud inscription Sargon describes himself as 'the subduer of (the land of) Judah, which lies far away' (*mušakniš māt Yaudu ša ašaršu rūqu*).[111] The claim that he made Judah submit does not reveal whether he did so by peaceful means or by military action.[112] Since this inscription presumably dates from 717/16, it has to refer to the campaign of 720.[113] Furthermore, one of the Nimrud letters mentions Judaean emissaries: 'the emissaries (*ṣīrānu*) of Egypt, of Gaza, of Judah, of Moab, of the Ammonites, entered Calah on the twelfth (with) their tribute (*madattu*) in their hands'.[114] The text is dated between 720 and 715,[115] and reflects Sargon's successful campaign of 720.

After the battle of Qarqar and the conquest of Samaria, the Assyrian army moved on to Philistia, where it conquered Gibbethon, Ekron, Gaza and Raphia. It is likely that Judah also became involved when the Assyrians went from Samaria to Philistia. As a result, Judah sub-

---

[110]   See Becking 1992: 56, for a similar explanation: 'In my opinion the deuteronomistic author of 2 Kgs 17:6b//18:11b, living at least a century after the events, was no longer aware of the double conquest of Samaria and consequently conflated all of the events and attributed them to one king.'

[111]   Nimrud inscription l. 8 (Winckler 1889: 168-173).

[112]   Dalley 1998: 85. The term *mušakniš* (< *kanāšu*), points to the imposition of Assyria's authority, but does not need to imply military conquest; Becking 1992: 55.

[113]   Na'aman 1994b; 1994a: 235; Frahm 1997: 231-232. I disagree with Becking (1992: 53-55), who connects the phrase of Sargon's subjugation of Judah with a campaign against Judah in 715. Becking's view is based on 2 Kgs 18:13, which dates the Assyrian military campaign against Judah in the fourteenth year of Hezekiah, which, according to Becking, was 715. However, the dating in 2 Kgs 18:13 is unreliable. According to 2 Kgs 18:2, Hezekiah reigned for 29 years; according to 2 Kgs 20:1-11, Hezekiah during a sickness coinciding with the siege of 701 was granted fifteen more years of reign; *ergo*, the campaign of Sennacherib was dated in Hezekiah's fourteenth year in 2 Kgs 18:13. This date, resulting from inner-biblical counting, cannot be trusted. Moreover, 2 Kgs 18:13 does not refer to a campaign of 715, but to the campaign of 701.

[114]   ND 2765, l. 34-39 (Saggs 2001: 219-221 = SAA 1 110); Saggs' translation.

[115]   Postgate 1974a: 118.

mitted to Assyria. It has been suggested that Isa 10:27b-32 reflects events from Sargon's campaign of 720 pertaining to Judah.[116] In my view, not only 10:27b-32, but also 10:5-15* and 10:24-25, reflect the situation of 720 (see below).

A disputed text is the so-called Azekah inscription,[117] which refers to an Assyrian assault against the Judaean city of Azekah, apparently mentions Hezekiah, and refers to a 'royal city of Philistines (Gath or Ekron),[118] which [Hezek]iah had captured and strengthened for himself'.[119] The Azekah inscription has been connected with Sargon's campaign of 720,[120] with Sargon's campaign against Ashdod in 711,[121] and with Sennacherib's campaign of 701.[122] Since the connection with 701 is the most likely,[123] I refer to this inscription under 4.1.7.

4.1.4   *Prophetic Words relating to 723-720 BCE*

Various prophetic words from First Isaiah can be connected with the events of 723-720 BCE: 14:29.31; 28:1-4; 10:5-15; 10:24-25; 10:27b-32.

Isa 14:29.31

> Do not rejoice, all you Philistines, that the rod that struck you is broken. For from the root of the snake will come forth an adder, and its fruit will be a flying fiery serpent. Wail, O gate; cry, O city; melt in fear, O Philistia, all of you! For smoke comes out of the north, and there is no straggler in its ranks.

This prophetic saying is to be dated after the events of 734-732 and before those of 723-720. The oracle reacts to the death of Tiglath-pileser in 727 BCE. Tiglath-pileser had been the first Assyrian king that invaded Philistia and proceeded as far as the border of Egypt, in 734. For this reason, he is appropriately designated as 'the rod that struck you (i.e. Philistia)'. Furthermore, with the campaigns of 733-732 he had broken the Syro-Palestinian resistance against Assyria's

---

[116]   Sweeney 1994; see also Younger 2002a: 292, and 2003: 238.
[117]   Na'aman 1974.
[118]   Younger 2002a: 238-239.
[119]   Na'aman 1974: 27.
[120]   Frahm 1997: 229-232; Fuchs 1994: 314-315.
[121]   Galil 1992: 61-63, and 1996: 98.
[122]   Na'aman 1974: 30-36, and 1994a: 245-247.
[123]   See Na'aman 1994a: 245-247; Younger 2003: 238-240.

hegemony led by Rezin of Damascus. When Tiglath-pileser died, Palestinian rulers perhaps fostered the hope that Tiglath-pileser's expansion would remain an exception. Some of them may have been ready to throw off the Assyrian yoke. This prophetic saying warns the Philistines however not to rejoice about Tiglath-pileser's death. This means that the prophecy warns against the hope that with the death of Tiglath-pileser Assyrian dominance in the region will come to an end. In reaction to this hope, the prophecy makes a clear political statement: the politics of expansion of Tiglath-pileser, reaching as far as Philistia, to the border of Egypt, will be continued by his successors. There is no reason for joy, only for lament, because the oppression will increase. The prophetic imagination already sees the Assyrian army approaching led by Tiglath-pileser's successor.

Apart from its explicit meaning, the prophecy has an implicit message. The word addressed to the Philistines implicitly warns the political leaders of Judah that the death of Tiglath-pileser does not mean that the Assyrian yoke has been broken. Similar hopes as attributed to the Philistines, may have been fostered in Judah. As in 734-732 BCE, the prophet advocates a policy of submission and rejects the anti-Assyrian politics. Shalmaneser V (727-722 BCE) who campaigned in Syria and conquered Samaria,[124] probably did not campaign against Philistia. His successor Sargon II, however, campaigned against Philistia in 720. Philistia was again submitted to Assyria and the cities Gibbethon, Ekron, Gaza and Raphia were conquered. Thus, 14:29.31 forms a prelude to the campaign of Sargon II in 720 BCE.

Isa 28:1-4

> Woe, proud garland of the drunkards of Ephraim, a fading flower is his glorious beauty, which is on the head of the fertile valley! See, the Lord has one who is mighty and strong; like a storm of hail, a destroying tempest, like a storm of mighty, overflowing waters. He hurls down to the earth with his hand, and tramples with feet the proud garland of the drunkards of Ephraim. And it will be like a first-ripe fig before the summer; whoever sees it, eats it up as soon as it comes to hand.

The 'garland', a wreath of flowers worn like a crown, probably symbolises the city of Samaria. The 'drunkards of Ephraim' represent the inhabitants of Samaria as being arrogant and overconfident. The image of drunkenness stands for being blind to reality out of misplaced self-

---

[124] Veenhof 2001: 254-255.

confidence.[125] The destruction of Samaria is announced. The agent of Yahweh, 'one who is mighty and strong', must be Assyria (cf. 7:20; 8:4; 10:5-6). Assyria will destroy Samaria and its inhabitants. As elsewhere in the prophetic oracles (e.g. 7:16 and 8:4), the promptness of the destruction is asserted (28:4).

Contrary to the prophecies connected with the events of 734-732, Samaria is no longer presented in connection with Damascus. The reason for this is that by 732 the Assyrians had dealt decisively with Damascus and Rezin, whereas Ephraim-Samaria remained a kingdom, although of a reduced size. Samaria was captured by Shalmaneser in 723/22, and by Sargon in 720. From the point of view of Isaiah's prophecies, the conquest of Samaria settled an old score. According to the announcement of 8:4, made in c. 733, the spoils of Samaria would be taken to Assyria. This finally happened in 723/22 and 720.

The word of 28:1-4 is likely to be connected with the events of 722-720, when, after Shalmaneser's death, Samaria joined a revolt against Assyria. During the revolt, led by Yau-bi'di of Hamath, the anti-Assyrian politics adopted by Samaria for some time probably appeared to be an attractive option. The prophecy of 28:1-4 however announces the disastrous outcome of this politics. The glory of Samaria is already fading away; soon Samaria will be swallowed by the Assyrians. As in the case of 14:29.31, the implicit meaning is to warn Judah against the adoption of anti-Assyrian politics. After Shalmaneser's death, for some years Assyria seemed unable to maintain its hegemony in the West. This was the moment that Samaria joined the rebellion, led by Yau-bi'di, and this probably was also the moment that the prophet Isaiah pointed out the disastrous outcome of these politics, emphasising once again that Samaria would be destroyed, and warning the Judaean politicians.

Storm and flood function as an image of destruction. Assyria is depicted with this kind of terminology elsewhere too (e.g. Isa 28:17-18). Images of natural disaster, such as storm and flood, are popular metaphors or similes for military invasions. The prophetic word is however more than a political assessment. It asserts that behind the political scene Yahweh governs the events: Yahweh orders Assyria to take action.

---

[125] See Oeming 1994: 3; cf. Job 12:24-25; Isa 19:13-14; Nah 3:11.

Whereas 28:1-4 can be regarded as a prophetic word announced during the rebellion of 722-720 BCE, the prophecies included in Isa 10* are to be interpreted as reflection on the events of 720, Sargon's campaign to the West, which also involved Judah.

Isa 10:5-15

I present Isa 10:5-15* in its earliest form, consisting of 10:5-9.15a:

> Woe, Assyria, my rod of anger, my club of fury! Against a godless nation I send him, and against the people of my wrath I command him, to take spoil and seize plunder, and to tread it down like the mire of the streets.
> But this is not what he thinks he should do, nor does this accord with his intentions, for it is in his heart to destroy, and to cut off many nations. He says:
> "Are my officials not all kings? Is not Calno like Carchemish?
> Is not Hamath like Arpad? Is not Samaria like Damascus?"
> Shall the axe vaunt itself over the one who wields it, or the saw magnify itself against the one who handles it?

This prophetic word is closely connected with the prophecies discussed above, but also adds a new perspective. On the one hand, Assyria is once again presented as Yahweh's agent, as in 7:20, 8:4, 28:1-4. Here, Assyria is presented as the agent of Yahweh sent against a 'godless nation', which refers to Ephraim/Samaria,[126] to trample it down (מִרְמָס 10:6; cf. רמס 28:3), and to take spoil and seize plunder (cf. 8:4). Assyria is ordered to carry out Yahweh's judgement against Ephraim/Samaria. Finally, the old bill has been paid off: Samaria is captured and plundered. Yahweh's commission of Assyria as formulated in 10:5-6 resembles the way Assyrian kings presented themselves as being commissioned by their god Aššur to punish the enemy and to conquer the world: '... the great Lord Aššur ... gave in my hand an 'angry sceptre' (šibirru ezzu) to smite the enemy, he entrusted me to spoil and pillage (ana ḫabāti šalāli) the land that had sinned against Aššur ... in order to expand the borders of Assyria ...'.[127] The principal difference is that Isaiah presents the powerful Assyrian king as an

---

[126] Cf. 28:1-4, where the image of the inhabitants of Samaria as being drunk points to their self-confidence and godlessness.

[127] Borger 1956: 98, Monument A r. 30-35; translation from Weinfeld 1998: 35.

agent of Yahweh, not of Aššur. This may be considered a response to Assyria's imperialistic ideology.[128]

The new perspective in 10:5-15* is Assyria's condemnation. Assyria is criticised for not behaving like an obedient rod in the hand of Yahweh, but having an agenda of its own. As described above, the conquest of Samaria was only one stage of Sargon's campaign to the West, which indeed was directed against 'many nations' (10:7).[129] The Assyrian conquest and annexation of many nations offended Yahweh.

However, why would the prophet care whether Assyria's measures against Ephraim involved many other nations as well? In my view, again Judah is implicitly present in the prophetic word. Whereas the prophecies against Philistia (14:29.31) and Samaria (28:1-4), implicitly warn the Judaeans not to yield to the temptation to adopt a politics of rebellion against Assyria, here the worldwide Assyrian conquest also involves Judah. As discussed above, Sargon's campaign of 720 affected Judah too. Certain actions made Sargon the 'subduer of the land of Judah'. Although Judah had not joined the rebellion, it became nevertheless involved, probably after the conquest of Samaria, before the invasion of Philistia. In 734, when Ahaz submitted to Assyria and paid tribute, no Assyrian army had entered Judah. In 720, probably for the first time in Judaean history an Assyrian army entered Judah.

In the previous prophetic words, Assyria's military actions were seen as having been ordered by Yahweh as a punishment for Judah's enemies (7:20; 8:1-4; 28:1-4). Judah's involvement in Assyria's military actions in 720 however led to a change of view: Assyria's expansion is condemned as a self-willed, arrogant, godless enterprise in 10:5-15*; 10:24-25; 10:27b-32.

Isa 10:24-25

> Thus says the Lord Yahweh of Hosts: O my people, who live in Zion, do not be afraid of Assyria when it beats you with a rod and lifts up its staff against you on the way to Egypt. For in a very little time the limit will be reached, and then my anger will be directed at their destruction.

---

[128] See Levine 2005: 411-427, esp. 414. I agree with Levine that material from First Isaiah from the Assyrian period in various ways reacts to the Assyrian imperialistic ideology.

[129] The series of six cities in 10:9 is to be connected with Sargon's campaign of 720; see Sweeney 1994: 466-467.

The oracle depicts Judah as suffering from Assyria's expansion while the latter marches from Phoenicia, through Philistia, along the *via maris*, to the border of Egypt. The Assyrian army took this road a number of times, but the connection with 720 is most likely.[130] First, Sargon's claim to have subdued Judah fits the expression of Assyria beating Judah with a rod and lifting up its staff against them. Moreover, the critical, negative depiction of Assyria equals that of 10:5-15* and 10:27b-32, not that of the prophecies connected with the events of 734-732. Assyria no longer is presented as Yahweh's agent sent to destroy Judah's enemies, but as a self-willed aggressor, whose aggression illegitimately affected Judah too.

The people of Jerusalem are encouraged with the typical phrase 'do not fear' (see the discussion of 7:4-9a above). As in 10:5-15*, Assyria is condemned for its behaviour toward Judah and Jerusalem in the context of its wider expansion. Once more, the emphasis on the imminence of the outcome of the announcement (cf. 7:16; 8:4; 28:4) functions as encouragement.

Isa 10:27b-32

> He has marched from [Samaria], come to Aiath, passed through Migron. At Michmash he stores his baggage. They have crossed over the pass: 'Geba will be our quarters for the night'. Ramah trembles, Gibeah of Saul has fled. Cry aloud, O Bat-Gallim! Listen, O Laishah! Answer him, O Anathoth! Madmenah is in flight, the inhabitants of Gebim flee for safety. This very day he will halt at Nob, he will shake his fist at the mount of daughter Zion, the hill of Jerusalem.

This saying refers to a military expedition of the Assyrians. Coming from Samaria, they approach Jerusalem from the north. Apparently, the army left the main road from Beth-El to Jerusalem in order to bypass fortified Mizpah, and approached Jerusalem along the central ridge.[131] This would mean that the aim was not to conquer Judah's fortified cities, but to quickly march to Jerusalem. At Nob (Mount Scopus) the army halted in order to intimidate the people of Jerusalem. The saying does not describe a huge army preparing for a siege of Jerusalem, but refers to a specific military expedition, aiming to in-

---

[130] The 'way to Egypt' refers to the coastal highway, along which Sargon in all probability marched on his way to Gaza and Raphia (see Hayes and Kuan 1991: 178).

[131] Blenkinsopp 2000a: 261; Sweeney 1994: 464; Wildberger 1972-82: 431.

timidate and quickly subjugate Jerusalem and Judah to Assyria.[132]
10:27b-32 probably describes the scene which made Sargon the 'subduer of Judah'. After the capture of Samaria, when the main army
headed for Philistia (Gaza and Raphia), Judah was involved too. Part
of the army quickly marched to Jerusalem, not to lay siege to it, but to
intimidate, to collect tribute, and to remind its king and leaders of Assyria's hegemony.

In 14:29.31 Isaiah announced that the Assyrian rule of Philistia
would not end with the death of Tiglath-pileser, but that his succes-
sor(s) would strengthen the bonds of Assyria's dominance. In 28:1-4
he announced that Yahweh would take action against Samaria through
the hand of the Assyrians. Both came true with the campaign of Sargon in 720. However, Sargon did not only conquer Samaria and secure Assyria's control over the Mediterranean seaports, but also
subdued Judah, with a display of power and intimidation. This provoked the question: If Assyria is Yahweh's agent, why then is Judah
also affected? The three prophetic words of Isa 10* can be read as attempts to solve this difficulty. 10:5-15* distinguishes between the
conquest ordered by Yahweh and the program of expansion set up by
Assyria itself. The point of 10:5-15* is that Sargon's conquest of Ephraim and Samaria was justified, whereas his submission of Judah was
illegitimate, against the will of Yahweh. 10:24-25 and 10:27b-32 furthermore criticise Assyria's display of aggression against Judah, and
10:25 makes explicit what was already implied in the *woe* of 10:5-
15*: Yahweh is going to punish Assyria. Although one could argue
that this announcement did not exactly come true, the violent death of
Sargon in 705 (see 4.1.7 below) in all likelihood added to the credibility of the prophet. At last, Yahweh had punished Sargon for his display of aggression against Judah and Jerusalem.[133]

---

[132]   Sweeney 1994: 464-465.
[133]   I would suggest connecting the earliest expansion of 10:5-15*, namely the rhetorical, literary additions of 10:13-14 and 15b to the original word of 10:5-9.15a (see
chapter 2.3.2), with the death of Sargon II in 705. The additions of 10:13-14.15b emphasise the hubris of the Assyrian king, and hence allude to his downfall. Furthermore, 10:13-14 contains motifs that react to the Assyrian royal ideology, e.g. the
motif of the removal of boundaries in 10:13 (see Machinist 1983a: 725); cf. also the
prophecy SAA 9 2.3, where Ištar of Arbela promises: 'I will abolish the boundaries of
all the lands and give them to you' (ii 15'-16').

4.1.5   The Historical Events of 716-711 BCE

Sargon consolidated Assyria's hegemony in the West and secured Assyria's trade interest. In 716, Assyrian forces marched to the Philistine coast. Sargon, in one of his inscriptions, states: 'I opened the sealed-off harbour of Egypt, mixed Assyrians with Egyptians and let them trade with each other.'[134] Sargon subjected territories as far as 'the city of the river of Egypt' and established an Assyrian trade colony near Gaza.[135] With the Assyrian army nearby, the Egyptian ruler Osorkon IV (Shilkani) presented a gift (*tāmartu*) consisting of 'twelve great horses whose like did not exist in Assyria'.[136] During Sargon's reign, the international trade with Egypt and Greece flourished. At this period, Judah cooperated with the Assyrians. Judah played a role in the international trade, and the Assyrians apparently felt free to send troops and traders down through Judah and through Philistine territory.[137] Despite their trading relations, the interest of dominating Philistia and Phoenicia kept a potential conflict between Assyria and the Cushite rulers of Egypt alive.

Troubles occurred in the Philistine city of Ashdod. According to Sargon's inscriptions, King Azuri of Ashdod planned rebellion and incited neighbouring kings against Assyria. Apparently without much result, for Sargon states that he replaced Azuri with Ahimiti, his brother.[138] This probably happened in 716 or 715.[139] The citizens of

---

[134]   See Kahn 2001: 9.

[135]   Both Tiglath-pileser (ITP: 178) and Sargon (Fuchs 1994: 88) claim to have set up trading stations on the border of Egypt, and to have appointed local Arabs to take charge of the operations.

[136]   Fuchs 1998: 28-29; see Younger 2003: 240. This gift illustrates the competition between the Cushites and the Assyrians. When the Cushite king Piye defeated the Egyptian rulers in 734, they brought him their finest horses as a mark of his lordship (see the stele of Piye, in: TUAT I/4: 570-571). Osorkon IV was one of them. After Shabaka's conquest of Egypt in 720, Osorkon IV was a vassal of Shabaka. In 716, however, he gave a similar gift of fine horses to Sargon, which marked his transfer to a new overlord. See Kahn 2001: 9; Schipper 1999: 156-157. Another Assyrian text mentions that 'Pir'ū, king of Egypt' sent a tribute of gold and precious stones to Sargon; this is also likely to be Osorkon IV, and this tribute is dated to 716 (Tadmor 1958: 78) or 715 (Fuchs 1998: 131).

[137]   Dalley 2004a: 389. For the relations between Judah and Assyria in this period, see Saggs 2001: 219-221 (ND 2765, l. 34-38) and 128 (ND 2608). A contingent of Judaean soldiers fought at the side of the Assyrians in a campaign against Urartu; see Dalley 2004a: 288.

[138]   Annals, l. 241-245 (Fuchs 1994: 132-133), Great Summary inscription, l. 90-93 (Fuchs 1994: 219).

[139]   Younger 2002a: 312-313.

Ashdod however did not accept Aḫimiti as their king and instead appointed a man called Iamani. This man, referred to in the Assyrian
texts as *ḫupšu*, 'a commoner', led a rebellion against Sargon, sometime between 715 and 712. According to Sargon's Nineveh prism, the
Ashdodites tried to muster support from local rulers and from 'Pir'ū',
presumably Shabaka, of Egypt.[140] They sent good-will gifts to Shabaka, and implored his alliance:

> To the k[ings] of the lands of Philistia, Judah, Edom and Moab, (and to
> those) who live at the sea, those who are (all) indebted to pay tribute
> and gifts to Aššur, my Lord, <they sent> (letters full of) deceitful and
> malicious words, to antagonise them against me. To Pharaoh, king of
> Egypt, a king that could not save them (*malku lā mušēzibīšunu*), they
> brought (*našû*) their goodwill gifts (*šulmānu*),[141] and kept imploring him
> for assistance (*erēšu kitra*).[142]

Iamani's reliance on Egypt, misplaced from the Assyrian point of
view, is described in ideological terminology. The rebels implored a
powerful king for assistance, offering him a payment for military aid
against Assyria. Sargon dealt with the rebellion of Ashdod in 712 or
711. Isa 20:1 says that Sargon sent his *tartānu*, which may imply that
he himself stayed in Assyria. This has been connected with a note in
the Eponym Chronicle, saying that the king stayed in the land in
712.[143] However, this may be unfounded, as the statement that the king
stayed in the land probably means that no campaign was conducted at
all. The campaign against Ashdod is therefore to be dated to 711.[144] Isa
20:1 nevertheless could be right that Sargon himself did not join the
campaign, but sent his *tartānu*. The Nineveh prism relates that Sargon
sent his troops on a military expedition to Ashdod; it is only in his
later inscriptions that Sargon claims that he personally went to Ashdod

---

[140] For the text see Fuchs 1998: 44-46 and 73-74. Kahn (2001: 4) and Younger
(2002a: 313-314) identify Pir'ū as Shabaka. Conversely, Fuchs (1998: 131) argues
that Pir'ū sending tribute in 715 (Shilkani/Osorkon IV) must be the same Pir'ū referred to here. However, the Assyrian texts refer to Shilkani/Osorkon IV as to Pir'ū in
the context of his paying tribute in order to demonstrate that the legitimate ruler of
Egypt submitted to Assyria. The Cushite rulers however had adopted this title too, so
that in the context of Iamani's request to Egypt, the Cushite king may very well be referred to as Pir'ū.

[141] The word *šulmānu/šulmannu* 'goodwill gifts' is often used with the connotation of 'bribe, inducement'.

[142] Translation based on Fuchs 1998: 44-46, 73-74 (fragment VIIb).

[143] For the Eponym Chronicle, see Millard 1994: 47, 60.

[144] Fuchs 1998: 83-87.

in order to end the rebellion.[145] From the Assyrian inscriptions it appears that Iamani at the approach of the Assyrian army fled to the border of Egypt and Ethiopia, where he received asylum from Shabaka. The Assyrians conquered Ashdod, Gath and Ashdod-Yam and turned them into an Assyrian province governed by Assyrian officials.[146] In 706, Shabatka (Shebitku), who had succeeded Shabaka, extradited Iamani and handed him over to the Assyrian king.[147] The Ashdod stele,[148] erected in Ashdod after the conquest of 711 BCE (and apparently destroyed during the anti-Assyrian revolt that broke out after Sargon's death in 705 BCE)[149] testifies to the Assyrian conquest of Ashdod.[150]

In Sargon's Nineveh prism, quoted above, Judah is mentioned in relation to the rebellion of Iamani. Apparently, Iamani had taken diplomatic efforts to incite local rulers, among them Hezekiah of Judah, to join his rebellion against Assyria. From the description in the Assyrian sources however it seems that neither the surrounding kings nor the Cushite king of Egypt actually came to his assistance. Apparently, Shabaka did not send him military aid, though he granted him asylum. There is no evidence of Assyrian measures taken against Judah in this period. This suggests that Hezekiah was not persuaded by the Ashdodite envoys to join the rebellion, and that the Assyrians had as yet no reason to take action against Judah.[151]

4.1.6   *Prophetic Material relating to 716-711 BCE*

The information that Sargon's *tartānu* undertook the campaign rather than Sargon himself (Isa 20:1) may be reliable.[152] Iamani had taken efforts to involve Egypt in his rebellion. Since the Cushite ruler of Egypt would be a powerful helper, it may have appeared an attractive

---

[145]   Great Summary inscription, l. 97-101 (Fuchs 1994: 348).

[146]   Great Summary inscription, l. 104-109 (Fuchs 1994: 220-221); Younger 2002a: 315.

[147]   See Sargon's Tang-i Var rock inscription; Frame 1999. The inscription confirms that Iamani was handed over to Assyria in 706, and identifies the Cushite king who extradited him as Shabatka (Shebitku). For the implications for the chronology of the Cushite dynasty, see Kahn 2001.

[148]   For the Ashdod stele, see Tadmor 1971.

[149]   Tadmor 1971: 192-195; Kapera 1976: 91-92.

[150]   Tadmor (1971: 195-197) assumed that the stele dealt with the Ashdod revolt and interpreted fragments I and III in this light. For fragment II, see Kapera 1976: 93.

[151]   So also Na'aman 1994a: 240; Younger 2003: 242-243.

[152]   Fuchs 1998: 45-46.

option for the Judaeans to join the rebellion. However, as far as we
know, Hezekiah did not join the rebellion, in agreement with Isaiah's
position.

Isaiah's symbolic action reported in Isa 20* predicted the Assyrian
victory over Egypt and Cush. Isaiah's appearing naked and barefoot
depicted the Cushites and Egyptians being taken away by Assyria as
deportees and captives. The report of Isa 20* is reliable for several
reasons. First, we know of other eye-catching public performances
with a symbolic meaning carried out by prophetic figures.[153] Second,
the crudeness of the act may suggest that the report of Isa 20* became
part of the Isaiah tradition at an early stage. Third, the message of Isa
20* resembles that of the prophecies relating to the period 705-701
BCE (see 4.1.8 below). The image of the captive Egyptians and
Cushites being led away barefoot and naked corresponds with the depiction of deportations of inhabitants of conquered cities and defeated
enemies on Assyrian reliefs.[154] Isaiah's symbolic action depicts the
Egyptians and Cushites in the context of the Ashdod rebellion. Yet it
is meant as a lesson for a different group of people, as appears from
20:5: 'And they shall be dismayed and confounded because of Cush
their hope and of Egypt their boast.' Who are the people that will be
dismayed and confounded? In my view, there are two possibilities.
They may be the leaders from Judah that regarded rebellion against
Assyria as an attractive option. Or they may be the political leaders of
Ashdod who sought the assistance of the Cushite king of Egypt (see
20:1). In the latter case, the implicit message would still be one for the
Judaeans: trusting in the Cushite king of Egypt against Assyria is
pointless.

4.1.7 *The Historical Events of 705-701 BCE*

Sargon's disgraceful death in 705 BCE on the battlefield in Anatolia
caused consternation in Assyria and led to revolts throughout the empire. The Chaldean prince Merodach-baladan returned to Babylon and
took the throne in 703. Although his reign lasted for nine months only,
he assembled some powerful allies, including Elam and several Arab

---

[153] An example is found in the report in the Mari letter ARM 26/1 206: a prophet
(*muḫḫû*) of Dagan devours a raw lamb in front of the city gate.
[154] See Oded 1979: 34-35, for examples of Assyrian reliefs on which captives or
deportees are pictured as being led away barefoot and/or naked.

tribes.[155] If the story of 2 Kgs 20:12-19 has a base in history, it is best situated in this period.[156] Among Western rulers, the rebellion seems to have been widespread. In the inscriptions of Sennacherib concerning 701, eight Western kings are mentioned that paid fourfold to Assyria, which indicates that they had stopped paying tribute after the death of Sargon and thus joined the revolt against Assyria. In addition to these eight kings, Lulî of Sidon and Tyre, Ṣidqā of Ashkelon, and Hezekiah of Judah, are mentioned as the rulers that persisted in their rebellion when the Assyrian army arrived in 701.

In Hezekiah's perspective, the time was ripe for throwing off the Assyrian yoke. First of all, the problems for Assyria seemed to be great, with so many rulers revolting supported by strong allies. Second, according to the thinking of the time, Sargon's violent death and the loss of his body which was not properly buried, showed that the gods had reversed Assyria's good fortune.[157] Third, the Cushite rulers of Egypt were ready to intervene in Palestinian affairs.[158] In all likelihood, Hezekiah had concluded an alliance with them to support him with military aid. Fourth, Hezekiah had much to gain by rebellion. At this time, the Kingdom of Judah had become relatively important, and Hezekiah was a strong king within the region. Hezekiah acted as overlord of Ekron, and perhaps of other Philistine cities as well, and presumably controlled part of the trade from Egypt via Philistia.[159] The huge punitive tribute Hezekiah was forced to pay in 701, indicates that Hezekiah had amassed a great wealth.[160]

---

[155] Brinkman 1984: 57.

[156] Na'aman 1994a: 244; Brinkman 1984: 57, note 268.

[157] Dalley (2004a: 391) even suggests that Sargon's disgraceful death excused his vassals from their oaths of loyalty. Because of the loss of his body, Sargon did not receive a proper royal burial. This was regarded a divine curse because of some grave offence committed by Sargon. Sargon's son Sennacherib distanced himself from his father in various respects: he replaced Sargon's new capital Dur-Sharukkin by Nineveh as the royal capital, and he was hesitant to present himself as Sargon's son in his inscriptions; see Frahm 1999: 82-83.

[158] See Schipper 1999: 217, for a general assessment of the Cushite interests in intervening in Palestine.

[159] Dalley 2004a: 393.

[160] Dalley (1998; 2004a) suggests that the Davidic dynasty was related by marriage to the Assyrian royal house. According to Dalley, the Assyrian queens Yabâ and Atalyā (or Atalia), the consorts of Tiglath-pileser III and Sargon II respectively, found at Nimrud (see Damerji 1999) are to be identified as Judaean princesses. The difficulties involved in this suggestion have been discussed by Younger 2002b and Achenbach 2002 (cf. also Frahm 2000: 492-493; 2002: 1114; Radner 1999: 433). Furthermore, Judah's political history of the late eighth century can be plausibly reconstructed without assuming a marital relationship between the Davidic dynasty and the

Sennacherib dealt with the revolt in the West in 701. The Assyrian version of the events is found in several inscriptions.[161] The information offered by these inscriptions must however be handled with care. First, the account does not present a chronological report of the events, but has a geographical, or topical, arrangement.[162] Second, the triumphal tone of the texts gives the impression that the campaign was successful in every respect and that Sennacherib completely mastered the situation. On closer reading however we find indications that Sennacherib experienced serious opposition and was obliged to negotiate on several occasions. The Assyrian inscriptions present the following geographical-topical sequence (references are to the Chicago Prism).[163]

Episode	Inscriptions
1	Dealings with Lulî of Sidon (ii 37-49)
2	Eight Western kings pay homage (ii 50-60)
3	Ṣidqā of Ashkelon captured and deported to Assyria (ii 60-68)
4	Conquest of territory north of Ashkelon (ii 68-72)
5	Dealings with Ekron (ii 73-iii 17) a. Nobles who had delivered Padî to Hezekiah ask Egypt-Cush for help b. Egyptian-Cushite army comes and is defeated near Eltekeh c. Eltekeh and Timnah conquered, nobles of Ekron executed d. Padî restored on throne
6	Dealings with Hezekiah (iii 18-49) a. 46 Judaean cities conquered, huge booty taken b. Hezekiah enclosed in Jerusalem c. Parts of Judaean territory given to Philistine kingdoms d. Hezekiah pays a huge tribute

---

Assyrian royal house. To mention the two most important cases, the events of 734-733 and the events of 701: 1) Dalley (1998: 88) comments with regard to the loyalty oath which Ahaz probably swore in 734: 'This oath-enforced bond, quite apart from the question of marriage alliances, explains why Judah did not resist Assyria, nor join Samaria and Damascus in their bid for independence'. 2) With regard to 701, Dalley (1998: 97) comments: 'Atalyā was almost certainly the mother of Sennacherib. If she was a Judaean directly related to Hezekiah, we have a special explanation for the tolerance shown to Hezekiah and to the cult of Yahweh by both Sargon and Sennacherib.' However, this special explanation is not necessary. Sennacherib's dealing with Judah in 701 was not exceptional: there are examples of similar practice 'especially in regions which lay just beyond provinces directly governed' (Dalley 1998: 92; cf. 97-98).

[161] For the Assyrian texts in transcription and translation, see Mayer 2003: 186-200.

[162] Knauf 2003: 142.

[163] For a commentary on the six episodes of the campaign, see Gallagher 1999: 91-142.

A historical reconstruction of the campaign results in a slightly different picture. The first target of the campaign was Sidon. The rebellious
king Lulî fled to Cyprus, and his capital it is claimed was conquered
without a fight. Sennacherib installed Ittobaal as the new king. The
rulers from Samsimuruna, Sidon, Arwad, Byblos, Ashdod, Ammon,
Moab and Edom, visited Sennacherib at Ushu (Old Tyre) and paid
homage.[164] The inscriptions state that the eight Western kings brought
'sumptuous gifts (and) their heavy greeting-presents fourfold'.[165] This
indicates these kings had withheld their tribute since the death of Sargon in 705, and now had to pay up for the past years.[166] Although they
had joined the revolt, Sennacherib offered them the opportunity to
submit and to avert an Assyrian invasion. This lenient attitude
benefited Sennacherib in various ways. The submission of these kings
meant that he had their armies at his disposal, it isolated the rulers per-
sisting in their rebellion, such as Hezekiah and Ṣidqā of Ashkelon, and
it saved the Assyrian army time.[167]

The next stage was the invasion of Philistia. The Assyrians conquered the coastal region ruled by Ashkelon, the largest and most
powerful Philistine kingdom at that time.[168] Ṣidqā, king of Ashkelon,
had refused to submit to Sennacherib at Ushu. Since the conquest of
Ashkelon itself is not claimed in the Assyrian inscriptions, the conquest of Ashkelon's northern territory was apparently enough to effectuate the surrender of Ṣidqā and his family. They were not killed, but
deported to Assyria. Presumably, the Ashkelonite king, realising that
his refusal to submit in Ushu had made his position impossible, surrendered after negotiations.[169]

It is difficult to decide what happened next. According to Knauf's
reconstruction the Assyrians bypassed Ekron and marched on to Tim-
nah, which was probably in Judaean hands. He suggests that Ekron
was not much of a threat to the Assyrians and that it was enough for
the moment to cut off the rebels from their Judaean ally.[170] This is possible, although it cannot be excluded that the Assyrians already at this
point had conquered Ekron and executed the rebellious nobles. What

---

[164] Mayer 2003: 175.
[165] Translation from Mayer 2003: 188.
[166] Gallagher 1999: 106-110.
[167] Gallagher 1999: 105-112.
[168] Knauf 2003: 142.
[169] Gallagher 1999: 127.
[170] Knauf 2003: 144.

seems certain, however, is that the remark of the reinstallation of Padî as king of Ekron (episode 5d, above) runs ahead of the events. It is highly unlikely that Hezekiah released his prisoner before the Assyrians had put him under severe pressure.[171]

The Assyrians invaded Judah and conquered 46 cities in the Shephelah and the Negev, including Lachish, where the Assyrian king had his headquarters. The conquest of the Judaean city of Azekah, as described in the Azekah inscription is best situated during this campaign as well.[172] The Assyrian inscriptions present the conquest of Judah as the climax of the campaign. A close reading indicates however that Sennacherib's victory was incomplete. There is a mysterious gap between episode 6a-b and episode 6c-d. Evidently, a great part of Judah was ravaged by the Assyrian army and massive booty was taken from the conquered areas (episode 6a).[173] Furthermore, Jerusalem was not besieged with attack and storming, but blockaded with several forts.[174] The goal of a blockade was to force the city to submission through starvation.[175] However, the fall of the city is not claimed. Episode 6c and 6d, instead, deal with the aftermath of Sennacherib's campaign: parts of Judah's territory were given to the Philistine kingdoms, and Hezekiah *afterwards* sent a huge punitive tribute to Nineveh. What is missing is the surrender of Hezekiah. Apparently, Hezekiah did not come to Lachish to do obeisance and present his tribute, but stayed in Jerusalem.[176] Only at the last moment did he accept submitting a huge tribute to Sennacherib, which was sent to Nineveh afterwards. The explanation that the king travelled faster than

---

[171] Knauf 2003: 144.

[172] For the inscription, also referred to as Sennacherib's Letter to God, see Na'aman 1974. Na'aman (1994a: 245-247) persuasively argues that the Azekah inscription refers to the campaign of 701. Similarly Mayer 2003: 170. Na'aman accepts that the Philistine city mentioned in this text is Ekron (not Gath).

[173] The Assyrian account claims that Sennacherib took a huge number of people and animals from Judah (205,105). Mayer (2003: 182) suggests this sum includes both people and cattle taken from all conquered territories, in Philistia and Judah. Others have suggested that something is wrong with the number.

[174] Mayer 2003: 179-181; Van der Kooij 1986: 97-98.

[175] See Gallagher 1999: 133-134, for examples. Mayer 2003: 181: 'Ultimately, the effects of building such forts were similar to the effects of full-scale siege but without the costs.'

[176] Gallagher (1999: 141) observes that the later Bulls inscriptions 1, 2, and 3 claim that Hezekiah submitted at Sennacherib's feet. This reflects the Assyrian ideal of a vassal's behaviour, but does not provide a reliable depiction of the historical events.

the tribute caravan,[177] is inadequate; the claim that Hezekiah sent tribute *after* Sennacherib had returned, is unique in the Assyrian inscriptions:[178]

> This Hezekiah, the fearsome splendour of my rule overwhelmed him, and he sent the Urbi[179] and his elite troops, which he had stationed in Jerusalem, his royal city, as reinforcement and had acquired as help, together with 30 talents of gold, 800 talents of silver, (... etc.), and also his (own) daughters, his palace women, singers male and female, after me to Nineveh, my royal city.[180]

The circumstances of Hezekiah's surrender are unknown. Although Jerusalem was not captured, Hezekiah gave in and sent his tribute to Nineveh. I suggest connecting Hezekiah's surrender with the outcome of the battle of Eltekeh. In the Assyrian account, the battle of Eltekeh is interwoven with the dealings with Ekron (episode 5) and positioned *before* the conquest of Judah. This has to do with the geographical-topical arrangement of the inscription: Phoenicia – Philistia – Judah. Furthermore, it makes for a better finale: Hezekiah's huge punitive tribute bestows more glory and honour on Sennacherib than the close victory at Eltekeh and negotiations at Ekron.[181] The Assyrian account only blames the nobles of Ekron for their alliance with Egypt.[182] Historically, this is unlikely, since Hezekiah, who held Padî captive in Jerusalem, acted as Ekron's overlord.[183]

The presentation of the events of episode 5 in the Assyrian account is not historically reliable.[184] If the Egyptian army had been in Philistia

---

[177]   Mayer 2003: 181.
[178]   Gallagher 1999: 132.
[179]   The meaning of [lú]*Urbi* is uncertain. Mayer (2003: 183-184) suggests reading *ubri* (metathesis), 'strangers', here: 'mercenaries'. Gallagher (1999: 136) mentions a suggestion of Tadmor: a West-Semitic derivation, ארב 'to lie in ambush', hence 'ambushers'. Elat (2000) takes up the earlier view that they are Arabs. As he points out, Merodach-baladan of Babylon was allied with certain Arab tribes ([lú]*Urbi* occur among the allies of Babylonia in the inscription of Sennacherib's campaign of 703; Luckenbill 1924: 25:1, 39-42, 54:52, 57:12). It is possible that Merodach-baladan's Arab allies cooperated with Hezekiah as well.
[180]   Chicago iii 37-49; Taylor iii 29-41. This translation follows Gallagher 1999: 136-140, and Borger, in: TUAT I: 390. The translation given by Mayer 2003: 189-190 ('... the Urbi and his elite troops ... ceased their services [*iršû baṭlāti*]. Together [*itti*] with 30 talents of gold, ..., he also sent his daughters ...'), has been proved wrong by Gallagher 1999: 136-140.
[181]   Knauf 2003: 144.
[182]   Gallagher 1999: 127.
[183]   Cf. Knauf 2003: 144.
[184]   Contra Gallagher 1999: 123-125.

before the Assyrians arrived, Ashkelon's king Ṣidqā would probably not have surrendered.[185] Furthermore, if the battle of Eltekeh had taken place at the point where it is put in the Assyrian account, Hezekiah's army would have joined the battle as well. It is thus more likely that the Egyptian army arrived later. They came to the aid of Hezekiah and Ekron; the arrival of the Egyptian army meant a relief for Hezekiah: the conquest of Judah was abandoned and his surrender postponed.[186]

Sennacherib claims to have defeated the Egyptians, but the wording of the inscriptions suggests it was a close victory. The victory is described in dry phrases, 'I fought with them and I defeated them', and instead of describing the pursuit and annihilation of the enemy forces, the inscription continues with the capture of two unimportant towns. This suggests that the battle ended in a close victory.[187] It was followed by negotiations, which took place near Ekron. Sennacherib showed no mercy to the nobles of Ekron: they were executed. After the retreat of the Egyptians, Hezekiah at last was forced to submit. As a result, Padî returned from Jerusalem and was reinstalled on the throne in Ekron. The Philistine kingdoms Gaza, Ekron, Ashdod received parts of Judah's territory.[188] Hezekiah had to pay a huge punitive tribute. The Assyrian army withdrew from the area, and Hezekiah's tribute was sent after Sennacherib to Nineveh. The outcome of 701 was disastrous for Judah.[189] Although Sennacherib's campaign was less easy-going than the inscriptions may suggest, the campaign certainly was effective.[190]

The biblical story concerning 701 in 2 Kgs 18:13-19:37 reflects a later view. It has been argued that 2 Kgs 18:13-19:37 can be read as an ongoing story, whose coherence is marked by the motif of the 'return' or 'withdrawal' of the Assyrian king.[191] This coherence does however not change the view that the composition is based on three

---

[185] So Knauf 2003: 144.
[186] My reconstruction largely agrees with that of Veenhof (2001: 266-267) and Knauf (2003).
[187] Gallagher 1999: 121; Knauf 2003: 146-147.
[188] This is sometimes explained as a reward for their loyalty, but it is more likely that Sennacherib, from a policy of 'divide and rule', strengthened the Philistine kingdoms at Judah's cost.
[189] According to Stern (2001: 130), all territory south of Jerusalem and the settlements in the Shephelah and the Negev were destroyed. See also Knauf 2003: 146; Mayer 2003: 184.
[190] Na'aman 1991a: 96.
[191] Van der Kooij 2000: 109.

different parts, conventionally referred to as A (18:13-16), B1 (18:17-
19:9a.36-37), and B2 (19:9b-35).[192] Whereas part A (18:13-16) is
based on an early historical report, B1 (18:17-19:9a.36-37) is a later
story, to be situated in the seventh century. Finally, B2 (19:9b-35) is a
later extension to the B1-story,[193] dating from the exilic period.[194]

2 Kgs 18:13-16 (part A) is based on an early report and contains
historical information. 1) Sennacherib captured the fortified cities of
Judah, but not Jerusalem. 2) Hezekiah was forced to submit. 3) Hezekiah paid a huge punitive tribute. The payment mentioned in 2 Kgs
18:14 partly corresponds to that of the Assyrian account. The early account does not conceal the fact that Hezekiah had brought Judah into a
disastrous situation: Judah's cities were captured, Hezekiah admitted
he had sinned, i.e. broken his loyalty oath by rebelling against Assyria, and the treasures, not only from the palace but also from the
temple were handed over to the Assyrian king.[195]

The first narrative account B1 (2 Kgs 18:17-19:9a.36-37) contains
various elements that reflect its retrospective character. It concludes
with the murder of Sennacherib (19:37), which happened in 681
BCE.[196] Furthermore, Taharqa is referred to as 'king of Cush' (19:9),
whereas he reigned from 689-664.[197] The story is to be understood
from its conclusion: the murder of Sennacherib. The narrative explains
Sennacherib's murder as Yahweh's wrath for the offence committed
by this king against Jerusalem.[198] Although the story presents a later,
seventh-century, perspective on 701, it may testify to some important
historical elements: at the moment Judah was invaded by the Assyrian
army and Jerusalem threatened, Hezekiah still counted on Egypt's assistance (see the speech of the Rabshakeh, 2 Kgs 18:21-24); and the

---

[192]   See Van der Kooij 2000: 108; Gonçalves 1986.
[193]   Van der Kooij 1986: 107-108.
[194]   Na'aman 2000; 2003.
[195]   The early account has been adapted in several ways. First, the dating in 18:13
is secondary (see note 113 above). Second, the moment of Hezekiah's surrender,
while Sennacherib was at Lachish, may be questioned, since this is not mentioned in
the Assyrian royal inscriptions. This element probably resulted from the inclusion of
part A in the ongoing composition of 18:13-19:37.
[196]   For this story, see chapter 6.1.2.
[197]   See Van der Kooij 2000: 113-116.
[198]   Van der Kooij 2000: 118.

Assyrian invasion of Judah was broken off when the news arrived that
Taharqa was coming with his army (2 Kgs 19:8-9a.36).[199]

The suggestion that Sennacherib reacted remarkably leniently to
Hezekiah's rebellion has to be reconsidered. Sennacherib's dealings
with the Kingdom of Judah were not lenient at all. Lachish and many
other cities were ravaged and plundered and many people were deported to Assyria. Hezekiah personally received milder treatment, but
he had to pay a huge price for his life and throne. Hezekiah's treatment is not without parallel. Rebellion of a ruler otherwise known as a
loyal vassal was sometimes regarded as an incident, a once-only mistake, for which the ruler was punished but not executed. This happened particularly in regions that lay just beyond directly governed
provinces.[200] From Ahaz's submission in 734 onwards, Judah had not
caused any trouble to Assyria. The Judaean kings were probably regarded as loyal vassals, and Hezekiah got away with a severe punishment, a reduction of land and a huge payment, but saved his life and
throne.

The depiction of Hezekiah in the Assyrian inscriptions has to be
understood from this outcome of the events. Since he had not been
executed as a rebel but stayed on the throne, the Assyrian inscriptions
do not depict him as a rebel. Instead of accusing him of breaking the
loyalty oath, he is described as 'Hezekiah, who did not submit to my
yoke'.[201] Various later inscriptions even seem to present Hezekiah as a
king that was subdued for the first time: 'I overthrew a vast district,
the land of Judah, and the strong and mighty Hezekiah, its king, I
made submit at my feet and he pulls my yoke'.[202] Hezekiah for the rest
of his reign remained submissive to Assyria; his successor Manasseh
is depicted in Assyrian sources as a loyal vassal.[203]

---

[199] According to this reconstruction, the 'report' (or 'rumour') of the arrival of the
Egyptian army (2 Kgs 19:7) was not fake, but sound, as is usually the case in the biblical historical books (1 Sam 2:24; 1 Sam 4:19; 2 Sam 4:4; 1 Kgs 2:28; 10:7).

[200] Dalley 1998: 92.

[201] Chicago Prism iii 18-19; Mayer 2003: 187, 189.

[202] Gallagher (1999: 130, note 13) argues that Hezekiah in these later inscriptions
(Bull inscriptions) is qualified as *šepṣu mitru* 'strong and tough' rather than *šepṣu
bēru* 'a notorious rebel' (cf. Mayer 2003: 194). Gallagher (1999: 142, note 71) points
out that the qualification *šepṣu mitru* 'strong and tough' only occurs in the inscriptions
of Sennacherib and that it refers to peoples that had not yet been subdued by Assyria.

[203] Some indications of Judah's pro-Assyrian attitude after 701 can be mentioned.
1) On a sculpture from Sennacherib's palace in Nineveh some soldiers, likely to be
Judaeans, are depicted among the royal bodyguard (Barnett 1998: I, 135 and II, 484).
This implies that the Judaeans were regarded as reliable allies (Dalley 2004a: 391-

4.1.8   *Prophetic Words relating to 705-701 BCE*

Many of the prophecies from First Isaiah that can be dated to the eighth century, relate to the circumstances of 705-701 BCE. This is sufficiently clear for 28:7b-10; 28:15-18; 29:15; 30:1-5*; 30:6-8; 31:1.3a, and also likely for 18:1-2; 19:1b-4; and 22:15-18. I will argue that the *woe*-sayings of 5:8-23* and 10:1-2 are also to be connected with this period.

The historical situation of 705-701 is of great importance for the understanding of these prophetic words. In Jerusalem, a controversy was going on as to whether or not to adopt a policy of rebellion against Assyria while relying on help from Egypt. At some point Hezekiah concluded an alliance with the Cushite king of Egypt, to support Judah in a revolt against Assyria. The Assyrian inscriptions accuse the leaders of Ekron of concluding an anti-Assyrian alliance with Egypt. However, Hezekiah acted as overlord of Ekron, since Ekron's king Padî had been taken prisoner to Jerusalem. This implies that Judah was involved in the alliance with Egypt too.[204] Prophetic words from Isaiah, connected with 705-701, reflect the policy of rebellion adopted by Judah and the diplomatic efforts Judah made to conclude an alliance with the Cushite overlords of Egypt (30:6-8; 30:1-2; 31:1.3a; 28:15-18). As argued above, the Assyrian inscriptions are silent about Judah's alliance with Egypt, because of the outcome of the events. Since Hezekiah was not executed as a rebel but bought off his life and throne, he was not depicted as a rebel in the Assyrian inscriptions.

Alliance with Egypt (Isa 30:1-8*; 31:1; 28:15-18; 18:1-2; 19:1b-4)
The alliance between Judah and Egypt was based on negotiations and consisted of a formal and binding agreement concerning military aid from Egypt, ruled by the Cushite (25th) dynasty, that was paid for by

---

392). 2) Ussishkin (1995: 289-303) argues that the Siloam tunnel was not built for defence purposes in preparation for 701, but as part of a prestigious royal building project influenced by the magnificent royal architecture in the main Assyrian cities, in particular Nineveh. Dalley (1998: 91; 2004a: 397-398) argues that the Siloam tunnel was an imitation on a small scale of Sennacherib's great irrigation constructions for his famous palace garden (cf. Knauf 2001).

[204]   Dalley (2004a: 391) suggests that on the Lachish relief Cushite soldiers are depicted: the people depicted as deportees from Lachish are identifiable as Judaeans, but the people being punished, 'grovelling in front of the king', are Cushite soldiers (for the pictures, Barnett 1998: II, 322-352).

Judah. Situations in which a less powerful king facing a military conflict with a stronger king asked another, equally strong ruler for help, occurred quite often. For the understanding of Isaiah's prophecies it is important to show how such political alliances were perceived. In the Assyrian royal inscriptions from the eighth and seventh century, we find two profoundly different perceptions of military alliances. When Assyria assists a smaller king who is in trouble, the alliance is presented in positive terms. The troubled king, often presented as a loyal vassal, is threatened by enemies. The king humbly implores the Assyrian king to help him and the Assyrian king comes to his aid and defeats the enemies. This is presented as a justified military intervention.[205] When however the alliance is concluded with another superpower, Urarṭu, Elam or Egypt, against Assyria, it is depicted in negative terms.[206] The negative depiction of anti-Assyrian alliances in the Assyrian royal inscriptions is explored here, because it closely resembles Isaiah's negative depiction of Judah's anti-Assyrian alliance with Egypt.

The Assyrian royal inscriptions present the following depiction of anti-Assyrian alliances. The ruler requesting assistance often is an Assyrian vassal and the alliance means a violation of his loyalty oath (adê) to Assyria. Out of fear of Assyria, the rebel king seeks for an alliance with a strong king. The agreement for military help against Assyria is not sanctioned by the gods but a purely human affair,[207] and therefore unreliable.[208] The alliance is further condemned by the claim that it was bought by a bribe.[209] The king supplying military assistance on request did not do so out of noble motives but only for his eco-

---

[205] See for examples and discussion, Oded 1993.

[206] Liverani (1982) has presented a description of this ideological complex.

[207] E.g. BIWA, Prism A ii 111-115: King Gyges, who 'did not heed the word of Aššur, but, his heart being proud, trusted in his own strength', sent his forces to assist Psammetichus, king of Egypt against Assyria; Sargon's Display inscription, l. 112-113 (Fuchs 1994: 222-223): 'Muttallu of Kummuh, wicked Hittite, who did not fear the command of the gods, plotter of evil, speaker of lies, trusted in Argišti, king of Urarṭu, an ally that could not save him.'

[208] The smaller king ran the risk that the stronger king, even after a payment, would *not* send military aid. See e.g. Sargon's Annals, l. 308-309 (Fuchs 1994: 153), where the rebel Merodach-baladan seeks the help of the king of Elam: 'this evil Elamite took the bribe, but being afraid of my weapons he turned around and told him: I am not coming'.

[209] Terms for the payment are ṭa'tu 'bribe' (e.g. Fuchs 1994: 153, Ann. l. 309; Luckenbill 1924: 42, l. 34), šulmānu 'greeting-gift' often as bribe, (e.g. Fuchs 1998: 46, l. 32), kadrû 'present', 'bribe' (e.g. Fuchs 1994: 153, Ann. 309), maḫīru 'exchange' (e.g. Borger 1956: 13, l. 33).

nomic advantage. The aim of the military assistance is help or rescue but this aim is never attained. The typical epithet of the helper-king is ally or helper 'that could not save him' (*lā mušēzibīšu*). The allied forces do not stand a chance against Assyria, because they put their trust on the wrong side. The rebel trusts in his own strength or in the military forces coming to his aid. The illegitimate and pointless character of the anti-Assyrian alliance is illustrated by the following passage from an inscription of Sennacherib:

> The Babylonians opened the treasury of the temple Esagila; they took the gold and silver of Marduk and Zarpanitu, the property of the temple of their gods, and they sent it as a bribe to Umman-menanu, king of Elam, a man who had no sense at all, saying: 'Gather your army, prepare your camp, hurry to Babylon, come to our aid, for you are our trust'.[210]

The Assyrian king, by contrast, trusts in his god.[211] Among the examples of anti-Assyrian alliances in the Assyrian royal inscriptions,[212] we find three cases where Palestine kings ask for assistance from Egypt: 1) Hanunu of Gaza received assistance from the king of Egypt: 'he (i.e. the king of Egypt) provided him Re'e, his [*tartānu*] as assistance, and he went into battle against me (i.e. Sargon). At the command of Aššur, my Lord, I defeated them, after which Re'e like a herdsman (Akk. *rē'û*) who has been robbed of his sheep, escaped completely alone'[213] (see 4.1.3). 2) The leaders of Ashdod and their king Iamani 'brought (*našû*) their goodwill gifts (*šulmānu*)[214] to Pharaoh, king of Egypt, a king that could not save them (*malku lā mušēzibīšunu*), and kept imploring him for assistance (*erēšu kitra*)'[215] (see 4.1.5). 3) The alliance of the rebels of Ekron with the Cushite king of Egypt, in 701 BCE:

> The high officials, the nobles, and the people of Ekron, who had thrown into chains Padî, their king, who was loyal to the treaty and oath with Assyria, and had handed him over like an enemy to Hezekiah, the Judaean, became afraid because of the pollution they had caused. They

---

[210] Luckenbill 1924: 42:31-38.

[211] See e.g. Borger 1956: 49, the inscription Nineveh A iii 27-29, 'they (the allied enemies) trusted in their own strength, I however trusted in the great gods, my lords'.

[212] Listed by Liverani 1982: 49-50.

[213] Fuchs 1994: 90, l. 53-55. Cf. also the Display inscription, l. 25-26 (Fuchs 1994: 197-198).

[214] *šulmānu/šulmannu* 'goodwill gifts', often in the sense of 'bribe' or 'inducement'.

[215] Translation based on Fuchs 1998: 44-46, 73-74, fragment VIIb.

requested help (*katāru*) from the kings of Egypt, troops, archers, chariots and the cavalry of the king of Cush, an army beyond counting, and they came to their assistance. Near Eltekeh their battle lines were drawn up against me, while they sharpened their weapons. Trusting to Aššur, my Lord, I fought with them and I defeated them.[216]

The Ekronites are pictured as criminals, who transgressed the treaty with Assyria by throwing King Padî who remained loyal to his oath into chains to Jerusalem. The army that came to their aid is depicted as numerically superior. Sennacherib, by contrast, is presented as trusting in his god.

In reality, anti-Assyrian alliances were of course as formal and binding as pro-Assyrian alliances.[217] However, as demonstrated above, the Assyrian royal inscriptions in ideological terms emphasise the illegitimate character of the anti-Assyrian alliances. The prophet Isaiah strongly opposed rebellion against Assyria and rejected an alliance with Egypt. He denounced his opponents by using terms and images that are to a great extent similar to the Assyrian descriptions of anti-Assyrian agreements. The prophetic sayings 28:15-18, 29:15, 30:1-5*, 30:6b-8 and 31:1, contain a range of elements that resemble the negative ideological depictions of the anti-Assyrian alliances as found in the Assyrian royal inscriptions. In 30:1-5* the policy of alliance with Egypt for help against Assyria is described as rebellion against Yahweh, which stresses the illegitimate character of the alliance:

> Rebellious sons—oracle of Yahweh—to carry out a plan, but without involving me, to make an alliance, but against my will, not to aid and not to profit, but to bring shame and disgrace.

The 'rebellious sons' are the political leaders of Judah.[218] Their rebellion consisted of the violation of the loyalty oath (*adê*) with Assyria.[219] 30:6b-8 criticises the economic basis of the agreement with Egypt:

> Through a land of trouble and distress, where lioness and lion roar, viper and serpent fly, they carry (נשא) their riches on the backs of donkeys, and their treasures on the humps of camels, to a people that cannot profit them (hi. לא יעל). Yes, Egypt is wind, and vain their aid (עזר), therefore I have called her, 'Rahab who sits still.' Go now, write it

---

[216] Chicago Prism ii 73-iii 3; Taylor Prism ii 69-79 (Mayer 2003: 186-191). For the text see Frahm 1997: 53-54 (cf. Luckenbill 1924: 31: ii 74-81; 69:22-25).

[217] Liverani 1982: 60-62.

[218] Ruppert 1986: 960.

[219] The loyalty oath (*adê*) was sworn not only by the gods of Assyria, but also by one's own gods, in the case of the Judaean kings: Yahweh; see Dalley 1998: 88, 98.

before them on a tablet, and inscribe it in a document, so that it may be
for the time to come as a witness forever.

Judah's riches and treasures are carried off to Egypt, but without any
profit. This equals the bribe for help against Assyria, as often mentioned in the Assyrian inscriptions. Furthermore, Egypt is referred to
as עַם לֹא יוֹעִילוּ, 'a people that cannot profit them'; 'profit' here means
'save'.[220] Egypt is 'a people that cannot save them', which resembles
the Assyrian expression the helper or king 'that could not save him'
(lā mušēzibīšu). The references to Egypt's help correspond to Assyrian terminology: עזר, 'to help' (30:7) resembles the Assyrian katāru,
'to come to aid',[221] whereas עֶזְרָה, 'help' in 31:1 equals Assyrian kitru,
'military aid':[222]

> Woe them that go down to Egypt for help (עֶזְרָה) and who rely on
> horses, but did not look to the Holy One of Israel nor consulted Yah-
> weh!

The denouncement of the rebels and their intended helper both in the
Assyrian inscriptions and in the sayings of Isaiah is dressed in similar
ideological cloths.

The presumed helper Egypt is described with contempt in Isaiah's
sayings, in particular in 28:15-18*:

> Because you have said, 'We have made a covenant with death, and with
> Sheol we have an agreement; when the overwhelming scourge passes
> through it will not come to us; for we have made lies our refuge, and in
> falsehood we have taken shelter', therefore thus says the Lord Yahweh:
> Look, I am about to lay a foundation stone on Zion, a massive stone,
> and I will make justice the line, and righteousness the plummet; but hail
> will sweep away the refuge of lies, and waters will overwhelm the shel-
> ter, your covenant with death will be annulled, your agreement with
> Sheol will not stand; when the overwhelming scourge passes through
> you will be beaten down by it.

This prophecy refers to Judah's anti-Assyrian alliance with Egypt.
First, the 'overwhelming scourge' is Assyria. The addressees, Judah's
political leaders (see 28:14), have made an alliance with a third party
in order to obtain protection against Assyria. From the historical con-

---

[220] The verb יעל hi. is used in parallelism with נצל hi. 'to save' (1 Sam 12:21; Prov
10:2; 11:4; Isa 44:9-10, 17; 47:12-13; 57:12-13). For a meaning similar to Isa 30:6,
see Prov 11:4 (riches do not profit, i.e. save, in the day of wrath, but righteousness delivers from death).
[221] Cf. Josh 10:4, 6; 1 Kgs 20:16; 1 Chron 12:19; 2 Chron 28:16; Ezek 32:21.
[222] Cf. Judg 5:23; Isa 20:6; Jer 37:7; Lam 4:17; Nah 3:9.

text, we know that this was the Cushite king of Egypt. This interpretation is confirmed by the parallels between 28:15 and 30:2. 28:15, 'we have made lies our refuge (מַחְסֶה)', corresponds to 30:2, 'to take refuge (חסה) in the protection of Pharaoh'. Furthermore, the references to 'treaty' and 'agreement' in 28:15 correspond to the alliance with Egypt referred to in 30:1.[223] The rejection of Egypt's help in 28:15, 17 as 'lies' and 'falsehood', resembles that of 30:7, 'vain and void'.

28:15-18 characterises the alliance with Egypt as a 'treaty with death'. This means that relying on Egypt against Assyria is a fatal mistake, which leads to certain death. 28:15 is a fictitious quotation by which the prophet ridicules his opponents through ironical language. In strong terms, Egypt's help is rejected, as in 30:7. There Egypt is called 'Rahab who sits still,' a power that comes to nothing, and whose help is worthless. Egypt is depicted as being totally unreliable, like the kings on whom the rebels trust in the Assyrian inscriptions. The terms 'death' and 'Sheol' (metaphorical language typical of prophetic oracles, cf. e.g. 7:4) characterise the pointlessness of the alliance with Egypt. In the Assyrian royal inscriptions, the Assyrian king is often cast in the role of the divine hero, the winner of the cosmic battle, such as Marduk or Ninurta, whereas the enemies are cast in the role of the powers of chaos, such as Tiamat.[224] It is likely that the terms chosen for Egypt in 28:15, 'death and Sheol' and in 30:7 'Rahab', likewise cast them in the role of the powers of chaos, the losers of the cosmic battle.[225]

In Isa 18:1-2 and 19:1b-4, Cush and Egypt are mentioned in passages that can probably be connected with the situation of 705-701. The saying of 18:1-2 describes the diplomacy of Cush as being in vain. The Cushite king allied himself with Judah and Philistine cities to assist them against Assyria, for a payment, but it will lead to nothing:

---

[223] Blenkinsopp 2000c: 474; contra Day 1989: 58-64.

[224] See Annus 2002: 94-101, for examples. Furthermore, in Sennacherib's inscription concerning 701, it is said of the Cushite-Egyptian forces that had come to the aid of Ekron, that 'they sharpened their weapons'. This alludes to Enuma Elish 4:92 (see Gallagher 1999: 120-121), where the divine powers allied with Tiamat are said to 'sharpen their weapons' before the battle with Marduk.

[225] Assyria, depicted as a raving storm in 28:15-18, the 'overwhelming scourge', is perhaps associated with the storm god, the cosmic hero. Egypt is associated with the forces that are to lose: Rahab (the West-Semitic counterpart of Tiamat), and Môt, the god of the underworld. On the association between Egypt with the underworld, see also SRronk 1999: 685; cf. Ps 87:4.

> Woe, land of whirring wings, in the region of the rivers of Cush, which
> sends envoys by the Nile in vessels of papyrus on the waters!

Similarly, 19:1b-4 announces the defeat of the Egyptians and their
subjection to a 'fierce king'. This probably refers to an Assyrian king.
The announcement resembles the message of Isa 20*. In both cases,
the background is the suggestion that Egypt's intervention in Palestine
will bring them into conflict with Assyria, and that Assyria as a result
will conquer Egypt. Although this only came true during the reigns of
Esarhaddon and Ashurbanipal, the prophecy makes sense in the context of 705-701 BCE.

Both in the Assyrian inscriptions and in Isaiah's sayings, the rebels
and their allies are depicted as being self-willed and self-confident.
The Assyrian royal inscriptions present anti-Assyrian agreements—
military aid in exchange for a payment—as not divinely sanctioned
but based on a wrong kind of trust.[226] A similar contrast between the
divine and the human sphere,[227] is found in 30:1-2 and 31:1.3a (cf. also
29:15). Egypt's help is searched for, but without Yahweh's consent.
The Judaeans trusted in Egypt's military force instead of in Yahweh.
It is foolish to seek human protection while opposing the will of
God.[228] This is, of course, a polemical point of view. The Judaeans
who advocated an alliance with Egypt surely did not agree that they
acted against Yahweh's will. They probably *had* consulted Yahweh
(cf. 28:7b-10). The suggestion that the controversy was between a
prophet who wanted to involve Yahweh in state politics, and his opponents operating as secular politicians, fails to recognise the polemical character of the prophetic sayings.[229] Moreover, in the ancient Near
East politics was too interwoven with religion for secular politics ever
to be spoken of at all.[230] However, accusing one's opponents of ignor-

---

[226] BIWA: 17, A i 56-57 / B i 55-56: 'He (the Cushite king Taharqa) forgot the
power of Aššur and Ištar, and the great gods, my lords, and trusted in his own strength
(var. wisdom)'.

[227] BIWA: 99, B v 35, concerning the Elamite king Teumman: 'Teumman who
did not respect the gods'.

[228] Høgenhaven 1989: 134.

[229] Contra Dietrich 1976; Barthel 1997. Høgenhaven (1989: 125) gives the following description: 'In particular, scholars have striven to reconstruct the prophetic vi-
sion(s) of a "religious" or "Yahwistic" policy, which, it is assumed, was advanced by
the prophets as an alternative to the "secular" politics usually conducted by the kings
of Israel and Judah.'

[230] The concept of secular, man-made politics occurs in ancient Near Eastern texts
as an example of what must be avoided. A well-known example is King Naram-Sin,
who according to the Cuthian legend blatantly ignored the will of the gods (for the

ing God's will or acting against God's will is a well-known motif in
ancient Near Eastern texts.[231] The alleged self-confidence of the opponents is contrasted with consulting Yahweh (31:1).[232]

Of course Assyria's enemies trusted in their own gods too, but according to the Assyrian point of view, rebellion against Assyria automatically implied alienation from the gods and trusting in oneself.
Similarly, in the political controversy of 705-701 in Judah, the advocates of each position based their views on what they regarded as
Yahweh's will. Both the Assyrian inscriptions and the Isaiah's
prophecies represent a partial point of view; those involved in the
agreement held a different opinion.

The prophet's opponents

From Ahaz's submission to Tiglath-pileser in 734 until Sargon's death
in 705, Judah did not rebel against Assyria. Yet, rebellion always was
a political option that presumably had its advocates among the
Judaean elite and political rulers. At least in 722-720 and c. 712 (4.1.3
and 4.1.5 above) rebellion may have seemed an attractive option.
Isaiah's prophetic words consistently imply that Judah should remain
loyal to Assyria. Evidently, a fierce political debate was going on in
Judah. In 705, following the death of Sargon, the time appeared to be
ripe for rebellion. At this stage, when the scales were tipped for rebellion, Isaiah's polemic became particularly harsh. In a series of critical
sayings, Isaiah detested his political opponents.

Who were Isaiah's opponents? First of all, conspicuously *not* included in the prophetic criticism, at least not explicitly so, is King
Hezekiah. Evidently, as the head of the Judaean state, Hezekiah ulti-

---

text, see Goodnick Westenholz 1997: 317). Naram-Sin's hubris was punished by the
gods. In this way, he learned that man must trust in the gods, not in human powers
(see Goodnick-Westenholz 1997: 264).

[231] E.g. Esarhaddon in his description of the struggle for the throne of Assyria,
qualifies in retrospect the actions of his brothers as being opposed to the will of the
gods: 'I (Esarhaddon) said to myself: Their deeds are arrogant, they trust in their own
plans. What will they do in their disregard of the gods?' (Borger 1956: 42). This is, of
course, Esarhaddon's point of view. His brothers would have described their deeds
quite differently.

[232] Cf. the oracles reported in the Mari letter ARM 26/1 199. Both the oracle from
Lupaḫum, *āpilum* of Dagan and that of a *qammatum* of Dagan of Terqa contain the
admonition: 'without consulting the god, the king shall not conclude a treaty!' The
historical situation was the conclusion of a treaty of peace between Zimri-Lim of Mari
and Ibalpiel of Eshnunna. The oracles show that the god Dagan of Terqa objected to
the treaty. Despite his objections, Zimri-Lim accepted the peace treaty with Ibalpiel.

mately took the decision to adopt a policy of rebellion. The reason why Hezekiah nevertheless is not mentioned in Isaiah's sayings will be discussed below. The people addressed in Isaiah's critical words can be found within the followings groups. Closely around the king stood 'the king's servants' (עַבְדֵי הַמֶּלֶךְ), court officials closely connected with, and dependent on, the king. A wider circle around the king formed the socio-political elite (שָׂרִים).[233] This group consisted of the upper part of the wealthy and upper-class elite of Judah, entangled in a common interest with the dynasty in Jerusalem and obtaining a firm footing at the royal court. The שָׂרִים can be considered an institution besides the king, which took part in the exercise of authority and power.[234] On the one hand we have the king's advisors, and on the other, the powerful leaders of Judah, who were in a position to exert pressure on the king.

Besides, 28:7b-10 deals with the religious experts, 'priest and prophet', who thanks to their access to the will of Yahweh, were in a position to authorise political decisions. Members of this last group are referred to in 28:7b-10:

> The priest and the prophet reel with strong drink, they are confused with wine, stagger with strong drink; they err in vision, stumble in giving verdict. All tables are covered with filth, vomit is everywhere. Whom will he (i.e. the priest) teach knowledge, and to whom will he (i.e. the prophet) explain the message? To those who are weaned from milk, taken away from the breast? For it is *ṣaw lāṣāw ṣaw lāṣāw qaw lāqāw qaw lāqāw*, a bit here, a bit there.

The saying accuses religious experts of being dazzled by drink, unable to advise the political decision-makers. Their advice and messages are only fit for small children; they talk stupidity. The criticism is to be understood as being not directed at priests and prophets in general, but at those religious experts that supported the anti-Assyrian policy. Whereas Isaiah, with his words, authorised a policy of loyalty toward Assyria, other religious experts authorised the opposed position of resistance against Assyria. Isaiah portrays these religious experts as being drunk. In this way, he insinuates that they sat at the table of the upper classes and spoke words the leaders of Judah wanted to hear. According to Isaiah, they speak in drunkenness, which means that their advice is unsound and their visions are unreliable. Their being

---

[233] See Rüterswörden 1985: 94-95.
[234] This characterisation is based on Niemann 1993.

drunk also suggests that they are blind to the real situation. In short, Isaiah accuses these priests and prophets of incompetence and of fraudulent, fake, divination.

Isaiah's denouncement of these priests and prophets has a parallel in the examples of Assyrian religious experts who accuse colleagues of incompetence and of fraudulent verdicts.[235] A message from the gods that was regarded as unacceptable could only be explained as a fraud. An example of this is found in the letter SAA 10 179 to King Esarhaddon. In this letter, Kudurru, an expert in divination, reports to the king how he became against his will involved in a conspiracy.[236] He states that he was forced to perform a divination: 'Will the *rab ša rēšē* take over the kingship?'.[237] Kudurru performed the divination, with a positive outcome. Since this outcome is, of course, unacceptable to the king, Kudurru continues: '[By the gods of the king], my [lord]: The extispicy [which I performed was] but a colossal fraud! (The only thing) [I was th]inking of (was), "May he not kill me." [Now th]en I am writing to the king, lest [the king my lord] hear about it and kill me.'[238]

Isaiah's reaction to the prophetic visions and priestly verdicts supporting a policy of rebellion was similar. Rebellion against Assyria posed a threat as great to the state of Judah, as a conspiracy against the king in Assyria. Any prophecy, verdict, or extispicy supporting it could be nothing but a fraud. It was a non-prophecy or a non-extispicy, produced either by force and from fear of being killed (SAA 10 179), or by religious experts too drunk to understand what they were talking about (28:7b-10). As Kudurru disqualifies his own extispicy, Isaiah ridicules the visions and verdicts of his colleagues who authorise the policy of rebellion. Isaiah claims that the policy of rebellion is not backed up with trustworthy divine messages. On the contrary, this policy is against Yahweh's will (30:1-2; 31:1).

---

[235] SAA 10 72, l. 6-17; 10 23 and 10 51. For the harsh competition and rivalry among the religious experts at the royal court of Assyria, see Van der Toorn 1998.

[236] For a historical reconstruction, see Nissinen 1998: 133-134.

[237] This title is often translated as 'chief eunuch', but Dalley (2001: 198-206) questions this, suggesting that *ša rēšē* does not necessarily mean eunuch, but can mean 'courtier', often pointing to relatives of the king placed in the highest offices (2001: 205).

[238] SAA 10 179, r. 19'-23' (Parpola's translation). The phrase 'but a colossal fraud', is a free rendering of *alla šāru meḫû*, 'nothing but wind and storm'; Nissinen 1998: 134.

Isaiah's main criticism is reserved for the political leaders advocating rebellion. They are criticised in 28:14-18*, 29:15, 30:1-5*, 30:6b-8, 31:1.3a (see above) and 5:8-23*, 10:1-2 (see below). The issue of rebellion against Assyria was not a calm discussion of pros and cons, but a deep controversy involving the issue of good versus bad leadership. From Isaiah's criticism against the political leaders it appears that their wrong policy in the eyes of the prophet makes them bad leaders. The rejection of the anti-Assyrian politics goes hand in hand with accusing the proponents of ignoring Yahweh and portraying them as robbers of the poor. Isaiah criticised his opponents on a political level for the attempt to conclude an alliance with Egypt, on a religious level for their self-willed ignorance of Yahweh's will,[239] and on a social level for violating justice and righteousness. These accusations can be grouped together, as they all form part of the same blackening of the political leaders.

Isaiah's rejection of a particular policy did not imply however the rejection of the state of Judah. Quite the contrary, according to Isaiah it was the political elite planning that threatened Judah's peace. Their policy of rebellion against Assyria posed a direct threat to the Judaean state. For this reason, Isaiah depicted his opponents as enemies of the state, who threatened Judah's well-being, the order protected by Yahweh. Internal enemies of the state figure also in the Assyrian prophecies. High officials who conspired against the king posed a threat to the Assyrian king, and hence to the well-being of Assyria. In various prophetic oracles, the gods promise to track down the disloyal officials and to punish them.[240] Disloyal Assyrian officials, as potential rebels, posed a threat to the Assyrian king and thus to Assyria.[241] Similarly, Judah's political leaders advocating rebellion, from Isaiah's point of view posed a threat to Judah's well-being. Both in Isaiah's prophecies and in the Assyrian prophecies, these people are depicted as enemies of the state.

---

[239] Rebellion also implied a transgression of the oath of loyalty to Assyria (the confession by Hezekiah 'I have sinned' in 2 Kgs 18:14 is to be understood against this same background). Although Isaiah does not explicitly mention the transgression of the oath of loyalty, he clearly presents the treaty with Egypt as against Yahweh's will and depicts the advocates of rebellion as sinful and wicked people.

[240] SAA 9 2.3, ii 9'-10'; 2.4, ii 31'-33'; 3.5, iv 22-30; see furthermore SAA 10 284, r. 4-9.

[241] See also SAA 10 2 and 10 112.

The prophetic announcements against the enemies of the state were not unrealistic. If a conspiracy against the Assyrian king was revealed, the participants were executed.[242] Similarly, the political leaders of a rebellious state were punished by the Assyrians. They were executed, as happened to the political leaders of Ekron in 701, or deported to Assyria. A similar fate for the political leaders of Judah is referred to in 28:18 'when the overwhelming scourge passes through you will be beaten down by it,' and more specifically in 22:15-18:

> Thus says the Lord Yahweh of Hosts: Come, go to that *sōkēn* (an official), [Shebna] (and say to him): What do you think you are doing *here*, and whom do you think you can rely on *here*, that you have cut out a tomb for yourself *here*? Look, Yahweh is about to hurl you away violently, O mighty man! He will seize firm hold on you, whirl you round and round, and throw you like a ball into a wide land. *There* you shall die, and *there* your splendid chariots shall lie, oh you disgrace to your master's house!

The focus of this oracle is the misplaced trust of the *sōkēn* addressed. The oracle emphasises that a policy of rebellion inevitably leads to punishment and deportation of the political elite to which the *sōkēn* belongs. The oracle announces the inevitable outcome of the revolt against Assyria: the deportation of the ruling class. The oracle depicts the *sōkēn* as feeling fine and safe in Jerusalem: he expects to enjoy a peaceful life and ultimately a peaceful end. The prophet however opens his eyes (22:17, Look!). Instead of dying in peace in his own country, the *sōkēn* will be taken into captivity to Assyria (22:18) and die on foreign ground. The background is the Assyrian policy to deport the political elite of a rebellious nation in order to break local resistance.

The *sōkēn*, later perhaps adequately identified as Shebna, was evidently a high-ranking royal official ('your splendid chariots', 22:18), involved in the political decision-making.[243] Remarkably, the final

---

[242] Cf. e.g. the Chronicle of Esarhaddon: 'In the eleventh year the king of Assyria put many of his magnates to the sword' (Grayson 1975a: 86:29; 127:27).

[243] The term *sōkēn* has been connected with the West-Semitic title *skn/sākinu*, denoting a high-ranking royal official (see Fox 2000: 178-182). Van Soldt (2002, esp. 827) pointed out that the *sākinu* of Ugarit was the highest official in the city-state, endowed with judicial authority, charged with the care for royal messengers, and functioning as a political stand-in if the king was unable to perform his political duties. The terminological parallel does not mean that the *sōkēn* in eighth-century Judah held the same position as the *sākinu* of Ugarit, but may confirm that the *sōkēn* addressed in 22:15-18 was a high-ranking royal official.

words of the oracle, 'oh you disgrace to your master's house!', dissociate the king from the policy of rebellion propagated by the *sōkēn* and
his colleagues. The expression 'your master's house' in an address to
a high official refers to the king and his dynasty.[244] The disastrous outcome of the policy of rebellion will be a disgrace to the king of Judah
and his dynasty, and the *sōkēn* is blamed for this. The king's dissocia-
tion from Isaiah's critical sayings will be explained below.

Isa 5:8-23* and 10:1-2

> [8] Woe them that join house to house, who add field to field,
> until there is no room left in the midst of the land!
> [11] Woe them that rise early in the morning in pursuit of strong drink,
> who linger in the evening to be inflamed by wine!
> [18-19] Woe them that drag iniquity along with cords of falsehood,
> who drag sin along as with cart ropes,
> who say, 'Let him make haste, let him speed his work that we may see
> it; let the plan of the Holy One of Israel hasten to fulfilment, that we
> may know it!'
> [20] Woe them that call evil good and good evil, who put darkness for
> light and light for darkness, who put bitter for sweet and sweet for bit-
> ter!
> [21] Woe them that are wise in their own eyes, and shrewd in their own
> sight!
> [22-23] Woe them that are heroes in drinking wine and valiant at mixing
> drink,
> who acquit the guilty for a bribe, and deprive the innocent of their
> rights!
> [10:1-2] Woe them that make iniquitous decrees, who write oppressive stat-
> utes, to turn aside the needy from justice and to rob the poor of my peo-
> ple of their right, that widows may be their spoil, and that they may
> make the orphans their prey!

The *woe*-sayings of 5:8-23* and 10:1-2 are usually interpreted as prophetic protest against a social crisis in the eighth century.[245] Blenkinsopp describes this presumed crisis as follows: 'This was a situation in
which the system of patrimonial domain was being undermined both
by the emerging state apparatus, hungry as always for land, and members of powerful families, a process eventuating in vast social changes
including the formation of latifundia and the prevalence of rent capi-

---

[244] Cf. Gen 44:4, 8; 2 Sam 12:8; 2 Kgs 10:2-3; Zeph 1:8-9.
[245] See Houston 2004: 130, with note 1.

talism.'[246] This interpretation is to be reconsidered. First, evidence for
a social crisis in the eighth century only stems from the prophetic
books,[247] and the conclusiveness of this evidence must be questioned.[248]
Second, the abuses criticised in Isa 5:8-23* and 10:1-2 are hardly
characteristic of eighth-century Judah but rather are of all times and
places.[249] Instead of relating the *woe*-sayings of 5:8-23* and 10:1-2 to
presumed inner-Judaean economic developments, I suggest to relate
them to the historical circumstances of the late eighth century. The
central issue in late eighth-century Judah was what position to adopt
toward Assyrian imperialism. Generally speaking, Assyrian imperialism put pressure on the Judaean society, as it led to 'an outflow of
precious metal and other valuables in tribute'.[250] This was however not
what the prophet complained about. What the prophet criticised was
the payment to Egypt: 'they carry their riches on the backs of don-
keys, and their treasures on the humps of camels, to a people that cannot profit them' (30:6). This payment probably had to be raised by
taxation, and since Isaiah regarded it as a waste of money, it was, in
his view, a robbery of the people. Furthermore, the period 705-701
probably saw a wartime economy, characterised by royal confiscation
and organised distribution.[251] The preparations for war were expensive.

I suggest connecting the *woe*-sayings of 5:8-23* and 10:1-2 with
the conflict of 705-701 between Isaiah and the political leaders of
Judah who advocated the rebellion against Assyria. Several arguments
can be mentioned. First, Isaiah elsewhere condemns the economic
burden of the rebellion (30:6). Second, the reproach of the hedonistic
lifestyle of the leaders (cf. 5:11) can be compared with the reproach of
the *sōkēn* in 22:15-18. According to 22:15-18, the *sōkēn* is wrong to
expect a peaceful lifetime and burial because of the policy of rebellion
which he supports. Similarly, the opulent lifestyle of the upper class is
despicable in the prophet's eyes, *because* of their politics of rebellion,

---

[246] Blenkinsopp 2000a: 213. See further Wildberger 1972-82: 183-202; Albertz
1994: I, 159-160 (1992: I, 248-249).

[247] Houston 2004: 131-132

[248] Becker 2004: 59; see also Houston 2004: 131-136.

[249] Cf. Neh 5:1-5, where in a fifth-century context exactly those features are described that are considered as characteristic of the social crisis in the eighth century.

[250] Houston 2004: 146; De Geus 1982: 56.

[251] The *lmlk*-seal impressions on jar handles have been interpreted as reflecting a
pre-war and wartime operation, kingdom-wide and controlled by the government; see
Halpern 1991: 21-27; cf. Fox 2000: 216-235.

which according to the prophet inevitably leads to war with Assyria.[252] Third, because of their policy of rebellion, Isaiah regards his opponents as wicked leaders and enemies of the state, and this is exactly how they are portrayed in 5:8-23* and 10:1-2.[253] True leadership, according to ancient Near Eastern values, means securing social justice and observing the will of the gods.[254] The Judaean leaders have failed in both respects: they acted against Yahweh's will and trusted in their own wisdom, and they committed crimes against social justice. In order to demonstrate that the political leaders had adopted the wrong political position, the prophet pictures them as having gone astray in every respect: they are accused not only of oppression of the poor and self-willed arrogance, but also of greed, dipsomania, hubris and impertinence. Isaiah does not present a description of the social problems of his time, but blackens a particular part of the ruling class. Fourth, a number of parallels between sayings that clearly deal with the political issue of 705-701 and the *woe*-sayings of 5:8-23* and 10:1-2 confirm this interpretation: the motif of drunkenness (5:11, 22; see 28:7b-10),[255] falsehood and iniquity instead of justice and righteousness (5:18; 10:1-2; see 28:15-18, esp. 28:16-17a), the notion of the self-willed leaders that do not care for Yahweh's will (5:19, 21; see 30:1-2; 31:1; 29:15), and the association of the opponents with the powers of darkness (5:20; see 29:15; 28:15).

The accusing of the political elite of corruption, oppression of the weak and injustice, is to be understood from the stand-point of the prophet's rejection of an alliance with Egypt. According to the prophet, a policy of rebellion meant a shift from security grounded in divine strength to security grounded in human might, bought at the cost of injustice and oppression.

A final issue to discuss is the absence of references to King Hezekiah in the critical sayings of Isaiah relating to 705-701. As the head of the political state Hezekiah was responsible for Judah's rebellion against Assyria, strongly rejected by Isaiah. Why then is he not mentioned in

---

[252] See Kratz 2003a: 81, 86, who argues with regard to the *woe*-sayings in Amos, directed against the elite of Samaria, that especially in critical circumstances (as it was uncertain when and how Assyria would strike back) the opulent lifestyle of the elite appeared all the more despicable to the prophet.

[253] Cf. Houston 2004: 141.

[254] Nissinen 2003d.

[255] Cf. also 28:1-4, where drunkenness is an image for self-willed arrogance.

the criticism? The suggestion that Isaiah did not bother to mention him because he was a weak king, not in control of the political decisions, is not convincing.[256] Quite the contrary, Hezekiah seems to have been a relatively strong king, who managed to stay on the throne even after the critical events of 701. The reason for Isaiah's not mentioning him must have been different. As argued above, Isaiah was loyal to the Judaean state; Judah's well-being was the whole point of his harsh polemics of 705-701. Since the king was the divinely appointed head of the state, it was hardly possible to criticise the king, at least not in a direct way, without becoming an enemy of the state oneself. Instead of blaming the king, Isaiah blamed those who advised him and put pressure on him. In this way, his criticism is directed at members of the upper class, the political leaders that advocated a policy of rebellion.[257]

The best way to criticise state politics without criticising the king himself is to blame the royal advisors.[258] An example of a prophetic oracle that similarly avoids direct criticism of the king is found in the Mari letter ARM 26/2 371. This letter reports prophetic words from the *āpilum* of Marduk of Babylon. According to the prophet, Išme-Dagan, the king of the Assyrian city Ekallatum, who was staying in Babylon under the protection of King Hammurabi in Babylon, had offended Marduk. The offence was that Išme-Dagan had sent goods and treasures from Marduk's temple in Babylon as a goodwill gift to the king of Elam. The prophet announced that Išme-Dagan would pay dearly for this robbery of Marduk.[259] Significantly, the prophetic message only addresses Išme-Dagan, not Hammurabi, the king of Babylon. This is remarkable, since it is hardly conceivable that Išme-Dagan could dispose of the possessions of the temple of Marduk without Hammurabi's consent. Although the representatives of the Marduk temple must have been furious at their own king Hammurabi, the prophet avoids direct criticism against him, but instead focuses on his protégé Išme-Dagan.[260]

---

[256] Contra Wildberger 1972-82: 1128.

[257] See in particular 22:18, where the *sōkēn* is accused of being a 'disgrace' to the house of his master, i.e. the king.

[258] Cf. Esarhaddon's 'Letter to the God', where the king of Šubria who neglected the command of Esarhaddon, his overlord, tries to excuse himself claiming: 'My princely counsellors told me unreliable lies' (Borger 1956: 103, ii 20; translation from Lanfranchi 2003: 100).

[259] ARM 26/2 371, see Roberts 2002b: 246-249; Nissinen 2003a: 73-74; Heimpel 2003: 64, 325.

[260] This text is further discussed in chapter 5.1.4.

Isaiah's criticism is mainly directed at the political leaders of Judah. The lack of direct criticism against the king agrees with Isaiah's role in 734-732 (cf. in particular 7:4-9a) and with the later picture of the prophet in the Hezekiah stories (2 Kgs 18-19). This implies that the prophet Isaiah, although being radically opposed to the politics of rebellion, did anything but reject Hezekiah or the Davidic dynasty.

4.1.9 *Evaluation*

In the first part of this chapter, I have discussed four episodes from the late eighth century and argued that the early prophetic material from First Isaiah is to be connected with these events. Apart from the revolt of Ashdod in c. 712 BCE (4.1.5) and the report of Isaiah's symbolic act attributed to this period (Isa 20*; 4.1.6), three periods stand out as situations to which Isaiah's prophecies relate: 734-732, 722-720 and 705-701 BCE. Significantly, Isaiah's prophecies are interconnected with exactly the three direct encounters between Judah and Assyria in the late eighth century: 734, 720 and 701 BCE. The main issue reflected in the prophecies of Isaiah is the perception of Assyria's imperialism. First, Isaiah saw Assyria as Yahweh's agent to destroy Judah's enemies. Second, he condemned Assyria for swallowing up Judah in its illegitimate, unlimited expansion. Third, he rejected rebellion against Assyria while trusting Egypt. This view implied that Yahweh himself would punish Assyria for its offences against Judah, but that rebellion against Assyria was a serious mistake. Isaiah's political assessment appeared to be correct, and this, in my view, made his words worth preserving.

4.2 *Historical Events in Assyria and Assyrian Prophecies*

The Assyrian prophetic oracles relate to historical situations of major importance. Although many of them contain clues for determining their historical background, some uncertainty has to be taken for granted.[261] The second part of this chapter explores the events to which the oracles relate and demonstrates that prophecy played a role at sev-

---

[261] Nissinen's statement '[m]ost of the prophecies are easily datable and can be more or less firmly associated with historical events' (2003a: 101), is too optimistic.

eral key moments during the reigns of Esarhaddon and Ashurbanipal. The first period to mention is 681 BCE: the death of Sennacherib and the subsequent struggle for kingship, between Esarhaddon and his brothers. These events have been dealt with in previous studies of the Assyrian prophecies.[262] In addition, seven further episodes from the reigns of Esarhaddon and Ashurbanipal will be explored as moments to which Assyrian oracles can be related.

Parpola and Nissinen have greatly contributed to the exploration of the historical background of the Assyrian prophecies.[263] Nissinen gave the following assessment of the prophecies to Esarhaddon: 1) the oracles of SAA 9 1 are proclaimed during Esarhaddon's war against his brothers in 681; 2) the oracles of SAA 9 2 deal with the stabilisation of Esarhaddon's rule and the restoration of the cults of the Babylonian gods; these oracles were probably delivered at the beginning of Esarhaddon's reign (680-679); 3) SAA 9 3 consists of oracles and cultic commentaries attached to Esarhaddon's enthronement ritual in Ešarra, the temple of Aššur in Assur, which took place at the end of the year 681.[264] In my view however the oracles of SAA 9 1 and 2 do not exclusively relate to the limited period of 681-679 BCE.[265] A first issue to reconsider is the date of the oracle collections. Parpola's suggestion that SAA 9 1 dates from 673, together with Esarhaddon's Nineveh A inscription,[266] may be correct. The suggestion that SAA 9 2 and 3 were composed as early as 680 (SAA 9 3) and 679 (SAA 9 2),[267] is however unlikely, since both contain references to events that took place later during the reign of Esarhaddon (see 4.2.3 below). Moreover, there is no compelling reason to assume that all oracles from a particular collection must relate to the same historical situation. On the contrary, it seems clear that they do not. This means that the individual oracles must be dated on the basis of clues provided by the oracles themselves, and that the (later) collections of oracles are to be dated independently.

---

[262] Weippert 1981: 92-99; Parpola 1997: LXVIII-LXXI; Nissinen 1998: 15-30.

[263] Parpola 1997; Nissinen 1998; 2003a: 97-101, 133-136.

[264] Nissinen 2003a: 101. Parpola (1997: LXVIII-LXIX), although allowing for some variation in dating between the various oracles of the collections, similarly attributes all oracles from SAA 9 1, 2 and 3 to 681-679 BCE.

[265] Cf. Weippert 2002: 37. I have argued in chapter 3.1.1, that SAA 9 3 is not a collection of oracles.

[266] Parpola 1997: LXIX-LXX.

[267] Parpola 1997: LXIX-LXX.

4.2.1 Esarhaddon's Rise to Power (681 BCE)

According to a common view, Esarhaddon ascended the throne of Assyria by the end of 681 after he defeated his elder brothers who had murdered Sennacherib and had rebelled against him (Esarhaddon) as the legitimate crown prince. This view is based on Esarhaddon's account of the events in the Nineveh A inscription.[268] However, this account is rarely approached with appropriate suspicion.[269] Granted that there is evidence to support Esarhaddon's claim that he was at some stage appointed as crown prince of Assyria,[270] a critical reading of his own report indicates that he lost his father's favour afterwards:

> Malicious gossip, slander and falsehood they (i.e. Esarhaddon's brothers) wove around me in a godless way, lies and insincerity. They plotted evil behind my back. Against the will of the gods they alienated my father's well-disposed heart from me, though in secret his heart was affected with compassion, and he still intended me to exercise kingship.[271]

The claim that Sennacherib, although his actions suggested otherwise, still intended Esarhaddon to become king, is suspicious. Once Esarhaddon had become king, Sennacherib's 'secret favour' could not be verified anymore, because he was dead. Esarhaddon's confession that he fell from his father's favour, however, is important from a historical point of view. This must have been a public fact that could not be concealed afterwards. The claim that Sennacherib in secret still favoured Esarhaddon attempts to neutralise his public misfortune. Historically, Esarhaddon's fall into disfavour was presumably the reason for his flight from Nineveh to save his life.[272] After his flight, Sennacherib was killed on 20 Tebet 681. Since Sennacherib was probably killed before Esarhaddon had been replaced as crown prince, Esarhaddon presumably was still the official crown prince.

---

[268] Borger 1956: 40-45.

[269] Parpola 1980: 175; Frahm 1997: 18; Porter 1993: 13-26; Nissinen 1998: 15-30. See Tadmor 1983: 38-41, for a more critical discussion of this passage. The inscription was composed in Adar (XII) 673/2 (Borger 1956: 64). It seems likely that the composition of the Nineveh A inscription is to be connected with the appointment of Ashurbanipal as crown prince of Assyria (Parpola 1997: LXIX-LXX).

[270] See Nineveh J l. 1 (Borger 1956: 68-69) and SAA 12 88, both undated. Parpola's identifycation of SAA 2 3 as succession-adê for Esarhaddon (Parpola 1987: 178-180) is questionable, since it rather seems to be an oath of loyalty to Sennacherib himself (see l. 1-4).

[271] Nineveh A i 26-31, Borger 1956: 41-42.

[272] Nineveh A i 32-40, Borger 1956: 42-43.

Although it is commonly accepted that Esarhaddon's brother Arda-
Mullissi was the offender, or one of the offenders, the murder of Sen-
nacherib cannot be considered a closed case. The letter SAA 18 100
(ABL 1091),[273] usually regarded as the main evidence, accuses
Esarhaddon's brother Arda-Mullissi of a plot to murder Sennacherib.
However, this letter was probably written afterwards, and sent to
Esarhaddon after he had prevailed in the conflict.[274] Besides, the letter
probably intended to discredit certain officials. For these reasons, the
letter must be treated with caution. It is clear that during Esarhaddon's
reign the official reading was that Arda-Mullissi (together with one or
more of his brothers) had killed Sennacherib. This official reading,
authorised by King Esarhaddon, is also echoed in other sources.[275] This
is, however, not the end of the matter. The Babylonian Chronicle refers to the murder of Sennacherib without identifying the murderer:

> Sennacherib, king of Assyria, was killed by his son in a rebellion. (...)
> The rebellion continued in Assyria (...). On the *twenty-eighth/eighteenth*
> day of the month Adar Esarhaddon, his son, ascended the throne in As-
> syria.[276]

Esarhaddon's Nin. A inscription, on the other hand, does not accuse
any of Esarhaddon's brothers in particular, but accuses them generally:

> After that, my brothers became frenzied and committed everything that
> both gods and men consider improper. They plotted evil and set up an
> armed rebellion in Nineveh against the will of the gods, and in their
> strife for exercising kingship they butted each other like young goats.[277]

---

[273] Previously edited by Parpola 1980: 180-181.

[274] The addressee is missing, but it may be assumed that it was King Esarhaddon.

[275] In the accounts from Berossus' Babyloniaca (third century BCE), Arda-
Mullissi is identified as the murderer as well: Ardumuzan/Adremelos (see Mayer
Burstein 1978: 24-25). Since Esarhaddon's vassals and allies would have had to promote his account of the events, the sources available to Berossus were anything but
impartial. Similarly, 2 Kgs 19:37 (Isa 37:38), mentioning Sennacherib's sons Adrammelech and Sharezer as the murderers, seems to be based on the official Assyrian
reading (see Mayer Burnstein 1978: 25). If Zawadzki (1990: 69-72) is right that traditions of the death of Queen Semiramis mirror the death of Sennacherib, the account of
Ctesias of Cnidos is of interest, because this ascribes the murder of Semiramis ('Sennacherib') to her son Ninyas, born from her second marriage ('Esarhaddon').

[276] Grayson 1975a: 81, l. 34-38; Grayson's translation.

[277] Nineveh A i 43-44, Borger 1956: 42. See also Tadmor 1983: 40.

The aim of this accusation is to discredit all his brothers,[278] leaving only Esarhaddon worthy of the kingship. It is difficult to ascertain who murdered Sennacherib. Evidently, it was not Esarhaddon himself, since he had fled from the Assyrian heartland. It is, however, very possible that someone belonging to Esarhaddon's faction killed Sennacherib; after all, Sennacherib's death was in the interests of Esarhaddon, since though fallen into disgrace, he still was the official crown prince. For this reason, I agree with Borger's suggestion:

> Die Unklarheiten in Asarhaddons Darstellung, wo merkwürdigerweise Asarhaddon seine älteren Brüder nicht einmal ausdrücklich des Vatermordes bezichtigt, sowie der Umstand, daß es Asarhaddon gelungen ist, sehr rasch am meisten von der Ermordung seines Vaters zu profitieren, lassen es doch zweifelhaft erscheinen, ob Asarhaddon wirklich ganz unschuldig am Tode seines Vaters gewesen ist.[279]

According to Esarhaddon's inscription (Nin. A i 45-47), the gods took Esarhaddon's side in the struggle for the throne:

> Giving me their firm positive answer, they constantly sent me this oracle of encouragement (*šīr takilti*): 'Go ahead, do not hold back! We will constantly go by your side; we will kill your enemies'.[280]

Although the 'oracle of encouragement' (*šīr takilti*) is the outcome of extispicy rather than a prophetic oracle,[281] it resembles the prophetic oracles that can be dated to the period of the struggle for the throne. Oracle 1.2 mentions Esarhaddon's succession to the throne and can be dated to before his accession:

> King of Assyria, fear not! I will deliver the enemy of the king of Assyria for slaughter. [...] your succession [I will keep] you safe and [...] you. I am the Gr[eat Lady, I am Ištar o]f Arbela (i 30'-37')

Ištar of Arbela assures Esarhaddon that she will keep him safe (*taqānu*) for succession (*ridûtika*, 'your succession').[282] By addressing

---

[278] Sennacherib's sons known by name are: Aššur-nadin-šumi (the eldest son; killed by the Elamites in 694), Arda-Mullissi, Aššur-šuma-ušabši, Aššur-ili-muballissu, and Nergal-šumu-x. Another son may be referred to in the biblical account (2 Kgs 19:37) as Sharezer; Frahm 2002: 1114-1115.

[279] Borger 1982-85: 392.

[280] Nineveh A i 60-62.

[281] Nissinen 1998: 33-34.

[282] Cf. Nineveh A i 18 (Borger 1956: 40), where Esarhaddon refers to the oath of loyalty enforced on all Assyrians, 'to protect my succession' (*aššu naṣār ridûtīya*). Parpola's reading 'É'-*re-du-te-ka* (*bīt ridûtīka*) is improbable. Of 'É' only two verticals are visible, which could represent many signs. The expression *bīt ridûti* does not

Esarhaddon as 'king of Assyria' and referring to his rivals as 'the enemy of the king of Assyria' the goddess makes clear that Esarhaddon
is the legitimate successor of Sennacherib. This fragment corresponds
with Nin. A i 38-40, where Esarhaddon states: the great gods provided
me a 'secure place' and 'protected me for the kingship'. Oracle 2.5
probably belongs to this period as well:

> Esarhaddon, fear not! I will put Assyria in order, I will appease the an-
> gry gods with Assyria, I will tear out the (...) of your enemies, I will
> shed the blood of the enemies of my king. I will protect my king. I will
> bring enemies in neckstocks and vassals with tribute before his feet. I
> am your father, I am your mother; I raised you between my wings. I
> will see you success! Fear not, Esarhaddon, I will place you between
> my arm and my forearm. In woe I will vanquish the enemies of my
> king. I will put Assyria in order, I will put the king[ship] of heaven in
> order (2 iii 19'-34').

The deity promises Esarhaddon to reconcile (*salāmu* D) the angry
gods with Assyria. The anger of the gods—caused by the rebellion
and the murder of Sennacherib—was perceived as the heavenly counterpart of the political unrest in Assyria, which is referred to as well.

Furthermore, Esarhaddon's mother Naqia appears in various oracles that can be situated in the period that Esarhaddon had fled Nineveh (1 v 8, v 13-20, 2 i 13', iv 28'). According to oracle 1.8, Naqia
had implored Ištar of Arbela to take Esarhaddon's side against his rival brothers. This may indicate that Naqia had sent someone to Arbela
to deliver her request to the goddess. The oracle is the following:

> I am the Lady of Arbela. To the king's mother: Because you implored
> me thus: 'Those of the right and the left you have placed in your lap,
> but my own offspring you made roam the wild,' Well then, fear not, o
> king! The kingship is yours, the power is yours!

Naqia's supplication contrasts the unfavourable fate of Esarhaddon
with the favourable position of his brothers. The phrase 'those of the
right and the left' refers to Esarhaddon's brothers, who at that time

---

go with a suffix (CAD s.v. *ridûtu*, 326-327), whereas *ridûtu* meaning 'royal succession' does (Borger 1956: 40, Nineveh A i 12, 18; BIWA: 36, Prism A iii 18). Hecker
(1986: 57) translates similarly: '[....] deiner Nachfolgeschaft'. The historical situation
renders the restoration *bīt ridûtīka* even more unlikely, since Esarhaddon did *not* stay
in the 'palace of succession', but had fled Nineveh (cf. Nissinen 1998: 20-21). See
also Weippert 2002: 40.

occupied honourable positions, at the right and left side of the king.[283] Esarhaddon, by contrast, was a refugee: he had fled from Nineveh. This supplication, referring to the situation after Esarhaddon's flight and before the death of Sennacherib, is answered by the announcement that Esarhaddon is the legitimate king. The final sentence of the oracle is Ištar of Arbela's reply to Naqia's request, directly addressed to her son Esarhaddon, addressed as 'king'. A second oracle addressing Naqia is 2.1. Here, the goddess Banitu speaks:

> I will put [.....] in order and consolidate the [throne/crown[284] of Esarha]ddon. [.......] we are the goddesses[285] [.........i]n Esagila [.....] Esarhaddon, king of Assyria. I will seize[286] [his enemies] and trample them [*under my foot*]. Fe[ar not], mother of the king ([*lā tapa*]*llihi ummi šarri*). (2 i 6'-14').

After the announcements that the goddess would bring order and that Esarhaddon's enemies would be destroyed, the oracle ends with the encouragement of Naqia.

In oracle 1.7, a deity promises to kill Esarhaddon's enemies: 'The weasels and shrews that have plotted (*dabābu*), I will cut them to pieces before his feet' (v 3-7). The degrading characterisation 'plotting weasels and shrews', refers to Esarhaddon's rival brothers and their supporters.[287] Esarhaddon is referred to in the third person. This suggests that the oracle is directed to Naqia, who is addressed in the enigmatic phrase 'You (fem.) are you, the king is my king!' (v 8-9). This probably means: *You*, Naqia, take care of yourself; *I* (the deity speaking) will take care of Esarhaddon.

A fourth oracle that refers to Naqia, is 2.6. The phrase [*l*]*ā tapallihi*, 'fear not!' (iv 28'), addresses a feminine subject, probably Naqia.[288] The goddess speaking is restored by Parpola in iv 8' as [^d*ur-*

---

[283] SAA 10 185:5-13 gives a description of Esarhaddon's appointment of Ashurbanipal as crown prince of Assyria and Šamaš-šum-ukin as crown prince of Babylon, and concludes: 'You have placed the first on your right, the second on your left side!' (Parpola's translation). From this phrase it may be inferred that oracle 1.8 'those of the right and the left' refers to Esarhaddon's rival brothers. Cf. SAA 9 3 iv 23-24, '[the ones at the right and] left side', probably referring to the high courtiers standing at both sides of the king.

[284] Cf. 1 iii 21; cf. 2 ii 5.

[285] Apparently, another goddess has presented herself as well.

[286] Weippert 2002: 42, translates: '[Auf seine Feinde] schlage ich ein'.

[287] Cf. Nineveh A i 28 (Borger 1956: 41) 'they (the brothers) plotted (*dabābu*) evil behind my back'. Both texts describe the actions of Esarhaddon's rivals as plotting, conspiring (*dabābu*).

[288] Parpola's completion 'mother of the king' is plausible.

k]*i-tú*, Ištar of Uruk. The following phrases can be read: '[*I am
Urk*]*ittu*, praise me! ... I will guard you ... Fear not! ... [I will pr]otect
you ... I will put your kingship in order'. Furthermore, Babylon is
mentioned (iv 4') and the god Aššur (iv 2', 29').[289]

The four oracles referring to Naqia, stem from various cities (Arbela, 1 v 25, and Assur, 2 i 14', are mentioned) and involve various
deities (Ištar of Arbela, 1 v 12, Banitu, 2 i 5', and probably [Urk]ittu,
2 iv 8').[290] It seems that Naqia actively searched for support for
Esarhaddon in various cities and from various deities. Some of the
oracles relate to Babylonia as well. The goddesses presenting themselves in oracle 2.1 express a concern with Esagila (2 i 9'); and in oracle 2.6, the goddess (probably Ištar of Uruk) perhaps refers to Esagila
and clearly to Babylon (2 iv 4'). All deities involved are presented as
being on Esarhaddon's side. The likeliest explanation is, that these
oracles belong to the period when Esarhaddon was not in the heartland
of Assyria. During his absence, his faction, in which his mother Naqia
played a prominent role, was striving for his cause. More insight into
these events is provided by a report from the Babylonian astrologer
Bel-ušezib (SAA 10 109). The letter, addressed to Esarhaddon early in
his reign, refers to the events of 681:

> [7'] I am Bel-ušezib, your servant, your dog, the one who fears you [....]
> [8'] the words which I heard in Nineveh as many as were available [....][291]
> [9'] Why has [the king not sum]moned the prophets and prophetesses
> (*raggimānu raggimātu*)?[292]
> [10'] I [who] with my own mouth blocked the exorcist[293] for the well-being
> of the crown prince my lord,[294]

---

[289] Weippert (private communication) proposes to read in iv 2' [d]MAŠ, 'Ninurta'
(instead of Aššur).

[290] For SAA 9 5 see chapter 3.1.1.

[291] For l. 7'-8' cf. SAA 10 110 (another letter by Bel-ušezib) r. 8-9, 'I am [a dog
of the king], my [lord, reporting] to the king, my lord, whatever I hear'. In line 9' a
new sentence begins.

[292] I propose to restore in l. 9' [LUGAL *la iš-ši*], as l. 16'. Instead of 'summon'
the translation 'pay attention to', is also possible (CAD s.v. *našû: ammīni re-e-ši la iš-
ši* 'why did he not pay attention to me?'). In either case, Bel-ušezib's complaint is that
the king has neglected the message of the prophets and prophetesses and of Bel-ušezib
himself, namely that Esarhaddon was to become king *in order to* rebuild Babylon and
to restore Esagila.

[293] The phrase is uncertain (CAD s.v. *parāku* follows Parpola). In this passage,
Bel-ušezib refers to his deeds for the benefit of Esarhaddon as crown prince. One of
his brave deeds apparently was that he personally, 'with his own mouth', countered
the spell of an exorcist against Esarhadon. This exorcist must have been someone different from the exorcist Dadâ mentioned in l. 14'.

¹¹' whom your [...] saved from being executed²⁹⁵ [...] to the 'city of confusion' (URU.*ašīt*[*i*]) [...],
¹²' regarding my murder and that of your servants [they plotted] every-
day,
¹³' and the sign (*ittu*) of kingship of my lord the crown prince Esarhaddon,
¹⁴' which I told to the exorcist Dadâ and the queen mother, saying:
'Esarhaddon
¹⁵' will rebuild Babylon and restore Esagila and [*honour?*] me'.
¹⁶' Why has the king until now not summoned me? And in [....]
¹⁷' he/they went [to]²⁹⁶ the 'city of confusion' (URU.*ašīti*), was this excellent structure/design (*šiknu*, i.e. of Esagila);
¹⁸' and as I told it to the crown prince my lord, it has been done to the
king my lord [....]'

This is part of a report dealing with the period right before Esarhaddon's accession, but the letter is written afterwards. Thus, the letter
describes a situation in which Esarhaddon was referred to as crown
prince (l. 10', 13', 18'), but at the moment of writing, Esarhaddon is
king (l. 16', 18'). Bel-ušezib claims that during the period that
Esarhaddon had fled Nineveh, he reported the words that he heard in
Nineveh, as many as were available. This seems to refer to the prophetic oracles that were delivered in favour of Esarhaddon, since Bel-
ušezib continues: 'why has [the king not] summoned the prophets and
prophetesses?'

Bel-ušezib emphasises that his striving for the well-being of crown
prince Esarhaddon brought great risks to him: he was nearly executed,
probably by Esarhaddon's brothers and their men, but he escaped to
the URU.*ašīti* (l. 11', again l. 17'). I suggest reading this as *āl ašīti*,
'the city of confusion',²⁹⁷ and taking it as a reference to Babylon.²⁹⁸ In

---

²⁹⁴ The second half of l. 10' should be taken with the first half.
²⁹⁵ Parpola's restoration [*al-li*]-*ka* at the beginning of l. 11' is improbable between
two verbal forms with an enclitic *ma*; instead, [*x x*]-*ka* is probably the subject of the
clause; *ú-še-zi-ba-am-ma* (*ezēbu* Š with suffix first person singular) needs a third person singular subject.
²⁹⁶ The preposition *ana* may be restored at the end of l. 16'.
²⁹⁷ URU.*a-ši-ti* is unlikely to be a form of *asi'tu* (*isītu*, *asa'ittu*), 'tower' (contra
Parpola, SAA 10 109), since the spelling *a-ši-ti* is not attested for *asi'tu*. Preceded by
the URU-determinative *asi'tu* means 'storehouse' according to CAD. Instead, it could
be taken as *āl ašīti*, 'city of confusion', referring to Babylon. The same expression occurs also in another letter, SAA 16 29, which similarly refers to Esarhaddon as crown
prince and addresses him as king. The author of this letter, Mardî, points to his loyalty
to Esarhaddon in the difficult period: 'I constantly prayed to [B]el, Nabû and Šamaš
for the king, my lord, saying: "May the crown prince, my lord, seize the royal throne
of his father's house! I am his servant and his dog, who fears him; may I see light un-

the following lines, an excellent design or structure (*šiknu*) is mentioned, which probably points to Esagila, again with a reference to the
āl ašīti, 'the city of confusion', Babylon. In Babylon Bel-ušezib received the *ittu*, the 'sign' that promised kingship to crown prince
Esarhaddon. He claims to have immediately reported it to the exorcist
Dadâ and the queen mother Naqia, leading figures of Esarhaddon's
faction in Nineveh.[299] The *ittu* was the following: 'Esarhaddon will rebuild Babylon and restore Esagila, and [*honour*] me'. The term *ittu*
can refer to a range of ominous signs; here it is likely to refer to an
oracle from Marduk. First, the deity appears to speak in the first person (*yā[ši]* 'me', l. 15'), which is an indication of prophecy. Furthermore, Bel-ušezib was familiar with prophetic oracles, judging from
the beginning of his report, and from another letter in which he quotes
a prophecy from Marduk.[300] Because this *ittu* concerns Babylon and
Esagila, it is likely to represent an oracle from Marduk as well. The
point of the passage is that Bel-ušezib explicitly connects the promise
of kingship with Babylon's restoration, and strongly argues that now
Esarhaddon has become king he should restore Esagila (see 4.2.2 below).[301]

Scholars have been surprised that the Babylonian cities did not revolt after Sennacherib was murdered, given their resistance to Assyrian dominance in preceding decades.[302] This may indicate that Babylon

---

der his protection".' Like Bel-ušezib, this Mardî had to flee, *ana libbi* URU.*i-si-ti* (l.
6). Here too URU.*i-si-ti* may be read as *āl išīti*, 'city of confusion' (with *isītu* as variant spelling of *išītu*, 'confusion'; cf. Luukko 2004: 74-75). Like Bel-ušezib, Mardî
fled to the 'city of confusion' (Babylon), in order to save his life during the struggle
for the throne in 681.

[298] *ešû* 'to confuse' is used in connection with cities (e.g. KAR 158 r. 111-112
'who tramples down the corners of the world, who throws all the cities into confusion', *a-šu-ú kalu ālāni*). See also *ešītu* 'confusion', 'political disorder', in the expression *ina ešīti māti* 'in the disordered state of the country' (CAD s.v. *ešītu*). After
Sennacherib's measures against Babylon in 689, including the deportation of Marduk
to Assyria, the city is described as *namûtu*, 'wasteland', and *karmu*, 'heap' (Borger
1956: 14). In oracle 2.3 (ii 24') the phrase *ina ṣēri lemni balli*, 'in the evil desert of
confusion', probably refers to Babylon too (see 4.2.2 below). Finally, a similar reference to Babylon is found in the letter SAA 10 169, where apparently king Esarhaddon
is quoted, as saying with respect to Babylon: 'The city was in ruins, and I have reset-
tled it and established its freedom!'

[299] This Dadâ apparently made a great career during the reigns of Esarhaddon and
Ashurbanipal; see Mattila 1999: 360.

[300] SAA 10 111 r. 23-26, introduced as *Bēl iqtabi umma akī*. For this oracle, see
4.2.3.

[301] SAA 10 109 l. 13'-15', cf. also l. 24', r. 14-15.

[302] See e.g. Porter 1993: 28-30.

and other Babylonian cities supported Esarhaddon in his fight for the throne.[303] Whereas the focus often is on Esarhaddon's initiative in Assyria's improved relations with Babylonia,[304] part of the initiative for this may have come from the Babylonian cities themselves. At least part of Babylonia took Esarhaddon's side in the conflict with his brothers.[305]

The precise moment of Esarhaddon's return to Assyria is unknown. A retrospective passage in oracle 3.5 probably refers to this moment. Ištar of Arbela rhetorically asks: 'did I not bend the four doorjambs of Assyria and did I not allow you (to enter)?' The later accounts of Esarhaddon's fight against his brothers, found in the Nineveh A inscription and in the prophetic text SAA 9 3.3 are heavily coloured with mythological motifs and do not present a historical picture.[306]

The reality of 681 BCE was that Esarhaddon's kingship started with a bitter fight. He and his faction were deeply involved in the bloodshed. Esarhaddon was supported by Naqia, Dadâ, Bel-ušezib, Mardî,[307] and others, who mobilised support for him in various cities and from various deities, including those of Babylonia. Historically, we only know the outcome of the fight for the throne: Esarhaddon defeated his rivals and acceded to the throne, two months after Sennacherib's death. These two months of war form the historical background for various oracles from the collections of SAA 9 1 and 2 (1.2, 1.7, 1.8, 2.1, 2.5 and 2.6, see above). In these oracles, the gods support Esarhaddon and encourage him, addressing him as the rightful successor whose enemies will be annihilated.

---

[303] It were presumably (some of) the Babylonian cities, in particular Babylon, that supported Esarhaddon in his struggle for kingship.

[304] E.g. Porter 1993: 6.

[305] See De Jong 2004.

[306] For mythological overtones in Esarhaddon's Nineveh A account, see Annus 2002: 100. The prophetic text SAA 9 3.3, furthermore, presents Aššur's intervention against Esarhaddon's rivals in mythological terms. I doubt whether the phrase 'I filled the river with their blood' (3.3 ii 23) can be de-mythologised into a 'battle at the riverbank' (Nissinen 1998: 26-27). The prophetic text SAA 9 3.3 (in relation to the account in the Nineveh A inscription) is discussed in chapter 6.2.1.

[307] See SAA 16 29.

4.2.2   Esarhaddon's Accession to the Throne and First Regnal Years

According to Esarhaddon's Assur A inscription (679 BCE), his accession was accompanied by all sorts of favourable omens, including prophetic oracles:

> Prophetic oracles (*šipir maḫḫê*) concerning the everlasting establishment of the foundation of my priestly throne, were constantly and regularly provided. Good omens in dreams and ominous utterances, concerning the establishment of the throne, and the duration of my reign, kept occurring to me. When I saw these favourable signs, I became confident and pleased.[308]

Various oracles can be connected with the period immediately after the accession.[309] Oracle 1.4 can be situated in this period. The deities Bel (Marduk), Ištar of Arbela, and Nabû promise Esarhaddon that the gods will support him as they before have supported him. Ištar of Arbela reminds Esarhaddon: 'I appeased Aššur with you' (ii 31'). Since no deteminative is used, Aššur may either stand for Assyria or the god Aššur.[310] Ištar has restored the disturbed relationship of Esarhaddon with Assyria/Aššur. In either case it refers to the period of trouble after the murder of Sennacherib: the war between members of the royal family and the bloodshed in Assyria. Thus, the oracle looks back at the events of 681. Both Bel (Marduk) and Ištar of Arbela make furthermore clear that Esarhaddon as the legitimate throne candidate, had

---

[308]   Assur A ii 12-26. This inscription was composed in 679 (Borger 1956: 6), not long after Esarhaddon's accession to the throne. A similar description is found in the later Nineveh A inscription, ii 6-7 (673 BCE): 'Prophetic oracles (*šipir maḫḫê*), messages of the gods and the goddess (i.e. Ištar), were constantly sent to me and encouraged my heart.'

[309]   The short oracle 1.3 may reflect the happy occasion of Esarhaddon's throne ascension: 'I (i.e. Ištar of Arbela) rejoice with Esarhaddon, my king! Arbela rejoices!' Furthermore, 1.9 probably relates to Esarhaddon's ascension. This fragment is not an oracle, but perhaps the introduction to an oracle that is lost: 'Well-being for Esarhaddon, king of Assyria! Ištar of Arbela has gone out to the desert and has sent an oracle of salvation to her calf in the city. [...] at [her] coming out [...].'

[310]   The parallel (partly restored) in 2 ii 3', 'I will [reconcile] Assyria with you' supports the interpretation of 'Assyria' (so Weippert 2002: 14, n. 55). However, for the motif of the reconciliation of the king with the god Aššur through Ištar's intermediation (so Parpola in SAA 9: 6), a parallel can be found in the prophecy of SAA 13 139, which refers to the reconciliation of Ashurbanipal with Bel (Marduk) upon the intercession of Mullissu (see Nissinen 2002: 16). In the latter case, the anger of Bel (Marduk) related to the violent events of the war between Šamaš-šum-ukin and Ashurbanipal (see 4.2.8).

been protected by the gods since he was born.[311] The gods had supported him, through the difficulties, until he became king, and they would keep on supporting him. The three gods speaking in this oracle in different words give a similar message: Esarhaddon will be protected in the future as he was in the past.

Furthermore, two oracles from the prophet La-dagil-ili, 1.10 and 2.3, can be dated at, or shortly after, Esarhaddon's accession, as is indicated by the references to his palace (1 vi 25-26, 2 ii 2, 9) and royal crown (2 ii 5):

> [I am the Lady of Arb]ela. [Esarhaddon, whos]e bosom [Ištar] of Arbela has filled with goodwill, could you not rely on the previous word that I spoke to you! Now you can rely on (this) later one as well, therefore praise me! When the day declines, let them hold torches. Praise me in front of (them). From my palace I will let go out trembling.[312] You shall eat safe food and drink safe water, and you shall be safe in your palace. Your son and grandson will exercise kingship in the lap of Ninurta.

> [I am the La]dy of Arbela. [Esarhaddon, king of] Assyria, [fear not!] .... Your enemies, as many [they are .....] your palace [....] I will [reconcile] Assyria with you. I will [pro]tect you by day and by dawn and [consolidate] your crown. Like a winged bird ov[er its young] I will chirp over you, go round and turn around you. Like a good puppy dog I will run around in your palace, and smell your enemies. I will keep you safe in your palace. I will make you overcome anxiety and trembling. Your son and your grandson will exercise kingship before Ninurta. The territories of the lands, I will give them to you in their totality. Mankind is deceitful; I am the one who speaks and acts, I am the 'noisy daughter',[313] I smell, catch and deliver (them)[314] to you. As for you to me:

---

[311] Cf. Nineveh A section 27 (Borger 1956: 39-40, l. 4-7), where Esarhaddon is referred to as 'the beloved of the Great Gods whom Aššur, Šamaš, Bel, Nabû, Ištar of Nineveh and Ištar of Arbela called to the kingship of Assyria when he was still a child'; see Nissinen 1998: 19.

[312] Translation suggested by Weippert (private communication) '[Z]ittern lasse ich [v]on meinem Palast ausgehen'. The meaning is that the goddess promises she will intimidate and deter the adversaries and enemies of Esarhaddon, so that the king will live in safety.

[313] Parpola (SAA 9) translates: 'I am the one who says and does. I will sniff out, catch and give you the "noisy daughter".' According to Parpola, "noisy daughter" is a metaphor for "corrupt men" ('daughter' means 'mankind' and 'noise' means 'corruption'). Nissinen (2003a: 113) translates: '... I am the one whose words and deeds are reliable. I am the one who sniffs out and captures the riotous people and gi[ves] them to you.' Weippert (2002: 42-44) objects to this interpretation. The passage reflects the energy and vigour of the goddess, Weippert translates: 'Ich bin es, die spricht (und) handelt! Eine Tatkräftige bin ich!'.

[314] No explicit object is mentioned, but clearly the king's enemies are indicated.

praise me! Collect these words of mine from Arbela in the inner quarter
of your palace. The gods of Esagila languish in the wild of confused
evil.[315] May two burnt offerings be quickly sent out to their presence, so
that they may come and announce your well-being.

In several ways these oracles differ from the ones to be situated in the
context of Esarhaddon's rise to power (4.2.1). The announcement of
divine actions against the enemy (Esarhaddon's rivals) is changed into
the general promise 'Your enemies, as many [they are]' (2 ii 1'). The
focus is on Esarhaddon's protection in his palace (1 vi 19-26; 2 ii 6'-
12'), the kingship of his progeny (1 vi 27-30; 2 ii 13'-14'), and praise
for the goddess (1 vi 13,18; 2 ii 21').[316]

An important issue in the first years of Esarhaddon's reign was the
restoration of Babylon.[317] Bel-ušezib, in his already mentioned letter,
emphasised the connection between Esarhaddon's kingship and Babylon's restoration.[318] The demand found in oracle 2.3, regarding
sacrifices to the suffering gods of Esagila, so that they will announce
Esarhaddon's *šulmu*, his well-being, is related to this issue.

In oracle 2.2 a deity, possibly Bel (Marduk),[319] promises Esarhaddon to protect him, and announces his *šulmu* (i 33').[320] The best preserved part of this oracle is as follows:

> Fe[ar not] Esarhaddon. [Like] a good [boat]man I will [k]eep [the ship]
> in a good quay;[321] as before, in future I will [go] around and protect [you
> as] your guard. [The guard over] the lands is very strong. [Sixty gods
> are standing at] my [right], sixty gods at my left. Esarhaddon, king of
> Assyria, I will vanquish yo[ur enemies]. [...] I am their Lord (i 15'-24').

---

[315]   The expression 'evil and confused desert' (*ṣēru lemnu ballu*) probably refers to
Babylon, see note 298 above.

[316]   If Parpola's restoration of the name La-dagil-ili in SAA 9 3 in iv 31 is correct,
this third prophecy of La-dagil-ili (3.5) probably relates to the early years of Esarhaddon's reign too (for this oracle, see chapter 5.1.4).

[317]   See Borger 1956: 16-26, episode 12-37; Borger 1972: 33-37.

[318]   SAA 10 109, 13-15, 24, r. 14-15.

[319]   Cf. the parallel with the 'sixty gods' in 1 ii 22', 25', where Bel (Marduk) is
speaking.

[320]   There may be a connection between oracle 2.3, demanding for sacrifices to the
gods of Esagila, so that they will announce Esarhaddon's *šulmu* and oracle 2.2 in
which a deity—possibly Bel (Marduk)—announces Esarhaddon's *šulmu*. Perhaps oracle 2.2 was spoken in reaction to the offerings that were required in oracle 2.3. For the
connection between the offering of sacrifices to the gods by the king and a message of
well-being (*šulmu*) for the king sent by the gods, see SAA 13 43 l. 1-4.

[321]   Similarly Weippert 2002: 42.

A clue for situating this oracle lies in the phrase 'as before, in the future I will [go] around and protect [you as] your guard'. The deity promises to protect Esarhaddon, as he did before. This refers to past events, presumably to the troublesome period in 681. The oracle itself thus belongs to a later stage. In the conflict over the succession, in 681, certain Babylonians had taken Esarhaddon's side.[322] Moreover, various Babylonian deities had supported Esarhaddon, and promised him kingship through prophetic oracles and other means.

However, one does not get owt for nowt. From the Babylonian perspective, Esarhaddon was to become king in order to restore Babylon and Esagila. This thought is adopted in Esarhaddon's Babylon inscription. The Babylon inscription describes the destruction of Babylon and the deplorable state of the city and its temples.[323] The inscription further narrates that when Marduk's heart became peaceful again, he appointed Esarhaddon as king in order to restore the evil situation: the state of destruction of Babylon and Esagila (Marduk's temple).[324] This is accompanied by favourable omens concerning the restoration of Babylon and Esagila.[325] These favourable omens resemble the *ittu* reported by Bel-ušezib (see 4.2.1 above). The earliest version of the Babylon inscription (Bab. A) is dated to 680.[326] It presents Esarhaddon as a typical Babylonian ruler and displays a pro-Babylonian tendency.[327]

During Sennacherib's reign the relation between Assyria and Babylonia had been disturbed, with as a climax Sennacherib's siege and capture of Babylon and the deportation of Marduk's statue to Assyria.[328] The Babylonian support of Esarhaddon indicates that the Babylonians considered him to be the likeliest candidate to turn their fate. This proved to be a right calculation: when Esarhaddon became king he soon started rebuilding activities in Babylon and the restoration of Esagila. The first copies of his Babylon inscription, dealing with the restoration of city and temple, date to 680, implying that the

---

[322] Cf. SAA 18 100 (ABL 1091), a Babylonian letter that connects certain Babylonians with Esarhaddon's side in the conflict of 681.

[323] It should however be kept in mind that 'language of destruction' in the royal inscriptions does not always correspond with reality; kings may claim to have utterly destroyed a city, whereas the real damage was limited; see Dalley 2005.

[324] Babylon A and D, Episode 11:9-13 (Borger 1956: 16).

[325] Borger 1956: 16.

[326] Porter 1993: 95; cf. 1993: 100.

[327] Porter 1993: 95-97.

[328] Porter 1993: 29 and 39.

work had been started by then.[329] Other Babylonian and Assyrian cities saw their sanctuaries restored as well.[330]

The oracles relating to Esarhaddon's first years as a king, confirm the impression that prophecy, though evidently supportive of the king, should not be regarded as merely royal propaganda. Besides the encouraging aspect, a demanding aspect has to be accounted for too (this will be explored in chapter 5).

4.2.3   *External Threat and Internal Instability (c. 675 BCE)*

SAA 9 2.4 in my view consists of various oracles which are introduced as divine words, ii 30', 38': 'Word of Ištar of Arbela, word of Queen Mullissu', 'word of Ištar [of Arbela] to [...]' (see chapter 3.1.1). The various words apparently stem from one prophetess: Urkittu-šarrat from Calah (iii 18'). As a heading to the words, ii 29' states: 'Thus you shall answer the disloyal ones'.[331] This may indicate that what follows is some sort of anthology. iii 7'-10' confirms that the divine words are meant as a reaction to anxious or disloyal people: 'How, how (to answer) those who to the many [....] men [say] thus: 'when the land becomes hostile, let us not stay in Calah and Nineveh!' The goddess reacts in ii 31'-34', 'I will look, I will listen, I will search out, and I will put the disloyal ones into the hands of my king', and in iii 11'-17':

> You, keep silent, Esarhaddon! I will choose the envoys of the Elamite and the Mannean. I will seal the writings of the Urarṭian. I will cut off the *heel*[332] of Mugallu. Whoever is lone, whoever is oppressed, fear not under the protection of Esarhaddon, king of Assyria.[333]

The references to the foreign nations are indicative of the oracle's date. Esarhaddon went on campaign against the Manneans in 675.[334] In

---

[329]   Porter 1993: 43, 169. For the text, see Borger 1956: 16-26.
[330]   Porter 1993: 61-62.
[331]   Or: 'This is how she (i.e. the goddess) answers the disloyal ones'.
[332]   The word *igbu* is understood by Parpola as a form of *eqbu* 'heel'.
[333]   The protective shadow (*ṣillu*) of the king is a common expression, see e.g. SAA 10 160, 43; 207, 20 and r. 3; 259 r. 10; 294 r. 22. The reassurance of these people to a great extent parallels the encouraging words of Isaiah addressed to the people of Zion (Isa 10:24-25) and to the 'weary' (Isa 28:12). Furthermore, Esarhaddon is presented by Ištar as the protective shadow of the lone and the oppressed, just as the ideal king and his officials are described as the protective rock and refuge of the people in Isa 32:1-2. Cf. Isa 14:32, also presented as an 'answer' to people.
[334]   Starr 1990: LIX-LX; queries SAA 4 28-34 and letters SAA 10 111 and 112.

674 he concluded a peace treaty with Urtaku, king of Uraṛṭu.[335] Furthermore, an expedition against Mugallu of Melid was undertaken in
675, which forced Mugallu to ask for peace.[336] These circumstances
provide an approximate date for this text, presumably shortly before
these events.

Preceding the campaign against the Manneans, the Babylonian
scholar Bel-ušezib wrote a letter to Esarhaddon (SAA 10 111), which
concludes with an oracle of Marduk announcing the defeat of the
enemies (r. 23-26): 'Bel has said: "Esarhaddon, king of Assyria (sits)
on the throne like Marduk-šapik-zeri, and while he is seated there I
will deliver all the countries into his hands".' Although Bel-ušezib is
uncertain with respect to the best military strategy in the war against
the Manneans (see SAA 10 111), he is convinced that Marduk has decided the destruction of Mannea.[337] Marduk-šapik-zeri is a former king
of Babylon (1081-1069 BCE). According to the oracle, Marduk regards Esarhaddon as the legitimate king of Babylon and ruler of the
world. This can be taken as an indication that important military campaigns were guided not only by technical divination, but also by prophetic oracles.

From the passage from 2.4 quoted above it appears that this period
was troubled by internal unrest as well. Internal turmoil was not restricted to the period just before Esarhaddon's accession. At various
points during his reign a threat of conspiracy or social instability occurred. A major uprising, led by a Babylonian called Ṣillaia, has been
dated to this period (c. 675/674).[338] One of the letters referring to this
conspiracy is by the already mentioned Bel-ušezib (SAA 10 112). After having assured the king he will have further successes in the war
against the Manneans (l. 3-27), the second part of the letter deals with
a conspiracy against the king, led by Šuma-iddin, the governor of
Nippur.[339] Bel-ušezib mentions various persons involved, among them
Ṣillaia. He advises the king to take immediate action, encouraging the
king as follows: 'The great gods said to Bel: "May it be in your power
to exalt and to abase". You are Marduk of the people; Bel destined

---

[335] Borger 1956: 58-59:26-33; Parpola and Watanabe (1988: XVII) refer to ABL
328 and 918.

[336] Esarhaddon Chronicle, Grayson 1975a: 126:15; Starr 1990: LVII-LVIII, queries SAA 4 1-12.

[337] For a commentary on this letter, see Fales and Lanfranchi 1981.

[338] Dietrich 1970: 39-50; Frame 1992: 84-88; Nissinen 1998: 138-139.

[339] SAA 10 112 r. 7-8.

your glori[ous ....] (to be) like destinies. [Let the king, my lord] act in
a way corresponding to Bel: abase the high and [exalt] the low.'[340]
Both in the oracles of 2.4 and in this letter of Bel-ušezib it is made
clear that the problems, external and internal, will be solved, and that
the king will rule to the benefit of the good people: 'Whoever is lone,
whoever is oppressed, fear not under the protection of Esarhaddon,
king of Assyria' (2.4 iii 16'-17').

4.2.4   *Ashurbanipal's Appointment as Crown Prince (672 BCE) and*
the War against Egypt

Esarhaddon's first campaign against Egypt of 674 was unsuccessful:
the forces of the Cushite king Taharqa defeated the Assyrian army.[341]
In the following years, the war against Egypt was a major issue. In my
opinion, two oracles from SAA 1 can be connected with this period:
1.1 and 1.6. Oracle 1.1 belongs to the time that Esarhaddon was already king of Assyria.[342] The first part of the oracle (i 6'-17') refers to
the past:

> What wind has risen against you whose wing I have not broken? Your
> enemies will roll before your feet like ripe apples. I am the Great Lady,
> I am Ištar of Arbela, who has cast your enemies before your feet. What
> words of mine that I spoke to you could you not rely upon?

Ištar refers to her deeds in the past, when she saved Esarhaddon from
his enemies. The interrogative *ayyu*, 'what wind' (i 6'), 'what words'
(i 15'), has a frequentative force. The goddess points out that she has
always saved Esarhaddon and let him prevail over his enemies. In the
second part of the oracle Ištar of Arbela stresses that she will support
Esarhaddon this time too: 'I will flay your enemies and give them to
you. I, Ištar of Arbela, will go before and behind you. Fear not!' (i 19-
24'). A further clue is provided in i 25, where Ištar says: 'you are in
cramp/stiffness' (*atta ina libbi muggi)'*. The word *mungu/mug(g)u*,
not often used, is also attested in a letter referring to Esarhaddon's
disease.[343] That Esarhaddon suffered from a disease is well-known.
Parpola has argued that he suffered from a rheumatoid disease of

---

[340] SAA 10 112 r. 29-33 (Parpola's translation).
[341] Babylonian Chronicle; Grayson 1975a: 84:16; see Tadmor 1983: 41-43.
[342] Contra Parpola 1997: LXVIII; Nissinen 1998: 25.
[343] SAA 10 37 r. 1, 7; Parpola 1983: 336-337. CAD *mangu/mungu* 'stiffness', 'pa-
ralysis'.

which stiffness was part. According to Parpola's reconstruction, Esarhaddon was seriously ill in 672 and 670, before he died of it in 669.[344] I would suggest that 672 makes most sense as a date for this oracle. Besides, the promise of the goddess to flay Esarhaddon's enemies, probably applies to foreign enemies.[345]

The second oracle to be situated in this period is 1.6. This oracle contains the announcement: 'I will take you safely across the river' (iv 3-4), which has been connected with Esarhaddon's crossing the Tigris in 681, referred to in Nin. A i 84-86.[346] However, the motif 'crossing the river' is common in Assyrian royal inscriptions,[347] and Weippert rightly states that this announcement could relate to any military campaign to the West.[348] The designation of Esarhaddon in this oracle as *aplu kēnu*, 'true heir' (iv 5-6 and [20]), does not point to the period before his ascension to the throne,[349] but is a royal epithet.[350] Oracle 1.6 is concerned with the consolidation of Esarhaddon's kingship, which suggests that he was already king. The oracle is likely to relate to one of the military campaigns undertaken by Esarhaddon. The text is as follows:

> I am Ištar of [Arbela]. Esarhaddon, king of A[ssyria], in Assur, Nineveh, Calah and Arbela I will give long days and everlasting years to Esarhaddon my king. I am your great midwife, I am your excellent wet nurse. I have established your throne under the great heavens for long days and everlasting years. In the (bed)room of gold in the midst of heavens I watch, I let a lamp of amber shine before Esarhaddon, king of Assyria, and I watch him like the crown of my head.
>
> Fear not, O king. I hereby say to you: I did not lie to you, but I gave you trust, and I will not let you come to shame. I will take you across the river in safety. Esarhaddon, true heir, son of Mullissu, angry dag-

---

[344] Parpola 1983: 230-236; see also Porter and Radner 1998: 146.

[345] On the Lachish relief soldiers are pictured as being cast down to be flayed (the figure is included in Parpola 1997: 28). According to Dalley (2004a: 391) these are Cushite soldiers (see note 204 above).

[346] Parpola 1997: 8, and Nissinen 1998: 25.

[347] For Esarhaddon, cf. Borger 1956: 112:10. According to Parpola (1997: LXIX) and Nissinen (1998: 25), it refers to Esarhaddon's crossing the Tigris before his final conquest of Nineveh (681 BCE).

[348] Weippert 2002: 37.

[349] Contra Nissinen 1998: 25.

[350] See Seux 1967: 43 note 47. The designation is used by various kings, among them Ashurbanipal (SAA 3 7 r. 8) and Nebuchadnezzar II (Langdon 1912: 10:5, 12:14, 44:1, 50:3).

ger[351] in my hand! I will destroy your enemies. Esarhaddon, king of Assyria, cup full of lye, double-bladed axe![352]
Esarhaddon, I will give you long days and everlasting years in Assur,
Esarhaddon, I will be your good shield in Arbela. Esarhaddon, tr[ue]
heir, son of Mullissu, I am constantly thinking of you, I have (always)
loved you intensely. By a lock of your hair I keep you in heaven. On
your right, I make smoke rise up, on your left, I kindle fire [....]

The oracle has two main themes: the protection of the king and consolidation of his kingship, and the king as a weapon in the hand of the
goddess that will conquer all the enemies. The middle part deals with
a military campaign to the West. The strong encouragement 'I did not
lie to you' makes sense if one assumes that a second campaign against
Egypt is in mind, after the defeat of 674.

If the oracles 1.1 and 1.6 date to the period immediately preceding
the campaign of 672 to Egypt, oracle collection 1 cannot date from
673.[353] This need not imply however that the connection between the
collection and the appointment of Ashurbanipal as crown prince in
672 (as suggested by Parpola) has to be given up. On the contrary, the
possible connection becomes even stronger. The oracles 1.1 and 1.6
take an important position within the collection: 1.1 at the beginning,
and 1.6 in the middle as the longest oracle. In 672, these two oracles
dealing with the campaign against Egypt, were combined with a series
of earlier oracles, into a collection which demonstrated the legitimacy
of Esarhaddon's kingship and his hegemony over the world. This collection was also supportive of Ashurbanipal's position as crown
prince of Assyria. Furthermore, the collection composed for the purpose of supporting Ashurbanipal's appointment as crown prince, also
contained the promise to the king, and the crown prince, that Egypt
would be defeated.

Significantly, in the oracle SAA 9 7, dealing with Ashurbanipal's
appointment as crown prince, the war against Egypt also takes a
prominent position. These words of Mullissu to Ashurbanipal can be
dated to before the ceremony of Ashurbanipal's appointment as crown

---

[351] The expression 'angry dagger' is disputed and uncertain; see Weippert 2002:
40-41; Nissinen 2003a: 108, note d.

[352] The suggestion to read GÍN as *pāšu*, 'blade', proposed by Langdon (1914:
131), refuted by Parpola, (1997: 8), and argued again by Weippert (2002: 41-42)
makes sense. The alternative is 'axe of two shekels' (so Parpola; Nissinen). The point
of the image is that Esarhaddon is a dangerous weapon in the hand of the goddess.

[353] See the suggestion of Parpola, mentioned in note 266 above.

prince. Mullissu promises to protect him in the palace of succession, and to keep him safe for the kingship (2-6):

> This is the word of Queen (?)[354] Mullissu: Fear not, Ashurbanipal! Thus: until I will do and give to you as I have promised, (namely) until you exercise the kingship over the sons of the bearded courtiers and the next generation of eunuch-*courtiers*,[355] I [will take ca]re of you in the palace of succession.

The passage that follows (lines 7-11) probably refers to an *adê* ceremony for Ashurbanipal:

> [Thus: ...] he shall gird [you] with the diadem [...][356] [thus: .... The king]s of the lands will say to one another: '[... let us] go, with regard to Ashurbanipal, the king (i.e. Esarhaddon) *has witnesses* [...].[357] [Like his fathers] decreed our fathers' and grandfathers' [fate]s,[358] may [now h]e judge between us.' [Mullis]su has said: '[The king]s of the lands, <you will show them the ways>,[359] you will set their feet upon the roads.'

---

[354] According to Parpola (1997: 38), the sign LUGAL ('king') here stands for 'queen'. I agree with Weippert that this is not entirely convincing. Weippert (1997: 155-156; 2002: 48-50) alternatively suggests taking *abat šarre/amāt šarri* as a technical term for 'appellation to the king'; he translates: 'Eine Petition/Appellation der Mullissu an den König ist dies'. Although the following prophecy is not a petition or appellation, according to Weippert (2002:50) the term was nevertheless used in order to draw the king's close attention to the prophecy. This explanation is not entirely convincing in my view.

[355] So Weippert 1997: 153.

[356] Weippert (1997: 154) quotes a restoration from Parpola which has not been adopted in Parpola's edition: [AD-*ka ina ri-š*]*a-ti*, '[Your father] will [joy]fully gird (your temples) with the royal headband'. Nissinen 2003a: 127: '[your father] will gird the diadem'. Cf. SAA 10 185: 7-9 'You (Esarhaddon) have girded a son of yours (Ashurbanipal) with the diadem and entrusted to him the kingship of Assyria.'

[357] The words [*ni*]-*il-lik ina* UGU followed by the name Ashurbanipal, are translated by Parpola (1997: 38), Nissinen (2003a: 127), and Weippert (2002: 51), as: 'let us go to Ashurbanipal'. In my view, [*ni*]-*il-lik* must not be taken with *ina muḫḫi*, since *alāku ina muḫḫi* means 'to march against'. Instead, the preposition *ina muḫḫi* is used in the context of the conclusion of the *adê* 'on behalf of' Ashurbanipal. Esarhaddon concluded the *adê* 'on behalf of' (*ina muḫḫi*) his son (cf. SAA 2 6:41-44). The gods normally act as witnesses to the loyalty oaths, but the phrase *ši-i-bi ra-ši ˹x˺* is obscure (cf. Weippert 2002: 51, note 214). This passage is likely to refer to the ceremony of the loyalty oath, taken by the vassal kings on behalf of the crown prince Ashurbanipal.

[358] Line 10 restore [*ki-i* AD.MEŠ(*abbū*)-*šu* NAM.ME]Š(*šīmāte*). See Weippert 2002: 51, for a slightly different restoration.

[359] Weippert (2002: 51) suggests reading the beginning of line 13 as [*a*]*t-ta ḫu-la-a-ni tu-saḫ-mil-šu-nu*. The first part [*a*]*t-ta ḫu-la-a-ni* is attractive, since it seems uncertain whether there is space for Parpola's restoration [*ta-pi-a*]*l* at the beginning, and since *ḫūlāne*, 'ways' makes for a good parallelism with *ḫarrānāte*, 'roads', in the following clause. However, I am not convinced by Weippert's reading *tu-saḫ-mil-šu-nu*,

This prophecy pictures Ashurbanipal as the future sovereign king who rules over his vassals. Ashurbanipal was appointed as crown prince in Iyyar (II) 672, on which occasion all Assyrians assembled in order to swear a loyalty oath.[360] The difference in dating indicates that the oath-taking ceremonies took at least several days.[361] Royal functionaries such as astrologers, haruspices, exorcists, physicians and augurs probably had already taken the loyalty oath on 15 and 16 Nissan (I).[362]

I am not convinced by Weippert's suggestion that lines 3-11 are a quotation of an earlier oracle delivered on Ashurbanipal's appointment as crown prince in the context of a later oracle sometime during Ashurbanipal's reign.[363] In my view, it is a prophecy consisting of two parts. Lines 1-13 refer to the *adê*-ceremony at Ashurbanipal's appointment as the crown prince. Lines 12-13 form a conclusion to this part, by taking up a prophecy within the prophecy. The reason for the extra prophetic formula '[Mullis]su has said' in line 12 can be easily explained. In lines 9-11, the goddess cites the vassal kings; in order to make clear that in lines 12-13 the goddess is speaking herself again, an extra speaking formula is inserted.[364]

The second part of the prophecy begins in line 14: 'Secondly, let me tell you ...', and deals with foreign affairs. Mullissu announces that she will deal exhaustively (*gamāru*)[365] with the Cimmerians like she did with Elam (line 14).[366] Further, she promises the defeat of Egypt (r. 1-5):

---

instead of Parpola's *tu-kal-lam-šú-nu* 'you will show them', as a second person singular of the perfect of *ḫamālu* Š. The phrase 'you made them plan ways' is paraphrased by Weippert as '[Die König]e der Länder *ließest* [d]u Wege *ins Auge fassen*', which seems a rather free rendering.

  [360] Prism A i 11-22 // F i 10-17 (BIWA: 15-16). The beginning of line 13 is problematic.

  [361] Most documents date the event to 18 Iyyar (II): Ashurbanipal's Prism F i 11 (BIWA: 15), Esarhaddon's Tarbiṣu-inscription A l. 40 (Borger 1956: 72), most versions of Esarhaddon's succession-*adê* (SAA 2 6:664); alternative dates are 12 Iyyar (Prism A i 12; BIWA: 15) and 16 Iyyar (SAA 2 6:664Q).

  [362] See SAA 10 6 and 7.

  [363] Weippert 1997: 156-157; 2002: 47-51.

  [364] The perfect form *taqṭibi* can be understood either as a performative '[Mullis]su hereby says ...' (cf. 1 iii 31'), or as referring to a promise previously made by Mullissu. In any case, lines 12-13 conclude the first part of the prophecy, and in line 14 the second part begins. The fact that the second part is marked as dealing with another subject (line 14), confirms that the first and second part of the oracle are on the same level: both contain divine promises for Ashurbanipal.

  [365] Parpola's translation of *a-ga-mar*, 'I will finish', is unlikely since a comparison is made with the case of Elam, which was settled with a peace treaty in 674.

  [366] For a correction of Parpola's reading, see Ivantchik 1993: 40-41.

> I will break the thorn, I will pluck the bramble[367] into a tuft of wool, I will turn the wasps into a squash. *Hallalatti enguratti!* You will say: what does it mean, *hallalatti enguratti*? *Hallalatti* I will enter Egypt, *enguratti* I will come out.

This passage is somewhat uncertain. The point of the first sentence is the promise that the goddess is going to turn something that is harmful (prickly) into something harmless (soft). In other words, she will take the sting out of Egypt. The meaning of the saying *hallalatti enguratti* is unknown.[368] The prophecy ends with Mullissu's assurance that she will take care of Ashurbanipal.[369]

The importance of the Egyptian affair is indicated elsewhere by an oracle quoted in a letter to king Ashurbanipal (SAA 10 174). The letter describes how Esarhaddon, when he marched out to Egypt in 671, was encouraged in the temple of Sîn outside the city of Harran with a prophetic oracle: two crowns, probably symbolising Upper and Lower Egypt, were placed on Esarhaddon's head, and he received the message 'You will go and conquer the world with it!' According to the author of the letter, this was exactly what happened: '[So he we]nt and conquered Egypt' (the letter is discussed in chapter 6.2.1).

4.2.5   *The Presumed Conspiracy of Sasî (671/670 BCE)*

The Assyrian official Nabû-reḫtu-uṣur in several letters reports to king Esarhaddon about an alleged conspiracy led by a man called Sasî.[370] Nabû-reḫtu-uṣur is convinced that the life of the king is threatened by the conspiracy headed by Sasî, which has its base in the city Harran.[371] Nissinen has suggested connecting the conspiracy revealed by Nabû-reḫtu-uṣur with a coup d'état of 671/70, the outcome of which is reflected by the Chronicle of Esarhaddon: 'In the eleventh year, the

---

[367] The sequence *a-šab-bir ma-a mur-din-nu* is perhaps better read as *a-šab-bir-ma a-mur-din-nu*.

[368] Suggestions in Parpola, SAA 9, 39; Weippert 1997: 154, note 27.

[369] 'You whose mother is Mullissu, fear not! You whose nurse is the Lady of Arbela, fear not! I will carry you on my hip like a nurse. I will place you (like) a pomegranate between my breasts. (.....) You, fear not, my calf that I rear.' (r. 6-11).

[370] Parpola's first edition of the letters is published in Nissinen 1998: 109-115. They are republished, with minor changes, as SAA 16 59-61, and in Nissinen 2003a: texts 115-117. Lambert's critical remarks concerning Parpola's edition in Nissinen 1998 (Lambert 2002b: 212) are not yet mentioned in the later editions.

[371] See Nissinen 1998: 127.

king of Assyria put many of his magnates to the sword.'[372] Nissinen
connected a range of further letters with this coup d'état, among them
SAA 10 179, in which the Babylonian scholar Kudurru writes to the
king that he was forced to perform the treasonous divination 'Will the
rab ša rēšē take over the kingship?' The divination was positive, but
Kudurru in his letter assures the king that the divination was not valid,
and begs the king to spare his life.[373] A difficulty with Nissinen's reconstruction is, that in 671/70 Sasî did not hold the office of *rab ša
rēšē* (a highest-rank military officer).[374] Who was the leader of the conspiracy: the *rab ša rēšē*, Sasî, or still someone else? The identity of the
'many magnates' that were executed in 670 is unknown. Not everyone
accused in a letter addressed to the king was also executed. Sasî, for
instance, accused by Nabû-reḫtu-uṣur, seems to have been still in
office during the reign of Ashurbanipal.[375] The letters of Nabû-reḫtu-
uṣur represent his subjective point of view.[376]

In Nabû-reḫtu-uṣur's letters prophecy plays a prominent role.[377] In
the first letter, SAA 16 59, he reports a prophetic oracle in favour of
Sasî, which the current editions present as follows:

> A slave girl of Bel-aḫu-uṣur [...] upon [...] on the ou[tski]rts of
> H[arran]; since Sivan (III) she has been enraptured and speaks a good
> word about him: 'This is the word of Nusku: the kingship is for Sasî; I
> will destroy the name and the seed of Sennacherib' (ABL 1217 r. 2'-
> 5').[378]

Uncertain are the reading H[arran],[379] and the translation 'enraptured'.[380] Yet, it is clear that the prophecy supports Sasî and announces

---

[372] Grayson 1975a: 86:29; 127:27. See Nissinen 1998: 108-153, in particular 128.
Cf. also Starr 1990: LXIII.
[373] See Nissinen 1998: 133-134. For the letter of Kudurru see also 4.1.8 above.
[374] Nissinen 1998: 147-150.
[375] Nissinen 1998: 145. Nissinen (1998: 135-150) analyses the evidence and cau-
tiously discusses various possibilities.
[376] More people were accused than were actually punished. Royal officials were
obliged by oath to report any (presumed) conspiracy. Many accusations probably
were merely based on rumours, but nevertheless reported, in order to fulfil the obligations to the king.
[377] For the background of the letters, see Nissinen 1998: 116-127.
[378] Taken from Nissinen 2003a: 171; cf. SAA 16 59.
[379] According to Lambert (2002b: 212), this reading is 'entirely wrong'. Lambert
suggests reading l[ú SA]G (*ša rēšēn*) 'royal official', which changes the phrase 'on
the outskirts of Harran', to 'in association with the royal official'. In this case, Nissinen's interpretation (1998: 123-124) is to be revised. However, it need not be doubted
that Harran was the centre, or one of the centres, of the conspiracy (see SAA 16 59
[ABL 1217] l. 8').

the death of Esarhaddon, 'the seed of Sennacherib'. In his letters Nabû-reḫtu-uṣur attempts to counter this oracle of Nusku by quoting and paraphrasing various prophetic oracles in favour of king Esarhaddon. The oracles serve as reinforcement of his advice to the king to take action against the people accused in his letters. In the same letter SAA 16 59, two oracles are quoted or paraphrased. The first is referred to as *dabābu* (word) of the goddess Nikkal:

> Hear me, O king my lord![381] The word of Nikkal[382] […] 'May the […] die! May […][383] [save] your life and the life of your family, may they be your father and your mother,[384] and may they li[ft up …]; you must not destroy your life, you must not […] the kingship from your hands.'
> Hear me, O king my lord! Do not dis[regard this] word of Nik[kal] (SAA 16 59 [ABL 1217] l. 8-12).

The second is only a fragment: 'Let me gather yo[ur …] [… you], stay in safety in your palace[385] […] until […] [may …] die, save your life!' (ABL 1217 r. 22-23). In Nabû-reḫtu-uṣur's second letter, SAA 16 60, we find paraphrases or quotations of four different oracles. The first is, again, presented as a *dabābu* (word), this time of the goddess Mullissu:

> Those who sin against [your father's goodness, yo]ur fa[ther's loyalty oath and] your loyalty oath, and who [plot against yo]ur [life], they (i.e. the gods) will [place them] in [your] hands,[386] [and you shall delete] their name from Assyria[387] and from [your pa]lace. This is the word of Mullissu; [the king my lord] should not be ne[glectful] about it (SAA 16 60 [CT 53 17] l. 5-9).[388]

---

[380] The interpretation of *sarḫat* as 'enraptured' (Parpola *apud* Nissinen 1998: 111, note 430; Nissinen 2003a: 172 note b) remains uncertain.

[381] Four times in these letters, the phrase 'Hear me, O king my lord' occurs in connection with a divine word (SAA 16 59 [ABL 1217] l. 8, 12; SAA 16 60 [CT 53 17] r. 18, left edge 1).

[382] Nikkal was the moon goddess, the spouse of Sin of Harran. Weippert (2003: 288) makes mention of a collation of ABL 1217 by K. Deller reading NIN.LÍL[!] 'Mullissu' instead of Nikkal in lines 5 and 8.

[383] Perhaps restore [Bel, Nabû and Mullissu], see SAA 16 60 [CT 53 17] r. 15'.

[384] Cf. SAA 9 2.5 'I am your father and your mother' (iii 26).

[385] Cf. SAA 9 1.10, 'You shall be safe in your palace' (vi 25-26); 2.3, 'I will keep you safe in your palace' (ii 11').

[386] Cf. SAA 9 2.4, 'I will search out, and I will put the disloyal ones into the hands of my king' (ii 32'-33').

[387] Cf. SAA 10 284, 'we (i.e. Ištar of Nineveh and Ištar of Arbela) shall root out from Assyria those who are not loyal to the king our lord'.

[388] This same oracle also occurs in the text SAA 16 61 (CT 53 938) l. 5-9. This text is a fragment resembling the second letter (SAA 16 60). There are only some minor differences between the two, see Lambert 2002b: 212.

A subsequent oracle of Ištar of Nineveh is quoted: 'Ištar of Nineveh says: 'I [...], I have done, I have [...] from [your] palace [...]' (SAA 16 60 [CT 53 107] 12-14). Further on apparently an oracle is paraphrased:

> Interrogate them! Let them tell you the [...] of the people who conspired with them, and let these people die! Fear not![389] Bel, Nabû and Mullissu are standing [with you].[390] Let the people die quickly and [save] your life (SAA 16 60 [CT 53 17] r. 13'-16').

It continues with 'Hear me, O king my lord! Sa[ve] your life!' (SAA 16 60 [CT 53 17] r. 18'-19'). Finally, an oracle of Bel (Marduk) is quoted, in which the god demands gold and precious stones: 'Hear me, O king [my lord]! Bel [...] to [...] "let *xx* [....] constantly bring gold and precious stones [...] safety for [...] that he/I may prolong your li[fe]. Take care of yourself".' (SAA 16 60 [CT 53 17] e. 1-2).

Nabû-reḫtu-uṣur reveals the presumed conspiracy to the king as he was obliged.[391] The prophecy supporting Sasî clearly is an example of a prophecy forbidden by the king.[392] Such a prophecy is high treason. Nevertheless, Nabû-reḫtu-uṣur does not picture it as pseudo-prophecy.[393] Although his speaking about an *amtu*, 'slave girl', may indicate that the prophecy was enforced and produced by illegitimate means, he nevertheless presents it as a real prophecy. Nabû-reḫtu-uṣur took the prophecy of Nusku very seriously,[394] for he attempted to counter it by paraphrasing from several oracles supportive of Esarhaddon.[395]

---

[389] 'Fear not!' often occurs in prophetic oracles. If a human author admonished the king not to fear, he would use the expression 'the king should not be afraid' (*šarru (lū) lā ipallaḫ*); Nissinen 2003b: 135. This confirms that the passage paraphrases a prophetic oracle.

[390] Cf. SAA 9 1.4, 'When your mother gave birth to you, sixty great gods stood with me (i.e. Bel) and protected you: Sin was at your right, Šamaš at your left, sixty great gods were standing around you and girded your loins' (ii 20'-26').

[391] Nissinen 1998: 116-118.

[392] See SAA 2 6 l. 116-117.

[393] Contra Nissinen 1998: 121, 151-152. A comparable case is 2 Kgs 9:1-13, where a prophet proclaims to the military commander Jehu: 'Thus says Yahweh, the God of Israel: I anoint you as king over the people of Yahweh, over Israel. You shall strike down the house of your master Ahab' (2 Kgs 9:6b-7a).

[394] So also Nissinen 1998: 150-151.

[395] Nissinen 1998: 121-122.

4.2.6 *Ashurbanipal's War against Mannea (c. 660 BCE)*

Ashurbanipal's fourth campaign, c. 660,[396] was directed against
Aḫšeri, king of Mannea,[397] who rebelled against Assyria. In the account of the war, we read:

> Ištar, who dwells in Arbela, delivered Aḫšeri, who did not fear my lord-
> ship, up to his servants, according to the word that she had said in the
> very beginning: 'I will, as I have said, take care of the execution of
> Aḫšeri, the king of Mannea.'[398]

The Assyrian records (Prisms A, B, and C) narrate that Aḫšeri was
killed in a revolt by his own people, in the wake of the Assyrian military threat, and that his body was desecrated.[399] This fulfilled Ištar's
prophecy. Aḫšeri's son Ualli became subject to Assyria's rule and the
case was settled. The phrase 'in the very beginning' probably refers to
the beginning of the campaign against Mannea. The oracular phrase
itself refers to an earlier oracle as well, 'as I have said'.[400] Ištar of Arbela announced that she would destroy king Aḫšeri of Mannea. This
encouraged Ashurbanipal to undertake the campaign. At the beginning
of the campaign Ištar of Arbela repeated her announcement: 'I will, as
I have said, take care of the execution of Aḫšeri, the king of Mannea'.
After the successful campaign, the oracle was inserted in the royal account, to demonstrate that Aḫšeri's death by the hand of his own people was the work of the goddess (see further chapter 6.2.1).

4.2.7 *Ashurbanipal's War against Elam (653 BCE)*

The war against the Elamite king Teumman in 653 is described in
Ashurbanipal's Prisms B and C.[401] The inscriptions narrate that
Teumman planned war against Assyria while Ashurbanipal celebrated
a festival of Ištar in Arbela. Ashurbanipal appealed to Ištar in prayer,
and the goddess answered him: 'Ištar heard my desperate sighs and
answered me: "fear not!" She encouraged my heart: "Because of the
prayer you sent up, your eyes filled with tears, I feel compassion".'[402]

---

[396] Nissinen 1998: 46-47; Starr 1990: LXXV, note 267.
[397] See SAA 4 267-269.
[398] Prism A iii 4-7; BIWA: 35.
[399] BIWA: 35.
[400] Nissinen 1998: 52.
[401] BIWA: 97-105. For the dating in 653, see Frame 1992: 123-124.
[402] Prism B v 47-49 // C vi 46-48 (BIWA: 100). The oracle is specified in a dream
report of a *šabrû*.

The answer was probably given in the form of a prophetic oracle. First, the goddess is presented as speaking. Second, the formula 'fear not' is used, particularly at home in prophetic oracles. Third, the combination of a supplication addressed to the goddess followed by the goddess' answer in the form of a prophetic oracle, is paralleled in oracle 1.8.[403] According to the royal inscriptions, in the same night Ištar's oracle of encouragement was specified by a dream, witnessed by a šabrû.[404] In this dream Ištar appears as a mighty warrior. She states that she will go to war and defeat Elam. Ashurbanipal, in the dream, responds that he will accompany her, but Ištar commands him to stay in Assyria and let her accomplish the task ahead. The dream report concludes with the following description: 'She sheltered you in her sweet embrace, she protected your entire body. Fire flashed in her face, and she went raging away, directing her anger against Teumman, king of Elam, who had made her furious.'[405]

The description has much in common with the prophetic oracles: Ištar's protection of the king, and the motif of divine war (the goddess fights for the king). Encouraged by the 'messages of the goddesses' and the 'unchanging message of Ištar',[406] Ashurbanipal fights against Elam: 'On the command of Aššur and Marduk, the great gods, my lords, who encouraged me with good omens, dreams, speech omens and prophetic messages (šipir maḫḫê), I defeated them in Tell Tuba.'[407]

Various further prophetic oracles relate to this episode. A similar sequence of Teumman's plotting, Ashurbanipal's prayer and Ištar's answer, is found in the literary text SAA 3 31 l. 7-r. 2, but Ištar's oracle is almost completely lost (l. 18-r. 2). When the Assyrians marched against Elam, Teumman took shelter in Susa. The Elamite army was crushed and Teumman was killed. The oracle SAA 9 8 probably announces these events:

> Words [concerning the Elam]ites:[408] As [Aššur?] says:[409] 'I have go[ne and I ha]ve come.' He said this five or six times, and after that: I have

---

[403] Nissinen 1998: 53. See further chapter 5.1.2.

[404] The šabrû 'visionary', 'dreamer' was closely related to maḫḫû and raggimu (see chapter 5.1.5).

[405] Translation by Nissinen 2003a: 148.

[406] Prism B v 77-79; BIWA: 103-104.

[407] Translation by Nissinen 2003a: 149.

[408] Weippert (2002: 51) suggests reading 'Words [of the ....]', whereby the person who delivers it is presented by a gentilic form –a-a ('Die Wörte [des ...] ...äers').

[409] L. 2 can be read as ki-i ᵈ[x-x] i-qab-bi. The insertion of any name is of course uncertain. The verbal forms are masculine (although that may not be conclusive). The

gone to the [j]avelin,[410] I have pulled out the snake which was inside it, I have cut it (in pieces) and I have destroyed the javelin. And thus: I will destroy Elam. Its army will be levelled to the ground. In this manner I will finish off Elam.

The fierce language, 'its army will be levelled to the ground' equals the description in Prism B v 96-99. The terms 'javelin' (*nar'antu*) and 'snake' (*ṣerru*) in all likelihood refer to Elam and Teumman respectively.[411] According to this imagery, Teumman is pulled out of his country and 'cut into pieces' (*batāqu*; cf. *nakāsu* in Prism B vi 3; C vi 134), and Elam is broken (*ḥapû* l. 8 and 9). Weippert interprets: 'Wie ich die *nar'antu* zertrümmert habe, werde ich das Land Elam zertrümmern'.[412] The oracle describes a symbolic act carried out by the deity. This resembles what Ashurbanipal writes in his letter to Aššur: 'in the assembly of his army you (i.e. Aššur) cut off his (i.e. Teumman's) head'.[413]

In a letter to Ashurbanipal by Nabû-bel-šumate (ABL 839),[414] referring to the events of 653, prophecy plays a role again. The letter, in a postscript, connects the defeat of Teumman with an oracle of Nabû and Marduk:

> Nabû (and) Marduk, your gods, have tied [your enemies] and placed them [unde]r your feet, saying: 'May he govern all the [land]s! Let him place a prin[ce] from amongst his servants to the governors[hip of El]am and let him place another in the Sealand!' [Bel] and Na[bû] have destroyed Elam *on your behalf* saying [....][415]

The author paraphrases an oracle in which political advice is included concerning the Assyrian rule of Elam and the Sealand.[416] Through the divine word, the writer advised the king to reorganise the rule over

---

restoration [*aš-šur*] is attractive (see chapter 3.1.1) and cf. Ashurbanipal's letter to Aššur (see note 413).

[410]   I follow Weippert (2002: 52), 'Zu der *nar'antu* bin ich hingegangen'; contra Parpola (SAA 9), 'I have come from the [m]ace'.

[411]   The snake was a prominent symbol in Elamite religion and art; Nissinen 2003a: 129.

[412]   Weippert 2002: 52.

[413]   Ashurbanipal's letter to Aššur, r. 6; Bauer 1933: 83. See also Prism A v 7-8: 'Teumman, whose head I had cut off (*nakāsu*) according to the instruction (*našpartu*) of Aššur'; BIWA: 47.

[414]   Published by Mattila 1987.

[415]   ABL 839 r. 11-18; translation based on Mattila 1987.

[416]   As a letter dealing with a political issue and concluding with an oracle, ABL 839 is best compared with SAA 10 111 (see 4.2.3).

Assyria and the Sealand by appointing princes as governors over these countries.[417]

4.2.8   *The War against Šamaš-šum-ukin (652-648 BCE)*

The cause of the war between Ashurbanipal and Šamaš-šum-ukin in 652-648 was the rivalry between Assyria and Babylonia in general and the rivalry between Ashurbanipal and his brother Šamaš-šum-ukin in particular.[418] Ashurbanipal, king of Assyria and sovereign of the Assyrian empire, was the overlord of his brother Šamaš-šum-ukin, who was governor of Babylonia. Ashurbanipal kept his brother on a tight rein,[419] but after eighteen years Šamaš-šum-ukin took his chance and revolted. Šamaš-šum-ukin was supported by several of the main Babylonian cities, the Chaldean and Aramaean tribes, the Sealand, and Elam.[420] After initial success of Šamaš-šum-ukin, the Assyrians began to win ground from 650 onwards in Northern Babylonia, the heart of the resistance. The siege of Babylon, Šamaš-šum-ukin's capital, from mid-650 onwards, marked the beginning of the end of the rebellion, even though it took two more years before Babylon fell and Šamaš-šum-ukin died in 648.[421] Ashurbanipal's Prism A offers a lengthy account of the war. It begins with a description of Šamaš-šum-ukin's rebellion, which is followed by a dream report in which the god Sin announces the destruction of the enemies:[422]

> At that time a *šabrû* was sleeping ... and had a dream: It stood written on the pedestal of Sin: 'Whoever has evil plans against Ashurbanipal and picks a quarrel with him—these people I will finish off with an evil death. I will make an end of their life with a swift sword, a rain of fire, famine and pestilence.' I (i.e. Ashurbanipal) heard this and trusted the word of Sin.[423]

The subsequent description of the war is presented as the outcome of this dream: the enemies of Ashurbanipal were annihilated by sword, fire, starvation and pestilence. The reason for presenting the war with the help of this schema of divine prediction and its outcome was to

---

[417]   Mattila 1987: 30.
[418]   See Frame 1992: 131-132.
[419]   See Frame 1992: 109-114 and 130.
[420]   Frame 1992: 133.
[421]   For a detailed survey of this course of events, see Frame 1992: 137-157.
[422]   Prism A iii 118-127 (BIWA: 40-41).
[423]   Translation by Nissinen 1998: 55.

justify the brutal facts: the civil war, the siege of Babylon, and the death of Šamaš-šum-ukin. Various prophetic texts serve the same purpose.

The prophetic text SAA 9 9 is dated by its colophon to Nisan (I) 650. This is in the midst of the war, three months before the siege of Babylon began.[424] The leitmotif of the prophecy is the life of Ashurbanipal.[425] The goddess speaking in the oracle (Ištar of Arbela or Mullissu) emphasises how hard she struggles for Ashurbanipal's life. SAA 9 9 is not an oracle written down immediately from the mouth of the prophetess, but a product of literary elaboration. It is a literary text in which a previously reported prophetic oracle has been reworked. This will be further explored in chapter 6.2.1. Several elements within the text are reminiscent of the original prophetic oracle that lies at its base. The colophon contains the expression *ša pî*, 'by mouth of', which points to an originally oral deliverance of the oracle. The middle part of the text contains phrases characteristic of prophetic oracles: 'My arms are strong and will not let you fall before the gods. My shoulders are ready and will keep carrying you.' And the goddess' announcement of the destruction of the enemy and the return of an enemy (probably Elam) to his country. Clearly, the goddess encourages Ashurbanipal in a difficult situation, and assures his survival. SAA 9 9 is not the only prophetic text relating to the war between Ashurbanipal and Šamaš-šum-ukin. Other examples are SAA 3 13, the Dialogue of Ashurbanipal and Nabû, and SAA 3 44, a composition of divine words. These texts can be qualified as literary texts reminiscent of oracular language. For this reason, they are discussed in chapter 6.2.2.

Because of the huge impact of the war, afterwards there was a strong need to justify what had happened. This is clear from the oracle reported in SAA 13 139.[426] From the reverse, it appears that the author of the report is Aššur-hamatu'a, a priest or a high temple functionary, probably in the temple of Ištar of Arbela. He added to the oracle the following remark: 'I implored Bel and prayed to him, and sent Nabû-šarru-uṣur, a tracker of my contingent.' The obverse contains an oracle of Bel (Marduk). Nissinen and Parpola suppose that Aššur-hamatu'a

---

[424] Babylon was besieged on IV-11 650, see the Šamaš-šum-ukin chronicle (Grayson 1975a: 19).

[425] 'Life', *balāṭu* in l. 8, 16, 20, 21, [25], cf. 6 and r. 3.

[426] SAA 13 139; corrected versions in Nissinen 2003a: 168; Nissinen and Parpola 2004.

instantly recorded the oracle when he heard it, then added a comment on the reverse and sent it to the king.[427] The oracle is the following:

> I [am] the Lord![428] I have entered and made peace with Mu[ll]issu. Ashurbanipal, king of Assyria, whom she raised: Fear not! [I] am the Lord! I have spared (him) for you (i.e. Mullissu). Ashurbanipal is in a country of loyalty. Him together with his country I have spared for you.[429] I left your city in peace and safety. Mercy and compassion [...] *about four lines broken away.*

Nissinen and Parpola (2004) relate this oracle to the return of Marduk's statue to Babylon (668), but it is more likely to be connected to the aftermath of the war against Šamaš-šum-ukin. Since none of Aššur-hamatu'a's letters is dated (SAA 13 138-142),[430] arguments for dating 13 139 are to be drawn from the content of the oracle quoted. The interpretation of Nissinen and Parpola is based on the word 'I have entered' (*ētarba*). Because *erēbu* 'to enter' is a technical term for the return of a divine statue to its temple, they state that it is 'virtually certain that *e-tar-ba* here refers to Bel's return to his (newly restored) temple in Babylon, Esaggil.'[431] This is however not convincing. First, *erēbu*, 'to enter', is used in various ways.[432] It is used, for instance, in descriptions of divine processions: whereas *aṣû* 'to go out' marks the beginning of a procession, *erēbu* 'to go in' marks its end. Descriptions of processions in letters often contain the expressions *ina šulmi* 'in peace' and *ina šalimti* 'in safety', to emphasise that the procession

---

[427] Nissinen and Parpola 2004: 212.

[428] The logogram EN stands for Bel, 'Lord', a designation of the Babylonian god Marduk.

[429] The form *artēanki* in l. 6 and 9 does not come from *riāmu* (contra lexicon SAA 13: 192), but from *rêmu* (*re'āmu*), 'to take pity', 'to have mercy'. CAD s.v. *rêmu*, 264: 'I have spared (him) for you (i.e. Mullissu). Ashurbanipal is in a country of safety/firmness. Him together with his country I have spared for you' (CDA gives *râmu* II 'to love'; and *râmu* III [Assyrian: *riāmu*] 'excuse/remit', Neo-Assyrian). Nissinen and Parpola 2004: 206: 'to grant/bestow' or 'remit/excuse' a thing requested or pleaded for. The verb takes a direct object denoting the thing granted or excused and an indirect object denoting the beneficiary. Mullissu is the indirect object, whereas Ashurbanipal (and his country) are the direct object. Thus, *artēanki* means 'I (Marduk) have spared (him, i.e. Ashurbanipal [direct object]) for you (Mullissu [indirect object])'. Nissinen and Parpola (2004: 207) translate: 'I have spared for you Ashurbanipal in a country of truth'. In my translation, I have followed the suggestion of CAD s.v. *rêmu*, 264: 'I am sparing (him) for you'.

[430] Radner 1998: 186-187.

[431] Nissinen and Parpola 2004: 202; also 216.

[432] See Pongratz-Leisten 1994: 159.

was untroubled.[433] This is what we find in the oracle too. There is no compelling reason to connect *ētarba* specifically with Marduk's return to Babylon in 668. Moreover, the oracle as a whole supports a different understanding. Marduk asserts: 'I have entered and made peace with Mullissu.' The result of this reconciliation is worked out in the next few lines. After that, Marduk concludes that he left Mullissu's city in peace and safety. Thus, Marduk says that he came to Mullissu's city, entered (*ētarba*), made peace, and left again (*attūṣi*). This is procession terminology, used in an imaginative way, which is of course possible in an oracle.

In the oracle Marduk describes how he made peace with Mullissu. The use of *salāmu* (G), 'to make peace', implies that Marduk was angry, but relented toward Mullissu. As a result, Ashurbanipal is encouraged (Fear not!). The explication of the reconciliation is that Marduk has spared Ashurbanipal and his country. This makes sense against the background of the events of 652-648. In SAA 9 9, the goddess Mullissu or Ištar of Arbela appears as an intercessor for Ashurbanipal in front of 'the assembly of the gods' (*puḫur ilāni*). Given the outcome of the events, the goddess' intercession was successful: Ashurbanipal survived and Šamaš-šum-ukin died. This is also the issue in the oracle of SAA 13 139. The oracle implies a heavenly scene to be understood as a council of the gods.[434]

The oracle reported in SAA 13 139 resembles other prophetic oracles in various ways: the god's presentation ('I am Bel'), the direct address of Ashurbanipal, and encouragement formula 'Fear not!'. The oracle of 13 139 is therefore likely to be a prophetic oracle as well. The theme of reconciliation appears in several other prophetic oracles. In four cases *salāmu* (D) 'to pacify', occurs; Ištar of Arbela promises to pacify Assyria and the angry gods, which means she will reconcile

---

[433] Cf. SAA 10 98:7-9: 'Aššur and Mullissu left (the temple) in peace (*ina šulmi*) and entered it in safety (*ina šalimti*)'. For further examples see Pongratz-Leisten 1994: 162-163; cf. Nissinen and Parpola 2004: 208.

[434] So Nissinen and Parpola 2004: 216. Marduk's statement 'I entered' means that he entered the gods' assembly. I disagree with Nissinen and Parpola (2004: 202-204) that this 'divine council' must be located in Esagila. That Esagila from the Babylonian perspective is the seat of the divine council (cf. Enuma Elish) does not prevent the Assyrian view that the seat of the divine council is Aššur's temple Ešarra. Since Marduk says that after the 'meeting' he left Mullissu's city, which is Assur, as Nissinen and Parpola (2004: 208) agree, the 'meeting' is to be located in Assur.

them through intercession.[435] Oracle 2.5 contains the phrase: 'I will put
Assyria in order (*taqānu* D) and reconcile (*salāmu* D) the angry gods
with Assyria'. The 'angry gods' parallel the social-political disorder.
In this oracle, to be situated during Esarhaddon's struggle against his
brothers for the throne, Ištar of Arbela promises Esarhaddon that she
will restore the order in Assyria and pacify the angry gods. This
closely corresponds to 13 139, where Marduk says he has put aside his
anger with result that Ashurbanipal and his country are safe. The verb
salāmu (G) often has a political meaning with the connotation of
voluntarily submitting to a superior power. Marduk's reconciliation
with Mullissu, the spouse of Aššur and 'mother' of Ashurbanipal,
implies the acknowledgement of Babylonia's subordination to
Assyria.[436] The main message is that Babylonia and Assyria have made
peace again. The likeliest historical background, therefore, is the war
against Šamaš-šum-ukin. After the violent events, the damaging of
Babylon and the interruption of the cult, the gods, Marduk in
particular, had to be reconciled.[437] The oracle reported in SAA 13 139
contains Marduk's message of reconciliation.

4.2.9   *Evaluation*

The second part of this chapter shows that the Assyrian prophecies
that have been recorded relate to political key events.[438] A first issue of
crucial importance is the divine legitimation of the king. Both in the
difficult circumstances of 681 (4.2.1) and during the events of 672
(4.2.4), the gods proclaimed through prophetic oracles that Esarhaddon and Ashurbanipal respectively, were the legitimate Assyrian
kings. Furthermore, the gods, through the prophetic voice, confirm

---

[435]   SAA 9 1.4 'I reconciled Aššur with you' (ii 31'); 2.3 'I will reconcile Assyria
with you' (ii 3'); 2.5 'I will put Assyria in order, and reconcile the angry gods with
Assyria' (iii 19'-20'); 2.6 '[I will re]concile ...' (iv 19'). For other attestations of
salāmu, cf. e.g. SAA 10 111 r. 19: 'Marduk is reconciled with the king, my lord'.

[436]   So Nissinen and Parpola 2004: 204. The rare spelling of Assyria as KUR-AŠ
('the single country'), in a word of Marduk, could be an implicit acknowledgement of
Assyria's hegemony over Babylonia (so Nissinen and Parpola 2004: 204-205). Nissinen and Parpola (2004: 202) further suggest that the writing of Marduk's name without divine determinative reflects the Assyrian view of Marduk's subordination to
Aššur.

[437]   The New Year festival was not celebrated in Babylon for three years because
of the war, see the Akītu-chronicle, Grayson 1975a: 132:18-23.

[438]   In this respect the Assyrian prophecies resemble the Mari prophecies; see Durand 1997: 132.

Assyria's superiority, whenever Assyria's hegemony is challenged by strong enemies, such as Elam and Egypt. Finally, the gods promise the protection of the king when his position is threatened, either by conspiracies, as in the case of Esarhaddon, or by an insurrection, as in the case of Ashurbanipal in 652-648.

4.3 *Conclusion*

It has been argued in this chapter that prophecy played a role in situations of crucial political importance. The prophetic sayings of Isaiah can be connected with various key moments of Judah's political history of the late eighth century, and the prophetic oracles from Assyria relate to several key moments of the times of Esarhaddon and Ashurbanipal. When we compare both sets of prophecies, some significant similarities can be discerned. On both sides, the claim that God or the gods govern the historical scene plays a prominent role. It is the deity who is in command and decides the course of the events. Furthermore, on both sides we find the deity's affirmation that he is on the king's side. The gods are presented as intervening in situations of crucial importance.

The prophetic material discussed in this chapter is basically pro-state. Both in the prophetic material from First Isaiah and in the Assyrian prophecies an ideal image functions as a frame of reference. In the Isaianic material, the ideal image pictures the people governed by the Davidic king in justice and righteousness as living a peaceful life under Yahweh's protection. In the Assyrian prophecies, the ideal image depicts the king as protected by the gods—in particular Ištar and Mullissu—himself the protector of his subjects; there is peace in the land, the rule of heaven and earth is in harmony, and Assyrian hegemony is unthreatened. In both cases the prophecies fiercely react against any challenge to the ideal situation, both external enemies and internal adversaries. Isaiah's conflict with the leading politicians of Jerusalem is to be seen in this light. Not only was there competition between the prophet and his opponents with regard to the issue of what foreign politics to adopt, but also the prophet saw their pro-Egyptian policy as a threat to Judah's well-being, challenging the ideal of a peaceful life. Isaiah's fierce reaction can be compared to the way in which action was taken in Assyria against those threatening the well-being of the king, which meant the well-being of the state. Isaiah fulminated against the Judaean leaders advocating rebellion precisely because he regarded their politics as a mortal threat to Judah's well-being. His loyalty to state and king serves as an explanation for the absence of any direct reference to King Hezekiah in his critical sayings.

This does not mean that prophecy was royal propaganda. Prophets were supportive of the state, but did not necessarily agree with every decision of the king. On the one hand, the prophetic material contains cases of divine encouragement of the king in threatening situations. Examples are Isaiah's prophecies in 734-732 (see 4.1.2) and the prophecies for Esarhaddon in 681 (see 4.2.1). On the other hand, there are cases of divine direction to the king either to undertake or to refrain from certain actions. Examples are the demand not to trust in the military aid of Egypt (see 4.1.8) and the demand to restore Babylon and Esagila (see 4.2.2). This leads to the conclusion that prophecy in Judah and Assyria to an important extent functioned in a similar way.

There is an important difference between Isaiah's prophecies and the Assyrian prophecies as well. Isaiah's critical sayings against Judah's political leaders (4.1.8) are characterised by a quite different tone of voice than the Assyrian prophecies, which are mostly encouraging. The Assyrian prophecies frequently announce the destruction of the king's enemies, but mainly consist of positive, beneficial promises to the king. Isaiah, on the other hand, although his ideal view of Judah's society is clear, formulates his messages mostly negatively: *against* Aram and Ephraim, *against* Assyria, and, in particular, *against* Judah's political leaders. As an explanation, two issues can be mentioned, apart from the obvious fact that prophecy found different expressions in different times and places. 1) The situation of late eighth-century Judah was quite different from that of seventh-century Assyria. Whereas the Assyrian prophecies were concerned with the well-being of the king and his divine legitimacy, in Judah the survival of the state was at stake. The Assyrian prophecies, at least the extant ones, focused on the king; Isaiah's prophecies addressed the king when he was threatened (Isa 7*), but otherwise took a somewhat broader perspective on the state of Judah. The difference in tone may reflect different circumstances. Whereas the Assyrian king, despite occasional troubles, marched victoriously throughout the Near East, Isaiah witnessed the political abolition of neighbouring political states and wanted to avoid a similar fate for Judah. 2) The prophetic material at our disposal is limited. The Assyrian prophecies stem mainly from the royal archives, so a royal focus should not surprise us. Isaiah's prophecies, on the other hand, were preserved probably because his political assessment proved to be right. The analysis of this chapter shows that prophetic oracles in Judah and Assyria functioned in a more or less similar way. However, the same prophetic phenomenon found different sorts of expressions. At the one end we have the Assyrian prophecies, mainly from the royal archives, with their positive tone, at the other end Isaiah's prophecies, in which a negative tone predominates. Somewhere in between there are, for instance, the Mari prophecies. Notwithstanding the difference in expression, the prophecies from Isaiah and the Assyrian prophecies demonstrate a similar phenomenon. Isaiah, in his prophecies, supported the king and the well-being of the state of Judah; and in the Assyrian oracles, the gods exercise their power on the king by making strong cultic demands on him. Even in Assyria, the king was not invulnerable. The same prophetic voice that encouraged and legitimised the king, could also formulate demands on him, or even choose the side of his adversaries, as will be elaborated in chapter 5.

CHAPTER FIVE

FUNCTIONS OF THE PROPHETS

5.1 *Prophets in Assyria*

In the first part of this chapter I will present the material from seventh-century Assyria pertaining to the question of the role, function and social location of the prophets. Whereas the focus is on Assyrian prophecy, other examples of ancient Near Eastern prophecy, in particular from Old Babylonian Mari, will be taken into account as well. The purpose of this section is to gain insight into Assyrian prophecy as a socio-religious phenomenon, by studying it from the following angles: terms and concepts, prophets within the cultic order, prophets within the political and social order, prophetic claims and criticism, and prophets among the diviners.

5.1.1 *Terms and Concepts*

Texts from the ancient Near East show a variation in prophetic designations. Letters from Old Babylonian Mari report about prophetic oracles delivered by persons referred to by the terms: *muḫḫûm* 'ecstatic', *āpilum* 'respondent', *assinnum* 'cult functionary', *qammatum*, of which the meaning is uncertain, and *ittātum* 'signs'.[1] One letter refers to the *nabûm* of the Hanaeans, either prophets or some other kind of diviners, who where gathered for a consultation.[2] The Zakkur Stele mentions *ḥzyn* 'seers', and *'ddn* 'visionaries' (?),[3] and the Deir 'Allā Plaster Text presents Balaam as *ḥzh 'lhn* 'seer of the gods'.[4] Finally, in

---

[1]   The term 'signs' is used in the phrase *ittātim* (*zikāram u sinništam*) *ašqi aštālma*, 'the signs (male and female) I caused to drink in order to make an inquiry' (ARM 26/1 207 4-6 and ARM 26/1 212 2'). For the terms and the different prophetic functions in Mari, see ARM 26: 386-396; Fleming 2004: 51-53.

[2]   ARM 26/1 216. Fleming (2004: 52-53) objects to the view that the *nabûm* performed extispicy. Their divinatory activity may have resembled that of the 'signs' (ARM 26/1 207 and 212).

[3]   Zakkur Stele l. 12, see Seow, in: Nissinen 2003a: 204-206. The meaning of *'ddn* (Seow: visionaries) is disputed; see also Lemaire 2001b: 95.

[4]   Combination I l. 1, see Seow, in: Nissinen 2003a: 209-210.

the Lachish ostraca, the term *hnb'* 'the prophet', appears.[5] In the Neo-Assyrian period two terms for prophetic figures are attested, namely *raggimu* and *maḫḫû*. Since the terms appear both in official documents and in daily correspondence, *raggimu* and *maḫḫû* may represent two different prophetic functions. In one text, an *adê*-treaty for crown prince Ashurbanipal, the terms appear side by side. This document obliges those who take the loyalty oath to report to the king any negative or possibly harmful word they hear concerning Ashurbanipal:

> Either from the mouth of his enemy or from the mouth of his ally, or from the mouth of his brothers (...), or from the mouth of your brothers, your sons, your daughters, or from the mouth of a *raggimu*, a *maḫḫû*, or a *šā'ilu amat ili*, or from the mouth of any human being at all.[6]

The enumeration of *raggimu*, *maḫḫû*, and *šā'ilu amat ili*, the last one being an 'inquirer of divine words', is part of the attempt to be all-inclusive.[7] The term *raggimu* may be a Neo-Assyrian innovation, but the traditional term *maḫḫû* stayed in use as well.[8] Given the variation in prophetic titles elsewhere in the ancient Near East there is no need to enforce an identification of the terms *raggimu* and *maḫḫû* in the Neo-Assyrian period. Instead, there may be some indication that *raggimu* denoted a somewhat different prophetic function from *maḫḫû*.[9]

Maḫḫû

The *maḫḫû* (Assyrian) or *muḫḫû* (Babylonian) is a prophetic figure well known from the Mari letters.[10] The term *muḫḫû*, which was in use from the Ur III period through the Old Babylonian and Middle Assyr-

---

[5]   Ostracon 3 r. 4 and 16 l. 5, see Seow, in: Nissinen 2003a: 214-218.

[6]   SAA 2 6:111-118. This text is an oath of loyalty for Ashurbanipal taken at the moment of his appointment as crown prince of Assyria. Whereas the Medes presented in this text as those taking the oath of loyalty have been commonly regarded as vassals of Assyria, Liverani (1995) argues that they were royal bodyguards.

[7]   SAA 2 6 contains several enumerations of persons. From the inclusion of prophets in the list of people that could be suspected of conspiring against the crown prince or the king, it follows that prophecy could also be used *against* the king. Since the king did not directly control the prophets, he needed to be informed about their words in order to root out any sign of disloyalty; Nissinen 1998: 160-161.

[8]   Weippert 2002: 32. Since *maḫḫû* is attested in Neo-Assyrian texts, MÍ.GUB.BA in SAA 9 10 s. 1 can be read as *maḫḫūtu* (contra Parpola 1997: XLVI). Nissinen's suggestion of *raggimu* as 'colloquial equivalent' of *maḫḫû* (2000b: 91) is unfounded.

[9]   Cf. Villard 2001: 65-66.

[10]   Durand 1988: 386-388, 398.

ian periods to the Neo-Babylonian time,[11] is commonly translated as 'ecstatic' or 'ecstatic prophet'.[12] In lexical lists and cultic and administrative texts, *muḫḫû* is regularly associated with other temple-figures, in particular those characterised by peculiar behaviour, such as *zabbu* 'frenzied one', *kalû* 'chanter', *assinnu* and *kurgarrû*, which are cult functionaries as well.[13] The term *maḫḫû* is furthermore attested in Neo-Assyrian texts.[14] The *maḫḫû* was known for his ecstatic, frenzied behaviour, both in Mari,[15] and in the Neo-Assyrian period.[16]

In the inscriptions of Esarhaddon and Ashurbanipal, the *maḫḫû* is mentioned several times in the expression *šipir maḫḫê* 'messages from the *maḫḫû*-prophets'. In Esarhaddon's inscriptions the *šipir maḫḫê* appear among the favourable signs which inaugurated his kingship (Assur A i 31-ii 26; Borger 1956: 2):

> Messages from the *maḫḫû*-prophets concerning the firm founding of the foundation of the throne of my priesthood until far-off days were sent to me constantly on a regular basis; good omens, through dreams and speech omens (*idāt dumqi ina šutti u gerrê*), concerning the firm founding of my throne and the long lasting of my reign, kept occurring to me.

---

[11] Attestations listed by Parpola 1997: XLV-XLVI, CIII, notes 221-223, 228.

[12] In Assyrian royal inscriptions derivatives of *maḫû* occur in the (negative) meaning 'to become crazy'. E.g. Borger 1956: 42, i 41, 'my brothers became mad'; 44, i 73, 'seeing my onslaught, they became mad'; BIWA Prism B i 81 and Prism E Stück 10 2, concerning Taharqa, 'he went out of his mind'. These may be allusions to Tiamat: '[Tiamat] went out of her mind, she lost her reason' (*maḫḫūtiš ītemi ušanni ṭēnša*; Enuma Elish iv 88). Note that CAD places *maḫḫūtiš emû* 'to become crazy', under *muḫḫūtu*, 'woman ecstatic', and *maḫḫūtiš alāku* 'to become crazy', under *maḫḫūtu* 'condition of an ecstatic'.

[13] See Nissinen 2000b: 93-94, notes 22-25. Maul (1992) suggests that *assinnu* and *kurgarrû* were figures associated with the cult of Ištar, who played a role in ritual activities. Maul explains the occasional negative references to these figures from people's fear of the powers (associated with witchcraft) these figures were believed to possess due to their being different (*contra* the explanation that these figures were homosexuals and transsexuals).

[14] SAA 2 6:117 (quoted above); various ritual texts, SAA 3 23:5; 34:28; 35:31; Farber 1977: 140-142:31, 59; and SAA 12 69:29: 'The brewers tak[e] 1 homer 5 litres (of barley) for the prophetesses (*maḫḫâte*)' (dating from 809 BCE).

[15] Nissinen (2000b: 92) mentions examples from the Mari prophecies, and one from a ritual text (cf. Durand and Guichard 1997: 52-58). Whereas the *muḫḫû* was characterised by ecstatic behaviour (Durand [1997: 123] qualifies *muḫḫû* as 'totalement fou'), the *āpilu* sometimes wrote to the king himself (ARM 26/1 194); for this difference, see Durand 1988: 386-392.

[16] See SAA 3 23:5, 'he wailed like a *maḫḫû*'. The cult of Ištar included ecstatic dancing and cultic activities. Whereas *assinnu* and *kurgarrû* in particular are connected with this (e.g. Gabbay 2003: 103-104), *muḫḫû* perhaps also took part in them.

When I saw these good signs (*ittātu*) my heart became confident, and my mood joyful.[17]

A similar passage from a later inscription, referring to the same period, includes the following description (Nineveh A ii 3-7; Borger 1956: 45):

Good portents (*idāt dumqi*) appeared to me in the sky and on earth; messages from the *maḫḫû*-prophets, messages from the gods and the goddess (Ištar) were constantly sent to me and encouraged my heart.[18]

In Ashurbanipal's inscriptions the expression *šipir maḫḫê* occurs in the episode concerning the campaign against the Elamite king Teumman, before the final battle (Prism B v 93-95, C vi 125-127; BIWA: 104):

On the command of Aššur and Marduk, the great gods, my lords, who encouraged me through good omens, dreams, speech omens (*ina ittāti damqāti šutti egerrê*), and messages from the *maḫḫû*-prophets, I defeated them in Tell Tuba.[19]

Finally, the expression occurs in Ashurbanipal's inscriptions dealing with the restoration of the cult of Ištar-Kidmuri (Prism T ii 14-19, C i 59-62; BIWA: 140-141):

She (Ištar) constantly instructed me through dreams (*ina šutti*) and messages from the *maḫḫû*-prophets to perfect her exalted divinity and to glorify her precious cult.[20]

In several cases *šipru*, without *maḫḫû*, refers to a divine message. Ashurbanipal's votive inscription mentions a *šipru* of Marduk to Ashurbanipal (*šipri ilūtika*, l. 24), in which Marduk announces the destruction of Ashurbanipal's enemy.[21]

These messages from the *maḫḫû*-prophets are related to dreams (*šuttu*), speech omens (*egerrû*), portents (*idu*), and signs (*ittu*); they were reported to the king. It may be that some of the prophetic mes-

---

[17] Cf. Nissinen 2003a: 143.
[18] Cf. Nissinen 2003a: 141.
[19] Cf. Nissinen 2003a: 149.
[20] Cf. Nissinen 2003a: 143-144.
[21] BIWA: 202. Cf. also Prisms B v 78-79, C vi 80-82 (BIWA: 103), relating to Ashurbanipal's campaign against Teumman: 'I relied on the decision of the bright Moon and the message (*šipru*) of Ištar, which cannot be changed'.

sages referred to in the passages quoted above, are in fact included in the corpus of SAA 9.[22]

Raggimu

The terms *raggimu* and *raggintu* (fem.) appear in administrative texts, letters, colophons of prophetic oracles, and in an *adê*-text.[23] In addition, the verb *ragāmu* is attested several times meaning 'to prophesy', 'to deliver an oracle'.[24] The precise meaning of the term *raggimu* is uncertain,[25] but may be associated with *ragāmu* meaning 'to call out', 'to proclaim', 'to claim', perhaps 'to announce'.[26] Thus, *raggimu* is associated with the public deliverance of a spoken message. A main characteristic of the *raggimu* was the oral deliverance of divine messages, the spoken word.

The *raggimu* and *maḫḫû* were related in many respects. Both functioned as mediators of the divine word, and both usually belonged to the temple personnel (see below). These shared features however do not imply that *raggimu* and *maḫḫû* were indistinguishable. Whereas the *maḫḫû* is clearly connected with ecstatic behaviour, this is much less clear for the *raggimu*.[27] Given the scantiness of the evidence, we

---

[22]   The suggestion of a complete identification between the *šipir maḫḫê* and the oracles from SAA 9 collections 1 and 2 (Parpola 1997: XLV; Nissinen 1998: 14-34) goes too far. For the *šipir maḫḫê* mentioned in the inscriptions of Esarhaddon, cf. chapter 4.2.2; for the *šipir maḫḫê* in Ashurbanipal's inscriptions concerning the campaign against the Teumman, cf. chapter 4.2.7.

[23]   SAA 7 9 r. i 23 (administrative text); SAA 10 109:9; 294 r. 31; 352:23, r. 1; SAA 13 37:7 (letters); SAA 9 3.5 iv 31; [6 r. 11]; 7:1; 10 s. 2 (colophons); SAA 2 6:116 (*adê*-treaty).

[24]   SAA 9 6 r. 11-12; SAA 10 352:22-25; SAA 13 37:7-10.

[25]   Weippert 2002: 33, note 130. *Raggimu* is a *parris*-form, which functions as agent noun from *ragāmu*. It denotes habitual and/or professional activities; Kouwenberg 1997: 59-61; cf. GAG § 55m.

[26]   See CAD s.v. *ragāmu*. The meaning 'to call out', 'to proclaim' may be understood as to raise one's voice to make an important announcement. In the Assyrian prophecies, the prophets both *proclaim* or *announce* the divine assistance of the king and *claim* provisions and properties from the king (e.g. SAA 9 3.5, delivered by a *raggimu* [3 iv 31], where Ištar demands food and drink from the king [3 iii 26-37]). Cf. Ugaritic *rgm* meaning 'to say, tell, announce, communicate, inform, to answer' (Del Olmo Lete and Sanmartín 2003: 732), with *rgm*, 'word, saying' also occurring in the phrase *rgm* DN 'the oracle of DN' (Del Olmo Lete and Sanmartín 2003: 734).

[27]   See Nissinen 2000b: 90-95, for an examination of the evidence for the ecstatic character and frenzied behaviour of the prophets. Whereas the *maḫḫû* clearly is associated with ecstatic behaviour, this is much less clearly the case for the *raggimu*. Nothing indicates that the *raggimu* delivered oracles in an ecstatic mood.

should refrain from either completely identifying *maḫḫû* and *raggimu*, or drawing a sharp distinction between them.[28]

Diglu

Parpola has suggested that the term *diglu* in various cases means 'vision', received by a prophet (*raggimu*),[29] but in my view this is based on a misconception. The word *diglu* (< *dagālu*) indicates the ability to see,[30] and in the cases where Parpola translates it as 'prophetic vision', an alternative interpretation might be preferable.

The first case is in the letter of Urad-Gula, SAA 10 294 r. 31-33, in Parpola's edition rendered as follows:

> [31] [*ina* IGI *x la*]-*a maḫ-rak el-li a-na* É.GAL *la-a tar-ṣa-ak* : LÚ.*ra-ag-gi-mu*
> [32] [*as-sa-'a-al*? SI]G₅? *la-a a-mur ma-aḫ-ḫur ù di-ig-lu un-ta-aṭ-ṭi*
> [33] [*ša* LUGAL *be-lí*]-*iá a-ma-ár-ka* SIG₅ : *na-as-ḫur-ka maš-ru-ú*

> [The king] is not pleased with me; I go to the palace, I am no good; [I turned to] a prophet (but) did not find [any hop]e, he was adverse and did not see much. [O king] my [lord], seeing you is happiness, your attention is fortune.

This interpretation is problematic for a number of reasons. The phrase *diglu untaṭṭi* does not mean 'he did not see much', 'being unable to offer any vision',[31] but '(my) eyesight is diminishing'.[32] Furthermore, the word *ma-aḫ-ḫur* is strange (SAA 10 glossary < *maḫāru*) and the translation 'he was adverse' or 'he was unresponsive'[33] is unlikely. With a different hyphenation r. 32 reads [*x x x x* SI]G₅? *la-a a-mur-ma aḫ-ḫur ù di-ig-lu un-ta-aṭ-ṭi* and can be translated as: 'I did not see [happi-

---

[28]   Villard (2001: 65-66) suggests that *maḫḫû* is the general Akkadian term for 'prophet', whereas the Old Babylonian *āpilum* and Neo-Assyrian *raggimu* are used in a somewhat more restricted way for recognised prophets that could be consulted.

[29]   Parpola 1997: XLVI-XLVII; followed by Nissinen 1998: 86-87; Pongratz-Leisten 1999: 81.

[30]   *Dagālu* can mean 'to look', 'to regard', or 'to wait for'. E.g. SAA 16 21 23-r. 2: 'Bel-eṭir and Šamaš-zeru-iqišu are astrologers, they watch (*i-da-gul*) the sky day and night'; SAA 18 142 r. 4, 'I am waiting (*ad-da-gal*) for the king, my lord'. Cf. CAD s.v. *diglu*: 'eyesight, gaze, sight (what is looked upon), wish, mirror'. Dream experiences are expressed with the verbs *amāru* and *naṭālu*, not with *dagālu*; cf. Durand 1988: 456; Butler 1998: 31-37.

[31]   So Nissinen 2003a: 162. Cf. Nissinen 1998: 87: 'lit. "he lacked a vision"'.

[32]   The term *diglu* with the verb *maṭû* is an expression for 'weak eyesight' (CAD s.v. *diglu*, 136). Parpola 1997: CIV, note 243, on *diglu untaṭṭi*: 'lit. "lacked/reduced vision"', comes close to this interpretation, if 'vision' is taken as 'eyesight'.

[33]   So Nissinen 2003a: 162.

ness] thereafter and my eyesight is diminishing.' In the context of complaining about his age (r. 30), Urad-Gula's lament that his eyes are getting worse makes sense. He emphasises that if he is not granted audience soon, it will be too late. The passage can be translated as follows:

> [...] I am not well received. (Whenever) I go to the palace, I am not good enough : a prophet [...]; I did not see [happiness] thereafter and my eyesight is diminishing. [O king] my [lord], seeing you is happiness : your attention is fortune.

Although the role of the *raggimu* is unclear in the alternative translation, this is because the immediately following text is lost. The symbol : before *raggimu* marks a connection between the preceding and following phrase, as in r. 33.[34] This means that the *raggimu* in some way has to do with the rejection of Urad-Gula at the palace. This alternative interpretation is significant for another reason as well. This passage has been presented as evidence for the practice of consulting prophets for personal affairs in seventh-century Assyria.[35] Although I do not exclude at all the possibility that in Assyria prophets were consulted for personal affairs,[36] the letter of Urad-Gula, in my view, cannot be used as evidence for this.

The term *diglu* furthermore occurs in the letter SAA 10 361 r. 2-3, in which a favourable dream is reported (l. 13'-r. 1). The term used for dream is *šuttu* (l. 14', 16'). The writer comments on his dream with the phrase *ma-a pa-an di-gi-li-ia an-ni-i-u šu-u ša ep-šá-ku-u-ni*. Parpola translates *pān digilīya* as 'contrary to my vision', but then one would have expected the term *šuttu*, 'dream' and a different preposition. Instead, the phrase can be understood as 'before my (own) eyes I have been treated in this way'.[37]

The other supposed occurrences of *diglu* as 'vision' are SAA 9 11 r. 6 and SAA 16 60:10 (61:10). In Parpola's edition, SAA 9 11 r. 6, [*m*]*ā ina digilīya p*[*ānī*], is translated as 'in my pr[evious] vision'.

---

[34]   The phrase before the symbol ('seeing you is good') is synonymous with the phrase following the symbol ('your attention is fortune'). Cf. SAA 10 102:1-3; 104 r. 5,13; 168:10, 169 r. 7; 207 r. 12; 290 r. 7; 294 r. 33; 316 r. 11; 322 r. 12; 324 10, r. 5.

[35]   Parpola 1997: XLVII; Nissinen 1998: 86-87; Pongratz-Leisten 1999: 80-81.

[36]   Charpin (2002: 33) may be right that in the ancient Near East prophecies addressed to people other than kings existed just as well, although this has hardly left any traces in the material preserved.

[37]   For this interpretation, see CAD s.v. *diglu*.

However, the restoration *p[ānī]* may be questioned,[38] and the phrase
can alternatively be read as 'at my glance/look […]'.[39] The final case
occurs in a letter to Esarhaddon, in which the author informs the king:
ina UD.6.KAM *ša Araḫšamnu diglu addagal*, translated by Parpola as
'on the sixth of Marchesvan (VIII), I had a vision', but alternatively as
'on the sixth of Marchesvan, I had a (close) look'.[40] This makes sense
in the context: the author reveals a conspiracy against the king, and
points out that he is forced by the oath of loyalty to report to the king
whatever he discovers that may harm the king.

The term *diglu* can be eliminated from the prophetic vocabulary.

5.1.2 Prophets within the Cultic Order

Prophets and the Cult

Various indications suggest that *maḫḫû* and *raggimu* usually belonged
to the temple personnel. First, lexical and omen texts associate both
maḫḫû and *raggimu* with other cultic functionaries.[41] In a Middle Assyrian text, *maḫḫû* and *maḫḫūtu* are listed as recipients of food among
other personnel of an Ištar temple.[42] SAA 9 3.5, concerning a banquet
for Ištar, and SAA 13 37:10 ('she has prophesied [in the] temple'), indicate that a *raggimu* could be associated with the temple as well. Furthermore, the deliverer of oracle 1.7 is called *šēlūtu ša šarri* 'votaress
of the king', a woman donated to the goddess by the king. The prophetess Ilussa-amur (oracle 1.5) is mentioned elsewhere as a recipient of
provisions.[43] This evidence suggests that prophets belonged to the
temple community.[44] Furthermore, the *maḫḫû* is connected with temple rituals,[45] and evidently played a role in the temple cult.[46]

---

[38] For *p[a]* the tablet merely shows two horizontal traces.
[39] SAA 9 11 is probably not a prophecy but a letter reporting a prophecy (r. 4-r.
13ff); r. 12 [*ina*] *re-še-ia* '[at] my head ...', is likely to refer to the deity.
[40] The form *a-da-gal* is normalised by Nissinen (2003a: 172, 175) as *addagal*
(perfect); *diglu* may be understood as reinforcing accusative of the same root.
[41] See Nissinen 2000b: 90-95.
[42] VS 19, 1 I 37-39 (Freydank 1974); see Nissinen 2003a: 185.
[43] Parpola 1997: L.
[44] Similarly, in Old Babylonian Mari prophets belonged to the temple; see Durand 1997: 127; Charpin 2002: 8; Fleming 2004: 46, 51: 'prophets maintained a formal affiliation with temples'.
[45] In an Assyrian text describing a ritual of Ištar and Dumuzi (Farber 1977: 128-
155), the *maḫḫû* plays a role in the ritual: 'for the frenzied men and women (*zabbu*)
and for the prophets and prophetesses (*maḫḫû*) you shall place seven pieces of bread.'
(l. 31, translation from Nissinen 2003a: 177). Two further texts connecting the *maḫḫû*

A large number of the oracles stems from Ištar of Arbela. However, Assyrian prophecy was not restricted to this goddess. The corpus of SAA 9 includes oracles from other deities too, and the oracles quoted or reported in letters and included in royal inscriptions balance the picture even more. Prophecy was not the exclusive domain of Ištar of Arbela. A variety of attestations rather suggests that all important deities could give oracles. In many oracles, Ištar—either as Ištar of Arbela or in some other manifestation—appears as a motherly figure, presented as nursing the king and as fighting for him. However, the Babylonian scholar Bel-ušezib appears to be familiar with oracles from Bel, the Babylonian god Marduk.[47] Marduk and Zarpanitu gave an oracle on their way to Babylon (SAA 10 24), the god Sin of Harran encouraged Esarhaddon, who was on his way to Egypt (SAA 10 174), and when affairs of the city of Harran are concerned, the Harranean deities Nikkal and Nusku speak (SAA 16 59-61).[48] Evidently, in a given situation, prophets spoke the word of the appropriate deity. The prominence of Ištar did not prevent prophets from acting in temples of other gods, or from speaking for other deities.[49]

The close connection between the cult of Ištar of Arbela and the phenomenon of Assyrian prophecy has been rightly stressed.[50] Yet, this connection was not an exclusive one.[51] The prominent position of Ištar among the deities present in the extant oracles can be explained in the following way. Almost all oracles are characterised by a royal interest, since it was because of this interest that prophetic oracles were preserved in the royal archives. This need not imply that Assyrian prophecy always was 'royal prophecy', but rather that royal interest functioned as a criterion for preservation. Since the goddess Ištar played a role of great importance in imperial ideology of the (late)

---

with temple rituals: LKU 51 r. 29-30 (a Neo-Babylonian ritual) and SAA 3 34:28//35:31 (the Marduk Ordeal; see Nissinen 2003a: 151).

[46]   A ritual text from Mari (Durand and Guichard 1997: 52-58) refers to a function of the *muḫḫû*, (see Nissinen 2003a: 81).

[47]   SAA 10 109 and 111.

[48]   See also Nissinen 2000b: 99.

[49]   Henshaw's view (1994: 162) that the *raggimu* is part of the temple personnel of Ištar of Arbela may be too narrow.

[50]   Parpola 1997: XLVII-XLVIII.

[51]   Weippert 2002: 35.

Sargonid era,[52] it is conceivable that she figures prominently in the prophetic oracles that were preserved according to the criterion of royal interest.[53] Prophets, however, were attached to temples of other deities too,[54] and if appropriate they spoke for other deities as well.

The following Assyrian prophets are known by name: Aḫāt-abīša,[55] a woman from Arbela (SAA 9 1.8), Bayâ,[56] a woman from Arbela (SAA 9 1.4, [2.2]), Dunnaša-āmur,[57] a woman from Arbela, *maḫḫūtu* (SAA 9 9, 10), Ilūssa-āmur,[58] a woman from Assur (SAA 9 1.5), Is-sār-bēlī-da''ini, a woman of unknown domicile, 'votaress of the king' (*šēlūtu ša šarri*),[59] (SAA 9 1.7), Issār-lā-tašīyaṭ,[60] a man from Arbela (SAA 9 1.1), Lā-dāgil-ili,[61] a man from Arbela (SAA 9 1.10, 2.3, perhaps 3.5, there referred to as *raggimu*), Mullissu-abu-uṣri, a *raggintu* probably from Assur (SAA 13 37), Mullissu-kabtat, a *raggintu* of unknown domicile (SAA 9 7), [...]-ḫussanni, a man from Assur (SAA 9 2.1), Quqî, a *raggimu*, from Šadikanni (SAA 7 9 r. i 20-24), Rēmutti-

---

[52]   Cf. Brown 2000: 51. Reiner (1985: 22) suggests that from the reign of Sargon II onwards, the goddess Ištar reappeared in Mesopotamian royal ideology in her role as protector of the king.

[53]   Van der Toorn (2000b: 79) gives a different, but not mutually exclusive, explanation: 'In Neo-Assyrian times, prophecy was a type of divination pertaining to the province of Ištar, as extispicy was a type of divination connected with the gods Šamaš and Adad.' Since Ištar was a goddess related to war, and since prophecy played a role of importance especially at times of crisis, it is not surprising that among the prophetic material oracles from Ištar relating to wars and crises take a prominent position.

[54]   Nissinen 2000b: 99. For examples, see SAA 13 37, a letter reporting a prophecy of Mullussi-abu-uṣri, probably from Ešarra, the Aššur temple in Assur; SAA 12 69, a decree for temple maintenance from Ešarra refers to various *maḫḫātu*.

[55]   Weippert (2002: 33) regards Aḫāt-abīša, 'Sister-of-her-father', as an 'Ersatzname'.

[56]   Bayā is a feminine name (cf. fem. determinative), but she is referred to as a 'male resident of Arbela'. Weippert explains this as a scribal mistake. However, if Parpola's restoration of the name MÍ.*ba-ia*]-ʾ*a*ʾ URU.*arba-il*-ʾ*a-a*ʾ in 2 i 35' is correct (which is uncertain) the case is more complicated. I doubt however whether the confusion warrants the conclusion that Bayā was castrated.

[57]   The name can be read as Dunnaša-āmur 'I have seen her strength' (Parpola 1997: IL) or as Dunqaša-āmur 'I have seen her goodness' (Weippert 2002: 34). Parpola suggested an identification with Sinqiša-āmur ('I have seen her distress').

[58]   With respect to the gender of Ilūssa-āmur, the confusions seems to be caused by the restoration of a masculine gentilic form, whereas there is no reason not to restore a feminine form: ᵘʳᵘŠÀ.URU-*a*[-*a-tú*], since Ilūssa-āmur clearly is a woman.

[59]   Issār-bēlī-da''ini was a hierodule, donated by the king to an Ištar temple.

[60]   Issar-lā-tašīyat, 'Do not neglect Ištar!' is a masculine name, however with a feminine determinative (Weippert 2002: 34). This may be due to a scribal error.

[61]   The name *la–da-gíl*–DINGIR, instead of 'the one who does not see god' (Parpola 1997: L), perhaps means 'would god not see?' In any case, since PNAE: 649-650, lists seven individuals with this name, it is unlikely to be an adoptive, prophetic name.

Allati, a woman from Dara-aḫuya, a mountain town (SAA 9 1.3), Sin-qīša-āmur, a woman from Arbela (SAA 9 1.2), Tašmētu-ēreš,[62] a [rag-gimu] from Arbela (SAA 9 6), and Urkittu-šarrat, a woman from Calah (SAA 9 2.4).

With regard to the possible confusion concerning the gender of some of these prophets, I tend to follow Weippert (2002: 33-34) rather than Parpola (1997: IL-L). Parpola also suggested that many of these prophets have a 'prophetic name', i.e. adopted names relating to their prophetic function.[63] It is true that the goddess Ištar is well represented in the names listed above. However, there is no clear indication that any of the names is to be seen as a 'prophetic name'.[64] Seven prophets come from Arbela, two from Assur, one from Calah, one from an un-known mountain town, and for the rest we do not know. Ištar of Ar-bela's prominent appearance in the oracles matches the prominence of residents of Arbela among the prophets.

The Assyrian prophets belonged to the community of devotees of Ištar and other major deities.[65] They had their nearest colleagues among visionaries and dreamers on the one hand, and ecstatic figures characterised by frenzied behaviour, on the other. The prophets were probably permanently attached to the temple.[66] Van der Toorn has ar-gued that the prophetic oracles reported in the Mari letters were regu-larly delivered in the sanctuary, in front of the statue of the deity that is presented speaking in the oracle. The prophet standing before the statue functioned as the deity's mouth. An oracle revealed to a prophet at the sanctuary could however be delivered outside the temple. In that case, in order to make clear whose word it concerned the prophet pre-sented himself as a messenger of the deity involved.[67]

In seventh-century Assyria, prophecy could be delivered within a temple setting as well. In SAA 13 37 (a letter), we read: 'Mullissu-

---

[62]   Parpola (1997: LII) explains Tašmētu-ēreš as 'Tašmetu desired'; Weippert (2002: 34) as 'Ich habe (ihn) von Tašmetu erbeten'.

[63]   Parpola 1997: XLVIII-LII.

[64]   The fact that a name is not attested elsewhere does not automatically make it a 'prophetic name'. Tašmetu-ereš is singularly attested, but names ending in -ereš are attested in combination with many other divine names. Names with the element -amur (the prophetesses Dunnaša-amur, Ilussa-amur, Sinqiša-amur) are paralleled by compa-rable names (see PNAE: Ilu-amur, Nabû-amur, Gabbu-amur, etc.; cf. Weippert 2002: 34). The name Remutti-Allati ('gift of Allati') is paralleled by names with the element Rēmūt followed by a divine name (PNAE: 1045-1049). For Lā-dāgil-ili see note 61.

[65]   Hilber 2005: 57-58.

[66]   So also Nissinen 2000b: 95-96.

[67]   Van der Toorn 2000a: 221-224.

abu-uṣri, the prophetess who conveyed the king's clothes to the land of Akkad, prophesied [in] the temple: "[The] throne from the te[mp]le [...]".' Two further prophetic oracles, SAA 13 139 and 144, are reported to the king by temple functionaries, which indicates that they were presumably delivered in a temple too.[68] In addition, two 'votaries', belonging to a temple, are connected with prophecy.[69] These indications show that there is no reason to assume a contrast in this respect between the situation in Old Babylonian Mari and seventh-century Assyria.[70] The temple remains the most likely, though perhaps not the exclusive, location where prophets were believed to receive, and often delivered, oracles.[71] When a prophet delivered a divine message at some other public place, such as the city gate, the idea may have been, as in Mari, that the message was previously revealed to him in the sanctuary.

Royal Supplication and Divine Reassurance

Assyrian texts reveal a connection between royal supplication and divine reassurance in the form of a prophetic oracle. The pattern is the following: the king, or someone in his stead, implores the god, whereupon the god gives a positive reaction to the supplication in the form of an oracle of encouragement.[72] The following examples can be mentioned:

1) The oracle SAA 9 1.8, where Ištar of Arbela says: 'To the king's mother: Because you implored me (*maḫāru*) thus: "Those of the right and the left you have placed in your lap, but my own offspring you made roam the wild," Well then, fear not, o king! The kingship is yours, the power is yours!'

---

[68]　See also Nissinen 2000b: 98.

[69]　SAA 9 1.7 and SAA 13 148.

[70]　Contra Van der Toorn 2000b: 82-83. See the criticism by Hilber 2005: 58-59.

[71]　Cf. SAA 13 37:10, cf. SAA 10 174:10-14. The formula 'I am god so-and-so', which frequently occurs in Assyrian oracles, is not often attested in the Mari prophecies. This formula prominently occurs in the oracles from the collections SAA 9 1 and 2, but not in any of the other oracles of SAA 9, nor in the oracles reported or quoted in letters and royal inscriptions (with the exception of SAA 13 139). Furthermore, the 'self-presentation' does not occur in oracles presented as the 'word' of a particular deity (SAA 9 2.4; 3.4; 3.5; 5-9). By contrast, the expression appears in SAA 3 13, l. 7, 'Pay a[ttent]ion, Ashurbanipal! I am Nabû!'. In l. 3, however, it is said that Ashurbanipal approached Nabû in the temple of Ištar of Nineveh. In this setting, Ashurbanipal hardly needed the identification in order to know that Nabû was speaking.

[72]　Hilber 2005: 66-74, and Nissinen 2003b: 146-154, give similar presentations.

2) Esarhaddon's inscription Nineveh A i narrates the events of 681:
the struggle between Esarhaddon and his brothers for the throne of
Assyria. In i 59-62, Esarhaddon's reaction to the wicked deeds of his
brothers is described: 'With raised hands I prayed to Aššur, Sin,
Šamaš, Bel, Nabû, Nergal, Ištar of Nineveh, and Ištar or Arbela, and
they accepted my words. Giving me their firm positive answer they
constantly sent me this oracle of encouragement: "Go ahead, do not
hold back! We go constantly by your side; we annihilate your enemies".'[73]

3) Texts from the reign of Ashurbanipal present a similar scene.
According to Prism B v, Ashurbanipal celebrated a festival of Ištar in
Arbela, when he heard that Teumman, the king of Elam, planned a
war against Assyria. Ashurbanipal reacted as follows: 'I approached
Ištar the most high. I placed myself before her, prostrated myself under her feet. My tears were flowing as I prayed to her divinity: "O
Lady of Arbela! (....)".'[74] The goddess replied to the supplication of
Ashurbanipal: 'Ištar heard my desperate sighs and said to me: "Fear
not!" She made my heart confident, saying: "Because of the prayer
you said with your hand lifted up, your eyes being filled with tears, I
have compassion for you".'[75]

4) The same episode is referred to in the text SAA 3 31. After
Teumman's evil plan is mentioned, we read: 'When I heard [this piece
of insolence], I opened my hands (in supplication) to [Ištar, the lady of
Arbela], saying: "I am Ashurbanipal, whom [your] own father, [Aššur,
engende]red. I have come to worship you; why is [Teu]mman fa[lling]
upon me?" [Ištar sa]id to me: "I myself [...] in the centre of [........]".'[76]

5) In SAA 3 13, the 'Dialogue between Ashurbanipal and Nabû'
we see a similar scene. The historical context is the war against
Šamaš-šum-ukin. In SAA 3 13 l. 19-22 Ashurbanipal is presented as
imploring Nabû: 'Ashurbanipal is on his knees, praying incessantly to
Nabû, his lord: "Please, Nabû, do not abandon me (.....) among those
who wish me ill!".' Nabû gives an encouraging response to this

---

[73]   Translation from: Nissinen 2003a: 139. The 'oracle of encouragement' probably is the outcome of extispicy (Nissinen 2003a: 142), but it is completely in line with
the prophetic messages that were also delivered in that period. The same episode is
presented from the perspective of the god Aššur in the prophetic text SAA 9 3.3.
Aššur refers to Esarhaddon's cry for help ('you opened your mouth, thus: hear me,
Aššur!'), and states that he listened ('I heard your cry'), and annihilated his enemies.
[74]   Translation from: Nissinen 2003a: 146.
[75]   Translation from: Nissinen 2003a: 147.
[76]   Translation from: Livingstone, SAA 3 31.

prayer: 'Fear not, Ashurbanipal! I will give you long life (....); my pleasant mouth shall ever bless you in the assembly of the great gods.'[77]

6) A final example to mention is from the Zakkur Stele. King Zakkur is threatened by a strong coalition of enemies who besiege him: 'But I lifted my hands to Baalshamayn, and Baalshamay[n] answered me, [and] Baalshamayn [spoke] to me [thr]ough seers and through visionaries [and] Baalshamayn [said], "F[e]ar not, for I have made [you] king, [and I will st]and with [you], and I will deliver you from all [these kings who] have forced a siege against you!".'[78]

Although most of the examples stem from royal inscriptions and do not directly witness a prophetic scene, they reflect the same practice attested in the first example mentioned, the prophetic oracle SAA 9 1.8. Behind the literary images, a standard procedure is visible: in a threatening situation, the king implores the deity who gives a response through an encouraging oracle, either by the mouth of a prophet or by other means. This procedure of supplication and reassurance once again points to a temple setting for the deliverance of prophetic oracles.[79] This prophetic response to (royal) supplication suggests that prophets functioned in a temple environment.[80]

5.1.3 *Prophets within the Political and Social Order*

Prophets and the Royal Court

There is no evidence for prophets staying at the royal court in Nineveh, but one text mentions a prophet among royal employees, SAA 7 9 r. i 20-24:

---

[77] Translation from: Livingstone, SAA 3 13. This response, which looks like a prophetic oracle, is introduced as the word of Nabû, spoken by a *zāqīqu*. *Zāqīqu/zīqīqu* is the name of a dream god, but can, according to Butler (1998: 83), occasionally denote 'a professional, who may have prophesied'.

[78] Translation from: Seow, in: Nissinen 2003a: 206.

[79] This procedure of supplication and reassurance occurs in a Late Babylonian ritual text. Following a supplication of the king, we read '...fear not! .... Bel [has heard] your prayer [...] He had enlarged your rule [...] He will enlarge your kingship ...' (translation from: Nissinen 2003a: 195). The high priest, the central figure of the ritual, assumes a divinatory role, but it is a 'prophetic oracle' reused within a ritual text; Nissinen 2003b: 158; Van der Toorn (2000b: 77) calls it a 'frozen' prophecy.

[80] See Hilber 2005: 53-61 and 74-75.

Nergal-mukin-aḫi, chariot owner; Nabû-šarru-uṣur, cohort commander of the crown prince; Wazaru, bodyguard of the queen mother; Quqî, prophet (*raggimu*); in all, four: the 'residences' of the Šadikannaeans.[81]

The passage is part of a lodging list that contains circa hundred names. It was probably compiled for a major event in Nineveh in which people from various parts of the empire took part.[82] The list includes mainly high officials, and the prophet Quqî occurs among three high-ranking officers, who were in the service of members of the royal family.[83] One may deduce from this that apparently a prophet could serve in a royal office.

It has been suggested that prophets joined military campaigns as part of the divinatory staff. This is possible, but clear evidence is lacking.[84] The prophetic material seems to suggest that Esarhaddon and Ashurbanipal received oracles at the start of, and in the course of, military campaigns, but it is not known where the prophets delivering these oracles were located.[85] There is no clear evidence for prophets delivering their oracles in the presence of the king, although this may have happened. The terminology in royal inscriptions pointing to the direct communication between deities and kings through the mouth of prophets is likely to be located in the sanctuary rather than in the king's court room (see 5.1.2 above).

The letter SAA 10 109 (discussed in chapter 4.2.1) urges the king to summon certain prophets and prophetesses. In my interpretation, Bel-ušezib complains that the king has neglected the message of prophets and prophetesses, reported by Bel-ušezib. In the difficult period, the prophets and prophetesses and Bel-ušezib have supported Esarhaddon in delivering and reporting favourable messages, which connected Esarhaddon's reign with the restoration of Babylon and Esagila. Bel-ušezib wants Esarhaddon now he has become king, to summon these prophets and prophetesses and Bel-ušezib himself, in order to closely investigate the matter and to set to work on the resto-

---

[81] Translation from: Nissinen 2003a: 152. For the reading Šadikannaeans, i.e. 'people from Šadikanni', a city on the river Ḫabur, see Nissinen 2003a: 152, note b.

[82] According to Nissinen (1998: 64) the occasion may have been a ceremony for the conclusion of the *adê*-treaty for Ashurbanipal at his appointment as crown prince.

[83] Nissinen 1998: 65.

[84] Nissinen (1998: 65) argues that it is conceivable that prophets, like haruspices, formed part of the divinatory staff that accompanied the army on campaign. The 'Epic of Zimri-Lim' seems to reflect prophetic activity during military campaigns (l. 137-142; Nissinen 2003a: 90).

[85] See Nissinen 2000b: 103, with note 73.

ration of Babylon and Esagila. In some cases, to be summoned by the king means to become part of the king's entourage, which is a mark of honour and reflects a good position (SAA 10 171; 284 r. 16). In other cases, the king summoned people in order to interrogate them (SAA 10 99 r. 6'-7'; 199 r. 21'-22') or to judge their case (SAA 10 160 33-35). In the case of SAA 10 109, the 'summoning' probably implies the king's investigation of the matter, in order to undertake the restoration of Babylon and Esagila. It is difficult to say whether the summoning of prophets and prophetesses, as requested by Bel-ušezib, was exceptional or something that more often happened.[86] There is no evidence for prophets delivering their oracles 'live' at the royal court in the presence of the king, but it cannot be excluded that this sometimes happened.[87]

One of the important capacities of prophetic inspiration was to legitimate a claim to the throne. The oracles from 681 BCE relating to Esarhaddon's rise to power, demonstrate that prophecy could play an important role in a situation of competing claims to the throne. The prophetic oracle quoted in the letter SAA 16 60 (ABL 1217) r. 4-5 apparently had a similar function: to legitimise Sasî's claim to kingship.[88] Presumably, this legitimising authority was employed in a further case as well, when a *raggintu* directed a Babylonian nobleman to be the

---

[86]   In Mari we find examples of prophets consulted by royal figures, such as Queen Šîbtu. In one case, King Zimri-Lim himself ordered Šîbtu to make a consultation (Charpin 2002: 19-22). Nissinen (2000b: 104) suggests that in Mari and in Assyria, palace women were in closer contact with prophets than male persons at court. However, with regard to the Assyrian prophecies, the only palace woman evidently in close contact with the prophets is Esarhaddon's mother Naqia, and only, in my view, during the turbulent events of late 681 (see chapter 4.2.1). This particular case does not warrant a general conclusion (cf. Fleming 2004: 49, on the situation in Mari).

[87]   Charpin (2002: 9, 16, 32), discussing the situation in Old Babylonian Mari, suggests that prophets often appeared before Zimri-Lim in the palace to present their oracles 'live'. According to Charpin, the evidence for this is lacking simply because such oracles were not recorded. I am not convinced by this suggestion. It seems that prophets normally delivered their oracles either in the temple or at a public spot like the city gate or the palace gate (ARM 26/1 206; ARM 26/2 371; in this last text nothing suggests that the *āpilum* of Marduk first tried to speak out the oracle in the presence of the king and only delivered it in the gate of the palace because he was not admitted to the palace; contra Charpin 2002: 27). Even in Mari itself, royal officials were stationed in order to report to the king every prophetic oracle that came to their knowledge (cf. Nissinen 2003a: 19; on the oath-enforced duty of royal officials to keep the king informed, see Durand 1991). This suggests that prophets did *not* normally deliver their oracles in the palace before the king. Similarly Fleming 2004: 50.

[88]   For the conspiracy of Sasî, see chapter 4.2.5.

substitute king (SAA 10 352, see below).[89] This kind of prophetic authority was, of course, of profound interest for the king, the crown prince, and any pretender to the throne. Furthermore, the prophetic function of expressing divine approval of a claim to kingship illustrates the public importance of the prophets, since their legitimising authority could influence public opinion. Furthermore, both in Mari and in seventh-century Assyria prophecy could function as a divine direction to the king in politics. A clear case is the ban on a peace treaty with Eshnunna, made particularly though not exclusively, by the god Dagan of Terqa.[90] In seventh-century Assyria, we find some examples of scholars making use of prophetic oracles in their political advice to the king.[91]

Prophets and the Public

In several Assyrian prophecies the 'public' is explicitly addressed. The prophecy labelled 2.4, in fact an anthology of divine words (see chapter 3.1.1), is presented as a response to the 'disloyal ones' (*lā kēnūti*), and contains the announcement 'I will speak to the multi[tudes]: listen! ....' (2 ii 34'-35'). The prophecy ends with the encouragement: 'Whoever is lone, whoever is oppressed, fear not in the protection of Esarhaddon, king of Assyria.'

The *šulmu*, 'oracle of salvation' in 3.2, is another example of a divine message to the public:

> [List]en, Assyrians! [The king] has vanquished his enemy, [you]r [king] has put his enemy [under] his foot, [from] sun[se]t [to] sun[ris]e, [from] sun[ris]e [to] sun[se]t!
> 'I will destroy [.....], [I will de]stroy [.....], [..............], I will deliver the Cimmerians into his hands,[92] and set the land of Ellipi on fire.'[93]

---

[89] Cf. Weippert 2002: 29.

[90] ARM 26/1 197, 199, 202; see Nissinen 2003d: 25-29.

[91] E.g. SAA 10 109, 111, 284; ABL 839 (Mattila 1987).

[92] Weippert (2002: 44) suggests reading the last word of ii 1 as *a-gam-m[ar]*, based in SAA 9 7 l. 14 *Gimir agammar* 'I wil finish off the land of the Cimmerians'. However, 3 ii 1 is different since it contains the expression 'into his hands'. Based on the parallel in 2 ii 33' 'I will deliver (*šakānu*) them into the hands of my king', Parpola's reading (*a-ʿšá-kan*ʾ) is preferable.

[93] Esarhaddon claims to have defeated the Cimmerians in 679 (Esarhaddon Chronicle, Borger 1956: 122), but they remained prominent among the enemies of Assyria during Esarhaddon's entire reign (Starr 1990: LIX); the land of Ellipi is mentioned in Monument text B, l. 20 (Borger 1956: 100); an expedition against the armies of Ellipi, the Medes and the Cimmerians was undertaken in 672 or later (Starr 1990: LXI). This implies that the divine announcement makes sense almost any time during

Aššur has given to him the totality of the four regions, from sunrise to
sunset. There is no king equal to him; he shines as bright as the sun.
This is the salvation oracle placed before Bēl Tarbāṣe (and) before the
gods.[94]

This unit consists of four elements: 1) an introduction addressing the
Assyrians, 2) divine speech, probably going back to a prophetic oracle, 3) a conclusion, which glorifies the king, as does the introduction,
4) some sort of colophon.[95] It seems to be a prophetic oracle in a reworked form. The promise of the deity to destroy Esarhaddon's enemies has become part of a broader setting in which the Assyrian
people are addressed. This illuminates an aspect of prophecy that often remains implicit: the encouragement of the king is at the same
time the encouragement of the people.

With regard to the situation in Mari, Fleming has argued that
prophets occasionally spoke at public festivals, for instance at a festival of Dagan, probably in Mari, where two *āpilum*-prophets publicly
denounced the Babylonians and their king Hammurabi in the voices of
Dagan of Tuttul and Belet-ekallim.[96] Generally speaking we know the
Assyrian prophets mainly through the oracles that have been preserved. However, a few letters grant us glimpses of public actions of
Assyrian prophets. Two particular events can be singled out and will
be presented here.

The first event is described in SAA 10 352. This letter mentions a
prophetess, *raggintu*, playing a role in the appointment of a substitute
king.[97] With the help of various letters that refer to this ritual, which
took place in Tebet (X) 671,[98] the events can be reconstructed as fol-

---

the reign of Esarhaddon. The first part of the unit however implies in my view that
Esarhaddon had already conducted several successful campaigns.

[94]   Or with Weippert (2002: 16), *šakānu* G as 'to issue', 'to pronounce': 'this is
the salvation oracle that was pronounced in front of Bēl Tarbāṣe and the gods'. My
translation of 3.2 largely follows Parpola's (SAA 9).

[95]   The prophetic text SAA 9 9 similarly consists of these four elements; see chapter 6.2.1.

[96]   ARM 26/1 209; Fleming (2004: 54) suggests that the verb *tebûm* 'rise' is
indicative of a public setting.

[97]   The substitute king ritual was performed in response to the occurrence of a lunar eclipse that portended the death of the king. The ruling king abdicated his throne
for a substitute king who, having ruled for a predetermined period (the danger period,
100 days), was put to death, after which the king ascended the throne again. See Parpola 1983: XXII –XXXII; Rochberg 2004: 77-78.

[98]   Parpola 1983: XXIII.

lows. In a letter to Esarhaddon, the chief exorcist Marduk-šakin-šumi suggested appointing a substitute king, although no lunar eclipse had occurred, and exclaimed in the same breath that the rebellious Babylonians should be dealt with (SAA 10 240 r. 14-25). This suggests that he already had a candidate in mind to take the role of substitute king. From a report of Mar-Issar, Esarhaddon's agent in Babylonia, it appears that Marduk-šakin-šumi punished the Babylonians by appointing a Babylonian nobleman, the son of a chief temple administrator, as substitute king instead of following the normal procedure to appoint an unimportant man (SAA 10 351). The sanctions against the allegedly rebellious Babylonians were carried out with the help of a *raggintu*, who publicly delivered an oracle to the intended substitute King Damqî: 'you will exercise the kingship' (l. 25).[99] A second oracle (r. 1-4) demonstrated Damqî's 'legitimacy' as king: 'The prophetess had also said to him in the assembly of the country (*ina puḫri ša māti*): "I have revealed the *polecat*, the ... of my lord, and placed (him) in your hands".'

This *raggintu* probably is the prophetess Mullissu-abu-uṣri, mentioned in SAA 13 37 as 'the one who took the king's clothes to Akkad'.[100] These clothes were used in the substitute king ritual, together with the royal throne, which this prophetess equally demanded (SAA 13 37).[101] Apparently, the public performance of the prophetess was part of the strategy developed by Esarhaddon's officials to punish the Babylonian noblemen by appointing Damqî as substitute king. The letter in which the performance of the prophetess is related (SAA 10 352) also reports to the king the death and burial of the substitute king and his queen. Here we have a case in which the prophetic function to legitimate a claim to kingship and the ritual of the substitute king are used as part of a show trial.

The second case of prophecy playing a role in a public performance relates to Esarhaddon's attempt to return the statue of Marduk to Babylon in 669 BCE.[102] Esarhaddon made great efforts to restore Babylon and in particular Marduk's temple Esagila (see chapter

---

[99] According to Nissinen (1998: 73) the oracle legitimises the unusual appointment.
[100] Von Soden 1956: 102; Landsberger 1965: 47, 49.
[101] Parpola 1983: XXIV.
[102] See Vera Chamaza 1996: 210-220.

4.2.2). Nevertheless, during his reign the New Year festival was not celebrated in Babylon, because the main statue of Marduk was still absent. Sennacherib had in all probability deported this statue to Assur, when he captured Babylon in 689 BCE.[103] During Esarhaddon's reign, this deported statue of Marduk was repaired and renewed,[104] a work requiring divine permission.[105] The 'new statue' was placed in the temple of Aššur, where it was 'born' and placed in front of its 'begetter' Aššur. In early 669 BCE, Esarhaddon attempted to return the statues of Marduk and his consort Zarpanitu to Babylon. The statues departed from Assur, and ten days later they arrived in Labbanat, a town at the Tigris on the border of Assyria with Babylonia.[106] Here the journey was interrupted by a curious incident, described in the letter SAA 10 24.[107] One of Ashurbanipal's servants involved in the transport suddenly mounted the sacred horse that pulled the chariot. When he was seized, he claimed to have been instructed by Bel and Zarpanitu to give the following message:[108] 'Babylon has become booty of Kurigalzu'.[109]

This curious sentence may be explained as follows. Kurigalzu is the name of a Kassite king,[110] and the phrase *ḫubtu* (plunder, captives) of Kurigalzu might allude to some past event in which Babylonian statues were taken off as booty. The oracle seems to warn against a robbery on the way to Babylon. This is at least how the oracle was explained by another person: 'I know that these [robb]ers are waiting [in Du]r-Kurigalzu' (r. 14-17). Whether he correctly explained the prophecy by taking the personal name Kurigalzu as standing for Dur-

---

[103] According to Vera Chamaza (1996: 96), Sennacherib's claim that the statues of the Babylonian gods were smashed is 'nur eine masslose Propaganda'.

[104] Vera Chamaza (1996: 217) proposes that the statues that had been damaged during the capture of Babylon in 689 were restored by Esarhaddon.

[105] SAA 3 33, a literary text in which the deceased Sennacherib (fictitiously) addresses Esarhaddon, probably relates to the renewal of Marduk's statue. According to Sennacherib, the gods wanted him to renew the statue, but his religious experts prevented him from doing so.

[106] Parpola 1983: 32-33.

[107] This text is not included in Nissinen 2003a.

[108] SAA 10 24 l. 7-9: 'He said: "The gods Bel and Zar[panitu] have ordered me thus: ...".'

[109] For this interpretation, see Vera Chamaza 1996: 219. The enigmatic phrase literally says 'Babylon on a tow rope, the booty of Kurigalzu'.

[110] There were at least two kings named Kurigalzu, both in the 14th century (see Brinkman 1976: 205-246). See further Grayson 1975a: 159-160, Chronicle 21, and 172-175, Chronicle 22. Various other prophecies also contain references to ancient Babylonian kings: SAA 10 111 r. 24, Marduk-šapik-zeri; SAA 3 44 r. 7, Išdu-kin.

Kurigalzu (Parsa), a town on the way to Babylon, we cannot know. In any case the divine message was taken seriously, since the journey was aborted.[111] It was Šamaš-šum-ukin who brought the statues back in 668 BCE.[112]

Although we cannot make out whether this was a case of sincere prophecy or part of a trick to keep Marduk in Assyria, the scene shows that 'spontaneous signs', including divine messages, were taken seriously. Part of the prophetic power, it seems, consisted of impressing the public by speaking the divine 'words of the gods'.

5.1.4 *Prophetic Claims and Criticism*

Prophetic Claims

Although prophets could play a role in temple rituals and cultic performances, we know them almost exclusively from their prophecies that survive in written form. The messages are characterised by a twofold nature. On the one hand, the gods encourage the king in troublesome situations. In chapter 4.2, I have discussed various episodes that can be regarded as the historical backgrounds to the Assyrian prophecies. In various situations the gods used the medium of prophecy to present to the king or crown prince a declaration of their support. On the other hand, the gods used prophets to present their claims to the king. In the Assyrian oracles we find divine claims for offerings (oracle 2.3), food for a banquet (oracle 3.5), property, such as torches (oracle 1.10), a throne (SAA 13 37 r. 6-7), a prayer-bowl (SAA 13 43:8-9), and a certain wooden object (SAA 13 144 r. 8-17).[113] The connection between promises and claims is made clear in the oracle SAA 9 3.5:

> As if I did not act or give you anything! Did I not bend the four door-jambs of Assyria and did I not allow you (to enter)? Did I not vanquish your enemy? Did I not catch your haters and your enemies like

---

[111] The servant mounting the sacred horse committed a sacrilege, but escaped because of the divine word he delivered.

[112] Grayson 1975a: 86:34-36; 127:35-36; see Frame 1992: 103-107. Both Ashurbanipal and Šamaš-šum-ukin claim to have returned Marduk. It was presumably Šamaš-šum-ukin who took Marduk into his temple and restored his cult. Ashurbanipal however presents himself as the benefactor of Marduk and Babylon.

[113] See also the instructions concerning the restoration of the cult of Ištar-Kidmuri, mediated by the *maḫḫû*-prophets to Ashurbanipal (see 5.1.1 above). The Mari prophecies display the same twofold character of promises of divine assistance on the one hand, and claims for gifts, booty, food, etc., on the other.

butterflies? And you, what have you given to me? [Fo]od for the banquet no[t …] food (?) for the temple; I [am depri]ved of my food, I am d[ep]rived of my cup. I look for their presence, I have cast my eyes on them. Truly, fix a one-seah dish of food and a one-seah flagon of good beer. Let me take vegetables and soup and let me put it in my mouth. Let me fill the cup and let me drink from it. Let me restore my charms![114]

The connecting principle is *do ut des*: after having given her support, Ištar expects generous gifts from the king.[115] The banquet Esarhaddon organised for Ištar of Arbela, described in his inscriptions,[116] may have followed this request.

As far as we can tell, prophets did not occupy high positions at the royal court. Not among the king's magnates, nor among the highest courtiers, nor among the king's "entourage" of religious experts do we find any prophets.[117] At the same time, it seems that prophets were less dependent on the favour of the king than specialists in other branches of divination and officials in the service of the king. Their occasionally demanding tone contrasts with the politeness with which even the highest functionaries address the king. The prophets had a double role: they encouraged the king by proclaiming divine assistance, and they requested of the king that he fulfil his (cultic) duties. The position of the prophets as servants of the deity enabled them to express demands to the king and even to criticise his behaviour.[118]

Prophetic Criticism
Ancient Near Eastern prophecy has often been regarded as *Heilsprophetie*, in contradistinction to the typical *Unheilsprophetie* of

---

[114] Nissinen (2003d: 11-12) relates the phrase 'Let me restore my charms' to SAA 9 9. There, the goddess describes how her exertions for the sake of Ashurbanipal affected her beautiful figure. Ištar's help, waging war against the enemies of the king, leads to her exhaustion. When the fight is over, the goddess needs to restore her beauty and charms, i.e. she needs the good (cultic) care of the king.

[115] For the same principle in Mari prophecies, see ARM 26/1 194, 198, 206, 217 and A 1121+ l. 7-11 (Lafont 1984). Nissinen (2003d: 15) uses the term 'Gegendienste'.

[116] See Borger 1956: 95:19-37, Esarhaddon organised a banquet for Ištar, because she had made him greater than his predecessors.

[117] Nissinen 2000b: 109. In seventh-century Assyria the king directly employed top-ranking religious experts, such as astrologers, haruspices, and exorcists, but not prophets (Parpola 1993: XXV-XXVI). In Mari, haruspices were in royal employment, not prophets (Sasson 1998: 116-119; Charpin 2002: 8, 22). For the Old Babylonian extispicy-diviners as advisers in royal service, see Jeyes 1989: 22-28, 34-36.

[118] Nissinen 2000b: 105.

the biblical prophets.[119] Nissinen however shows in his study 'Das kritische Potential in der altorientalischen Prophetie', that ancient Near Eastern prophecy contains critical aspects.[120] According to ancient Near Eastern values, the king was responsible for the cultivation of the cults of the gods and the preservation of their temples. Furthermore, the king had to secure justice, i.e. to maintain a just order in his land and to provide justice for his subjects. With respect to these duties, the gods were believed to control the king, and they could do so, *inter alia*, through the prophets. Nissinen discusses various examples of prophetic oracles containing reproaches directed against kings who failed to fulfil their duties. The purpose of the reproaches was obviously to receive compensation for the neglect. Examples of prophetic reproaches dealing with cultic neglect stem both from the Mari letters and from the Assyrian prophecies.[121] Prophets, both in Mari and in Assyria, were in a position to critically examine the activities of the king and to remind him of his duties. With respect to the king's duties regarding the maintenance of justice, we find examples of admonitions in the oracles reported in the Mari letters.[122] One comes from an oracle delivered by Abiya, the *āpilum* of Adad of Aleppo: 'Thus says Adad: [...] Now hear a single word of mine: If anyone cries out to <you> for judgement, saying: "I have been wr[ong]ed," be there to decide his case; an[swer him fai]rly. [Th]is is what I de[sire] from you.'[123]

According to Nissinen, that such admonitions are missing from the Assyrian prophecies need not imply that these prophets were not interested in the king's social duties. Securing the well-being of the poor and the weak was part of the ideal image of the king in Mesopotamia, throughout the ages, including the Assyrian period.[124] Both in Mari and

---

[119] Cf. Nissinen 2003d: 1-2.
[120] Nissinen 2003d: 1-32.
[121] See Nissinen 2003d: 4-14. For Mari, see ARM 26/1 198, 214, 215, 219; for Assyria, see SAA 13 144 and SAA 9 3.5 (the demand in oracle 2.3, discussed by Nissinen 2003d: 12-13, is a claim, not a reproach).
[122] Nissinen (2003d: 14-23) discusses ARM 26/1 194, A 1121+, and A 1968.
[123] A 1968 l. 6'-11'; translation from: Nissinen 2003a: 22.
[124] According to Nissinen (2003d: 22-23), it is possible that the Assyrian prophets in fact admonished the king to fulfil his social duties, but that these oracles were not preserved, since the criterion of preservation of the extant corpus seems to be the confirmation of the king's legitimacy. It is however equally possible that it was at this point not part of the prophetic task to remind the king of his social duties, important though these were. Nissinen (2000b: 105) may be right to suggest that not too sharp a distinction should be made between 'cultic' and 'social' criticism.

Assyria, divine claims, put forward by prophets, could be either material (goods, treasures) or immaterial (justice, praise).[125]

In addition to the texts discussed by Nissinen, I would like to draw attention to two further letters from Mari, ARM 26 371 and ARM 26 206. The sharpest criticism directed at a king in a prophetic oracle is in the Mari letter ARM 26 371:[126]

> The *āpilum* of Marduk stood in the gate of the palace shouting repeatedly: "Išme-Dagan will not escape the hand of Marduk. He (Marduk) will tie up the net and he (Išme-Dagan) will be caught in it". This is what he repeatedly shouted in the gate of the palace, but [nobody] spoke to him. Likewise he stood in the gate of Išme-Dagan, and in the assembly of the whole land he was shouting repeatedly: "You went to the ruler of Elam to establish peaceful relations, you delivered the treasure of Marduk and the city of Babylon to the ruler of Elam in order to establish good relations. You used up my silos and stores, but did not return my favour. And now you depart for Ekallatum! He [who] removes my treasure, should not ask for its addition!" [This] is what he [repeatedly shouted] in the assembly of the [whole] land, but [nobody] spoke to him.

This scene takes place in Babylon, where Išme-Dagan, king of Ekallatum (a city in Assyria), who is gravely ill, stays as protégé of King Hammurabi. Išme-Dagan sent goods and treasures from Marduk's temple in Babylon as a goodwill gift to the ruler of Elam. Marduk, by mouth of his *āpilum* furiously announced that Išme-Dagan would pay dearly for this. The oracle addresses Išme-Dagan, not Hammurabi. This is remarkable, as it is inconceivable that Išme-Dagan could dispose of the possessions of the Marduk temple without Hammurabi's consent. Implicitly, the oracle criticises the politics of Hammurabi.[127] The furious tone of the oracle betrays a temple community that stood helpless against the decision of Hammurabi to use temple possessions for the sake of Išme-Dagan.[128] In this case, the temple interest, repre-

---

[125] In the oracle 1.4 three different deities present themselves, reminding Esarhaddon of what they did for his benefit, and submitting their demand. Bel (Marduk): 'pay attention to me' (ii 29'), Ištar of Arbela and Nabû: 'praise me' (ii 33'; 39'). The demand 'praise me' also occurs in the oracle from Ištar of Arbela, 1.10 (vi 18).

[126] Not discussed by Nissinen 2003d. For the text, see Nissinen 2003a: 73-74.

[127] Charpin 2002: 27.

[128] See Heimpel 2003: 64, for the historical reconstruction. Išme-Dagan of Ekallatum, gravely ill, went to Hammurabi of Babylon for help. He left his throne to Mut-Aškur, his son. Atamrum, king of Allahad, assisted by a party of Ekallateans, put a certain Hammutar on the throne as his puppet-king. Atamrum himself was however a vassal of Elam. So, Išme-Dagan sent a precious gift to Elam, to obtain an Elamite or-

sented by the prophet, was far removed from the royal interest, and it may well be that the 'assembly of the whole land' rather sympathised with the king and his protégé, Išme-Dagan. This, it seems, is indicated by the final sentence: 'this he shouted repeatedly, but nobody spoke to him'. The reported oracle shows something else too. The representatives of the Marduk temple must have been just as angry with their own king, Hammurabi. The *āpilum* avoids however addressing the divine criticism directly against Hammurabi, but instead focuses on his client, Išme-Dagan.

In one case (ARM 26/1 206) a prophet announced the occurrence of a specific disaster:

> To [my lord] speak! [Your] servant [Yaqqim-Addu] (says),
> 'A *muḫḫûm* [of Dagan] came to me and [spoke to me] as follows: He (said), "S[urely, what] shall I eat that belongs to Z[imri-Lim]? [Give me] one lamb and I shall eat."
> [I gave] him one lamb, and he ate it alive in front of the city gate. And I assembled the elders in front of the city gate of Saggaratum, and he spoke as follows: He (said), "A devouring will occur. Give orders to the cities to return the taboo (i.e. sacred things). They must expel from the city anyone who committed an act of violence. And for the well-being of your lord, Zimri-Lim, you will clothe me in a garment."
> This he said to me, and for the well-being of [my] lord I clothed [him] in a garment. Herewith [I *sent*] you the directive/oracle (*têrtum*) he told me, [and] I have written to [my lord]. And he did not mention his directive/oracle to me in private. He gave his directive/oracle before the assembled elders.'[129]

The *muḫḫûm*, as reported in this letter, announced a disaster and underscored it with a symbolic act. There is a word-play between his eating (*akālu*) of the lamb and the 'devouring' (*ukultu*) that will take place. A disaster is announced, but with the purpose of averting it; if the right action is undertaken, it will not happen. A god is angry, a devouring (an epidemic) may occur, but if the god is appeased, nothing bad will happen.

This final example shows that the categories *Heilsprophetie* and *Unheilsprophetie* are inadequate. Prophets could announce a specific

---

der to Atamrum to remove Hammutar from the throne of Ekallatum. Since he stayed in Babylon, Išme-Dagan had to request Hammurabi to provide him with the treasures he needed. Hammurabi decided to take them from the temple of Marduk.

[129] ARM 26/1 206; Nissinen 2003a: 38; cf. Heimpel 2003: 256; Roberts 2002b: 228-231.

disaster, but with the purpose of averting it.[130] By announcing a disaster, a prophet did not stand in opposition to the establishment, but served the interest of king and state. He revealed otherwise hidden knowledge concerning a threat to the general well-being. If the predicted outcome was successfully averted, this did not make such a prophecy false. Rather, a prophet protecting society by revealing a threatening disaster was only doing his job.[131]

Encouragement of the king takes a prominent position in ancient Near Eastern prophecy, especially in the Assyrian prophecies. However, declarations of support are sometimes accompanied by divine claims. Furthermore, both in Mari and in Assyria we see, that if such claims were not granted or if a king had otherwise not fulfilled his duties, the gods, through their prophets, could reproach him. More drastically, the prophecy of encouragement could be turned upside down. Whereas normally the gods encouraged the king and announced the annihilation of his enemies, the announcements of annihilation could also be directed *against* the king as part of a declaration of divine support to his adversary. An example of such a prophecy is reported in a letter by Nabû-reḫtu-uṣur, concerning Esarhaddon's presumed adversary Sasî.[132] Although kings forbade this kind of prophecy, it was nevertheless possible.[133] The same prophetic voice that encouraged and legitimised the king, could also formulate demands on him, or even choose the side of his adversaries. The fact that prophets functioned within the existing order did not mean that they always agreed with

---

[130] Similarly, negative apodoses to omens are formulated as if a disaster is going to happen, but likewise with the purpose of averting it, by performing the appropriate apotropaic ritual. For these *namburbi*-rituals, see Maul 1994.

[131] Tiemeyer (2005) surveys prophetic foreknowledge serving as guidelines for rulers in the ancient world in their decision-making and relates this to Mesopotamian divination. She shows that prophecy and other forms of divination must be understood in the light of the Near Eastern belief that the future was predictable and that the predicted future was alterable. Prophecy was used by political decision-makers, and when a disastrous course of events was revealed, by prophecy or other means, people sought to change the decisions of the gods, through rituals, magic, and supplication.

[132] SAA 16 59 r. 4-5; see chapter 4.2.5.

[133] Nissinen 2003d: 24-25, pointing to the *adê*-text SAA 2 6:108-122.

the king and his politics.[134] The interest of the cosmic and social-political order could transcend the interests of an individual king.[135]

Prophets in the ancient Near East did more than speaking pleasant words to those who paid and fed them. A recent study counts the prophets among the *Vertreter des Herrschaftswissens*.[136] This qualification means that the prophets were part of a broader system of divination, and that their access to the will of the gods enabled the king in his assertion of power.[137] Prophets were part of the system, which means that they spoke and acted for the benefit of social and cosmic stability.[138] At the same time, however, *within* this order, the prophets stood at a certain distance from the king. They were also used by gods to serve the particular interest of the cults and they functioned as the mouthpiece of the gods for reproaching kings failing to fulfil their duties. The prophets served the state interest but not necessarily the king's particular interests. This implies that the categories of *Heilsprophetie* and *Unheilsprophetie* are better abandoned from descriptions of prophecy in the ancient Near East.

5.1.5   *The Prophets among the Diviners*

Prophecy as a Form of Divination

Prophecy was a branch of divination among others.[139] The various kinds of ancient Near Eastern divination are commonly divided into two categories: 1) inductive, technical divination, represented mainly by astrologers, haruspices and exorcists, and 2) non-inductive, non-technical, intuitive divination, represented by prophets, dreamers and visionaries.[140] It may however be questioned whether this distinction is entirely adequate. As was the case with the so-called technical forms of divination, prophetic oracles could also be delivered both spontane-

---

[134] So also Charpin 2002: 28: 'aussi bien à Babylone qu'à Mari, les prophéties étaient toujours favorables au roi local, mais pas nécessairement à sa politique du moment'. See for some examples from Mari, Charpin 1992: 22-25; Roberts 1997a.

[135] Cf. the Old Babylonian oracle of Adad, lord of Kallassu: 'I, the lord of the throne, territory and city, can take away what I have given!' (l. 21-23; translation from: Nissinen 2003a: 19).

[136] See Pongratz-Leisten 1999; Nissinen 2003d: 29-31.

[137] Nissinen 2003d: 30.

[138] Nissinen (2003d: 30) points out that no ancient Near Eastern prophet rejected the institution of kingship or announced the collapse of the society or state he was part of.

[139] E.g. Van der Toorn 1987: 67; Nissinen 2004: 21-22.

[140] See Rochberg 2004: 47-48; Nissinen 2004: 21-22; Bottéro 2001: 125-126.

ously and on request.[141] The various forms of divination were to a great extent complementary to each other and were practiced side by side.[142] Furthermore, Van der Toorn mentions various examples of 'technical oracles' and 'prophetic oracles' that are hardly distinguishable from each other with regard to their formulation,[143] and points out that the texts often do not explain through what particular form of divination a certain oracle was obtained. He concludes that some cooperation between various forms of divination, or even a transfer of divinatory roles, should not surprise us, since people in the ancient Near East were generally more interested in the message than in the mode of its transmission.[144] The outcome was more important than the means.

Although prophets had a role of their own, the purpose of prophecy corresponded at least to an important extent with the purpose of divination in general. All branches of divination shared a common ideological basis and were grounded in the belief that the gods communicated with humans and that the decisions of the heavenly world affected earthly circumstances. In first millennium Assyria, the role of divination in state politics was particularly important.[145] Divination served as a help for decision-making, as assurance, and as prediction. Prophetic oracles were used by political decision-makers, as were the results of extispicy and astrology. The references to prophetic oracles in the inscriptions of Esarhaddon and Ashurbanipal show that prophecy occupied an established role among other forms of divination.[146]

Prophecy and Dreams

Prophecy probably was most closely related to divination through dreams.[147] As a counterpart to *raggimu*, the designation for a person

---

[141] See SAA 9 1 v 14; Durand 1982; 1997: 125.

[142] Van der Toorn 1987: 70-71.

[143] Van der Toorn 1987: 68-70.

[144] Van der Toorn 1987: 71. Cf. also Charpin 2002: 11: 'la prophétie n'a pas un statut particulier', since prophetic oracles were treated like the "événements fortuits", such as eclipses and meteorological phenomena: the gods were believed to send their messages through multiple forms.

[145] Cancik-Kirschbaum 2003: 43-44.

[146] So Nissinen 2000a: 266. With regard to Old Babylonian Mari, Fleming (2004: 46) suggests that 'prophets were not of the highest social rank, but they were integrated into the core institutions of the Mari kingdom'.

[147] Van der Toorn 1987: 71-73; Grabbe 1995: 145-148. Butler (1998: 15) distinguishes between three kinds of prognostic dreams in Akkadian sources: 1) Message-dreams containing a clear statement that requires no interpretation. The main charac-

able to receive message-dreams was *šabrû*. In a lexical list *raggimu* and *šabrû* are equated.[148] A *šabrû* is mentioned in Ashurbanipal's Prisms as the recipient of a dream reinforcing a preceding (prophetic) oracle.[149] Elsewhere, *šabrû* occurs in connection with *maḫḫû* and *zabbu* (ecstatic).[150] The *šabrû* is perhaps best understood as a 'visionary'.[151] Both in dreams and in prophecy, a human being functioned as a medium of the divine message. Although there is a terminological distinction between orally mediated divine words (*amātum, dabābu, dibbu*, etc),[152] and dreams (*šuttu*),[153] it is not always clear, when quoted in a royal inscription, whether a certain report is an oracular message or a dream message.

It has been suggested that dreams were less strictly connected with 'specialists' than prophecies, since non-specialists could apparently receive message-dreams as well.[154] The dream that set the stage for the narration of the war against Šamaš-šum-ukin was received by 'a man' (*ištēn etlu*).[155] In addition, Ashurbanipal's Prisms mention a message-dream received by the Lydian king, Gyges,[156] and one received by the whole Assyrian army.[157] Although the reliability of these dream-

---

teristic of a message-dream is that a (divine) figure gives an unequivocal message to the dreamer. 2) Symbolic-message dreams which have to be decoded (mainly recorded in Mesopotamian epics). 3) Dream omens which are interpreted from Dream Books. It is the direct-message dreams that closely resemble prophetic oracles.

[148] MSL 12 6.2, l. 134; see Nissinen 2003a: 187-188. According to Henshaw (1994: 140-143), dreamers and dream-interpreters were related to temples.

[149] B v 50 // C vi 50 and K 2652:25; BIWA: 100, 102.

[150] In various city omen texts, *šabrû* occurs in association with *maḫḫû* and various other cultic figures (CT 38 4:87-88, see Parpola 1997: CIII, note 222; Nissinen 2003a: 189-191). In LKA 29d ii 2, *šabrû* occurs in juxtaposition with *zabbu*: 'Let the *zabbu* speak to you, let the *šabrû* repeat it to you'. This phrase may suggest that the *šabrû* sometimes repeated or clarified ecstatic utterances.

[151] The term *šabrû* 'dreamer' is to be distinguished from *šabrû* 'administrator'. The suggestion that *šabrû*, 'dreamer', derives from *barû* Š 'to reveal (in a dream)' (Nissinen 1998: 56) is questioned by Weippert 2002: 32-33, note 130.

[152] Cf. also Cancik-Kirschbaum 2003: 48; Charpin 2002: 8, notes 8-11.

[153] Cancik-Kirschbaum 2003: 48.

[154] E.g. Parpola 1997: XLVII. For the practice of incubation in Mesopotamia, see Zgoll 2002.

[155] A iii 118 (BIWA: 40-41). The earlier reading by Streck (1916 II: 32), *ištēn šabrû*, is to be rejected (contra Nissinen 1998: 55). The designation *ištēn etlu* is frequently attested in the context of dreams, but usually as the designation of the figure appearing in a dream; see Kvanvig 1988: 414-422.

[156] A ii 95-110, B ii 93-iii 4, C iv 1-14, F ii 10-20; BIWA: 30-31.

[157] A v 95-103; BIWA: 50.

accounts should be doubted,[158] they may reflect the phenomenon of people claiming to have received divine message-dreams concerning state matters.[159]

Prophets and Scholars

Although the boundaries between the various forms of divination were not always sharply perceived, a distinctive feature was that some forms of divination were more learned than others. It is possible that prophets received some sort of training,[160] but this must have been very different from the intensive scribal education in the ancient lore.[161] In the Assyrian period, five 'expert disciplines' can be distinguished, that of *ṭupšarru* 'scribe, celestial diviner',[162] *bārû* 'haruspex', *āšipu* 'exorcist', *asû* 'physician', and *kalû* 'lamentation chanter'.[163] Experts in one or more of these five disciplines are designated as *ummânu* 'scholar'.[164] The scholars learned their expertise at scribal schools, located at the main temples of the major cities of Assyria and Babylonia.[165]

Whereas most scholars, as religious specialists, were affiliated with temples,[166] we know most about the top-ranking scholars obtaining a position at the royal court, in the first half of the seventh century. The Sargonid kings employed Assyrian and Babylonian scholars for their own protection, and by extension for the protection of the state.[167] It was held that the gods constantly sent messages pertaining to all aspects of the king's behaviour. These scholars were engaged in reporting omens to the king, performing rituals, chants, extispicy, applying medicines, and assisted the king in the face of the supernatural with their respective technologies. Scholars who were summoned to the king's entourage were specifically employed to this end and repre-

---

[158]   See Butler 1998: 17.
[159]   As is also the case in the letters SAA 10 361 and 365.
[160]   Cryer 1991: 83.
[161]   Nissinen 2000b: 109.
[162]   The complete title was *ṭupšarru enūma Anu Ellil*, 'celestial diviner'.
[163]   Brown 2000: 33; cf. SAA 7 1, where these five disciplines are mentioned, followed by various designations of foreign experts in divination. See Parpola 1993: XIII-XXVII; Starr 1990: XXX-XXXV.
[164]   See Parpola 1993: XIII-XXVII. According to Brown (2000: 34-36), in the Assyrian period no strong hierarchy consisted between the five disciplines, each being of approximately equal worth.
[165]   Brown 2000: 41-42; Van der Toorn 2007: 54-67. For an introduction to scholarly divination, Rochberg 2004: 44-65 and 210-224.
[166]   Van der Toorn 2007: 59.
[167]   Rochberg 2004: 77; Brown 2000: 36-42.

sented the main experts in the various disciplines. The duty of these scholars in direct royal employment, described as "keeping the watch of the king" and as "standing before the king", was probably more prestigious than temple employment.[168] The status and power of scholars at the royal court was considerable,[169] but entirely dependent on royal favour. Even the highest scholar had no easy access to the king, but had to write to him.[170] Their complete dependence on the favour of the king,[171] led to intense competition and rivalry among the scholars in the king's entourage.[172]

In the Assyrian period scholarly forms of divination reached a high scientific standard. The scholars had profound knowledge of the traditional literature of their respective fields and a high level of literacy.[173] From various allusions it appears that the scholars in royal service were seen as the successors of the mythical antediluvian sages, the *apkallu*.[174] Just as these legendary sages were believed to have served and guided the ancient kings, and imparted all wisdom to the Mesopotamians, so the scholars served and guided Esarhaddon and Ashurbanipal, and imparted the very same wisdom to the king.[175]

Thus, whereas prophets, as far as we can tell, are to be located in a temple environment, scholars, at least during the reigns of Esarhaddon and Ashurbanipal, often were directly employed by the royal court.[176] In contrast to the five scholarly disciplines, prophecy did not emanate from guilds of scientifically trained diviners, but concerned, as it seems, mainly temple functionaries who were believed to have the

---

[168] Brown (2000: 41) notes that scholars that were part of the royal entourage could also be associated with temples, either as part of the temple personnel or as royal agents.

[169] On the relation between the king and his scholars, see Pongratz-Leisten 1999: 293-319.

[170] Brown 2000: 44-45.

[171] Brown (2000: 49-50) criticises Parpola's view of an 'inner circle' of the top-ranking scholars and an 'outer circle' of scholars still important but not residing in Nineveh (1993: XXV-XXVI). Brown prefers the concept of the king's entourage, consisting of all scholars in royal employment. Entrance to this circle depended on one's level of education and descent.

[172] Brown 2000: 46-47.

[173] Nissinen 2000b: 108.

[174] Nissinen 2000b: 109; Rochberg 2004: 181-185.

[175] Brown 2000: 46; Parpola 1993: XVII-XIX.

[176] The situation in Old Babylonian Mari was rather similar: whereas the prophetic figures belonged to the temple personnel, the *bārû* (haruspices) were employed by the king; see Sasson 1998: 116-118; Charpin 2002: 8, 22. Fleming (2004: 56) qualifies the *bārûm*-diviners as 'royal officials with career opportunities almost without limit'.

ability to speak with the voice of the deity.[177] Practising this form of divination probably did not include a profound literary training. In the later part of the Assyrian period, many top rank scholars were in the direct employment of the king; there is no evidence of prophets taking a similar position. Finally, the scholars are exclusively male, and often stem from specific families; among the prophets, women take a prominent position, and nothing is known about 'families of prophets' in the Assyrian period.

Status of the Prophets

Prophets differed from scholars with regard to social standing and political position and often with regard to gender. Prophets it seems were not directly employed by the king, and did not belong to the entourage of the king. Although their oracles could influence the political decision-making, and in general were taken seriously by the king,[178] the prophets were not in a position to advise the king in political matters.[179] However, at times, in particular at critical moments, the prophets functioned as an important alternative, when their oracles became ground or help for political decision-making. The prophetic function of proclaiming divine legitimation of a throne pretender was not under full royal control and prophetic oracles could include critical elements. The prophetic authority, usually employed for the king's benefit, could also be used against him.[180]

5.2   Isaiah among the Prophets in Judah and Israel

A fundamental problem for a survey of prophecy in Judah and Israel is the nature of the sources. The books of the Old Testament do not merely describe prophetic activity, but rather present views on prophecy, interpretation of prophetic activity, and reflection on prophecy. The gap between literary sources and historical reality cannot be easily bridged. Yet, a description of prophecy as a socio-historical phe-

---

[177]   Cf. also Weippert 2003: 286-287.

[178]   It has been suggested that the Assyrian prophets enjoyed a (somewhat) higher status than the prophets in Old Babylonian Mari (Nissinen 2000b: 103; Huffmon 2000: 62). In my opinion, the arguments presented so far are inconclusive; a broader study is needed to come to any firm conclusion on this point.

[179]   Nissinen 2000b: 108.

[180]   Cf. Cancik-Kirschbaum 2003: 52, note 98.

nomenon in Judah and Israel is impossible without the use of the Old Testament. The problem is how to use the Old Testament material for a description of Israelite prophecy in a plausible and valid way. In order to solve this, two scholarly enterprises must be distinguished: the analysis of the portrayals of the prophets in the books of the Old Testament on the one hand, and the reconstruction of prophecy as a socio-historical phenomenon in Judah and Israel on the other.[181] After a section on terms and concepts, 5.2.2 deals with prophets in the Old Testament, and 5.2.3 with prophets in Judah and Israel. Finally, 5.2.4 discusses the prophetic function of Isaiah.

5.2.1 *Terms and Concepts*

In the Old Testament we find the following designations for figures that may be considered prophets: *nābî'*, *ḥōzeh*, *rō'eh*, *'îš hā'ĕlōhîm*, and *qōsēm*.[182] The term *nābî'* is the most frequently attested by far. A recent suggestion to interpret *nābî'* as an active form, meaning 'the one who invokes (the gods)',[183] has been critically reviewed by Huehnergard,[184] who argued in favour of the earlier understanding of *nābî'* as a passive, meaning 'the called one'.[185] The terms *ḥōzeh*, from חזה 'to see', and *rō'eh*, from ראה 'to see', are usually translated as 'seer'. The term *'îš hā'ĕlōhîm* means 'man of God'. Finally, *qōsēm*, from קסם, 'to divine, predict, decide', denotes a certain type of diviner, but it is difficult to be more precise. In the Old Testament the lexical

---

[181] Cf. Nissinen's proposal (2004: 31) to distinguish between 'ancient Hebrew prophecy' on the one hand and 'biblical prophecy' on the other. In earlier contributions to the study of Israelite prophecy such a distinction has not often been adequately made; see Collins 1993: 13-14.

[182] These five terms are discussed by Gonçalves (2001: 144-171, for a comprehensive overview of the terms in the Old Testament). My analysis is restricted to these terms, although they cannot be completely distinguished from, e.g. *ḥolēm* 'dreamer', and some of those listed in Deut 18:10-11.

[183] So Fleming 1993a; 1993b, based on evidence from Mari and Emar. In texts from Mari and Emar, the word *nabûm* is attested, indicating a group of religious personnel. Fleming interprets it as 'those who invoke the gods in prayer, blessing, or divinatory/oracular inquiry', and suggests a similar active etymology for the Hebrew *nābî'*: the Israelite prophets in origin invoked the name of Yahweh for power and guidance (1993b: 221-224). Fenton (1997: 33-36) argues similarly: *nābî'* is 'speaker'.

[184] Huehnergard 1999: 88-93. Huehnergard points out that the attestations of *nabûm* in Mari and Emar may equally represent passive forms ('those who are called'). Fleming (2004: 61-64) replies to Huehnergard's objections, again in favour of an active understanding of *nābî'*.

[185] Müller 1984: 140-141.

groups of נבא, חזה, ראה and קסם are regularly used interchangeably and in connection with each other.[186]

From a certain stage onwards, the terms *nābî'*, *ḥōzeh*, and *rō'eh* were used as synonyms. The various terms are used without much distinction, in 2 Kgs 17:13 *nābî'* and *ḥōzeh*,[187] in Isa 29:10 *nābî'* and *ḥōzeh*,[188] and in 30:10 *ḥōzeh* and *rō'eh*.[189] Furthermore, at a certain stage *nābî'* became the standard designation for prophetic figures,[190] as is confirmed by the definition of 1 Sam 9:9b, 'for the one who is now called a prophet (*nābî'*) was formerly called a seer (*rō'eh*)'.[191] The title *ḥōzeh* is found mostly in Chronicles, where the *ḥōzîm* are presented among the temple musicians.[192] The Chronicler does not carefully distinguish between 'seers' and 'prophets', neither between *nābî'* and *ḥōzeh*, nor between *ḥōzeh* and *rō'eh*.[193] Outside Chronicles, *ḥōzeh* is always used in connection with other terms for 'prophet': *nābî'* (2 Sam 24:11; 2 Kgs 17:13; Isa 29:10; Amos 7:12-14), *rō'eh* (Isa 30:10), and *qōsēm* (Mic 3:7). The terms *rō'îm*, *ḥōzîm*, and *nābî'*, although originally perhaps not complete equivalents, often function as synonyms in the Old Testament.[194]

The term *'îš hā'ĕlōhîm* 'man of God' is a somewhat different case. It is used exclusively for individual males, and always positively.[195] The designation *'îš hā'ĕlōhîm* occurs in a range of relatively late instances,[196] but also in traditions that may be of an earlier origin, which present the *'îš hā'ĕlōhîm* as gifted with supernatural knowledge and

---

[186] Gonçalves 2001: 144-145.

[187] 2 Kgs 17:13 is a late addition, from a nomistic editor (cf. 2 Chron 24:19; Neh 9:26, 29-30, 34).

[188] In Isa 29:10 *nābî'* and *ḥōzeh* appear as glosses.

[189] Cf. Fenton 1997: 30. In Isa 30:9-11, the people are depicted as disobedient to Yahweh. They reject his word and they order the prophets not to prophesy 'what is right', but delusion and deception.

[190] Stökl 2004: 30; Johnson 1962: 9.

[191] See Fenton 1997: 23-42.

[192] According to Schniedewind (1995: 187), the Chronicler portrays the heads of the Levitical clans as *ḥōzîm*, because of their role as temple musicians and singers.

[193] Stökl 2004: 26-29. In 2 Sam 24:11, Gad is described as 'the *nābî'* Gad, David's *ḥōzeh*', but he is referred to as *ḥōzeh* in 1 Chron 21:9; 29:29; 2 Chron 29:25. Jehu is referred to as *nābî'* in 1 Kgs 16:7, but as *ḥōzeh* in 2 Chron 19:2. In 2 Chron 33:18, the 'seers' replace the 'prophets' of 2 Kgs 21:10. Cf. Fenton 1997: 30, for the Chronicler's use of *rō'eh* as based on 1 Sam 9.

[194] See also Waschke 2004: 63.

[195] Gonçalves 2001: 158-159.

[196] E.g. Moses (in Deut 33:1; Josh 14:6; Ezra 3:2; 1 Chron 23:14; 2 Chron 30:16); David (Neh 12:24, 36; 2 Chron 8:14).

power.[197] In the stories concerning Elijah and Elisha the title *'îš ha'ĕlōhîm* occurs mostly where Elijah or Elisha acts in supernaturally powerful ways.[198] In the biblical traditions 'man of God' is often synonymous with 'prophet'.[199] It may be that *'îš ha'ĕlōhîm* is a general, honorific title reflecting the powers attributed to (prophetic) figures rather than denoting a specific type of prophet.[200]

The term *qōsēm* mostly appears in passages criticising the (religious) establishment. The *qōsĕmîm* are mentioned together with other (religious) functionaries, such as the *ḥōzîm*, or as representatives of the religious establishment.[201] In Deut 18:10 and 14 the *qōsēm* is mentioned among religious practitioners that are not allowed to exist in Israel. Despite the claim of Deut 18 that the *qōsĕmîm* were originally foreign to Israel, it seems rather clear that the *qōsĕmîm* were part of the religious establishment in Judah and Israel.[202] They are usually related to prophetic figures, but precisely what kind of divination they practised is difficult to ascertain.

The terms *nābî'*, *ḥōzeh* and *rō'eh* may originally have denoted different prophetic figures, but the differences cannot be recovered. The term *nābî'* is most frequently used, not only in late contexts but also in relatively early traditions concerning the prophets, such as the prophetic groups described in 1 Sam 10 and 19, and the prophet Nathan, who is closely connected to the fortunes of the Davidic dynasty (2 Sam 7, 12; 1 Kgs 1).[203] In the texts, the *ḥōzeh* denotes a prophetic figure, associated with the *nābî'*, which also forms part of religious establishment.[204] The *rō'eh*, furthermore, denotes a prophetic figure as-

---

[197] Petersen (1981: 43-50) describes the *'îš ha'ĕlōhîm* as leader of the 'sons of the prophets', a peripheral prophetic cult. However, only in the case of Elisha is a connection between the title *'îš ha'ĕlōhîm* and the prophetic group apparent (2 Kgs 4:38-40; 5:22; 6:1-6).

[198] Petersen 1981: 42.

[199] Wilson 1980: 140. See 1 Kgs 13:18; 2 Kgs 5:8; Elisha in 2 Kgs 4:40; 5:13-14; 6:12, 15. Cf. Fenton 1997: 30, suggesting that *'îš ha'ĕlōhîm* is 'a general term and often interchangeable with *nābî'*.'

[200] For this position, cf. Schniedewind 1995: 47-49.

[201] Isa 3:2; 44:25; Jer 27:9 (referring to Judah's neighbours); Jer 29:8; Ezek 13:9, 22:28, Mic 3:7; Zech 10:2. Forms of קסם or derivatives often occur in combination with forms or derivatives of חזה or נביא / נבא; see Gonçalves 2001: 165-166.

[202] Cryer 1994: 256-257.

[203] Stökl (2004: 18) suggests that since Nathan is consistently designated *nābî'* in Samuel, Kings and Chronicles, this is likely to go back to a relatively early tradition.

[204] Apart from 2 Kgs 17:13 and Isa 29:10, the terms *nābî'* and *ḥōzeh* are used in combination in 2 Sam 24:11, where Gad is designated as 'the prophet, David's seer'. In Amos 7:12, Amaziah addresses Amos as *ḥōzeh* to which Amos replies in 7:14 'I

sociated with *ḥōzeh* and *nābî'*. Apart from Chronicles, *rō'eh* occurs in Isa 30:10, as synonym of *ḥōzeh*,[205] and in 1 Sam 9. In 1 Sam 9, two narrative strands have been combined: one concerning a locally based clairvoyant, *'îš hā'ĕlōhîm* (9:6-8) and the other concerning a *rō'eh*, an itinerant seer who comes to officiate at the sacrifice.[206]

Attempts to uncover different origins of the terms have not been convincing, in my view. It has been suggested that the term *nābî'* was originally connected with Northern traditions and was imported into Judah in the seventh century where it was used almost interchangeably for the typically southern term *ḥōzeh*.[207] However, the term *nābî'* is well-rooted in Judaean tradition, appearing in Isa 8:3 (*nĕbî'â*, commonly dated to the eighth century), the earliest part of the Hezekiah legends concerning 701 (2 Kgs 19:2),[208] the Nathan-David traditions,[209] and the Lachish ostraca. Furthermore, *ḥōzeh* can hardly be regarded as *the* Judaean term for 'prophet' before *nābî'* came in use. Only Gad is mentioned a *ḥōzeh*,[210] and Amos in Amos 7:12 (see 5.2.2 below). Besides, the term is used in connection with Balaam, and in the Zakkur Stele,[211] which makes it even less typically Judaean. It is hardly possible to make plausible distinctions between *nābî'*, *ḥōzeh*, and *rō'eh*.[212] A basic similarity between these figures is however discernable: all prophetic figures functioned as intermediaries between the human and the divine world.[213] Not only is it impossible to strictly separate between various prophetic figures, but also the prophetic figures cannot be completely distinguished from other cultic functionaries. One has to reckon with a considerable overlap, between the various prophetic figures discussed here, and also between prophetic figures and other practitioners of divination.

---

am no *nābî'*, nor a *ben nābî'*.' The logic of the dialogue implies that the terms at least to some extent are parallel (for Amos 7:10-17, see 5.2.2 below).

[205] So Gonçalves 2001: 170.
[206] Fenton 1997: 27-30.
[207] So Petersen 1981: 53-69, 70, 99, followed by Stökl 2004: 24.
[208] I.e. the so-called B1-story, dating from the seventh century; see chapter 6.1.2.
[209] See note 203 above.
[210] According to Gonçalves (2001: 169), the earliest title of Gad was *nābî'* (1 Sam 22:5), and the designation 'David's seer' was probably added under influence from Chronicles.
[211] Num 24:4, 16; Deir 'Allā plaster texts, combination I l. 1; Zakkur Stele l. 12.
[212] Cf. Grabbe 1995: 117.
[213] Grabbe 1995: 82; Johnson 1962: 30.

5.2.2   *Prophets in the Old Testament*

Most traditions concerning prophets in the Old Testament are not descriptions of how prophecy actually was, but a reflection of prophecy based on later perceptions. Images of the prophets in the Old Testament, although not complete imagination, should not be taken as descriptions of prophecy in Judah and Israel.

In the Old Testament we find two very different images of 'the prophets' (*hannĕbī'îm*). According to the first image, the prophets are servants of Yahweh; they urged the people to amend their ways, announced Yahweh's punishment over Judah and Israel, and functioned as mediators of the law. According to the second image, the prophets are liars, who with their false messages of peace deceived the people and caused the punishment of Judah and Jerusalem.[214] This contrast is not between two different types of prophets but two different characterisations of the prophets. As I will argue in this section, these characterisations of the prophets are ideological constructs retrojected onto Israel's and Judah's past. Neither image of 'the prophets' was a complete invention; both derive from real prophetic activity. Behind the image of the prophets as false and deceptive smooth talkers, one can see the prophetic function of encouraging king and people in a threatening situation. The image of the false prophets is a caricature of the prophetic function of guarding the safety and well-being of king and people. Behind the image of the prophets as Yahweh's servants warning the people, one discerns the prophetic function to remind the addressee of his duties and criticising behaviour that poses a threat to the well-being of the state. This image of the prophets equally is a caricature.

In this section, the origin of the two images of the prophets will be explained. First I discuss the biblical traditions in which individuals are portrayed as delivering prophecies of judgement but nevertheless not as prophets. The logic behind these traditions is, in my view, that at a certain stage the political and religious establishment was depicted as evil and corrupt, and the prophets were conceived as part of the establishment. Therefore, true bearers of the word of Yahweh were deliberately not called prophets. This view of the prophets as part of a wicked and corrupt establishment, furthermore, led to the image of the prophets as being false and deceptive. Finally, at a later stage, the true

---

[214]   Both images of the prophets are worked out below.

bearers of the word of Yahweh, began to be designated again as prophets.

Individual against Establishment

In the prophetic books we find individuals portrayed as delivering prophecies of judgement against a hostile establishment. In various cases these figures are deliberately not called prophets, in order to distinguish them from the prophets that were part of the religious establishment. Yet, these figures were commissioned by Yahweh to prophesy. The examples stem from the books of Amos, Jeremiah, Micah, Zephaniah, and Ezekiel.

The first example is found in Amos 7:10-17, the story of the confrontation between Amos and Amaziah the priest. Amos is accused of conspiracy against the state, because he said: 'Jeroboam shall die by the sword, and Israel will go into exile.' Because of this the priest Amaziah expels him from the land: 'seer (*hōzeh*), go, be off to the land of Judah, earn your bread there, and prophesy there; but never again prophesy at Bethel, for it is the king's sanctuary, and it is a temple of the kingdom' (7:12-13).[215] To this, Amos gives his famous reply: 'I am no prophet (*nābî'*), nor a prophet's son (*ben nābî'*); but I am a herdsman, and a dresser of sycamore trees, Yahweh took me from following the flock, and said to me, Go, prophesy (*nb' ni.*) to my people Israel.'

It has been often argued that Amos rejected the title *nābî'* and *ben nābî'*, but that he might have accepted another title for himself, like *hōzeh*, which he does not reject explicitly, or *rō'eh*.[216] This however misses the point of the story, which is that Amos is a farmer, commissioned by Yahweh to prophesy.[217] He is not a prophet, the story wants

---

[215] The words of Amaziah (7:12) are often translated as advice to the prophet: 'O seer, go, flee away to the land of Judah'. However, the phrase *běrah lěkā* should be translated as 'be off', 'make yourself scarce'. Amos is expelled, with exactly the same words as with which Balak chases off Balaam in Num 24:11, 'Now be off to your home!' (cf. Dijkstra 2001: 126). After Balaam has failed to do the job Balak hired him for—i.e. to curse the people of Israel—Balak chases him off and denies him any reward for his services (Num 24:11). The cases of Balaam and Amos are similar: 1) Both are supposedly taken into royal service to perform a prophetic role. 2) Both do the opposite of what they were supposed to do. 3) Both are chased off, expelled by official order. 4) Both are denied any reward or payment. Perhaps *hōzeh* in Amos 7:12 is inspired by Num 24:4, 16, where Balaam's activity is described with חזה.

[216] Zobel 1985: 293-298.

[217] Amos' commission, 'Yahweh took me from following the flock', resembles David's commissioning as ruler in 2 Sam 7:8 (see Dijkstra 2001: 126-127). This may

us to believe. For if he had been a prophet, he would have been part of the corrupt establishment, which was to collapse because of its wickedness, which Amos, being an outsider, had already announced.[218] The words of Amaziah make, indirectly, clear what prophets in reality were supposed to do. Prophets were often connected with the sanctuary, shared in the royal supplies of the temple, proclaimed the wellbeing of the king, thereby encouraging the people, and were public figures of importance. Amos does not deny that this is the function of a prophet, but denies he is a prophet. Not being a prophet, Amos is commissioned by Yahweh to prophesy, in opposition to the hostile and godless establishment.

A second example is found in Jeremiah 26. In this story, three individuals are presented: Jeremiah (especially in 26:12), Micah (26:18) and Uriah (26:20), who are commissioned by Yahweh to prophesy (*nb'* ni.) but who are nevertheless not called prophets. They are positioned in contrast to a hostile and godless establishment, of which the prophets as officials are part.[219] In the Septuagint version of Jeremiah, representing *grosso modo* an earlier edition of the book than the longer Masoretic version,[220] the designation 'prophet' (προφήτης) for Jeremiah is used very restrictively.[221] In particular when Jeremiah is

---

underscore that Amos is presented as being commissioned by Yahweh, but not really as a prophet.

[218] A new perspective is presented in Amos 3:7, 'Surely, the Lord Yahweh does nothing without revealing his secret to his servants the prophets'. According to this view, Amos was a true prophet (*nābî'*), who prophesied doom according to what he had heard and seen in the heavenly council. This passage is part of a later redaction of the Amos tradition, adding a new perspective to the story of Amos 7:10-17 (cf. Dijkstra 2001: 123).

[219] The priests and prophets (Jer 26:7, 8, 11 and 16). In the Septuagint of Jeremiah, the *nĕbî'îm* in their depiction as bad guys are often, but not always, rendered interpretatively as ψευδοπροφῆται; see Gonçalves 2001: 176; and Schöpflin 2002a: 280, with note 131.

[220] See in particular the work of Tov 1972; 1981; 2001. Carroll (1986: 50-55) observed that in the later edition, the *persona* of Jeremiah is considerably enlarged.

[221] In the Septuagint version, Jeremiah is presented as prophet to the nations (1:5, 28:59 [MT 51:59]). Furthermore, he is presented as prophet within ch. 44-51 (49:2 [M. 42:2]; 50:6 [M. 43:6]; 51:31 [M. 45:1]), which is the part of the book dealing with the fall of Jerusalem and its aftermath. In these narratives Jeremiah is the only prophet present on the scene. He is not opposed to other prophets; see Carroll 1986: 78-79; and Gonçalves 2001: 175-176.

opposed to 'the prophets' the Septuagint version tends to present him not as a προφήτης (*nābî'*), but as bearer of the divine word.[222]

A third passage is Mic 3:5-8, where the prophets are presented as part of a corrupt establishment.[223]

> Thus says Yahweh concerning the prophets who lead my people astray, who cry 'Peace' when they have something to eat, but declare war against those who put nothing into their mouths. Therefore it shall be night to you, without vision, and darkness to you, without revelation. The sun shall go down upon the prophets, and the day shall be black over them; the seers shall be disgraced, and the diviners put to shame; they shall all cover their lips, for there is no answer from God.
> But as for me, I am filled with power (with the spirit of Yahweh)[224] and with justice and might, to declare to Jacob his transgression and to Israel his sin.

The prophets are denounced as being corrupt, and doom is announced for the wicked establishment and the people. The speaker, depicted in 3:8, is commissioned by Yahweh to declare the wickedness of the people and to prophesy judgement. He is deliberately not called a prophet, in order to distinguish him from 'the prophets', condemned in 3:5-7.[225]

A similar depiction is found in Zeph 3:1-5, where the establishment of Jerusalem—the officials, judges, prophets and priests—is strongly rejected. Again, the speaker of the words of Yahweh to which this passage belongs is not presented as a prophet but as a bearer of the word of Yahweh (Zeph 1:1).

A final example is the presentation of Ezekiel, not as *nābî'*, but as 'mortal', ordered by Yahweh to prophesy (*nb'* ni.).[226] This is particularly significant where Ezekiel prophesies against 'the prophets' (Ezek 13:1-16), and where he denounces the establishment: officials, priests and prophets (Ezek 22:23-28).[227]

---

[222] In the later edition, represented by the Masoretic text, Jeremiah is called *nābî'* 27 more times. As Carroll (1986: 61-62, 79) points out, it is characteristic of the later tradition that Jeremiah could be designated as prophet without being confused with the prophets condemned in the tradition.

[223] Mic 3:1-12 condemns the establishment as a whole, both the political and the religious leaders.

[224] This is often considered a later addition; see Wagenaar 2001: 119, 261.

[225] So also Carroll 1992: 81; Gonçalves 2001: 174-175.

[226] Ezekiel is presented in this way throughout the book (29 times).

[227] Although in Ezek 38:17 the image of the prophets of old as Yahweh's servants appears, and Ezekiel is indirectly referred to as *nābî'* (2:5; 33:33), the presentation of Ezekiel as a 'mortal' commissioned to prophesy, functions to distinguish him from

Evidently, there is some variation between these five examples. Whereas Amos in 7:14 explicitly denies he is a prophet, in Micah and Zephaniah the term is not used for designating the speaker presented, and the cases of Jeremiah and Ezekiel are somewhat ambiguous. However, in these traditions a similar motif is at stake: an individual, truly commissioned by Yahweh to prophesy (doom) is presented as bearer of the divine word, but the designation prophet is not used. The reason for this was to distinguish this bearer of Yahweh's word from the prophets, who are, according to these traditions, part of the wicked establishment. The difference between a *nābî'* and someone presented as commissioned to prophesy (*nb'* ni.) may seem subtle. However, this subtle difference in terminology functions to express a clear ideological difference. The individuals commissioned by Yahweh to prophesy are portrayed as standing in opposition to a corrupt and evil establishment. Although they are presented as the real spokesmen of Yahweh, they are *not* called prophets, in order to distinguish them from their opponents: the wicked establishment, formed by the king, the officials, the priests, *and* the prophets. This image of Yahweh's real spokesmen who prophesy doom against a corrupt establishment is first of all a literary portrayal that has been included in several prophetic books.

Scholars have discussed the question whether these figures were prophets or not. Auld proposes that the so-called classical prophets were not prophets in their own estimation, but fierce opponents of the prophets instead. Only much later were they called prophets.[228] Gonçalves, on the other hand, argues that these individuals prophesying doom represent a *particular type* of prophet. In Gonçalves' view, alongside the various types of prophets such as *nābî'*, *ḥōzeh*, and *rō'eh* there existed another type: 'Yahweh's mouth-pieces'. They did not belong to any professional class of prophets. Most of the writing prophets, according to Gonçalves, belong to this type.[229] This vindicates the traditional view that the 'writing prophets' (whether or not the label *nābî'* is appropriate) represent a particular type of prophet.

'the prophets', who are part of the wicked establishment. For the presentation of the figure Ezekiel in the book, see De Jong 2007.

[228] Auld 1983; Auld's view is adopted by Carroll (1983), who argues that these spokesmen of Yahweh were not prophets, but poets. For an overview of the discussion raised by Auld, see Dijkstra 2001: 107-110.

[229] Gonçalves 2001: 178.

They are conveniently called the 'free prophets', in order to distinguish them from the so-called professional prophets,[230] and the supposed antagonism between the professional prophets or cult prophets on the one hand, and the free prophets on the other, is taken as a point of departure for the exegesis of the biblical prophetic books.[231]

A fundamental objection to this view is that it takes the portrayal of characters in the prophetic books as reliable depictions of historical figures belonging to a distinct type of prophet. This jump from literature to history is, in my view, problematic. Instead of taking the concept of the great prophets or classical prophets as a point of departure, first the relation between the prophetic books and the 'historical prophets' must be explored from case to case. We have a series of books which share the feature that they are presented as the words or vision of a particular prophetic figure after whom they have been named. The books are not only hugely different from each other, but also is it clear in most cases that the content of the book in its entirety cannot be attributed to one hand, let alone to that of the figure mentioned in the heading. Even if at the basis of each book there stands a prophetic figure (which cannot be taken for granted) the relation between 'prophet' and 'book' might be different from case to case.

In chapters 2 and 4, the prophetic material from the eighth century has been analysed and discussed within its historical background. The prophetic profile emerging from the material is not that of a 'classical prophet', but rather of what one could call a Judaean exponent of ancient Near Eastern prophecy (see 5.2.4 below). Apart from various particular traits, the prophet Isaiah shared many essential similarities with the prophets from Mari and Assyria. It was in the later development of the Isaiah tradition that the prophet Isaiah came to be depicted as a figure prophesying the irrevocable doom of his society, thereby conforming to the image of 'classical prophet'.[232]

---

[230] E.g. Lang (1980: 33) defines the common distinction between three types or classes of prophets as the prophetic groups, the professional prophets or cult/temple prophets, and the free prophets. A first question is whether 'prophetic groups' and 'temple prophets' formed clearly distinguished categories. A second question is, whether the 'free prophets' represent a historical category at all.

[231] Schöpflin (2002a: 280-282) gives an overview of this position. Nissinen (2004: 23) objects: 'The often-made dichotomy between free, charismatic prophets and the so-called cultic or court prophets should no longer be upheld as a fundamental, generally applicable distinction'; see also Pohlmann 1994: esp. 337.

[232] Similarly Collins 1993: 13. For a similar view, concerning Jeremiah, see Van der Toorn 2007: 190-193.

Furthermore, the concept of the 'free prophets' as a historical category underestimates the ideological character and purpose of the prophetic books. Instead of concluding that in late monarchic Judah and Israel certain individuals were active who prophesied doom in Yahweh's name but were nevertheless not *nĕbī'îm*, one should ask whether perhaps in the later depiction of this period, when the downfall of the states of Israel and Judah had to be explained, certain individuals were portrayed as delivering prophecies of judgement against a hostile establishment, and whether these figures were perhaps deliberately not called *nĕbī'îm*, in order to distinguish them from the *nĕbī'îm*, who were part of the religious establishment.

The events of the early sixth century—the fall of Jerusalem, the desecration of the temple, the end of the monarchy and the political state, and the exile of part of the population—were a huge disaster. Prophets, as is discernible from various caricatural depictions,[233] had encouraged king and people in the name of Yahweh that things would end up all right. The encouragement of the prophets during moments of crisis was based on the conviction that Yahweh would protect Judah and Jerusalem, its king and temple. The events of the early sixth century were thus also a failure of prophecy.[234] The prophets had not been able to prevent the collapse of the state, and neither had its other protectors: the king, the officials and the priests. As part of the reflection on the disastrous events, certain individuals were depicted as being commissioned by Yahweh to prophesy doom. They are presented in contrast to a hostile and godless establishment of which the prophets were part, and for this reason these figures were deliberately not called prophets.

Subsequently, the view of the prophets as part of a corrupt establishment led to the image of the prophets as false and deceiving liars. As such, the prophets were blamed for the disaster that befell Israel and Judah. At a somewhat later stage, a different development occurred: the development of the image of the prophets as Yahweh's servants. This image built on the depiction of individuals commis-

---

[233] Cf. e.g. Jer 6:14; 8:11; 14:13; 23:17; 27:9, 14, 16; 37:19.

[234] For a general depiction of the religious crisis caused by the events of 586 BCE and the various theological explanations that followed the events, see Pohlmann 2002. Cf. also Roberts 1977a concerning Ps 74:9. According to Roberts, Ps 74:9 testifies to a general loss of the credibility of prophecy due to the failure of the encouraging prophecies of 'peace' (cf. also Lam 2:9b and Ezek 7:26). For a similar view, see Johnson 1962: 66-75.

sioned by Yahweh to prophesy doom, and by this time they are explicitly called prophets (see below).[235]

The Image of the Prophets as False and Deceptive Smooth Talkers

The development of the image of the prophets as false and deceptive
smooth talkers, followed from reflection on the events of the early
sixth century.[236] These events, as mentioned above, implied the failure
of prophecy. Of course, prophets had sometimes been wrong before.
However, such prophetic mistakes had not led to an image of 'the
prophets' as being generally untrustworthy. The fact that such an image developed in the sixth century is to be explained from reflection
on the disastrous events. According to the thinking of the time, the
disasters that had befallen Judah were explained as a divine punishment.[237] The disastrous events were interpreted as being due to Yahweh's anger: Yahweh had punished his people because of their
wickedness. As part of this interpretation, a caricature of the prophets
was made as deceivers of the people.

Reflection on the disastrous events of the sixth century found different expressions. One variant was blaming the prophets. The prophets, as it was judged in retrospect, had encouraged king and people
and proclaimed the well-being of the state, *despite* the grave sins of
the people. Instead of warning the people of the coming disaster, the
prophets had falsely encouraged them. From there, it was only a small
step to conclude that the falseness of the prophets had caused the disaster:[238] the prophets had deceived the people, they had lied,[239] they had
led the people astray,[240] and because of their sins Judah and Jerusalem

---

[235]   This later development is reflected by Amos 3:7 and the later (Masoretic) version of Jeremiah. In these later traditions, Amos and Jeremiah could be referred to as
nābî' without being confused with the prophets condemned in the tradition (see Carroll 1986: 61-62, 79).

[236]   The image of 'the prophets' as deceiving liars occurs in Jer 2:8; 4:9; 5:13, 31;
6:13; 8:10; 14:13-18; 23:9-37; 26:7-16; 27:9-18; 29:1, 8, 15; 37:19; Ezek 13:1-16;
22:28 (and to some degree in Mic 2:6, 11; 3:5-11; Zech 13:1-6). See also Gonçalves
2001: 150-152.

[237]   Van der Toorn 1985: 56: in the ancient Near East 'calamities are conceived as
divinely contrived punishments'.

[238]   Their actions, attitudes and techniques are frequently depicted as being 'false'
(שֶׁקֶר). Various passages refer to the prophets as the guilty party *par excellence* (e.g.
14:13-16; 23:9-40), even as the cause of evil in society as such (23:15). Their falseness caused the collapse of society; cf. Carroll 1986: 73.

[239]   Jer 5:31; 14:14; 23:16, 26, 30-32; 27:10, 14, 16; Ezek 13:2, 6-9, 23; 22:28.

[240]   Jer 23:32; Lam 2:14; Ezek 13:10.

were punished.[241] The image of the prophets as false and deceiving liars is particularly prominent in the book of Jeremiah. Here, the criticism of the prophets is put into the mouth of Jeremiah who, initially, when he appears in opposition to the prophets, is portrayed as not being a prophet himself. Jeremiah is portrayed as an individual commissioned by Yahweh to prophesy his words of doom over the king, the nation, and not least the prophets.[242]

The Image of the Prophets as True Servants of Yahweh
The other characterisation of the *nĕbī'îm* is marked by the designation 'servants of Yahweh'.[243] As 'servants of Yahweh' the prophets are presented as belonging to a past stage of the history of Israel and Judah, until the end of Judah as a state. The passages referring to the prophets as Yahweh's servants have different accents.

First, within the book of Jeremiah we find the following picture of the prophets as Yahweh's servants: Yahweh has continuously, i.e. from Moses till the end, in the sixth century, sent his servants the prophets to the people, in order to urge them to turn from their evil ways, but the people refused to listen.[244]

Second, 2 Kings presents the prophets as predicting the harsh punishment Yahweh is going to bring over Israel and Judah (2 Kgs 17:23; 21:10-14; 24:2; cf. Ezek 38:17). In this respect, the prophets are part of the narrative framework: the end of the states of Israel and Judah is narrated by means of the pattern 'prediction and fulfilment'.

Third, the prophets are described as mediators of Yahweh's law. As stated in 2 Kgs 17:13, where Yahweh warns the people: 'keep my commandments and my statutes, in accordance with all the law that I commanded your ancestors and that I sent to you by my servants the

---

[241] Jer 14:13-16; 23:15, 16-22; 27:14-15; 28:15-16; Lam 4:13.

[242] Although the image of the false prophets took flight in the sixth century and later, prophets as such did not disappear. The figures Haggai and Zechariah look remarkably similar to the prophets criticised and caricatured in other prophetic books (see Ezra 5:1-2; Hag 2:2-9; Zech 7:1-5; 8:9). On the other hand, the tradition of the prophets harming the people is maintained in some late passages as well: Zech 13:2-6 foresees a time in which Yahweh's people are finally saved *from* the prophets.

[243] The image of the prophets as Yahweh's servants occurs in 2 Kgs 9:7; 17:13, 23; 21:10; 24:2; Ezra 9:11; Jer 7:25; 25:4; 26:5; 29:19; 35:15; 44:4; Ezek 38:17; Dan 9:6, 10; Amos 3:7-8; Zech 1:6. See also Gonçalves 2001: 152-153.

[244] Jer 7:25-26; 25:4-6; 26:4-5; 29:18-19; 35:15; 44:4-6 (cf. Judg 6:8-10; 2 Chron 24:19; 36:15-16; Neh 9:26, 30; Zech 7:12). A similar picture, without the designation 'Yahweh's servants', is found in 2 Kgs 17:13 (connected with the image of the prophets as mediators of the law).

prophets'.[245] Here the prophets are portrayed as successors of Moses, mediator of the law *par excellence*.[246]

As is the case with the image of the prophets as deceiving liars, the image of the prophets as servants of Yahweh has a connection with the prophetic practice. This image of the prophets is based on the critical tone of voice that was part of the prophetic function. However, as in the case of the prophets as false prophets, it is a one-dimensional picture, aiming to explain the disasters that had befallen Israel and Judah. The disasters were seen as divine punishment brought upon Judah due to the sinful behaviour of the people: they had stubbornly refused to listen to the prophets who had urged them to refrain from their evil ways and to obey Yahweh. This image presents the prophets as something of the past, from Moses to Jeremiah, and it is therefore an exilic or post-exilic construct.

Connection of the Two Images

Both images, that of the prophets as deceiving liars and that of the prophets as Yahweh's true servants, give the strong impression that they refer to the prophets in general. It is never stated that *some* prophets were liars but that *others* were truly sent by Yahweh. In their depiction as false prophets, the prophets are blamed for the disaster. In their depiction as Yahweh's servants, on the other hand, the prophets are excused for what had happened. In this context, the disaster was seen as the result of the persistent rejection of the prophets sent by Yahweh. These two traditions must have developed independently. Furthermore, they occur independently of each other. Although both images occur in the book of Jeremiah, they are nowhere really connected.[247]

---

[245] See further Deut 18:15-19; Ezra 9:10; Dan 9:5-6, 10-11; Zech 1:6.

[246] Explicitly so in Deut 18:15-19.

[247] In Jer 26 'the prophets' seem to appear both as Yahweh's servants (26:5-6), and as bad guys, 'the priests and the prophets' taking a leading role in demanding Jeremiah's execution (26:7-16). However, the image of the prophets as notorious bad guys has been introduced into the story at a later stage. In 26:2, 8, Jeremiah addresses the people of Judah; in 26:9 'all the people gathered against Jeremiah'. The *people* wanted to kill him, whereas the *officials* decided there was no ground for execution (cf. 26:24). The priests and the prophets were only secondarily introduced into the story taking over the role as bad guys, since they had come to be Jeremiah's proverbial adversaries (cf. Köckert 2000: 91). Furthermore, in Jer 29 (Septuagint ch. 36) the prophets as deceiving liars appear in 29:8-9 (cf. also 29:15-23), whereas the image of the prophets as Yahweh's servants occurs in 29:19. However, 29:16-20 is part of a later edition of the book and misses in the Septuagint.

It is only Deut 18:9-22 that brings both images together, on the one hand the 'prophet like Moses', a true spokesman of Yahweh (18:15-19), and on the other hand prophets speaking in the name of other gods or speaking presumptuously in Yahweh's name (18:20-22). Deut 18:9-22 is a redefinition of prophecy, which aims to create some order in the variety of prophetic images by bringing the two images of the *nĕbī'îm* under a common denominator.

The dichotomy of cultic prophets prophesying peace, and true prophets—or bearers of the divine word—prophesying doom, is part of the biblical portrayal of the prophets, but does not apply to prophecy as a socio-historical phenomenon. In Judah and Israel, as elsewhere in the ancient Near East, the prophetic function included both encouragement of king and people, announcements of the annihilation of the enemies, criticism of the king or the political leaders, and political direction. When a prophet announced a disaster, he did not stand in opposition to the state, but functioned as guardian of the well-being of the state. The image of the prophets as oppositional figures predicting the irrevocable downfall of society is a product of later reflection. Such predictions make no sense within a system of divination, aiming at the well-being of state, king and people. Understood as reflection on the events, the 'predictions' make sense.

5.2.3   *Prophets in Judah and Israel*

The claim for the existence of prophets in Judah and Israel is sustained by references to prophetic figures and prophecy in texts from ninth-seventh century Syria-Palestine, such as the Zakkur Stele, and the Deir 'Allā plaster texts, and in particular references to prophets in the Lachish ostraca.[248] In order to uncover prophetic practice in Judah and Israel, one must attempt to glimpse behind the scenes of the biblical depictions of prophecy. In the following, a description is given of some main aspects of the prophetic practice in Judah and Israel.

---

[248]   For the texts, see Lemaire 2001b; and Seow, in: Nissinen 2003a: 201-218.

Prophets as Part of the Religious Establishment

As was the case elsewhere in the ancient Near East, prophecy in Judah and Israel represented one form of divination among others.[249] Prophecy is mentioned among other forms of divinatory practice, such as 'dreams, Urim, and prophets (*nĕbī'îm*)' in 1 Sam 28:6, and 'prophets (*nĕbī'îm*), seers (*ḥōzîm*), diviners (*qōsĕmîm*)' in Mic 3:6-7. In Isa 3:2-3, the prophet (*nābî'*), diviner (*qōsēm*), 'skilful magician' and 'expert enchanter' are counted among the pillars of society. Jer 29:8 mentions prophets (*nĕbī'îm*), diviners (*qōsĕmîm*), and dreams. Whereas in the redefinition of prophecy in Deut 18:9-22, 'the *nābî'* raised up by Yahweh' stands in complete opposition to all sorts of diviners, in reality prophecy was a form of divination.[250] The view that prophecy, dreams, and the so-called priestly oracle (Urim) were genuinely Israelite, whereas all other forms of divination were imported from neighbouring nations, is to be rejected.[251] The range of specialists mentioned in Jer 27:9, prophets, diviners, dreamers, soothsayers, and sorcerers, presented as the religious specialists of Judah's neighbour states, probably existed in Judah and Israel as well.[252]

The biblical depiction suggests that in Judah and Israel prophecy was the principal and most important form of divination. However, this outstanding role of prophecy may be partly due to a later perception of the past. Although prophecy was an important form of divination in Judah and Israel, prophets certainly were not the only religious specialists active.

The biblical picture suggesting that prophetesses only played a marginal role may be misleading too. A few women are explicitly called 'prophetess'. Miriam (Exod 15:20) and Deborah (Judg 4:4) were prophetesses. It may be significant that both are associated with singing about Yahweh's annihilation of his enemies (Exod 15:20-21; Judg 5).[253] Other prophetesses are Huldah, who is consulted by the

---

[249] Nissinen 2004: 21; Barstad 1993a: 47; Long 1973: 489; cf. Kitz 2003.

[250] Cryer 1994: 242.

[251] Cryer 1994: 229-262.

[252] For prophets, diviners and dreamers, see 5.2.1; for soothsayers and sorcerers in Judah, see e.g. Mic 5:11 (Wagenaar 2001: 194-195, 308). Cryer (1994: 295-305) furthermore suggests that extispicy was practised in Israel, whereas astrology was not practised (1994: 321-322). However, the absence of an extensive apparatus of astrological specialists need not imply that astronomical and meteorological phenomena did not play a role in Israelite divination.

[253] In Judg 5, Deborah is presented as a prophetic figure (5:7, 12). The phrase 'Deborah, speak a chant!' (דַּבְּרִי שִׁיר) in 5:12 casts her in the role of a prophet who, be-

high Judaean officials (2 Kgs 22:14; 2 Chron 34:22), and Noadiah, among the opponents of Nehemiah (Neh 6:14).[254] Finally, an anonymous prophetess appears in Isa 8:3-4 (see 5.2.4 below). These limited examples seem to contrast with the situation in Old Babylonian Mari and seventh-century Assyria, where we find references to many prophetesses. However, the biblical veil may hide a different situation. Ezek 13 contains a harangue against the prophets, who are accused of misleading the people (13:1-16). This is followed by a passage directed against the 'daughters of your (i.e. Ezekiel's) people', who are equally accused of deceiving the people (13:17-23). Their characterisation as women 'who act as prophets (נבא hitp.) of their own accord', 13:17 (cf. 13:23), indicates they can be seen as prophetesses, although this label is not used. Apparently, in later biblical tradition the label 'prophetess' was used with restraint, and the role of female prophets was played down.[255]

Traditionally, a clear-cut distinction was made between prophets and priests. Priests, it was held, occupied an institutionalised office and defended the interest of the establishment, whereas prophets were seen as occupying a charismatic office and representing the oppositional voice. This distinction was based on a presumed contrast between the so-called 'free prophets', and the religious establishment, represented by priests (and cult prophets). However, this priest-prophet dichotomy must be rejected.[256] Both prophets and priests are to be counted among the religious specialists.[257] Presumably, there was not a watershed between 'priestly divination' (technical divination), and 'prophetic divination' (intuitive divination).[258] Sometimes prophets

---

fore the battle begins, delivers an oracle of victory in which the deity announces that the enemy will be destroyed. See further note 303.

[254] On these prophetesses, see Fischer 2002: 158-188 and 255-273.

[255] Fischer 2002: 26. The use of official terms for female diviners was perhaps suppressed to some extent; cf. Exod 22:18; 1 Sam 28:8.

[256] Petersen (1981: 9-15) shows that the prophet as ideal-type of charismatic leader does not fit the situation in ancient Judah and Israel. A dichotomy between *Charisma* (the free prophets characterised by inspiration and vocation) and *Amt* (the establishment of those occupying the priestly office), is to be rejected. So Cryer 1991; Van der Toorn 1996a: 306; Grabbe 1995: 65; and Grabbe and Ogden Bellis (eds) 2004, especially Ben Zvi 2004: 9-11, 21-22; Zevit 2004: 189-217.

[257] Cryer 1991: 81; cf. Henshaw 1994: 25, for the functions of the *kōhēn*; Van der Toorn 1996a: 302-306, for the Levites as cult personnel.

[258] For technical divination (often associated with priests) by means of Urim and Thummin (binary lots), see Exod 28:30; Lev 8:8; Num 27:21; Deut 33:8; 1 Sam 14:41 (LXX); 28:6; Ezra 2:63; Neh 7:65 (Cryer 1994: 273-276). In addition, ephod and

may have used technical means by performing divination, and perhaps some people played a double role as priest and prophet.[259] A range of practitioners of divination and religious specialists existed. The expression 'priests and prophets' in the Old Testament is often used as characterising the religious establishment in general.[260]

The various religious specialists, such as seers, prophets, and priests, are regularly depicted in close relation to cult and sanctuary.[261] Prophets, although not necessarily all of them, were associated with the cult and attached to sanctuaries.[262] Prophets were not exclusively bound to temples, given the examples of prophets active during a military expedition or being consulted at home. Yet, a common practice seems to have been to visit a prophet at the sanctuary to which he was attached.[263] Furthermore, as argued by Husser, 1 Sam 3 reflects the practice of prophetic initiation in the temple.[264]

Various texts, closely associating prophets with priests, suggest that prophets as much as priests belonged to the temple personnel in Jerusalem.[265] A clear reference to the presence of prophets in the temple is given by Lam 2:20, part of a lament over Jerusalem: 'Should priest and prophet be killed in the sanctuary of Yahweh?' Furthermore, Jer 35:4 refers to a room in the temple where the sons of Hanan, 'the man of God', resided. Apparently, Hanan was a prophetic figure, and his 'sons' perhaps were members of a prophetic order.[266] Prophets were

---

teraphim functioned as a means of divination, see Judg 17-18; 1 Sam 23:6-12; 30:6-8 (for ephod, Cryer 1994: 277-282; for teraphim, Van der Toorn 1990; 1996a: 218-225).

[259] See Cryer 1994: 250. Cf. 2 Sam 15:27, where David addresses the priest Zadok הֲרוֹאֶה אַתָּה, 'are you not a seer?'

[260] Stökl 2004: 15. Mentioned in juxtaposition to the king and the officials (the political leaders), the priests and the prophets represent the religious establishment, in distinction to the common people (see e.g. 2 Kgs 23:2; Jer 2:8, 26; 4:9; 6:13; 8:1, 10; 13:13; 18:18; 29:1; 32:32; Ezek 7:26; Mic 3:11; Zeph 3:4).

[261] Hilber 2005: 28-29.

[262] Van der Toorn 2007: 183.

[263] 1 Sam 3:19-21; 1 Sam 10:5 (which according to Hilber 2005: 27, suggests that the prophets participated in a cultic celebration at the 'high place'). 1 Kgs 19:10 mentions both the destruction of Yahweh's altars and the killing of his prophets; in 1 Kgs 18:30 the prophet Elijah restores the destroyed altar of Yahweh at Mount Carmel; this also was where Elisha could be found (2 Kgs 4:23-25).

[264] Husser (1994: 147-151, and 156), suggesting that '[l]e néophyte est ainsi guidé dans le deux phases du processus prophétique qui fait de lui un médiateur: entendre-proclamer' (1994: 149).

[265] See e.g. Jer 5:31; 14:13-18; 23:11, 33-34; 26:7-16; Lam 2:20; 4:13; Zech 7:3 (cf. also 2 Kgs 10:19). Similarly, Gonçalves 2001: 148-149, 166-168.

[266] See furthermore Hilber 2005: 28.

linked to sanctuaries and sometimes also performed in the cult.[267] At the time of the restoration governed by Zerubbabel, prophets and priests were co-operating in the project to restore the temple. Haggai and Zechariah are described as members of a company of prophets with official connections with the cult.[268]

The suggestion that *ḥōzeh* can be seen as a 'court prophet',[269] is not convincing in my view. The *ḥōzeh* is found among the religious officials, first and foremost within a temple setting.[270] The prophetic stories in the Old Testament give the impression that prophets in Judah and Israel had easy access to the king (e.g. 1 Kgs 1:23). The stories depict prophets as delivering their oracles in the presence of the king. Although there is no clear evidence for prophets residing at the royal quarters,[271] the many direct encounters between prophets and kings suggest that in this respect the situation in Judah and Israel was different from that in seventh-century Assyria. However, various stories concerning the late Monarchic period give a somewhat different picture. In 2 Kgs 19:1-7, Hezekiah sends his officials to consult the prophet Isaiah; and in various stories concerning Jeremiah, royal officials likewise appear as a mediating party between prophet and king (e.g. Jer 36-38). These stories may suggest that access to the king was *not* as self-evident as the prophetic stories dealing with earlier periods suggest. Yet it seems that prophets in Judah and Israel could function as advisors to the king. At least, since prophets were believed to be able to determine the divine will, their words could play a role in the political decision-making.[272]

---

[267] See Hilber 2005: 37-39. See e.g. 1 Sam 9:11-24, where a seer is pictured as taking a leading role in the cult; in 2 Kgs 10, where Jehu, intending to abolish the Baal cult, pretends to organise a great sacrifice for Baal, he gathers 'all the prophets of Baal and all his priests' (10:18). The prophets of Baal were part of the cultic personnel.

[268] See Ezra 5:1-2; Hag 2:1-3; Zech 7:1-5; 8:9. Cf. Hilber 2005: 34.

[269] Schniedewind 1995: 38-40.

[270] The figure Balaam in the Deir 'Allā plaster texts is not in royal service (contra Schniedewind 1995: 39); the reference to *ḥzyn* in the Zakkur Stele is to be understood within a temple setting (see 5.1.2 above); Gad's title '*ḥōzeh* of David' (2 Sam 24:11) is probably secondary, influenced by Chronicles (so Gonçalves 2001: 169). This leaves only the references to the '*ḥōzeh* of the king' in 1 Chron 25:5; 2 Chron 29:25; 35:15; these figures are connected with the temple service as well.

[271] 1 Kgs 18:19 mentions prophets that 'eat at Jezebel's table'. This reflects a position of high esteem with the queen (or, in other cases the king), or simply refers to food rations provided by the royal court, rather than permanent residence at the royal court (cf. 2 Sam 19:29; 1 Kgs 2:7).

[272] See Tiemeyer 2005.

Prophetic Activity

Prophets were believed to be able to determine Yahweh's will, Yahweh's secret purposes, and to speak authoritatively in Yahweh's name.[273] Their oracles were believed to reflect the decisions taken in the divine council, and their intimate knowledge about the divine will proved their divine commission.[274] Prophets received divine messages by various means and communicated these to addressees.[275] Furthermore, they sought Yahweh's will in certain matters on request. Finally, they could call upon the name of Yahweh for the sake of the people: prophets functioned as intercessors.[276]

According to biblical description, a prophetic 'word' or 'vision' could be requested from a prophet.[277] At least occasionally, prophets received rewards or gifts for a consultation,[278] as was also the case elsewhere.[279] In the Old Testament, a distinction is made between 'prophets' receiving rewards and occupying an official function in the cult, and individuals commissioned by Yahweh to prophesy doom not affiliated with the wicked establishment (see 5.2.2 above). This is a later ideological view, which indirectly confirms the prophetic practice: it was common to reward prophets for their service and prophets were part of the religious system.

Prophets could be consulted for securing the welfare of individuals, social units, or corporate personalities, like the city of Jerusalem or the kingdom of Judah. Prophets are often consulted with regard to important state matters, either by the king himself,[280] or by royal officials on behalf of the king.[281] The importance of the availability of the pro-

---

[273] See Nissinen 2002.

[274] Nissinen 2002: 4-5.

[275] Grabbe 1995: 107.

[276] Cf. e.g. 1 Kgs 13:6; 17:17-24; 2 Kgs 4:33; 6:17-18; Jer 27:18.

[277] Ezek 7:26; Zech 7:3. The expression 'to enquire of Yahweh' (דרשׁ אֶת יהוה) often involves the consultation of a prophet (e.g. 1 Kgs 22:5-8; 2 Kgs 3:11; 8:8; 22:13-14, 18; Isa 31:1).

[278] See Num 22:7; 1 Sam 9:7-8; 1 Kgs 13:7; 14:2-3; 2 Kgs 4:42; 5:15; 8:8; Amos 7:12; Mic 3:5, 11.

[279] The Mari letters confirm that prophets (occasionally) received rewards or gifts for their oracles. ARM 25 142:12-15: 'one *ḫullum* ring of silver for the prophet (*muḫḫûm*) of Adad, when he delivered an oracle to the king' (translation from: Nissinen 2003a: 89). For further examples, Nissinen 2003d: 7, note 25; Charpin 2002: 17-18. For the texts, see Nissinen 2003a: 83-89. For examples from later periods, see Nissinen 2003a: 185, a Middle Assyrian food rations list, and 192-193, a Neo-Babylonian list of temple offerings.

[280] E.g. 1 Kgs 22:1-28; 2 Kgs 3:11; 8:8; 22:13-14; cf. 1 Sam 28:6-7.

[281] E.g. 2 Kgs 19:1-7; Jer 21:1-7; 37:3-10.

phetic consultation for determining God's will is illustrated in laments
over the lack of prophetic inspiration at times of crisis:

> Our signs we have not seen; There is no longer a prophet; And there is
> not anyone with us who knows "How long?" (Ps 74:9);
> Guidance is no more, and her prophets obtain no vision from Yahweh
> (Lam 2:9b);
> Disaster comes upon disaster, rumour follows rumour; they shall keep
> seeking a vision from the prophet; instruction shall perish from the
> priest, and counsel from the elders (Ezek 7:26).

This *topos* in laments is illustrative of the prophetic function of guid-
ing and guarding the state by determining and revealing Yahweh's
will.

Prophets not only were consulted but also delivered messages
without request. Prophets held a mediating position between the people and the divine, and both sides, so to speak, could take the initiative
for communication. The prophetic means most often mentioned is the
divine word (דְּבַר יהוה).[282] The divine word was more than just a message: it was believed to be powerful and effective.[283] Other prophetic
means include the vision (חָזוֹן),[284] dream (חֲלוֹם),[285] prediction (קֶסֶם),[286] and
furthermore the אוֹת, the 'sign', which underscored the prophetic message. In the Old Testament we find several kinds of prophetic signs. A
sign could be a foretold event that, when it happened, 'proved' a certain prophecy.[287] Furthermore, an act performed by a prophet, carrying

---

[282] See Schmidt 1974: 116-123.

[283] See 1 Sam 3:11; 1 Kgs 12:15; Isa 55:1-11; Jer 1:11-12; Ezek 13:6. In 1 Kgs
22:11, Zedekiah attempts to secure victory (cf. 2 Kgs 13:17). Hos 12:11 depicts the
prophets as Yahweh's instrument in fashioning the future; their actions and words
have creative and destructive power (cf. Prov 29:18).

[284] E.g. 1 Sam 3:1; Prov 29:18; Jer 14:14; 23:16; Lam 2:9; Ezek 7:26; 13:16; Hos
12:11; Mic 3:5-7. In some cases the term מַרְאָה 'vision' is used as a synonym of חָזוֹן
(Num 12:6; 1 Sam 3:15).

[285] The dream is sometimes described as a prophetic means (Num 12:6; Jer 23:27,
28, 32; Jer 29:8; Joel 3:1), and sometimes as the means of a type of diviner closely related to, but distinct from, the prophet (Deut 13:2-6; 1 Sam 28:6, 15; Jer 27:9; Zech
10:2).

[286] In various cases, the prophets are accused of making 'void, false predictions',
which implies that 'making predictions' was part of the prophetic activity (Jer 14:14;
Ezek 13:6, 9, 23; 22:28; Mic 3:6, 11). In other cases, those making 'predictions' are
described as a particular type of diviner, related to, but distinct from, the prophet (Isa
3:2; Jer 27:9; 29:8; Mic 3:7; Zech 10:2).

[287] E.g. Exod 3:12; 1 Sam 2:34; 1 Sam 10:1-13; 2 Kgs 19:29; Isa 7:14; Jer 44:29-
30. Cf. Deut 13:2-3; Judg 6:17; Ps 74:9; Isa 44:25; Jer 10:2. Cryer (1994: 283) describes this as follows: 'A secondary prophecy accompanies the "primary" one, so
that when the secondary prophecy is "fulfilled", one has reason for faith in the "pri-

a symbolic meaning, could be designated as a 'sign'.[288] Thirdly, it is related that some prophets performed supernatural, miraculous signs. The legends relating the supernatural power of prophetic figures are suggestive of the popular belief that prophets held special powers.[289]

The question of whether Israelite prophecy was ecstatic in character has been answered affirmatively in recent studies.[290] Persons in a trance may exhibit either behaviour that resembles symptoms of ill-ness, or behaviour consisting of coherent and rational actions and ut-terances, depending on social role expectations.[291] Although it is unwarranted to ascribe all prophetic oracles automatically to ecstatic experiences, there is no reason to categorically deny such experiences to the Israelite prophets either.[292] The biblical texts in general display much less interest in the phenomenon of prophecy, than in the prophe-cies resulting from it.[293] Yet, the similarity in designation of insane persons on the one hand and of ecstatically and prophetically inspired persons on the other, may be telling. The case of Saul provides a good example. Saul's ecstatic behaviour together with the prophets (1 Sam 10:6), his behaviour in the battle against the Ammonites (1 Sam 11:6), and his jealous behaviour towards David (1 Sam 19:9), are described with a similar expression: 'the spirit of Yahweh overwhelmed him'. Such designations reflect a belief in spirit possession: apparent altera-tions in the personality were interpreted as being caused by the influence of a spirit.[294] This explained both pathological behaviour and

---

mary" one'. According to Cryer, this is paralleled in the Mesopotamian practice of pairing one sort of divination with another. Cf. Van Soldt 1992.

[288] E.g. Isa 20:3; Ezek 4:3.

[289] E.g. Isaiah in 2 Kgs 20:9-11. The term אוֹת is not used for the miracles per-formed by Elijah and Elisha, but it is used for Moses' signs in Egypt.

[290] Michaelsen 1989: 34-35. Holm (1982: 7) defines prophetic ecstasy as 'differ-ent states of consciousness that are characterised by unusual achievements, peculiar experiences and odd behaviour.'

[291] Michaelsen 1989: 35-37; Wilson 1979: 321-337.

[292] Grabbe 1995: 111. See Michaelsen 1989: 29-33, 38-52, for a critique of Parker's view that Israelite prophecy was *not* familiar with possession trance or ec-stasy (Parker 1978 distinguishes between non-prophetic possession trance and proph-ecy).

[293] See however Husser 1994: 129-200, esp. 156, 199, for an attempt to illuminate the prophetic experience of receiving 'visions'. He concludes that the prophetic vision (ḥāzôn) appeared during the night and was more or less equivalent to what elsewhere is referred to as 'dream' (ḥălôm). The ḥāzôn represents 'un état onirique propre à l'expérience prophétique', different from ordinary or allegorical dreams (1994: 268-269).

[294] Michaelsen 1989: 53.

(prophetic) trance behaviour.[295] The similarity in terminology between (prophetic) ecstasy and madness is supported by the phenomenon that within a particular culture the same behaviour can be regarded either as 'acceptable' or as 'pathological'.[296] Thus, in Israel, as elsewhere, the attitude towards prophets was ambivalent.[297] A certain degree of strangeness could be regarded as a mark of contact with the spiritual world.[298] In Hos 9:7 the *nābî'* is paralleled with the 'man of the spirit'. The connection between prophetic inspiration and the 'spirit of Yahweh' is clear.[299] Yet, the Old Testament material suggests that prophets delivered their oracles in a rather straightforward and intelligible way. The ecstatic mood did not preclude prophets from delivering clear messages.[300]

In certain cases, the prophetic consultation apparently involved inducement of the prophets' characteristic behaviour,[301] aiming to bring forth an experience that was seen as the influx of the divine spirit. Music was a stimulus to achieving the prophetic mood.[302] A connection between prophecy and music, especially in a cultic setting, is indicated in several ways.[303]

---

[295] Michaelsen 1989: 48.

[296] Michaelsen 1989: 32. Roberts (1971) discusses the expression 'hand of Yahweh' and its ancient Near Eastern counterpart, often designating a 'disastrous manifestation of the supernatural power'. Roberts derives the specific use of this expression as applying to prophets from the general designation. He argues that the prophetic state was associated with illness, such as the delirious raving of a person with fever. Both in Hebrew and in Akkadian, the same verb is used for both prophetic and mad behaviour: *nb'* (hitp.) and *maḫû* (N).

[297] Fenton 1997: 36.

[298] Fenton 1997: 31.

[299] Num 11:29; 1 Sam 10:10; 19:20; 1 Kgs 18:12; 22:22-24; 2 Kgs 2:15; 2 Chron 20:14; Neh 9:30; Ezek 37:1; Zech 7:12.

[300] Similarly, Hilber 2005: 31: 'ecstatic behaviour by Mari prophets did not preclude rational speech'.

[301] In 1 Kgs 22:5-7, the enquiry for the word of Yahweh implies gathering and consulting the prophets. Apparently, the characteristic behaviour of the prophets was promoted (1 Kgs 22:10-12).

[302] 1 Sam 10:5-12; 2 Kgs 3:11-19.

[303] Three points may be mentioned. First, singers, musicians and dancers played a role in the temple cults, both in Mesopotamia and in Judah and Israel (Henshaw 1994: 84-134, esp. 116-118; Mazar 2003: 126-132, esp. 131) and 1 Sam 10:5 suggests that prophetic figures could take part in these activities too. Second, the phenomenon of 'cultic prophecy' in the Psalms, for which a strong case has been made by Hilber 2005, confirms the connection between prophets and music and singing in the pre-exilic cult. Third, the Levitical singers in Chronicles are presented as in continuity with the 'cult prophets' of pre-exilic Israel; this presentation was possible since prophets of earlier times were known to have made use of music, and were associated with musicians and singers playing a role in the temple cults; Williamson 1982a: 166.

In the Old Testament, prophets sometimes appear in groups. We find descriptions of a 'band of prophets' in 1 Sam 10:5 and 10, a 'group of prophets' in 1 Sam 19:20, and in particular the expression 'sons of the prophets'.[304] In various cases, the leader of such a group is referred to as 'father'.[305] In several further instances the prophets are described as a collective as well.[306] These descriptions can be taken as evidence for the existence of prophetic groups in Judah and Israel. Several texts suggest a relation between the group activity of prophets and military threat. At least, the 'sons of the prophets' were involved in the Aramaean campaigns under the Omri and Jehu dynasties, issuing instructions and predicting successful outcome (1 Kgs 20).[307] The operation in groups did not exclude individual activity. Individual prophets functioned as spokesmen of a prophetic collective,[308] and someone belonging to a prophetic collective could perform a specific task.[309]

The Prophetic Message
In the ancient Near East, prophets play a significant role at moments of national importance, such as political-military crises caused by an enemy threat, wars, and internal power conflicts. Particularly in the midst of a struggle for the throne, a conspiracy or a coup d'état, prophecy could function as a means of divine legitimation of a throne pretender. This was the case in Judah and Israel too.[310] A clear example of this prophetic function is 2 Kgs 9:1-13, where a prophet proclaims the kingship for Jehu, a military officer: 'Thus says Yahweh: I anoint you king over Israel' (9:3, 6, 12).[311] Divine election of the one, however means divine rejection of his adversary. The prophetic function of encouragement by announcing divine support went together with

---

[304]   1 Kgs 20:35; 2 Kgs 2:3, 5, 7, 15; 4:1, 38; 5:22; 6:1; 9:1; cf. Amos 7:14; Jer 35:4.

[305]   1 Sam 10:12; 2 Kgs 2:12. Cf. Kgs 6:1.

[306]   1 Kgs 18:4, 13; 1 Kgs 22:6, 10-12.

[307]   Blenkinsopp (1995: 136) also suggests a connection between the prophetic groups referred to in 1 Sam 10 and 19 and the wars against the Philistines.

[308]   Zedekiah (1 Kgs 22:11, 24-25), Pashhur (Jer 20:1-6), Hananiah (Jer 28:1-17).

[309]   In 2 Kgs 9:1-7, Jehu is anointed as king by 'a member of the company of prophets'.

[310]   Noort (1977: 109) concludes: 'Sowohl in Mari als auch in Israel ergeht der Gottesbescheid in einer Krisissituation.' See Noort 1977: 104, for a characterisation of Israelite priests and prophets as 'Gottesbefrager in Kriegsituationen'.

[311]   See further 1 Sam 9-10; 16:1-13; 1 Kgs 1:11-40; 11:29-32.

announcements of destruction of the enemies and divine legitimation of war.[312]

Prophets encouraged king and people at times of national disaster especially during military threat.[313] Two examples of prophetic oracles relating to Israel's wars with Aram may be quoted here. The first is that of Zedekiah son of Chenaanah, who had made for himself iron horns, and proclaimed: 'Thus says Yahweh: with these you shall gore the Aramaeans until they are destroyed.'[314] The second example is that of Elisha who ordered King Joash of Israel to take a bow and arrows and to draw the bow. Elisha laid his hands on the king's hands and ordered him to shoot through the east window (see 2 Kgs 13:15-17a). After that, Elisha proclaimed: 'Yahweh's arrow of victory, the arrow of victory over Aram! For you shall smite the Aramaeans in Aphek until they are destroyed.'[315] In both cases, the prophetic act symbolises the victory. Zedekiah and Elisha carry out exactly the same prophetic function: in a critical situation they promise the king that Yahweh is on his side and that he will defeat his enemy with help of Yahweh. It is the narrative composition that presents Zedekiah as false and Elisha as a true prophet. For our survey it is irrelevant whether later tradition labelled a prophet as false or true. More important is that these examples indicate how prophets acted.

The reference to a *nābî'* in Lachish ostracon 3 may be mentioned here too: 'As for the letter of Tobiah the servant of the king, which came to Shallum the son of Jaddua from the prophet, saying, "Beware!"—your serv[ant] has sent it to my lord.'[316] According to a common interpretation, the letter of Tobiah contained a message of the *nābî'*, which began with the word השמר 'Be careful!' or 'Beware!'.[317] Based on similar warnings within a prophetic oracle (2 Kgs 6:9; Isa 7:4), Barstad has suggested that the prophetic message, recorded in a

---

[312] These two sides of the prophetic coin are echoed in Mic 3:5: the prophets, 'who cry "Peace" when they have something to eat, but declare war against those who put nothing into their mouths'. Here the prophets are presented as being corrupt: they declare divine favour to those who pay them and divine war against those who do not. In this way, the prophets are depicted in analogy to corrupt judges, whose verdicts are bought by bribes (Mic 3:11; 7:3). In Micah, this is part of the image of the corrupt establishment, which functions as an explanation of the disasters of the sixth century.

[313] 1 Kgs 20:13-28; 22:5-12; 2 Kgs 3:11-20; 6:9-10; 19:1-7; cf. also 1 Sam 13:8-12; 28:5-6.

[314] 1 Kgs 22:11.

[315] 2 Kgs 13:17b.

[316] Lachish ostracon 3 r. 3-5, translation from: Seow, in: Nissinen 2003a: 214-215.

[317] Rüterswörden 2001: 187.

written document (the letter of Tobiah), can be seen as proof of 'prophetic engagement in a critical war situation'.[318] This, then, would be
another example of supportive prophecy in a critical situation, and furthermore, another example of a prophetic message that was written
down, and perhaps sent around.[319]

Apart from encouraging king and people, prophets also delivered
divine criticism. The critical prophetic voice served the following purposes. First, prophets reminded the addressee (often the king) of his
duties, and pointed out his shortcomings with regard to the gods.
Many Old Testament stories of encounters between prophets and
kings echo this prophetic function. Second, since the well-being of the
state was a prophetic concern, prophets harshly denounced persons
they perceived as enemies of the state (see 5.2.4 below).

In several cases, prophets announce the occurrence of a specific
disaster.[320] The purpose of the announcement is to avert the disaster by
undertaking the right action. The prophecy of Micah as presented in
Jer 26:17-19, however fictitiously, may be reminiscent of this. In this
narration of the confrontation between Jeremiah and the people, some
of the elders remind the people that more than a century ago, during
the reign of Hezekiah, Micah prophesied as follows: 'Zion shall be
plowed as a field; Jerusalem shall become a heap of ruins', and according to the elders, Hezekiah responded to this prophecy by entreat-
ing the favour of Yahweh (וַיְחַל אֶת־פְּנֵי יהוה), which means: he appeased
Yahweh. The disaster announced by Micah was averted by the right
action taken by the king.[321] In announcing a disaster, a prophet did not
stand in opposition to the establishment, but served the interest of king
and state. He revealed otherwise hidden knowledge concerning a
threat to the well-being, with the purpose to avert it.

---

[318]   Barstad 1993b: 9. See also Rüterswörden 2001: 188; Lemaire 2001b: 112-113.
[319]   This interpretation seems to be the best explanation for the occurrence of the
words *l'mr hšmr* (r. 4-5). For a different view, see Hoftijzer 1986: 87-89.
[320]   See the example of ARM 26/1 206, in 5.1.4 above.
[321]   Another example of a cancelled prediction is found in the story of 2 Kgs 20:1-
11, where Hezekiah's prayer successfully changes the prophecy announcing his death
into a prophecy announcing fifteen more years to live. Again, this does not make the
initial prophecy 'false'. Instead, it confirms the belief that rituals and prayers could
revoke announcements of a specific disaster; cf. Tiemeyer 2005: 349.

5.2.4   *The Prophet Isaiah*

The Historical Isaiah

This section explores to what extent Isaiah fits into the description of
the prophetic practice in Judah and Israel as outlined above. The present survey is based on the material from First Isaiah that can be attributed to the eighth century (see chapter 2 and chapter 4.1). From a
sceptical point of view, the historicity of the prophet Isaiah is not beyond doubt, since the name יְשַׁעְיָהוּ, 'Yahweh is salvation', could be regarded as a late, theological construct.[322] This view however is to be
rejected. First, Isaiah's name is attested in Isa 7:2-3a, an early introduction to the oracles of 7:4-9a and 7:14b.16. In addition, his name is
found in the earliest layer of Isa 20. Furthermore, Isaiah appears as
nābî' in the so-called B1-version of the Hezekiah story (2 Kgs 18:17-
19:9a.36-37),[323] which dates from the seventh century BCE.[324] According to this story, the high royal officials consulted the prophet Isaiah
on behalf of King Hezekiah, and Isaiah delivered an oracle of encouragement. This is a plausible scene and it is quite unlikely that Isaiah is
a completely invented figure.[325] Instead, the image of Isaiah in 2 Kgs
19:1-7 is presumably based on prophetic material from the eighth century. Sometime during the seventh century Isaiah became a highly es-
timated figure, who was associated with the announcement of the
rescue of Jerusalem and the violent death of Sennacherib. Thus, in all
likelihood, in late eighth-century Jerusalem a prophetic figure lived
and worked called Isaiah.

Isaiah's Activity

Isaiah functioned as a prophet by delivering oracles. Apart from prophetic oracles, the early material includes critical sayings that represent Isaiah's contribution to the political controversy going on at the
time. Furthermore, the early material contains several reports of sym-

---

[322]   For an analysis of the name, see Williamson 2006: 12. The theme of Yahweh's
salvation is prominent throughout the book of Isaiah.

[323]   2 Kgs 19:2. I am not convinced by Gonçalves' suggestion (2001: 173) to delete
the word *nābî'* from the B1-story. In 2 Kgs 19:1-7 Isaiah acts as an official prophet,
playing an encouraging role in a situation of crisis, which makes the designation *nābî'*
wholly appropriate.

[324]   See chapter 6.1.2.

[325]   Nor is it a completely historical scene. Van der Kooij (2000: 113-114) points
out that the oracle of Isaiah in 2 Kgs 19:6-7 is not a real prophetic word but a literary
creation.

bolic acts performed by Isaiah that underscored his message. At two points in time, Isaiah wrote down an inscription on a tablet. According to 8:1-2, he wrote down the saying '(to) Maher-shalal-hash-baz', which indicated the imminent conquest and spoliation of Aram and Israel by Assyria, and according to 30:8, he wrote down the symbolic name 'Rahab who sits still', which indicated the inability of Egypt and Cush to save Judah from Assyria.

Furthermore, in Isa 20* Isaiah himself is depicted as a symbol: he walked around naked and barefoot as a symbol of the terrible fate of Egypt and Cush.[326] In addition, 8:3 describes that Isaiah had sexual intercourse with a prophetess (*nĕbî'â*).[327] When she conceived, Isaiah called his son Maher-shalal-hash-baz, which again indicated the imminent conquest of Aram and Israel by Assyria. There is no indication that the prophetess was Isaiah's wife.[328] Both the prophetess and the child become part of the prophetic message, an important political message in a critical situation.[329]

Various scholars have argued that 8:1-4 is best understood within a temple setting. At least one of the two witnesses mentioned in 8:2 was a priest, and the temple provides the most logical place for the public display of this prophecy written on a large tablet.[330] Two further texts indicate that Isaiah is to be associated with the temple. First, the imagery in the vision of Isa 6 suggests a scene placed in the temple of Jerusalem. Second, the description of 2 Kgs 19:2-7 (part of the B1-story) presupposes that Isaiah was consulted in the temple, where the prophet is requested to 'lift up a prayer' for the people of Jerusalem.[331]

---

[326] In the Mari letters, prophetic figures are sometimes referred to as 'signs' (*it-tātum*); cf. Durand 1982. A further example is found in the Epic of Zimri-Lim: 'Zimri-Lim (...) the prince of the land saw his sign (*ittu*), the prophet (*āpilum*): "The king goes forth with forceful heart! Adad shall go at his left side, Erra, the mighty one, at his right side".'; l. 137-142, translation from Nissinen 2003a: 90; cf. Nissinen 2000a: 263-264.

[327] The designation *nĕbî'â* implies she was a prophetess in her own right; so Gonçalves 2001: 156; Fischer 2002: 194-196.

[328] Gonçalves 2001: 156; Grabbe 1995: 114.

[329] Fischer 2002: 203.

[330] Van der Toorn 2007: 180; Fischer 2002: 204-206; cf. Wildberger 1972-82: 317-318. The oracle of 30:7 may also have been put on display in the temple. For an example of a prophecy displayed on the pedestal of the god Sin in a temple (as part of a dream report), see Ashurbanipal's Prism A iii 118-127 (BIWA 40-41, 233).

[331] Hezekiah goes to the temple (19:1) and there summons his high officials to consult the prophet, probably in the temple. Furthermore, the words נשא תפלה בעד 'to lift up a prayer for someone' (19:4), further only occur in Jer 7:16; 11:14, where Yahweh forbids Jeremiah to intercede for the people. In both cases the context sug-

Isaiah was greatly concerned with Judah's well-being, and his function may be described as guardian of the well-being of the state. On two instances in First Isaiah, the 'ancient prophetic message' is expressed. In 28:12: 'This (i.e. Zion) is the resting place—give rest to the weary; this is the place of repose'; and in 30:15: 'Thus says the Lord Yahweh, the Holy One of Israel: In sitting and rest you shall be saved; In quietness and in trust shall be your strength.' In my view, this 'prophecy of old' (presented by the later literary context as being superseded because of the people's disobedience) represented Isaiah's position. Isaiah aimed at Judah's well-being, but he did not merely announce 'peace' (as do 'the prophets' in their depiction as deceiving liars in the book of Jeremiah). Rather, Isaiah indicates how Judah's well-being is to be achieved: by heeding social justice (28:12), and by maintaining a submissive stance towards Assyria (30:15). Isaiah's concern for Judah's welfare further comes to the fore in the encouraging oracles addressed to king and people (e.g. 7:4-9a, 10:24-25), and the announcements of disaster and threatening words against Judah's enemies and oppressors (e.g. 7:14b.16; 8:1-4; 10:5-15*).

Isaiah contributed to the political issues of his time, especially with regard to the question of what position to adopt towards Assyria. Isaiah strongly rejected a policy of alliance with the Cushite rulers of Egypt aiming at rebellion against Assyria. His opponents are to be found among the political leaders of Judah, and among the religious experts, such as the priests and prophets (see chapter 4.1.8). It is not unreasonable to assume that Isaiah too was one of the leading religious specialists in Jerusalem. For three decades, until 705 BCE, the kings Ahaz and Hezekiah remained submissive to Assyria, in conformity with the position advocated by Isaiah.[332]

In various important respects Isaiah fits the description of prophetic practice in Mesopotamia and in Judah and Israel as presented above. The eighth-century prophetic material is however particularly stamped

---

gests that such intercession-prayers took place in the temple (cf. 7:1, 10, 14; 11:15). The תְּפִלָּה-prayer, a ritual prayer is particularly associated with the temple cult (Gerstenberger 1988: 611). Furthermore, when in the B2-extension to the story (2 Kgs 19:9b-35) Hezekiah himself takes the intercession prayer before Yahweh, he does so in the temple (19:14-19).

[332] That Isaiah reputedly was able to write (8:1; 30:8) confirms that he was a figure of some importance. According to Young (1998b: 419-420), the literary segment of monarchic Israel and Judaean society consisted of scribes, priests and the upper class.

by Isaiah's critical contribution to the controversy of 705-701. Isaiah's critical sayings as such do not make him a fundamentally different type of prophet, since criticism was part of the prophetic repertoire both in Judah and Israel and in Mesopotamia. However, the dominant critical tone gives Isaiah a particular profile.

Isaiah into Politics

Isaiah's prophetic function cannot be disconnected from the historical events of the final decades of the eighth century BCE, described in the first part of chapter 4. Isaiah was concerned with Judah's well-being, which, in his view, depended on submission to Assyria. Isaiah held that Yahweh himself would deal with Assyria, and he radically rejected the policy of alliance with the Cushite rulers of Egypt as being unwarranted and godless. From 734-705 BCE the Judaean kings Ahaz and Hezekiah followed the political line advocated by Isaiah. Even before 705, the temptation to join the anti-Assyrian forces may at times have been strong in Judah. In c. 713-711, during the revolt of Ashdod against Assyria, the Asdodites put diplomatic pressure on the neighbouring states, including Judah, to join the rebellion. The alliance with the Cushite king of Egypt, concluded by Iamani of Ashdod, may have added to the attractiveness of rebellion. However, Judah was not involved in the measures taken by Sargon, so if there had been an intention to revolt, it was called off in time, and the kingdom of Judah survived. This may have been partly due to the actions of Isaiah. According to the report of Isa 20*, the prophet Isaiah displayed a vehement reaction to the anti-Assyrian policy: he walked around naked in Jerusalem, symbolising the fate of Egypt and Cush.

The violent death of Sargon II in 705 led to rebellion in the Assyrian empire. Hezekiah sought the assistance of the Cushite rulers of Egypt in order to rebel against Assyria. The earlier policy of submission, advocated by Isaiah, was at last overruled by a strong 'now or never' feeling, and the desire to throw off the Assyrian yoke (see chapter 4.1.7). In 705 and the following years the political controversy in Jerusalem was at its height. Isaiah rejected the policy of rebellion. He criticised the alliance with the Cushite rulers of Egypt as being doomed to failure and accused the political and religious establishment of Jerusalem of bad leadership, from a political, social, and cultic point of view. In the saying of 28:7b-10, Isaiah ridiculed some of his colleagues. Through the sarcastic depiction of his opponents' words, Isaiah intended to undermine the position they supported: rebellion against Assyria. He pictured them as being drunk and blind to the divine will, to which he himself, as he claimed, had access. We do not know how the opponents ridiculed in 28:7b-10 in their turn depicted Isaiah, but perhaps equally harshly.[333]

There are no examples of comparable controversies among prophets from Mari and Assyria, but it is clear that prophetic oracles could play a role in political advice that competed with opposite views.[334] The clash between Isaiah and his opponents among the political elite and religious experts in Jerusalem, finds a parallel in the sometime harsh competition between scholars at the royal court of Assyria.[335] In 28:7b-10, Isaiah accuses his colleagues ('priest and prophet') of incompetence, exactly as Assyrian scholars occasionally did.[336] Furthermore, his contemptuous depiction of the political elite as bad leaders is to some extent comparable to Assyrian scholars accusing colleagues or high officials of conspiracy against the king.[337] Diviners holding back the results of their investigations or using their skills for the king's adversary were disloyal to the king and therefore regarded as enemies of the state.[338] Similarly, Isaiah exposes the political leaders advocating rebellion as enemies of the state. He does so mainly by using a form of speech that may be called the prophetic *woe*-saying. This form of speech, which refers to Yahweh in the third person, is not found among the prophetic words from Mesopotamia and may be typically Judaean (see also chapter 4.3). However, despite the use of different forms of speech, Isaiah's prophetic function was similar to that of the Assyrian prophets: both functioned as guardians of the well-being of the state and fiercely turned against those perceived as enemies of the state. A notorious aspect of Isaiah's criticism is that it never explicitly targets Hezekiah, although Hezekiah was ultimately

---

[333] Cf. Jer 29:26-27.

[334] See SAA 16 59, a letter by Nabû-reḫtu-uṣur, in which a prophecy from Nusku against Esarhaddon is countered by a prophecy from the goddess Nikkal in favour of Esarhaddon; see chapter 4.2.5. For Mari, see e.g. ARM 26 199 (Nissinen 2003a: 30-32). This letter reports various prophetic oracles from Dagan of Terqa warning Zimri-Lim not to conclude a peace treaty with Ešnunna; it seems that the goddess Diritum approved of such a treaty and that Dagan through a prophetic oracle warned her not to trust the messages from Ešnunna (see Charpin 1992: 23-25).

[335] For the competition and rivalry, see Brown 2000: 239-243; Van der Toorn 1998.

[336] See SAA 10 23, 51, 72.

[337] See SAA 10 2, 112, 179, 284.

[338] See Koch-Westenholz 1995: 66-67.

responsible for the political decision Isaiah abominated (see chapter 4.1.8). The absence of references to the king confirms that Isaiah, although radically opposing rebellion, did not at all reject the Davidic monarchy or the state of Judah. The furious tone of voice has everything to do with his concern for the well-being of Judah, its king and people.

Isaiah among the ancient Near Eastern Prophets

The main elements of ancient Near Eastern prophecy appear to be part of Isaiah's messages too: 1) Oracles of encouragement with declarations of divine support (7:4-9a; 10:24-25); 2) Announcements of the downfall and annihilation of the enemies (Aram-Damascus, Ephraim-Samaria, Assyria); 3) Political relevance: Isaiah's words pertained to the main political issue of his time, and could be—and, from Isaiah's point of view should be—used for the political decision-making; 4) Guarding the well-being of the state: Isaiah strongly turned against what he perceived as disastrous policy, namely rebellion against Assyria. He exposed those advocating this policy as enemies of the state.

Two further elements repeatedly occurring in the prophetic material, although not specifically 'prophetic', contribute to Isaiah's ancient Near Eastern profile: 1) Within Isaiah's prophetic words, 'the enemies' are always depicted as being self-willed and arrogant. Not only the external enemies, Aram-Damascus and Ephraim-Samaria (in the words of 734-732), and Assyria (in the words connected with 720) are presented in this manner, but also the internal enemies, the political leaders advocating rebellion (in the sayings of 705-701). Although the offences differ from case to case, the 'bad guys' are consistently depicted as being self-willed and arrogant. They are presented as acting against Yahweh's will. Whereas the prophet is Yahweh's spokesman, the bad guys have completely gone astray and are alienated from the divine will. This favourite rhetorical strategy of Isaiah is a common ancient Near Eastern motif used for sharply criticising one's opponents. The speaker self-evidently assumes that he speaks in accordance with the will of the gods, whereas the opponents or enemies are alienated from the divine will and arrogantly trust in their own power. 2) A further recurrent element within the Isaianic material is the emphasis on the imminence of fulfilment of the announcements (see 7:16; 8:4; 10:25; 18:5; 28:4). Repeatedly, the prophet emphasised that the events announced would take place soon. In the case of 7:16

and 8:4 the prophet assigned a time-limit. In this respect, Isaiah's announcements fulfilled a function elsewhere fulfilled by other forms of divination.[339]

The prophet Isaiah belonged to the religious system. The importance of the values of justice and righteousness in his message and the notion of Yahweh's kingship,[340] suggest that he was influenced in particular by the temple traditions.

5.3   Conclusion

5.3.1   Limitations

The first part of this chapter describes the prophetic functioning in the ancient Near East, focusing on seventh-century Assyria. In the second part, after an analysis of various biblical images of the prophets, an attempt has been made to describe the main aspects of the prophetic practice in Judah and Israel, followed by a survey on the prophetic function of Isaiah. The study of the function of the prophetic figures is complicated due to the character of the sources. The material pertaining to prophets and prophecy from the ancient Near East has been preserved by chance and cannot be expected to give a more than partial picture of the prophetic practice. Based on the extant material, the prophetic contribution in Mari seems to have been somewhat broader and more diverse than that in seventh-century Assyria. However, the greater part of the Assyrian prophecies that have been preserved was archived for a particular purpose: legitimation of the ruling monarchs. Perhaps it was not so much the role of the prophets that was more narrowly defined in Assyria in comparison with Mari, but the criterion of preservation. In the case of Isaiah, the prophetic material is heavily stamped by the main political issue of his time: Assyria's imperialism and Judah's political stance *vis-à-vis* Assyria. Isaiah's oracles and sayings were probably preserved exactly because of their political relevance. We therefore know Isaiah as a prophet connected with political key moments in the later eighth century. Our insight into the function of prophets is based on material that was never preserved or collected

---

[339]   See Roberts 1977a; Starr 1990: XVI. The 'time limit' (*adānu*) functions as indication for the realisation of a portent, or, in the case of Isaiah, an announcement.

[340]   See Wagner 2006.

with the intention of offering a full picture of prophetic practice as it was.

5.3.2 *Essential Similarity*

Despite this complication, some conclusions may be drawn. First, the analysis of the prophetic function presented in this chapter, suggests that prophecy both in Assyria and in Judah and Israel was part of the same phenomenon which may be designated as prophecy in the ancient Near East. The following characteristics can be mentioned:

*   Prophecy was one form of divination among others. The various forms of divination share a similar ideological basis: the decisions of the divine world, affecting the course of events on earth, can be known through divination in its different forms.
*   Both in Judah and Israel, and in Assyria and Mari we find different terms for prophetic figures. Although the prophetic figures might have differed from each other, they were part of more or less the same phenomenon.
*   Prophets served as functionaries of a deity. In their function as mouthpiece of the deity, they delivered messages from the divine world to a third party, often the king; that is, prophecies that were recorded are mostly messages for the king.
*   Among the prophetic figures we find both men and women.
*   Prophets are sometimes referred to in the plural, operating as a group, but often they spoke or acted individually.
*   Prophets were often connected with the cult and associated with the temple. Although prophets for the delivery of divine messages were not exclusively bound to the temple, the main institutional embodiment of prophecy seems to have been the temple.
*   A hallmark of prophetic activity was a kind of ecstatic behaviour, which included the performance of symbolic acts. Yet, generally speaking, prophetic oracles are clear and intelligible messages.
*   Prophetic oracles often contained divine assurance: declarations of divine assistance and announcements of annihilation of the enemies. These oracles of encouragement pertain especially to situations of political-military crisis. Furthermore, prophecy functioned to legitimate throne candidates by announcing divine support.

- In return for his help, the deity also formulates demands for the addressee (again, mostly the king). Divine demands could relate to both material and immaterial matters. Neglect of the divine expectations led to prophetic reproach; criticism was part of the prophetic repertoire.
- Prophetic announcements of disaster with the aim of averting it by taking the right action—a ritual or a prayer—functioned as warnings.
- Since the prophetic oracles were held to reflect the decisions taken in the divine council, they could be used as help or as a basis for political decision-making. Sometimes, perhaps as the exception rather than as the rule, prophets functioned as royal advisors.
- Prophets could be consulted by the king or by someone on his behalf, and perhaps were consulted by ordinary people too.
- Prophets, at least occasionally, were paid or rewarded for their services.
- The king did not exercise full control over the prophets.
- Prophets at least partly had a public function: encouragement of the king probably was also intended to encourage the people, and the formulation of divine demands and criticism probably gained strength because of its public character. To some extent prophets served a public function as opinion-makers.
- Prophets functioned as guardians of the well-being of the state. They were part of the religious establishment.

The prophet Isaiah as described in 5.2.4 above, essentially conforms to this set of characteristics. Prophecy in late monarchic Judah, Old Babylonian Mari and seventh-century Assyria can be seen as variants of the larger phenomenon of prophecy in the ancient Near East, and Isaiah can be described as a Judaean exponent of ancient Near Eastern prophecy.

My interpretation of prophecy departs from the traditional understanding of biblical prophecy. I have argued that the classical prophets do not form a distinct historical class of prophets, but a particular characterisation of prophets (5.2.2). Furthermore, the historical Isaiah as discussed in 5.2.4 does not fit the stereotypes of the classical prophets at all. Whereas the particularity of biblical prophecy mainly is to be found in the literary and theological development of the prophetic heritage, the prophetic practice in Judah and Israel in many respects resembled that of the ancient Near East, represented by Mari and Assyrian prophecy. The prophet Isaiah is to be counted among the ancient Near Eastern prophets.

5.3.3   *Significant Difference*

The discussion of prophecy and the depiction of Isaiah as a prophetic figure has also revealed various important differences between prophecy in Judah and Israel on the one hand and in Assyria on the other.

First, a difference in speech-forms may be noted. One of the main speech-forms used by Isaiah was the *woe*-saying. This form, which refers to Yahweh in the third person and addresses the adversaries, is not found among the prophetic words from Mesopotamia. However, behind the different forms of speech lies similar ideology. Both the Assyrian prophets and Isaiah functioned as guardians of the state and fiercely turned against those perceived as enemies of the state. Since most of the extant Assyrian prophecies were preserved because of their outspoken support for Esarhaddon and Ashurbanipal, the enemy of the state figuring in these oracles is the enemy of the king: disloyal officials or illegal throne pretenders. The words of Isaiah to be situated in 705-701 BCE criticise the anti-Assyrian policy adopted and present the advocates of this position as enemies of the state. Although the king figures much less prominently in Isaiah's messages, the words are nonetheless relevant to state matters.

Second, the words to be attributed to Isaiah on the whole seem to have a more critical outlook than the prophecies from Mesopotamia. This difference may be due to the different circumstances. Isaiah considered the policy of rebellion adopted in 705 BCE as disastrous for the state of Judah. He furiously opposed this policy, picturing those who advocated it as enemies of the state, with the intention of bringing about a political change and averting Assyria's wrath.[341]

Third, it seems that in general prophets in Judah and Israel at least in certain situations played a more important role in the public sphere

---

[341] This position makes sense in the light of the fate of other countries in Syria-Palestine. According to Sennacherib's inscriptions, at the start of his third campaign a range of rulers came to Ushu to do obeisance to him. These rulers had to pay up fourfold, which means that they had stopped their payment of tribute during the previous years too. These rulers had been rebellious, like Hezekiah, but resumed a submissive stance in time (see chapter 4.1.7). Isaiah wanted Judah to do the same.

than the Assyrian prophets did. The impression of prophecy being of major importance in Judah and Israel and of lesser importance in Assyria, is, as we have seen, partly due to the character of the sources. The prominence of prophecy in Judah and Israel may be an exaggeration of the biblical record, whereas the Assyrian prophets may have been more manifest than the extant sources suggest. This however may not be the full explanation. The difference between the prophets in Judah and Israel and those in Assyria is partly to be explained as resulting from the huge differences between the Israelite/Judaean and the Assyrian society. Assyria's society, particularly in the late eighth and seventh century, was characterised by a far-reaching differentiation. To mention just one point: the Assyrian king employed a considerable number of religious specialists, the so-called scholars. They were experts in the several branches of ancient lore, such as astrology, extispicy, and exorcism, and stood in daily correspondence with the royal court. Prophets, it seems, did not belong to the entourage of the king. Although it is reasonable to suggest that at times of national crisis, prophets had a more direct access to the king, normally the king was guided by his scholars, who could, of course, be influenced themselves by prophetic oracles. Since Judah's society was much less differentiated, prophets may have had a more direct influence on the king and public opinion.

To go one step further, it may well be that prophets in Judah and Israel to some extent played a role comparable to that of the scholars in seventh-century Assyria. Isaiah's raving at his opponents resembles the antagonism that at times existed between Assyria's foremost religious specialists, the scholars. In their function as royal advisors, they occasionally accused colleagues of incompetence, deceit and involvement in a conspiracy against the king.[342] This may, to some extent, be comparable to Isaiah's function in eighth-century Judah.[343]

It has been suggested that in contrast to the prophets in Judah and Israel, prophets in Mari and Assyria had no personal authority but only acted as the mouthpiece of the gods.[344] Although this supposed difference is difficult to substantiate on the level of prophetic practice,

---

[342] For some examples see SAA 10 2, 23, 51, 72, 112, 179, 284.

[343] Cf. Sasson 1998: 118-119, who argued that from a *functional* point of view (or, with regard to their social position), the Israelite-Judaean prophets can be paralleled with the *bārûm* in Mari, rather than with the *āpilum* or the *muḫḫûm*.

[344] Nissinen 2003d: 13.

it seems to be valid on the level of the reception of prophetic oracles. Whereas the Assyrian prophets remained in relative obscurity—their names were recorded but they do not seem to have become well-known public figures—Isaiah's star rose rather quickly. The words attributed to Isaiah were preserved as independent collections, whereas the collection tablets from Nineveh contain oracles from different prophets (see chapter 6). Furthermore, the emergence of stories in which the prophet Isaiah figured, and the expansion of a prophetic tradition attributed to him, miss their counterpart for the Assyrian prophets.[345] With regard to the development of stories and legends, it is rather a figure like the wise scribe, Ahiqar from the Aramaic Ahiqar story,[346] with whom Isaiah as a legendary figure may be compared. Thus, the social standing of prophetic figures and their posthumous fame may to some extent have depended on the kind of society in which they operated. It is only to be expected that within grand-scale Assyrian society of the seventh century with its tradition of scientific-religious specialists trained in ancient lore, prophets occupied a somewhat different position from that found in the small-scale society of eighth-century Judah, where scholarly tradition was still at an elementary stage.

---

[345]   The figure of Balaam son of Beor is a good example of this development. For the author of the Deir 'Allā plaster inscriptions, Balaam son of Beor was a figure of the past, to whom a legendary tradition was attributed. For the Balaam inscription, see, e.g. Weippert 1991; Dijkstra 1995; Lemaire 2001: 96-101; Seow in: Nissinen 2003a: 207-212.

[346]   See Koch-Westenholz 1995: 63, for the suggestion that this story might spring from the Assyrian period, as an illustration of the competition and rivalry among the king's scholars. See also the literary self-depiction of the Assyrian scholar Urad-Gula, SAA 10 294. Cf. Van der Toorn 1998.

CHAPTER SIX

FROM PROPHECY TO LITERATURE

This chapter explores the early stages of development of the Isaianic material and compares it with the development of the Assyrian prophecies. In the first part it will be argued that a substantial revision of the Isaianic material can be situated in the late seventh century during the reign of Josiah. The revision was carried out against the background of the decline of Assyria's power and its loss of grip on Syria-Palestine, which fuelled an anti-Assyrian, nationalistic spirit. Those responsible for the revision believed that the events of their time, Assyria's decline and Judah's relative independence under Josiah, proved the prophet Isaiah right. The revision of the Isaianic material turned the prophet Isaiah into a mouthpiece of state ideology, glorifying the reign of Josiah as an ideal time. This development of the Isaiah tradition will be explored from two angles. First, from the angle of the early prophetic material: through the revision, the prophetic material developed into literature. Second, from the angle of the revision material: the revision has a literary character, but resembles or imitates the prophetic genre. It can be qualified as a literary derivative of prophecy or pseudo-prophecy.

In the second part of this chapter I discuss the prophetic material from seventh-century Assyria,[1] from the same two angles. First, the development of prophecy that becomes literature will be explored. The texts to be discussed in this respect consist of prophetic oracles that once were orally delivered and afterwards found their way into literature. Examples of this development include the formation of oracle collections, the inclusion of oracles in royal inscriptions, and the elaboration of oracles into literary texts. Second, the phenomenon of literary texts deriving from prophecy will be discussed. This concerns texts that are literary in origin but that closely relate to the genre of

---

[1] Among the other examples of prophecy becoming literature, the Deir 'Allā plaster inscriptions take an important position. Weippert (1991: 177-178) refers to them as a literary collection, providing an analogy to the Assyrian collection tablets of SAA 9 1 and 2.

prophetic oracles. These texts may be regarded as literary derivatives of prophecy. In addition, some attention will be paid to a handful of texts that may be designated as pseudo-prophecy or pseudo-predictions. These are literary imitations of prophecy.

This chapter will conclude that there is a strong analogy between the Isaiah tradition and the Assyrian prophetic texts with regard to their respective development. The first parallel concerns the phenomenon of prophecy becoming literature. In both cases we find originally orally delivered oracles that were documented, preserved, and included in collections or compendia. In both cases we see examples of prophecy finding its way into literature, in the form of elaborations of oracles or as prophetic texts. Whereas oracles originally referred to a specific situation, secondarily they became part of a broader perspective. The second parallel relates to the phenomenon of literary derivatives of prophecy. In both cases we see texts that are literary in origin that resemble or imitate the prophetic genre. In both cases these texts provide interpretations of historical events by means of the thesis that it is God—be it Aššur, Ištar, or Yahweh—who decides the course of the events. Both the Assyrian texts and the revised Isaiah tradition express a close relationship between the king and the gods. The texts depict an ideal situation in which the reign of the king is in complete agreement with the will of the gods and, in this way, represent official ideology.

6.1   The Development of the Isaiah Tradition in the Seventh Century

6.1.1   The Hypothesis of a Seventh-Century Revision

The suggestion of a late seventh-century revision of the Isaianic material was put on the exegetical agenda by Hermann Barth,[2] and has played a role ever since in the study of First Isaiah (see chapter 1.1.2). The suggestion makes sense for the following reasons.

1) It is commonly agreed that the Isaianic material, the prophetic heritage from the eighth century, was developed and expanded during the exilic and post-exilic periods. It is likely that this process of development already started as early as the pre-exilic period. Instead of passing from the eighth century to the sixth, scholars should take into

---

[2]   Barth 1977.

account the seventh century as a stage in the development of the Isaiah tradition.[3]

2) A range of passages from First Isaiah reflects, as will be argued below, the circumstances of the late seventh century.[4] The passages are characterised by two motifs: (a) the downfall and destruction of Assyria, and (b) the restoration of Judah, in particular the appointment of a new Davidic king. Both aspects are presented as the work of Yahweh. These passages are likely to be of a pre-exilic origin. The motif of the downfall and destruction of Assyria reflects the historical situation of the late seventh century. Since the Isaiah tradition has its roots in the Assyrian period it is reasonable to understand 'Assyria' as Assyria (not as a *chiffre* for some later empire), in particular where Assyria is portrayed as a political-military superpower.[5] Furthermore, the passages focusing on the reign of the ideal king (9:1-6, 11:1-5 and 32:1-2) are likely to be pre-exilic as well because of their connection with the Davidic kingship ideology and their interest in human kingship.[6]

3) The passages under examination are to be attributed to a later, seventh-century, revision of the Isaiah tradition, because they cannot be plausibly related to the earliest layer, consisting of prophetic material relating to historical episodes of the late eighth century. There are essential differences, with regard to both form and content, between the eighth-century material and the seventh-century revision. Whereas the eighth-century material goes back to prophetic words that initially were orally delivered, the revision material consists of scribal texts without any oral background. Furthermore, whereas the eighth-century material describes Assyria as the current superpower, the seventh-century revision focuses on Assyria's downfall. This difference will be elaborated in 6.1.5.

4) Any reconstruction of the development of the Isaiah tradition is necessarily hypothetical. In this chapter however I hope to demon-

---

[3]   See in particular Barthel 2003: 135.

[4]   The list of texts I attribute to the seventh-century revision (Isa 9:1-6; 10:10-11.16-19.26a.27a.33-34; 11:1-5; 14:24-27.28.32; 18:1-6; 30:27-33; 31:4-5.8-9; 32:1-2; see chapter 2.4) to a significant extent corresponds with that of Barth, Clements, and others; see chapter 1.1.2. In this chapter, I proceed with the hypothesis of a seventh-century revision of the Isaiah tradition by presenting my analysis of this revision.

[5]   Höffken 2004: 133-134.

[6]   Williamson 1998a: 10-11.

strate that the late seventh-century revision of the Isaiah tradition is
more than just an attractive possibility, by taking the following steps:

First, I discuss the earliest version of the story of Hezekiah and
Sennacherib (6.1.2), because here we find portrayals of the prophet
Isaiah and Assyria that clearly date from the seventh century. It will
be argued that the seventh-century revision of the Isaiah tradition continued the development started by this story, which makes the late
seventh century a plausible setting for the revision.

In the second place, I present the historical circumstances of the
seventh century, focusing on the reign of Josiah (6.1.3). It will be
shown not only that the motifs of the revision fit the situation of the
late seventh century, but also that Josiah's reign is otherwise marked
as well as a 'new beginning', just as is the case in the passages portraying the reign of the ideal king.

The third step is an analysis of the passages attributed to the seventh-century revision, which demonstrates that they form a thematically coherent and consistent whole (6.1.4). Furthermore, it is
plausible that the Isaianic material was revised in the form of three
compilations (see chapter 2.4).

Fourth, as will be argued in 6.1.5, the texts attributed to the seventh-century revision bear a clear redactional imprint. It will be argued that they cannot belong to the same level as the eighth-century
prophetic material.

Fifth, the traditio-historical background of the revision is found in
the state ideology of monarchic Judah (6.1.6). This supports a) the
pre-exilic provenance of the revision; b) the likelihood of a scribal
origin of the revision; c) the difference between the seventh-century
revision and the eighth-century prophetic material, since the latter is
less close to the imagery of Judah's state ideology.

Finally, it will be shown that the development of the Isaiah tradition in the seventh century and later, from a historical point of view
followed a logical course (6.1.7). These steps show, in my view, that
the suggestion of a seventh-century revision is the most plausible explanation for the earliest stages of development of the Isaiah tradition.

6.1.2   *The Story of Hezekiah and Sennacherib*

Clements was the first to point out a close connection between the Hezekiah stories (2 Kgs 18-20, Isa 36-39) on the one hand,[7] and the presumed seventh-century redaction of the Isaiah tradition on the other.[8] For the argument of this chapter, the connection is relevant. One part of the Hezekiah stories, dealing with Jerusalem's deliverance, is often labelled the B1-story (2 Kgs 18:17-19:9a.36-37; the term B1 is explained below). This story dates, as we will see, from the seventh century. The story provides insight into the seventh-century image of the prophet Isaiah, the view of Assyria, and Judah's state ideology of the time. Furthermore, as will be demonstrated, the revision of the Isaiah tradition, to be situated in the late seventh century, in important respects corresponds to the seventh-century reception of 701 as it appears in the B1-story. The relevance for the present survey is the following. Since the B1-story dates from the seventh century, and since the material from First Isaiah on which the first part of this chapter focuses can be seen as being in continuity with the B1-story, the suggestion to regard this material as a seventh-century revision of the Isaiah tradition becomes substantiated.

According to a well-known view, the story of Hezekiah and Sennacherib (2 Kgs 18-19) consists of three different parts, which have been labelled part A (18:13-16), B1 (18:17-19:9a.36-37), and B2 (19:9b-35).[9] Although the account as a whole can be read as an ongoing story,[10] it clearly consists of three distinct parts.[11] Whereas part A contains an early account of the events of 701 (see chapter 4.1.7), 18:17-19:37 presents a later literary account. The earliest part of this literary account is the so-called B1-story, which dates from the seventh century BCE. The passage 19:9b-35 (B2) is a later extension to the B1-story,[12] which in all likelihood dates from the sixth century.[13] For the present purpose I concentrate on the B1-story. This story nar-

---

[7]   The relationship of the two parallel versions and the question of which version is primary has been the subject of ongoing debate. Gonçalves (1999) argues that the version of 2 Kings is older; see also Van der Kooij 2000: 107, note 1.

[8]   Clements 1980b; 1991. Neither Barth (1977) nor Vermeylen (1977-78) discusses this connection. Cf. Barth 1977: 4, note 5.

[9]   See particularly Gonçalves 1986: 351-354 and 355-487.

[10]   See Van der Kooij 2000: 107-111, esp. 109; Smelik 1992: 101-123.

[11]   Van der Kooij 2000: 107-108.

[12]   Van der Kooij 2000: 108-109; Van der Kooij 1986: 107-108.

[13]   Na'aman 2000; 2003; Clements 1991; Gonçalves 1986: 480.

rates the threat posed to Jerusalem in 701 and the city's rescue through
Yahweh's intervention. The climax of the story is the murder of Sennacherib, back in Assyria (19:37), which happened in 681 (see chapter
4.2.1). According to the story, Sennacherib was murdered in his country because he offended Yahweh and threatened Jerusalem.[14] This can
be shown by an outline of the story:

18:17-35	The Rabshakeh boasts on behalf of Sennacherib and threatens Jeru-salem: - Egypt cannot save Jerusalem - Yahweh cannot save Jerusalem
19:1-5	Hezekiah reacts in shock; the prophet Isaiah is consulted
19:6-7	Isaiah delivers a prophecy of encouragement: - Sennacherib will return to Assyria because of a rumour he hears - He will die violently in his own country
19:8-9a.36-37	Thus it happens: - Rumour of the coming of Taharqa of Cush causes Sennacherib's retreat - In Assyria he is murdered by his sons

The murder of Sennacherib is presented as Yahweh's punishment for
an offence committed in 701: Sennacherib's threat to Jerusalem and
insult of Yahweh.[15] The connection between the events of 701 and 681
makes sense in light of the logic of the time: a negative fate for a king
was seen as a sign of divine wrath for a grave offence.[16] Yahweh punished Sennacherib because of his arrogant provocation.[17]

It was of course a bold claim that Sennacherib's death in 681, in the
temple of his own god and by the hands of his own sons, was due to
Yahweh's intervention.[18] In my view, the events of 701 could only be
re-interpreted this way if the concept of Yahweh as sovereign king of
the earth protecting Zion against enemy threat, already existed. The
fact that Jerusalem was spared in 701 of course added to Jerusalem's
status, and the re-interpretation of the events in the Hezekiah story
(B1) may have given an impulse to the belief of Jerusalem's inviola-

---

[14]   Van der Kooij 2000: 118; cf. Clements 1994: 242-243.
[15]   Van der Kooij 2000: 118.
[16]   The inscription of Nabonidus explains Sennacherib's murder as Marduk's re-
venge for Sennacherib's violence against Babylon in 689 (Babylon Stele l. 1'-41';
Schaudig 2001: 515-516, 523); see Van der Kooij 2000: 118.
[17]   See 2 Kgs 19:4, 6. Ollenburger (1987: 79) points out that arrogance towards
Yahweh is the proverbial sin according to the Zion tradition.
[18]   2 Kgs 19:7b, 'I will cause him to fall by the sword in his own land'.

bility. Nevertheless, this re-interpretation of the events was only possible because the belief that Yahweh protected Zion, and by implication Jerusalem, already existed.[19]

Since the view of 701 as expressed in the B1-story was provoked by the violent death of Sennacherib in 681, the story should be dated not too long after Sennacherib's death, around the middle of the seventh century BCE.[20] The story presents an image of the prophet Isaiah as a supportive figure, who encouraged Hezekiah and the people of Jerusalem in the threatening circumstances of 701. Furthermore, it presents an image of the Assyrian superpower headed by Sennacherib, as being arrogant and offensive towards Yahweh; Yahweh however frustrates the Assyrian campaign and causes the violent death of Sennacherib. Finally, the story is revealing regarding Judah's state ideology, in presenting Hezekiah as a pious king and Yahweh as sovereign king of the earth, who protects Jerusalem and punishes those that threaten her.

The B1-story shows points of connection with the Isaiah tradition. First, the B1-story can to some extent be seen as being in continuity with the eighth-century Isaianic material. The B1-story contains motifs and themes that play an important role in the earlier prophetic sayings attributed to Isaiah. At the heart of both the B1-story and the critical sayings of Isaiah lies the conviction that only Yahweh can save. The boast of the Rabshakeh closely resembles that of Assyria in Isa 10:8-9.13-14 (cf. in particular 2 Kgs 18:34 and Isa 10:8-9). Further points of resemblance are the scornful depiction of Egypt as a worthless ally (2 Kgs 18:21, 24; Isa 28:15-18; 30:1-5*.6b-8; 31:1.3a) and the criticism of Judah's plan (עֵצָה) to rebel against Assyria (2 Kgs 18:20; Isa 29:15; 30:1-2). A huge difference however is that Isaiah's criticism of 705-701 is put into the mouth of the enemy, and that it is through a rumour about the Cushite king of Egypt that Yahweh saves Jerusalem. Furthermore, there is tension between Isaiah's critical sayings relating to 705-701 (28:7b-10.15-18; 30:1-5*; 31:1.3a) and the

---

[19]   Contra Clements 1980b: 83-84; Amit 2003: 367; Wanke 1966a: 93-99. Since Jerusalem in 701 BCE was blockaded but not assaulted by storm and frontal attack (see Van der Kooij 1986: 93-109), it is quite unlikely that the events of 701 led to the invention of the *Völkerkampf*-motif and the concept of Jerusalem's inviolability.

[20]   Gonçalves 1986: 440-441; Van der Kooij 2000: 116-117. Furthermore, as Van der Kooij (2000: 114) shows, the B1-story plays with the role of Egypt/Cush. Whereas the Rabshakeh boasts that Egypt cannot save Jerusalem, the mere rumour of the coming of Taharqa, king of Cush, suffices for the Assyrian retreat. Taharqa's title 'king of Cush' points to the seventh-century provenance of the B1-story, since Taharqa was king from 689-664 BCE.

portrayal of Isaiah in the B1-story. Yet, Isaiah's role in the B1-story is in complete agreement with his role during the Syro-Ephraimite crisis, reflected by the oracles of 7:4-9a, 14b.16, 8:1-4 (see chapter 4.1.2). The composer of the B1-story may have been familiar with the prophetic words attributed to Isaiah, but used them in a creative way for his own purposes. In the B1-story, the prophetic role is incorporated into a perspective of state ideology, with Yahweh as sovereign king of the earth and Hezekiah as his pious king. Isaiah is depicted as a supportive, encouraging prophet. This is *not* in complete disagreement with the eighth-century Isaiah tradition, as appears from the oracles relating to 734-732.[21] The difference in outlook from his critical sayings of 705-701 can be explained as resulting from the development of a seventh-century reinterpretation of the events of 701, which half a century later cast Isaiah in a prophetic role in conformity with the current state ideology.

Whereas the B1-story can be dated round the mid seventh century, a revision of the Isaiah material is best situated in the late seventh century. This late seventh-century revision is consistent with the perspective of the B1-story. Whereas the punishment of Assyria in the B1-story is restricted to the frustration of the campaign and the violent death of Sennacherib, the revision of the Isaiah tradition expands this to a general destruction of Assyria. This development reflects the historical situation of the late seventh century. The gradual decline of Assyria's power and its loss of grip on Syria-Palestine reinforced an anti-Assyrian view in Judah. Furthermore, a significant similarity in outlook between the B1-story and the revision of the Isaiah tradition lies in the portrayal of Isaiah. In both traditions, the figure of Isaiah has become a mouthpiece of the official, royal perspective. In the B1-story, Isaiah encourages the king ('do not fear', 2 Kgs 19:6) and announces rescue and an evil fate for the aggressor. In the revision of the Isaiah tradition, the destruction of Assyria makes room for a Judaean king, presented as an ideal ruler, which effectively makes the prophet Isaiah a spokesman for the glorification of the king. I like to emphasise that this portrayal of Isaiah is not inappropriate, as it is in agreement with the role of prophets in the ancient Near East in general and with Isaiah's role during the Syro-Ephraimite crisis in particular. The incorporation of Isaiah within a royal ideological perspective however

---

[21]   Contra Smelik 1992: 126; Blenkinsopp 2000b: 21.

meant a limitation of the prophetic role to that of supporter of the king and his politics. In reality, prophets were more than that, as appears from the evidence from Mari, Assyria, and, not least, from Isaiah's sayings from 705-701. Significantly, a similar process of narrowing down the prophetic role to that of mouthpiece of the royal perspective is apparent in Assyria, as will be shown in the second part of this chapter. Both the B1-story and the seventh-century revision of the Isaiah tradition are marked by a royal ideological perspective. This suggests that both are likely to originate from a (royal) scribal milieu, just as most of the prophetic texts from Assyria.[22]

The B1-story is important for the discussion of a seventh-century revision of the Isaiah tradition. The B1-story brings us to the mid-seventh century and offers glimpses of the seventh-century image of Isaiah, of Assyria, and of the state ideology. The revision of the Isaiah tradition is consistent with the B1-story, but goes one step further, in the light of the historical developments of the late seventh century, to which we turn presently. Because of this continuity, the B1-story offers considerable support to the plausibility of a late seventh-century revision of the Isaiah tradition.

6.1.3 *History of the Seventh Century and the Reign of Josiah*

The International Scene

After Sennacherib's campaign of 701 Hezekiah reverted to a submissive stance towards Assyria, in which his successors followed.[23] In the seventh century, Judah went through a process of recovery, enjoying the economic prosperity shared by the entire region under Assyrian rule.[24] During his long reign, Manasseh was submissive to Assyria and apparently considered a loyal vassal by both Esarhaddon and Ashurbanipal.[25] Judah's dependence on Assyria implied sharing in the *pax Assyriaca* and profiting from international trade.[26]

---

[22] Cf. Van der Kooij's suggestion (2000: 117) that the B1-story was composed by members of the intellectual elite in Jerusalem.

[23] Evans 1980: 166.

[24] Lipschits 2005: 10-11; Finkelstein 1994.

[25] Manasseh occurs in Esarhaddon's inscriptions in a list of twenty-two kings characterised as 'kings of the Ḫatti-lands and the sea-coast' (Borger 1956: 60, Nineveh A-F v 55). These kings transported materials and treasures to Nineveh for the building of a palace. A similar reference to the 'kings of the Ḫatti-lands and the sea-coast', relating to the building of an Assyrian trade centre in Phoenicia, probably includes Manasseh again (Borger 1956: 48, Nineveh A ii 65-82). In Ashurbanipal's in-

Esarhaddon and Ashurbanipal conducted several military campaigns against Taharqa, ruler of the Cushite (25th) Dynasty,[27] whose
policy of interference in Palestine and Phoenicia brought him into
conflict with Assyria (see chapter 4.2.4).[28] After the successful campaign in 671, local rulers of Lower Egypt were brought under Assyrian rule. Among them was Necho I (671-664) of Sais.[29] After Taharqa
re-established his rule in the Delta region, Ashurbanipal defeated him
during his first campaign (667 BCE). Afterwards, Delta rulers that had
taken the side of Taharqa were punished by Ashurbanipal, but
Necho's position was strengthened by his appointment as governor of
Memphis.[30] When Taharqa's successor Tanwetamun invaded Egypt
and took Memphis,[31] Necho opposed him but was killed. In his second
campaign to Egypt (664/663) Ashurbanipal conquered Thebes. Tanwetamun fled Nubia and the 25th dynasty of Egypt ended.[32] Necho's
son Psammetichus I ascended the throne as a vassal of Assyria. He
succeeded in extending his rule to the entire Delta, and by 656 he had
brought Upper and Lower Egypt under his control.[33] Officially an Assyrian vassal he effectively founded the Saite (26th) Dynasty.[34] Psammetichus became increasingly independent and at a certain point
ceased paying tribute to Assyria.[35] Yet, he apparently remained an ally
of Assyria, and there is no evidence of hostility between the two kingdoms.[36] Assyria was preoccupied with Babylonia and Elam and did not
take action against Psammetichus but accepted him as king of Egypt.[37]

---

scriptions Manasseh appears again in a list of the same twenty-two kings, who joined
Ashurbanipal's first campaign against Taharqa (BIWA: 212, Prism C ii 60-67).

[26]   Lipschits 2005: 11.
[27]   For the Cushite (25th) dynasty, see Morkot 2000; Schipper 1999: 199-228;
Kitchen 1986: 378-398. For the reign of Taharqa, see Török 1997: 171-184.
[28]   Schipper 1999: 218-221.
[29]   Lipschits 2005: 21-22.
[30]   Taylor 2000: 359; Onasch 1994: 151-154; Lipschits 2005: 22.
[31]   For the reign of Tanwetamun, see Török 1997: 184-188.
[32]   Onasch 1994: 91-145, 154-158; Schipper 1999: 223-224; Lipschits 2005: 23.
[33]   Schipper 1999: 228; Lipschits 2005: 23-24.
[34]   Taylor 2000: 371. For this dynasty, see Kitchen 1986: 399-408.
[35]   Psammetichus' detachment from Assyria is reflected in an inscription of
Ashurbanipal referring to Psammetichus as 'who had thrown off my yoke' (Prism A ii
114-115; BIWA: 31). Cf. Onasch 1994: 158. This however did not lead to Assyrian
sanctions.
[36]   Lipschits 2005: 24.
[37]   Schipper 1999: 229.

Due to gaps in our sources the political events of the second half of the seventh century are difficult to reconstruct.[38] At the point where the Babylonian Chronicle resumes (626 BCE), Assyria no longer is a supreme imperial force, but a monarchy struggling for survival.[39] It is difficult to ascertain at which point Assyria had to give up its rule of Syria-Palestine. The last clear evidence of Assyrian rule dates from the 640s,[40] but it is mostly assumed that Assyria's control over Syria-Palestine ended after the death of Ashurbanipal (631).[41] The years following his death are marked by a struggle for the throne in Assyria. In the mean time, the Chaldean Nabopolassar became king of Babylonia, and Assyrian efforts to defeat him failed. In 623, the Assyrian prince Sin-šar-iškun eliminated his rival Sin-šum-lišir and acceded to the throne in Assyria. However, he was not able to restore Assyria's supremacy. Assyria's withdrawal from Syria-Palestine is usually connected with this troubled period (c. 630-623).[42]

Na'aman has suggested that after Assyria withdrew from the region, Egypt established its rule in Syria-Palestine as a 'successor state'. In his view, Egypt inherited Assyria's territory beyond the Euphrates in exchange for military aid in the war against the Babylonians and the Medes.[43] This explains why Psammetichus in 616 and 610,[44] and Necho II in 609 came to the aid of the Assyrians.[45] Despite Egyptian support, Assyria was overrun by its enemies. After the cities Assur and Nineveh had fallen, the last Assyrian king, Assur-uballiṭ for some years held out in Harran. Necho II came to his aid, but Assur-uballiṭ was defeated in 609, which ended the Assyrian empire.[46]

---

[38] The archives of the second part of Ashurbanipal's reign (640 BCE onwards) are not preserved. The Assyrian Eponym Canon breaks off at 648 BCE, and the Babylonian Chronicle has a lacuna between 669 BCE (accession of Šamaš-šum-ukin) and 626 BCE (accession of Nabopolassar); see Grayson 1975a: 10, 86-88.

[39] Stern 2001: 131.

[40] Stern 2001: 4.

[41] For the dating, see Na'aman 1991c: 243-267; Lipschits 2005: 13, with note 39.

[42] Na'aman 1991b: 38.

[43] Na'aman 1991b: 33-41; cf. Lipschits 2005: 27-29.

[44] See Smith 1991: 108; but cf. Lipschits 2005: 25, note 99.

[45] Na'aman 1991b: 38-40; Schipper 1999: 230.

[46] Veenhof 2001: 275-276; Lipschits 2005: 17-20. Dalley (2003: 25-28) challenges the view of the 'end' of the Assyrian empire and the 'beginning' of the Babylonian empire. In her view, Nabopolassar and his successors continued the tradition of the late Assyrian kings and regarded themselves as heirs to their throne. Dalley is right that the Assyrians did not completely disappear from the scene, but the Assyrian empire evidently was brought to an end (Kühne 2002). Cf. Nabopolassar's view on his achievements: 'The Assyrian, who had, because of the wrath of the gods, ruled the

Josiah's Reign: Territorial Expansion and Religious Reform

Earlier studies describe Josiah's reign (640/39-609 BCE) as a golden age characterised by huge territorial expansion and great religious reform, but more recently it has been argued that this picture needs correction.[47] When Assyria withdrew from Syria-Palestine in the last third of the seventh century, Egypt established its rule in the region.[48] The view that after Assyria's withdrawal Josiah took advantage of the political vacuum by expanding his kingdom in all directions, does not hold.[49] According to Na'aman's reconstruction, under Josiah, Judah's northern border was extended a little northward from the Geba-Mizpah line to the Bethel-Ophrah line.[50] However, it is unlikely that the northward expansion extended as far as to the Samarian hill country.[51] Furthermore, expansions to east, south, and west are unlikely or uncertain.[52] The overall situation suggests that Josiah's territorial achievements were modest.[53]

The image of Josiah as a reformer king whose religious reformation was a decisive stage in the development of Israelite religion, needs reconsideration too. Whereas part of the description of Josiah's reform in 2 Kgs 23 is likely to go back to an early source,[54] the portrayal of Josiah's actions as a religious reformation and the supposed link with the book of Deuteronomy, belong to a later editorial stage.[55] It has been suggested that within 2 Kgs 23:4-20 distinction can be made between purification or reorganisation of the Jerusalem temple cult on the one hand, and measures pertaining to cult centralisation and the

---

land of Akkad and who had oppressed the people of the land with his heavy yoke (...), with the mighty strength of Nabû and Marduk my lords, I chased them (the Assyrians) out of the land of Akkad and caused (the Babylonians) to throw off their yoke' (translation Al-Rawi 1985: 5, i 28-ii 5).

[47] In particular Na'aman 1991b, recently updated by Lipschits 2005: 135-140.

[48] Na'aman 1991b: 40; Lipschits 2005: 27.

[49] Na'aman 1991b: 41-51; Lipschits 2005: 136, with note 7.

[50] Na'aman 1991b: 25; Lipschits 2005: 135.

[51] Lipschits 2005: 137-138.

[52] Na'aman 1991b: 41-50; Lipschits 2005: 135-140; cf. also Schipper 1999: 232.

[53] Na'aman 1991b: 55-58; Lipschits 2005: 136. In the reconstruction of Judah under Josiah, town lists from the book of Joshua (Josh 15:21-62; 18:21-28), play an important role (Lipschits 2005: 135-136, with note 3; Na'aman 1991b: 8-13). De Vos (2003: 527-528, 532-533) however argues that the basic layer of Josh 15:21-62; 18:21-28, is to be connected with the reign of Manasseh.

[54] See Knoppers 1994: 176-181 and especially Hardmeier 2000: 116-145.

[55] Uehlinger 1995: 71, note 64; Würthwein 1976: 414-415.

abolition of 'high places' on the other.[56] Various literary-critical studies have shown that the early account of Josiah's reform deals with the
purification and reorganisation of the temple cult, whereas a later
composer/editor inserted additions concerning the illegitimate character of the 'high places' (23:5.8-9.13-14.19-20) and references to
specific kings (Manasseh, 23:12; Solomon, 23:13; Jeroboam, 23:15).[57]
The early account was more or less the following:[58]

> [4*] The king commanded the high priest Hilkiah, the priests of the second
> order, and the guardians of the threshold, to bring out of the temple of
> Yahweh all the vessels made for Baal, for Asherah, and for all the host
> of heaven; he burned them outside Jerusalem in the fields of the Kidron.
> [5*] He deposed the *kĕmārîm*-priests whom the kings of Judah had or-
> dained (to make offerings) to the sun, the moon, the constellations, and
> all the host of the heavens.
> [6*] He brought out the image of Asherah from the house of Yahweh, out-
> side Jerusalem, to the Wadi Kidron, and burned it at the Wadi Kidron.
> [7] He broke down the houses of the *qĕdēšîm* that were in the house of
> Yahweh, where the women did weaving for Asherah.
> [11] He removed the horses that the kings of Judah had dedicated to the
> sun, at the entrance to the house of Yahweh, by the chamber of the
> eunuch Nathan-Melech, which was in the precincts; then he burned the
> chariots of the sun with fire.
> [12*] The altars on the roof (of the temple), which the kings of Judah had
> made, the king broke in pieces.

Uehlinger has shown that most of the measures mentioned in this account from a religious-historical point of view can be plausibly situated in a late seventh-century context.[59] Although the precise content
of the account remains a matter for debate,[60] the measures mentioned

---

[56] See particularly Uehlinger 1995: 71-74. In a similar way, Hardmeier makes a
distinction between a 'great' and a 'small' reform (2000: 124-136).

[57] Arneth 2001: 206-207, with note 52; Würthwein 1976: 418.

[58] I am grateful to Arie van der Kooij (Leiden) for giving me his analysis of 2
Kgs 23:4-20 (unpublished), which generally resembles the view presented here.

[59] Uehlinger 1995: 74-83. For a general analysis supporting the credibility of
Josiah's measures and their religious-political significance, see Na'aman 2006b.

[60] Cf. Uehlinger (1995: 83, note 116) doubting the early provenance of 23:4*;
Hollenstein (1977: 325-335), reducing the early account to 23:4, (5), 11-12. Hardmeier (2000: 116-145) plausibly distinguishes between an early source reflecting a
'small' cult reform (23:4-15*) and the later elaboration of 2 Kgs 22-23, which turned
the small reform into a great reform. According to Hardmeier, the early source consisted of 23:4aβb, 5-7*, 8b, 10a, 11-15* (see 2000: 145). I am not convinced by
Hardmeier's view (2000: 123) that the references to the former Judaean kings (verses
5, 11, 12) belong to the secondary redaction. In contradistinction to the negative refer-

in verses 5, 11 and 12 have been plausibly connected with a temple 'reform' under Josiah.[61] Significantly, it is exactly in these verses that the actions of Josiah are presented in contrast to the deeds of his predecessors, 'the kings of Judah'. The account does not simply contain a series of measures, but to some extent presents a programme. Josiah discontinued various practices that were introduced by his predecessors.

Broadly speaking, Josiah's reform can be understood as the elimination of cultic practices that had lost plausibility in the light of major changes on the political map and the accompanying economic and cultural reorientation.[62] However, an explanation of the reform out of purely economic motives downplays its religious and political significance.[63] The measures reflect a restriction of the state cult to the service of Yahweh. The contrastive references to 'the kings of Judah' point to the innovative character of the measures. Josiah abolished certain cultic elements that had been introduced into the Jerusalem temple cult by his predecessors. This reorientation is likely to be connected with the discontinuation of Assyrian rule.[64] The reform account presents to some extent Josiah's cultic measures as the mark of a new era, which coincided with a new political situation of relative independence. The new era was contrasted with the preceding period, characterised by Assyrian supremacy and cultic innovations of 'the kings of Judah' that had now been abolished. This is not to say that these cultic practices had been imposed on Judah by Assyria,[65] nor that the reform account is anti-Assyrian propaganda.[66] Rather, the measures represent a new orientation exclusively focusing on Yahweh as the national god. The reform is anti-Assyrian only in an indirect way: the demand of exclusive loyalty to the Assyrian king and his god Aššur secured by the loyalty oath was turned into an exclusive loyalty to

---

ences to former kings in verse 12 (Manasseh), 13 (Solomon), 15 (Jeroboam), and 19 (the kings of Israel), these references to the Judaean kings are of a more neutral tone.

[61] Uehlinger 1995: 74-83.
[62] Uehlinger 1995: 80.
[63] Arneth 2001: 208-209, note 61; Na'aman 2006b: 140-141, 165-166. Contra Uehlinger 1995: 80.
[64] Cf. Na'aman 2006b:140-141, who points out that Josiah took these measures after Assyria failed to suppress a revolt in Babylonia and a civil war had broken out.
[65] The view that the Assyrians imposed their cults on the people they subjected, has been refuted by Cogan 1993; Smelik 1997; Holloway 2002.
[66] Contra Arneth 2001.

Yahweh.[67] By contrasting Josiah's cultic measures to the deeds of his predecessors, who had been under Assyrian dominion, the account presents Josiah's reign as a new era.

Josiah's Reign: Ambitions and Ideology

Josiah's reign was, in all likelihood, perceived as a glorious time. First of all, Assyria lost its supremacy and withdrew from Syria-Palestine. With the collapse of Assyrian rule Judah regained part of its political independence. It has been suggested that after Assyria's withdrawal, Egypt established its rule in Syria-Palestine.[68] However, since Egypt's main interest lay in the coastal areas of Philistia and Phoenicia,[69] Josiah had room to manoeuvre. For two decades (c. 630-610) Judah enjoyed a relative freedom and independence, which ended with the reign of Necho II (see below). The collapse of Assyrian dominion and regaining of independence were the ingredients of the portrayal of Josiah's reign as a glorious time.[70] However small the territorial achievements, Josiah's political ambitions may have been considerable.[71] A boost to nationalistic ideology fuelled the hope, however unrealistic, of a Judaean takeover of regions abandoned by the Assyrians. It is quite likely that at this stage, the image of the Davidic king as the guardian of justice and righteousness and overlord of the surrounding nations was popular, and that the hope of a 'Great Israel' was blooming.[72]

The early account of Josiah's reform can be understood from a similar perspective. This account presents the deeds of Josiah in contrast to that of his predecessors and hence characterises Josiah's reign

---

[67]   This view concurs to some extent with the thesis of Otto (1998), that the covenant theology of Deuteronomy and Exodus originated from an application of the *adê* (loyalty oath) with the Assyrian king to Yahweh. Otto situates this development, the transfer of exclusive loyalty from the Assyrian king to Yahweh, during the reign of Josiah, and suggests a connection with the reform. See Otto 1998: 42-50, 60-63.

[68]   Na'aman 1991b: 33-41; cf. Lipschits 2005: 27-29.

[69]   Lipschits 2005: 25-29, 137. During the reign of Psammetichus I, Egypt's rule of Palestine was restricted to Philistia and the Negev; Schipper 1999: 230-233.

[70]   The ending of vassalage was of course advantageous: Judah did not have to pay tribute and to provide levies any more.

[71]   Sweeney 1996b: 110, with note 20. If Hardmeier (2000: 121-145) is correct that the early source of 2 Kgs 23 included Josiah's destruction of the altar of Bethel (23:15*), this may show that Josiah aimed to exert religious authority over part of the former kingdom of Israel. For a similar view, see Na'aman 2006b: 141, 165.

[72]   See the royal ideology as expressed in Psalms 2 and 72, and the image of Solomon as 'sovereign over all the kingdoms from the Euphrates to the land of the Philistines, even to the border of Egypt' (1 Kgs 4:21). Cf. Finkelstein 2003: 89, 91.

as a new and felicitous era. The relative political freedom following the Assyrian withdrawal was enough to portray Josiah's reign as a new beginning: the yoke of the oppressor had been broken, a new king ruled in glory. This is precisely the perspective of the revision of the Isaiah material to be situated in this period, as will be shown in the following section.

When Necho II ascended the throne (610 BCE) the political situation changed.[73] Necho's efforts to intensify Egyptian rule in Syria-Palestine involved Judah too.[74] Josiah's death, described in 2 Kgs 23:29, can be understood in the light of the changes in Egyptian policy:

> In his (i.e. Josiah's) days Pharaoh Necho king of Egypt went up to the king of Assyria,[75] to the river Euphrates. King Josiah went to meet him (וַיֵּלֶךְ לִקְרָאתוֹ), but as soon as he (Necho) saw him, he killed him, at Megiddo (וַיְמִיתֵהוּ בִמְגִדּוֹ כִּרְאֹתוֹ אֹתוֹ).

The view that Josiah tried to block off the Egyptian army that came to the aid of the Assyrians, and that he lost his life in battle (cf. 2 Chron 35:20-24) is unlikely. First of all, 2 Kgs 23:29 does not refer to a battle.[76] Furthermore, Josiah had no reason to attempt to stop Necho passing through, since Judah was not threatened and would not stand a chance against Egypt.[77] Another interpretation is preferable.[78] In 610 Necho had succeeded Psammetichus. On his way to the Euphrates to aid the Assyrians, he took the opportunity to let Palestine rulers make obeisance to him, and perhaps to make them join his army with their troops. Josiah went to Megiddo because he was obliged to pay his respects to Necho, but as he appeared before him, Necho had him exe-

---

[73]   Lipschits 2005: 25.

[74]   Schipper 1999: 233; Lipschits 2005: 29.

[75]   The expression עלה עַל here not means 'to march against', but 'to come up to'. According to the Babylonian Chronicle, the Egyptians came to the aid of the Assyrians (Grayson 1975a: 19, 96).

[76]   As Schipper (1999: 235) points out, וַיֵּלֶךְ לִקְרָאתוֹ in most cases is not used in a military sense. If used in a military sense, it denotes the marching out of the army, not a military clash. Schipper concludes that it 'sicherlich nicht zu Kampfeshandlungen gekommen ist'.

[77]   Williamson (1982b; 1987) argues that 2 Chron 35:20-25 goes back to an earlier source, according to which Josiah died while opposing Necho in battle (cf. however the criticism by Begg 1987; Na'aman 1991b: 54, note 69). Even if this is accepted, it must be questioned whether this source is reliable or rather a digression of 2 Kgs 23:29-30. On the other hand, if Josiah *did* attempt to block off Necho's army, it confirms the overconfident and nationalistic mood that characterised his reign.

[78]   Following Na'aman 1991b: 51-55.

cuted. The motive for this probably was Necho's dissatisfaction with the amount of freedom Josiah had taken. Josiah had taken advantage of the power vacuum following the Assyrian retreat by strengthening his kingdom and perhaps modestly expanding it. His political ambitions and the nationalistic propaganda that thrived irritated the Egyptian king.[79] With Josiah's execution, Necho showed that under his rule the bonds of vassalage would be tightened. This was not an incident but part of Necho's vassal policy. After the war of 609, Necho set up his quarters in Riblah and from there probably established his rule over the Levant.[80] Jehoahaz of Judah, who had succeeded his father Josiah, was ordered to Riblah. Necho took him prisoner to Egypt and he appointed Eliakim, another son of Josiah, to the Judaean throne (2 Kgs 23:33-34). To conclude, Josiah's death can be seen in light of the clash between Judah's political ambitions and nationalist ideology, and Necho's policy of tightening his grip on Syria-Palestine.

6.1.4 Themes and Motifs of the Seventh-Century Revision

The prophetic sayings of Isaiah relate to various episodes of the late eighth century (see chapter 4.1). It is likely that these words were preserved in writing and kept in an archive in Jerusalem.[81] The Isaianic material was presumably preserved in the form of several small collections of oracles and sayings,[82] each of which pertained to a particular period: 1) the prophetic words of Isa 7*, 8* and 17:1b-3 relate to 734-732 BCE; 2) the words of Isa 10* and 14:29.31; 28:1-4 relate to 720 BCE; 3) the words of Isa 28-31*, 18-19*, 22*, and 5:8-23*; 10:1-2 relate to 705-701 BCE.

The initial written accounts of Isaiah's words may have involved some editorial activity.[83] However, I focus on what may be regarded as a first substantial revision of the Isaiah material. In my view, such a revision can be detected and attributed to the late seventh century.

---

[79] Cf. Na'aman 2006b: 165-166.

[80] Lipschits 2005: 32. Cf. 2 Kgs 23:33.

[81] See Nissinen 2005: 170-172. On archives, or a library, in Jerusalem, see Davies 1998: 62; Na'aman 2006a; and particularly Van der Toorn 2007: 82-89, 175-178 and 182-184. In Van der Toorn's view, prophetic oracles were part of the material preserved in the temple archive.

[82] See Davies 2000: 72-76; Knauf 2000: 3. For the existence of other kinds of collections, cf. Prov 25:1.

[83] Cf. Van der Toorn 2007: 112-113. An example may be 10:5-15*: the original word of 10:5-9.15a was at an early stage extended to 10:5-9.13-15 (see chapter 2.3.2).

This section contains a survey of the textual material from First Isaiah that reflects the circumstances of the late seventh century and can be attributed to a revision of the Isaiah tradition. The material is characterised by two central themes: the destruction of Assyria carried out by Yahweh, and the reign of a new Judaean king. After this thematic survey, section 6.1.5 deals with the redactional character of this material, focusing on the seventh-century material as a revision of the earlier, prophetic material. Finally, in section 6.1.6 the traditio-historical background of the revision is explored.

The present discussion of the seventh-century revision builds on, and corroborates, the suggestion of the three compilations, discussed in chapter 2.4. The discussion is not repeated here, but the three compilations are briefly described.

Each compilation begins with a dating formula followed by a passage in which the commission of the prophet is described: compilation 1 begins with 6:1-8; compilation 2 with 14:28-32; compilation 3 with 20:1-5*. Furthermore, each compilation adapts a series of prophetic words to which some commentaries are added: compilation 1 adapted the prophetic words of 7:2-3a.4-9a, 14b.16, 20; 8:1-4; 17:1b-3 and added as commentary 8:9-10 and 17:12-14. Compilation 2 adapted the prophetic words of 28:1-4; 10:5-15*, 24-25, 28-32 and added as commentary 14:24-27; 10:11, 16-19, 26a.27a, and 33-34. Compilation 3 adapted the prophetic words of 28:7b-18*; 29:15; 30:1-8*, 15; 31:1.3a; 18:1-2; 19:1b-4; 22:15-18; 5:8-23*; and 10:1-2 and added as commentary 18:1-6; 30:27-33, and 31:4-5.8-9. Finally, each compilation ends with a passage portraying the ideal king: compilation 1 with 9:1-6; compilation 2 with 11:1-5 and compilation 3 with 32:1-2.

The revision thus consisted of the adaptation of existing prophetic material, to which was added some commentary, an introduction dealing with the prophetic commission, and a conclusion portraying the ideal king. The three compilations, consisting of prophetic material presented in a literary garb, are to be regarded as a new, seventh-century, edition of the prophetic texts attributed to Isaiah.[84]

---

[84] This view of a seventh-century edition of the prophetic material attributed to Isaiah corresponds with the general depiction of literary productivity by Van der Toorn 2007: 123-128 (expansion explained as an activity in the context of a new edition), 175-178, 182, 188, 203.

Destruction of Assyria

The first motif of the revision is the destruction of Assyria through Yahweh's intervention (9:3-4; 10:16-19; 10:33-34; 14:25; 30:31-33; 31:8-9). Yahweh destroys Assyria; no human agent is mentioned. The principal means of destruction is fire: Yahweh burns Assyria down.[85] Furthermore, he smites Assyria with a rod (30:31) and raises a whip against Assyria (10:26).[86] 30:27-33 in particular describes Yahweh's violent intervention, by means of fire, cloudburst, tempest and hailstones (30:27-28a, 30). Other motifs of destruction are the imagery of Assyria as wood or trees being destroyed by Yahweh (10:18-19; 10:33-34), Yahweh breaking the yoke (9:3), removing the burden (10:27), and breaking and trampling the Assyrians (14:25).

In Assyrian imperialistic ideology the 'yoke', *nīru*, is an important metaphor.[87] In Assyrian inscriptions 'the yoke', either that of the king or that of the god Aššur, always is the Assyrian yoke depicting Assyria's dominion.[88] The 'yoke' in Isa 9:3, 10:27, and 14:25b,[89] similarly reflects Assyria's dominion. However, in these texts the Assyrian yoke is not just thrown off, but 'broken' (9:3) and 'destroyed' (10:27). This can be regarded as counter-ideology to the Assyrian yoke imagery.[90]

An important aspect of these texts is the fundamental difference between Yahweh and Assyria. Assyria is wood, Yahweh a mighty axe (10:34); Assyria is not destroyed by man, but by the sword of someone not a man (31:8). Assyria is powerless against the might of Yah-

---

[85] The words used are 'fire' (9:4; 10:16, 17; 30:27, 30, 33), a 'fire' that 'consumes' (10:17; 30:27, 30), 'fire' and 'furnace' (אור and תַּנּוּר in 31:9). Cf. also the connection of 'light' (אור in 9:1 and 10:17) with the fire motif.

[86] For עור po. 'to set in motion', 'to arouse', cf. Akk. *êru* D (*kakki*) 'to waken, to arouse (weapons)'.

[87] From Tiglath-pileser III onwards, the yoke-metaphor occurs with increasing frequency in the inscriptions of the Assyrian kings, indicating Assyria's worldwide dominion (see Ruwe and Weise 2002). By contrast, of the Neo-Babylonian kings only Nabonidus uses the yoke-metaphor in this way (see Vanderhooft 1999: 25, note 75).

[88] In the inscriptions of Tiglath-pileser, Sargon and Sennacherib the yoke-metaphor is used for people who have been brought under Assyrian dominion. In the inscriptions of Esarhaddon and Ashurbanipal, the motif of 'throwing off the yoke', indicating rebellion against Assyria, occurs as well. In various contexts the yoke is imposed on people, they drag it, they are submitted to it, and, occasionally, are accused of throwing it off. See Ruwe and Weise 2002: 281-291.

[89] Whereas 9:3 and 10:27 belong to the revision, 14:25b could be a later elaboration based on 9:3 and 10:27 and added when 14:24-27 received its present position separate from the material of Isa 10.

[90] Ruwe and Weise 2002: 297-301.

weh. When Yahweh takes action Assyria falls (10:34; 31:8). The contrast between Yahweh and Assyria is manifest in the use of חתת: Assyria is deadly afraid of the voice of Yahweh (מִקּוֹל יהוה יֵחַת; 30:31),
but Yahweh is not at all afraid of Assyria voice (מִקּוֹלָם לֹא יֵחַת; 31:4).

Assyria's destruction is set in an international perspective. Yahweh's actions against Assyria are presented as integral part of his
worldwide rule. Yahweh's dealing with Assyria (14:24-25; 30:30-33;
31:8-9) is connected with his worldwide authority and supremacy over
the world of the nations (14:26-27; 30:27-29; 31:4-5). 8:9-10 and
17:12-14 can be understood in this light too. These passages, describing the fate of the enemy nations, are marked by an international perspective too. Assyria's 'roar' (הֲמוֹן 31:4) resembles that of the nations
(הֲמוֹן 17:12). Both Assyria and the nations are deadly afraid of Yahweh
(חתת 30:31; 31:9 and 8:9), and both Assyria and the nations flee when
Yahweh intervenes for the sake of his people (נוס 31:8 and 17:13).
Yahweh's dealing with Assyria is part of his worldwide dealing with
enemies threatening Judah.

8:9-10 and 17:12-14 leave open the identity of 'the nations' involved, for the following reason. These passages comment on the prophetic material of 7:4-9a, 7:14b.16 (8:9-10) and 17:1b-3 (17:12-14).
Since these prophecies deal with Aram-Damascus and Ephraim-
Samaria as Judah's enemies, they are implied in the commentary of
8:9-10 and 17:12-14 as well. Furthermore, however, as part of the
seventh-century revision of the Isaiah tradition, 8:9-10 and 17:12-14
apply to Assyria too.[91] This becomes evident in 9:1-6, which likewise
belongs to the revision of the Isaianic material relating to 734-732. In
9:3-4, the enemy is not specified either, but the description leaves no
doubt that Assyria is in mind. The message is that all aggressors will
be dealt with in like manner. From the perspective of the eighth-
century prophetic material, this means Aram and Ephraim; from the
seventh-century point of view this means Assyria.

In the descriptions of the fate of Judah's enemies, focusing on Assyria, the so-called *Völkerkampf*-motif figures prominently.[92] Assyria
is cast in the role of the 'enemy nations' typical of the *Völkerkampf*-
motif. This motif, part of the Jerusalem cult traditions of the monarchic period is applied to Assyria (see 6.1.6 below). The seventh-
century revision presents Yahweh's actions against Assyria as demon-

---

[91]   Cf. Van der Kooij 1990: 7-8.
[92]   For this motif, see Steck 1972: 17-19; Janowski 1989: 185-187.

strating his worldwide dealings. His intervention follows from the protection of his abode Zion, and, by extension, Jerusalem (31:4-5), that is threatened by the aggressors. This traditio-historical background may explain why the Assyrian downfall is located in the land of Judah, more precisely in Zion and Jerusalem (14:24-25; 31:8-9). A central conviction of these texts is that Yahweh governs the international scene. Important in this respect is the reference to Yahweh's plan. This plan, which involves his dealing with the whole world, will be executed; no one can block it off. Yahweh's plan is contrasted with the evil plans of the nations, which are annulled by Yahweh (14:24, 26-27; 8:10). Yahweh's plan for Assyria is part of his plan concerning the whole world (14:24-27).

Assyria's punishment is followed by a joyous celebration of the Judaean people. The disappearance of the Assyrians leads to a cultic celebration, in 30:27-33 (verses 29, 32) and in 9:1-4. The motif of 'happiness' (שִׂמְחָה) occurs in 9:2 and 30:29. In 9:2 this is qualified as happiness *before Yahweh* (שָׂמְחוּ לְפָנֶיךָ), corresponding with the joyous celebration of 30:29, 32. The celebration is compared to 'the joy of the harvest', and the happiness of dividing booty.[93] Both in 9:3 and 10:26 the fate of Midian functions as an image to emphasise the terrible destruction of Assyria. According to 9:3, Yahweh has crushed Assyria's power 'as on the day of Midian', whereas in 10:26, Yahweh raises a whip against Assyria 'like the slaughter of Midian at Rock Oreb'. 9:3 and 10:26 present parallel phrases marked by a similar ideology. The defeat of Midian functions in a similar way in Psalm 83, a hymnal expression of the *Völkerkampf*-motif.[94] In this psalm, 'the enemies' conspire against 'Yahweh's people' in order to 'wipe them out as a nation' (83:3-6). Mentioned are Judah's neighbours, e.g. Edom, Moab, Ammon and the Philistines, and 'also Assyria has joined them' (83:9). After the description of the threat posed to Yahweh's people, there follows in verses 10-13:

> Do to them as you did to Midian, as to Sisera and Jabin at the Wadi Kishon, who were destroyed at En-dor, who became dung for the ground. Make their nobles like Oreb and Zeeb, all their princes like Zebah and Zalmunna, who said, 'Let us take the pastures of God for our own possession.'

---

[93] The shared point is the reaping or collecting of both harvest and booty.
[94] Weber (2000: 72-75) dates this psalm to the Assyrian period.

Both in 9:3 and 10:26 and in Psalm 83, the focus is on Yahweh's intervention: he is to destroy the enemy nations that threaten his people
as he once destroyed Midian. In both cases, Yahweh's violent intervention is rooted in his position as sovereign king of the world (Ps
83:19). It seems clear from 9:3, 10:26 and Psalm 83 that, at least by
the late seventh century, the destruction of Midian served as a paradigm for the terrible fate of Judah's enemies.

Judah's Restoration

In addition to the motif of Assyria's destruction, the seventh-century
revision is characterised by the theme of Judah's restoration. The main
aspect of Judah's restoration is the reign of a new king, in 9:5-6, 11:1-
5, and 32:1-2. Here as well, it is Yahweh who achieves this.[95] By
eliminating Assyria, Yahweh creates room for a new Judaean king.
Significantly, the king is presented only after Yahweh has broken the
power of Assyria: 9:5-6 follows 9:1-4, 11:1-5 follows 10:33-34, and
32:1-2 follows 31:8-9. In 9:1-6, the connection between Assyria's removal and the new king's rule is marked by the parallel of 9:3 and
9:5: after the Assyrian yoke is removed from the *shoulder* (9:3), authority is put on the new king's *shoulder* (9:5). In the case of 10:33-34
and 11:1-5, there is a syntactical connection: first, Yahweh cuts down
the majestic Lebanon (i.e. Assyria, 10:33-34), then the shoot of Jesse
comes out (11:1, *wĕqatal*) on whom Yahweh lets his spirit rest.[96] Finally, in 31:8-9 and 32:1-2, although there is no syntactical connection, the sequence is similar. According to 31:9, Assyria's rock (סֶלַע),
its king, shall pass away in terror, and its functionaries (שָׂרִים) shall
flee. In 32:1-2, the Judaean king and his officials (שָׂרִים) are like a protective rock (סֶלַע). 32:1-2 continues 31:8-9: after Yahweh has cleared
the way by eliminating Assyria, there is room for a new Judaean
king.[97]

Whereas Yahweh brings about Assyria's destruction, the new king
is described as an ideal king, who rules in justice and righteousness.
The king rules in conformity with Yahweh's governance, as the ex-

---

[95]   This is explicated in 9:6b, 'this the zeal of Yahweh Zebaoth will do'. The demonstrative זֹאת refers to the infinitives of 9:4-5, that are presented as Yahweh's actions; Ruwe and Weise 2002: 298-299.

[96]   Beuken 2002: 18, 22.

[97]   Furthermore, the beginning of 32:1-2, the exclamation *hēn*, reacts to the exclamation *hôy* of the *woe*-sayings that figure prominently in the compilation concluded by 32:1-2.

ecutor of Yahweh's just rule (11:2-3), as Yahweh's deputy.[98] Where
Yahweh smites Assyria with a rod (30:31), the righteous king smites
the oppressors with the rod of his mouth (11:4). Furthermore, the just
rule of the king conforms to Yahweh's standards with respect to the
care for the weak. In 14:32, Zion is presented as a refuge for the needy
founded by Yahweh, and in 30:29, Yahweh is referred to as the 'Rock
of Israel'. Similarly, the ideal king is a hiding place and a shelter for
his people, and a rock (32:1-2). The king is the rightful heir to the
throne: he represents the continuation of the throne and the kingdom
of David (9:6). According to 11:1 the king is not only descended from
the house of David, but a new David himself.[99] Furthermore, the king
is presented as wise, pious, and righteous. He is attentive to Yahweh's
will and executes Yahweh's standards. He is powerful and a guardian
of the peace.

Whereas Yahweh is presented as sovereign king governing the
world, the ideal king is presented as ruling his people. 11:4 distinguishes between two categories: the poor and needy protected by the
king, and the wicked and oppressor eliminated by him.[100] The ideal
king protects the poor and the meek.

6.1.5 The Redactional Character of the Revision

Literary Character of the Revision
In contrast to the eighth-century prophetic material which goes back to
orally delivered words, the texts belonging to the revision do not have
an oral background, but are literary in character. The three compilations are to be regarded as literary compositions, originating from a
scribal milieu. The eighth-century material is the written record of
prophetic words that originally were orally delivered. The texts belonging to the revision, by contrast, do not seem to have an oral background.

---

[98] Williamson 1998b: 259.
[99] Williamson 1998a: 55; 1998b: 259. In ancient Near Eastern language, a (royal)
descendant could be referred to as 'sprout', 'shoot', or 'offshoot'; for examples, see
Barth 1977: 70, note 304. The metaphor of the king as a shoot or branch was popular
(cf. Jer 23:5), because it suggested the antiquity of the dynasty (Weinfeld 1995: 65-
66). The 'shoot' that grows out (11:1, Josiah) forms a contrast with the 'branches'
(Assyria) that Yahweh will cut (10:33).
[100] See chapter 2.3.2. For the contrast, cf. Ps 10:2; 37:14; 82:4; 147:6; Isa 25:4;
Prov 29:7.

The revision material of compilation 1 consists of 8:9-10; 17:12-14 and 9:1-6. None of these can be regarded as (going back to) a prophetic word addressed to a third party. 8:10 is a construct of three phrases from the earlier material (7:5, 7, 14b), a product of scribal activity; 9:1-4 addresses Yahweh and thus can hardly be regarded a prophecy; 17:12-14 may look like a *woe*-saying, but it does not address a specified subject. All three texts contain a phrase with first person plural forms (8:10; 9:5; 17:14). These phrases function as explanations: the aggressive plan of the enemies will come to nothing, 'for God is with us' (8:10); the aggressive enemies will be chased off by Yahweh; 'this is the fate of those who despoil us' (17:14); the people have gone from darkness to light, 'for a child has been born to us' (9:5). This is not reminiscent of prophetic style, but rather of a hymnal style. The first-plural references are based on the name 'Immanuel', which occurs in the prophecy of 7:14b.16. In the seventh-century revision, this prophecy is interpreted as the announcement of the destruction of Judah's enemies (8:9-10; 17:12-14) and of the glorious reign of a new king (9:5-6). The events of the late seventh century are presented as the outcome of Isaiah's prophecy and Josiah is glorified as the announced son Immanuel.

The revision texts of compilation 2 consist of 14:28.32; 14:24-27; 10:11; 10:16-19; 10:26a.27a; 10:33-34 and 11:1-5. The passages that respond to the earlier prophecies of 10:5-9.15a; 10:24-25; 10:28-32, provide a commentary in which Yahweh is referred to in the third person: 10:16-19; 10:26a;[101] 10:33-34 and 11:1-5. The theme is that Yahweh strikes Assyria (whereas in the earlier prophecies Assyria is accused of its self-willed 'striking') and that Assyria's brutal rule is changed for a glorious reign of the ideal king. Within 14:24-27, we find divine speech, not as a prophecy, but as an oath sworn by Yahweh. In verses 26-27 the oath is explained: every event in the world happens according to Yahweh's plan (cf. 8:10; 17:14).

The revision texts of compilation 3, 18:1-6; 30:27-33; 31:4-5.8-9 and 32:1-2, focus on the role of Yahweh: his violent intervention and his protection of Zion and Jerusalem. 18:1-6 is a reworking of earlier, prophetic material (18:1-2, 4). The portrayal of Yahweh's epiphany in 30:27-33 begins with *hinnê*, which reminds of Yahweh's interventions announced in the earlier prophetic words included in this compilation,

---

[101]   10:27a is a different case: it adds a new 'prophecy' through the formula 'on that day'.

28:16 *hinĕnî* and 19:1b *hinnê*.[102] 30:27-33 gives a third person description in mythological dress of Yahweh's violent intervention. It is true that in verse 29 the people or Judah are addressed as part of the contrast between Assyria's destruction and the joyful celebration at Zion, but this does not make 30:27-33 a prophecy. 31:4-5.8-9, although introduced (31:4a) and concluded (31:9b) as a divine word, is a literary text. Not only is Yahweh referred to in the third person throughout, but more importantly, the 'word' does not have an addressee. Furthermore, 31:4-5.8-9 is a literary unity (see chapter 2.2.4), which elaborates on the earlier prophetic word of 31:1.3a. In addition, 32:1-2 explicitly relates to 31:9: the rock that passes away in terror (i.e. the Assyrian king) is succeeded by a king who is like a rock that provides protection (i.e. Josiah). In this way, 32:1-2 is also presented as fulfilment of 28:16: the stone in Zion is interpreted as the new king. In order to mark this connection, 32:1 *hēn* alludes to 28:16 *hinĕnî*. The exclamation *hēn* in 32:1 furthermore responds to the exclamation *hôy*, which prominently figures in the early material included in the third compilation. The *hēn*-passage provides a positive counterpart to the critical *hôy*-sayings addressed to the bad leaders. In order to complete the contrast, the 'leaders' are presented together with the ideal king, in 32:1. Neither 31:4-5.8-9 nor 32:1-2 contains an addressee; instead, the passages describe Yahweh's intervention and the glorious situation established thereafter.

In general, the revision texts respond to the earlier prophetic words. Whereas the earlier material is likely to go back to prophecies and sayings that were orally delivered, the revision texts are to be seen as scribal products. As far as these texts are presented as prophecy, it is a form of literary prophecy. Each compilation concludes with a portrayal of the ideal king. In the second part of this chapter (6.2.3) it will be shown that a similar feature occurs in literary prophecies of Mesopotamia. Some of these texts too conclude with a portrayal of the ideal king, which is fictitiously presented as part of a prophecy. A predictive style is used, but it contains glorification of the current king.

Contrast and Coherence
The revision poses two thematic contrasts to the earlier material. The first is the juxtaposition of Yahweh's rule (revision) with Assyria's

---

[102] In 19:1b, the coming (בוא) of Yahweh is referred to as well as in 30:27. Contrary to 30:27-33, 19:1b-4 and 28:15-18 are likely to go back to prophetic oracles.

rule (early material). Whereas in the prophetic words Assyria is presented as a powerful entity, in the revision Assyria has become powerless. This difference, which causes a huge difficulty if the texts are
regarded as all belonging to the same level, can easily be explained
from a difference in historical circumstances between the late eighth
and the late seventh century BCE. In the eighth-century material Assyria figures as a rod that strikes; in the revision Assyria is the one that
is struck by Yahweh.

The second contrast is found in the opposition between the ideal
king in the revision, and the bad leaders criticised in the earlier material. Again, it is difficult to explain both sets of texts on the same
level. In the critical sayings of Isaiah the king is not explicitly referred
to. The reason for this is, that Isaiah, although harshly opposed to
Judah's state policy of 705-701, did not reject Hezekiah. Isaiah supported the king of Judah, as appears from his oracles pertaining to
734-732, and when he rejected Judah's policy, he did not reject the
king but focused his criticism on the political leaders advocating
rebellion. In the light of this position it is highly unlikely that Isaiah
announced the reign of a new Judaean king. Read as eighth-century
prophecy, the portrayals of the ideal king (9:5-6; 11:1-5; 32:1-2)
would imply a rejection of the current king, and this was not part of
Isaiah's message. Both contrasts are worked out.

Yahweh contra Assyria
The main connection between the prophetic material and its revision is
that Assyria from the one that strikes others (prophetic material) becomes the one that is struck (revision). Whereas Assyria is the agent
of Yahweh's anger in 7:20; 8:1-4; 10:5-15*; 28:1-4, in the revision it
becomes the victim of his anger. This retribution is marked by the
adoption of similar terminology:

- In 28:15.18 Assyria is a destroying 'whip' (שׁוט) for the bad leaders of
  Judah, whereas in 10:26 Yahweh raises a 'whip' (שׁוט) against Assyria to
  strike it.
- In 10:24 Assyria smites the people of Zion with a rod and in 14:29 As-
  syria smites the Philistines, whereas in 30:31 Yahweh smites Assyria.
- In 20:5 the people who see Assyria's powerful actions will be afraid
  (חתת), whereas in 30:31; 31:9 (cf. 8:9) Assyria is afraid.
- In 10:5-15* Assyria is the rod of Yahweh's anger, an instrument of
  Yahweh, an axe and saw in his hand (in 7:20 a razor), whereas in 10:34
  Assyria becomes the victim of Yahweh's saw.

- In 14:29.31 the Philistines are forbidden to celebrate the death of the Assyrian king: 'do not rejoice because the rod that struck you is broken'; but in a context of similar terminology describing the end of Assyria's dominance (the 'rod of the oppressor' is 'crushed', 9:3) happiness is appropriate (9:2; 30:29).
- An important element of Assyrian imperialism is looting (8:1-4, 10:6, 10:13). By contrast, Yahweh's intervention not only puts an end to the enemies' looting of Judah (17:14), but also brings 'happiness as with dividing loot' (9:3).

Clearly, both perspectives cannot belong to the same layer; either Assyria is active as a superpower (whether presented as Yahweh's instrument or not), or Assyria's power has come to an end. The best explanation is that the first view of Assyria belongs to the eighth century and the second to the late seventh century.

It is true that already in the Isaianic material a threat is posed to Assyria, in the prophecies of 10:5-15* and 10:24-25. In 10:5, the threat is implied in the exclamation *hôy*, and in 10:25 Yahweh announces: 'For in a very little time the limit will be reached, and then my anger will be directed at their destruction'. This unspecified announcement got a partial fulfilment with the violent death of Sargon II (705 BCE). However, it was only the late seventh-century perspective that considered this announcement as having come true, and expanded on the theme of Assyria's destruction. At this later stage the theme of Yahweh's punishment of Assyria was elaborated:

- In 10:5-15*, Assyria was accused for following its own 'mind' (10:7), which is now contrasted with Yahweh's superior mind, 14:24.
- In 10:5-15* Assyria went astray by turning a specific task into a worldwide expansion; this is contrasted with Yahweh's worldwide authority (14:26-27).
- In 10:5-15* Assyria is no more than Yahweh's instrument (cf. also 31:3a). This contrast between 'man' and 'God' is substantiated in the revision: Yahweh destroys Assyria (e.g. 31:8).

In this respect, the revision does not so much contrast with the earlier prophecies of 10:5-15* and 10:24-25, but expands on them. Threat and announcement are elaborated into clear descriptions of Yahweh's destruction of Assyria as part of his worldwide governance. Again, the two perspectives, although not entirely contrastive, are too different to be explained as on the same level.

Ideal King versus Bad Leaders

Judah's restoration is characterised by values that form a marked contrast to the description of the bad leaders in the polemic sayings of the late eighth century. The rule of the ideal king is characterised by 'justice and righteousness' in 9:6, 11:4-5, and 32:1. It is clear from his critical sayings that Isaiah accuses his opponents of neglecting exactly these values. In the oracle of 28:15-18, accusing the rulers of bad leadership, Yahweh's standard of justice and righteousness is introduced as a contrast to the standards of the bad leaders (28:17).

The values of justice and righteousness are closely connected with the protection of the poor and the weak. The bad leaders are accused in 10:2: 'the poor of my people are robbed of their right'. This is contrasted by 14:32, which presents Zion as a refuge founded by Yahweh for 'the poor of his people'. Furthermore, whereas the bad leaders provide a hiding place and a shelter that are false (28:15-18), the ideal king and his officials provide true shelter (32:2). In particular 32:1-2 directly responds to the critical sayings against the bad leaders. In 28:16 Yahweh announces that he is about to 'lay a foundation stone in Zion'. This meant, originally, that Yahweh would provide a secure refuge at Zion, characterised by justice and righteousness, in contrast to the false and deceptive shelter of the bad leaders. However, in the context of the seventh-century revision of the Isaiah tradition, 28:16 was read as announcing the reign of a new king, which according to this revision, was fulfilled with Josiah's reign (32:1-2). If both perspectives were to be on the same level, one would expect criticism of the current king, which is however absent. Instead, for the revisers, the 'new king' of 32:1-2 is the then current king, Josiah.

Yahweh's Plan

Yahweh's plan is opposed to all human planning and plotting. In the revision, Yahweh is pictured as king of the world whose plans are superior to all human plans (14:24-27). This poses a contrast to the plans of the human beings criticised in Isaiah's prophecies: the enemies of Ahaz (7:5-6), the bad leaders (5:19; 29:15; 30:1), Egypt (19:3), and Assyria (10:6-7). None of these plans came true, because they were opposed to Yahweh's will. Evidently, already the prophetic sayings point to the failure of these plans (7:7; 10:5.15; 19:3; 28:18). The revision however takes two further steps: first, in contrast to all the plans that fail there stands Yahweh's superior plan for the world which comes true (14:24-27), and second, the rule ('counsel and might') of the ideal king is based on, and in accordance with, the plan of Yahweh (9:5; 11:2). Whereas the view of Yahweh's superior, worldwide plan is entirely in agreement with the prophetic material, the second step, the rule of the ideal king as based on, and in accordance with, Yahweh's plan, clearly adds a new perspective. The most likely explanation for this new step is that it belongs to a different stage.

As has been argued in the discussion of the three compilations (chapter 2.4), each passage concerning the ideal king echoes the prophetic material included in the compilation it concludes, but also expands on it. Although the portrayals of the ideal king are presented as the logical outcome of Isaiah's prophecies, and in fact are attributed to Isaiah through the seventh-century revision, they can, in themselves, hardly be characterised as prophecy. 9:1-6, 11:1-5, and 32:1-2, marked by a perspective of royal ideology, are examples of pseudo-prophecy.

6.1.6 *Traditio-Historical Background of the Josiah Revision*

State Ideology of Monarchic Judah
The seventh-century revision of the Isaianic material originates from a scribal milieu and is characterised by a perspective of state ideology, as will be argued in this section.[103] The state ideology of monarchic Judah may be formulated as follows.[104] Yahweh dwells in Zion as sovereign king of the earth and the Judaean king, the son of David, is the legitimate executor of Yahweh's rule. He is Yahweh's deputy, whose government is seen as running parallel to Yahweh's governance.[105] Yahweh's kingship is grounded in his deeds of creation, that is, his victory over the powers of chaos, and in his securing of a stable world. Yahweh protects the order against cosmic and historical forces.[106] The

---

[103] For the scribes in late monarchic Judah, see Van der Toorn 2007: 76-89.

[104] With 'state ideology' I mean the tradition-complexes centred around 'Zion' and 'David'. The precise relationship between these complexes is difficult to establish. Ollenburger (1987: 59) regards 'David' and 'Zion' as the central symbols of two closely related but nevertheless distinguished tradition-complexes. For the Zion tradition, see Dekker 2004: 208-233; Ollenburger 1987: 15-19; Steck 1972: 13-25; Roberts 2002c; Albertz 1994 I: 132-138. For the David tradition, see Albertz 1994 I: 116-122; Roberts 1973. The origin of Judah's state ideology has been a subject of persistent debate. It is generally agreed however that it existed in the Assyrian period.

[105] Ollenburger 1987: 30-31.

[106] Ollenburger 1987.

enemy kings and hostile nations that threaten the order, can be typified as the waters of chaos (Ps 46:3-7; 48:6-8, also in Isa 17:12-13).[107] The values that secure the order against the threats of chaos are justice and righteousness; Yahweh's maintenance of justice and righteousness allows the world to thrive.[108] The king on the throne of David is held to be directly appointed by Yahweh; his rule accords with Yahweh's governance of the earth. The Davidic king is furthermore regarded as the 'son of Yahweh' (Ps 2:2-8; 89:27; 110:3; cf. Isa 9:5). As Yahweh's deputy, the king secures justice and righteousness: he guards the rights of the poor and delivers the weak from the hand of the oppressors.[109] From Yahweh's dwelling in Zion, it followed that Zion and by extension Jerusalem was a place of special protection (cf. Isa 14:32). Zion is the refuge *par excellence* against the forces of chaos, either in terms of the primeval waters or the enemy kings.[110] Zion's privileged status as a divinely protected place led to the belief that Zion and by extension Jerusalem could not be harmed.[111] Violating Zion was an offence against the order destined by Yahweh.[112]

Psalms
The link of the seventh-century revision with the state ideology of Jerusalem appears from resemblances with Psalms in which the Jerusalem traditions are expressed. The main examples include the Zion Psalms (Ps 46; 48; 76), the Royal Psalms (Ps 2; 18; 20; 21; 72; 89;[113] 101; 110), the Enthronement Psalms (Ps 24; 47; 93; 96-99), and various others (Ps 29; 59; 65; 68; 82; 83; 108).[114] Without attempting to be exhaustive, I present the important parallels.

---

[107] Roberts 2002c: 679.
[108] Roberts 2002c: 680-681.
[109] Roberts 2002c: 682-683.
[110] Roberts 2002c: 685.
[111] Cf. Ps 46:6, 48:4, 76:3-4, Mic 3:11; see Ollenburger 1987: 66; Van der Toorn 1996b: 51.
[112] The belief in the inviolability of Zion and by extension Jerusalem, was not unique to the state cult ideology of Judah. Main cults of the Mesopotamian cities had as their central conviction that the holy temples represented the midst of the earth, the dwelling-place of the city god as Lord or as Lady of the world. Because of the presence of the god, the temple and the city were divinely protected places. See Van der Toorn 1996b; Maag 1980: 332-336; Clements 1980b: 77-78.
[113] Ps 89 is likely to date from the exilic period, but contains references to pre-exilic royal traditions; cf. Day 2004: 226, 240.
[114] For the pre-exilic provenance of these Psalms, see Day 2004: 225-237; Seybold 1986: 108-114; Steck 1972: 9-10.

1) The portrayal of Yahweh as sovereign king of the world in 14:26, resembles the expression in Ps 47:3 (similarly Ps 83:19; 97:9; 108:6), 'Yahweh the most high is the great king of the world'. Yahweh's rule clashes with the wicked plans of the nations of the world (Ps 2:1-3; 21:12; 89:10-11.22-23), which is resembled in 8:9-10 and 17:12-14. The 'wicked plan' implies aggression against Zion, but Yahweh subdues and destroys the aggressors and annuls their plans (Ps 47:4; 83:2-19; 97:9; 108:7-14).

2) Yahweh defeats the powers of chaos. The image of powerful, roaring waters occurs in Ps 89:11, 'You crushed Rahab like a carcass, you scattered your enemies with your mighty arm'. Yahweh brings these powers to a stop by rebuking them (נער/גְּעָרָה Ps 18:16; 68:31; 76:7), which is paralleled in Isa 17:13. The enemy nations are identified with the defeated power of chaos. The roar of the waters, just as the uproar of the nations, is eliminated by Yahweh (Ps 46:3-4, 7; 59:7, 15; 65:8; 83:3; terms המה or הָמוֹן), as it is in Isa 17:12-14 and 31:4. Both Ps 18:10 and Isa 31:4 describe Yahweh's violent intervention with ירד, 'to come down'.

3) One of the principal means with which Yahweh destroys the enemies is fire, see Ps 18:9, 13-14; 21:10; 29:7; 46:10; 68:3; 83:15; 97:3. The fire motif figures prominently in the revision of the Isaiah material too: Isa 9:4; 10:16-17; 30:30.33; 31:9. The term 'furnace' (תַּנּוּר) appears both in Ps 21:10 and Isa 31:9 as a means of destruction of the enemies.

4) Yahweh is the light of his people, in Ps 18:29; 76:5; 89:16; 97:4, 11, and paralleled in Isa 9:1; 10:17, over against the darkness of the enemy. Both in Ps 18:29 and Isa 9:1, a light-darkness contrast is made. Connected with this is the motif of 'rescue in the morning' (Ps 46:6; 59:7,15, 17; 101:8), which is also found in Isa 17:14.[115]

5) The people of Yahweh joyfully celebrate the defeat of the enemies that threatened them. The motif of their happiness (שׂמח; שִׂמְחָה) is found in Ps 21:2.7; 46:5; 48:11; 68:4; 97:8 and furthermore in Isa 9:2 and 30:29; or, with the related term גיל 'to exult', in Ps 21:2; 48:12; 65:13; 89:17; 97:8 and Isa 9:2. Related to the 'joy' is the motif of dividing spoil, which occurs in Ps 68:13 and in Isa 9:3.

6) The values of justice and righteousness, which are closely connected with the protection of the poor and the weak (Ps 18:27; 72:2.4),

---

[115] See Janowski 1989: 180-191, relating this motif to the Jerusalem cult tradition.

are a principal motif both in these Psalms and in the revision (9:5-6; 11:1-5; 32:1). The image of the righteous king and his just rule is the focus of Isa 11:1-5 and Psalm 72.[116]

7) In 14:32, the special character of Zion is emphasised: 'Yahweh has founded Zion, and the needy among his people will find refuge in her'. The motif of divine foundation of Zion and the protective character of Zion as the place where Yahweh dwells and from which the king as Yahweh's executor rules, is found in the Psalms (Ps 2:6; 20:2; 48; 76; 78:68-69; 87; 110).[117] The motif of the divine foundation of Zion-Jerusalem reflects the special status attached to Jerusalem and its temple. The motif of divine foundation is similarly attested for important cities such as Babylon and Nineveh. The supreme role of these cities is presented as a cosmic arrangement: the city is portrayed as a cosmic datum, like the stars, the mountains or the sea. As a consequence, challenging the supremacy of the city is madness, as much as an attempt to defy nature and the elements.[118] In particular in the seventh century when Jerusalem had become an important city, traditions concerning its special status prospered.[119] The revision of the Isaiah tradition can be seen in the light of the outburst of nationalistic ideology during the reign of Josiah. The state ideology of monarchic Jerusalem is the background to the revision of the Isaianic material.[120]

---

[116] See Wagner 2006: 208-212, on the 'צדק-Tradition' of pre-exilic Jerusalem, and 213-217, on Isa 9:6 in connection with Ps 72:1-7.

[117] For the motif of the gods as the founders of temples and cities, see Hurowitz 1992: 332-337; Bolin 2003: 172-175; Weinfeld 1998: 33.

[118] Bolin 2003: 175.

[119] Steiner 2003a: 79: 'It was the only town in the wide region that had not been taken by the mighty Assyrians. It had grown to huge dimensions, mainly because of the many refugees fleeing to this "safe haven". All economic and political power of the country was concentrated within its walls. This "special status", in so many respects, could have given rise to a change in religious significance and importance as well.'

[120] Barth (1977: 272-323) suggests a fourfold traditio-historical background for the revision. 1) First and foremost, Barth identifies the influence from the Jerusalem cult traditions, such as the *Völkerkampf* motif, royal ideology, epiphany and intervention of Yahweh, the motif of Yahweh's fire at Zion, and Zion as refuge. 2) Furthermore, Barth proposes influence from 'altisraelitisch-altjudäische Traditionen' (1977: 228-229), evident in a 'gesamtisraelitische Interesse', such as the motifs of the throne of David and the 'Day of Midian' (9:4). 3) Barth sees the influence of the wisdom tradition; and 4) Barth discerns a 'prophetische Prägung' of the Josiah revision. However, Barth's second point, the 'gesamtisraelitische Interesse' pertains to elements that, by the seventh century, had become integrated in the traditions of the state ideology. The ideal of a great Israel under Davidic rule had become part of the Jerusalem tradition, and Psalm 83 testifies that in the Assyrian period the tradition of Midian's destruction was integrated into the Jerusalem cult tradition (Barth [1977: 176, note

Ideal King

In 9:5-6, 11:1-5 and 32:1-2 the ideal king is depicted as a Davidic king (9:6; 11:1), as son and child (9:5), as new shoot or branch (11:1) and as a guardian of justice and righteousness.[121] In each passage the ideal king is characterised by his exceptional qualities, which in general terms resembles the portrayal of the king for instance in Psalms 2 and 110. Although the reference to the king as 'son' in 9:5 does not necessarily mean 'son of Yahweh' (as in Ps 2:6), the king is portrayed in 9:5-6 in conformity with the Davidic ideology.[122] The king is presented as Yahweh's agent, whose rule inaugurates and maintains God's ideal for Judah.[123] The rule of the king closely coincides with Yahweh's rule. This explains why in 32:2, the reign of the king and his officials is depicted in imagery normally used to depict Yahweh's role towards his people (e.g. the king as refuge and protective rock).[124] The royal names of 9:5, indicating the almost godlike appearance of the king, can be understood from the close association between Yahweh and the ideal king as well. These names 'wonderful decider',[125] 'mighty god',[126] 'eternal father',[127] and 'prince of peace',[128] are to be understood against

---

237] acknowledges that at the time of Josiah the Jerusalem cult tradition was 'in altisrealitische-landjudäischem Sinne neuakzentuiert'). Barth's third point, the wisdom tradition, may be correct, but does not detract from the state ideological traditions either. The main motif in this respect is Yahweh's plan (e.g. Isa 14:26), which points to his position as the sovereign king. The motif of Yahweh as sovereign king whose plan governs the earth, belongs to state ideology. Barth's final point, the 'prophetische Prägung' of the revision, may be disputed. A revision of prophetic material is not necessarily prophetic itself. As far as the revision is prophetic, it is a form of literary prophecy, which originated from a scribal milieu. To conclude, the principal traditio-historical background of the revision is the Jerusalem state ideology.

[121] Williamson (1998a: 30-72) makes a strong case for the pre-exilic character of the three ideal king passages, 9:1-6, 11:1-5 and 32:1-5 (in my opinion to be restricted to 32:1-2, see chapter 2.2.4).

[122] See Williamson 1998a: 35-42. Williamson (1998b: 255-257) points out that 9:5-6 is close to 2 Sam 7:12-17 and Ps 72. Barth (1977: 169-170) argues that 9:5-6 refers to a historical king (not to a messianic figure), and that the names have general parallels in the Jerusalem cult ideology, e.g. 2 Sam 23:5, Ps 20:5; 21:5; 45:7; 72:3-5.

[123] Williamson 1998a: 35, 50.

[124] Williamson 1998a: 66.

[125] The term יוֹעֵץ is to be understood as 'planner', 'decision-maker'. The title means: 'he who takes decisions, based on divine (secret) knowledge'; cf. Wildberger 1972-82: 381-382; Wagner 2006: 223.

[126] Or 'godlike hero' (cf. Ezek 32:21). This title resembles the Assyrian royal epithet *ilu qarrādu*; Seux 1967: 108; Carlson 1974: 134; Wagner 2006: 224.

[127] De Boer (1955: 58) suggests understanding father as 'he who makes decisions' and eternal as 'with regard to the future'. See further Wagner 2006: 224.

a background of ancient Near Eastern royal titulary.[129] The three passages must be connected with each other, for two reasons. First, each
of them forms the conclusion to a compilation of earlier, prophetic
material in a revised form (see chapter 2.4). Second, all three of them
present the king as being in close association with Yahweh.

The ideal king passages are different in outlook from the eighth-
century prophecies—both from the encouraging oracles (such as 7:4-
9a), and from the critical sayings—and are clearly marked by royal
ideology. The thesis of this chapter is, that the ideal king is most plausibly identified as Josiah. The suggestion that the words 'shoot' and
'branch' (11:1) refer to Josiah as a juvenile king (cf. 2 Kgs 22:1) is to
be rejected, since 'shoot' and 'branch' simply mean descendant.[130]
However, behind the expression 'stump (גֵּזַע) of Jesse' (11:1) one
might suspect a reference to the murder of Josiah's father Amon (2
Kgs 21:23). The tree of David was cut, but from the stump a new
branch came out: Josiah. He is presented as a second David, his reign
as a new beginning.[131] This at least fits the ideology of Josiah's reign.
The identity of the king is not explicitly revealed, because the portrayals of the ideal king are presented as prophecies of Isaiah. The fiction
of the revision is that the prophet Isaiah announced the glorious reign
of Josiah.

---

[128] According to Wagner (2006: 225) this echoes the Assyrian word for king
(šarru); the 'prince of peace' forms a counter-image to the Assyrian kingship characterised by military expansion and war.
[129] Wagner (2006: 227) concludes that the names can be understood as deriving
from Assyrian royal epithets, but the parallels he mentions (2006: 222-225) are to
some extent rather general. In addition, various glorifying descriptions from Ashurbanipal's court poetry may be mentioned, as a general parallel to Isa 9:5-6: 'representative', 'deputy' of Aššur (SAA 3 1 r. 8, 26:1), 'warrior king' (šarru qarrādu, SAA 3
27:4); 'May eloquence, understanding, justice and righteousness be given to him as a
gift! (...) Ashurbanipal is the [representative] of Aššur, the creation of his hands. May
the great gods make firm his reign, may they protect the life [of Ashurba]nipal, king
of Assyria! May they give him a straight sceptre to extend the land and his people!
May his reign be renewed, and may they consolidate his royal throne for ever!' (SAA
3 11:8, 15-18); 'creation of Aššur [and] Šamaš (...) the vast in understanding, the
fa[thomless] mind, the competent, the ord[erly], the wizard, (...) the king of righteousness' (SAA 3 25 r. 17'-23'). Translations based on Livingstone SAA 3.
[130] See the discussion and criticism of this view in Williamson 1998a: 53, note 41.
[131] Cf. Williamson 1998a: 70.

6.1.7   *The Josiah Revision*

Evaluation

The reign of Josiah provides the most plausible setting for a revision of the Isaiah tradition. During the seventh century Jerusalem became an important city, the economic, political and social centre of Judah,[132] and Judah had developed into a centralised state.[133] The B1-story reveals the views prevailing in seventh-century Jerusalem: Yahweh had protected his city against the Assyrian aggression, and punished Sennacherib for his offences. In c. 630-623, Assyria lost its dominion of Syria-Palestine and Judah enjoyed several decades of relative independence during Josiah's reign. The reform account 2 Kgs 23:4-7*.11-12* shows that the reign of Josiah in contemporary ideology was presented as a period of revival. The account portrays Josiah's measures of purification and reorganisation of the Jerusalem temple as the opposite of what his predecessors, 'the kings of Judah', had done.[134] During Josiah's reign Judah probably had the ambition of enlarging its territory and extending its rule over (parts of) the former Northern Kingdom. The political ambitions were supported by political-ideological propaganda, in which Josiah was presented as the new David (cf. 11:1).[135]

The hope, ambitions and ideology of the time provide a plausible setting for the revision of the Isaianic material.[136] The two main topics of the revision, the liberation of Judah from the Assyrian yoke and the independent rule of a Judaean king, both point to the time of Josiah.[137] The ideological message of the revision is that the reign of Josiah was a turn for the good: through Yahweh's intervention a troubled period was brought to an end and a new time began characterised by the

---

[132]   Steiner 2003a: 75-79; 2001: 109-111; Geva 2003; Reich and Shukron 2003; Killebrew 2003: 335-338.

[133]   Na'aman 1991b: 23-33.

[134]   Whereas the B1-story from the mid-seventh century and the revision of the Isaiah tradition from the late seventh century are best located in the circles of the royal court, the early reform account can be associated with temple circles.

[135]   E.g. Laato 1992: 364; Sweeney 2001: 238; cf. Christensen 1984. In general terms I agree with the ideas presented in these studies. However, Laato and Sweeney are, in my view, too confident with regard to the biblical description of Josiah's reform, and take too much from the prophetic books as pre-exilic material.

[136]   See Barth 1977: 174-175, 205 with note 12, 228, 237, and 255.

[137]   This is Barth's main argument and it has not lost its plausibility (1977: 176-177, 250-260); cf. similarly, Collins 1993: 38-39.

reign of a new king. The theme of a new and glorious time after a period of trouble is a prominent feature in royal ideology.[138]

Logic of the Development of the Isaiah Tradition
The revisers of the Isaiah tradition believed that the historical events
of their time, Assyria's retreat and Judah's relative independence under Josiah, proved Isaiah right. Through their revision they attempted
to show that Isaiah's words had been fulfilled. Isaiah's prophecies
against Assyria (10:5-9.15a, 10:24-25) were believed to be fulfilled
with Assyria's withdrawal from Syria-Palestine and the grave troubles
it was facing at home. Furthermore, the announcements concerning
the son Immanuel (7:14b.16) and the foundation stone at Zion (28:16)
were applied to Josiah. Finally, according to the revisers, history had
proved that Isaiah was right not to trust in Egypt but to leave things to
Yahweh: it was Yahweh who put an end to Assyria's oppression
thereby creating room for a new and independent Judaean king. Yahweh had not only caused Sennacherib's retreat in 701 and his violent
death in Nineveh (the B1-story), but also the decline and fall of the
empire as a whole.[139]

The purpose of the seventh-century revision was to provide ideological support for the position of Josiah and to add to the glory of
Yahweh and his king. In the revision, Josiah's kingship is glorified not
so much in terms of political expansion or in terms of cultic reform,
but in terms of his legitimacy as Yahweh's deputy and in terms of social justice. These are the particular accents of the Josiah revision. The
revision can be regarded as promoting state ideology, but with specific
accents emphasising the close ties between Yahweh and his king.[140]

In the seventh century, the authority of 'Isaiah the prophet' was ris-
ing. At that time, Isaiah had won the reputation of having been right,
and the preserved oracles and sayings attributed to him were re-edited
as part of a Josiah revision, emphasising Assyria's downfall and glorifying Yahweh and his king. This is reflected both by the revision of
the prophetic material attributed to him, and from his role in the B1-
story. In the seventh century, the image of the prophet Isaiah was un-

---

[138] With regard to Josiah, this theme is apparent in the early account of the reform
(2 Kgs 23:4-15*) and in the revision, in particular in Isa 9:1-6. This theme appears
prominently in the so-called literary prophecies, which will be discussed in 6.2.3.

[139] Cf. Clements 1980b: 83.

[140] Barth (1977: 230-231, with note 34) proposes a liturgical setting for the Josiah
revision (the use of the prophetic tradition for liturgical purposes).

ambiguous: both in the Hezekiah story and in the revision the prophet is portrayed as a supporter of king and state.

The image of Isaiah changed drastically in the later period, due to the disastrous events of the sixth century. The disasters caused a profound political and religious crisis,[141] as they falsified the current state ideology.[142] Afterwards the catastrophe was interpreted, explained and justified in theological terms.[143] Significant parts of the biblical prophetic books can be understood as resulting from this kind of interpretation, explanation and justification of what had happened. Many texts from the prophetic books present the disastrous events as the result of Yahweh's punishment of the sins of his people. These texts are better regarded as the product of reflection rather than as the message of the 'classical prophets'.[144] The general concepts of 'blame to all' and 'total punishment' implying the collapse of the social order, are difficult to imagine at a time when society, temple, cult, and king, were functioning. The concept of a complete destruction of a corrupt society is likely to be of a retrospective character. Importantly, theological explanation and justification of historical events occur not only in the Old Testament, but also in the literature of the ancient Near East.[145] Experiences of misfortune were afterwards explained in theological terms. Reflection followed historical events, which were explained, interpreted or justified. It is unlikely that in the preaching of the 'classical prophets' reflection preceded the events, whereas in the rest of the ancient Near East it followed the events (see also the discussion of the 'classical prophets' in chapter 5.2.2).

The sixth-century catastrophe did not mean the end of the Isaiah tradition, but a new and decisive step in its development. In response to the disastrous events the Isaiah tradition underwent a transformation, through which the prophetic image and his message became revised and adapted to the new situation.[146] The deployment of Isaiah's authority for a theological explanation of the sixth-century disasters was a crucial step in the development of the Isaiah tradition into the later book. Characteristic of the exilic reworking of the Isaiah tradition

---

[141] Pohlmann 2002: 40-60, esp. 40-41. The ideological crisis can be grasped from e.g. Psalms 74 and 79.
[142] Steck 1972: 46-51.
[143] Pohlmann 2002: 43-48.
[144] Pohlmann 2002: 48-50.
[145] Van der Toorn 1985: 56.
[146] Collins 1993: 39-40.

was first the view that, like Israel, Judah too had been punished for its sins, and second the generalisation of specific criticism against Isaiah's opponents, the leading class of Jerusalem, applying it to the people as a whole. In particular Isaiah's sayings against his political opponents were a useful handle for retrospective explanations for the disasters that had befallen Judah.

I discern a development of the Isaiah tradition consisting of three stages prior to Second Isaiah. First is the prophetic material from the later part of the eighth century. This material contains both an encouraging, supportive component and a critical component (comparable to prophecy elsewhere in the ancient Near East). As a second stage, I discern a literary revision of the Isaianic material, to be dated to the late seventh century. This revision is in continuity with the supportive component of Isaiah's prophecies and provides a positive counterpart to his critical sayings. Thirdly, an exilic reworking of the Isaiah tradition sought to explain the disasters that had befallen Judah as Yahweh's punishment of the grave sins of the people. As a result, Isaiah was turned into a prophet of judgement. This reworking took up and expanded the critical sayings of Isaiah, and provided a negative counterpart to his encouraging prophecies. Each stage, the eighth-century prophetic words, the seventh-century royal-ideological revision, and the exilic reworking, closely related to the historical events of the time.

This survey supports the view that the origins of prophetic literature are to be found in the last two centuries of the Judaean monarchy, but that it is from the exilic period onwards that literary prophecy increasingly took flight.[147] Whereas Isaiah's message was recorded in the eighth century and literarily developed in the seventh, it was only the exilic redaction that the Isaiah tradition explicitly presented itself as a written tradition (Isa 8:16).

---

[147] Van Seters 2000: 88; similarly Collins 1993: 16, 37-40. I also agree with Clements (1997: 9) that 'it is the rise and fall, and subsequent re-establishing after 587 BCE, of the cult ideology of Jerusalem that explains the peculiar shifts and apparent incongruities in the book (i.e. the book of Isaiah).'

6.2 *Assyrian Prophecy in Literature*

The development of Assyrian prophecies has been described by Nissinen as follows:

> Under Esarhaddon and Ashurbanipal, Assyrian prophecy apparently developed from spoken performance into an established written tradition that became a source of intellectual inspiration and scholarly interpretation. ... The process was too short to bear fruit comparable to the blossoming of the prophetic literature in the Hebrew Bible; nevertheless, this development already demonstrates the initial phases of emergence of prophetic books.[148]

Previous surveys of the development of Assyrian prophecies have been restricted to the so-called oracle collections (SAA 9 1 and 2). In the section 6.2.1, I adopt a broader approach: apart from the formation of oracle collections, I discuss some examples of oracles referred to in letters, the inclusion of oracles in royal inscriptions, and the development of oracles into literary texts. In this way, I explore the different ways in which prophetic oracles that once were orally delivered afterwards found their way into literature.

In section 6.2.2, I deal with another group of texts, namely texts of literary origin closely resembling prophetic oracles. These texts, from seventh-century Assyria, can be considered as literary derivatives of prophecy. There are close connections between the oracles that found their way into literature (discussed in 6.2.1) and the literary derivatives of prophecy (discussed in 6.2.2). SAA 9 9, a prophetic oracle in a literary garb (6.2.1), is particularly close to SAA 3 13, a literary derivative of prophecy (6.2.2). SAA 3 44, a literary text resembling the prophetic genre (6.2.2) shares important traits with SAA 9 3.3, which is part of a literary reworking of prophecies (6.2.1). From seventh-century Assyria we have on the one hand prophetic oracles that enjoyed a second life as part of a collection or in a literary, elaborate form, and on the other hand texts that were produced that were literary in origin, but that adopted or imitated the prophetic genre. These two sets of texts, which because of their shared characteristics should be studied together, evidence the development from prophecy into literature in seventh-century Assyria.

A final group of texts, discussed in 6.2.3, consists of examples of literary texts containing pseudo-predictions. These texts include imita-

---

[148]   Nissinen 2000a: 254; similarly Weippert 2002: 35.

tions of prophecy. They deploy a predictive, prophetic form for expressing a royal ideological perspective. Unlike the texts discussed in
6.2.1 and 6.2.2, the texts discussed in the third subsection date from
different periods and can be regarded as exponents of the 'stream of
tradition'.[149] Several of these texts were known, probably well-known
in scribal circles, in the Assyrian period, in particular during the reigns
of Esarhaddon and Ashurbanipal. This additional set of texts is taken
into account in order to provide a counterpart to the seventh-century
revision of the Isaiah tradition as a literary phenomenon.[150]

The discussion of the phenomenon of prophecy becoming literature
is thus not restricted to the Assyrian prophetic oracles, but also takes
some literary texts into account. I have chosen this broad approach for
two reasons. First, there is as will be demonstrated a close relation between reworked oracles (6.2.1) and literary derivatives of prophecy
(6.2.2); these two kinds of texts form part of a similar phenomenon,
and must not be discussed in isolation from each other. The second
reason pertains to the comparative purpose of this chapter. In 6.1 the
revision of the Isaiah tradition was approached from two angles: the
prophetic material being revised and the literary-redactional character
of the revision. To the first aspect, the material discussed in 6.2.1
forms a counterpart, whereas 6.2.2 and 6.2.3 form a counterpart to the
second aspect.

6.2.1   *The Prophetic Oracles*

This section explores the literary afterlife of the Assyrian oracles.
Originally, oracles are part of the situational communication between
god and man (in the oracles at our disposal mostly the king). Oracles
belong to specific moments and relate to particular, often critical,
situations. They were written down, at least occasionally, in order to
facilitate their communication to the king.[151] In the case of the Mari
prophecies, the process of recording the prophetic oracles remained
mostly limited to this initial stage. These prophecies are reports of

---

[149]   For this term, see Oppenheim 1977: 13.
[150]   See the discussion in chapter 1.2.3, on the importance of comparative study of
prophecy as a *literary phenomenon*, with the reference to Grabbe 1995: 94.
[151]   Pongratz-Leisten 1999: 267-268; Nissinen 2000a: 239-242, 268-269. It is furthermore possible that oracles sometimes were recorded after deliverance, for the sake
of remembrance or later checking.

newly received oracles that were recorded in letters to the king.[152] Most of the Assyrian oracles, however, are preserved as secondary records.[153] After the oracles had been used in the political decision-making, they could be preserved for memory in a written document. At least during the reigns of Esarhaddon and Ashurbanipal, prophetic oracles were written down for a second time. Whereas oracles originally belonged to a particular situation, at a secondary stage they were dissociated from their original context and divinatory frame and became part of a new constellation of meaning. The oracles exceeded their original, situational perspective and became part of a wider perspective, looking back on a longer episode of connected events.[154] Thus, after deliverance Assyrian prophetic oracles sometimes served a longer-term purpose. This second stage is characterised by editorial selection and stylisation of the oracles. Prophecies were reused for new situations and became part of the written tradition.[155] As part of this process, I will discuss the collections of oracles, some examples of oracles referred to in letters, oracles included in royal inscriptions, and the oracles integrated into literary texts.

Collections of Oracles

The corpus of Assyrian prophecies contains two compendia of oracles (SAA 9 1 and 2) and a fragment of a third one (SAA 9 4).[156] The texts are compilations of previously delivered and recorded oracles. The compilations seem to imply that the divine promises made in the oracles were regarded as being still operative. As part of a collection, the oracles transcended the original historical situations and received a more generally applicable meaning.[157] The compendia are not to be

---

[152] Parker (1993: 60) however argues that authors sometimes took considerable freedom in formulating the prophetic oracles they reported. Schart (1995) mentions examples of Mari letters reporting prophecy that show traces of reworking or reshaping of the oracles by the author of the letter. Furthermore, among the Mari texts an example has been found of a prophetic oracle included within a literary text: the Epic of Zimri-Lim (see Nissinen 2003a: 90).

[153] The Assyrian material contains a few examples of firsthand records of prophecy. Several letters to the king report a prophetic oracle in order to inform the king. Within the SAA 9 corpus, texts 6, 10 and 11 can be regarded as containing reports of oracles, either as part of a letter or as an independent report.

[154] Pongratz-Leisten 1999: 283; Van der Toorn 2007: 15.

[155] Nissinen 2003a: 98; Nissinen 2000a; Van der Toorn 2000b.

[156] SAA 9 3 is not a collection of prophetic oracles (see chapter 3.1.1 and below).

[157] Nissinen 2000a: 254; Schart 1995: 92.

seen as mere anthologies, but rather as compositions.[158] The oracles included enjoyed a second life, as part of a more general perspective, illustrating the close relation between king and gods.

The first collection (SAA 9 1) has as its theme the divine protection
of Esarhaddon against all enemies, internal and external, that threaten
his royal position. The annihilation of the enemies and the protection
of Esarhaddon's kingship is referred to in almost every oracle. A crucial referential point is the intervention of Ištar in the struggle for the
throne of Assyria as the example *par excellence* of Esarhaddon's divine protection. At the same time, various oracles emphasise that just
as the gods have protected Esarhaddon in the past (i.e. in the struggle
for the throne), they will protect him against his enemies in future (i
15'-16'; ii 34'-37'; vi 7-12). The combination of oracles concerning
the struggle for the throne (e.g. 1.8) and from later moments of
Esarhaddon's reign (e.g. 1.1, 1.6) emphasises that Esarhaddon in all
his actions is guarded and protected by the gods. The final sentence of
the last oracle (1.10), 'Your son and your grandson shall rule as kings
on the lap of Ninurta', which had its original setting shortly after
Esarhaddon's accession to the throne, may indicate the compositional
purport of the compendium. Parpola suggested to connect SAA 9 1
with the Nineveh A inscription (673), and to regard both texts as being
connected with Ashurbanipal's appointment as the crown prince in
672 BCE.[159]

The second collection (SAA 9 2) has as its main theme the stabilisation and consolidation of Esarhaddon's reign. Recurrent motifs are
the reconciliation with the gods, and the care for Babylon and the
Babylonian gods. Parpola's suggestion that this composition may be
related to Esarhaddon's Assur A inscription (679 BCE) is unlikely.[160]
Alternatively, the composition of collection 2 may be connected with
a version of Esarhaddon's Babylonian inscription.[161]

---

[158]   There is no evidence that the compendia functioned as a source of oracles for
other compositions, such as royal inscriptions (contra Cancik-Kirschbaum 2003: 42).
[159]   Parpola 1997: LXIX-LXX. See for this also chapter 4.2.4.
[160]   Parpola 1997: LXIX-LXX. SAA 9 2 is unlikely to date from before 675, as appears from unit 2.4, discussed in chapter 4.2.3.
[161]   For the dating of Esarhaddon's inscriptions, see Porter 1993: 169-176. If the
proposed connection with the Babylon inscription makes sense, it is perhaps with the
later C/F version (674 or later).

In both compendia the oracles are presented with uniform colo-phons.[162] The uniform presentations betray an editorial hand. To what extent the oracles themselves have been edited is difficult to deter-mine. Since many of them are considerably longer than the average length of oracles reported in letters, it might be suspected that they were embellished by the composers of the collections.[163] The oracles cannot self-evidently be taken as the *ipsissima verba* of the prophets. On the other hand, the great variety in address of Esarhaddon, the in-troduction of the deity, and references to past and future, suggests that they were to some extent merely reproduced. In any case, the oracles were presumably carefully arranged. Although the editing may have been limited, the oracles are displayed in a new, compositional garb.

Quotations of Oracles in Letters

In various letters addressed to the king prophetic oracles have received a second life. These letters do not report a new prophetic oracle, but refer to, or quote from, an earlier oracle. The purpose of a quotation or paraphrase of prophetic oracles in letters is to support the author's standpoint before the king. The divine word is used secondarily as an argument. A main characteristic is that no reference is made to the in-termediary, the prophet or prophetess, as is normally the case when a new oracle is reported. Only the content of the oracle, formulated in condensed wording, matters. These quotations from, or references to, prophetic oracles mean a reuse or a recycling of prophecy. The prophecies are secondarily adapted to a new situation.

In the letter SAA 10 109 Bel-ušezib reminds Esarhaddon that it was he who reported an oracle in which Esarhaddon's kingship was announced and again quotes from the oracle (13'-15'): 'Esarhaddon will rebuild Babylon and restore Esagila and [*honour*] me'. The rea-son for this reminder is that Bel-ušezib wants Esarhaddon to pay attention to the request.

In the letter SAA 10 111, Bel-ušezib quotes from an oracle of Mar-duk concerning Esarhaddon's supremacy (r. 23-26). The letter as a whole deals with the war against Mannea, and concludes with the quo-tation: 'Bel has said: "Esarhaddon, king of Assyria (sits) on the throne

---

[162] SAA 9 1: *ša pî*, 'from the mouth of', followed by a personal name and city name; separated from the oracle and the following oracle with single rulings. SAA 9 2: *issu pî*, 'from the mouth of', followed by a personal name and city name; separated from the following oracle by a single ruling.

[163] For this view, see Villard 2001: 75-78.

like Marduk-šapik-zeri, and while he is seated there I will deliver all the countries into his hands".' The original oracle probably did not relate to the Mannean war, but presented Esarhaddon as legitimate king of Babylon and supreme ruler of the world. Bel-ušezib applied the oracle to a new situation.[164]

In the letter SAA 10 284, Nabû-nadin-šumi, a high-ranking scholar, reminds the king of a prophecy of Ištar of Nineveh and Ištar of Arbela: 'We shall root out from Assyria those who are not loyal to the king, our lord!' On the basis of this prophecy, Nabû-nadin-šumi urges the king concerning a presumed troublemaker: 'really, let him be rooted out from Assyria'. The letter does not contain an exact quotation of an oracle but a concise paraphrase.[165] The author uses the divine announcement to reinforce his standpoint that a supposed troublemaker should be punished. The original oracle is lifted from its original situation and adapted to a new one.

The royal official Nabû-reḫtu-uṣur in various letters warns Esarhaddon against a supposed coup d'état (SAA 16 59-61). He quotes or paraphrases several prophetic oracles in favour of the king, which he apparently had at his disposal. These quotations or paraphrases, fluently integrated into the argument, serve as reinforcement of his position that the supposed rebels must be immediately executed (for the oracles, see chapter 4.2.5).

These cases show that prophetic oracles were used secondarily in support of one's position and could be applied to new circumstances.[166] The formulation of the prophecies was probably adapted to serve a new purpose.

In addition to these examples, one case may be mentioned in which the quotation of an oracle has become integrated into a letter with a literary-ideological purpose. In the letter SAA 10 174 (dated to 667 BCE), Marduk-šumu-uṣur the chief haruspex reminds Ashurbanipal of an oracle of the god Sin of Harran to his father Esarhaddon, announcing the conquest of Egypt (l. 10-16). This text is an exposition of the

---

[164] A similar re-use of a prophetic oracle is found in the letter ABL 839 (published by Mattila 1987).

[165] The goddesses' address to Esarhaddon as 'the king, our lord' (r. 6) must be Nabû-[nadin]-šumi's formulation, as this is how functionaries address the king.

[166] The flexibility with which authors applied oracles to certain events is comparable to the flexible dealing with astrological omens in letters that attempt to give the king good news; for this, see Lanfranchi 1989: 111.

ideology supporting Ashurbanipal's kingship, focusing on the divine favour of his dynasty, in the form of a letter:

> [1-6] To the king, lord of kings, my lord, and Aššur, the highest [god], [who] by his holy and unchangeable command [... has ordered] a thousand years of life for the king, my lord: your servant Marduk-šumu-uṣur. [May] Sin and Šamaš [attend to] the health of the king, my lord! May Nabû and Marduk [give] name and seed to the king, my lord! May the Lady of Nineveh and Ištar of Arbela guide [you] like a mother and sister!
> [7-9] Aššur, in a dream, called the grandfather of the king, my lord, a sage. The king, lord of kings (i.e. Ashurbanipal), is an offspring of a sage and Adapa: you have surpassed the wisdom of the Abyss and all scholarship.
> [10-16] When the father of the king, my lord, wen[t] to Egypt, a temple of cedar was bu[ilt] outside the city of Harran. Sin was seated upon a staff, with two crowns on (his) head, and (the god) Nusku stood before him. The father of the king, my lord, entered; he placed (the crowns) on his head (and it was said to him): 'You will go and conquer the world with it!' [So he we]nt and conquered Egypt. The king, the lord of kings (i.e. Ashurbanipal), will conquer the rest of the countries [which] have not submitted to Aššur and Sin.
> [17-23] [May] Aššur, Sin, Šamaš, Adad, Bel and Nabû, Ninurta, [Nergal] and Nusku, Ištar of Nineveh, Ištar of Arbela [give] an everlasting throne, a l[ong] reign, [...] peace and prosperity [...], arrow [...]. (*break*)
> [r.] [...] your [royal] fathers [...] come before the king, lord of kings [...] a thousand years, Aššur and the [great] gods [...] the king, the sun of the people [...] Aššur [...] witness [...] to fear you [...] before Aššur and the great gods [....].[167]

The introduction (l. 1-6) is remarkable: not only the king but also the god Aššur is addressed. The blessing formula differs from that of the other letters by the same writer (cf. SAA 10 173, 175-177). The second part (l. 7-9) refers to a dream of Sennacherib and applies this to Ashurbanipal: since Sennacherib was called a sage (*apkallu*) by Aššur, Ashurbanipal is an offspring of a sage (Sennacherib), and hence an offspring of Adapa, legendary sage and ancestor of the sages.[168] The next part (l. 10-16) refers to an incident from Esarhaddon's reign. On campaign to Egypt, he received a supportive divine message in the temple of Sin of Harran (see chapter 4.2.4). Marduk-šumu-uṣur reminds Ashurbanipal that it happened as predicted (Esarhaddon de-

---

[167] Translation from Parpola in: SAA 10 174.
[168] For the motif of the Sargonid king as sage, see Pongratz-Leisten 1999: 309-316.

feated Taharqa in 671), and extrapolates this to Ashurbanipal: Ashurbanipal will conquer the rest of the world that has not yet submitted to
Assyria. This is a free use and far-reaching application of the earlier
divine announcement. The fourth part (l. 17-23) contains blessings for
Ashurbanipal. Finally, the partially preserved reverse glorifies Ashurbanipal's kingship, in reference to the reign of his predecessors. The
writer of this letter uses a dream and a divine message, probably a
prophetic oracle, in order to serve his purposes. He wants to emphasise the close bond between the gods, and Ashurbanipal and his
forefathers, and the divine favour bestowed on the royal dynasty and
on Ashurbanipal in particular.

Oracles included in Royal Inscriptions
The royal inscriptions of Ashurbanipal contain various (prophetic)
oracles integrated into the chain of events. The primary purpose of
these oracles is to show that the actions of the Assyrian king were in
agreement with the will of the gods. A hidden intent may be to legitimise the violent actions of the Assyrians that follow in the narration. It
has been argued that the oracles included in royal inscriptions serve a
new purpose.[169] Originally, prophetic oracles belonged to the situational communication between god and king and were connected
with specific circumstances. At a second stage however some oracles
found their way into the royal inscriptions. These messages were not
repeated for their own sake, but functioned as support for the overall
demonstration of the close bond between the king and the gods and of
the divine order behind the king's achievements. However, the au-
thenticity of these oracles cannot be taken for granted; they could be
free reformulations or literary imitations of oracles.[170]

Prism A iii 4-10 (BIWA: 35), a word (*amātu*) of Ištar of Arbela announcing the death of Aḫšeri: 'I will, as I said, take care of the execution of Aḫšeri, the king of Mannea' (see chapter 4.2.6), called by
Nissinen a reminder of a divine promise.[171] Whereas the report of the
death of Aḫšeri also occurs in the F, B and C versions, the prophecy
of Ištar is found only in the (late) A version. Only at this late stage
was the death of Aḫšeri presented as the outcome of a promise made

---

[169]   Pongratz-Leisten 1999: 283.
[170]   Nissinen 1998: 58-60.
[171]   Nissinen 1998: 52.

by Ištar and carried out by her. Aḫšeri's servants, who actually killed him, are portrayed as agents of Ištar.

Prism A vi 107-117 (also F, T; BIWA: 57-58), a word (*amātu*) of Nanaya announcing her return to Uruk:

> Nanaya, who 1635/1630/1535 years (ago) became angry, went away and settled down in Elam in a place unworthy of her; in those days she and the gods, her fathers, appointed me to the kingship of the lands. She entrusted me with the returning of her godhead (saying): 'Ashurbanipal will take me away from evil Elam and bring me back to Eanna'. (This) word, her (their) divine command that she (they) had spoken since distant days, she (they) now revealed to the coming generation. I grasped the hands of her great divinity, and she, heart full of joy, took the shortest way to Eanna.[172]

This conforms to a prediction-fulfilment pattern, which to a great extent resembles the literary predictions (see 6.2.3 below). It is likely to be an *ex eventu* prediction composed by a scribe.

Prism B v 29-45 (C vi 22-44; BIWA: 99-100). Confronted with a threat from the Elamite king Teumman, Ashurbanipal supplicates Ištar of Arbela. He presents himself as a pious worshipper of the goddess and blames Teumman. Ištar of Arbela gives an encouraging reply: 'Fear not! (...) Because of the prayer you said with your hand lifted up, your eyes being filled with tears, I have compassion for you'.[173] The oracle of encouragement was confirmed by a dream received by a visionary. In the dream, Ištar of Arbela appeared as a divine warrior, ready for battle. To Ashurbanipal she gave the following order: 'You stay here in your place! Eat food, drink beer, make merry and praise my godhead, until I go to accomplish that task, making you attain your heart's desire. You shall not make a wry face, your feet shall not tremble, you shall not even wipe the sweat in the tumult of war!'[174] The goddess makes clear that Ashurbanipal is under divine protection, and that she herself will destroy the Elamites.[175] To what extent this goes back to an actual prophecy and dream-report is uncertain.

Ashurbanipal's votive inscription to Marduk (l. 24-26) contains a message (*šipru*) of Marduk announcing the defeat of the enemy (BIWA: 202):

---

[172] Translation based on Nissinen 1998: 40.
[173] Nissinen 2003a: 147.
[174] Nissinen 2003a: 147-148.
[175] Nissinen (1998: 54) points out that Ištar's order to Ashurbanipal to remain inactive conforms to the ancient Near Eastern war ideology.

> According to your divine message, which you sent, saying thus: 'I will scatter (or disperse) the band [of ....] Sandakšatru, his son, his own offspring, which they had appointed in his position, I [....]'. When I heard this, I praised Marduk, the Hero, and the name of Eru[...]

Ashurbanipal received a message from Marduk in which the god, speaking in the first person, announced his intervention in an important political issue. Sandakšatru, a loyal vassal of Assyria, had been replaced by his son in a rebellion against Assyria. Marduk presents himself as the one who governs the international scene.

As far as these oracles are scribal adaptations or creations, they evidence the transition from prophecy into literature in seventh-century Assyria.

Oracles that received Literary Elaboration

Among the texts from seventh-century Assyria we find several cases of prophetic oracles that have been elaborated into larger texts. These texts are important examples of the development of prophecy into literature. The first three cases are only dealt with briefly. The last two cases, in my view the best examples, are more fully discussed.

1) Within SAA 9 2 the unit 2.4 is included as if it were one oracle. However it seems to consist of various oracles, which are introduced as divine words (ii 30'; 38'). The opening (ii 29') functions as a heading to the divine words: 'Thus you shall answer the disloyal ones',[176] which may indicate that what follows is some sort of anthology (cf. chapter 3.1.1; chapter 4.2.3).[177]

2) SAA 3 47 is a divine message secondarily copied on an archival tablet and characterised as a 'message (šipirtu) of Ninurta'. The divine message may go back to a prophetic oracle that originally was orally delivered. The divine message is largely lost, but it is clear that Ninurta is very angry.[178] The dating of this message is unknown. The reason for Ninurta's anger remains a matter of speculation.[179] Whatever it was, it was something the addressed king was supposed to solve, as this would be the intent of the message.[180] The message was probably

---

[176] Also possible: 'This is how she (i.e. the goddess) answers the disloyal ones'.

[177] For a prophetic word secondarily presented as an 'answer' to be given to certain people, cf. Isa 14:32.

[178] L. 6-9: 'I am in distress, I am angry and furious [...] I am in distress [....] I am angry [....] I am furious in my temple'.

[179] Cf. the discussion of various suggestions in Pongratz-Leisten 1999: 230-232.

[180] A parallel may be found in the oracle of Ištar of Arbela in SAA 9 3.5, where the goddess in harsh words poses her demands to the king.

at a later stage expanded and reworked in a literary style and preserved on an archival tablet. SAA 3 47 contains various features indicating its literary character, such as the lengthy designation of the
royal addressee: 'S[ay] to the prince, [my] outstretched hand, to the
one who has received sceptre, throne, and [regnal insignia], to the
governor, appointed by my own hand'.[181] The classification of the message as *šipirtu* of Ninurta (r. 3') may go back to the scribe.[182] The secondary copy of the divine message on a library tablet shows that
Ashurbanipal regarded Ninurta's message as of importance.

3) SAA 9 5 is a divine word (*abutu*) of Ištar of Arbela. The text is a
literary derivation of prophecy, comparable to SAA 9 3.4 (see below).
Ištar of Arbela appears as intercessor for Esarhaddon, mobilising divine support for him (see chapter 3.1.1).

4) The text SAA 9 9 will be presented in full because of its importance as literary text containing a prophetic oracle in an elaborate
form. It consists of four elements: introduction, main part, blessing,
and colophon:

> [1-7] [Oracle of protection][183] of Mullissu, [...] of the Lady of Arbela!
> [They] are the strongest among all gods. They [lov]e and constantly be-
> stow their love [upon] Ashurbanipal, the creation of their hands. They
> [encou]rage him (literally his heart) for the sake of his life.
> [8-28] I roam the wild desiring your life. I continually cross rivers and seas,
> I continually pass mountains and tops, I continually cross all rivers.
> Droughts and showers devastate me, they ruin my charming figure. I am
> exhausted, my whole body is restless.[184] I have pleaded for your life in
> the assembly of all the gods. My arms are strong and will not let you
> fall before the gods. My shoulders are ready and will keep carrying you.
> For you, with my l[ip]s I keep desiring your life. [.......] your life. You
> shall surpass the life of [...] [...] Nabû, may your lips rejoice! [In the
> assembly of] all the [gods I incessantly ple]ad for your well-being. I
> roam the wild [desir]ing [your life]. [In woe I will r]ise and slau[ghter]
> your enemy. [...] will retur[n] to his country. *c. 4 lines lost*
> *reverse: space of c. 8 lines, not inscribed.*
> [1'-3'] May Mullissu and the Lady of Arbela keep Ashurbanipal, the crea-
> tion of their hands, alive for [e]ve[r]! *blank line*

---

[181] See further Pongratz-Leisten 1999: 229-230.

[182] The message is followed by a colophon, which has been qualified as an abbreviated form of a standard Ashurbanipal-colophon; see Hunger 1968: no. 319.

[183] Nissinen (2003a: 130-131) follows Parpola's restoration [*kidin*]*nu*, and interprets this as 'oracle of protection', see 131, note a. *Kidinnu* can also be interpreted as
'promise of protection'.

[184] For this interpretation, see Weippert 2002: 53.

[4'-7'] By mouth of Dunnaša-amur [a woman from Arbe]la. Nis[an] 18, eponymy of Bel-šadu'a, governor of Tyre (650). *Rest of tablet not inscribed.*

SAA 9 9 is a literary text in which a prophetic oracle has been incorporated. Both the colophon and several phrases in the main part indicate that the text goes back to a prophetic oracle. The colophon contains the prophetic formula *ša pî* ('by mouth of'). Phrases characteristic of oracles in the main part are: 'my arms are strong and will not let you fall before the gods. My shoulders are ready and will keep carrying you,' and the announcement of the destruction of the enemy. Based on the colophon, the oracle can be dated to 650 BCE, in the midst of the war between Ashurbanipal and his brother Šamaš-šum-ukin.[185]

In its present form however it is not an oracle report but a literary text. This is clear from the shape of the tablet,[186] its beautiful inscription,[187] and the framing of the introduction and conclusion in hymnal rather than oracular language. The main part of the text contains divine speech, but is an oracle in an elaborate form. The goddess speaking, either Ištar of Arbela or Mullissu, emphasises how hard she struggles for Ashurbanipal's life. It has been noted that the goddess models her quest for Ashurbanipal's life on the quest for life of Gilgameš.[188] The following parallels can be discerned.

i) Gilgameš' wandering searching for life after the death of Enkidu, is recurrently expressed as *rapādu ṣēra*, 'roaming the wild', e.g. tablet 9 l. 1-5:

> Gilgameš was weeping bitterly for his friend Enkidu, roaming the wild. 'I shall die, and shall I not then be like Enkidu? Sorrow has entered my heart. I am afraid of death, so go roaming the wild.'[189]

Gilgameš' roaming the wild, out of fear for death, is paralleled by the goddess' roaming the wild, for the benefit of Ashurbanipal's life.

ii) Gilgameš faces great troubles and hardships on his quest for life:

---

[185] For the oracle and its historical setting, see chapter 4.2.8.

[186] Parpola 1997: LIII.

[187] Parpola 1997: LXI. According to Weippert (1981: 72, note 2), the language of this text is a 'stark assyrisierendem Neubabylonisch'.

[188] Parpola in SAA 9: 41; already Zimmern 1910: 168-171.

[189] Translation based on George 2003: 666-667. Cf. Gilgameš' statement: 'I grew fearful of death and so roam the wild' (tablet 10 l. 62, 139, 239; George 2003: 680-681, 686-687, 692-693).

I thought, I will go and find Ūta-napišti the Far-Away (...). I went journeying through all the lands. Time and again I passed over arduous mountains, and time and again I crossed all the seas. My face did not have enough of sweet sleep, I scourged myself by going sleepless.[190]

The constant passing over mountains (*etēqu šadî*) and crossing of seas (*ebēru tiāmtu*) is repeated in SAA 9 9, as well as the motif of sleeplessness (*dalāpu*). Because of the hardships suffered, both Gilgameš and the goddess look exhausted.[191]

iii) Finally, Gilgameš finds Ūta-napišti, 'he who stood in the assembly of the gods and found life,'[192] but Ūta-napišti disappoints him: 'But now, who will bring the gods to assembly for you, so you can find the life you search for?'[193] Gilgameš will not find the eternal life, for this can only be granted by the assembly of the gods, and there is no one to gather the gods on Gilgameš' behalf. By contrast, the goddess encourages Ashurbanipal: 'I have pleaded for your life in the assembly of all the gods.'

The allusions to the Gilgameš epic are more than a literary device. Gilgameš' quest for life is provoked by, and contrasts with, the death of his friend Enkidu. Likewise, the quest for Ashurbanipal's life mirrors the death of his brother Šamaš-šum-ukin. The parallel becomes even stronger when it is noted that Gilgameš and Enkidu are described as brothers too.[194] Moreover, in both cases it is the gods that decide on the life and death of the brothers. When Gilgameš and Enkidu become too audacious together, the gods decide that one of them must die; this is Enkidu.[195] Similarly, the gods have ordained Šamaš-šum-ukin's

---

[190] Tablet 10 l. 250-255; translation by George 2003: 692-693.

[191] See tablet 10, l. 40-45, 113-118, 213-218: 'Why are your cheeks hollow, your face sunken, your mood wretched, your features wasted? ... Why is your face like one who has travelled a distant road? Why is your face burnt by frost and sunshine, and you roam the wild?' (George 2003: 680-681, 684-685, 690-691).

[192] Tablet 9 l. 75-76 (George 2003: 670-671).

[193] Tablet 11 l. 207-208 (George 2003: 716-717).

[194] In tablet 3 l. 127-128 Gilgameš' mother Ninsun says: 'I myself hereby adopt Enkidu, whom [I love], as a son, let Gilgameš in [brotherhood] treat Enkidu with favour!' (George 2003: 580-581). Cf. tablet 6 l. 149-150 'they stepped back and prostrated themselves before Šamaš, both the brothers sat down' (George 2003: 628-629, 'both of them (then) sat down together', but cf. his note 35). And cf. tablet 7 l. 139, where Gilgameš is called Enkidu's 'friend' and 'brother'; George 2003: 640-641.

[195] The gap at the beginning of tablet 7 can be partly filled with help of the Hittite version (Stefanini 1969). Here, Enkidu relates his dream to Gilgameš, in which he saw the assembly of the gods, deciding that one of the two friends must die: Enkidu.

death and Ashurbanipal's life.[196] The text skilfully ties up the fate of
Ashurbanipal and Šamaš-šum-ukin with that of Gilgameš and Enkidu.
The leitmotif of SAA 9 9 is the life of Ashurbanipal,[197] which through
the Gilgameš-parallel mirrors the death of Šamaš-šum-ukin.

Since the text as a whole is a scribal piece of work, a literary text,
the allusions to Gilgameš are to be attributed to the composer rather
than to the prophetess of the oracle.[198] Whereas the colophon situates
the original oracle in 650 BCE in the midst of the war, the text in its
reworked form, including the allusions to Gilgameš, is best situated
after the death of Šamaš-šum-ukin in 648 BCE. The focus on the life
of Ashurbanipal, which as I have argued mirrors the death of his
brother, reflects the outcome of the war: the death of Šamaš-šum-ukin.
However, although the outcome of the events of 648 was known to the
composer, he maintained the perspective of the original oracle, of 650
BCE. The promises of the original oracle were fulfilled, but the oracle
had not become meaningless. Through reworking it received a more
general meaning: the glorification of the king and the goddesses protecting him. Furthermore, SAA 9 9 probably served as a justification
of the violent events. The war between the two brothers ended with
the death of Šamaš-šum-ukin, and the military actions against Babylon
caused an interruption of the religious cult (the *akītu* festival was not
celebrated for three years). SAA 9 9 and other Assyrian texts that retrospectively describe this period (e.g. SAA 3 13 and SAA 3 44, see
6.2.2 below) refer to the gods' decisions and adhesions that are to be
understood as attempts to justify what had happened (see also SAA 13
139, discussed in chapter 4.2.8). By maintaining the perspective of
650 BCE, the outcome of the events, Ashurbanipal's life and Šamaš-
šum-ukin's death, is presented as the decision of the gods.

5) The text SAA 9 3 consists of two main parts, which are separated from each other by a double ruling.[199] The first part is a tripartite
text focused on the god Aššur and the king (3.1, 3.2, 3.3). The second
part contains two units that are both presented as an *abutu* (word) of

---

[196] According to Prism A iv 46-52, the gods threw Šamaš-šum-ukin into the fire;
Frame 1992: 153-154.

[197] See the word *balāṭu* in l. 8, 16, 20, 21, [25], cf. 6 and r. 3'.

[198] Contra Weippert 2002: 52.

[199] Parpola, regarding SAA 9 3 as one 'covenant-text', belittles the importance of
the double ruling: 'we do not know what it stood for' (1997: LXIV). This is however
contradicted by his own comment on the double ruling in SAA 9 1: 'the text before it
differed in nature from the rest of the tablet' (1997: LVI).

Ištar of Arbela (3.4, 3.5). The first part is a ceremonial-cultic text. The units 3.2 and 3.3, labelled as *šulmu*, 'message of well-being' (ii 8-9; ii 26), are embedded in a description of a ceremony for Aššur (i 14-26) and an *adê*-ceremony (ii 27-32). The purpose is the exaltation of Esarhaddon as victorious king and Aššur as king of the gods. The Aššur-cycle is a literary text, not a compilation of prophetic oracles.[200]

The unit 3.1 is badly fragmented. It contains a blessing, '[Hail t]o heaven and earth, [hai]l to Ešarra, [hail] to Esarhaddon, king of Assyria!' (i 9-11), and perhaps a description of a procession or ritual in the city of Assur. The unit 3.2 seems to contain a prophetic oracle (i 35-ii 2) incorporated in a frame that refers to king and god in the third person. The language of the frame-text is hymnal.[201] In this respect, 3.2 is best compared to SAA 9 9, which also is an oracular text incorporated into a hymnal framework.

> [List]en, Assyrians! [The king] has vanquished his enemy, [you]r [king] has put his enemy [under] his foot, [from] sun[se]t [to] sun[ris]e, [from] sun[ris]e [to] sun[se]t!
> 'I will destroy [.....], [I will de]stroy [.....], [..............], I will deliver[202] the Cimmerians into his hands, and set the land of Ellipi on fire'. Aššur has given to him the totality of the four regions, from sunrise to sunset. There is no king equal to him, he shines as bright as the sun.[203]

The unit ends with the description: 'This is the message of salvation (*šulmu*) placed[204] before Bel-Tarbāṣi,[205] and before the gods.'

In unit 3.3, the god Aššur looks back at the struggle for the throne of Assyria between Esarhaddon and his brothers in 681 BCE:

> At this moment these (well-known) rebels[206] incited against you, came out against you and surrounded you, you opened your mouth, thus: "hear me, Aššur!" I heard your cry. I issued forth as a fiery glow from the gate of heaven, to throw down fire and have it devour them,[207] while

---

[200]   This is confirmed by the absence of a reference to a prophetic figure in this part of the text.

[201]   Cf. SAA 3 4 [r. i 3'], r. ii 13' 'Hear, O world, the praise of Queen Nanaya!'.

[202]   Weippert (2002: 44) proposes the meaning 'to finish', 'to settle'.

[203]   My translation of 3.2 largely follows Parpola's (SAA 9).

[204]   For a different interpretation, see Weippert 2002: 16; cf. note 210 below.

[205]   On this name, see note 211 below.

[206]   For *sar-sar-a-ni*, 'rebels', see Nissinen 2003a: 120-121, note a; Weippert 2002: 45-46.

[207]   Here I follow Parpola's interpretation. For a discussion of this phrase, see Parpola's annotations in SAA 9 and Weippert 2002: 44-45 (cf. also Nissinen 2003a: 121, note e). Weippert takes ii 10-18 as a quotation from an earlier oracle and ii 20-23 as

you are standing in their midst. I took (them) from your presence, I put
them on a mountain and I rained stones and fire on them. I slaughtered
your enemies and filled the river with their blood. Let them see it, let
them praise me for what I am: Aššur, Lord of the gods.

In this text, the god Aššur is presented speaking, just as in other texts
of this period (SAA 3 44, 45, 46, see below). The same episode is described in Esarhaddon's Nineveh A inscription.[208] There, Esarhaddon
is presented as the legitimate successor to Sennacherib, threatened by
his elder brothers who want to take the throne of Assyria. In the
inscription the brothers are typified as 'rebels' too.[209] Esarhaddon prays
to the gods—Aššur is mentioned first—who listen to him, and who
order him to march to Nineveh, while they accompany him. Esarhaddon claims that from his place of refuge he marched back to Nineveh
without taking preparations, not minding the cold weather, and thanks
to Ištar even without a real fight (i 63-86). The Assyrians chose the
side of Esarhaddon, the rebels made off to a far-away land, and
Esarhaddon peacefully entered Nineveh and ascended the throne.

At first sight the perspective of Aššur in SAA 9 3.3 seems to be
quite different from that of the Nineveh A inscription. However, both
texts serve a similar goal. In reality, a bitter fight had taken place between Esarhaddon and his brothers (see chapter 4.2.1), and Esarhaddon was far from innocent. One way to wipe out this blot was by
presenting the events as if no blood had been shed, as does the Nineveh A inscription. Before a civil war broke out, Ištar made the Assyrians of the enemy camp join Esarhaddon's side, which left the rebel
brothers in isolation. They are described as corrupt criminals,
Esarhaddon as being totally innocent. The other way to wipe out
Esarhaddon's violent actions was to make the god Aššur responsible
for the bloodshed, as does the prophetic text 3.3. Both texts serve a
similar ideological goal. Both the Nineveh A inscription and SAA 9
3.3 reflect a later view of the events of 681. In 3.3, the episode of the
fight for the throne is summarised from the perspective that it was
Aššur who governed the scene and who decided the course of history.

----

its fulfilment, but I regard the text as a whole as retrospective (apart from the concluding appeal to praise Aššur).

[208] Borger 1956: 40-45.

[209] Nineveh A i 46, 82, ḫammā'e, 'rebels'.

In the concluding words, some sort of colophon, the text is typified thus: 'This is the message of salvation (*šulmu*), that is (placed) before the *ṣalmu*.'[210] Like 3.2, this unit is qualified as *šulmu*, a message of salvation. After this follows a colophon that refers to the first part of the tablet as a whole, 3.1, 3.2 and 3.3: 'This *adê*-tablet of Aššur enters in front of the king on a *cushion*. Fragrant oil is sprinkled, sacrifices are made, incense is burnt. In front of the king it is read aloud' (*ina pān šarri isassiū*). The units 3.1, 3.2 and 3.3 together are qualified as 'tablet of the *adê* of Aššur'.[211]

The two following two units, presented as *abutu* of Ištar of Arbela (3.4 and 3.5), are of different kinds. 3.4 is a description of an *adê*-ritual hosted by Ištar of Arbela on behalf of the king. Although Ištar appears speaking, it is not a prophetic oracle, but a prophetic text (comparable to SAA 9 5). 3.5 is formulated as a prophetic oracle. Ištar of Arbela directly addresses Esarhaddon, reminding him of what she has done for him, and demanding food and drink for a banquet. The end of the oracle probably includes a divine promise for the king. Furthermore, the unit ends with a reference to a prophet (*raggimu*), no doubt suggesting that this prophet delivered the preceding oracle (3.5). Yet, the oracle is remarkably long, and part of it may contain a description of past events hardly expected in a prophetic oracle (iv 3-13). 3.5 probably is a prophetic oracle in a somewhat elaborate form.

SAA 9 3 as a whole is a literary compilation.[212] The prophetic oracles preserved in this text (within 3.2 and 3.5) are reworkings of oracles that previously had been orally delivered and reported, and afterwards were inserted in an elaborate form into a new context. This compiled text shows that prophetic texts and reused oracles were closely related. On the one hand, prophetic oracles received a second life in a reworked form (3.2, 3.5). On the other hand, texts were pro-

---

[210] Differently Weippert 2002: 16, with note 63: 'Dies ist das Heilsorakel, das vor der Statue ergangen ist'. For the meaning of *ṣalmu*, see note 211 below.

[211] The expression *adê ša Aššur* means *adê* sworn to, and guarded by, Aššur (see Prism A ix 72; BIWA: 68, and cf. *adê ilānī rabûti*, in Watanabe 1987: 10-23). It is a loyalty oath for Esarhaddon taken by the Assyrians. The first *šulmu* (3.2) is placed before Bēl-Tarbāṣi, 'the Lord of the courtyard'. The courtyard of Ešarra was the place where oath-swearing ceremonies were held (see SAA 1 76, 13-r. 7). The second *šulmu* (3.3) is placed before the *ṣalmu*. The *ṣalmu* is either the statue of Aššur or, as Dalley (1986: 99) argues, a divine symbol on which loyalty oaths were sworn.

[212] The reason for this combination may be found in the shared reference to a loyalty oath (*adê*) for King Esarhaddon (ii 27; ii 36, iii 11, 14). So also Villard 2001: 80.

duced that were literary in origin, but closely resemble the genre of
prophetic oracles (3.3, 3.4).

6.2.2   *Literary Derivatives of Prophecy*

In this section, I discuss four texts from seventh-century Assyria that
can be qualified as literary derivatives of prophetic oracles. Although
these texts bear close resemblance to the genre of prophetic oracles,
they are unlikely to go back to orally delivered words. Instead, they
can be qualified as literary compositions.

SAA 3 13

SAA 3 13 is a fictive dialogue between Ashurbanipal and the god
Nabû, situated in the temple of Ištar of Nineveh. Although in part
strongly reminiscent of oracular language, SAA 3 13 probably is a literary text.[213] The text shares important similarities with SAA 9 9, and
it is quite likely that both belong to the same historical context.[214] Like
SAA 9 9, SAA 3 13 focuses on the life of Ashurbanipal (SAA 3 13 l.
2, 18, 21, 24, r. 5), which is threatened. Ashurbanipal, in a threatening
situation, went to the temple of Ištar of Nineveh to implore Nabû for
support. This can be related to the war with Šamaš-šum-ukin. Ashurbanipal implored Nabû's help against his 'ill-wishers' and 'adversary',
which refers to Šamaš-šum-ukin and his supporters (l. 2, 6, 22, r. 3, 4,
5, 9). SAA 3 13 can be regarded as a literary representation of a scene
that actually may have taken place at some point during the war
against Šamaš-šum-ukin. The lines 24-26, which read like a prophetic
oracle, are introduced as a word of Nabû, spoken by a *zāqīqu*:[215]

> A *zāqīqu* answered from the presence of Nabû, his lord: Fear not,
> Ashurbanipal! I will give you long life, I will entrust pleasant breezes
> with your soul; my pleasant mouth shall ever bless you in the assembly
> of the great gods.[216]

After a response of Ashurbanipal (r. 1-5), a similar divine speech is
given, which concludes the text (r. 6-11)

---

[213] Pongratz-Leisten (1999: 75) qualifies this text as a 'literarische Kreation in
Anlehnung an die Gattung der Prophetensprüche'.

[214] Cf. Parpola 1997: LXXI. For the similarities between SAA 9 9 and SAA 3 13,
see Hilber 2005: 70-74.

[215] *Zāqīqu/zīqīqu* denotes a ghost or a dream god. According to Butler (1998: 83),
it may occasionally denote 'a professional, who may have prophesied'.

[216] Translation from: Livingstone SAA 3.

You were a child, Ashurbanipal, when I left you with the Queen of Nineveh; you were a baby, Ashurbanipal, when you sat in the lap of the Queen of Nineveh! (...) Your ill-wishers, Ashurbanipal, will fly away like *pollen* on the surface of the water. They will be squashed before your feet like *burbillātu* insects in spring! You, Ashurbanipal, you will stand before the great gods and praise Nabû![217]

SAA 3 13 is reminiscent of oracular language, but composed as a literary text. Both SAA 9 9 and SAA 3 13 attest to the importance of divine encouragement of Ashurbanipal during the war against Šamaš-šum-ukin. Both texts maintain the perspective of the time of the war; SAA 9 9 through the colophon, SAA 3 13 through the divine promise that Ashurbanipal's enemies will be destroyed. Yet, both texts were probably composed after the events, and *ex eventu* present the outcome of the war as according to the will of the gods. Since SAA 3 13 probably is a literary text imitating oracular language—contrary to SAA 9 9, containing an elaborate oracle in literary dress—it is discussed here. The correspondences between both texts show however that literary elaborations of prophetic oracles and literary texts imitating the oracular style were intimately related.

SAA 3 44

SAA 3 44, 45 and 46 are to be qualified as compositions of divine words.[218] Here, I present SAA 3 44 as a whole, for two reasons. First, it is one of the best examples from seventh-century Assyria of prophecy as literature. Second, it is an important text that has not received the attention it deserves.[219] In Livingstone's edition three of the horizontal rulings dividing the different sections of this composition are erroneously omitted.[220] With the rulings in place, the text appears to consist of some 27 sections, divided into three main parts (l. 1-15, l. 16-r. 2,

---

[217] Translation from: Livingstone SAA 3.

[218] Contra Livingstone (1989: XXX) who shares these texts among the 'letters from gods'. This category applies to SAA 3 41-43, but not to 44-47. In the latter texts, the divine voice does not quote from, or respond to, a royal report. These texts are not divine letters but compositions of divine words.

[219] This text is discussed by Pongratz-Leisten (1999: 249-260). Her discussion is helpful, but not without problems. Her presentation of the text is based on Livingstone's edition in which several rulings are missing. Besides, she regards the text as a 'letter from God', which it is not in my view. She divides the text into 'historical descriptions', 'legitimation formulae', and 'commands to cultic service'.

[220] From inspection of the tablet it appears that horizontal rulings are to be added directly after line 15, directly after line 32, and directly preceding r. 11. These rulings were noted in CT 35 13-14 (albeit the ruling preceding r. 11 is somewhat unclear).

and r. 3-29'). The three parts are separated from each other by empty sections: sections 6 and 17. I have included the two empty sections in my numbering, because this is in agreement with the numbering as it appears on the tablet: the sections 1, 2, 3, 12, 13, and 14 are numbered on the tablet, which shows that the empty section 6 was counted as well.[221] The numbering of sections on the tablet demonstrates that SAA 3 44 is a deliberately composed text. In the presentation of the text below, the section numbering is in the first column.

Part I (l. 1-15) mainly deals with accusations against Šamaš-šum-ukin. The accusations against Šamaš-šum-ukin (sections 1, 3 and 5) are presented in contrast to Ashurbanipal, who is pious and just (sections 2 and 4). Part II (l. 16-32 and r. 1-2) focuses on the divine measures taken against Šamaš-šum-ukin (sections 7-9), which are identified as deeds of Ashurbanipal at the command of the god (sections 10-14). Finally, part III (r. 3-29') deals with the exaltation of Ashurbanipal (sections 18, 27'), who is presented as obedient and pious (sections 25', 26'), in contrast to Elam and Šamaš-šum-ukin, who suffer a terrible fate (sections 19, 20). The text concludes with a divine promise of support (r. 26'-27'): everyone who rebels against Ashurbanipal will be punished like Šamaš-šum-ukin.

In the composition, different perspectives have been combined. First, we find a range of words referring to Šamaš-šum-ukin in the third person, which deal with divine actions against him (sections 3, 5, 7, 8, 9, 15, and 20). These sections deal with Šamaš-šum-ukin's transgressions and punishment. Ashurbanipal is not addressed here (only referred to once in line 8); rather, the god explains the cruel events that have happened from a sin-punishment perspective. Second, we find words that address Ashurbanipal in the second person, emphasise his deeds, and deal with the defeat of enemies and restoration of cults in general terms (sections 2, 4, 10, 11, 12, 13, 14, 18, 19, 24', 25', 26'). These sections do not mention Šamaš-šum-ukin, but in general terms deal with Ashurbanipal's privileged position: he takes care of the divine cults, rules the people, and defeats the enemies. The enemies are consistently referred to in the plural (l. 11, 22-23, 26, 29, r. 1-2, 4, 6). Only in part III is there some specification: Elam is mentioned (r. 5), the [*land of Akkad*] (r. 20'), and 'those gods' (r. 23'). Ashurbanipal's actions against Babylonia and Elam are an exponent of his

---

[221] For this numbering, see CT 35 Plate 14 (mistakenly indicated as reverse).

royal and military supremacy in general. Third, the sections 1, 11 and 27', deliberately positioned at beginning, middle and end of the composition, combine the two perspectives and shape the text into a meaningful composition. In the following presentation, the material combining the two perspectives (sections 1, 11, 27') is marked as type A; the words addressed to Ashurbanipal are marked as type B; and the words referring to Šamaš-šum-ukin are marked as type C.

Evidently, the text was composed out of divergent material. A clear indication for this consists of the suffixes that in their present context miss an antecedent: *'their* cities', *'their* booty' (*-šunu*, l. 22-23), *'his* warriors' (*-šu*, l. 24), *'his* predecessor' (*-šu*, r. 7). The demonstrative *'those* gods' (*šá-a-tu-[nu]*, r. 23') has no clear antecedent either.

		PART I.	
1	1	By my great support, with which I gave [you] confid[ence, ...]	A
	2	who rival with you [for the kingship ....]	
	3	Because of these evil deeds [which Šamaš-šum-u]kin committed against you,	
	4	I pulled out the foundations of his royal throne, over[threw] his reign and [comma]nded the destruction of the entire land of Akkad.	
2	5	To perfect the shrines of the great gods, to renew [...] the offerings,	B
	6	to venerate my divinity (and) a good reign of [....] I decreed as your fate.	
3	7	As for Šamaš-šum-ukin, who did not keep my *adê*	C
	8	but sinned against the kindness of Ashurbanipal, my beloved king,	
	9	I confined him in harsh prisonment and bound [.....]	
	10	I placed nose-ropes on his magnates and [led] them to [...?] presence.	
4	11	To give kings military support, to overthrow enemies, to resettle [....] sanctuaries,	B
	12	I appo[inted you] as the shepherd of justice of the subjects of Enlil.	
5	13	Of ruining his life and destroying the land of Akkad, the words of the gods, which [......]	C
	14	Šamaš-šum-ukin [*neglected*] my lordly curse with which I had cursed him,	
	15	and did not take seriously good [couns]el regarding his life [.....].	
6		empty section	
		PART II.	
7	16	[.....] he aroused [the anger of] all the gods	C
	17	and [....] performed evil deeds which were to cost him his life.	
8	18	[As for Šamaš-šum-ukin], who carried off the property of the gods,	C

	19	[..... I] decreed his fate as evil.	
9	20	Because of these evil deeds [which] he kept on perpetrating,	C
	21	at my command²²² his own gods became angry, abandoned him, and took to foreign parts.	
10	22	At the command of my great divinity you conquered their cities	B
	23	and took their heavy booty as plunder from them to Assyria.	
11	24	By my great support you brought about the defeat of his warriors.	A
	25	The rest you [handed over] to me alive, in Nineveh, city of your lordship you killed them with weapons.	
12	26	I sent before you my fierce weapons to defeat your enemies.	B
13	27	At the mention of your name, which I made great, your troops go victoriously wherever there is fighting with weapons.	B
14	28	Because of your in[cessant] prayers and supplications [with which] you beseeched my great divinity,	B
	29	I stood at your side and [poured out the blood] of your enemies.	
15	30	[....] of [..........] the citizens of Assyria	C
	31	[...............] him	
	32	and [.....................] his kingship.	
16	r. 1	[..... who had not] kept [my *adê*] and had sin[ned against] your [ki]ndness,	B
	2	you [took] with your hands like sheep, and slaughtered like lambs.	
17		empty section	
		PART III.	
18	3	In the enactment of my utterance, the [Igigi] and Anunnaki pay attention to his command!	B
	4	All the kings seated on thrones bow down [before] you and kiss your feet.	
19	5	I smashed the [bo]ws of Elam, and strengthened your bow.	B
	6	I made your weapons stronger than those of all (your) enemies.	
20	7	I decreed for him [the fate] of his predecessor Išdu-kin, king of B[abyl]on,	C
	8	and in his time his people were seized by famine; they chewed leather straps.	
	9	I made [.....] to seize the people of Akkad,	
	10	and I made them eat each other's flesh [....].	
21-23	11'-18'	break of approximately 8 lines, 3 sections	
24	19'	[You .... the word of] my [great] divinity,	B

---

²²² Livingstone's reading [*b*]*i-tu-u-a* is strange (*bītu*, locative, and suffix; literally 'in my house', translated 'on my account'). Pongratz-Leisten (1999: 252) adopts Livingstone's reading, but takes it with the previous line ('Wegen jener üblen Taten, die er immer wieder beging gegen mich'), which is unconvincing too. I adopt Bauer's suggestion: [*qí*]-*bi-tu-u-a*, 'auf mein [G]eheiß' (1933: 79, 81).

	20'	eased my [*angry* heart and made *the land of Akkad* conclude peace] with me.	
25	21'	[.....] forgiveness and [...] are in my hands.	B
	22'	I spoke to you with my divine word and you acted.	
26	23'	I commissioned you to renew those gods and [to prov]ide for their shrines.	B
27	24'	They heard (this) in their assembly, blessed your kingship,	A
	25'	and commended your good deeds greatly in my presence.	
	26'	[Any oth]er enemy who does not fear my great divinity,	
	27'	I will deliver into your hands in like manner.	
	28'	You sent a tablet of good tidings and peace	
	29'	to the presence of my [god]head!	
	30'	[Co]py of the words [of ......]	

Pongratz-Leisten has shown that the text bears a literary character.[223] SAA 3 44 contains many parallels with Ashurbanipal's royal inscriptions relating to 652-648 BCE: Prism C (647 BCE) and particularly Prism A (643 BCE).[224] SAA 3 44 must have been composed after the war, just as the royal inscriptions. Its purpose probably was the same as that of the accounts of the war in the Prisms C and A: legitimisation and justification of the violence, the suffering of the people of Babylon, and the sacrilege committed against the gods of Babylon. The events are narrated from a divine point of view. It is explained that the god destined everything as it happened: the fate of Ashurbanipal was to be king (l. 5-6), for Šamaš-šum-ukin an evil fate was destined (l. 19). The concrete actions against Babylon and Šamaš-šum-ukin are presented as actions of the god. The main point of the text is the contrast between Ashurbanipal and Šamaš-šum-ukin.[225] Because Ashurbanipal is pious and good, the deity supports him and grants him victory. By contrast, because Šamaš-šum-ukin committed evil and violated the will of the gods, the deity decreed his fate as evil and caused his death. The contrast between life (Ashurbanipal) and death (Šamaš-šum-ukin), which plays an important role in SAA 9 9 and SAA 3 13, appears also in SAA 3 44. Here, the focus is on Šamaš-šum-ukin losing his life: 'ruining his life' (l. 13), not taking seriously

---

[223] Pongratz-Leisten 1999: 254-255.

[224] Pongratz-Leisten 1999: 249-251. A remarkable element, pointed out by Pongratz-Leisten (1999: 256) is that both Prism A and SAA 3 44 include Elam within the Šamaš-šum-ukin episode; in both cases the reference to Elam is immediately followed by the motif of Babylon suffering from a famine.

[225] Cf. Pongratz-Leisten 1999: 259.

good counsel regarding his life (l. 15), he 'performed evil deed which were to cost him his life' (l. 17).

The deity speaking in this text probably is Aššur.[226] The closest counterpart to SAA 3 44 is in fact SAA 9 3.3. Both texts are literary derivatives of prophecy; both present an account of major historical events from a divine perspective (681 BCE and 652-648 BCE respectively); and in both accounts, the deity speaking takes full responsibility for the violent events. In SAA 9 3.3, the god Aššur makes clear that it was he who annihilated Esarhaddon's rivals. Similarly, in SAA 3 44 it is the god who is responsible for the destruction of Babylon. Here too, it is likely to be Aššur, who, after the events, asserts that it was he who decreed and acted. In both cases, violence and bloodshed among members of the royal family took place, which afterwards needed justification; this is the purpose of SAA 9 3.3 and SAA 3 44.

In r. 30', '[co]py of the words [of/that] ....', the preceding text is qualified as 'words' (*dibbī*). This term is more often used to indicate divine words. In SAA 9 8 line 1, 'words (*dibbī*) [concerning the Elam]ites', and in SAA 9 2.3 22'-23', 'these words of mine (*dibbīya*) from Arbela, collect them inside your palace'. The term *dibbī* was thus used to indicate divine oracles. Although SAA 3 44 is a literary composition, the term *dibbī*, suggests as if the text consists of divine oracles. Furthermore, at the end of the text, r. 26'-27', the perspective changes from past to future: '[any oth]er enemy who does not fear my great divinity, I will deliver into your hands in like manner.' This is a divine declaration of support, often found in prophetic oracles. The fate of Šamaš-šum-ukin and his allies is turned into an example, precisely as was the case with SAA 9 1, where the divine support of Esarhaddon in his struggle for the throne was broadened to divine support of Esarhaddon against whatever enemy would rise against him.

SAA 3 45

SAA 3 45 is a composition of divine words of encouragement relating to Ashurbanipal's war against Teumman.[227] The deity speaking probably is Aššur. His words addressed to the Assyrian king are separated from each other by horizontal rulings. The king is consistently ad-

---

[226] So also Livingstone, SAA 3; Pongratz-Leisten 1999: 249.
[227] It cannot be a reply to Ashurbanipal's account of the battle, because it contains announcements concerning the war.

dressed in the second person. In the first section, Aššur states he made Ashurbanipal supreme king, honoured by all other kings. The second section (l. 6'-8') is as follows:

> [The magnates] of Elam tremble and shake b[efore you]. [By] your [... and] the good fate which I decreed for you, [you will sm]ite [her], and her governors will sway to and fro like reeds in the tempest.[228]

In the next section, a contrast is made between Ashurbanipal, whose closeness to Aššur is emphasised, and 'they', perhaps the Elamites, who have taken something to Elam and have sinned. Text 45 is substantially shorter than 44, it consistently addresses the king in the second person, and it clearly refers to the future. It could be a written oracle, sent to the king before the events actually took place.

SAA 3 46

SAA 3 46 is a fragment of a text similar to 3 44. In Livingstone's restored reading, the text begins as 3 44, '[By the support] of my great divinity, with which [I gave you confidence]'. In the first section, Aššur formulates his commission of the Assyrian king to conquer a disobedient land (l. 1-3). In the second section, Aššur states that at his command the entire world has become subjected to Assyria; the rulers of the earth come to Ehursaggalkurkurra to honour Aššur and his king. Since Ehursaggalkurkurra is the chapel of Aššur in his temple Ešarra in the city of Assur,[229] it can be regarded as certain that the deity speaking here is Aššur.[230] In the third section, the Assyrian king is addressed: 'I desired you, I picked you out for shep[herdship .... and *sent* you with] mighty weapons, sharp arrows, and flaming [*swords*] to fell [*my*] enemies.'[231] In this text, Aššur defines the commission of his king: to fell the enemies, to conquer the disobedient land, to rule the world, so that all rulers come to Assur to revere Aššur's supreme divinity.

The four texts discussed in this section are characterised by a perspective that is broader than that of individual oracles. This is a feature they share with the oracles that were elaborated into literary texts, discussed in 6.2.1. Both the reworked oracles and the literary derivatives

---

[228] Translation from: Livingstone, SAA 3: 113.
[229] George 1993: 100.
[230] Contra Grayson (1983: 147-148) who suggests Šamaš is the divine speaker.
[231] Translation from: Livingstone, SAA 3: 114.

of prophecy testify to the phenomenon of prophecy finding its way
into literature. Furthermore, both served similar purposes: to emphasise the close relationship between king and god, and to present episodes of major political importance as being governed by the gods.

6.2.3   *Literary Predictions*

In this section I present five examples of literary predictions. These
texts contain announcements of events that will take place in future,
but are in fact *ex eventu* compositions that fictitiously use prediction
as a form (these texts are introduced in chapter 3.3). With these examples I like to show how the form of prediction—divine announcement
of future events—was used within literary texts, in order to provide a
counterpart to the seventh-century revision of the Isaiah tradition.

Marduk Prophecy
This text consists of two main parts.[232] In the first part, mostly in the
past tense,[233] Marduk relates about three periods he spent abroad, in the
land of Ḫatti, in Assyria, and in Elam.[234] The first two journeys function as an introduction in which Marduk presents himself as a traveller
who leaves and returns as he wishes. The third journey forms the main
topic of the text: Marduk's stay in Elam. The second part of the text,
in the future tense, deals with the glorious reign of the Babylonian
king who takes Marduk back from Elam to Babylon.

Marduk presents himself as: 'I am Marduk, the great Lord ... The
one who roams about all the lands, from sunrise to sunset, am I (i 7-
12).' The first illustration of this is his stay in the land of Ḫatti (i 13-
19): 'I gave the command that I go to Ḫatti (...). I stayed there for 24
years and I established the trade of the Babylonians'. In the next section, Marduk relates his return to Babylon. The beginning of this sec-

---

[232]   For the text, see Borger 1971: 5-13.
[233]   Sommerfeld 1982: 188, note 2.
[234]   Usually, this is interpreted as referring to three deportations of Marduk's
statue, by the Hittite king Mursilis (1594), the Assyrian king Tukulti-Ninurta I (c.
1243-1207), and the Elamite king Kudur-Naḫḫunte (1155). Whereas the third journey
to Elam, the main topic of the text, indeed reflects the deportation of the statue by
Kudur-Naḫḫunte, followed by its return under Nebuchadnezzar I, the precise historical background of the first two journeys is a matter of debate. According to Dalley
(1997: 165-166), it is uncertain whether Mursilis took Marduk's statue to Ḫatti, and, if
he did, when it was returned; furthermore, the statue deported by Tukulti-Ninurta was
still in Assyria when Kudur-Naḫḫunte deported Marduk's statue to Elam. Evidently,
there was more than one statue (Dalley 1997: 163-166).

tion poses a problem. In Borger's edition the fragmented lines run: ....
⌈E₁₁⌉ (*ilâm*)-*ma* .... DIB⌈?⌉-*ma*,[235] which Borger restores and translates as
'[ein König von Babel?] stand auf, und fasste? [meine Hand?]'.[236] This
is possible but not convincing. First, no Babylonian king from this period is known that took Marduk back from Ḫatti. Moreover, in the
final lines of this section Marduk states: 'I returned home' (i 35). This
is strange if a king already brought him home. The description of
Marduk's return (i 35-37) has a parallel in the section that follows,
where Marduk returns from his stay in Assyria (i 15'-17'). There no
king is involved either: Marduk himself returned from Assyria. For
this reason the common interpretation of i 23-25 is unlikely. The Marduk Prophecy does not contain a sequence of kings, but a sequence of
travels. Only in the case of the third journey is a king involved: the
king whose reign is idealised in the second part of the composition
(see below). The second illustration of Marduk as a traveller deals
with his sojourn in Assyria, described in remarkably positive terms.[237]
The first two journeys set the stage for the main topic: Marduk's stay
in Elam and his return to Babylon. The introduction concludes with
the following self-presentation: 'I am Marduk, the great prince ....
Who has ever undertaken such a journey? From the place where I
went, I returned.[238] I was in command!' (i 18'-21'). Marduk asserts that
he returned as he went; as yet no king is mentioned.

Marduk's stay in Elam is described as follows: 'I went to Elam, all
the gods went (with me). I was in command!' (i 22'-23'). The absence
of the gods in Babylonia results in chaos and disaster. The temple
cults are discontinued, people get sick and die, morals fall short,
crimes abound (i 24'-ii 11). The section ends with Marduk's desire to
go home: 'I fulfilled my days, I fulfilled my years. Then I longed for
my city Babylon and Ekur-Sagila (i.e. Esagila). I called all the goddesses together. I commanded: Bring your tribute, O you lands, to
Babylon' (ii 12-17). Marduk's stay in Elam is described in much more
detail than the first two journeys. Furthermore, the deplorable situation
of Babylon after the gods had left is depicted. Finally, Marduk does
not conclude with 'I returned home', but 'I longed for (*libbi wabālu*)
my city Babylon and Ekur-Sagila'.

---

[235] Borger 1971: 6.
[236] Borger 1971: 16.
[237] Most remarkable in this respect is the phrase 'I blessed Assyria' (i 12').
[238] Cf. Sommerfeld 1982: 188, note 2.

The second part of the text contains a glorifying description of the reign of king who brings Marduk back to Babylon (Nebuchadnezzar I)

> A king of Babylon will arise. He will renew the temple of wonders, Ekur-Sagil. The plans of heaven and earth he will draw in Ekur-sagil. He will change its height. He will establish tax exemption for my city Babylon. He will grasp my hand and bring me forever in my city Babylon and in Ekur-Sagil.

This describes a reversal of fortune in reaction to the deplorable situation that was created because of Marduk's absence. Various subsequent sections refer to cultic restorations and divine blessings of the reign of this king. The deeds of the king include the restoration of the procession ships of Marduk (ii 28-33) and Nabû (2'-8'), the restoration of Ekur-Gišnugal, the temple of Sîn and Ningal of Ur (Assur iii 9'-16'), of Ekur-Egalmah, the temple of Ištar of Isin (Assur iv 6-7), and the return of Anu to his temple in Dēr (iii 25'-30'). Each section ends with a blessing of the king, such as: '[This prince] will experience divine grace. [The years] of his reign will be long' (Assur iii 7'-8'); 'This prince will be powerful; he will not have rivals' (Assur iv 4); 'This prince will rule the lands in their totality' (iii 20').

Further actions of the king include gathering the dispersed (Assur iv 5), feeding the land with abundance of crops (iv 12), and gathering the dispersed land and making its foundation firm (iv 21-22). The reign of this king is idealised, by the reversal of the deplorable situation described earlier. Evil will turn to good and people will live harmoniously together. In the final section Marduk states 'I have reconciled all the gods with him. He will destroy Elam, he will destroy its cities, he will [destroy] its strongholds.' The fourth column contains a listing of products, perhaps an offering list for Marduk's cult, and concludes: '(every) month, day and year ... I will bless him'.

The background of this text is, in all likelihood, the reign of Nebuchadnezzar I. In his inscriptions the return of Marduk's statue from Elam is a prominent topic.[239] The statue was deported to Elam by Kudur-Nahhunte, who put an end to the Kassite dynasty in Babylon (c. 1155 BCE). One inscription contains a prayer of Nebuchadnezzar: 'O lord of Babylon, how long will you dwell in the land of the enemy? ... Turn your face back to Esagila!' Marduk answers: 'by my own

---

[239] For the inscriptions of Nebuchadnezzar I, see Frame 1995: 11-35.

mouth I spoke to you ...: Take me [from E]lam to Babylon!'.[240] In general, the inscriptions present Marduk as being in command, Elam as the evil enemy, and Nebuchadnezzar as the superior king who reversed the deplorable state of affairs.[241] Since the main theme of the Marduk Prophecy is concurrent with the inscriptions of Nebuchadnezzar, it is likely that this text was composed during his reign.[242]

The text probably was composed during the reign of Nebuchadnezzar I, but various later Assyrian kings seem to have had a particular interest in its theme. One of the pious deeds described in the text has a parallel in the inscriptions of Esarhaddon. According to iii 25'-30', 'the Great King of Dēr (Ištaran) ... he (i.e. the king) will grasp his hand, and bring him in Dēr and Ekur-dimgalkalamma forever'. This closely resembles a phrase repetitively occurring in Esarhaddon's inscriptions, which presents Esarhaddon as 'the one who brought Great Anu (Ištaran) in his city Dēr and in his temple Edimgalkalamma and let him dwell in his dais forever.'[243] Furthermore, Esarhaddon's Babylon inscription presents a sequence of motifs similar to the Marduk Prophecy: 1) absence of the Babylonian gods (the gods ascended to heaven)[244] led to chaos (Babylon episodes 7 and 9); 2) when the days of absence were fulfilled (*malû*, ii 12; Babylon episode 10b:19) a reversal takes place: a king is commissioned to restore and renew Esagila;[245] 3) the gods are brought back,[246] Babylon's tax exemption (*zakûtu*) is restored,[247] and the dispersed Babylonians are gathered by the king.[248] Furthermore, Esarhaddon's inscriptions often mention the

---

[240] See Frame 1995: 18, l. 8-10, 13-17. Another text describes the conquest of Elam under Kudur-Naḫḫunte and Marduk's absence as a disastrous period (text 6 in Frame's numbering). Furthermore, two texts that belong together describe Marduk's anger with Babylon and his leaving to Elam and his pity and return to Babylon (text 8 and 9 in Frame's numbering).

[241] For the reign of Nebuchadnezzar I, see also Roberts 1977b; Lambert 1964.

[242] This concurs with the colophon of the text, reconstructed by Borger, which refers to 'the copy from Babylon' (see Borger 1971: 13).

[243] Esarhaddon, Uruk A 20-21 (Borger 1956: 74). See further Borger 1956: 25 36:c:8, 122 C E Chr., 84 42ff; Frame 1995: 176:10, 178:19-20, 183:20-21; Glassner 2004: 201:44-45; 209:6.

[244] Marduk Prophecy i 25'; Babylon episode 8a:45-46; b:14.

[245] Marduk Prophecy ii 19-24; Babylon episode 26c:18-28 'Esagila I built ... anew, I made it greater, higher and more beautiful than before. I made it shining like the stars'.

[246] Marduk Prophecy ii 26-27; 'the looted statues of the gods I have returned to their places from Assyria and Elam' (Babylon episode 36c:5-9).

[247] Marduk Prophecy ii 24-25; Babylon episode 37a:37.

[248] Marduk Prophecy Assur iv 5; Babylon episode 37a:22. The motif of long reign and prosperous time occurs in Marduk Prophecy iii 6'-10'; Babylon episode 39.

return of Marduk to Esagila (which actually took place in 668 BCE). Ashurbanipal, in his inscriptions, continued the themes of the completion of Esagila and the return of Marduk to Babylon. In addition, during his reign the wars with Elam were a principal concern. The destruction of Elam, referred to in the Marduk Prophecy (iii 22'-24'), is the topic of a prophecy from the reign of Ashurbanipal: 'I will destroy Elam' (ḫepû, SAA 9 8:8-9; as in iii 22'-24').

For Esarhaddon and Ashurbanipal, the restoration of Esagila and the return of Marduk, and the enmity with Elam, were interrelated. They presented themselves as patron of the Babylonian cults in order to bind Babylonia to Assyria and to prevent it from forging an alliance with Elam. Because of these concerns, Esarhaddon and Ashurbanipal probably were profoundly interested in the Marduk Prophecy. The Marduk Prophecy as we have it, may result from an elaboration during the reign of Esarhaddon or Ashurbanipal. Part of the Assyrian elaboration may have been the remarkably positive description of Marduk's stay in Assyria: 'I blessed Assyria' (i 12') and an extension of the description of the actions and blessings of the ideal king.

The Marduk Prophecy was never intended as a real prophecy, but as a glorification of the 'king of Babylon', Nebuchadnezzar, later probably applied to the Assyrian kings Esarhaddon and Ashurbanipal.

Šulgi Prophecy

The Šulgi Prophecy is badly preserved.[249] The narrator is Šulgi, a Sumerian king of the third dynasty of Ur (at the end of the third millennium), who is presented as a deified king: ^dŠulgi.[250] In the first lines, Šulgi presents himself as someone who has received divine knowledge: 'I am (god) Šulgi, beloved of Enlil and Ninlil; the hero Šamaš has spoken to me, Ištar my lady has revealed (this) to me' (i 1-4). From the perspective of Šulgi, the text deals with the future, and is presented as a divine revelation. King Šulgi describes himself as king of the earth, and as founder of Nippur. He furthermore states: 'When I spoke, the gods would listen to me. At my own expense,[251] I built this wall and made it firm' (6'-9'). The reference to 'this wall' suggests that the Šulgi Prophecy presents itself as a wall inscription, which

---

[249]   For the text, see Borger 1971: 13-15.

[250]   Šulgi also appears in Mesopotamian chronicles as one of the deified kings; see Glassner 2004.

[251]   So Foster 1993: 270.

means that the text (fictitiously) claims to be of ancient provenance and was placed into the wall of Nippur during Šulgi's reign.[252]

In the extant fragment of the third column, Šulgi refers to a ruler who will 'walk around in "woe!" and "alas!",' apparently because he was negligent to the citizens of Nippur and Babylon and did not provide justice for them (11'-16'). The following fragments describe a terrible period to come. A ruler will endure misery. During his reign fighting and war will not cease. Brother will devour brother, there will be complete chaos. Furthermore, 'the possessions of Babylon will go to Subartu (i.e. Assyria) and the land of Assyria. The king of Babylon will deliver to Assur the possessions of his palace to the ruler of Assur. For ever and ever Baltil (i.e. Assur) ...' The fragment of column v seems to continue the description of the deplorable situation of Babylonia: 'friend will slay friend with a weapon, companion will destroy companion with a weapon, [the lands] will be totally destroyed' (5-7). Furthermore, Nippur will be destroyed (9). Finally, however, 'At the command of Enlil the reign of the king of Babylon will come to an end' (13-15). The final part of the fragment (v 19-30) describes a reversal of the disastrous situation. A new king will carry out a restoration: he will rebuild the sanctuaries of the gods and maintain the (food)offerings of the great gods. He will rebuild the temples of Nippur and Isin (19-28).

The Šulgi Prophecy in some important respects resembles the Marduk Prophecy: a divine speaker presents himself and gives a self-description by way of introduction; the main topic is introduced—the picture of a deplorable situation—and subsequently a reversal of fortune during the reign of a restorer-king is predicted. The Šulgi Prophecy is literary fiction too. Šulgi is depicted as narrating a revelation of the gods concerning the future. It is difficult to ascertain to which events the text alludes. The most distinctive element is the transportation of the Babylonian (royal) possessions to Assyria. Borger suggested a connection with Tukulti-Ninurta I's conquest of Babylon (1225 BCE) and his robbing of the royal palace.[253] It is impossible to establish how long, according to the Šulgi Prophecy, the period of chaos continued, and to identify the restorer king. He could be Nebuchadnezzar I again, but this is uncertain. In any case, it is likely that the text was composed with a particular king in mind, whose identity

---

[252] Borger 1971: 22.
[253] Borger 1971: 23.

escapes us. Its rather general character however made this text applicable to later kings as well. It is conceivable that Assyrian kings such as Esarhaddon and Ashurbanipal had an interest in this text too, as it deals with the ideal image of the king as protector/restorer of the Babylonian cults. In particular Esarhaddon, according to his own inscriptions, went to great lengths attempting to reverse the deplorable cultic situation of Babylonia.

Uruk Prophecy

The Uruk Prophecy is known from a single tablet from Uruk written between the fifth and third century.[254] The obverse contains 24 lines, but only their ends have been preserved; the reverse contains 18 lines, which have been almost entirely preserved. The reverse presents a sequence of eleven kings, of which the second and tenth are most specifically described.[255]

king 2 (r. 3-7)	king 10 (r. 11-15)
[Aft]er him (i.e. king 1) a king will arise. He will not provide justice for the land. He will not make the right decisions for the land.	After him (i.e. king 9) a king will arise *in Uruk.* He will provide justice for the land. He will make the right decisions for the land. *He will establish the rites of the cult of Anu in Uruk.*
The old protective goddess of Uruk he will take away from Uruk and make her dwell in Babylon. He will make dwell in her sanctuary a protective goddess not belonging to Uruk and dedicate to her people not belonging to her. He will impose a heavy tribute on the people of Uruk. He will lay Uruk waste, fill the canals with silt, and abandon the cultivated fields.	The old protective goddess of Uruk he will take away from Babylon and make her dwell in Uruk, in her sanctuary. He will dedicate to her people belonging to her. He will rebuild the temples of Uruk, he will restore the sanctuaries. He will renew Uruk. He will rebuild the gates of Uruk with lapis-lazuli. He will fill the canals and the cultivated fields with plenty and abundance.

The likeliest identification of these two kings is with Erība-Marduk (c. 770) and Nebuchadnezzar II (605-562).[256] Nebuchadnezzar in his inscriptions claims to have restored the cult of Ištar of Uruk: 'I reinstalled the original cultic features and the former rites of Ištar of Uruk.

---

[254] Beaulieu 1993: 44.
[255] Translations from: Beaulieu 1993: 43.
[256] This was proposed by Hunger and Kaufman 1975. Lambert (1978: 10-12) and Goldstein (1988) propose alternative interpretations, but Beaulieu (1993: 44-49) makes a convincing case for the earlier interpretation.

I returned to Eanna its beneficent protective goddess (*lamassu*)'.[257] This is confirmed by an inscription of Nabonidus:

> Ištar of Uruk ... whose cult the Urukaeans changed during the reign of Erība-Marduk ... left Eanna in anger to dwell in a place not her dwelling. They made dwell in her cella a protective goddess not belonging to Eanna. He[258] appeased Ištar, re-established her shrine for her ... the inappropriate Ištar he removed from Eanna and returned Innin (i.e. Ištar) to Eanna, her sanctuary.[259]

It appears that the protective goddess (*lamassu*) and Ištar of Uruk are identical. According to the Uruk Prophecy, things went wrong under the reign of Erība-Marduk when the statue of Ištar was taken to Babylon and an illegal substitute took its place. Nebuchadnezzar however put an end to this deplorable situation.

Whereas king 1, from the Sealand, and king 3, a bad king without any specification, are difficult to identify, the interpretation followed here is supported by r. 8 (following king 3): 'Idem, idem, idem, idem, idem, he will take the property of the land of Akkad to the land of Subartu (i.e. Assyria).' This can be taken as an ingenious summary of the Assyrian domination of Babylonia, from Tiglath-pileser III to Ashurbanipal.[260] The king that will reverse the evil situation and restore the cult of Uruk, is Nebuchadnezzar II. The text however mentions one more king: '[Af]ter him a king, his son, will arise in Uruk and rule the four quarters. He will exercise [ruler]ship? and kingship in Uruk. His dynasty will endure forever. [The king]s of Uruk will exercise rulership like the gods'. That Amel-Marduk, Nebuchadnezzar's son, reigned for only two years and was not very successful need not hinder this interpretation. The glorifying depiction of Nebuchadnezzar suggests that the text was composed during his reign. The final passage is to be read as a divine promise. The text ends with a real prediction aiming to legitimate and support the predicted rule of the son of the good king.[261]

---

[257] Langdon 1912: Nebukadnezar nr. 9, ii 50-59.

[258] This must be Nebuchadnezzar. The passage refers to a predecessor of Nabonidus. Theoretically, it could refer to Nabopolassar, but that king in his inscriptions does not mention any building activities or the return of a cultic statue to Uruk.

[259] Schaudig 2001: 516-517, 523-524. Translation from Beaulieu 1993:45

[260] So Beaulieu 1993: 47.

[261] See Kaufman 1977: 224-225; cf. Heintz (1992) who discusses this text from the angle of 'royal messianism'.

Beaulieu has argued that the text in its present form shows a concern from a later period. The first phrase in the description of Nebuchadnezzar's restoration, 'He will establish the rites of the cult of Anu in Uruk', in Beaulieu's view betrays a third-century interest.[262] Whereas the basic layer of the text focuses on the contrast between Erība-Marduk and Nebuchadnezzar with respect to the cult of Ištar, the later edition presents Nebuchadnezzar as an exemplary ruler of the past, who restored the cults of Uruk and rebuilt her temples. The purpose of this was to gain support for the restoration of the Anu cult of Uruk in the Seleucid period; the newly edited Uruk Prophecy aimed to show the Seleucid rulers the proper royal conduct towards the city of Uruk.[263]

If this is correct, the Marduk Prophecy and the Uruk Prophecy present analogous cases. Both were composed during the reign of a king who was glorified as the restorer of the Babylonian cult, Nebuchadnezzar I and Nebuchadnezzar II respectively. Both texts probably were at a later stage reedited from later interest, seventh-century Assyria and Seleucid Uruk respectively. In the re-edition, the restorer king becomes a model for the contemporary ruler. The Uruk Prophecy in its final shape supports the establishment of the cult of Anu as reorganised in the third century and presents the ruler who will promote this cultic revival as a new Nebuchadnezzar (II).[264] Likewise, the Marduk Prophecy presents the king who will stimulate the restorations of the Babylonian cults as a new Nebuchadnezzar (I). A final similarity may be proposed. The first line of the obverse of the Uruk Prophecy ends with the word 'my signs'. This might suggest that the Uruk Prophecy like the Marduk Prophecy has a deity as its narrator.[265]

Dynastic Prophecy

The Dynastic Prophecy is known from a single, fragmentary tablet.[266] The Dynastic prophecy contains descriptions of the reigns of unnamed kings cast in the form of predictions. Whereas scholars agree on the identification of most of the kings mentioned, the identity of the final king poses a problem.

---

[262] Beaulieu 1993: 48-49.

[263] Beaulieu (1993: 49-50) mentions Antiochus I as the most probable candidate.

[264] Beaulieu 1993: 49. Beaulieu tentatively suggests that the Uruk Prophecy may have been cast as an oracle of Anu.

[265] Cf. Beaulieu 1993: 49. This may have been Anu or Ištar of Uruk.

[266] Editions by Grayson 1975b and Van der Spek 2003: 311-324.

The text starts with an introduction. Although much of it is lost, it seems that the narrator claims to have received information from the gods, consisting of unalterable predictions, which he has left to posterity.[267] In vi 17 the narrator is identified as Munnabtum. This name may refer to Munnabitum, a Babylonian astrologer who worked for the seventh-century Assyrian kings Esarhaddon and Asurbanipal. The Dynastic prophecy is a text from the early Hellenistic period in which a seventh-century Babylonian scholar fictitiously reveals the future.[268]

The predictions begin in column i 7', with *ár-kat* U$_4$-*mu* 'in later time', later of course from the fictitious standpoint of Munnabitum in the seventh century. The first set of predictions deals with the Babylonian takeover of the Assyrian empire. The column ends with a horizontal ruling. The next part, ii 1'-10', points to a king who reigns for three years, probably Neriglissar (559-556), whose son (Labaši-Marduk) will not succeed in ruling the land. After another horizontal ruling, the text continues with the seventeen-years reign of a usurper who establishes the 'dynasty of Harran'. This refers to Nabonidus, whose reign is judged as bad: 'He will plot evil against Akkad' (ii 16'). The following section describes the takeover by a king of Elam. This refers to Cyrus,[269] whose reign is evaluated as 'That king will be stronger than the land and all the lands [will bring him] tribute. During his reign Akkad [will live] in security.' (ii 22'-24').[270] In the next column, on the reverse, a king is mentioned who, after a reign of two years, is murdered by a eunuch. His successor reigns for five years. This must refer to Arses, murdered by the eunuch-general Bagoas, and succeeded by Darius III. The latter is predicted to suffer a setback against the Macedonians (see below).

Since there is a 200-years gap between the end of the obverse (column ii) dealing with Cyrus, and the beginning of the reverse dealing with Arses, the suggestion that an entire column, both on obverse and reverse is lost, makes good sense.[271] Grayson's column iii on the reverse is in fact column v, and columns iii and iv dealing with the kings

---

[267] Van der Spek 2003: 318. Longman's view that the introduction is cast in first-person speech (1991: 152, 162-163) has no firm ground.

[268] Van der Spek 2003: 323-324.

[269] Cf. Potts 1999: 306-311, for Cyrus, 'king of Anšan' as an 'Elamite' king.

[270] Translation Van der Spek 2003: 316, with discussion p. 319-320. Van der Spek argues convincingly that the description of the reign of Cyrus is positive (contra Grayson). Dijkstra (2002: 75) opts for a positive evaluation as well.

[271] Lambert 1978: 12-13.

between Cyrus and Arses are probably missing.[272] The reign of Darius III is described as follows:

> Five years [he will exercise] king[ship]. Troops of the land of Hani
> [......] will set out [.........] [his] troop[s *the will defeat*;] booty from
> him they will take [and his spoils] they will plunder.[273]

This refers to the defeat of Darius III against the Macedonians. The immediately following passage, which ends the preserved part of column v, has bewildered scholars:

> Later [his] tr[oops ....] he will assemble and his weapons he will ra[ise
> (...)] Enlil, Šamaš, and [Marduk?] will go at the side of his army [(...)]
> the overthrow of the Hanaean troops he will [bring about]. Its/their[274]
> extensive booty he will car[ry off] [and] into his palace he [will bring
> it]. The people who had [experienced] misfortune [will enjoy] well-
> being. The heart of the land [will be happy]. Tax exemption [*he will
> grant to the Babylonians*].[275]

The difficulty of this passage is that it appears to claim that Darius III after an initial setback against the Macedonians decisively defeated them. As a real prophecy it could make sense, but as part of a series of *vaticinia ex eventu* it is hardly intelligible.

In Grayson's opinion, the final column of the text contains a de-scription of the reigns of three further kings.[276] This column is badly damaged, but four horizontal rulings are visible, which mark five dif-ferent sections. According to Grayson, the first three sections describe the reigns of Seleucus I, Philip Arrhidaeus and Alexander IV.[277] From this understanding of the text, the apparent 'prediction' of Darius' vic-

---

[272]   Van der Spek 2003: 311-312, 316, 320.

[273]   Column v 8-13. Translation based on Van der Spek 2003: 317. The term Hani (*ha-ni-i*), 'Hanaeans', occurs in various Hellenistic chronicles: Chronicle concerning Darius III and Alexander l. 6' (Van der Spek 2003: 301-305); Arabia Chronicle l. 4'; Diadochi Chronicle l. 36; Antiochus and India Chronicle l. 12'; Invasion of Ptolemy III Chronicle l. 6', and the Babylonian king list of the Hellenistic period l. 8 (see on the website of Livius.org, 'chronicles', texts in preparation, Bert van der Spek). In the Hellenistic period the term Hani/Hanaeans apparently is a designation of Mac-edon/Macedonians, or by extension Greeks and Macedonians (Van der Spek 2003: 305). Dalley (2004b: 431) suggests for *ha-ni-e* the reading *ha-li-i*, 'Hellenes'.

[274]   The text has *šillatsu* 'his booty' (i.e. the booty taken from him/it). I suggest to explain –*šu* either as a mistake for –*šunu*, or 'its booty' as *ad sensum* referring to the booty taken from the Hanaean army.

[275]   Column v 13-23. Translation based on Van der Spek 2003: 317.

[276]   Grayson 1975b: 26-27, with note 14.

[277]   Grayson 1975b: 17. Grayson assumes that these kings are described negatively and that the Dynastic Prophecy is 'a strong expression of anti-Seleucid sentiment'. This is however based on a badly damaged passage.

tory over the Macedonians cannot be explained. On the one hand, it is highly unlikely that the author of the text falsified the outcome of the battle of Gaugamela, and on the other, if the chain of *vaticinia ex eventu* continues, Darius' victory cannot be explained as a real prediction.[278]

To come to a convincing solution, the following points must be mentioned.[279] First, the passage concerning the defeat of the Macedonians makes sense only as a real prophecy. It clearly forms a climax to the succession of reigns, highly comparable to the climaxes in the literary prophecies discussed above. The expression of the favour of the gods—'Enlil, Šamaš, and [Marduk[?]] will go at the side of his army'— is very different from the dry description of the reigns of previous kings.[280] Furthermore, the 'Hanaeans' are only referred to as an enemy power. No king of the Hanaeans is mentioned at all; the Hanaeans merely are the enemies that are to be destroyed. The passage in my view must be a real prediction concerning a glorious king who will defeat the Macedonians.

The final column need not contradict this interpretation. As far as we can judge, the sections of the last column are remarkably short. At least two sections are significantly shorter than any of the sections on the preceding columns, and arguably too short to describe the reigns of further kings.[281] Perhaps this column did not contain descriptions of further dynasties, but described aspects of the rule of the glorious king (introduced in the final part of column v) and his sons.[282] By analogy, in the Marduk Prophecy the glorious deeds and prosperous years of the restorer king are described in the final part of the text, divided over various sections. And even if column vi contained a description of further kings, it could be part of the prophecy, presenting the dynasty of

---

[278] Grayson 1975b: 26: 'The problem, of course, is how to reconcile the defeat of the Hanaeans with historical fact—the victory of Alexander at Gaugamela! For this I have no answer.'

[279] For an overview of solutions proposed, see Van der Spek 2003: 326-332.

[280] So also Van der Spek 2003: 331.

[281] It may be observed that in the rest of the text, the horizontal rulings separate the successive dynasties, not the individual reigns.

[282] The fragments of the final column accord with this. L. 8 [...] *ippuš*[uš], cf. perhaps i 23' ('he will build the palace of Babylon'); l. 9 Dt-stem of *elēlu* 'they will be purified'; l. 10 'and he will seize the land'; l. 12 *i-bé-el-lu* 'and they will rule' (see Van der Spek 2003: 314).

the glorious king described in column v as everlasting. A comparable ending is found in the Uruk prophecy.[283]

Who is this glorious king? Van der Spek suggests he is a future, yet unknown king who is expected to defeat the Hanaean army. This however presupposes the introduction of a new figure in v 13: 'Later [his] troops [he (sc. the yet unknown saviour king)] will assemble ...'. This does not seem very likely. Furthermore, in this interpretation the climax of the text is a reminder to Alexander: like the dynasties of As-syria, Babylonia and Persia, 'later' (but soon!) Alexander's power will reach its end, when a new king comes and destroys his army.[284] How-ever, Alexander is not even mentioned in the text; the Macedonians are merely referred to as an enemy power to be destroyed. The most likely solution therefore is that the prophecy concerning the glorious king still refers to Darius III. This is the most natural reading of the extant passage of column v. The *vaticinia ex eventu* extend to v 13. The author knows that Darius reigned for five years, and that he was defeated by the Macedonians (v 6-13). At this point the prophecy be-gins, predicting that Darius will return and assisted by the great gods will decisively destroy the Macedonian enemies.[285] According to this interpretation, the text must have been written in the eight-months pe-riod between the battle of Gaugamela (331) and Darius' death (330). This is assuredly a short period of time, but a piece of ideological sup-port for the dethroned Darius makes of course most sense soon after his defeat and his flight to Gutium. After a reign of five years, Darius lost his kingship, but as this text predicts, he will return and defeat the Macedonians. An indication that the text does not accept the Macedo-nian takeover as the establishment of a new dynasty, is that no king of the Macedonians is mentioned. They are merely described as an en-emy power, soon to be thrown out.

The climax of the Dynastic Prophecy consists of the supportive promise to Darius III that the Babylonian gods will assist him in his fight against the Macedonians. The text is probably written shortly af-ter his defeat at Gaugamela, when some people still had hope that he

---

[283]   '[Af]ter him a king, his son, will arise in Uruk and rule the four quarters. He will exercise [ruler]ship[?] and kingship in Uruk. His dynasty will endure forever. [The king]s of Uruk will exercise rulership like the gods.' (see above).

[284]   Van der Spek 2003:331-332.

[285]   Whereas the *vaticinia ex eventu* are introduced with *ár-kat* U_4-*mu* 'in later time' (i 7'), the real predictions are introduced with *arkānu* 'later' (cf. Van der Spek 2003: 318).

would come back to destroy the Macedonians, to regain the throne, and to establish an everlasting dynasty, protected by the gods.[286]

Various scholars have pointed out that the depictions of the ideal king in the literary prophecies resemble the portrayals of the ideal king as found in the Old Testament.[287] Whereas Nissinen, in this respect, refers to Jer 23:5-6 and Zech 6:12-13, the ideal king passages from First Isaiah, Isa 9:1-6, 11:1-5 and 32:1-2, can be mentioned as well.[288] This is not to claim that these biblical passages are dependent on the Akkadian literary prophecies.[289] Rather, the idealising portrayals of a king, in First Isaiah and in the Akkadian literary prophecies, share a more general *topos*. It is a general characteristic of royal ideology to present the king as a restorer of long-time lapses, and his reign as a period during which a deplorable situation reverted to a glorious time. However, two further features may be mentioned that are shared by the ideal king passages from Isaiah and those from the Akkadian literary predictions: first, their literary character and second, the anonymity of the ideal king. Both the texts from First Isaiah that form part of the seventh-century revision and the Akkadian literary predictions are literary, scribal products.[290] Furthermore, both take the form of divine or prophetic announcements—predictions concerning the future—and for that reason, the ideal king remains unidentified. Both can be seen as a form of pseudo-prophecy. The *Heilszeit* is characterised by a symbiosis between the king and the gods. The purpose of these texts is to glorify the reign of a particular king and to provide divine legitimacy for his actions.

---

[286] This interpretation is supported by the general impression the text gives. Whereas most of the kings are described in neutral terms, three of them receive explicit value judgements. Nabonidus is depicted as a bad king ('he will plot evil against Akkad'), Cyrus receives explicit praise ('During his reign Akkad [will live] in security') and the glorious king (Darius III) is also expressly depicted as a good ruler (I do not agree with Van der Spek's restoration in v 6). This means that the Persian dynasty is generally depicted in positive terms. The glorious reign of Cyrus put an end to the bad reign of Nabonidus. Similarly, the glorious (future) reign of Darius III will put an end to the Macedonian intrusion (cf. Van der Spek 2003: 325).

[287] Nissinen 2003c: 141; Höffken 1977; Beaulieu 1993: 51; Weinfeld 1998: 28.

[288] Cf. Höffken 1977: 69, note 50.

[289] The Marduk, Šulgi, Uruk and Dynastic Prophecies are predominantly concerned with events in Babylonia and show a cultic concern. An important theme is the connection between the absence of the deity with the failure of legitimate and correct rule, and the return of the deity with restoration (Ellis 1989: 175).

[290] Höffken (1977: 69) rightly points at this characteristic, but in my view is wrong to exclude Isa 9:1-6 and 11:1-5 from this (1977: 69, note 50).

Literary Prediction in the Song of Erra

A final example of literary prediction stems from the Song of Erra.[291] The date of this composition is debated,[292] but it was popular in the Assyrian period and later.[293] The song narrates how the god Erra, after Marduk has left his dwelling, causes a terrible ravage. Erra ruthlessly goes on the warpath against mankind in general and against Babylonia in particular. His advisor Išum attempts to keep the butchering within limits. Marduk abandons his throne, thereby leaving the world to chaos and the people to destruction.[294] The chaos and destruction are vividly depicted in tablet 4. Erra formulates his ambitions of worldwide ravage (4:131-136) as follows:

> Sea people shall not spare sea people, nor Subartian (spare) Subartian, nor Assyrian Assyrian. Nor shall Elamite spare Elamite, nor Kassite Kassite. Nor shall Sutean spare Sutean, nor Gutian Gutian. Nor shall Lullubean spare Lullubean, nor country country, nor city city. Nor shall tribe spare tribe, nor man man, nor brother brother, and they shall slay one another. But afterwards a man of Akkad shall rise up (*tebû*). He will fell them all and shepherd all of them.[295]

After this, Erra's destructive ambitions are carried out (4:139-150). Tablet 5 pictures the gods as being horrified by the terrors. Erra explains to them that it is thanks to Išum that there are some people left. Išum advises Erra to calm down: he has shown his power and the gods will serve him. Erra settles in Emeslam, his dwelling in the temple in Kutha, and Išum restores the order: 'Išum, in a loud voice, spoke the

---

[291] See Cagni 1969.

[292] Suggestions range from the eleventh to the seventh century. Von Soden (1971: 255-256) proposes the date of 764 BCE. His argument is mainly based on tablet 4:52-62, dealing with disturbances in Uruk. Lara Peinado (1989: 114-115) dates the composition to the eleventh century, when the Suteans ravaged the Babylonian cities and connects the deplorable period of chaos with the reign of the usurper Adad-apla-iddina. However, the term 'Suteans' may have been incorporated to lend an air of antiquity and hence authority to the song (Dalley 2000: 282). An eighth-century date may be likely (although older material may have been incorporated), since, as Dalley (2000: 284) points out, the family to which the author (Kabti-ilani-Marduk, son of Dabibi) belongs, is first attested in 765 BCE. A phrase from the song (5:35, 'then the governors of all cities, every one of them, haul their heavy tribute into Šuanna') has a parallel in Merodach-baladan II's cylinder inscription l. 34 (Brinkman 1984: 49, note 230). Besides, the Suteans often occur in Sargon's inscriptions as archaising term for nomadic plunderers that threaten civilisation (see Fuchs 1994: 459; Heltzer 1981: 96-97).

[293] Machinist 1983b: 221.

[294] For Marduk's motive to leave his throne, see Machinist 1983b: 222 and Lara Peinado 1989: 112.

[295] Translation based on Dalley 2000: 308-309.

sign (*ittu*), he conveyed the instruction concerning the scattered people of Akkad, 5:23-38:

> May the reduced people of the land become numerous again. May the short man and the tall man go along its paths. May the weak man of Akkad fell the strong Sutean. May one man drive way seven (of them) as if they were flocks!
>
> You shall make their towns into ruins and their hills into wildernesses. You shall bring their heavy spoils into Šuanna (i.e. Babylon). You shall bring the country's gods who were angry safely back into their dwellings. You shall let Šakkan and Nissaba descend into the country.[296] You shall let the mountains bear their wealth and the sea its produce. You shall let the meadowlands, which have been devastated, bear their produce!
>
> Then let the governors of all cities, every one of them, haul their heavy tribute into Šuanna. Let the temples, which were allowed to become damaged, lift their heads (up) as high as the rising sun. Let the Tigris and Euphrates bring the waters of abundance. Let the governors of all cities, every one of them, deliver up to the provider of Esagila and Babylon![297]

This 'oracle' (*ittu*) of Išum corresponds with Erra's announcement that after the destruction 'a man of Akkad' will bring about a reversal: the announcement that 'the man of Akkad will fell them all' (4:136) resembles the announcement that 'the weak man of Akkad will fell the strong Sutean' (5:27).[298] Furthermore, the middle part of Išum's speech (5:29-34) is a second-person address, which in all likelihood addresses the very same person: the 'man of Akkad' who will rule as king of Babylon. The song ends with a description of the ideal king, who will carry out the restoration. This king is again referred to in Išum's final words: 'Let the governors of all cities (…) deliver up to the provider of Esagila and Babylon!' (5:38). The provider (*zānin Esagila u Bābili*), a royal epithet,[299] must be the restorer king.[300]

The Song of Erra shares some important themes with the literary predictions discussed above. The absence of Marduk from his throne leads to chaos and destruction, but after a deplorable situation, a reversal of fortune takes place, carried out by a Babylonian king. The

---

[296] The disappearance of Šakkan (god of cattle) and Nissaba (goddess of grain) to heaven, which is paralleled in the Marduk Prophecy i 25' (Borger 1971: 7), indicates a disastrous situation; their descent into the land marks the reversal of fortune.

[297] Translation based on Dalley 2000: 310-311.

[298] In both cases *maqātu* (Š) 'to fell' is used.

[299] See Seux 1967: 372-375.

[300] Similarly Van der Toorn 2007: 42.

song contains a similar pseudo-prophetic element.[301] Since the composition as a whole is presented as a divine revelation, the prediction of a new Babylonian king is presented as a divine announcement.[302]

The Song of Erra has been qualified as a mythologisation of specific historical circumstances.[303] The song describes the events of an interregnum during which Erra is in power with Marduk's consent.[304] A clue to what this meant at the historical level may be found in the description at the beginning of the fourth tablet: 'You (Erra) changed your divine nature and made yourself like a man'. Erra in the shape of a braggart wandered around in Babylon instigating the people to revolt and make havoc. This probably is the mythologisation of a rebellion in Babylon, which led to chaos and destruction.[305] The absence of Marduk may reflect the situation of a deportation of Marduk's statue. His absence creates room for Erra with devastating consequences.[306] The end of the song pictures the recovery of Babylonia after a deplorable and troubled period, including the restoration of its royal dynasty and victory over its enemies.[307]

6.2.4   *Function and Purpose of the Texts*

6.2.1 dealt with the reuse and literary afterlife of the Assyrian prophetic oracles. Most of the extant oracles are preserved in a secondary shape. These oracles, not surprisingly, to a great extent resemble an official royal ideological point of view. From oracles directly reported in letters however we know that this was not necessarily the case. The

---

[301]   Dalley 2000: 315, with note 52.

[302]   See tablet 5:42-46 (Dalley 2000: 311). The song is presented as a divine revelation to Kabti-ilani-Marduk, the 'compiler' of the song. According to Van der Toorn (2007: 42) the name of the compiler/author is mentioned because, being presented as a prophecy, the text needed the name of the 'prophet'.

[303]   Machinist 1983b: 221; Lara Peinado 1989: 110.

[304]   Lara Peinado (1989: 115) argues that Marduk plays an indirect role, but nevertheless appears as sovereign and supreme king of gods and people. It is Marduk who permits and justifies Erra's actions.

[305]   Machinist 1983b: 221.

[306]   The disastrous situation during Erra's rule is analogous to the motif of the 'wrong Ištar' in the temple of Uruk and the accompanying deplorable situation in the Uruk Prophecy. The absence of the right god and presence of the wrong god on the throne necessarily led to chaos and terror. Misfortune is more often explained as the work of Erra; e.g. in a royal inscription of Nabuchadnezzar I, a military setback against Elam is described as: 'Against the will of the gods, the god Erra, (most) powerful of the gods, smote my [war]riors', see Frame 1995: 20, r. 10b-11.

[307]   Cf. Lara Peinado 1989: 116.

same prophetic voice that encouraged and legitimised the king could also make demands on him or even choose the side of his adversaries. The phenomenon of 'royal prophecy' is the result of the development of prophecy under royal auspices. Through reuse and elaboration, the prophetic oracles were lifted out of their original situational character.

In 6.2.2, various texts were discussed that can be seen as literary derivatives of prophecy. The texts closely resemble the genre of prophetic oracles, but bear from the outset a literary character. In these texts, divine legitimation and support of the king is an important theme. Furthermore, as is particularly apparent from SAA 3 44, these compositions are marked by an episodic perspective that is broader than the situational perspective of prophetic oracles. The oracles that received a literary development (6.2.1) closely resemble the literary derivatives of prophecy (6.2.2). Both sets of texts share the same themes and purposes. The development of prophetic oracles, such as the formation of oracle collections, must therefore not be regarded as an isolated phenomenon but as part of the broader development of prophecy becoming literature. The third section (6.2.3) dealt with the literary predictions. In these texts the concept of divine legitimation and commissioning of the king is an important theme. Furthermore, these texts have a particular agenda: the glorification of the reign of the king.[308]

All texts discussed in the second part of this chapter are characterised by an official, ideological point of view. They illustrate the close bond between king and god and in this way glorify the reign of the king and emphasise that the gods govern the historical scene.

6.3   Conclusion

6.3.1   Prophecy in Literature

This chapter dealt with the reuse, development and expansion of prophecy: the prophetic words of Isaiah and the Assyrian prophecies. At both sides, the development took on similar forms. Both in Assyria and in Judah we have to reckon with prophetic oracles that were recorded and documented. Whereas the primary documentation of prophetic oracles and sayings served their communication, we see on

---

[308]   Ellis 1989: 172.

both sides a further development. Prophecy, at least in some cases, was preserved in archives. This was certainly the case in Assyria; for the Judaean side this is plausible. The secondary development of prophecy in Judah and Assyria took on similar forms.

A first similarity is found in the reapplication, republication, re-working, and elaboration of prophetic oracles. Prophetic oracles were republished and preserved in the form of collections.[309] Prophetic material was furthermore elaborated: literary reworking of the archived material was undertaken. A second point of similarity relates to the composition of new texts that resembled or imitated the form and genre of prophecy. Both the seventh-century revision of the Isaiah tradition and several texts from seventh-century Assyria (6.2.2) can be seen as literary derivatives of prophecy. Furthermore, the examples of literary prediction (6.2.3) are characterised by a pseudo-prophetic, predictive style, similar to that of the revision of the Isaiah tradition. Both the literary predictions and the revision of the Isaiah tradition contain depictions of the reign of the ideal king. This is a general ancient Near Eastern theme.[310] However, the revision of the Isaiah tradition and the literary predictions share one more trait: the ideal king remains anonymous. This is because the reign of the ideal king is presented as something of the future, in prophetic, predictive veil.

With regard to the textual format an important difference may be pointed out. On the Assyrian side, we have discussed various forms of literary afterlife of the prophetic oracles (6.2.1), the literary derivatives of prophecy (6.2.2) and the literary predictions (6.2.3). These different examples of the phenomenon of 'prophecy in literature' however are all found in separate texts. On the Judaean side we have seen similar developments, which as part of the revision of the Isaiah tradition are found within one and the same text. The Isaiah tradition in its revised form probably consisted of three compilations, which took the form of three separate documents. Each compilation was to some extent a hybrid text; much more than the Assyrian texts dis-

---

[309] Cf. Knauf 2000: 3, comparing the prophecies of Isa 7* and 8*, as 'die Sammlung "734"' with the oracle collections of SAA 9. According to Knauf, both had a similar function: 'die gegenwärtige Politik durch den Rückblick auf ihre göttlich abgesegneten Anfänge zu legitimieren', and a similar *Sitz im Leben*: 'das Staatsarchiv'.

[310] A common pattern in ancient Near Eastern tradition is that a king is presented as the one under whose reign a deplorable situation came to an end after which a joyful period began. This relates to the divine mandate of the king, since it is the gods that initiate the beatific time; the king is executor of their decisions.

cussed in this chapter. From its earliest literary development onwards the Isaiah tradition became an expanding and enlarging tradition.

6.3.2 *Development of Prophecy and Royal Ideology*

Both in Judah and Assyria we discern the phenomenon of prophecy becoming incorporated into a royal ideological perspective. Examples of this development on the Judaean side are the B1-story of Hezekiah in which the prophet Isaiah figures, and the late seventh-century revision of the Isaiah tradition. On the Assyrian side, this applies to virtually all the texts discussed in 6.2.1 and 6.2.2. Prophecy in transmission could take the form of 'royal prophecy'. This development is of course not too surprising, since prophecy in the ancient Near East often was supportive of the king. However this development constricted prophecy to one, though admittedly main, aspect. In the process of preservation, transmission, reuse and reworking, prophecy became tightly connected with the royal perspective. In practice, prophecy had a broader function: as one of the means of the gods to support *and* to criticise the conduct of the king. Divine support of the king was not self-evident in the ancient Near East.[311] Although prophets functioned within the existing order and can be qualified as guardians of the state, this did not mean that they always agreed with the king and his politics. The interest of the cosmic and social-political order transcended the interests of the individual king. The gods could even go as far as taking the side of the king's adversary. In the *development of prophecy* however, god and king became inextricably connected. The elaborate prophecies and literary derivatives of prophecy emphasise and glorify the close bonds between king and god. Through this development, prophecy became captured in a royal, ideological perspective. The official ideological stamp of the literarily developed prophecies, in Judah and Assyria, is likely to indicate the provenance, purpose and function of the literary reworking of the prophecies. The development of prophetic oracles into collections, elaborated texts, royal inscriptions, and literary compilations occurred under royal auspices and served a royal interest. Its aim was to support and glorify the ruling king by expressing the close connection between the gods and the

---

[311] The relationship between god and king was one of mutual obligations, a *quid pro quo* contract. The gods' long-term concern was with the state not with the individual king. See Ellis 1989: 176-182.

king. The king enjoyed divine support and divine authority. The late seventh-century revision of the Isaiah material is to be understood from this perspective as well, in relation to the royal ideology concerning Josiah.

In the ancient Near East, the king was held to create order and to represent religious, political and moral authority.[312] Idealising portrayals of the king and his reign were a common phenomenon,[313] in Assyria,[314] as well as in Judah.[315] According to the ideal image, the king was endowed with great wisdom and understanding. He was able to give wise counsel, to discern the words that were in the heart and to determine true and false. The king's duty to establish justice and righteousness implied to protect the weak and the poor and to abolish evil and oppression from the land.[316] The ideal images of the king in the revision of the Isaiah tradition and in the Assyrian texts are exponents of ancient Near Eastern royal ideology. An additional similarity between the ideal king passages of the Isaiah revision and the Akkadian literary-predictive texts is that both present a nameless king. On both sides, as I have argued, specific kings were intended. The anonymous idealisation of the king followed from the prophetic, predictive style of the texts. Both in the Assyrian texts and in the Isaiah revision, the people share in the blessings of the rule of the ideal king. In Isa 9:1-6 and 11:4 the people are explicitly referred to, whereas in 32:1-2 they are obviously implied since the king is like a protective rock for his people. On the Assyrian side, the people are explicitly referred to as the profiting party in SAA 9 2.4; SAA 9 3.2; SAA 3 44, l.

---

[312]   Baines 1998: 50.

[313]   Baines 1998: 49. Lambert (1998: 69-70) argues that kingship in the ancient Near East was 'messianic', since according to the ideal image, the king was to bring about messianic blessing.

[314]   E.g. the idealising depiction of Ashurbanipal's reign in the letter SAA 10 226, 5-r. 3: 'There is a fine reign: days of security, years of justice, very heavy rains, massive floods, low prices. ... Old men dance, young men sing. Women and girls are happy and rejoice. ... The king my lord pardons him whose crimes condemned to death. ... Those who have been ill for many days have recovered. The hungry have been satisfied, parched ones have been anointed with oil, the naked have been clothed with garments.' Translation from: Lambert 1998: 69-70.

[315]   E.g. the royal Psalms; see further Weinfeld 1995: 45-74, esp. 59.

[316]   Weinfeld 1995: 45-74; Kramer 1974: 173-174. In the ancient Near East, 'justice and righteousness' denote the divine order of the cosmos, which was to be upheld and to adhered to in all aspects of life. The king was commissioned as patron *par excellence* of order and justice. Attributing 'justice and righteousness' to the king is part of the ideal picture, which stressed the bond between human and divine authority; see Nell 2000: 144-146.

12 ('I appo[inted you] as the shepherd of justice of the subjects of Enlil');[317] and in portrayals of the ideal king in the Marduk Prophecy, the Uruk Prophecy, the Dynastic Prophecy and the Song of Erra.

6.3.3 Historical-Theological Perspective

Characteristic of the literary development of prophecy is a broadening of perspective. Whereas prophetic oracles relate to particular situations, as described in chapter 4, in a developed form they are characterised by a more comprehensive perspective. Once the outcome of the events is known, the events retrospectively are perceived from a broader view. In distinction from the situational view of the prophetic oracles, the perspective of the elaborated texts and literary derivatives of prophecy can be called the episodic view. On the Assyrian side, the following episodic views prominently occur: 1) The struggle for the throne of Assyria after the death of Sennacherib, from the subsequent perspective of Esarhaddon as legitimate heir to the throne and ever-winning king. 2) The (cultic) restoration of Babylon from the perspective that the gods had chosen Esarhaddon as king in order to bring about the reversal of a deplorable situation. 3) The rivalry between Ashurbanipal and Šamaš-šum-ukin, from the perspective of the former as a pious, god-fearing king and the latter as a rebel justly punished by the gods. 4) The Elamite wars, or the Babylonian-Elamite wars, fought by Ashurbanipal.

Whereas prophetic oracles often were delivered in a critical situation, the literarily developed texts look back at longer episodes. In the literary-predictive texts the time perspective is still more comprehensive. The Uruk Prophecy for instance focuses on a time-span from Erība-Marduk (c. 770) to Nebuchadnezzar II (605-562). The seventh-century revision of the Isaianic material presents an episodic view of the period of Assyrian oppression from the late eighth to the late seventh century. The three compilations are characterised by extrapolations and generalisations similar to those found in the Assyrian material. In the first compilation, the prophecies concerning the destruction of Judah's enemies Aram and Ephraim are broadened in such a way as to include Assyria as well. In the second compilation, a particular confrontation with Assyria—Sargon's campaign of 720 BCE—becomes a paradigm for Assyrian imperialism in general. And in the

---

[317] In contrast to the terrible fate of the people of Šamaš-šum-ukin (l. 13, r. 8-10).

third compilation, the polemic words relating to a particular crisis in Judaean politics become a more general portrayal of ideal leadership. The episodic perspective, characteristic of prophecy in its developed forms, is also found in the Assyrian royal inscriptions.[318] In the same line of thinking lies the connection between the violent death of Sennacherib (681 BCE) and Sennacherib's campaign of 701, which forms the basis of the B1-story of Hezekiah (6.1.2). This shared characteristic indicates that both the literary development of prophecy and the composition of prophetic texts are to be situated in a (royal) scribal milieu.

---

[318] See Pongratz-Leisten 1999: 240-245; examples of the episodic perspective in the inscriptions of Ashurbanipal are the presentation of the wars against the Arabs in connection with the war against Šamaš-šum-ukin, and the interconnection between the wars against Elam and Babylonia (Prism C).

CONCLUSION

CHAPTER SEVEN

SUMMARY AND CONCLUSIONS

7.1 *Aim and Focus of the Study*

This study offers a comparison between parts of First Isaiah and the Assyrian prophecies. In the comparative study of prophecy, placing a prophetic book at the centre of a comparative investigation is a new approach. This approach has recently been anticipated by scholars who have put forward the Assyrian prophecies, in particular the oracle collections, as the ancient Near Eastern counterpart to the prophetic books. Manfred Weippert, for instance, remarked concerning the Assyrian oracle collections: 'Dies sind Bibliotheksexemplare, die man *mutatis mutandis* mit den Prophetenbüchern des Alten Testaments vergleichen kann' (Weippert 2002: 35). The essential question here is of course what lies behind the words *mutatis mutandis*, or, put differently, what are the conditions for a valid and fruitful comparison of the Assyrian prophecies with the biblical prophetic books? The present study attempts to create the conditions for a comparison between parts of the book of Isaiah and the Assyrian prophecies.

The main purpose of this study is the comparison of the Isaiah tradition in its earliest form and the prophetic material from seventh-century Assyria (part II, chapters 4, 5, and 6). Before the comparison is worked out, the material is investigated in its own right (part I, chapters 2 and 3).

7.2 *The Isaiah Tradition in the Assyrian Period*

Chapter 2 explores the origin and earliest development of the Isaiah tradition. According to a recent view, the book of Isaiah is to be seen as a literary product of the Persian (or even Hellenistic) period. It is generally acknowledged that the Isaiah tradition underwent a complex development in the course of time: new material was added at various stages and existing material was reworked and reinterpreted. First

Isaiah, therefore, is not an anthology of pre-exilic material supplemented by later elaborations, but part of an extensively edited literary
compilation containing divergent material from several ages. The earliest material within the book of Isaiah stems from the Assyrian period
and is to be found within the first part of the book. However, any
claim to date material from First Isaiah to the Assyrian period must be
proven. My exegetical assessment of the Isaiah tradition in the Assyrian period contains three main aspects: historical clues within First
Isaiah; distinguishing between the profiles of the early material and
the later (exilic) reworking of the Isaiah tradition; and the early forms
and format of the eighth-century prophetic and the seventh-century
revision material.

7.2.1   *Historical Clues*

A point of departure in the search for material belonging to the Assyrian period can be found in references to historical entities and circumstances of the eighth and seventh centuries. Some of the examples are
the names Ephraim and Samaria, in oracles predicting the downfall of
Northern Israel, references to the Cushite empire as a political and
military power, and references to Assyria as a political-military superpower.

The main issue in Judah in the later part of the eighth century was
the question of whether or not to resist Assyrian imperialism. In the
periods 734-732, 722-720, and 713-711 BCE, several of Judah's
neighbour states resisted Assyrian dominance, and in 705-701 BCE
Judah attempted to liberate itself from Assyria's rule. Furthermore,
Assyrian campaigns close to, or in, the land of Judah took place in
734, 720, 711, and 701 BCE. Material from First Isaiah that can be
connected with these major events can be confidentially dated to the
eighth century. The most secure ground for identifying the earliest
stratum within First Isaiah are the political issues of the late eighth
century. The earliest layer of the Isaiah tradition, in my assessment,
consists of prophetic words relating to particular, historical contexts
from the later part of the eighth century. The material can be essentially related to three episodes:

- The Syro-Ephraimitic crisis of 734-732 BCE, to which are related the oracles against Ephraim and Aram, included within Isa 7-8 (7:2-3a.4-9a; 7:14b.16; 7:20; 8:1-4) and in 17:1b-3.
- Sargon's campaign of 720 BCE, to which are related the oracles announcing a threat against Philistia and Samaria (14:29.31 and 28:1-4) and the oracles condemning Assyria's imperialism within Isa 10 (10:5-9.13-15; 10:24-25; 10:27b-32).
- The controversy of whether or not to rebel against Assyria, trusting in Egypt's military aid. This played a role in c. 713-711 BCE (Isa 20*) and reached a climax in 705-701 BCE. Related to this are the words against the Judaean leaders within Isa 28-31 (28:7b-10; 28:14-18*; 29:15; 30:1-5*.6b-8; 31:1.3a) and the critical oracles of 18:1-6*; 19:1-4; 22:15-18. Furthermore, the *woe*-sayings of 5:8-23* and 10:1-2 can be associated with this period as well.

It is likely that the oracles and sayings relating to these different moments of the late eighth century were initially preserved in the form of collections.

A second identifiable layer of the Isaiah tradition consists of passages dealing with the destruction of Assyria and the restoration of Judah. In the descriptions it is emphasised that it is Yahweh who carries out Assyria's destruction (10:16-19; 10:26a.27a; 10:33-34; 14:24-27; 30:27-33; 31:4-5.8-9), as part of his dealings with all the nations of the world (14:26-27; 30:27-28; cf. 8:9-10; 17:12-14; 18:1-6). Closely related to the theme of Assyria's destruction is that of Judah's restoration: the reign of a new Judaean king, who is authoritative and righteous, in 9:1-6, 11:1-5 and 32:1-2. The themes of Assyria's downfall and the reign of the ideal king are two sides of the same coin, as both result from Yahweh's intervention. These passages in all likelihood date to the Assyrian period. Yet they clearly differ from the eighth-century prophetic material. They can be regarded as the product of a revision of the Isaiah tradition in the late seventh century.

7.2.2   *Different Profiles*

A fundamental difference can be perceived between the Isaiah tradition in the Assyrian period—the eighth-century prophetic material and the seventh-century revision—on the one hand, and the later transformation of the Isaiah tradition on the other. In particular within Isa 6-8 and 28-32, the prophetic material and its first revision can be distinguished from a later elaboration that put a decisive mark on these chapters. Isa 6-8 and 28-32 in their basic literary version represent textual complexes in which the earlier Isaiah tradition is extensively reworked and in which a new view of Isaiah's prophetic ministry is presented.[1] These literary complexes represent a thorough reworking of the Isaiah tradition in the light of the events of the early sixth century. The suggestion that the disastrous events of the early sixth century left their mark on the Isaiah tradition is not new (e.g. Clements 1980c). However, in my view this mark was much more decisive than scholars have previously acknowledged. The disastrous events of the sixth century led to a profound reconsideration of the past. Far from being given up, the Isaiah tradition was thoroughly reworked to get it into line with a new view of Israel's past and to use the authority of the figure of Isaiah as a spokesman of the new view. This view was essentially that the destruction of Judah and Jerusalem was the result of Yahweh's punishment because of the sinful disobedience of the people.

Among the strategies deployed for connecting this new view with the earlier material, we see first the historical analogy that just as Northern Israel was punished for its sins, so Judah had to be punished as well. Early prophetic material dealing with the punishment of Ephraim-Samaria (e.g. 8:1-4; 28:1-4) was extended with later texts dealing with the punishment of Judah and Jerusalem (e.g. 8:5-8; 29:1-4). A second strategy was the generalisation of the specific criticism against Isaiah's opponents, the leading class of Jerusalem, so as to apply it to the people as a whole. Isaiah's criticism against Judah's leaders advocating rebellion against Assyria (sayings within Isa 28-31*) was turned into criticism against the people of Judah for their sinful disobedience (Isa 28-32). It was this transformation of the Isaiah tradition, presumably in the sixth century, which created the image of Isaiah as a prophet of judgement. The eighth-century prophetic material within First Isaiah and its earliest elaboration in the Assyrian period however are distinctly different from what is supposedly the main characteristic of biblical prophecy: the proclamation of unconditional

---

[1]   By the basic literary versions of Isa 6-8 and 28-32, I mean the units of 6:1-11, 7:1-17 and 8:1-18 on the one hand, and 28:1-22, 29:1-16, 30:1-17, 31, and 32:1-14, on the other, without taking into account the material that can be considered as representing later, post-exilic, editions.

judgement. The eighth-century prophetic material is partly marked by positive aspects (e.g. Isa 7*; 8*; 28:12*; 30:15*), and the critical sayings address a quite specific group of people; furthermore, the seventh-century revision is of an unambiguously positive tone. Isa 6-8 and 28-32 in their basic literary versions however present the positive message as a superseded stage: the positive message was rejected and what remains is the preaching of judgement, applied to the people as a whole. This transition must not be projected onto the prophetic biography, but is to be taken as an indication of the different stages of development of the Isaiah tradition.

7.2.3 The Format of the Isaiah Tradition in the Assyrian Period

The exegetical analysis of chapter 2 led to the following suggestion: the eighth-century prophetic material from First Isaiah received a seventh-century revision in the form of three compilations, which presented the earlier material in a literary garb. The eighth-century prophetic material can be connected with three historical periods, 734-732, 723-720 and 705-701 BCE. This corresponds exactly to the three encounters between Assyria and Judah in the later part of the eighth century: in 734 BCE when Ahaz paid tribute to Tiglath-pileser (chapter 4.1.1), in 720 BCE when Sargon became the 'subduer of the land of Judah' (chapter 4.1.3), and in 701 BCE with the campaign of Sennacherib against Judah (chapter 4.1.7). It seems likely that the material relating to each period was preserved in the form of a collection of prophetic words, and that each of these collections received a revision in the late seventh century. Each compilation consisted of the following elements:

- A dating formula, followed by an account demonstrating Isaiah's commission.
- A series of eighth-century prophetic words, with seventh-century comments added.
- A portrayal of the reign of an ideal king (9:1-6, 11:1-5, 32:1-2).

Notwithstanding later redactional developments, the contours of the three compilations are discernable: compilation 1 consisted of Isa 6:1-9:6*; compilation 2 of Isa 10:5-11:5; and compilation 3 of Isa 28-32*.[2]

---

[2]   All three compilations originally contained some additional material, which has been relocated in the course of development of the Isaiah tradition. Compilation 1

Compilation 1 includes prophetic oracles that originally dealt with the events of 734-732 BCE: Tiglath-pileser's campaigns to Philistia and Damascus, and the Syro-Ephraimite crisis. Its theme is that the enemy aggression against Judah will come to nothing. Compilation 2 includes prophetic words that originally referred to Sargon's campaign of 720 BCE. Its theme is that Assyria will be punished for its self-willed imperialism. Compilation 3 includes the prophetic material dealing with the issue of rebellion against Assyria, relating to the period 705-701 BCE, and the campaign of Sennacherib. Its theme is that it is senseless to trust Egypt for military support against Assyria, since it is Yahweh, and no human hand, that saves Judah from the Assyrian oppression.

Each compilation concludes with a portrayal of the ideal Judaean king. In each case the portrayal of the ideal king corresponds to the nature of the compilation it concluded. The presentation of the ideal king in 9:1-6 adopts the style of the earlier prophetic words included in this compilation. In 9:5 the king is presented as: 'For a child has been born to us, a son given to us.' This resembles the birth announcements in 7:14b.16 and 8:3-4, according to which the son to be born was a hopeful sign. 9:5 echoes the terminology of 7:14b and 8:3. Both in the prophetic oracles and in the description of the ideal king, the son's name plays a crucial role. 11:1-5 forms the conclusion to the second compilation. The way in which the ideal king operates in 11:1-5 forms a contrast with the brutal actions of Assyria described in Isa 10*. In contrast to the pride, self-satisfaction and godlessness of the Assyrian king stands the wisdom and piety of the ideal king. The Assyrian king boasts, 'by the strength of my hand I have done it, and by my wisdom, for I have understanding' (10:13a). The ideal king, by contrast, is endowed with the spirit of Yahweh, a 'spirit of wisdom and understanding, a spirit of counsel and might, a spirit of knowledge and the fear of Yahweh' (11:2). In contrast to the brutal power of Assyria, 'the stick' (10:5, 15), the ideal king rules with authority, 'the stick of his mouth' (11:4). Compilation 3 concludes with 32:1-2, another portrayal of the ideal king. Again, the depiction of the ideal king is closely related to the material incorporated in this compilation. Apart from the king, the officials (*śārîm*) are mentioned: 'See, a king

---

also contained 17:1b-3* and 17:12-14; compilation 2 also contained 14:24-27; 14:28-32; and 28:1-4; and compilation 3 also contained the earliest layers of Isa 18-22, i.e. 18:1-6; 19:1b-4; 20:1-5*; 22:15-18, and the *woe*-sayings of 5:8-23* and 10:1-2.

will reign in righteousness, and princes will rule with justice'. This forms a contrast to the image of the wicked leaders in the polemic words of Isaiah. In 28:15, the leaders are accused of having made lies their refuge and falsehood their shelter; 28:17-18 announces that the leaders, together with their deceptive refuge (Egypt), will fall down. By contrast, in the portrayal of the ideal situation in 32:1-2, both the king and the leaders are presented as a hiding-place and a shelter.

Finally, the three compilations presumably began with a dating formula, followed by an account relating Isaiah's prophetic commission by Yahweh. In each case, a scene is described that anticipates the events to which the prophetic material included in the compilation refers. Isa 6:1 situates the commission of Isaiah 'in the year that King Uzziah died'. This prefigures the reign of Ahaz and the troubles he has to face, whereas the following vision portrays Yahweh as a mighty king ready to intervene on the stage. The dating of 14:28, 'in the year that King Ahaz died', resembles that of 6:1. This prefigures the reign of Hezekiah. The early material from Isa 14 is to be connected to the Assyria-cycle of Isa 10. If, as I argue, 14:28-32 is understood as the beginning of the second compilation, it makes an inclusion with 11:1-5. With the dating formula of 14:28, the seventh-century reviser changed the meaning of the following oracle, 14:29.31. By relating it to the death of Ahaz and the rule of Hezekiah, he presented Hezekiah as a strong king who dominated the Philistines, in terms similar to 11:1, where the ideal king (Josiah) is depicted. The third compilation may have begun with a dating formula analogous to that of the other compilations. Isa 20 originally began with a dating resembling that of 6:1 and 14:28: 'In the year that the *tartānu*, commissioned by King Sargon of Assyria, campaigned against Ashdod, Yahweh spoke to Isaiah.' This refers to the period 712-711, when the city of Ashdod rebelled against Assyria. Isa 20:1-5* prefigures the issue of Judah's rebellion of 705-701, and anticipates the disastrous outcome. Therefore, the rebellion of Ashdod and Isaiah's symbolic act (20:1-5*) form a suitable point of departure for the third compilation. The following schema of the three compilations may be produced:

	Compilation 1 Isa 6-9* (+ 17*)	Compilation 2 Isa 10-11* (+ 14*, 28:1-4)	Compilation 3 Isa 28-32* (+ 18-22*, 5:8-23*, 10:1-2)
Dating, prophetic commission	6:1-8	14:28-32	20:1-5*
Early prophetic words	7:2-9a, 7:14b.16, 7:20, 8:1-4, 17:1b-3	28:1-4, 10:5-15*, 10:24-25, 10:27b- 32	28:7b-18*, 29:15, 30:1-8*, 30:15, 31:1.3a, 18:1-2, 19:1b-4, 22:15-18, 5:8-23*, 10:1-2
Comments	8:9-10, 17:12-14	14:24-27, 10:11, 10:16-19, 10:26- 27, 10:33-34	18:1-6, 30:27-33, 31:4-5.8-9
Portrayal of ideal king	9:1-6	11:1-5	32:1-2

The revision of the prophetic material into three compilations, post-dates the time of Isaiah, and is best situated in the late seventh century. In each of the compilations the reversal of fortune plays an important role: the aggressor (Assyria) is destroyed and a new Judaean king rules in glory. The portrayals of the ideal king, which form a climax to the compilations, presumably are indicative of the purpose of the revision. It is argued in chapter 6 that the ideal king in all likelihood is Josiah, and that the revision of the earlier prophetic material was undertaken during his reign (640/39-609 BCE). In the late seventh century the figure of Isaiah was associated with the promise that Judah would be liberated from Assyrian domination, though not through rebellion. The situation during Josiah's reign was regarded as proving the prophet right. The oracles attributed to Isaiah, which had been preserved, were edited and republished in the light of the new situation. The destruction of Assyria and the political restoration of Judah under Josiah are presented as both resulting from Yahweh's intervention, which, as is suggested, had already been announced by the prophet Isaiah. In this way, Isaiah's reputation served the glorification of the political situation under Josiah.

7.3   The Assyrian Prophecies

As a counterpart to the Isaiah tradition in its earliest stages I have taken the prophetic material from seventh-century Assyria. Reasons for giving priority to the Assyrian prophecies over other extra-biblical prophecies are the relative abundance of prophetic material from seventh-century Assyria, the integration of prophetic material into the literature of that period, and the closeness in time to the earliest stages of the Isaiah tradition.

In order to set the stage for a comparison this material is laid out in chapter 3. An attempt is made to apply clear and distinctive categories to the textual material. In this respect, my analysis sometimes differs from that of others.[3] In addition to the Assyrian prophecies in a strict sense, two further sets of texts are introduced: literary derivatives of prophecy that stem from seventh-century Assyria, and various examples of texts containing literary predictions. This is motivated by two factors. Firstly, most of the Assyrian prophecies are preserved in a secondary form (see chapter 6.2.1), and it is shown that in their secondary forms, prophetic oracles come close to literary texts deriving from prophecy (see chapter 6.2.2). Because of this closeness it is appropriate to study both sets of texts in relation to each other. Secondly, in order to provide a counterpart to the seventh-century revision of the Isaiah tradition, characterised by a usage of a prophetic-predictive style, examples of literary texts resembling the prophetic-predictive style have been taken into account as well.

7.4 *Prophecy in its Historical Setting*

In chapter 4 a comparison is carried out between the Isaianic material and the Assyrian prophecies with regard to the interrelation of prophecy and historical events. Both in eighth-century Judah and in seventh-century Assyria, prophecy played a role in situations of crucial political importance. Prophetic sayings of Isaiah can be connected with various key moments in the reigns of Ahaz and Hezekiah, and prophetic oracles from Assyria relate to several key moments in the times of Esarhaddon and Ashurbanipal. As a background to the prophetic material from First Isaiah, four moments from the political history of eighth-century Judah have been highlighted: Tiglath-pileser's

---

[3]   Parpola for instance presents SAA 9 3 as an oracle collection, whereas I regard it a compilation of different texts, some of them based on oracles, others deriving from prophecy. Furthermore, SAA 9 9 is not a report of a prophetic oracle, but a prophetic oracle reworked in a literary garb.

campaigns to Philistia and Syria-Palestine in 734-732 BCE and the Syro-Ehpraimic crisis (Isa 7*; 8*; 17*); Sargon's campaign against the West in 720 BCE, including an expedition against Judah which bestowed on him the title 'subduer of the land of Judah' (Isa 14:29.31; 28:1-4; 10*); Sargon's campaign against Ashdod in 711 BCE (Isa 20:1-5*); Judah's rebellion against Assyria in 705-701 BCE and Sennacherib's campaign of 701 BCE (Isa 28-31*; 18-22*; 5:8-23* and 10:1-2). The Assyrian prophecies can be related to eight different moments from the reigns of Esarhaddon and Ashurbanipal: Esarhaddon's rise to power (681 BCE); Esarhaddon's accession to the throne and his first regnal years; external threat and internal instability (c. 675 BCE); Ashurbanipal's appointment as crown prince and the wars against Egypt (672 BCE); the presumed conspiracy of Sasî (671/670 BCE); Ashurbanipal's wars against Mannea (c. 660 BCE); Ashurbanipal's war against Elam (653 BCE); the war against Šamaš-šum-ukin (652-648 BCE).

The prophecies present the gods—Yahweh in the Isaianic prophecies, Ištar and other deities in the Assyrian prophecies—as intervening in situations of crucial importance. It is claimed that the gods govern the historical scene. They are in command and decide the course of events. Furthermore, in both sets of prophecies we find the deity's affirmation that he is on the king's side to support him. The prophetic oracles and words are essentially supportive of the state. Both in the Isaianic material and in the Assyrian prophecies an ideal image functions as a frame of reference. In the Isaianic prophecies the ideal image pictures the people governed by the Davidic king in justice and righteousness and living a peaceful life under Yahweh's protection. The Assyrian prophecies reflect the ideal image of the king as protected by the gods, in particular Ištar and Mullissu, himself the protector of his subjects; there is peace in the land, the rules of heaven and of earth are in harmony, and Assyria's rule is unthreatened. Both in Judah and in Assyria, prophecies fiercely respond to any challenge to the ideal situation, posed either by external or by internal enemies. Isaiah's harsh words against the leading politicians of Jerusalem are to be understood in this light. Not only was there antagonism between the prophet and his opponents with regard to the issue of what politics to adopt vis-à-vis Assyria, but also the prophet saw their anti-Assyrian policy as a threat to Judah's well-being, challenging the ideal of a peaceful life. In the critical words relating to 705-701, Isaiah therefore depicted the Judaean leaders who advocated rebellion as enemies of the state. In the Assyrian prophecies, rebels and conspirators threatening the well-being of the king are equally depicted as enemies. Since according to official ideology, the well-being of the Assyrian king was to a great part identical to the well-being of the state, the prophetic fulminations against those threatening the well-being of the king in Assyria resemble Isaiah's fulminations against the Judaean leaders. On both sides, prophets functioned as guardians of the state, denunciating what they perceived as threats posed to the well-being of the state. Isaiah's loyalty to the Judaean state and king may furthermore serve as an explanation for the absence of direct references to Hezekiah in his critical sayings.

Prophecy was however not simply royal propaganda. Prophets were supportive of the state but did not necessarily agree with every decision of the king. Apart from divine encouragement of the king in threatening situations, the prophecies contain examples of divine direction to the king either to undertake certain actions, or to refrain from them.

An important difference between Isaiah's prophecies and the Assyrian prophecies is their tone of expression. Whereas the Assyrian prophecies mainly consist of positive, beneficial promises to the king, Isaiah formulates his messages mostly negatively: *against* Aram and Ephraim (734-732), *against* Assyria (720), and, in particular, *against* Judah's political leaders (705-701). The difference is however relative. First of all, the Assyrian prophecies equally contain negative components, as they frequently announce the gruesome destruction of the king's enemies, whereas behind Isaiah's negative formulations figures an ideal view of Judah's society. Isaiah's prophecies are supportive of the well-being of the state of Judah; and in the Assyrian oracles, the gods exercise their power on the king by making cultic demands on him. As for an explanation for the difference in tone between Isaiah's prophecies and those from Assyria, one may point to the different circumstances of late eighth-century Judah on the one hand and seventh-century Assyria on the other. Whereas the Assyrian prophecies are concerned with the well-being of the king and his legitimacy, in Judah the survival of the state was at stake. Whereas the Assyrian prophecies focus on the king, Isaiah's prophecies address the king when he is threatened, but otherwise take a broader perspective on the state of Judah. Isaiah witnessed the abolition of neighbouring

political states and saw a similar fate threatening Judah. He wanted to
prevent Judah's downfall, but the politics he supported was abandoned
in 705 BCE. Because of this his criticism became even more ruthless,
given the weight of the matter at stake. Isaiah furiously opposed the
policy of rebellion, portraying those who advocated it as enemies of
the state, with the intention of bringing about a political change and
averting Assyria's wrath.

Related to this is the difference in the prophetic form of speech.
One of the major forms of speech deployed by Isaiah is the *woe-
saying*. This form is not found among the prophetic words from
Mesopotamia. Yet behind the different forms of speech lie similar
ideologies. Both the Assyrian prophets and Isaiah functioned as
guardians of the state and fiercely turned against those perceived as
enemies of the state.

Although prophecy found different expressions in different times
and places, the prophecies from Isaiah and the Assyrian prophecies
are exponents of a similar phenomenon.

7.5 *Functions of the Prophets*

Chapter 5 deals with the functions of the prophetic figures in Judah
and Assyria. The first part of this chapter describes the prophetic functioning in the ancient Near East, with a focus on seventh-century Assyria. In the second part, after an analysis of various biblical images of
the prophets, the main aspects of the prophetic practice in Judah and
Israel are described, followed by a survey of the prophetic functions of
Isaiah. Based on the available evidence, the main characteristics of the
phenomenon of prophecy, both in Judah and Israel and in Assyria, can
be summarised as follows:

- Prophecy was one form of divination. All divination shared the
  ideological basis that the decisions of the gods, affecting the
  course of events on earth, could be known through divination.
  Isaiah portrays his opponents as practitioners of divination (28:7b-
  10), and also appears to be a practitioner of divination himself (cf.
  e.g. Isaiah's defining of time-limits in 7:16; 8:4; 10:25; 28:4).
- Throughout the ancient Near East different terms for prophetic
  figures were in use. The prophetic figures, although they may have

differed from each other, shared as their main characteristic that they functioned as a mouthpiece of the deity.

- Among the prophetic figures we find both men and women (cf. 'the prophetess' in Isa 8:3-4). Prophets are sometimes referred to in the plural, operating as a group, but often they spoke or acted individually. Isaiah, as far as we can see, operated individually, but not in isolation.

- Prophets were often connected with the cult and associated with the temple. Although prophets for the delivery of divine messages were not exclusively bound to the temple, the main institutional embodiment of prophecy seems to have been the temple.

- A hallmark of prophetic activity was a kind of ecstatic behaviour, which included the performance of symbolic acts. Symbolic acts performed by Isaiah have been recorded in Isa 8:1-4; 20:1-5*; 30:6b-8. However, generally speaking, prophetic oracles, including those of Isaiah, are clear and intelligible messages.

- Oracles of encouragement pertain especially to situations of political-military crisis (e.g. Isa 7:4-9a; 10:24-25). One of their functions was to legitimate throne candidates by announcing divine support. The oracles often contain divine assurance: declarations of divine assistance and announcements of annihilation of the enemies (e.g. Isa 7:16; 7:20; 8:4; 17:1b-3; 28:1-4).

- In return for his or her help, the deity could formulate demands on the addressee (again, mostly the king). Divine demands related to both material and immaterial matters. Neglect of the divine expectations led to prophetic reproach; for this reason, criticism was part of the prophetic repertoire. Isaiah's prophecies include both a harsh reproach of Assyria for its self-willed imperialism and a harsh reproach of Judah's political leaders for advocating rebellion against Assyria.

- Since the prophetic oracles were held to reflect the decisions taken in the divine council, they could be a help or a basis for political decision-making. Prophets could be consulted by the king or by someone on his behalf. Isaiah interfered with the political decision-making of his time, or attempted to do so, and seems to have been an important voice during the reigns of Ahaz and Hezekiah.

- The king did not have full control over the prophets. Prophets at least partly had a public function: encouragement of the king probably was also intended to encourage the people, and the for-

mulation of divine demands and criticism gained strength because
of its public character. To some extent prophets served a public
function as opinion-makers.

- Prophets functioned as guardians of the state; they were part of the
  religious establishment. This applies to Isaiah as well.

Prophecy in late monarchic Judah can be seen as a variant of the larger phenomenon of prophecy in the ancient Near East. The prophet
Isaiah can be counted among the ancient Near Eastern prophets. The
historical Isaiah was not a 'classical prophet' in the traditional sense.
It is even questionable whether the 'classical prophets' represent a historical category at all, rather than a biblical *image* of prophets (5.2.2).
Isaiah resembled prophets elsewhere in the ancient Near East in that
he was principally supportive of the Judaean state (which does not
mean however that 'Heilsprophet' is a felicitous characterisation of
Isaiah, as is argued in 5.1.4).

A difference between Judah and Assyria with regard to the prophetic function appears to have been that prophets in Judah and Israel
generally speaking played a more important role in the public sphere
than the Assyrian prophets did. The impression that prophecy was of
major importance in Judah and Israel and of lesser importance in Assyria, is partly due to the character of the sources. This however may
not be the full explanation. The difference between the prophets in Israel and Judah and those in Assyria may be partly explained as resulting from the huge differences between the Judaean and the Assyrian
societies. In the late eighth and seventh century, Assyria was characterised by a far-reaching differentiation. The Assyrian king employed
a great number of religious specialists. They were experts in the various branches of ancient lore, such as astrology, extispicy, and exorcism. Prophets did not belong to the entourage of the Assyrian king.
Although it is reasonable to suggest that at times of national crisis
prophets had more direct access to the king, normally the king was
guided by his scholars, although they could, of course, be influenced
themselves by prophetic oracles. Since Judah's society was much less
differentiated, prophets may more often have had a more direct
influence on the king and public opinion. Prophets in Judah and Israel
to some extent played a role comparable to that of scholars in seventh-
century Assyria.

With regard to the prophetic reputation, there is also a difference between Isaiah and his Assyrian counterparts. Whereas the Assyrian prophets remained in relative obscurity, Isaiah's star rose quickly. The words attributed to Isaiah were preserved as independent collections, whereas the collection tablets from Nineveh contain oracles from different prophets. Furthermore, the emergence of stories in which the prophet Isaiah figured and the expansion of a prophetic tradition attributed to him, have no counterpart among the Assyrian prophets. Thus, the social standing of prophetic figures and their posthumous fame may to some extent have depended on the kind of society in which they operated. It is reasonably to suspect that within the grand-scale Assyrian society with its tradition of scientific-religious specialists trained in ancient lore, prophets occupied a somewhat different position from those in the small-scale society of eighth-century Judah, where a scholarly tradition was in a more elementary stage.

7.6 *From Prophecy to Literature*

Chapter 6 deals with the reuse, reworking and development of the prophetic words of Isaiah and that of the Assyrian prophecies. For the Isaianic side, I have adopted the suggestion of a late seventh-century revision of the eighth-century prophetic material. A range of passages from First Isaiah reflects the circumstances of the late seventh century.[4] These passages are characterised by two motifs—the downfall and destruction of Assyria and the reign of a new Davidic king—which are both presented as being the work of Yahweh. Although both motifs are likely to date to the Assyrian period, they are essentially different, with regard to form and content, from the eighth-century prophetic material. The reign of Josiah (640/39-609 BCE) provides the most plausible setting for a revision of the Isaiah tradition. Both motifs, Judah's liberation from the Assyrian yoke and the independent rule of a Judaean king, make most sense in this time. Furthermore, Josiah's reign is otherwise marked as a 'new beginning' as well. The traditio-historical background of the revision is found in the state ideology of monarchic Judah. The hope, ambitions and ideology of Josiah's reign provide a plausible setting for the revision of the

---

[4] In my estimation: 9:1-6; 10:11.16-19.26a.27a.33-34; 11:1-5; 14:24-27.28.32; 18:1-6; 30:27-33; 31:4-5.8-9; 32:1-2.

Isaianic material. The ideological message of the revision is that the reign of Josiah was a turn for the good: through Yahweh's intervention a troubled period was brought to an end and a new time had begun characterised by the reign of an ideal king.

Both in Assyria and in Judah we are dealing with prophetic oracles that were recorded and documented. Whereas the primary documentation of prophetic oracles and sayings presumably was for the sake of communication, we see on both sides a further development. Prophecy was, at least in some cases, preserved in archives. This is certain for seventh-century Assyria and plausible for eighth-century Judah. The secondary development of prophecy in Judah and Assyria took on similar forms. A first parallel is found in the reapplication, republication, reworking, and elaboration of prophetic oracles. Prophetic oracles were republished and preserved in the form of collections: on the Assyrian side the oracle collections, on the Judaean side the presumed collections of Isaianic prophecies pertaining to particular moments of Judah's history. Furthermore, prophetic material was elaborated and received a literary reworking. For Isaiah's prophecies, this consisted of the seventh-century revision of the eighth-century prophetic material. A second parallel relates to the composition of texts that resemble or imitate the form and genre of prophetic oracles. Both the seventh-century revision of the Isaiah tradition and several texts from seventh-century Assyria can be qualified as literary derivatives of prophecy. Furthermore, the various examples of literary texts from Mesopotamia marked by a prophetic-predictive style, in imitation of prophecy, provide a counterpart to the revision of the Isaiah tradition as *literary* 'prophecy'. The co-existence in Assyria of collections and literary elaborations of prophetic oracles, literary texts deriving from prophecy, and the examples of literary prediction, demonstrates that the development of the Isaiah tradition as 'prophecy becoming literature' was not without parallel.

With regard to the textual format a significant difference can be pointed out. On the Assyrian side, the various literary manifestations of prophecy—oracles in a literary reworking, literary derivatives of prophecy, or literary predictions—all occur in separate documents. Similar developments to be perceived on the Judaean side however appear in one and the same text. The Isaiah tradition in its revised form probably consisted of three compilations, which took the form of three separate documents. Each of these was to some extent a hybrid text, much more than the Assyrian texts. The Isaiah tradition from its earliest literary development onwards became an expanding and increasing tradition. Related to this probably is the difference that the words attributed to Isaiah were preserved as independent collections, whereas the collection tablets from Assyria contain oracles from different prophets.

Both in Judah and Assyria we discern the phenomenon of prophecy becoming incorporated into a perspective of royal ideology. Examples of this development on the Judaean side are the B1-story of Hezekiah (see 6.1.2) and the seventh-century revision of the Isaiah tradition. On the Assyrian side, this applies to virtually every text discussed in 6.2.1 and 6.2.2. Prophecy in transmission served a royal interest. In *practice*, prophecy had a broader function, being one of the means by which the gods not only supported but also criticised the conduct of the king. The interest of the cosmic and social-political order transcended the interests of the individual king and the gods could even go as far as taking the side of the king's adversary. In the *development of prophecy* however god and king became inextricably connected. The elaborate prophecies and literary derivatives of prophecy emphasise and glorify the close bonds between king and god. Through this development, prophecy became captured in a royal ideological perspective. The official ideological stamp of the literarily developed prophecies in Judah and Assyria is likely to be indicative of the provenance, purpose and function of the literary reworking of the prophecies. The development of prophetic oracles served a royal interest. Its aim was to support and glorify the ruling king by expressing the close connection between the gods and the king. The king enjoyed divine support and divine authority. The late seventh-century revision of the Isaiah material is to be understood from this perspective as well, in relation to the royal ideology concerning Josiah.

In the ancient Near East, the king was held to create order and to represent religious, political and moral authority. Idealisations of the king and his reign were a common phenomenon. Both the literary prophecies and the revision of the Isaiah tradition contain depictions of the reign of the ideal king, in accordance with this general ancient Near Eastern tradition. The revision of the Isaiah tradition and the examples of literary prediction share one further trait: the ideal king remains anonymous. This is of course because in both cases the reign of the ideal king is presented as something of the future, in prophetic, predictive veil. On both sides however it is a literary form of prediction, since a specific king is intended.

Characteristic of prophecy in a developed form is a broadening of perspective. Prophetic oracles relate to particular situations, but in a developed form they are characterised by a more comprehensive perspective. In retrospect, the events are perceived from a broader view. Distinguished from the *situational* view of the prophetic oracles, stands the *episodic* view shared by the prophecies in elaborated form and literary derivatives of prophecy. In the literary predictions the time perspective is even more considerable, often comprehending several centuries. The revision of the Isaianic material similarly presents an episodic view of the period of the Assyrian oppression of Judah ranging from the eighth to the seventh century. The compilations are characterised by extrapolations and generalisations similar to those found in the Assyrian material. In the first compilation, the prophecies concerning the destruction of Judah's enemies Aram and Ephraim are broadened in such a way as to include Assyria, the later enemy, as well. In the second compilation, a specific moment of confrontation with Assyria, Sargon's campaign of 720, becomes a paradigm for Assyrian imperialism in general. And in the third compilation, the polemic words relating to a particular crisis in Judaean politics, become a more general portrayal of ideal leadership. A similar episodic perspective is found in the Assyrian royal inscriptions. In the same realm lies the B1-story of Hezekiah (see 6.1.2), in which Sennacherib's campaign of 701 BCE is reinterpreted in the light of his violent death in 681 BCE. This shared characteristic can be taken as support for the view that the literary development of prophecy and the composition of prophetic texts are best situated in a (royal) scribal milieu.

7.7   *Overview*

Recently, Manfred Weippert gave a clear characterisation of biblical prophecy in relation to ancient Near Eastern prophecy:

> Das Eigentümliche der israelitisch-judäischen Prophetie (insbesondere der 'Schriftprofeten') ist m.E. ... in erster Linie ein redaktionelles Phänomen, das eine Welt überdeckt, die der altorientalischen ähnlicher gewesen ist als die uns vorliegenden Texte suggerieren.[5]

---

[5]   Weippert 2003: 286.

The present study confirms this view. The main conclusion of this study is, that the earliest stages of the Isaiah tradition, i.e. the prophetic material from the eighth century and its earliest revision in the seventh century, to a great extent correspond with the prophetic material of seventh-century Assyria. Three aspects of comparison have been worked out:

1) Prophetic oracles relate to particular historical circumstances, and prophets sought to interfere in events of major political importance.

2) Prophets served as mouthpieces of the gods; through their prophets the gods both supported the king and put their demands on him. With regard to both aspects, prophets functioned as guardians of the well-being of the state.

3) Prophecies were recorded, in collections and otherwise, and in some cases became the subject of reworking and elaboration. Furthermore, literary texts resembling or imitating prophecy emerged. The various manifestations of prophecy in literature served a royal interest.

This conclusion is of importance for Old Testament exegesis. As a counterweight to newer methods that focus on synchronic reading and literary analysis of the biblical prophetic books, this study deals with the Isaiah tradition within a wider setting of ancient Near Eastern prophecy. The linkage between the prophetic books and the phenomenon of ancient Hebrew prophecy must not be abandoned. The exploration of the origins and earliest development of the Isaiah tradition, however difficult, remains part of the exegetical agenda, and the study of the book of Isaiah from a historical interest remains a rewarding enterprise. The conclusion of this study is furthermore of importance for the study of prophecy. The earliest layer of the Isaiah tradition, the eighth-century prophetic material, does not resemble the characteristics of prophecy of judgement; and the prophetic figure behind these prophecies and sayings cannot be described as a 'classical prophet'. The distinctive features of biblical prophecy are, as I have argued, mainly to be found in the literary and redactional development of the prophetic heritage, whereas the prophetic practice in Judah and Israel in many respects resembled that of the ancient Near East, represented by Mari and Assyrian prophecy. The historical Isaiah is to be counted among the ancient Near Eastern prophets.

SCHEMA OF THE DEVELOPMENT OF THE ISAIAH TRADITION			
ASSYRIAN PERIOD			
Prophetic Material	Material going back to prophetic activity in the eighth century preserved in the form of three collections		
	Collection 1 relating to 734-732	Collection 2 relating to 723-720	Collection 3 relating to 705-701
	7:2-9a*, 7:14b.16, 7:20, 8:1-4, 17:1-3*	10:5-15*, 10:24-25, 10:27b-32, 14:29-31*, 28:1-4	28:7b-10, 28:12*, 28:14-18*, 29:15, 30:1-8*, 30:15*, 31:1.3a, 18:1-2, 4, 19:1b-4, 22:15-18, 5:8-23*, 10:1-2
Josiah Revision	Revision of the prophetic material in the seventh century taking the form of three compilations (new material in bold)		
	Compilation 1	Compilation 2	Compilation 3
introduction	**6:1-8**	**14:28-32**	**20:1-5***
prophetic material and comments	7:2-9a*, 7:14b.16, 7:20, 8:1-4, **8:9-10** 17:1-3*, **17:12-14**	28:1-4, **14:24-27,** 10:5-15*, **10:16-19** 10:24-25, **10:26-27**, 10:27b-32, **10:33-34**	**18:1-6**, 19:1b-4, 22:15-18, 5:8-23*, 10:1-2, 28:7b-10, 28:12*, 28:14-18*, 29:15, 30:1-8*, 30:15*, **30:27-33,** 31:1.3a, **31:4-5.8-9**
conclusion	**9:1-6**	**11:1-5**	**32:1-2**
BABYLONIAN PERIOD AND LATER			
Exilic Edition	Transformation of the Isaiah tradition based on reflection on the disasters of 586 BCE, growing out into a substantial literary complex		
	Edition of Isa 6-9	6:1-11, 7:1-17, 8:1-18, 9:1-20	
	Edition of Isa 28-32	28:7-22, 29:1-4, 9-10, 13-16, 30:1-17, 31:1-5.8-9, 32:1-2.9-14	
	Further texts	E.g. 1:2-8, 22:1-14	
Successive Later Editions	New complexes, redaction of existing texts, and additional material of Second and Third Isaiah in successive redactional stages		
Final Editions	Final additions and redactions and coming into being of the book of Isaiah		

BIBLIOGRAPHY

Achenbach, R. 2002, Jabâ und Ataljā – zwei jüdische Königstöchter am assyrischen Königshof. Zu einer These von Stephanie Dalley, *BN* 113, 29-38

Ackroyd, P. 1982, Isaiah 36-39: Structure and Function, in: W.C. Delsman (ed.), *Von Kanaan bis Kerala: Festschrift J.P.M. van der Ploeg*, AOAT 211, Neukirchen-Vluyn, 3-21

——1984, The Biblical Interpretation of the Reigns of Ahaz and Hezekiah, in: W.B. Barrick and J.R. Spencer (eds), *In the Shelter of Elyon. Essays on Ancient Palestinian Life and Literature in Honor of G.W. Ahlström*, JSOTSup 31, Sheffield, 247-259

Albertz, R. 1992, *Religionsgeschichte Israels in alttestamentlicher Zeit*, 2 vols, Göttingen

——1994, *A History of Israelite Religion in the Old Testament Period*, 2 vols (English translation J. Bowden), London

Albrektson, B. 1967, *History and the Gods*, Lund

Al-Rawi, F.N.H. 1985, Nabopolassar's Restoration Work on the Wall *Imgur-Enlil* at Babylon, *Iraq* 47, 1-13

Alt, A. 1950, Jesaja 8,23-9,6: Befreiungsnacht und Krönungstag, in: W. Baumgartner et al. (eds), *Festschrift A. Bertholet*, Tübingen, 29-49 (repr. *Kleine Schriften zur Geschichte des Volkes Israel* II, Munich 1953, 206-225)

Amit, Y. 2003, Jerusalem in Bible and Archaeology: When Did Jerusalem Become a Subject of Polemic, in: A.G. Vaughn and A.E. Killebrew (eds), *Jerusalem in Bible and Archaeology. The First Temple Period*, SBLSS 18, Atlanta, 365-374

Anbar, M. 1993, Mari and the Origin of Prophecy, in: A.F. Rainey (ed.), *kinattūtu ša dārâti: Raphael Kutscher Memorial Volume*, Tel Aviv, 1-5

Annus, A. 2002, *The God Ninurta in the Mythology and Royal Ideology of Ancient Mesopotamia*, SAAS 14, Helsinki

Arneth, M. 2001, Die antiassyrische Reform Josias von Juda. Überlegungen zur Komposition und Intention von 2 Reg 23,4-15, *ZABR* 7, 189-216

Asurmendi, J.M. 1982, *La Guerra Siro-Efraimita. Historia y Profetas*, Valencia

Auld, A.G. 1983, Prophets through the Looking Glass: Between Writings and Moses, *JSOT* 27, 3-23

Baines, J. 1998, Ancient Egyptian Kingship: Official Forms, Rhetoric, Context, in: J. Day (ed.), *King and Messiah in Israel and the Ancient Near East. Proceedings of the Oxford Old Testament Seminar*, JSOTSup 270, Sheffield, 16-53

Baker, H.D. (ed.) 2000, *The Prosopography of the Neo-Assyrian Empire*, vol. 2/I, Helsinki

Barnett, R.D. et al. 1998, *Sculptures from the Southwest Palace of Sennacherib at Nineveh*, vol. 1 text, vol. 2 plates, London

Barstad, H.M. 1993a, No Prophets? Recent Developments in Biblical Prophetic Research and Ancient Near Eastern Prophecy, *JSOT* 57, 39-60

——1993b, Lachish Ostracon III and Ancient Israelite Prophecy, *ErIsr* 24, 8-12

——2000, Comparare necesse est? Ancient Israelite and Ancient Near Eastern Prophecy in a Comparative Perspective, in: M. Nissinen (ed.), *Prophecy in its Ancient Near Eastern Context. Mesopotamian, Biblical and Arabian Perspectives*, SBLSS 13, Atlanta, 3-12

Barth, H. 1977, *Die Jesaja-Worte in der Josiazeit. Israel und Assur als Thema einer produktiven Neuinterpretation der Jesajaüberlieferung*, WMANT 48, Neukirchen-Vluyn

Barthel, J. 1997, *Prophetenwort und Geschichte. Die Jesajaüberlieferung in Jes 6-8 und 28-31*, FAT 19, Tübingen

——2003, Das Problem des historischen Jesaja, in: I. Fischer et al. (eds), *Prophetie in Israel. Beiträge des Symposiums 'Das Alte Testament und die Kultur der Moderne' anlässlich des 100. Geburtstags Gerhard Von Rads*, ATM 11, Münster, 125-135

Barton, J. 1995, *Isaiah 1-39*, OTG, Sheffield

Bauer, T. 1933, *Das Inschriftenwerk Assurbanipals*, I. Teil: Keilschrifttexte, II. Teil: Bearbeitung, Leipzig

Beaulieu, P.-A. 1993, The Historical Background of the Uruk Prophecy, in: M.E. Cohen et al. (eds), *The Tablet and the Scroll. Near Eastern Studies in Honor of William W. Hallo*, Bethesda, 41-52

Becker, J. 1968, *Isaias – der Prophet und sein Buch*, Stuttgart

Becker, U. 1997, *Jesaja – von der Botschaft zum Buch*, FRLANT 178, Göttingen

——1999, Jesajaforschung (Jes 1-39), *TRu* 64, 1-37 and 117-152

——2001, Der Prophet als Fürbitter: zum literarhistorischen Ort der Amos-Visionen, *VT* 61, 141-165

——2003, Das Problem des historischen Jesaja, in: I. Fischer et al. (eds), *Prophetie in Israel. Beiträge des Symposiums 'Das Alte Testament und die Kultur der Moderne' anlässlich des 100. Geburtstags Gerhard Von Rads*, ATM 11, Münster, 117-124

——2004, Die Wiederentdeckung des Prophetenbuches. Tendenzen und Aufgaben der gegenwärtigen Prophetenforschung, *BTZ* 21, 30-60

Becking, B. 1992, *The Fall of Samaria. A Historical and Archaeological Study*, SHANE 2, Leiden

Begg, C.T. 1987, The Death of Josiah in Chronicles: Another View, *VT* 37, 1-8

Ben Zvi, E. 1991, Isaiah 1,4-9, Isaiah, and the Events of 701 BCE in Judah. A Question of Premise and Evidence, *SJOT* 5, 95-111

——2000, Introduction: Writings, Speeches, and the Prophetic Books – Setting an Agenda, in: E. Ben Zvi and M.H. Floyd (eds), *Writings and Speech in Israelite and Ancient Near Eastern Prophecy*, SBLSS 10, Atlanta, 1-30

——2003, The Prophetic Book: A Key Form of Prophetic Literature, in: E. Ben Zvi and M.A. Sweeney (eds), *The Changing Face of Form Criticism for the Twenty-First Century*, Grand Rapids, 276-297

——2004, Observations on Prophetic Characters, Prophetic Texts, Priests of Old, Persian Period Priests and Literati, in: L.L. Grabbe and A. Ogden Bellis (eds), *The Priests in the Prophets. The Portrayal of Priests, Prophets and Other Religious Specialists in the Latter Prophets*, JSOTSup 408, London, 19-30

Ben Zvi, E. and Floyd, M.H. (eds) 2000, *Writings and Speech in Israelite and Ancient Near Eastern Prophecy*, SBLSS 10, Atlanta

Berges, U. 1998, *Das Buch Jesaja. Komposition und Endgestalt*, HBS 16, Freiburg

Beuken, W.A.M. 1997, Isaiah 30: A Prophetic Oracle Transmitted in Two Successive Paradigms, in: C.C. Broyles and C.A Evans (eds), *Writing and Reading the Scroll of Isaiah. Studies of an Interpretive Tradition*, vol. 1, VTSup 70-1, Leiden, 369-397

——2000, *Isaiah Part II, vol. 2: Isaiah chapters 28-39*, HCOT (English translation B. Doyle), Leuven

——2002, 'Lebanon with its Majesty shall fall. A Shoot shall come forth from the Stump of Jesse' (Isa 10:34-11:1): Interfacing the Story of Assyria and the Image of Israel's Future in Isaiah 10-11, in: F. Postma, K. Spronk, and E. Talstra (eds), *The New Things. Eschatology in Old Testament Prophecy. Festschrift for H. Leene*, Maastricht, 17-33

——2003, *Jesaja 1-12*, HTKAT (German translation U. Berges), Freiburg

Biggs, R.D. 1967, More Babylonian "Prophecies", *Iraq* 29, 117-132

——1969, Akkadian Oracles and Prophecies, in: J.B. Prichard (ed.), *Ancient Near Eastern Texts Relating to the Old Testament* (3rd edition), Princeton, 605-607

——1985, The Babylonian Prophecies and the Astrological Traditions of Mesopotamia, *JCS* 37, 86-90

——1987, Babylonian Prophecies, Astrology, and a New Source for "Prophecy Text B", in: F. Rochberg-Halton (ed.), *Language, Literature, and History: Philological and Historical Studies Presented to Erica Reiner*, New Haven, 1-14

Blenkinsopp, J. 1995, *Sage, Priest, Prophet: Religious and Intellectual Leadership in Ancient Israel*, LAI, Louisville

——1996, *A History of Prophecy in Israel* (2nd edition), Louisville

——2000a, *Isaiah 1-39. A New Translation with Introduction and Commentary*, AB, New York

——2000b, The Prophetic Biography of Isaiah, in: E. Blum (ed.), *Mincha. Festgabe für Rolf Rendtorff zum 75. Geburtstag*, Neukirchen-Vluyn, 13-26

——2000c, Judah's Covenant with Death (Isaiah XXVIII 14-22), *VT* 50, 472-483

Bloch, M. 1970, Two Strategies of Comparison, in: A. Etzioni and F.L. DuBow (eds), *Comparative Perspectives: Theories and Methods*, Boston, 39-41

Blum, E. 1996, Jesajas prophetisches Testament. Beobachtungen zu Jes 1-11. Teil I, *ZAW* 108, 547-568

——1997, Jesajas prophetisches Testament. Beobachtungen zu Jes 1-11. Teil II, *ZAW* 109, 12-29

Boer, P.A.H. de 1955, The Counsellor, in: M. Noth and D.W. Thomas (eds), *Wisdom in Israel and in the Ancient Near East. Presented to H.H. Rowley*, VTSup 3, Leiden, 42-71

Bolin, T.M. 2003, The Making of the Holy City: On the Foundations of Jerusalem in the Hebrew Bible, in: T.L. Thompson (ed.), *Jerusalem in Ancient History and Tradition*, JSOTSup 381, London, 171-196

Borger, R. 1956, *Die Inschriften Asarhaddons, Königs von Assyrien*, AfOB 9, Graz

——1971, Gott Marduk und Gott-König Šulgi als Propheten: Zwei prophetische Texte, *BiOr* 28, 3-24

——1972, Review of B. Landsberger, Brief des Bischofs von Esagila an König Asarhadon, *BiOr* 29, 33-37

——1982-5, Historische Texte in akkadischer Sprache aus Babylonien und Assyrien, in: O. Kaiser (ed.), *Texte aus der Umwelt des Alten Testaments. Band I. Rechts- und Wirtschaftsurkunden, Historisch-Chronologische Texte*, Gütersloh, 354-410

——1996, *Beiträge zum Inschriftenwerk Assurbanipals: die Prismenklassen A, B, C, = K, D, E, F, G, H, J und T sowie andere Inschriften; mit einem Beitrag von Andreas Fuchs*, Wiesbaden

Bosshard-Nepustil, E. 1997, *Rezeptionen von Jesaja 1-39 im Zwölfprophetenbuch*, OBO 154, Freiburg

Bottéro, J. 2001, *Religion in Ancient Mesopotamia* (English translation T.L. Fagan), Chicago

Brinkman, J.A. 1976, *Materials and Studies for Kassite History*, Chicago

——1984, *Prelude to Empire: Babylonian Society and Politics, 747-626 B.C.*, Philadelphia

Brown, D. 2000, *Mesopotamian Planetary Astronomy-Astrology*, CM 18, Groningen

Broyles, C.C. and Evans, C.A. (eds) 1997, *Writing and Reading the Scroll of Isaiah. Studies of an Interpretive Tradition*, 2 vols, VTSup 70, Leiden

Brueggemann, W. 1998, *Isaiah 1-39*, WBC, Louisville

Butler, S.A.L. 1998, *Mesopotamian Conceptions of Dreams and Dream Rituals*, AOAT 258, Münster

Cagni, L. 1969, *L'epopea di Erra*, Rome

Cancik-Kirschbaum, E. 2003, Prophetismus und Divination – Ein Blick auf die Keilschriftlichen Quellen, in: M. Köckert and M. Nissinen (eds), *Propheten in Mari, Assyrien und Israel*, FRLANT 201, Göttingen, 33-53

Carlson, R.A. 1974, The Anti-Assyrian Character of the Oracle in Is. IX 1-6, *VT* 24, 130-135

Carr, D. 1993, Reaching for Unity in Isaiah, *JSOT* 57, 61-80

——2005, *Writing on the Tablet of the Heart. Origins of Scripture and Literature*, Oxford

Carroll, R.P. 1983, Poets not Prophets. A Response to "Prophets through the Looking Glass", *JSOT* 27, 25-31

——1986, *Jeremiah: A Commentary*, OTL, Philadelphia

——1992, Night without Vision: Micah and the Prophets, in: F. García Martínez et al. (eds), *The Scriptures and the Scrolls: Studies in Honour of A.S. van der Woude*, VTSup 49, Leiden, 74-84

Charpin, D. 1992, Le contexte historique et géographique des prophéties dans les textes retrouvés à Mari, *The Canadian Society for Mesopotamian Studies Bulletin* 23, 21-31

——2002, Prophètes et rois dans le Proche-orient Amorrite, in: D. Charpin and J.-M. Durand (eds) *Florilegium Marianum VI, Recueil d'études à la mémoire d'A. Parrot*, Mémoires de NABU 7, Paris, 7-38

Charpin, D. et al. (eds) 1988, *Archives épistolaires de Mari I/2*, ARM 26/2, Paris

Christensen, D.L. 1984, Zephaniah 2:4-15: A Theological Basis for Josiah's Program of Political Expansion, *CBQ* 46, 669-682

Clements, R.E. 1980a, *Isaiah 1-39*, NCB, Grand Rapids

——1980b, *Isaiah and the Deliverance of Jerusalem: A Study of the Interpretation of Prophecy in the Old Testament*, JSOTSup 13, Sheffield

——1980c, The Prophecies of Isaiah and the Fall of Jerusalem in 587 B.C., *VT* 30, 421-436

——1982, The Unity of the Book of Isaiah, *Int* 36, 117-129

——1989, Isaiah 14,22-27. A Central Passage Reconsidered, in: J. Vermeylen (ed.), *The Book of Isaiah. Le Livre d'Isaïe: les oracles et leurs relectures: unité et complexité de l'ouvrage*, BETL 81, Leuven, 253-262

——1991, The Prophecies of Isaiah to Hezekiah concerning Sennacherib. 2 Kings 19.21-34 // Isa. 37.22-35, in: R. Liwak and S. Wagner (eds), *Prophetie und geschichtliche Wirklichkeit im alten Israel. Festschrift für S. Herrmann*, Stuttgart, 65-78

——1994, The Politics of Blasphemy. Zion's God and the Threat of Imperialism, in: I. Kottsieper et al. (eds), *"Wer ist wie du, Herr, unter den Göttern?" Studien zur Theologie und Religionsgeschichte Israels. Festschrift für O. Kaiser*, Göttingen, 231-246

——1997, Zion as Symbol and Political Reality. A Central Isaianic Quest, in: J. van Ruiten and M. Vervenne (eds), *Studies in the Book of Isaiah. Festschrift W.A.M. Beuken*, BETL 132, Leuven, 3-17

——2000, The Prophet as an Author: the Case of the Isaiah Memoir, in: E. Ben Zvi and M.H. Floyd (eds), *Writings and Speech in Israelite and Ancient Near Eastern Prophecy*, SBLSS 10, Atlanta, 89-102

——2002, Isaiah: A Book without an Ending? *JSOT* 97, 109-126

Cogan, M. 1993, Judah under Assyrian Hegemony. A Reexamination of Imperialism and Religion, *JBL* 112, 403-414

Cohen, M.E. 1988, *The Canonical Lamentations of Ancient Mesopotamia*, 2 vols, Potomac

Cole, D.P. 1994, Archaeology and the Messiah Oracles of Isaiah 9 and 11, in: M.D. Coogan et al. (eds), *Scripture and Other Artifacts. Essays on the Bible and Archaeology in Honor of Ph.J. King*, Louisville, 53-69

Cole, S.W. and Machinist, P. (eds) 1998, *Letters from Priests to Kings Esarhaddon and Assurbanipal*, SAA 13, Helsinki

Collins, T. 1993, *The Mantle of Elijah. The Redaction Criticism of the Prophetical Books*, Sheffield

Conrad, E.W. 1985, *Fear Not Warrior. A Study of 'al tîrā' Pericopes in the Hebrew Scriptures*, Chico

Cooper, J. 2000, Assyrian Prophecies, the Assyrian Tree, and the Mesopotamian Origins of Jewish Monotheism, Greek Philosophy, Christian Theology, Gnosticism, and Much More, *JAOS* 120, 430-444

Cornelius, I. 1989, The Lion in the Art of the Ancient Near East: A Study of Selected Motifs, *JNSL* 15, 53-85

Cryer, F.H. 1991, Der Prophet und der Magier. Bemerkungen anhand einer überholten Diskussion, in: R. Liwak and S. Wagner (eds), *Prophetie und geschichtliche Wirklichkeit im alten Israel. Festschrift für S. Herrmann*, Stuttgart, 79-88

——1994, *Divination in Ancient Israel and its Near Eastern Environment. A Socio-Historical Investigation*, JSOTSup 142, Sheffield

Dalley, S. 1985, Foreign Chariotry and Cavalry in the Armies of Tiglath-Pileser III and Sargon II, *Iraq* 47, 31-48

——1986, The God ṣalmu and the Winged Disk, *Iraq* 48, 85-101

——1997, Statues of Marduk and the Date of *Enūma eliš*, *AoF* 24, 163-171

——1998, Yabâ, Atalyā and the Foreign Policy of Late Assyrian Kings, *SAAB* 12, 83-98

——2000, *Myths from Mesopotamia* (revised edition), Oxford

——2001, Review of R. Mattila, *The King's Magnates*, SAAS 11 (Helsinki 2000), *BiOr* 58, 197-206

———2003, The Transition from Neo-Assyrians to Neo-Babylonians: Break or Continuity? in: I. Eph'al et al. (eds), *Hayim and Miriam Tadmor Volume. Eretz-Israel. Archaeological, Historical and Geographical Studies* 27, Jerusalem, 25-28

———2004a, Recent Evidence from Assyrian Sources for Judaean History from Uzziah to Manasseh, *JSOT* 28, 387-401

———2004b, Review of: A. Kuhrt, *'Greeks' and 'Greece' in Mesopotamian and Persian Perspectives*, The Twenty-First J.L. Myres Memorial Lecture (Oxford 2002), in: *Ancient West and East* 3/2, 430-431

———2005, The Language of Destruction and its Interpretation. Paper given at the 4th International Congress of the Archaeology of the Ancient Near East, Berlin, *BaghM* 36, 275-285

Damerji, M.S.B. 1999, *Gräber assyrischer Königinnen aus Nimrud*, Mainz

Davies, Ph.R. 1998, *Scribes and Schools: The Canonization of the Hebrew Scriptures*, LAI, Louisville

———2000, "Pen of Iron, Point of Diamond" (Jer 17:1): Prophecy as Writing, in: E. Ben Zvi and M.H. Floyd (eds), *Writings and Speech in Israelite and Ancient Near Eastern Prophecy*, SBLSS 10, Atlanta, 65-81

Day, J. 1989, *Molech: A God of Human Sacrifice in the Old Testament*, UCOP 41, Cambridge

———2004, How Many Pre-exilic Psalms are there? in: J. Day (ed.), *In Search of Pre-exilic Israel. Proceedings of the Oxford Old Testament Seminar*, JSOTSup 406, London, 225-250

Dearman, J.A. 1996, The Son of Tabeel (Isaiah 7.6), in: S.B. Reid (ed.), *Prophets and Paradigms. Essays in Honour of G.M. Tucker*, JSOTSup 229, Sheffield, 33-47

Deck, S. 1991, *Die Gerichtsbotschaft Jesajas: Charakter und Begründung*, Würzburg

Deist, F.E. 1989, The Prophets: are we heading for a paradigm switch? in: V. Fritz, K.-F. Pohlmann, and H.-C. Schmitt (eds), *Prophet und Prophetenbuch. Festschrift für O. Kaiser*, BZAW 185, Berlin, 1-28

Dekker, J. 2004, *De Rotsvaste Fundering van Sion. Een Exegetisch Onderzoek naar het Sionswoord van Jesaja 28,16*, Zoetermeer

Del Olmo Lete, G. and Sanmartín, J. (eds) 2003, *A Dictionary of the Ugaritic Language in the Alphabetic Tradition*, 2 vols, Leiden

Dietrich, M. 1970, *Die Aramäer Südbabyloniens in der Sargonidenzeit 700-648*, AOAT 7, Neukirchen-Vluyn

Dietrich, W. 1976, *Jesaja und die Politik*, Munich

———1999, Jesaja – ein Heilsprophet? Review of Uwe Becker, *Jesaja – von der Botschaft zum Buch* (Göttingen 1997), *TRu* 64, 324-337

Dijkstra, M. 1980, *Gods voorstelling: Predikatieve expressie van zelfopenbaring in oudoosterse teksten en Deutero-Jesaja*, Kampen

———1995, Is Balaam also among the Prophets? *JBL* 114, 43-64

———2001, 'I am neither a prophet nor a prophet's pupil'. Amos 7:9-17 as the Presentation of a Prophet like Moses, in: J.C. de Moor (ed.), *The Elusive Prophet. The Prophet as a Historical Person, Literary Character and Anonymous Artist*, OtSt 45, Leiden

———2002, 'He who calls the Eras from the Beginning' (Isa 41:4): From History to Eschatology in Second Isaiah, in: F. Postma, K. Spronk, and E. Talstra (eds), *The New Things. Eschatology in Old Testament Prophecy. Festschrift for H. Leene*, Maastricht, 61-76

Dion, P. 1970, The "Fear Not" Formula and Holy War, *CBQ* 32, 565-570

Dobbs-Allsopp, F.W. 1993, *Weep, O Daughter of Zion: A Study of the City-Lament Genre in the Hebrew Bible*, BibOr 44, Rome

Donner, H. 1986, *Geschichte des Volkes Israel und seiner Nachbarn in Grundzügen. 2. Von der Königszeit bis zu Alexander dem Großen*, GAT 4/2, Göttingen

Duhm, B. 1922, *Das Buch Jesaja* (4th edition; [1]1892), Göttingen

Durand, J.-M. 1982, In Vino Veritas, *RA* 76, 43-50

——1988, Archives épistolaires de Mari I/1, *ARM* 26/1, Paris

——1991, Précurseurs syriens aux protocoles néo-assyriens: considérations sur la vie politique aux Bords-de-l'Euphrate, in: D. Charpin and F. Joannès (eds), *Marchands, Diplomates et Empereurs, études sur la civilisation mésopotamienne offertes à Paul Garelli*, Paris, 13-72

——1997, Les prophéties des textes de Mari, in: J.-G. Heintz (ed.), *Oracles et prophéties dans l'antiquité. Actes du Colloque de Strasbourg 15-17 juin 1995*, Paris, 115-134

Durand, J.-M. and Guichard, M. 1997, Les Rituels de Mari, in: *Florilegium marianum III*, Mémoires de NABU 4, 19-82

Eidevall, G. 1993, Lions and Birds as Literature: Some Notes on Isaiah 31 and Hosea 11, *SJOT* 7, 78-87

Elat, M. 2000, Arguments for the Identification of the [lú]Urbi in Assyrian Royal Inscriptions, in: G. Galil and M. Weinfeld (eds), *Studies in Historical Geography and Biblical Historiography. Presented to Zecharia Kallai*, VTSup 81, Leiden, 232-238

Ellermeier, F. 1968, *Prophetie in Mari und Israel*, Herzberg

Ellis, M. deJong 1979, Akkadian Literary Texts and Fragments in the University Museum, *JCS* 31, 216-231

——1987, The Goddess Kititum Speaks to King Ibalpiel: Oracle Texts from Ishchali, *MARI* 5, 235-266

——1989, Observations on Mesopotamian Oracles and Prophetic Texts: Literary and Historiographic Considerations, *JCS* 41, 129-146

Emerton, J.A. 2001, Some Difficult Words in Isaiah 28.10 and 13, in: A. Rapoport-Albert and G. Greenberg (eds), *Biblical Hebrew, Biblical Texts, Essays in Memory of M.P. Weitzman*, JSOTSup 333, Sheffield, 39-56

Etzioni, A. and DuBow, F.L. 1970, Introduction, in: A. Etzioni and F.L. DuBow (eds), *Comparative Perspectives. Theories and Methods*, Boston, 1-16

Evans, C.D. 1980, Judah's Foreign Policy from Hezekiah to Josiah, in: C.D. Evans, W.W. Hallo, and J.B. White (eds), *Scripture in Context: Essays on the Comparative Method*, Pittsburgh, 157-178

Fales, F.M. 1982, The Enemy in Assyrian Royal Inscriptions: 'The Moral Judgement', in: H.-J. Nissen and J. Renger (eds), *Mesopotamien und seine Nachbarn: politische und kulturelle Wechselbeziehungen im Alten Vorderasien vom 4. bis 1. Jahrtausend v.Chr.*, part 2, RAI 25, Berlin, 425-435

Fales, F.M. and Lanfranchi, G.B. 1981, *ABL* 1237: The Role of the Cimmerians in a Letter to Esarhaddon, *East and West* 31, 9-33

——1997, The Impact of Oracular Material on the Political Utterances and Political Action of the Sargonic Dynasty, in: J.-G. Heintz (ed.), *Oracles et prophéties dans l'antiquité. Actes du Colloque de Strasbourg 15-17 juin 1995*, Paris, 99-114

Farber, W. 1977, *Beschwörungsrituale an Ištar und Dumuzi*, Wiesbaden

Fenton, T.L. 1997, Deuteronomistic Advocacy of the *Nābî'*: 1 Samuel 9 9 and Questions of Israelite Prophecy, *VT* 47, 23-42

Finkelstein, I. 1994, The Archaeology of the Days of Manasseh, in: M.D. Coogan et al. (eds), *Scripture and Other Artifacts. Essays on the Bible and Archaeology in Honor of Ph.J. King*, Louisville, 169-187

——2003, The Rise of Jerusalem and Judah: the Missing Link, in: A.G. Vaughn and A.E. Killebrew (eds), *Jerusalem in Bible and Archaeology. The First Temple Period*, SBLSS 18, Atlanta, 81-102

Fischer, I. 2002, *Gotteskünderinnen: zu einer geschlechterfairen Deutung des Phänomens der Prophetie und der Prophetinnen in der Hebräischen Bibel*, Stuttgart

Fleming, D.E. 1993a, *Nābû* and *Munabbiātu*: Two New Syrian Religious Personnel, *JAOS* 103, 175-183

——1993b, The Etymological Origins of the Hebrew *nābî'*: The One Who Invokes God, *CBQ* 55, 217-224

——2004, Prophets and Temple Personnel in the Mari Archives, in: L.L. Grabbe and A. Ogden Bellis (eds), *The Priests in the Prophets. The Portrayal of Priests, Prophets and Other Religious Specialists in the Latter Prophets*, JSOTSup 408, London, 44-64

Fohrer, G. 1960, *Das Buch Jesaja*, vol. 1, Stuttgart

Foster, B.R. 1993, *Before the Muses: An Anthology of Akkadian Literature*, 2 vols, Bethesda

Fox, N.S. 2000, *In the Service of the King. Officialdom in Ancient Israel and Judah*, MHUC 23, Cincinnati

Frahm, E. 1997, *Einleitung in die Sanherib-Inschriften*, AfOB 26, Vienna

——1999, Nabû-zuqub-kēnu, das Gilgameš-Epos und der Tod Sargons II., *JCS* 51, 73-90

——2000, Iapa', in: H.D. Baker (ed.), *The Prosopography of the Neo-Assyrian Empire*, vol. 2/I, Helsinki, 492-493

——2001, Wie 'christlich' war die Assyrische Religion? Parpola's Edition der assyrische Prophetien, *WO* 31, 31-45

——2002, Sîn-aḫḫē-erība, in: H.D. Baker (ed.), *The Prosopography of the Neo-Assyrian Empire*, vol. 3/I, Helsinki, 1113-1127

——2003, Images of Ashurbanipal in Later Tradition, in: I. Eph'al et al. (eds), *Hayim and Miriam Tadmor Volume. Eretz-Israel. Archaeological, Historical and Geographical Studies* 27, Jerusalem, 37-48

Frame, G. 1992, *Babylonia 689-627 B.C. A Political History*, Istanbul

——1995, *Rulers of Babylon from the Second Dynasty of Isin to the End of the Assyrian Domination, 1157-612 BC*, RIMB vol. 2, Toronto

——1999, The Inscription of Sargon II at Tang-I Var, *Or* 68, 31-57

Franklin, N. 1994, The Room V Reliefs at Dur-Sharrukin and Sargon II's Western Campaigns, *TA* 21, 255-275

Freydank, H. 1974, Zwei Verpflegungstexte aus Kar-Tukulti-Ninurta, *AfO* 1, 55-89

Fuchs, A. 1994, *Die Inschriften Sargons II. aus Khorsabad*, Göttingen

——1998, *Die Annalen des Jahres 711 v.Chr.: nach Prismenfragmenten aus Ninive und Assur*, SAAS 8, Helsinki

Gabbay, U. 2003, Dance in Textual Sources from Ancient Mesopotamia, *Near Eastern Archaeology* 66, 103-104

Gadd, C.J. 1954, The Prism Inscriptions of Sargon, *Iraq* 16, 178-182

Galil, G. 1992, Conflicts between Assyrian Vassals, *SAAB* 6, 55-63

——1996, *The Chronology of the Kings of Israel and Judah*, SHCANE 9, Leiden

Gallagher, W.R. 1999, *Sennacherib's Campaign to Judah. New Studies*, SHCANE 18, Leiden

George, A.R. 1993, *House Most High. The Temples of Ancient Mesopotamia*, Winona Lake

——2003, *The Babylonian Gilgamesh Epic. Introduction, Critical Edition and Cuneiform Texts*, vol. 1, Oxford

Gerstenberger, E.S. 1988, *pll*, in: G.J. Botterweck, H. Ringgren, and H.-J. Fabry (eds), *Theologisches Wörterbuch zum Alten Testament* VI, Stuttgart, 606-617

Geus, J.K. de 1982, Die Gesellschaftskritik der Propheten und die Archäologie, *ZDPV* 98, 50-57

Geva, H. 2003, Western Jerusalem at the End of the First Temple Period in Light of the Excavations in the Jewish Quarter, in: A.G. Vaughn and A.E. Killebrew (eds), *Jerusalem in Bible and Archaeology. The First Temple Period*, SBLSS 18, Atlanta, 183-208

Ginsberg, H.L. 1968, Reflexes of Sargon in Isaiah after 715 BCE, *JAOS* 88, 47-53

Gitay, Y. 1991, *Isaiah and his Audience. The Structure and Meaning of Isaiah 1-12*, SSN 29, Assen

——1997, *Prophecy and Prophets: the Diversity of Contemporary Issues in Scholarship*, Semeia Studies, Atlanta

Glassner, J.-J. 2004, *Mesopotamian Chronicles*, SBLWAWS 19, Atlanta

Goldstein, J.A. 1988, The Historical Setting of the Uruk Prophecy, *JNES* 47, 43-46

Gonçalves, F.J. 1986, *L'Expédition de Sennachérib en Palestine dans la Littérature Hébraïque Ancienne*, PIOL 34, Louvain-La-Neuve

——1999, 2 Rois 18,13-20,19 par Isaïe 36-39: encore une fois, lequel des deux livres fut le premier? in: J.-M. Auwers and A. Wénin (eds), *Lectures et Relectures de la Bible. Festschrift P.-M. Bogaert*, BETL 144, Leuven, 27-55

——2001, Les "Prophètes Ecrivains" etaient-ils des NBY'YM? in: P.M.M. Daviau et al. (eds), *World of the Aramaeans I, Biblical studies in honour of P.-E. Dion*, JSOTSup 324, Sheffield, 144-185

Goodnick Westenholz, J. 1997, *Legends of the Kings of Akkade*, MC 7, Winona Lake

Gordon, R.P. 1993, From Mari to Moses: Prophecy at Mari and in Ancient Israel, in: H.A. McKay and D.J.A. Clines (eds), *Of Prophets' Visions and the Wisdom of Sages. Essays in Honour of R.N. Whybray*, JSOTSup 162, Sheffield, 63-79

——1995, A Story of Two Paradigm Shifts, in: R.P. Gordon (ed.), *'The Place is Too Small for Us'. The Israelite Prophets in Recent Scholarship*, SBTS 5, Winona Lake, 3-26

Gosse, B. 1988, *Isaïe 13,1-14,23 dans la tradition littéraire du livre d'Isaïe et dans la tradition des oracles contra les nations*, OBO 78, Freiburg

Grabbe, L.L. 1995, *Priests, Prophets, Diviners, Sages: A Socio-Historical Study of Religious Specialists in Ancient Israel*, Valley Forge

——2000, Ancient Near Eastern Prophecy from an Anthropological Perspective, in: M. Nissinen (ed.), *Prophecy in its Ancient Near Eastern Context. Mesopotamian, Biblical and Arabian Perspectives*, SBLSS 13, Atlanta, 13-32

Grabbe, L.L. and Haak, R.D. (eds) 2001, *'Every City shall be forsaken': Urbanism and Prophecy in Ancient Israel and the Near East*, JSOTSup 330, Sheffield

Grabbe, L.L. and Ogden Bellis, A. (eds) 2004, *The Priests in the Prophets. The Portrayal of Priests, Prophets and Other Religious Specialists in the Latter Prophets*, JSOTSup 408, London

Gray, J.B. 1912, *The Book of Isaiah I-XXXIX*, ICC, Edinburgh

Grayson, A.K. 1975a, *Assyrian and Babylonian Chronicles*, Locust Valley

——1975b, *Babylonian Historical-Literary Texts*, Toronto

——1980, Histories and Historians of the Ancient Near East: Assyria and Babylonia, *Or* 49, 140-194

——1983, Literary Letters from Deities and Diviners, *JAOS* 103, 143-148

——1996, *Assyrian Rulers of the Early First Millennium BC II*, 858-745 BC, RIMA vol. 3, Toronto

Greßmann, H. 1914, Die literarische Analyse Deuterojesajas, *ZAW* 34, 254-297

Guillaume, A. 1938, *Prophecy and Divination among the Hebrews and Other Semites*, London

Haldar, A. 1945, *Associations of Cult Prophets among the Ancient Semites*, Uppsala

Hallo, W.W. 1966, Akkadian Apocalypses, *IEJ* 16, 231-242

——1990, Compare and Contrast: the Contextual Approach to Biblical Literature, in: W.W. Hallo et al. (eds), *The Bible in the Light of Cuneiform Literature: Scripture in Context 3*, ANETS 8, Lewiston, 1-30

——1997, Ancient Near Eastern Texts and their Relevance for Biblical Exegesis, in: W.W. Hallo (ed.), *The Context of Scripture I. Canonical Compositions from the Biblical World*, Leiden, XXIII-XXVIII

Hallo, W.W. (ed.) 1997, *The Context of Scripture I. Canonical Compositions from the Biblical World*, Leiden

——2000, *The Context of Scripture II. Monumental Inscriptions from the Biblical World*, Leiden

Hallo, W.W. et al. (eds) 1983, *Scripture in Context II: More Essays on the Comparative Method*, Winona Lake

——1990, *The Bible in the Light of Cuneiform Literature: Scripture in Context III*, ANETS 8, Lewiston

Halpern, B. 1991, Jerusalem and the Lineages in the Seventh Century BCE: Kinship and the Rise of Individual Moral Liability, in: B. Halpern and D.W. Hobson (eds), *Law and Ideology in Monarchic Israel*, JSOTSup 124, Sheffield, 11-107

Hardmeier, C. 1979, Gesichtspunkte pragmatischer Erzähltextanalyse. "Glaubt ihr nicht, so bleibt ihr nicht" – ein Glaubensappell an schwankende Anhänger Jesajas, *WD* 15, 33-54

——1981, Jesajas Verkündigungsabsicht und Jahwes Verstockungsauftrag in Jes 6, in: J. Jeremias and L. Perlitt (eds), *Die Botschaft und die Boten. Festschrift für H.W. Wolff*, Neukirchen-Vluyn, 235-251

——1986, Jesajaforschung im Umbruch, *VF* 31, 3-31

——2000, König Joschija in der Klimax des DtrG (2Reg 22f.) und das vordtr Dokument einer Kultreform am Residenzort (23,4-15*), in: R. Lux (ed.), *Erzählte Geschichte. Beiträge zur narrativen Kultur im alten Israel*, BTS 40, Neukirchen-Vluyn, 81-146

Hartenstein, F. 1997, *Die Unzugänglichkeit Gottes im Heiligtum. Jesaja 6 und der Wohnort JHWHs in der Jerusalemer Kulttradition*, WMANT 75, Neukirchen-Vluyn

Hawkins, J.D. 2004, The New Sargon Stele from Hama, in: G. Frame (ed.), *From the Upper Sea to the Lower Sea. Studies on the History of Assyria and Babylonia in honour of A.K. Grayson*, Leiden, 151-164

Hayes, J.H. and Irvine, S.A. 1987, *Isaiah, the Eighth Century Prophet: His Times and his Preaching*, Nashville

Hayes, J.H. and Kuan, J.K. 1991, The Final Years of Samaria (730-720 BC), *Bib* 72, 153-181

Hecker, K. 1986, Assyrische Propheten, in: M. Dietrich et al. (eds), *Texte aus der Umwelt des Alten Testaments. Band II. Religiöse Texte 1*, Gütersloh, 55-63

Heimpel, W. 2003, *Letters to the King of Mari: A New Translation, with Historical Introduction, Notes and Commentary*, MC 12, Winona Lake

Heintz, J.-G. 1969, Oracles prophétiques et "guerre sainte" selon les Archives royales de Mari et l'ancien Testament, in: T.C. Vriezen (ed.), *Congress Volume: Rome 1968*, VTSup 17, Leiden, 112-138

——1990, *Bibliographie de Mari [1933-1988]*, Wiesbaden

——1992, Royal Traits and Messianic Figures: A Thematic and Iconographical Approach, in: J.H. Charlesworth et al. (eds), *The Messiah. Developments in Earliest Judaism and Christianity*, Minneapolis, 52-66

——1992-8, Bibliographie de Mari, *Akkadica* 77 (1992), 1-37; *Akkadica* 81 (1993), 1-22; *Akkadica* 86 (1994), 1-23; *Akkadica* 91 (1995), 1-22; *Akkadica* 96 (1996), 1-22; *Akkadica* 104/105 (1997), 1-23; *Akkadica* 109/110 (1998), 1-21

——1997, La 'fin' des prophètes bibliques? Nouvelles théories et documents sémitiques anciens, in: J.-G. Heintz (ed.), *Oracles et prophéties dans l'antiquité. Actes du Colloque de Strasbourg 15-17 juin 1995*, Paris, 195-214

Heltzer, M. 1981, *The Suteans*, Naples

Henshaw, R.A. 1994, *Female and Male. The Cultic Personnel. The Bible and the Rest of the Ancient Near East*, Princeton Theological Monograph Series 31, Allison Park

Herbert, A.S. 1973, *The Book of the Prophet Isaiah. Chapters 1-39*, CBC, Cambridge

Herrmann, S. 1965, *Die prophetischen Heilserwartungen im Alten Testament*, Stuttgart

Herzog, Z. and Singer-Avitz, L. 2004, Redefining the Centre: the Emergence of State in Judah, *TA* 31, 209-244

Hesse, F. 1955, *Das Verstockungsproblem im Alten Testament: eine frömmigkeitsgeschichtliche Untersuchung*, BZAW 74, Berlin

Hilber, J.W. 2003, Psalm CX in the Light of Assyrian Prophecies, *VT* 53, 353-366

——2005, *Cultic Prophecy in the Psalms*, BZAW 352, Berlin

Höffken, P. 1977, Heilszeitherrschererwartung im babylonischen Raum. Überlegungen im Anschluß an W 22 307.7, *WO* 9, 57-71

——1980, Notizen zum Textcharakter von Jesaja, *TZ* 36, 321-337

——2000, Bemerkungen zu Jesaja 31,1-3, *ZAW* 112, 230-238

——2004, *Jesaja. Der Stand der theologischen Diskussion*, Darmstadt

Hoffmann, A. 1972, Jahwe schleift Ringmauern – Jes 45,2αβ, in: J. Schreiner (ed.), *Wort, Lied und Gottesspruch: Festschrift für J. Ziegler. Teil II. Beiträge zu Psalmen und Propheten*, FzB 2, Echter, 187-196

Hoffmann, H.W. 1974, *Die Intention der Verkündigung Jesajas*, BZAW 136, Berlin

Hoftijzer, J. 1986, Frustula Epigraphica Hebraica, in: H.L.J. Vanstiphout (ed.), *Scripta Signa Vocis. Studies about Scripts, Scriptures, Scribes and Languages in the Near East, presented to J.H. Hospers*, Groningen, 85-93

Hoftijzer, J. and van der Kooij, G. 1976, *Aramaic Texts from Deir 'Alla*, DMOA 19, Leiden

Hoftijzer, J. and van der Kooij, G. (eds) 1991, *The Balaam Text from Deir 'Alla Re-Evaluated. Proceedings of the International Symposium held at Leiden, 21-24 August 1989*, Leiden

478 BIBLIOGRAPHY

Høgenhaven, J. 1988, *Gott und Volk bei Jesaja: eine Untersuchung zur biblischen Theologie*, Leiden
——1989, Prophecy and Propaganda. Aspects of Political and Religious Reasoning in Israel and the Ancient Near East, *SJOT* 3, 125-141
——1990, The Prophet Isaiah and Judaean Foreign Policy under Ahaz and Hezekiah, *JNES* 49, 351-354
Holladay, W.L. 1999, Text, Structure, and Irony in the Poem on the Fall of the Tyrant, Isaiah 14, *CBQ* 61, 633-645
Hollenstein, H. 1977, Literarkritische Erwägungen zum Bericht über die Reformmassnahmen Josias 2 Kön. XXIII 4ff., *VT* 27, 321-336
Holloway, S.W. 2002, *Aššur is King! Aššur is King! Religion in the Exercise of Power in the Neo-Assyrian Empire*, CHANE 10, Leiden
Holm, N.G. 1982, Ecstatic Research in the 20th Century – An Introduction, in: N.G. Holm (ed.), *Religious Ecstasy*, Uppsala, 7-26
Houston, W. 2004, Was There a Social Crisis in the Eighth Century? in: J. Day (ed.), *In Search of Pre-exilic Israel. Proceedings of the Oxford Old Testament Seminar*, JSOTSup 406, London, 130-149
Huehnergard, J. 1999, On the Etymology and Meaning of Hebrew *NĀBÎ'*, *ErIsr* 26, 89-95
Huffmon, H.B. 1968, Prophecy in the Mari letters, *BA* 31, 101-124
——1992, Prophecy: Ancient Near Eastern Prophecy, *ABD* 5, 477-482
——2000, A Company of Prophets: Mari, Assyria, Israel, in: M. Nissinen (ed.), *Prophecy in its Ancient Near Eastern Context. Mesopotamian, Biblical and Arabian Perspectives*, SBLSS 13, Atlanta, 47-70
Hummel, H.D. 1957, Enclitic *mem* in Northwest Semitic, especially Hebrew, *JBL* 76, 85-104
Hunger, H. 1968, *Babylonische und assyrische Kolophone*, AOAT 2, Neukirchen-Vluyn
——1976, *Spätbabylonische Texte aus Uruk*, Band 1, Berlin
Hunger, H. and Kaufman, S.A. 1975, A New Akkadian Prophecy Text, *JAOS* 95, 371-375
Hurowitz, V. 1992, *I Have Built You an Exalted House. Temple Building in the Bible in Light of Mesopotamian and Northwest Semitic Writings*, JSOTSup 115, Sheffield
Husser, J.-M. 1994, *Le songe et la parole: étude sur le rêve et sa fonction dans l'ancien Israël*, BZAW 210, Berlin
Hutter, M. 1996, *Religionen in der Umwelt des Alten Testaments I: Babylonier, Syrer, Perser*, Stuttgart
Irvine, S.A. 1990, *Isaiah, Ahaz, and the Syro-Ephraimitic Crisis*, Atlanta
——1993, Problems of Text and Translation in Isaiah 10.13bb, in: M.P. Graham, W.P. Brown, and J.K. Kuan (eds), *History and Interpretation. Essays in Honour of J.H. Hayes*, JSOTSup 173, Sheffield, 133-144
Irwin, W.H. 1977, *Isaiah 28-33. Translation with Philological Notes*, BibOr 30, Rome
Ishida, T. 1977, *The Royal Dynasties in Ancient Israel: A Study on the Formation and Development of Royal-Dynastic Ideology*, BZAW 142, Berlin
Ivantchik, A. 1993, Corrigenda aux textes akkadiens mentionnant les Cimmériens, *NABU*, 40-41

Janowski, B. 1989, *Rettungsgewißheit und Epiphanie des Heils. Das Motiv der Hilfe Gottes "am Morgen" im Alten Orient und im Alten Testament. Band 1: Alter Orient*, WMANT 59, Neukirchen-Vluyn

Janzen, W. 1972, *Mourning Cry and Woe Oracle*, BZAW 125, Berlin

Jenkins, A.K. 1989, The Development of the Isaiah Tradition in Isaiah 13-23, in: J. Vermeylen (ed.), *The Book of Isaiah. Le Livre d'Isaïe: les oracles et leurs relectures: unité et complexité de l'ouvrage*, BETL 81, Leuven, 237-251

Jeremias, J. 1994, Das Proprium der alttestamentlichen Prophetie, *TLZ* 119, 483-494

——1996, Die Anfänge der Schriftprophetie, *ZTK* 93, 481-499

Jeyes, U. 1989, *Old Babylonian Extispicy: Omen Texts in the British Museum*, UNHAII 64, Istanbul

Johnson, A.R. 1962, *The Cultic Prophet in Ancient Israel* (2nd edition), Cardiff

Jones, B.J. 1993, Isaiah 8.11 and Isaiah's Vision of Yahweh, in: M.P. Graham, W.P. Brown, and J.K. Kuan (eds), *History and Interpretation. Essays in Honour of J.H. Hayes*, JSOTSup 173, 145-159

Jong, M.J. de 2004, 'Fear Not, O King!' The Assyrian Prophecies as a Case for a Comparative Approach, *JEOL* 38 (2003-2004), 113-121

——2007, Ezekiel as a Literary Figure and the Quest for the Historical Prophet, in: J. Tromp and H.J. de Jonge (eds), *The Book of Ezekiel and Its Influence*, Aldershot, 1-16

Joosten, J. 2001, La prosopopée, les pseudo-citations et la vocation d'Isaïe (Is 6,9-10), *Bib* 82, 232-243

Joüon, P., S.J. and Muraoka, T. 1996, *A Grammar of Biblical Hebrew*, 2 vols, Rome

Kahn, D. 2001, The Inscription of Sargon II at Tang-I Var and the Chronology of Dynasty 25, *Or* 70, 1-18

Kaiser, O. 1981, *Das Buch des Propheten Jesaja. Kapitel 1-12*, ATD 17 (5th edition), Göttingen

——1983, *Der Prophet Jesaja. Kapitel 13-39*, ATD 18 (3rd edition), Göttingen

——1989, Literarkritik und Tendenzkritik. Überlegungen zur Methode der Jesajaexegese, in: J. Vermeylen (ed.), *The Book of Isaiah. Le Livre d'Isaïe: les oracles et leurs relectures: unité et complexité de l'ouvrage*, BETL 81, Leuven, 55-71

——1994, *Grundriß der Einleitung*, vol. 2, Gütersloh

Kaltner, J. and Stulman, L. (eds) 2004, *Inspired Speech: Prophecy in the Ancient Near East, Essays in Honor of H.B. Huffmon*, JSOTSup 378, London

Kang, S.M. 1989, *Divine War in the Old Testament and in the Ancient Near East*, BZAW 177, Berlin

Kapera, Z.J. 1976, The Ashdod Stele of Sargon II, *FO* 17, 87-99

Kaufman, S.A. 1977, Prediction, Prophecy, and Apocalypse in the Light of New Akkadian Texts, in: A. Shinan (ed.), *Proceedings of the Sixth World Congress of Jewish Studies* I, Jerusalem, 221-228

Keel, O. 1977, *Jahwe-Visionen und Siegelkunst*, Stuttgart

Kellermann, D. 1987, Frevelstricke und Wagenseil: Bemerkungen zu Jesaja v 18, *VT* 37, 90-95

Keulen, P. van 1996, *Manasseh through the Eyes of the Deuteronomists. The Manasseh Account (2 Kings 21:1-18) and the Final Chapters of the Deuteronomistic History*, OtSt 38, Leiden

Kilian, R. 1977, Der Verstockungsauftrag Jesajas, in: H.-J. Fabry (ed.), *Bausteine biblischer Theologie. Festgabe für G.J. Botterweck*, BBB 50, Bonn, 209-225

——1983, *Jesaja 1-39. Erträge der Forschung*, Darmstadt

Killebrew, A.E. 2003, Biblical Jerusalem: An Archaeological Assessment, in: A.G. Vaughn and A.E. Killebrew (eds), *Jerusalem in Bible and Archaeology. The First Temple Period*, SBLSS 18, Atlanta, 329-346

Kitchen, K.A. 1986, *The Third Intermediate Period in Egypt (1100-650 B.C.)* (2nd revised edition) Warminster

Kitz, A.M. 2003, Prophecy as Divination, *CBQ* 65, 22-42

Knauf, E.A. 2000, Vom Prophetinnenwort zum Prophetenbuch: Jesaja 8,3f im Kontext von Jesaja 6,1-8,16, *Lectio Difficilior. European Electronic Journal for Feminist Exegesis* 2, 1-9

——2001, Hezekiah or Manasseh? A Reconsideration of the Siloam Tunnel and Inscription, *TA* 28, 281-287

——2003, Sennacherib at the Berezina, in: L.L. Grabbe (ed.), *"Like a Bird in a Cage": The Invasion of Sennacherib in 701 BCE*, JSOTSup 363, London, 141-149

Knierim, R. 1968, The Vocation of Isaiah, *VT* 28, 47-68

Knoppers, G. 1994, *Two Nations under God: The Deuteronomistic History of Solomon and the Dual Monarchies, vol. 2: The Reign of Jeroboam, the Fall of Israel, and the Reign of Josiah*, HSM 53, Atlanta

Koch, K. 1995, *Die Profeten, vol. 1. Assyrische Zeit* (3rd edition), Stuttgart

Koch-Westenholz, U. 1995, *Mesopotamian Astrology. In Introduction to Babylonian and Assyrian Celestial Divination*, Copenhagen

Köckert, M. 2000, Zum literargeschichtlicher Ort des Prophetengesetzes Dtn 18 zwischen dem Jeremiabuch und Dtn 13, in: R.G. Kratz and H. Spieckermann (eds), *Liebe und Gebot: Studien zum Deuteronomium*, FRLANT 190, Göttingen, 80-100

——2003, Das Problem des historischen Jesaja, in: I. Fischer et al. (eds), *Prophetie in Israel. Beiträge des Symposiums 'Das Alte Testament und die Kultur der Moderne' anlässlich des 100. Geburtstags Gerhard Von Rads*, ATM 11, Münster, 105-116

Kooij, A. van der 1986, Das assyrische Heer vor den Mauern Jerusalems im Jahr 701 v.Chr., *ZDPV* 102, 93-109

——1990, *Abraham, Vader van/voor een Menigte Volkeren. Gen. 17, 4-5 in het Hebreeuws, alsmede in de Griekse, Aramese en Syrische Vertaling*, Leiden

——2000, The Story of Hezekiah and Sennacherib (2 Kings 18-19). A Sample of Ancient Historiography, in: J.C. de Moor and H.F. van Rooy (eds), *Past, Present, Future. The Deuteronomistic History and the Prophets*, OtSt 44, Leiden, 107-119

Kouwenberg, N.J.C. 1997, *Gemination in the Akkadian Verb*, SSN 32, Assen

Kramer, S.N. 1940, *Lamentation over the Destruction of Ur*, AS 12, Chicago

——1974, Kingship in Sumer and Akkad: The Ideal King, in: P. Garelli (ed.), *Le Palais et la Royauté. Archéologie et Civilisation*, RAI 19, Paris, 163-176

Kratz, R.G. 1991, *Kyros im Deuterojesaja-Buch: redaktionsgeschichtliche Untersuchungen zu Entstehung und Theologie von Jes 40-55*, FAT 1, Tübingen

——1997, Die Redaktion der Prophetenbücher, in: R.G. Kratz and T. Krüger (eds), *Rezeption und Auslegung im alten Testament und in seinem Umfeld*, OBO 153, Fribourg, 9-27

——2003a, Die Worte des Amos von Tekoa, in: M. Köckert and M. Nissinen (eds), *Propheten in Mari, Assyrien und Israel*, FRLANT 201, Göttingen, 54-89

——2003b, Das Neue in der Prophetie des Alten Testaments, in: I. Fischer et al. (eds), *Prophetie in Israel. Beiträge des Symposiums 'Das Alte Testament und die Kultur der Moderne' anlässlich des 100. Geburtstags Gerhard Von Rads*, ATM 11, Münster, 1-22

Kraus, H.-J. 1982, *Geschichte der historisch-kritischen Erforschung des Alten Testaments* (3rd edition), Neukirchen-Vluyn

Kselman, J. 1985, The Social World of the Israelite Prophets: A Review Article, *RSRev* 11, 120-129

Kuehne, H. 2002, Thoughts about Assyria after 612 BC, in: L. Al-Gailani Werr et al. (eds), *Of Pots and Plans. Papers on the Archaeology and History of Mesopotamia and Syria presented to D. Oates*, London, 171-175

Kvanvig, H.S. 1988, *Roots of Apocalyptic: the Mesopotamian Background of the Enoch Figure and of the Son of Man*, WMANT 61, Neukirchen-Vluyn

Laato, A. 1988, *Who is Immanuel? The Rise and the Foundering of Isaiah's Messianic Expectations*, Aabo

——1992, *Josiah and David Redivivus. The Historical Josiah and the Messianic Expectations of Exilic and Postexilic Times*, CBOTS 33, Almqvist

——1998, *'About Zion I will not be silent'. The Book of Isaiah as an Ideological Unity*, CBOTS 44, Stockholm

Lafont, B. 1984, Le roi de Mari et les prophètes du dieu Adad, *RA* 78, 7-18

Lambert, W.G. 1964, The Reign of Nebuchadnezzar I: A Turning Point in the History of Ancient Mesopotamian Religion, in: W.S. McCullough (ed.), *The Seed of Wisdom. Essays in Honour of T.J. Meek*, Toronto, 3-13

——1970, Review of: B. Albrektson, *History and the gods*, *Or* 39, 170-177

——1978, *The Background of Jewish Apocalyptic*, London

——1998, Kingship in Ancient Mesopotamia, in: J. Day (ed.), *King and Messiah in Israel and the Ancient Near East. Proceedings of the Oxford Old Testament Seminar*, JSOTSup 270, Sheffield, 54-70

——2002a, Review of Simo Parpola, *Assyrian Prophecies*, SAA 9 (Helsinki 1997), *AfO* 48/49, 208-211

——2002b, Review of Martti Nissinen, *References to Prophecy in Neo-Assyrian Sources*, SAAS 7 (Helsinki 1998), *AfO* 48/49, 211-212

——2004, Mesopotamian Sources and Pre-exilic Israel, in: J. Day (ed.), *In Search of Pre-exilic Israel. Proceedings of the Oxford Old Testament Seminar*, JSOTSup 406, London, 352-365

Landsberger, B. 1965, *Brief des Bischofs von Esagila an König Asarhaddon*, MKNAW, afd. Letterkunde 28:6, Amsterdam

Lanfranchi, G.B. 1989, Scholars and Scholarly Tradition in Neo-Assyrian Times: A Case Study, *SAAB* 3, 99-114

——2003, Ideological Implications of the Problem of Royal Responsibility in the Neo-Assyrian Period, in: I. Eph'al et al. (eds), *Hayim and Miriam Tadmor Volume. Eretz-Israel. Archaeological, Historical and Geographical Studies* 27, Jerusalem, 100-110

Lang, B. 1980, W*ie wird man Prophet in Israel? Aufsätze zum Alten Testament*, Düsseldorf

Langdon, S. 1912, *Die neubabylonischen Königsinschriften*, VAB 4, Leipzig

——1914, *Tammuz and Ishtar*, Oxford

Lara Peinado, F. 1989, El Mito de Erra y los Infortunios de Babilonia, *Historia* 16/161, 109-116

Lemaire, A. 1996, Les Textes prophétiques de Mari dans leurs Relations avec l'Ouest, in: J.-M. Durand (ed.), *Amurru 1. Mari, Ébla et les Hourrites. Dix ans de traveaux*, vol. 1, Paris, 427-438

——1997, Oracles, propaganda et littérature dans les royaumes araméens et transjordaniens, in: J.-G. Heintz (ed.), *Oracles et prophéties dans l'antiquité. Actes du Colloque de Strasbourg 15-17 juin 1995*, Paris, 171-193

——1999, Traditions amorrites et bible: le Prophétisme, *RA* 93, 49-56

——2001a, Introduction, in: A. Lemaire (ed.), *Prophètes et Rois. Bible et Proche-Orient*, Paris, 11-18

——2001b, Prophètes et Rois dans les Inscriptions Ouest-Sémitiques (IXe-VIe Siècle AV. J.-C.), in: A. Lemaire (ed.), *Prophètes et Rois. Bible et Proche-Orient*, Paris, 85-115

——2004, Hebrew and West Semitic Inscriptions and Pre-exilic Israel, in: J. Day (ed.), *In Search of Pre-exilic Israel. Proceedings of the Oxford Old Testament Seminar*, JSOTSup 406, London, 366-385

Lemaire, A. (ed.) 2001, *Prophètes et Rois. Bible et Proche-Orient*, Paris

Levine, B.A. 2005, Assyrian Ideology and Israelite Monotheism, *Iraq* 67, 411-427

Levine, L.D. 2003, Observations on "Sargon's Letter to the Gods", in: I. Eph'al et al. (eds), *Hayim and Miriam Tadmor Volume. Eretz-Israel. Archaeological, Historical and Geographical Studies* 27, Jerusalem, 111-119

L'Heureux, C.E. 1984, The Redactional History of Isaiah 5.1-10.4, in: W.B. Barrick and J.R. Spencer (eds), *In the Shelter of Elyon. Essays on Ancient Palestinian Life and Literature in Honor of G.W. Ahlström*, JSOTSup 31, Sheffield, 99-119

Lindblom, J. 1962, *Prophecy in Ancient Israel*, Oxford

Lipschits, O. 2005, *The Fall and Rise of Jerusalem. Judah under Babylonian Rule*, Winona Lake

Liverani, M. 1982, kitru, katāru, *Mesopotamia* 17, 43-66

——1995, The Medes at Esarhaddon's Court, *JCS* 47, 57-62

Livingstone, A. 1989, *Court Poetry and Literary Miscellanea*, SAA 3, Helsinki

Long, B.O. 1973, The Effect of Divination Upon Israelite Literature, *JBL* 92, 489-497

Longman, T. (III) 1991, *Fictional Akkadian Autobiography: A Generic and Comparative Study*, Winona Lake

López, G. 1995, *tôrāh*, in: H.-J. Fabry and H. Ringgren (eds), *Theologisches Wörterbuch zum Alten Testament* VIII, Stuttgart, 597-637

Loretz, O. 1992, Die Entstehung des Amos-Buches im Licht der Prophetien aus Mari, Assur, Ishchali und der Ugarit-Texte. Paradigmenwechsel in der Prophetenbuchforschung, *UF* 24, 179-215

Luckenbill, D.D. 1924, *The Annals of Sennacherib*, OIP 2, Chicago

Luukko, M. 2004, *Grammatical Variation in Neo-Assyrian*, SAAS 16, Helsinki

Maag, V. 1980, Kosmos, Chaos, Gesellschaft und Recht nach archaisch-religiösem Verständnis, in: V. Maag (H.H. Schmid and O.H. Steck [eds]), *Kultur, Kulturkontakt und Religion. Gesammelte Studien zur allgemeinen und alttestamentlichen Religionsgeschichte*, Göttingen, 329-341

Machinist, P. 1983a, Assyria and Its Image in the First Isaiah, *JAOS* 103, 719-738

——1983b, Rest and Violence in the Poem of Erra, *JAOS* 103, 221-226

Malamat, A. 1966, Prophetic Revelations in New Documents from Mari and the Bible, in: O. Eissfeldt (ed.), *Volume du Congrès: Genève 1965*, VTSup 15, Leiden, 207-227

——1980, A Mari Prophecy and Nathan's Dynastic Oracle, in: J. Emerton (ed.), *Prophecy – Essays for G. Fohrer*, BZAW 100, Berlin, 68-82 (repr. *Mari and the Bible*, Leiden 1998, 106-121)

——1989, *Mari and the early Israelite Experience*, Oxford

——1997, The Cultural Impact of the West (Syria-Palestine) on Mesopotamia in the Old Babylonian Period, *AoF* 24, 310-319

——1998, *Mari and the Bible*, SHANE 12, Leiden

Margalit, B. 1994, Rise and Fall of Zakkur, King of Hamath-and-Lu'ash, *NABU*, 13-14

Mattila, R. 1987, The Political Status of Elam after 653 B.C. According to *ABL* 839, *SAAB* 1, 27-30

——1999, Dādāia, in: K. Radner (ed.), *The Prosopography of the Neo-Assyrian Empire*, vol. 1/II, Helsinki

——2000, *The King's Magnates: A Study of the Highest Officials of the Neo-Assyrian Empire*, SAAS 11, Helsinki

Maul, S.M. 1992, *Kurgarrû* und *assinnu* und ihr Stand in der babylonischen Gesellschaft, in: V. Haas (ed.), *Außenseiter und Randgruppen. Beiträge zu einer Sozialgeschichte des Alten Orient*, Konstanz, 159-171

——1994, *Zukunftsbewältigung: eine Untersuchung altorientalischen Denkens anhand der babylonisch-assyrischen Löserituale (Namburbi)*, BaghF 18, Mainz am Rhein

Mayer Burstein, S. 1978, *The Babyloniaca of Berossus*, SANE 1/5, 24-25

Mayer, W. 1983, Sargons Feldzug gegen Urartu – 714 v.Chr. Text und Übersetzung, *MDOG* 115, 65-132

——1995, *Politik und Kriegskunst der Assyrer*, ALASP 9, Münster

——2003, Sennacherib's Campaign of 701 BCE, in: L.L. Grabbe (ed.), *"Like a Bird in a Cage": The Invasion of Sennacherib in 701 BCE*, JSOTSup 363, London, 168-200

Mazar, A. 2003, Ritual Dancing in the Iron Age, *Near Eastern Archaeology* 66, 126-132

McFadden, W.R. 1983, Micah and the Problem of Continuities and Discontinuities in Prophecy, in: W.W. Hallo et al. (eds), *Scripture in Context II: More Essays on the Comparative Method*, Winona Lake, 127-146

McNutt, P.M. 1999, *Reconstructing the Society of Ancient Israel*, LAI, London

Melugin, R.F. and Sweeney, M.A. (eds) 1996, *New Visions of Isaiah*, JSOTSup 214, Sheffield

Menzel, B. 1981, *Assyrische Tempel, Band 1. Untersuchungen zu Kult, Administration und Personal; Band II. Anmerkungen, Textbuch, Tabellen und Indices*, Studia Pohl: Series Maior 10/I/II, Rome

Menzies, G.W. 1998, To What Does Faith Lead? The Two-Stranded Textual Tradition of Isaiah 7.9b, *JSOT* 80, 111-128

Mettinger, T.N.D. 1999, Seraphim, in: K. van der Toorn, B. Becking and P.W. van der Horst (eds), *Dictionary of Deities and Demons in the Bible* (2nd edition), Leiden, 742-744

Michaelsen, P. 1989, Ecstasy and Possession in Ancient Israel: A Review of Some Recent Contributions, *SJOT* 3, 28-54

Millard, A. 1985, La prophétie et l'écriture: Israël, Aram, Assyrie, *RHR* 202, 125-144

——1994, *The Eponyms of the Assyrian Empire 910-612 BC*, SAAS 2, Helsinki

Mittmann, S. 1989, "Wehe! Assur, Stab meines Zorns" (Jes 10,5-9.13aβ-15), in: V. Fritz, K.-F. Pohlmann, and H.-C. Schmitt (eds), *Prophet und Prophetenbuch. Festschrift für O. Kaiser*, BZAW 185, Berlin, 111-132

Morkot, R. 2000, *The Black Pharaohs: Egypt's Nubian Rulers*, London

Mosis, R. 1981, *jāsad*, in: G.J. Botterweck and H. Ringgren (eds), *Theologisches Wörterbuch zum Alten Testament* III, Stuttgart, 668-682

Mowinckel, S. 1933, Die Komposition des Jesajabuches Kap. 1-39, *AcOr* 11, 267-292

Müller, H.-P. 1974, Glauben und Bleiben. Zur Denkschrift Jesajas Kapitel vi 1-viii 18, in: D. Lys et al. (eds), *Studies on Prophecy: A Collection of Twelve Papers*, VTSup 26, Leiden, 25-54

——1984, *nābî'*, in: G.J. Botterweck, H. Ringgren, and H.-J. Fabry (eds), *Theologisches Wörterbuch zum Alten Testament* V, Stuttgart, 140-163

Na'aman, N. 1974, Sennacherib's "Letter to God" on his Campaign to Judah, *BASOR* 214, 25-39

——1986, Historical and Chronological Notes on the Kingdoms of Israel and Judah in the 8th century BC, *VT* 36, 71-92

——1991a, Forced Participation in Alliances in the Course of the Assyrian Campaigns to the West, in: M. Cogan and I. Eph'al (eds), *Ah, Assyria .... Studies in Assyrian History and Ancient Near Eastern Historiography Presented to Hayim Tadmor*, ScrHier 33, Jerusalem, 80-98

——1991b, The Kingdom of Judah under Josiah, *TA* 18, 3-71

——1991c, Chronology and History in the Late Assyrian Empire (631-619 BC), *ZA* 81, 243-267

——1994a, Hezekiah and the Kings of Assyria, *TA* 21, 235-254

——1994b, The Historical Portion of Sargon II's Nimrud Inscription, *SAAB* 8, 17-20

——2000, New Light on Hezekiah's Second Prophetic Story (2 Kgs 19,9b-35), *Bib* 81, 393-402

——2003, Updating the Messages: Hezekiah's Second Prophetic Story (2 Kings 19.9b-35) and the Community of Babylonian Deportees, in: L.L. Grabbe (ed.), *"Like a Bird in a Cage": The Invasion of Sennacherib in 701 BCE*, JSOTSup 363, London, 201-220

——2006a, The Temple Library of Jerusalem and the Composition of the Book of Kings, in: A. Lemaire (ed.), *Congress Volume Leiden 2004*, VTSup 109, Leiden, 129-152

——2006b, The King Leading Cult Reforms in his Kingdom: Josiah and Other Kings in the Ancient Near East, *ZABR* 12, 131-168

Nell, P.J. 2000, Social Justice as Religious Responsibility in Near Eastern Religions: Historic Ideal and Ideological illusion, *JNSL* 26/2, 143-153

Nielsen, K. 1989, *There is Hope for a Tree. The Tree as Metaphor in Isaiah*, JSOTSup 65, Sheffield

Niemann, H.M. 1993, *Herrschaft, Königtum und Staat. Skizzen zur soziokulturellen Entwicklung im monarchischen Israel*, FAT 6, Tübingen

Nissinen, M. 1991, *Prophetie, Redaktion und Fortschreibung im Hoseabuch*, AOAT 231, Neukirchen-Vluyn

——1993, Die Relevanz der neuassyrischen Prophetie für das Studium des Alten Testaments, in: M. Dietrich and O. Loretz (eds), *Mesopotamica – Ugaritica – Biblica*, AOAT 232, Neukirchen-Vluyn, 217-258

——1996, Falsche Prophetie in neuassyrischer und deuteronomistischer Darstellung, in: T. Veijola (ed.), *Das Deuteronomium und seine Querbeziehungen*, Helsinki, 172-195

——1998, *References to Prophecy in Neo-Assyrian Sources*, SAAS 7, Helsinki

——2000a, Spoken, Written, Quoted, and Invented: Orality and Writtenness in Ancient Near Eastern prophecy, in: E. Ben Zvi and M.H. Floyd (eds), *Writings and Speech in Israelite and Ancient Near Eastern Prophecy*, Atlanta, 235-272

——2000b, The Socioreligious Role of the Neo-Assyrian Prophets, in: M. Nissinen (ed.), *Prophecy in its Ancient Near Eastern Context. Mesopotamian, Biblical and Arabian Perspectives*, SBLSS 13, Atlanta, 89-114

——2002, Prophets and the Divine Council, in: U. Hübner and E.A. Knauf (eds), *Kein Land für sich allein: Studien zum Kulturkontakt in Kanaan, Israel/Palästina und Ebirnâri für M. Weippert*, OBO 186, Göttingen, 4-19

——2003a, *Prophets and Prophecy in the Ancient Near East*; with contributions by C.L. Seow and R.K. Ritner; ed. P. Machinist, SBLWAW 12, Atlanta

——2003b, Fear Not: A Study of an Ancient Near Eastern Phrase, in: E. Ben Zvi and M.A. Sweeney (eds), *The Changing Face of Form Criticism for the Twenty-First Century*, Grand Rapids, 122-161

——2003c, Neither Prophecies nor Apocalypses: The Akkadian Literary Predictive Texts, in: L.L. Grabbe and R.D. Haak (eds), *Knowing the End from the Beginning. The Prophetic, the Apocalyptic and their Relationships*, JSPSup 46, London, 134-148

——2003d, Das kritische Potential in der altorientalischen Prophetie, in: M. Köckert and M. Nissinen (eds), *Propheten in Mari, Assyrien und Israel*, FRLANT 201, Göttingen, 1-32

——2004, What is Prophecy? An Ancient Near Eastern Perspective, in: J. Kaltner and L. Stulman (eds), *Inspired Speech: Prophecy in the Ancient Near East, Essays in Honor of H.B. Huffmon*, JSOTSup 378, London, 17-37

——2005, How Prophecy became Literature, *SJOT* 19, 153-172

Nissinen, M. (ed.) 2000, *Prophecy in its Ancient Near Eastern Context. Mesopotamian, Biblical and Arabian Perspectives*, SBLSS 13, Atlanta

Nissinen, M. and Parpola, S. 2004, Marduk's Return and Reconciliation in a Prophetic Letter from Arbela, in: H. Juusola et al. (eds), *Verbum et Calamus. Semitic and Related Studies in Honour of the Sixtieth Birthday of Professor Tapani Harviainen*, StudOr 99, Helsinki, 199-219

Noort, E. 1977, *Untersuchungen zum Gottesbescheid in Mari: die 'Mariprophetie' in der alttestamentlichen Forschung*, AOAT 202, Neukirchen-Vluyn

Noth, M. 1956, *Geschichte Israels* (3rd edition), Göttingen

——1957, Geschichte und Gotteswort im Alten Testament, in: H.W. Wolff (ed.), *Gesammelte Studien zum Alten Testament*, Munich, 230-247 (originally published as *Bonner akademische Reden* 3, Krefeld 1949)

Nötscher, F. 1966, Prophetie im Umkreis des Alten Israel, *BZ NF* 10, 161-197

Oded, B. 1972, The Historical Background of the Syro-Ephraimite War Reconsidered, *CBQ* 34, 153-165

——1979, *Mass Deportation and Deportees in the Neo-Assyrian Empire*, Wiesbaden

——1991, "The Command of the God" as a Reason for Going to War in the Assyrian Royal Inscriptions, in: M. Cogan and I. Eph'al (eds), *Ah, Assyria .... Studies in Assyrian History and Ancient Near Eastern Historiography Presented to Hayim Tadmor*, Scripta Hierosolymitana 33, Jerusalem, 223-230

——1993, Ahaz's Appeal to Tiglath-Pileser III in the Context of the Assyrian Policy of Expansion, in: M. Heltzer, A. Segal, and D. Kaufman (eds), *Studies in the Archaeology and History of Ancient Israel in Honour of M. Dothan*, Haifa, 63-71

O'Connell, R.H. 1994, *Concentricity and Continuity: The Literary Structure of Isaiah*, JSOTSup 188, Sheffield

Oeming, M. 1994, *śākar*, in: H.-J. Fabry and H. Ringgren (eds), *Theologisches Wörterbuch zum Alten Testament* VIII, Stuttgart, 1-5

Oesch, J.M. 1994, Jes 1,8f und das Problem der 'Wir-Reden' im Jesajabuch, *ZTK* 116, 440-446

Ollenburger, B.C. 1987, *Zion, the City of the Great King: A Theological Symbol of the Jerusalem Cult*, JSOTSup 41, Sheffield

Olyan, S.M. 2006, Was the "King of Babylon" Buried Before His Corpse Was Exposed? Some Thoughts on Isa 14,19, *ZAW* 118, 423-426

Onasch, H.-U. 1994, *Die Assyrischen Eroberungen Ägyptens. Teil 1: Kommentare und Anmerkungen*, ÄAT 27, Wiesbaden

Oppenheim, A.L. 1977, *Ancient Mesopotamia. Portrait of a Dead Civilization*, revised by E. Reiner, Chicago

Otto, E. 1998, Die Ursprunge der Bundestheologie im alten Testament und im Alten Orient, *ZABR* 4, 1-84

——2000, Political Theology in Judah and Assyria. The Beginning of the Hebrew Bible as Literature, *SEÅ* 65 (*Festschrift T.N.D. Mettinger*), 59-76

Parker, S.B. 1978, Possession Trance and Prophecy in Pre-exilic Israel, *VT* 28, 271-285

——1993, Official Attitudes toward Prophecy at Mari and in Israel, *VT* 43, 50-68

——1994, The Lachish Letters and Official Reactions to Prophecies, in: L.M. Hopfe (ed.), *Uncovering Ancient Stones. Essays in Memory of H.N. Richardson*, Winona Lake, 65-78

Parpola, S. 1980, The Murderer of Sennacherib, in: B. Alster (ed.), *Death in Mesopotamia*, Mesopotamia 8 (RAI 26), Copenhagen, 171-182

——1983, *Letters from Assyrian Scholars to the Kings Esarhaddon and Assurbanipal. Part II: Commentary and Appendices*, AOAT 5/2, Neukirchen-Vluyn

——1987, Neo-Assyrian Treaties from the Royal Archives of Nineveh, *JCS* 39, 161-189

——1993, *Letters from Assyrian and Babylonian Scholars*, SAA 10, Helsinki

——1997, *Assyrian Prophecies*, SAA 9, Helsinki

Parpola, S. and Watanabe, K. 1988, *Neo-Assyrian Treaties and Loyalty Oaths*, SAA 2, Helsinki

Pedersén, O. 1986, *Archives and Libraries in the City of Assur. A Survey of the Material from the German Excavations. Part II*, Uppsala

Perlitt, L. 1989, Jesaja und die Deuteronomisten, in: V. Fritz, K.-F. Pohlmann, and H.-C. Schmitt (eds), *Prophet und Prophetenbuch. Festschrift für O. Kaiser*, BZAW 185, Berlin, 133-149

Petersen, D.L. 1981, *The Roles of Israel's Prophets*, JSOTSup 17, Sheffield

——2000, Defining Prophecy and Prophetic Literature, in: M. Nissinen (ed.), *Prophecy in its Ancient Near Eastern Context. Mesopotamian, Biblical and Arabian Perspectives*, SBLSS 13, Atlanta, 33-44

Peursen, W.Th. van 1996, Guarded, Besieged or Devastated? Some remarks on Isaiah 1:7-8, with special reference to 1QIsa[a], *Dutch Studies in Near Eastern Languages and Literature* 2, 101-110

Pfeiffer, R.H. 1955, Oracles Concerning Esarhaddon, in: J.B. Prichard (ed.), *Ancient Near Eastern Texts Relating to the Old Testament* (2nd edition), Princeton, 449-451

Podella, T. 1996, *Das Lichtkleid JHWHs. Untersuchungen zur Gestalthaftigkeit Gottes im Alten Testament und seiner altorientalischen Umwelt*, FAT 15, Tübingen

Pohlmann, K.-F. 1994, Erwägungen zu Problemen alttestamentlicher Prophetenexegese, in: I. Kottsieper et al. (eds), *"Wer ist wie du, Herr, unter den Göttern?" Studien zur Theologie und Religionsgeschichte Israels. Festschrift für O. Kaiser*, Göttingen, 325-341

——2002, Religion in der Krise – Krise einer Religion. Die Zerstörung des Jerusalemer Tempels 587 v. Chr., in: J. Hahn (ed.), *Zerstörungen des Jerusalemer Tempels. Geschehen – Wahrnehmung – Bewältigung*, WUNT 147, Tübingen, 40-60

Polley, M.E. 1980, Hebrew Prophecy within the Council of Yahweh, Examined in its Ancient Near Eastern Setting, in: C.D. Evans, W.W. Hallo, and J.B. White (eds), *Scripture in Context: Essays on the Comparative Method*, Pittsburgh, 141-156

Pongratz-Leisten, B. 1994, *Ina šulmi īrub: Die kulttopographische und ideologische Programmatik der akītu-Prozession in Babylonien und Assyrien im 1. Jahrtausend v.Chr.*, BaghF 16, Mainz

——1999, *Herrschaftswissen in Mesopotamien. Formen der Kommunikation zwischen Gott und König im 2. und 1. Jahrtausend v. Chr.*, SAAS 10, Helsinki

Porter, B.N. 1993, *Images, Power, and Politics: Figurative Aspects of Esarhaddon's Babylonian Policy*, MAPS 208, Philadelphia

——2000, The Anxiety of Multiplicity: Conceptions of Divinity as One and Many in Ancient Assyria, in: B.N. Porter (ed.), *One God or Many?* Casco Bay, 211-271

Porter, B.N. and Radner, K. 1998, Aššur-aḫu-iddina, in: K. Radner (ed.), *The Prosopography of the Neo-Assyrian Empire*, vol. 1/I, Helsinki

Postgate, J.N. 1974a, *Taxation and Conscription in the Assyrian Empire*, Rome

——1974b, Royal Exercise of Justice under the Assyrian Empire, in: P. Garelli (ed.), *Le Palais et la Royauté*, RAI 19, Paris, 417-426

Potts, D.T. 1999, *The Archaeology of Elam. Formation and Transformation of an Iranian State*, Cambridge

Prichard, J.B. (ed.) 1969, *Ancient Near Eastern Texts Relating to the Old Testament*, (3rd edition; [2]1955; [1]1950), Princeton

Provençal, P. 2005, Regarding the Noun שרף in the Hebrew Bible, *JSOT* 29, 371-379

Radner, K. 1998, Aššūr-hamātū'a, in: K. Radner (ed.), *The Prosopography of the Neo-Assyrian Empire*, vol. 1/I, Helsinki, 186-187

——1999, Atalia, in: K. Radner (ed.), *The Prosopography of the Neo-Assyrian Empire*, vol. 1/II, Helsinki, 433

Radner, K. (ed.) 1998, *The Prosopography of the Neo-Assyrian Empire*, vol. 1/I, Helsinki

——1999, *The Prosopography of the Neo-Assyrian Empire*, vol. 1/II, Helsinki

Reade, J.E. 1972, *The Neo-Assyrian Court and Army: Evidence from the Sculptures*, *Iraq* 34, 87-112

Reich, R. and Shukron, E. 2003, The Urban Development of Jerusalem in the Late Eighth Century B.C.E., in: A.G. Vaughn and A.E. Killebrew (eds), *Jerusalem in Bible and Archaeology. The First Temple Period*, SBLSS 18, Atlanta, 209-218

Reiner, E. 1985, *Your Thwarts in Pieces Your Mooring Rope Cut. Poetry from Babylonia and Assyria*, Michigan

Rendtorff, R. 1984, Zur Komposition des Buches Jesaja, *VT* 34, 295-320

——1989, Jesaja 6 im Rahmen der Komposition des Jesajabuches, in: J. Vermeylen (ed.), *The Book of Isaiah. Le Livre d'Isaïe: les oracles et leurs relectures: unité et complexité de l'ouvrage*, BETL 81, Leuven, 73-82

——1996, The Book of Isaiah: A Complex Unity, Synchronic and Diachronic Reading, in: R.F. Megulin and M.A. Sweeney (eds), *New Visions of Isaiah*, JSOTSup 214, Sheffield, 32-49

Renz, J. 1995, Terror und Erosion: Ein Beitrag zur Klärung der Bedeutungsbreite der Wurzel *ḥtt*, in: M. Weippert and S. Timm (eds), *Meilenstein. Festgabe für H. Donner*, ÄAT 30, Wiesbaden, 204-224

Renz, T. 1999, *The Rhetorical Function of the Book of Ezekiel*, VTSup 76, Leiden

Reventlow, H. Graf von 1987, Das Ende der sog. "Denkschrift" Jesajas, *BN* 38/39, 62-67

Ringgren, H. 1982, Prophecy in the Ancient Near East, in: R. Coggins et al. (eds), *Israel's Prophetic Tradition: Essays in Honour of P.R. Ackroyd*, Cambridge, 1-11

——1983, Akkadian Apocalypses, in: D. Hellholm (ed.), *Apocalypticism in the Mediterranean World and the Near East*, Tübingen, 379-386

Roberts, J.J.M. 1971, The Hand of Yahweh, *VT* 21, 244-251

——1973, The Davidic Origin of the Zion Tradition, *JBL* 92, 329-344

——1975, Divine Freedom and Cultic Manipulation in Israel and Mesopotamia, in: H. Goedicke and J.J.M. Roberts (eds), *Unity and Diversity: Essays in the History, Literature, and Religion of the Ancient Near East*, Baltimore, 181-190

——1977a, Of Signs, Prophets, and Time Limits: A Note on Psalm 74:9, *CBQ* 39, 474-481

——1977b, Nebuchadnezzar I's Elamite Crisis in Theological Perspective, in M. deJong Ellis (ed.), *Essays on the Ancient Near East in Memory of J.J. Finkelstein*, Hamden, 183-187

——1987, Yahweh's Foundation in Zion (Isaiah 28:16), *JBL* 106, 27-45

——1997a, Blindfolding the Prophet: Political Resistance to First Isaiah's Oracles in the Light of Ancient Near Eastern Attitudes towards Oracles, in: J.-G. Heintz (ed.), *Oracles et prophéties dans l'antiquité. Actes du Colloque de Strasbourg 15-17 juin 1995*, Paris, 135-146

——1997b, Whose Child Is This? Reflections on the Speaking Voice in Isaiah 9:5, *HTR* 90, 115-129

——2002a, *The Bible and the Ancient Near East. Collected Essays*, Winona Lake

——2002b, The Mari Prophetic Texts in Transliteration and English Translation, in: J.J.M. Roberts, *The Bible and the Ancient Near East. Collected Essays*, Winona Lake, 157-253

——2002c, The Enthronement of Yhwh and David. The Abiding Theological Significance of the Kingship Language of the Psalms, *CBQ* 64, 675-686

——2004, The Context, Text, and Logic of Isaiah 7.7-9*, in: J. Kaltner and L. Stulman (eds), *Inspired Speech: Prophecy in the Ancient Near East, Essays in Honor of H.B. Huffmon*, JSOTSup 378, London, 161-170

Rochberg, F. 2004, *The Heavenly Writing: Divination, Horoscopy, and Astronomy in Mesopotamian Culture*, New York

Rösel, M. 2003, Inscriptional Evidence and the Question of Genre, in: E. Ben Zvi and M.A. Sweeney (eds), *The Changing Face of Form Criticism for the Twenty-First Century*, Grand Rapids, 107-121

Ruppert, L. 1986, *srr*, in: G.J. Botterweck, H. Ringgren and H.-J. Fabry (eds), *Theologisches Wörterbuch zum Alten Testament* V, Stuttgart, 957-963

Russell, J.M. 1999, *The Writing on the Wall: Studies in the Architectural Context of Late Assyrian Palace Inscriptions*, Winona Lake

Rüterswörden, U. 1985, *Die Beamten der israelitischen Königszeit: eine Studie zu śr und vergleichbaren Begriffen*, BWANT 117, Stuttgart

——2001, Der Prophet in den Lachish-Ostraka, in: C. Hardmeier (ed.), *Steine – Bilder – Texte. Historische Evidenz außerbiblischer und biblischer Quellen*, Arbeiten zur Bibel und ihrer Geschichte 5, Leipzig, 179-192

Ruwe, A. and Weise, U. 2002, Das Joch Assurs und *jhwh*s Joch. Ein Realienbegriff und seine Metaphorisierung in neuassyrischen und alttestamentlichen Texten, *ZABR* 8, 274-307

Saggs, H.W.F. 1978, *The Encounter with the Divine in Mesopotamia and Israel*, London

——2001, *The Nimrud Letters, 1952*, Cuneiform Texts from Nimrud V, London

Sass, B. 1993, The Pre-Exilic Hebrew Seals: Iconism versus Aniconism, in: B. Sass and C. Uehlinger (eds) *Studies in the Iconography of Northwest Semitic Inscribed Seals*, OBO 125, Fribourg, 194-256

Sasson, J.M. 1998, About 'Mari and the Bible', *RA* 92, 97-123

Schart, A. 1995, Combining Prophetic Oracles in Mari Letters and Jeremia 36, *JANESCU* 23, 75-93

Schaudig, H. 2001, *Die Inschriften Nabonids von Babylon und Kyros' des Grossen samt den in ihrem Umfeld entstandenen Tendenzschriften: Textausgabe und Grammatik*, AOAT 256, Münster

Schipper, B.U. 1998, Wer war "So', König von Ägypten" (2 Kön 17,4)? *BN* 92, 71-84

——1999, *Israel und Ägypten in der Königszeit: die kulturellen Kontakte von Salomo bis zum Fall Jerusalems*, OBO 170, Freiburg

Schmidt, W.H. 1974, *dābar*, in: G.J. Botterweck and H. Ringgren (eds), *Theologisches Wörterbuch zum Alten Testament* II, Stuttgart, 101-133

——1977, Die Einheit der Verkündigung Jesajas. Versuch einer Zusammenschau, *EvT* 37, 260-272

Schmitt, A. 1982, *Prophetischer Gottesbescheid in Mari und Israel: eine Strukturuntersuchung*, BWANT 114, Stuttgart

Schmökel, H. 1951, Gotteswort in Mari und Israel, *TLZ*, 55-56

Schniedewind, W.M. 1995, *The Word of God in Transition. From Prophet to Exegete in the Second Temple Period*, JSOTSup 197, Sheffield

Schöpflin, K. 2002a, *Theologie als Biographie im Ezechielbuch. Ein Beitrag zur Konzeption alttestamentlicher Prophetie*, FAT 36, Tübingen

——2002b, Ein Blick in die Unterwelt (Jesaja 14), *TZ* 58, 299-314

Seebaß, H. 1995, Jesaja, Jesaja (Buch), in: M. Görg and B. Lang (eds), *Neues Bibel-Lexikon* vol. 2, Zürich, 314-318

Seitz, C.R. 1991, *Zion's Final Destiny. The Development of the Book of Isaiah: a Reassessment of Isaiah 36-39*, Minneapolis

——1992, Isaiah, book of (First Isaiah), *ABD* 3, New York, 472-507

Seux, M.-J. 1967, *Épithètes royales Akkadiennes et Sumériennes*, Paris

Seybold, K. 1986, *Die Psalmen: eine Einführung*, Stuttgart

Sheppard, G.T. 1985, The Anti-Assyrian Redaction and the Canonical Context of Isaiah 1-39, *JBL* 104, 193-216

Shipp, R.M. 2002, *Of Dead Kings and Dirges. Myth and Meaning in Isaiah 14:4b-21*, Academia Biblica 11, Atlanta

Shupak, J. 1990, Egyptian 'Prophecy' and Biblical Prophecy: did the phenomenon of prophecy, in the biblical sense, exist in ancient Egypt? *JEOL* 31 (1989-1990), 5-40

Smelik, K.A.D. 1992, King Hezekiah advocates true prophecy. Remarks on Isaiah xxxvi and xxxvii // II Kings xviii and xix, in: K.A.D. Smelik, *Converting the Past. Studies in Ancient Israelite and Moabite Historiography*, OtSt 28, Leiden, 93-128

——1997, The New Altar of King Ahaz (2 Kings 16): Deuteronomistic Re-interpretation of a Cult Reform, in: M. Vervenne and J. Lust (eds), *Deuteronomy and Deuteronomic Literature. Festschrift C.H.W. Brekelmans*, BETL 133, Leuven, 263-278

——1998, The Representation of King Ahaz in 2 Kings 16 and 2 Chronicles 28, in: J.C. de Moor (ed.), *Intertextuality in Ugarit und Israel*, OtSt 40, Leiden, 143-183

Smith, M. 1952, The Common Theology of the Ancient Near East, *JBL* 71, 135-148

Smith, M.J. 1991, Did Psammetichus I die Abroad? *OLP* 22, 101-109

Soldt, W.H. van 1992, A Note on Old Babylonian *lū ittum*, 'Let Me Remind You', *ZA* 82, 30-38

——2002, Studies on the *sākinu*-Official (2). The functions of the *sākinu* of Ugarit, *UF* 34, 805-828

Sommerfeld, W. 1982, *Der Aufstieg Marduks: Die Stellung Marduks in der babylonischen Religion des zweiten Jahrtausends v. Chr.*, AOAT 213, Neukirchen-Vluyn

Spek, R.J. van der 2003, Darius III, Alexander the Great and Babylonian Scholarship, in: W. Henkelman and A. Kuhrt (eds), *A Persian Perspective. Essays in Memory of Heleen Sancisi-Weerdenburg*, Achaemenid History 13 (Leiden), 289-346

Spieckermann, H. 1982, *Juda unter Assur in der Sargonidenzeit*, FRLANT 129, Göttingen

Spronk, K. 1999, Rahab, in: K. van der Toorn, B. Becking and P.W. van der Horst (eds), *Dictionary of Deities and Demons in the Bible* (2nd edition), Leiden, 684-686

Stansell, G. 1996, Isaiah 28-33: Blest Be the Tie that Binds (Isaiah Together), in: R.F. Melugin and M.A. Sweeney (eds), *New Visions of Isaiah*, JSOTSup 214, Sheffield, 68-103

Starr, I. 1990, *Queries to the Sungod. Divination and Politics in Sargonid Assyria*, SAA 4, Helsinki

Steck, O.H. 1972, *Friedensvorstellungen im alten Jerusalem: Psalmen, Jesaja, Deuterojesaja*, ThSt 111, Zürich

——1985, *Bereitete Heimkehr: Jesaja 35 als redaktionelle Brücke zwischen dem ersten und dem zweiten Jesaja*, SBS 121, Stuttgart

——1989, Tritojesaja im Jesajabuch, in: J. Vermeylen (ed.), *The Book of Isaiah. Le Livre d'Isaïe: les oracles et leurs relectures: unité et complexité de l'ouvrage*, BETL 81, Leuven, 361-406

——1996, *Die Prophetenbücher und ihr theologisches Zeugnis. Wege der Nachfrage und Fährten zur Antwort*, Tübingen

Stefanini, R. 1969, Enkidu's Dream in the Hittite "Gilgamesh", *JNES* 28, 40-47

Steiner, M.L. 2001, *Excavations by Kathleen M. Kenyon in Jerusalem 1961-1967, vol. 3. The Settlement in the Bronze and Iron Ages*, London

——2003a, Expanding Borders: The Development of Jerusalem in the Iron Age, in: T.L. Thompson (ed.), *Jerusalem in Ancient History and Tradition*, JSOTSup 381, London, 68-79

——2003b, The Evidence from Kenyon's Excavations in Jerusalem: a response essay, in: A.G. Vaughn and A.E. Killebrew (eds), *Jerusalem in Bible and Archaeology. The First Temple Period*, SBLSS 18, Atlanta, 347-363

Stern, E. 2001, *Archaeology of the land of the Bible II. The Assyrian, Babylonian and Persian periods, 732-332 BCE*, ABRL, New York

Stökl, J. 2004, Who really "was also among the prophets?" A Study of the Use of the Hebrew terms נָבִיא, רֹאֶה, and חֹזֶה in Ancient Hebrew (unpublished M.St. thesis), Oxford

Streck, M. 1916, *Assurbanipal und die letzten assyrischen Könige bis zum Untergange Niniveh's*, 3 vols, VAB 7, Leipzig

Sweeney, M.A. 1988, *Isaiah 1-4 and the Post-Exilic Understanding of the Isaianic Tradition*, BZAW 171, Berlin

——1994, Sargon's Threat against Jerusalem in Isaiah 10,27-32, *Bib* 75, 457-470

——1996a, *Isaiah 1-39: with an introduction to prophetic literature*, FOTL 16, Grand Rapids

——1996b, Jesse's New Shoot in Isaiah 11: A Josianic Reading of the Prophet Isaiah, in: R.D. Weis and D.M. Carr (eds), *A Gift of God in Due Season. Essays on Scripture and Community in Honor of J.A. Sanders*, JSOTSup 225, Sheffield, 103-118

——2001, *King Josiah of Judah. The Lost Messiah of Israel*, Oxford

Tadmor, H. 1958, The Campaigns of Sargon II of Assur: A Chronological-Historical Study, *JCS* 12, 22-40 and 77-100

——1966, Philistia under Assyrian Rule, *BA* 29, 86-102

——1971, Fragments of an Assyrian Stele of Sargon II, in: M. Dothan, *Ashdod II-III. The Second and Third Seasons of Excavations* 1963, 1965. *Soundings in 1967*, vol. 1 Texts, vol. 2 Figures and Plates ('*Atiqot*. English Series, vols IX-X), Jerusalem, vol. 1, 192-197, vol. 2, plates XCVI and XCVII

——1975, Assyria and the West: the Ninth Century and its Aftermath, in: H. Goedicke and J.J.M. Roberts (eds), *Unity and Diversity: Essays in the History, Literature and Religion of the Ancient Near East*, Baltimore, 36-48

——1981, The Five Empires: a Note on a Propagandistic Topos, *AJP* 102, 330-339

——1982, The Aramaization of Assyria: Aspects of Western Impact, in: H.-J. Nissen and J. Renger (eds), *Mesopotamien und seine Nachbarn: politische und kulturelle Wechselbeziehungen im Alten Vorderasien vom 4. bis 1. Jahrtausend v. Chr.*, part 2, RAI 25, Berlin, 449-470

——1983, Autobiographical Apology in the Royal Assyrian Literature, in: H. Tadmor and M. Weinfeld (eds), *History, Historiography and Interpretation: Studies in Biblical and Cuneiform Literatures*, Jerusalem, 36-57

——1994, *The Inscriptions of Tiglath-Pileser III King of Assyria. Critical Edition, with Introduction, Translation and Commentary*, Jerusalem

Tadmor, H. and Cogan, M. 1979, Ahaz and Tiglath-Pileser in the Book of Kings: Historiographical Considerations, *Bib* 60, 491-508

Tallqvist, K.L. 1914, *Assyrian Personal Names*, Helsingfors

Talmon, S. 1978, The 'Comparative Method' in Biblical Interpretation: Principles and Problems, in: W. Zimmerli (ed.), *Congress Volume: Göttingen 1977*, VTSup 29, Leiden, 320-356

Tate, M.E. 1996, The Book of Isaiah in Recent Study, in: J.W. Watts and P.R. House (eds), *Forming Prophetic Literature. Essays on Isaiah and the Twelve in Honour of J.D.W. Watts*, JSOTSup 235, Sheffield, 22-56

Taylor, J. 2000, The Third Intermediate Period (1069-664 BC), The Late Period (664-332 BC), in: I. Shaw (ed.), *The Oxford History of Ancient Egypt*, Oxford, 330-394

Tiemeyer, L.-S. 2005, Prophecy as a Way of Cancelling Prophecy – The Strategic Uses of Foreknowledge, *ZAW* 117, 329-350

Tomasino, A.J. 1993, Isaiah 1.1-2.4 and 63-66, and the Composition of the Isaianic Corpus, *JSOT* 57, 81-98

Toorn, K. van der 1985, *Sin and Sanction in Israel and Mesopotamia: a Comparative Study*, SSN 22, Assen

——1987, L'oracle de victoire comme expression prophétique au Proche-Orient ancien, *RB* 94, 63-97

——1988, Echoes of Judaean Necromancy in Isaiah 28,7-22*, *ZAW* 100, 199-217

——1990, The Nature of the Biblical Teraphim in the Light of the Cuneiform Evidence, *CBQ* 52, 203-222

——1994, Parallels in Biblical Research: Purposes of Comparison, in: D. Assaf (ed.), *Proceedings of the Eleventh World Congress of Jewish Studies. Division A: the Bible and Its World*, Jerusalem, 1-8

——1996a, *Family Religion in Babylonia, Syria and Israel: Continuity and Change in the Forms of Relgious Life*, SHCANE 7, Leiden

——1996b, Een Pleisterplaats voor de Goden. Het verschijnsel 'Heilige Stad' in het Oude Nabije Oosten, in: K.D. Jenner and G.A. Wiegers (eds), *Jeruzalem als Heilige Stad. Religieuze Voorstelling en Geloofspraktijk*, Leidse Studiën van de Godsdienst 1, Kampen, 38-52

——1998, In the Lion's Den: the Babylonian Background of a Biblical Motif, *CBQ* 60, 626-640

——2000a, From the Oral to the Written: The Case of Old Babylonian Prophecy, in: E. Ben Zvi and M.H. Floyd (eds), *Writings and Speech in Israelite and Ancient Near Eastern Prophecy*, SBLSS 10, Atlanta, 219-234

——2000b, Mesopotamian Prophecy between Immanence and Transcendence: A Comparison of Old Babylonian and Neo-Assyrian Prophecy, in: Nissinen (ed.), *Prophecy in its Ancient Near Eastern Context. Mesopotamian, Biblical and Arabian Perspectives*, SBLSS 13, Atlanta, 71-87

——2007, *Scribal Culture and the Making of the Hebrew Scripture*, Cambridge MA and London

Török, L. 1997, *The Kingdom of Kush. Handbook of the Napatan-Meroitic Civilization*, Leiden

Tov, E. 1972, L'incidence de la critique textuelle sur la critique littéraire dans le livre de Jérémie, *RB* 79, 189-199

——1981, Some Aspects of the Textual and Literary History of the Book of Jeremiah, in: P.-M. Bogaert (ed.), *Le Livre de Jérémie: le prophète et son milieu, les oracles et leur transmission*, Leuven, 145-167

——2001, *Textual Criticism of the Hebrew Bible* (2nd revised edition), Minneapolis

Uehlinger, C. 1995, Gab es eine joschijanische Kultreform? Plädoyer für ein begründetes Minimum, in: W. Groß (ed.), *Jeremia und die "deuteronomistische Bewegung"*, BBB 98, Weinheim, 57-89

——1998, "...und wo sind die Götter von Samarien?" Die Wegführung syrisch-palästinischer Kultstatuen auf einem Relief Sargons II in Ḫorṣābād/Dūr-Šarrukīn, in: M. Dietrich and I. Kottsieper (eds), *"Und Mose schrieb dieses Lied auf": Studien zum Alten Testament und zum alten Orient. Festschrift für O. Loretz*, AOAT 250, Münster, 739-776

Ussishkin, D. 1995, The Water Systems of Jerusalem during Hezekiah's Reign, in: M. Weippert and S. Timm (eds), *Meilenstein. Festgabe für H. Donner*, ÄAT 30, Wiesbaden, 289-307

Vanderhooft, D.S. 1999, *The Neo-Babylonian Empire and Babylon in the Latter Prophets*, HSM 59, Atlanta

Vanel, A. 1974, Tabe'el en Is 7,6 et le roi Tubail de Tyr, in: D. Lys (ed.), *Studies on Prophecy: A Collection of Twelve Papers*, VTSuppl 26, Leiden, 17-24

Van Seters, J. 2000, Prophetic Orality in the Context of the Ancient Near East: A Response to Culley, Crenshaw, and Davies, in: E. Ben Zvi and M.H. Floyd (eds), *Writings and Speech in Israelite and Ancient Near Eastern Prophecy*, SBLSS 10, Atlanta, 83-88

Vaughn, A.G. and Killebrew, A.E. (eds) 2003, *Jerusalem in Bible and Archaeology. The First Temple Period*, SBLSS 18, Atlanta

Veenhof, K.R. 2001, *Geschichte des alten Orients bis zur Zeit Alexanders des Grossen*, GAT 11 (German translation H. Weippert), Göttingen

Vera Chamaza, G.W. 1996, *Die Omnipotenz Aššurs: Entwicklungen in der Aššur-Theologie unter den Sargoniden Sargon II, Sanherib und Asarhaddon*, AOAT 295, Münster

Vermeylen, J. 1977-8, *Du prophète Isaïe à l'apocalyptique*, 2 vols, Paris

Vieweger, D. 1992, "Das Volk, das durch das Dunkel zieht ..." Neue Überlegungen zu Jes (8:23aβb) 9,1-6, *BZ NF* 36, 77-86

Villard, P. 2001, Les Prophéties à l'Époque Néo-Assyrienne, in: A. Lemaire (ed.), *Prophètes et Rois. Bible et Proche-Orient*, Paris, 55-84

Von Beckerath, J. 1999, *Handbuch der ägyptischen Königsnamen* (2nd edition), Mainz

Von Rad, G. 1933, Die falschen Propheten, *ZAW* 51, 109-121

——1958, Das judäische Königsritual, in: *Gesammelte Studien zum Alten Testament*, Munich, 205-213

——1960, *Theologie des Alten Testaments II. Die Theologie der prophetischen Überlieferungen Israels*, Munich

Von Soden, W. 1956, Beiträge zum Verständnis der neuassyrischen Briefe über die Ersatzkönigriten, in: K. Schubert (ed.), *Vorderasiatische Studien. Festschrift für V. Christian*, Vienna, 100-107

——1971, Etemenanki vor Asarhaddon, *UF* 3, 253-263

——1985, *Einführung in die Altorientalistik*, Darmstadt

Vos, J.C. de 2003, *Das Los Judas. Über Entstehung und Ziele der Landbeschreibung in Josua 15*, VTSup 95, Leiden

Vriezen, T.C. 1969, The Study of the Old Testament and the History of Religion, in: T.C. Vriezen (ed.), *Congress Volume: Rome 1968*, VTSup 17, Leiden, 1-24

Wagenaar, J.A. 2001, *Judgement and Salvation. The Composition and Redaction of Micah 2-5*, VTSup 85, Leiden

Wagner, T. 2005, Ein Zeichen für den Herrscher – Gottes Zeichen für Ahas in Jesaja 7,10-17, *SJOT* 19, 74-83

——2006, *Gottes Herrschaft. Eine Analyse der Denkschrift (Jes 6,1-9,6)*, VTSup 108, Leiden

Wanke, G. 1966a, *Die Zionstheologie der Korachiten in ihrem traditionsgeschichtlichen Zusammenhang*, BZAW 97, Berlin

——1966b, אוֹי und הוֹי, *ZAW* 78, 215-218

Waschke, E.-J. 2004, Der *Nābî'*. Anmerkungen zu einem Titel, *leqach* 4, 59-69

Watanabe, K. 1987, *Die adê-Vereidigung anlässlich der Thronfolgeregelung Asarhaddons*, BaghMB 3, Berlin

Watts, J.D.W. 1985, *Isaiah 1-33*, WBC 24, Waco

——1987, *Isaiah 33-66*, WBC 25, Waco

Watts J.W. et al. (eds) 1996, *Forming Prophetic Literature: Essays on Isaiah and the Twelve in Honor of J.D.W. Watts*, JSOTSup 235, Sheffield

Weber, B. 2000, Psalm 83 als Einzelpsalm und als Abschluss der Asaph-Psalmen, *BN* 103, 64-84

Wegner, P.D. 1992, Re-Examination of Isaiah IX 1-6, *VT* 42, 103-112

Weinfeld, M. 1977, Ancient Near Eastern Patterns in Prophetic Literature, *VT* 27, 178-195

——1995, *Social Justice in Ancient Israel and in the Ancient Near East*, Jerusalem

——1998, Jerusalem – A Political and Spiritual Capital, in: J. Goodnick Westenholz (ed.), *Capital Cities: Urban Planning and Spiritual Dimensions*, Bible Lands Museum Jerusalem Publications 2, Jerusalem, 15-40

Weippert, M. 1972, "Heiliger Krieg" in Israel und Assyrien: kritische Anmerkungen zu Gerhard Von Rads Konzept des "Heiligen Krieges im alten Israel", *ZAW* 84, 460-493

——1973, Menahem von Israel und seine Zeitgenossen in einer Steleninschrift des assyrischen Königs Tiglathpileser III. aus dem Iran, *ZDPV* 81, 26-53

——1976-80, Israel und Juda, in: D.O. Edzard (ed.), *Reallexikon der Assyriologie* V, Berlin, 200-208

——1981, Assyrische Prophetien der Zeit Asarhaddons und Assurbanipals, in: F.M. Fales (ed.), *Assyrian Royal Inscriptions: New Horizons*, Rome, 71-115

——1982, De herkomst van het heilsorakel voor Israël bij Deutero-Jesaja, *NTT* 36, 1-11

——1985, Die Bildsprache der neuassyrischen Prophetie, in: H. Weippert, K. Seybold, M. Weippert, *Beiträge zur prophetischen Bildsprache in Israel und Assyrien*, OBO 64, Freiburg, 55-93

——1988, Aspekte Israelischer Prophetie im Lichte verwandter Erscheinungen des Alten Orients, in: G. Mauer and U. Magen (eds), *Ad bene et fideliter seminandum. Festgabe für K. Deller*, AOAT 220, Neukirchen-Vluyn, 287-319

——1991, The Balaam Text from Deir 'Allā and the Study of the Old Testament, in: J. Hoftijzer and G. van der Kooij (eds), *The Balaam Text from Deir 'Alla Re-Evaluated. Proceedings of the International Symposium held at Leiden 21-24 August 1989*, Leiden, 151-184

——1997, "Das Frühere, siehe, ist eingetroffen ...": über Selbstzitate im altorientalischen Prophetenspruch, in: J.-G. Heintz (ed.), *Oracles et prophéties dans l'antiquité. Actes du Colloque de Strasbourg 15-17 juin 1995*, Paris, 147-169

——2001a, "Ich bin Jahwe" – "Ich bin Ishtar von Arbela": Deuterojesaja im Lichte der neuassyrischen Prophetie, in: B. Huwyler et al. (eds), *Prophetie und Psalmen: Festschrift für K. Seybold*, AOAT 280, Münster, 31-59

——2001b, Prophetie im Alten Orient, in: M. Görg and B. Lang (eds), *Neues Bibel-Lexikon*, vol. 3, Zürich, 196-200

——2002, "König, fürchte dich nicht!" Assyrische Prophetie im 7. Jahrhundert v. Chr., Review article of S. Parpola, *Assyrian Prophecies*, SAA 9 (Helsinki 1997), *Or* 71, 1-54

——2003, Review of M. Nissinen, References to Prophecy in Neo-Assyrian Sources (Helsinki 1998); idem (ed.), *Prophecy in Its Ancient Near Eastern Context* (Atlanta 2000), *Or* 72, 282-288

Werlitz, J. 1992, *Studien zur Literarkritischen Methode. Gericht und Heil in Jesaja 7,1-17 und 29,1-8*, BZAW 204, Berlin

Werner, W. 1982, *Eschatologische Texte in Jesaja 1-39*, Würzburg

——1988, *Studien zur alttestamentlichen Vorstellung vom Plan Jahwes*, BZAW 173, Berlin

Wildberger, H. 1965-82, *Jesaja 1-39*, 3 vols, BKAT 10, Neukirchen-Vluyn

Williamson, H.G.M. 1982a, *1 and 2 Chronicles*, NCB, Grand Rapids

——1982b, The Death of Josiah and the Continuing Development of the Deuteronomistic History, *VT* 32, 242-247

——1987, Reliving the Death of Josiah: A Reply to C.T. Begg, *VT* 37, 9-15

——1994, *The Book Called Isaiah. Deutero-Isaiah's Role in Composition and Redaction*, Oxford

——1998a, *Variations on a Theme: King, Messiah and Servant in the Book of Isaiah*, Carlisle

——1998b, The Messianic Texts in Isaiah 1-39, in: J. Day (ed.), *King and Messiah in Israel and the Ancient Near East. Proceedings of the Oxford Old Testament Seminar*, JSOTSup 270, Sheffield 1998, 238-270

——2004, In Search of the Pre-exilic Isaiah, in: J. Day (ed.), *In Search of Pre-exilic Israel. Proceedings of the Oxford Old Testament Seminar*, JSOTSup 406, London, 181-206

——2006, *A Critical and Exegetical Commentary on Isaiah 1-27. Vol. 1: Commentary on Isaiah 1-5*, ICC, London

Willis, J.T. 1993, Textual and Linguistic Issues in Isaiah 22,15-25, *ZAW* 105, 377-399

Wilson, R.R. 1979, Prophecy and Ecstasy: A Reexamination, *JBL* 98, 321-337

——1980, *Prophecy and Society in Ancient Israel*, Philadelphia

Winckler, H. 1889, *Die Keilschrifttexte Sargons*, Band 1, Leipzig

Wolff, H.W. 1977, Die eigentliche Botschaft der klassischen Propheten, in: H. Donner et al. (eds), *Beiträge zur alttestamentlichen Theologie. Festschrift für W. Zimmerli*, Göttingen, 547-557

Wong, G.C.I. 1995, On 'Visits' and 'Visions' in Isaiah XXIX 6-7, *VT* 45, 370-376

——1999, Is 'God with us' in Isaiah VIII 8? *VT* 49, 426-431

Würthwein, E. 1952, Der Ursprung der prophetische Gerichtsrede, *ZTK* 49, 1-16

——1976, Die josianische Reform und Deuteronomium, *ZTK* 73, 395-423

Young, I.M. 1998a, Israelite Literacy: Interpreting the Evidence. Part I, *VT* 48, 239-253

——1998b, Israelite Literacy: Interpreting the Evidence. Part II, *VT* 48, 408-422

Younger, K.L. Jr 2002a, Recent Study on Sargon II, King of Assyria: Implications for Biblical Studies, in: M.W. Chavalas and K.L. Younger Jr (eds), *Mesopotamia and the Bible. Comparative Explorations*, Grand Rapids

——2002b, Yahweh at Ashkelon and Calah? Yahwistic Names in Neo-Assyrian, *VT* 52, 207-218

——2003, Assyrian Involvement in the southern Levant at the End of the Eighth Century B.C.E., in: A.G. Vaughn and A.E. Killebrew (eds), *Jerusalem in Bible and Archaeology. The First Temple Period*, SBLSS 18, Atlanta, 235-264

Zawadzki, S. 1990, Oriental and Greek Tradition about the Death of Sennacherib, *SAAB* 4, 69-72

Zehnder, M.P. 1999, *Wegmetaphorik im Alten Testament. Eine semantische Untersuchung der alttestamentlichen und altorientalischen Weg-Lexemen mit besonderer Berücksichtigung ihrer metaphorischen Verwendung*, BZAW 268, Berlin

Zevit, Z. 2004, The Prophet Versus Priest Antagonism Hypothesis: Its History and Origin, in: L.L. Grabbe and A. Ogden Bellis (eds), *The Priests in the Prophets. The Portrayal of Priests, Prophets and Other Religious Specialists in the Latter Prophets*, JSOTSup 408, London, 189-217

Zgoll, A. 2002, Die Welt im Schlaf sehen – Inkubation von Träumen im antiken Mesopotamien, *WO* 32, 74-101

Zimhoni, O. 1990, Two Ceramic Assemblages from Lachish Levels III and II, *TA* 17, 3-52

Zimmern, H. 1910, Gilgameš-Omina und Gilgameš-Orakel, *ZA* 24, 166-171

Zobel, H.-J. 1974, *hôj*, in: G.J. Botterweck and H. Ringgren (eds), *Theologisches Wörterbuch zum Alten Testament* II, Stuttgart, 382-384

——1981, *ja'ᵃqo(ô)b*, in: G.J. Botterweck and H. Ringgren (eds), *Theologisches Wörterbuch zum Alten Testament* III, Stuttgart, 752-777

——1985, Prophet in Israel und Juda, *ZTK* 82, 281-299

ABBREVIATIONS

General Abbreviations

Akk.	Akkadian
app. crit.	*apparatus criticus* of the *Biblia Hebraica Stuttgartensia,* [4]1990
BCE	Before the Common Era
c.	circa
cf.	*confer*, compare
ch.	chapter(s)
conj.	conjecture
DN	divine name
e.	edge (of tablet)
ed./eds	editor(s)
e.g.	*exempli gratia*, for the sake of example
esp.	especially
et al.	*et alii*, and others
etc.	*et cetera*, and the rest
f.	forthcoming (in print or to be published)
f.	following, i.e. the following verse
fem.	feminine
hi.	*hip'il*
hitp.	*hitpa'el*
ho.	*hop'al*
i.e.	*id est*, that is
l.	line(s)
LXX	Septuagint
masc.	masculine
MT	Masoretic Text
ni.	*nip'al*
p.	page
pi.	*pi'el*
PN	personal name
po.	*po'lel*
ptc.	participle
r.	reverse (of tablet)
repr.	reprinted (in)
s.	side (of tablet)
sec.	section
s.v.	*sub voce*, under the entry
var.	variant
vol./vols	volume(s)

Biblical Books

Gen	Genesis
Exod	Exodus
Lev	Leviticus
Num	Numbers
Deut	Deuteronomy
Josh	Joshua
Judg	Judges
1 Sam	1 Samuel
2 Sam	2 Samuel
1 Kgs	1 Kings
2 Kgs	2 Kings
1 Chron	1 Chronicles
2 Chron	2 Chronicles
Ezra	Ezra
Neh	Nehemiah
Job	Job
Ps	Psalms
Prov	Proverbs
Song	Song of Solomon
Isa	Isaiah
Jer	Jeremiah
Lam	Lamentations
Ezek	Ezekiel
Dan	Daniel
Hos	Hosea
Joel	Joel
Amos	Amos
Ob	Obadiah
Mic	Micah
Nah	Nahum
Hab	Habakkuk
Zeph	Zephaniah
Hag	Haggai
Zech	Zechariah
Mal	Malachi

Sigla for Cited Textual Sources and Reference Works

ABL	*Assyrian and Babylonian Letters*, R.F. Harper, London 1892-1914
AHw	*Akkadisches Handwörterbuch*, 3 vols, W. Von Soden, Wiesbaden 1965-1981
ARM 26/1	*Archives épistolaires de Mari I/1* (Archives royales de Mari 26/1), J.-M. Durand, Paris 1988
ARM 26/2	*Archives épistolaires de Mari I/2* (Archives royales de Mari 26/2), D. Charpin et al., Paris 1988
BIWA	*Beiträge zum Inschriftenwerk Assurbanipals*, R. Borger, Wiesbaden 1996

CAD	*The Assyrian Dictionary of the Oriental Institute of the University of Chicago*, A.L. Oppenheim et al. (eds), Chicago 1956 –
CDA	*A Concise Dictionary of Akkadian* (2nd corrected printing), J. Black, A. George, and N. Postgate, Wiesbaden 2000
CT	*Cuneiform Texts from Babylonian Tablets in the British Museum*, London 1896 –
GAG	*Grundriß der akkadischen Grammatik* (3rd edition), W. Von Soden, Rome 1995
HAE	*Handbuch der Althebräischen Epigraphik, Band I. Die Alt- hebräischen Inschriften*, J. Renz, Darmstadt 1995
ITP	*The Inscriptions of Tiglath-Pileser III King of Assyria*, H. Tadmor, Jerusalem 1994
JM	*A Grammar of Biblical Hebrew*, 2 vols, P. Joüon, S.J. and T. Muraoka, Rome 1996
KAI	*Kanaanäische und Aramäische Inschriften*, 3 vols., H. Donner and W. Röllig, Wiesbaden 1964
KAR	*Keilschrifttexte aus Assur religiösen Inhalts*, 2 vols, E. Ebeling, Leipzig 1919-1923
KB	*The Hebrew and Aramaic Lexicon of the Old Testament. The New Koehler Baumgartner in English*, 4 vols, translated and edited under the supervision of M.E.J. Richardson, Leiden 1994-1999
LKA	*Literarische Keilschrifttexte aus Assur*, E. Ebeling, Berlin 1953
LKU	*Literarische Keilschrifttexte aus Uruk*, A. Falkenstein, Berlin 1931
MSL 12	Materials for the Sumerian Lexicon, *The Series lú = ša and Related Texts*, M. Civil, Rome 1969
PNAE	*The Prosopography of the Neo-Assyrian Empire*, S. Parpola, K. Radner and H.D. Baker (eds), Helsinki 1998 –
SAA 1	*The Correspondence of Sargon II, Part 1. Letters from Assyria and the West*, S. Parpola, Helsinki 1987
SAA 2	*Neo-Assyrian Treaties and Loyalty Oaths*, S. Parpola and K. Watanabe, Helsinki 1988
SAA 3	*Court Poetry and Literary Miscellanea*, A. Livingstone, Helsinki 1989
SAA 4	*Queries to the Sungod. Divination and Politics in Sargonid Assyria*, I. Starr, Helsinki 1990
SAA 7	*Imperial Administrative Records, Part 1. Palace and Temple Administration*, F.M. Fales and J.N. Postgate, Helsinki 1992
SAA 8	*Astrological Reports to Assyrian Kings*, H. Hunger, Helsinki 1992
SAA 9	*Assyrian Prophecies*, S. Parpola, Helsinki 1997
SAA 10	*Letters from Assyrian and Babylonian Scholars*, S. Parpola, Helsinki 1993
SAA 12	*Grants, Decrees and Gifts of the Neo-Assyrian Period*, L. Kataja and R. Whiting, Helsinki 1995
SAA 13	*Letters from Priests to Kings Esarhaddon and Assurbanipal*, S.W. Cole and P. Machinist, Helsinki 1998
SAA 16	*The Political Correspondence of Esarhaddon*, M. Luukko and G. Van Buylaere, Helsinki 2002
SAA 18	*The Babylonian Correspondence of Esarhaddon and Letters to Assurbanipal and Sin-šarru-iškun from Northern and Central Babylonia*, F. Reynolds, Helsinki 2003

TUAT   *Texte aus der Umwelt des Alten Testament*, O. Kaiser et al. (ed.),
                Gütersloh 1984 –

Abbreviations used in the Bibliography

ÄAT	Ägypten und Altes Testament
AB	Anchor Bible
ABD	*Anchor Bible Dictionary*, D.N. Freedman (ed.), 6 vols, New York 1992
ABRL	The Anchor Bible Reference Library
AcOr	*Acta orientalia*
AfO	*Archiv für Orientforschung*
AfOB	Archiv für Orientforschung: Beiheft
AJP	*American Journal of Philology*
ALASP	Abhandlungen zur Literatur Alt-Syrien-Palästinas und Mesopotamiens
ANETS	Ancient Near Eastern Texts and Studies
AOAT	Alter Orient und Altes Testament
AoF	Altorientalische Forschungen
ARM	Archives royales de Mari
AS	Assyriological Studies
ATD	Das Alte Testament Deutsch
ATM	Altes Testament und Moderne
BA	*The Biblical Archaeologist*
BaghF	Baghdader Forschungen
BaghM	*Baghdader Mitteilungen*
BaghMB	Baghdader Mitteilungen: Beiheft
BASOR	*Bulletin of the American Schools of Oriental Research*
BBB	Bonner biblische Beiträge
BETL	Bibliotheca ephemeridum theologicarum lovaniensium
Bib	*Biblica*
BibOr	Biblica et Orientalia
BiOr	*Bibliotheca orientalis*
BKAT	Biblischer Kommentar, Altes Testament
BN	*Biblische Notizen*
BTS	Biblisch-Theologische Studien
BTZ	*Berliner Theologische Zeitschrift*
BWANT	Beiträge zur Wissenschaft vom Alten und Neuen Testament
BZ (NF)	*Biblische Zeitschrift (Neue Folge)*
BZAW	Beihefte zur Zeitschrift für die alttestamentliche Wissenschaft
CBC	Cambridge Bible Commentary
CBOTS	Coniectanea biblica Old Testament Series
CBQ	*Catholic Biblical Quarterly*
CHANE	Culture and History of the Ancient Near East
CM	Cuneiform Monographs
DMOA	Documenta et Monumenta Orientis Antiqui
ErIsr	*Eretz-Israel*
EvT	*Evangelische Theologie*
FAT	Forschungen zum Alten Testament
FO	*Folia Orientalia*

FOTL	The Forms of the Old Testament Literature
FRLANT	Forschungen zur Religion und Literatur des Alten und Neuen Testament
FzB	Forschung zur Bibel
GAT	Grundrisse zum Alten Testament
HBS	Herders biblische Studien
HCOT	Historical Commentary on the Old Testament
HSM	Harvard Semitic Monographs
HTKAT	Herders theologischer Kommentar zum Alten Testament
HTR	*Harvard Theological Review*
ICC	International Critical Commentary
IEJ	*Israel Exploration Journal*
Int	*Interpretation*
JANESCU	*Journal of the Ancient Near Eastern Society of Columbia University*
JAOS	*Journal of the American Oriental Society*
JBL	*Journal of Biblical Literature*
JCS	*Journal of Cuneiform Studies*
JEOL	*Jaarbericht Ex Oriente Lux*
JNES	*Journal of Near Eastern Studies*
JNSL	*Journal of Northwest Semitic Languages*
JSOT	*Journal for the Study of the Old Testament*
JSOTSup	Journal for the Study of the Old Testament: Supplement Series
JSPSup	Journal for the Study of the Pseudepigrapha: Supplement Series
JTS	*Journal of Theological Studies*
LAI	Library of Ancient Israel
MAPS	Memoirs of the American Philosophical Society
MARI	*Mari. Annales de recherches interdisciplinaires*
MC	Mesopotamian Civilizations
MDOG	*Mitteilungen der deutschen Orient-Gesellschaft*
MHUC	Monographs of the Hebrew Union College
MKNAW	Mededelingen der Koninklijke Nederlandse Akademie van Wetenschappen
NABU	*Nouvelles assyriologiques brèves et utilitaires*
NCB	New Century Bible
NTT	*Nederlands Theologisch Tijdschrift*
OBO	Orbis Biblicus et Orientalis
OIP	The University of Chicago Oriental Institute Publications
OLP	*Orientalia lovaniensia periodica*
Or (NS)	*Orientalia (New Series)*
OTG	Old Testament Guides
OTL	Old Testament Library
OtSt	Oudtestamentische Studiën
PIOL	Publications de l'Institut Orientaliste de Louvain
RA	*Revue d'assyriologie et d'archéologie orientale*
RAI	Rencontre Assyriologique Internationale
RB	*Revue biblique*
RHR	*Revue de l'histoire des religions*
RIMA	Royal Inscriptions of Mesopotamia, Assyrian Periods
RIMB	Royal Inscriptions of Mesopotamia, Babylonian Periods
RSRev	*Religious Studies Review*

SAA	State Archives of Assyria
SAAB	*State Archives of Assyria Bulletin*
SAAS	State Archives of Assyria Studies
SANE	Sources from the Ancient Near East
SBLSS	Society of Biblical Literature: Symposium Series
SBLWAWS	Society of Biblical Literature: Writings from the Ancient World Series
SBS	Stuttgarter Bibel-Studien
SBTS	Sources for Biblical and Theological Study
ScrHier	Scripta Hierosolymitana
SEÅ	*Svensk exegetisk årsbok*
SHANE	Studies in the History of the Ancient Near East
SHCANE	Studies in the History and Culture of the Ancient Near East
SJOT	*Scandinavian Journal of the Old Testament*
SSN	Studia semitica neerlandica
StudOr	Studia orientalia
TA	*Tel-Aviv*
ThSt	Theologische Studiën
TLZ	*Theologische Literaturzeitung*
TRu (NF)	*Theologische Rundschau (Neue Folge)*
TZ	*Theologische Zeitschrift*
UCOP	University of Cambridge Oriental Publications
UF	*Ugarit-Forschungen: Internationales Jahrbuch für die Altertums-kunde Syrien-Palästinas*
UNHAII	Uitgaven van het Nederlands Historisch-Archaeologisch Instituut te Istanbul
VAB	Vorderasiatische Bibliothek
VF	*Verkündiging und Forschung*
VT	*Vetus Testamentum*
VTSup	Supplements to Vetus Testamentum
WBC	World Biblical Commentary
WD (NF)	*Wort und Dienst (Neue Folge)*
WMANT	Wissenschaftliche Monographien zum Alten und zum Neuen Testament
WO	*Die Welt des Orients*
WUNT	Wissenschaftliche Untersuchungen zum Neuen Testament
ZABR	*Zeitschrift für altorientalische und biblische Rechtsgeschichte*
ZAW	*Zeitschrift für die alttestamentliche Wissenschaft*
ZDPV	*Zeitschrift des deutchen Palästina-Vereins*
ZTK	*Zeitschrift für Theologie und Kirche*

INDEX OF TEXTS (SELECTION)

1   *Bible*

2 *Cuneiform texts*

For the references to textual sources, see Sigla for Cited Textual Sources and Reference Works

2.1 *Mari*

2.2   Babylonia

2.2.1   Literary Compositions

2.2.2   Inscriptions of Babylonian Kings

2.2.3   Babylonian Chronicle

2.3   Assyria

2.3.1   Inscriptions of Assyrian kings

2.3.2   *State Archives of Assyria (SAA)*

2.3.3 *Other Assyrian Letters*

3 *West-Semitic texts*

INDEX OF SUBJECTS